DECEMBER 8, 1941

DECEMBER 8, 1941

MacARTHUR'S
PEARL HARBOR

WILLIAM H. BARTSCH

Texas A&M University Press
College Station

The paper used in this book meets the minimum requirements
of the American National Standard for Permanence
of Paper for Printed Library Materials, Z39.48-1984.
Binding materials have been chosen for durability.

Library of Congress Cataloging-in-Publication Data

Bartsch, William H., 1933–
    December 8, 1941 : MacArthur's Pearl Harbor / William H. Bartsch.
        p. cm.—(Texas A&M University military history series ; no. 87)
    Includes bibliographical references and index.
    ISBN 1-58544-246-1
    1. World War, 1939–1945—Campaigns—Philippines.   2. World War, 1939–1945—
Aerial operations, Japanese.   3. World War, 1939–1945—Aerial operations, American.
4. MacArthur, Douglas, 1880–1964.   I. Title.   II. Series: Texas A&M Universtiy
military history series ; 87.
    D767.4B37   2003
    940.54'25—dc21   2002152713

The author wishes to thank Eugene Eisenberg for his donation of John D. Shaw's
painting, *They Fought with What They Had,* for use on the jacket cover of this
book. The author also wishes to acknowledge the men represented in the painting. They are personnel of the 19th Bomb Group. Shown in the foreground
(*left to right*): Lt. Henry Godman, Sgt. Meyer Levin, Sgt. James Halkyard, Lt. Joseph
Bean (*kneeling*), Capt. Colin Kelly, Sgt. John Wallach, Sgt. J. W. DeLahanty, Pfc.
Robert Altman, Pfc. W. Money (*on bumper*). Shown on the Jeep (*left to right*):
Lt. William Bohnaker, Lt. Edward Jacquet, Lt. Harl Pease Jr., Lt. Jack Heinzel,
Lt. Don Robins (*kneeling*).

This book is dedicated to the memory of

Lt. Col. Kirtley J. Gregg, USAAF
(December 25, 1901–April 21, 1942)
and
Col. William R. Burt, USAF (Ret.)
(August 4, 1914–January 8, 2001)

The inability of an enemy
to launch his air attack on these islands
is our greatest security.

—Douglas MacArthur, commanding general,
U.S. Army Forces in the Far East, to visiting British
admiral Tom Phillips during a conference chaired
by Adm. Thomas Hart, Manila, December 5, 1941

Contents

DECEMBER 8, 1941

Foreword

My first contact with the author was in 1977 when he wrote me while researching his book *Doomed at the Start*. We corresponded over the next ten years, his letters asking many questions about my experiences as an Army Air Corps pursuit pilot stationed in the Philippine Islands at the start of World War II, and my answers describing my memories of the events and of my experiences during that chaotic period in our nation's history. We became friends during the ensuing years and this new book is a greatly expanded report of the events of those early days of World War II in the Philippine Islands, which he has aptly entitled *December 8, 1941: MacArthur's Pearl Harbor.*

A person's view of any unusual event, chaotic occurrence, accident, or, as in this case, the opening days of a war, is myopic, limited to what he heard or saw. Other people on the scene will report what they saw, and each person will offer a different version of what happened. Confusion so often prevails.

I was particularly impressed with the meticulous way in which Bill Bartsch conducted his research. He has taken all the stories related by the many participants, checked and cross-checked them, and pieced together the big picture of the opening day of World War II in the Philippine Islands. The result was surprising even to me—who was there in what I thought was the very center of all that was happening. So much more was going on, on a much grander scale than I had seen or imagined.

In *Doomed at the Start,* Bill told the graphic story of the pursuit pilots in the Philippine Islands during the military buildup that took place the preceding year and the day of the Japanese strike on Clark Field, December 8, 1941.

In this volume he traces the evolution of our military and national policies toward defending American interests in the Philippines in the face of mounting evidence of Japanese military expansion in the Southwest Pacific, using national and international sources of information. He also covers the development of Japanese plans to expand into the Southwest Pacific and to neutralize American military forces in the Philippines.

In October, 1940, I was a first lieutenant assigned to the 20th Pursuit Squadron—a trained, combat-ready unit of our regular Army Air Corps—stationed at Hamilton Field, California. We had just begun receiving new aircraft, the Curtiss P-40, the latest pursuit plane in the Army Air Corps's inventory, and were in the midst of a transition and training program on the new aircraft.

One Monday morning, we received orders to prepare for transfer to an overseas station. We were given just six days. After feverishly preparing our squadron for deployment in the short time allotted, we departed Hamilton Field the following Friday afternoon for San Pedro Harbor and embarked the next morning on the USS *Washington*. It was then that we learned we were en route to the Philippine Islands as the first aerial reinforcements for the U.S. Army's Philippine Department.

We arrived in Manila thirty days later and were assigned to Nichols Field. In contrast to the urgency that accompanied our departure from Hamilton Field, we found a complacent, business-as-usual atmosphere. We soon settled into the routine of life in the tropics: working during the morning hours and taking time off during the hot, humid afternoons. At that time, the U.S. Army Air Corps in the islands consisted of the 4th Composite Group, with the 3d Pursuit Squadron flying P-26A aircraft at Nichols Field, the 28th Bomb Squadron flying B-10Bs, and the 2d Observation Squadron flying O-19Es and O-46As at Clark Field. These squadrons were not fully manned, and they were flying old, obsolete aircraft that had been transferred from squadrons in the states as those squadrons received newer aircraft models. None of these 4th Composite Group squadrons had any combat capability. My squadron was given eight of the 3d Squadron's P-26As and we flew those eight aircraft more in the next thirty days than all the P-26As in the islands had been flown during the whole preceding year.

Two weeks later, the 17th Pursuit Squadron—another trained, combat-ready outfit—arrived from Selfridge Field. Shortly after Christmas, we received P-35As that had been sold to Sweden and then comandeered and sent to us to use as interim aircraft. In February, 1941, the 4th Composite Group received twenty-four new pilots, and thirty-nine more arrived in May—all recent graduates of stateside flight training schools. Six members of the February group and eight of the May arrivals were assigned to my 20th Pursuit Squadron.

Families were evacuated back to the states, and our training took on added emphasis as we began working a full-day schedule. Our work hours and training load became more purposeful as we began a program to train these new pilots who had come straight from flight school with no pursuit experience and no training in combat tactics. A shipment of new P-40B aircraft arrived in April. My squadron received the first twenty-five of the new planes, but we were forced to ground them for two months while we awaited the arrival of Prestone coolant for the engines. The 20th was moved to Clark Field when new construction was begun to upgrade the facilities at Nichols.

When our squadron commander was transferred to the 4th Composite Group headquarters in early May to serve as operations officer, I was selected to replace him. I was immensely proud to have been chosen and was determined to be the very best commander possible. Our training program intensified as we received another shipment of ninety-six new pilots in June, twenty of whom were assigned to my squadron. That brought us up to our authorized wartime strength of forty-eight pilots.

As the situation deteriorated and war with Japan seemed more imminent, our training became even more concentrated as we took steps to prepare Clark Field for the expected enemy attack. We built revetments around the airfield's perimeter to protect our aircraft, and we dug slit trenches for the protection of our personnel. I became concerned when I learned that the guns on our new planes had never been fired and that there was a severe shortage of .50-caliber ammunition for aircraft machine guns in the islands. None could be spared for gunnery training, and, as a result, none of the guns in the brand-new P-40s assigned to our pursuit squadrons were ever fired before the war started.

While we were concentrating on our training and preparing for a war that appeared ready to erupt at any moment, we knew little of the planning and strategic decisions being made by Gen. Douglas MacArthur's U.S. Army Forces in the Far East (USAFFE) headquarters and by the Far East Air Force (FEAF) headquarters in Manila, or for that matter by the War Department and the Air Staff at Army Air Forces headquarters in Washington. However, we occasionally received hints of intensive diplomatic and strategic moves taking place at the national level. In late November, we were ordered to stop all training flights and to assume a constant state of readiness for an expected attack by Japanese planes based on Formosa. We continued in that advanced state of readiness until the Japanese attacked on December 8, 1941.

The author, after conducting exhaustive research, has woven with extraordinary talent the strands of diplomatic, national, and international activity as they influenced the development of military strategy on both the Japanese and American sides. Within this framework he then covers the experiences of individuals caught up in the consequences of the decisions made at higher levels. It is a fascinating bit of history.

JOSEPH H. MOORE
Lieutenant General, USAF (Retired)
Former Commander, 20th Pursuit Squadron
Clark Field, Philippines, December 8, 1941

Preface

Twenty-five years ago I began research on the experiences of army pursuit pilots of the Far East Air Force in the ill-fated Philippines campaign of 1941–42. After thirteen years of effort, the results were published as *Doomed at the Start* in 1992. During my research I also became familiar with the experiences of the bomber crews who shared Clark Field with the pursuit pilots on December 8, 1941, as well as those of the men operating the radar unit at Iba to the west, providing early warning of the approaching Japanese attack force on that fateful day.

In 1951, Walter D. Edmonds related the story of what happened at Clark Field on December 8 in his now-classic book on the Army Air Forces in the air war in the Philippines and Dutch East Indies in 1941–42. However, his account of the December 8 attack was, in many ways, not complete. He excluded the experiences of the Air Warning Company operating the radar unit at Iba, for example, as well as those of the antiaircraft regiment and two tank battalions that attempted to engage the Japanese bombers and fighters over Clark Field. The experiences of the Japanese airmen who carried out the attack were also left out of the account. Furthermore, Edmonds made no attempt to present the air defense planning for the Philippines or to discuss the decisions made by the War Department and Army Air Forces headquarters in 1939–41. The latter helps us understand *why* the December 8 disaster occurred. Equally excluded were the plans and strategies of the Japanese high command in Tokyo and on Formosa for the attack on the Philippines.

In pointing out these gaps in Edmonds's presentation, I do not mean to criticize him. His guidance from the Army Air Forces called for him to write an account of the personal experiences of the men involved in the first six grim months of the air war in the Southwest Pacific. He was not asked to consider higher-level War Department and Army Air Forces headquarters planning and decision making or to include the Japanese side of the story. Edmonds, after all, was a well-known novelist, not a military historian. His highly readable account was my introduction to the subject and triggered my desire to know more.

Another person was responsible for developing my interest in what was happening at Army Air Forces headquarters that set the stage for the events in the Philippines on December 8, 1941. In the early 1980s, retired colonel William R. Burt was researching prewar Army Air Forces and War Department records at the National Archives to provide documentation for the book he was planning on his experiences in 1940–41 as an aide to Maj. Hoyt S. Vandenberg in the Air Corps's Plans Division. Colonel Burt's focus was on tracing Vandenberg's efforts in early 1941 to introduce an aerial defense system for the Philippines based on lessons learned from the Battle of Britain. When he learned of my research on the events of the December 8 attack, he invited me to join him as he dug through the records of the Army Air Forces' headquarters and the War Department's War Plans Division in an effort to track the developments that ultimately led to the July, 1941, decision to build up army airpower in the Philippines, but with an emphasis on offensive, rather than defensive, capabilities. Colonel Burt wanted to trace the Philippines' aerial reinforcement question all the way up to the president's level in seeking to identify why Vandenberg's proposal to develop a Battle of Britain–type defense was rejected.

Yet, if I related the story only from the American side—however comprehensively—I would be leaving out the Japanese and the answers to several important questions. How was the decision to attack the Philippines as the opening phase of their so-called southern operations made? What strategy did they formulate to that end? What roles did the Japanese army and navy air forces play in the strategy that was developed? What were the experiences of individual Japanese in the air attack that opened hostilities?

In seeking to answer these questions, I was obliged to examine Japanese-language sources, given the paucity of information on this subject in English. Fortunately, I had already corresponded with most of the surviving Zero pilots regarding their personal experiences in the Clark and Iba attacks, as well as the preparations they had made on Formosa for the aerial offensive. This information was augmented by published personal accounts in books and magazine articles that were translated for me. To understand the course of development of the southern strategy, especially the Philippines operation, I referred to published Japanese accounts, including the relevant volumes of the official war history, the *Senshi Sosho*.

This, then, is an account of what transpired on both sides from late 1940 through the traumatic attack on the Philippines—a commonwealth under the United States—that opened the Pacific War. It is told from three levels of experience: that of individual combatants following orders from above; of staff officers in the Philippines, on Formosa, and in Japan and Washington planning and supporting the projected combat operations; and of the senior military officers and political leaders in Washington and Tokyo who made the decisions that led to the opening of hostilities in the Pacific and the Far East on December 8, 1941. As in *Doomed at the Start,* however, the focus of the story is on the first level: the junior officers and enlisted men ordered to train for and engage in combat. They were on the receiving end. In the case of the Americans, it was their first experience of war.

Ironically, there has been a deluge over the past sixty years of books (not to mention two movies) covering every conceivable aspect of the Pearl Harbor attack that occurred just ten hours earlier, yet no one to date has given any book-length treatment to the "other Pearl Harbor," as I term it, despite its significance to the course of the Pacific War.

Was the December 8 attack on Clark and Iba Fields really another Pearl Harbor? If judged on the *nature* of the attack, the answer is no. It was not a "sneak attack," as was the one on Hawaii (although it was originally planned for just three and one-half hours after the Pearl Harbor attack in the hope that word would not get to the Philippines in time to alert the Americans there). However, in terms of its *strategic significance,* the answer is a resounding yes! As planned by the Imperial Navy, the Pearl Harbor attack was purely a one-shot operation aimed at preventing the U.S. Pacific Fleet from intercepting Japanese invasion forces assigned the mission of seizing the resource-rich colonies of British Malaya and the Dutch East Indies. The loss of five battleships (but no aircraft carriers) at Pearl Harbor had little impact on the course of the Pacific War and cannot be equated with the near-destruction of the largest force of warplanes outside the United States—on which hung the fate of Washington's deterrent strategy against Japan, or, failing that, of effective opposition to Japanese operations against the Philippines.

Acknowledgments

This story is mainly based on the personal experiences of hundreds of individuals, Americans and Japanese alike. Fortunately, I started my research in the mid-1970s, when most were still alive. I thus was able to learn of their prewar and December 8 experiences via correspondence, telephone conversations and interviews, narratives they prepared for me, and diaries and prewar correspondence to their families they shared with me. This direct input expanded my knowledge of their activities and those of other participants derived from interviews conducted in 1945 for the preparation of Walter D. Edmonds's 1951 epic, *They Fought with What They Had*. Almost all of them are gone now.

Singling out particular individuals from this group for an expression of gratitude is not easy. On the American side, the help of individual pursuit pilots has been acknowledged earlier in my book *Doomed at the Start,* but for the bomber crews included in this volume, I would particularly like to thank Ray Teborek, Ed Jacquet, Edson "Spon" Sponable, and Mel McKenzie for long years of assistance rendered in relating their experiences. Among the Japanese participants in this story, I am particularly indebted to the late Hideki Shingō for four years of faithful responses (up to the time of his death in 1982) to my unending questions about Zero fighter preparations and operations during the attack he led on Clark Field.

An important contribution was made by all those Far East Air Force personnel who did not survive the war, having been killed either in combat or in accidents or having lost their lives in prisoner of war (POW) camps or on hell ships taking them to Korea, Formosa, or Japan. Some were able to relate their experiences to fellow POWs who interviewed them for the record, such as Capt. William Priestley, who managed to bury his material (later exhumed) before he himself perished on a hell ship. Others sent letters home detailing their activities and feelings in 1940–41. They would be surprised to know how their innermost thoughts have now become part of history! I am highly indebted to their families for sharing such personal material with me.

In this connection, I would particularly like to thank the widow (since deceased), daughter, and grandson of Maj. Kirtley J. Gregg for making available his correspondence to his wife that opened the door for me on the goings-on at the staff level in the Philippine Department Air Force (PDAF) and its successors from November, 1940, to November, 1941. Additional inside information on PDAF activities in 1941 was gleaned from letters of Gregg's colleague, Maj. Bill Maverick. I am indebted to his daughter, Laura Maverick Griswold, for making copies for me. By the same token, I would like to thank Miriam Pachacki, widow of 28th Bomb Squadron pilot Ted Fisch, for making available copies of all of his 1941 letters to her that capture his feelings and those of the other frustrated senior pilots in his squadron.

For the inside picture of what was going on in Washington at Army Air Forces headquarters in 1940–41, I owe a debt of gratitude to Col. William R. Burt, USAF (Ret.). He developed my interest in understanding how the decisions of the Air Staff and Maj. Gen. Henry H. "Hap" Arnold, with whom he was serving at the time, shaped the future for air force officers and men stationed in the Philippines. It was with great sadness that I learned he passed away just before I completed this manuscript.

Others to whom I am indebted were facilitators in my effort to gain knowledge of the events covered rather than direct or indirect contributors of personal experiences. In this category, I wish to acknowledge the assistance of Duane Reed at the Air Force Academy Libraries for years of unstinting support in obtaining documentary material in the Academy's collections, particularly on the Air War Plans Division's Air Annex to the 1941 Victory Program. Just as they did for *Doomed at the Start,* Edward Boone and his successor, James Zobel, archivists at the MacArthur Memorial in Norfolk, Virginia, responded to my every request for the USAFFE records kept in its archives. The George C. Marshall Foundation in Lexington, Virginia, proved to be an unexpectedly valuable source of records not found elsewhere, and I am indebted to its staff for help in obtaining them during my visit there. Roger G. Miller, a historian at the Air Force History Support Office, helped me with useful background information on General Brereton, a personage in whom we share great interest. Another historian with a keen interest in the U.S. Army in the Philippines, Richard B. Meixsel at James Madison University, unfailingly responded to particular queries I had about the prewar situation at Clark Field, including the base's physical characteristics.

On the Japanese side, I am grateful to my old friend Osamu Tagaya, one of the foremost authorities on Japanese aerial operations in World War II, who during the last year of manuscript preparation came up with additional Japanese-language materials, published and unpublished, that filled the gaps in my efforts to present the Japanese experience and helped me resolve many vexing questions on the subject. I am also indebted to Masaru Nakai (the real name of Shirō Mori) for giving me permission to use material from his book gleaned from interviews that gave me an inside picture of planning for the Philippines attack conducted at the Eleventh Air Fleet headquarters on Formosa. Similarly, I am grateful to Masa-aki Shimakawa, since deceased, for allowing me to quote extensively on his experiences in training for and participating in the Clark Field attack as related in his published wartime memoir.

I wish to thank Lt. Gen. Joe Moore, another old friend, for writing the foreword to this book and for sharing with me his 1941–42 Philippines experiences over the past twenty-five years. I am indebted to Gene Eisenberg and artist John Shaw for the cover illustration. Gene commissioned the work and has kindly given Texas A&M University Press permission to use the painting for that purpose. Thanks are also due to Dale Wilson for his meticulous editing of the manuscript for publication.

PROLOGUE

"Seize This Golden Opportunity!"

When Gen. George C. Marshall reported to his office in the Munitions Building in Washington, D.C., on September 1, 1939, after being sworn in as the new chief of staff of the U.S. Army, a memo prepared eleven days earlier by the War Plans Division (WPD) was waiting on his desk. It called for Marshall to make an immediate decision on future military policy toward the Philippines, a commonwealth of the United States since 1935. Three options were identified: Was the War Department to recommend that the United States maintain the status quo, withdraw its forces from the Philippines to a new defense line in the Pacific along the 180th meridian (area of Midway Island), or reinforce the islands in order to maintain a dominant U.S. position in the western Pacific?[1]

But Marshall's mind was focused on the situation in Europe rather than in the Pacific. The startling news that day was that Germany had suddenly launched a massive invasion of Poland. For the present, the question of defense of the Philippines would have to take a backseat to the more pressing concerns Marshall faced at home in the wake of Hitler's lightning attack.

The WPD—the War Department's influential "think tank"—wanted a decision on the Philippines question that would resolve its long-running disagreement with the Navy Department on the issue. Under War Plan Orange, which constituted the agreed upon army-navy position on Philippines defense in the event of a Japanese attack, the Philippine garrison's mission was to hold Manila Bay as a base for the U.S. Pacific Fleet and a relief force.[2]

The navy had traditionally sought a strong naval base in the Philippines and the army defenses necessary to protect it, but the army regarded the islands as a military liability rather than an asset and for that reason opposed reinforcing them—particularly after the 1934 U.S. decision to grant the Philippines independence in 1946. The army's policy was to maintain its existing strength, especially for providing protection for the harbor defenses in Manila Bay, but "to go to no further expense for permanent improvements unless thereby ultimate savings will result."[3]

Beginning in the mid-1930s, defense of the Philippines meant primarily *air* defense, given the rapid growth of airpower as a destructive force in warfare during the period. The army had maintained a composite group of warplanes for Philippines defense since 1920, but by the 1930s its aircraft were primarily discards from Hawaiian and continental U.S. air bases that were becoming increasingly obsolete at the end of the decade. A War Department Air Board created in March, 1939, to recommend fundamental policies governing the tactical and strategic use of the Army Air Corps had concluded in its report six months later that "no further consideration" should be given to strengthening the Philippines' air defenses given the existing national policy of no modernization or expansion of army forces there. It accepted that the Japanese could seize the Philippines before the United States could reinforce the garrison. Consequently, it deemed the Philippines garrison "a sacrifice force" and declined to study air defense requirements for the islands.[4]

While the Air Board report conformed to the War Department's position on defense of the Philippines, the Plans Division of the Office of the Chief of the Air Corps (OCAC) was heading in an opposite direction. On September 1, 1939—just before the release of the Air Board's report—Lt. Col. Carl A. Spaatz, the division chief, signed a memorandum for the attention of Maj. Gen. Henry H. Arnold, the Air Corps chief, that developed an ambitious airpower strategy for the Philippines diametrically opposed to War Department policy and the position of the Air Board, three of whose five army members were War Department staff officers.[5]

The author of this heretical report was a forty-year-old West Point graduate brought to the Plans Division in the summer of 1939 by Spaatz following completion of his one-year assignment to the Army War College (AWC) in 1938–39. Spaatz had given Capt. Hoyt S. Vandenberg an assignment that summer to prepare one of five secret studies for determining Air Corps requirements in connection with implementation of the Air Board's report. In preparing his report, Vandenberg drew on the work he had done at the AWC as the Air Corps member of the committee on military policy in the western Pacific, with special emphasis on the Philippines. He had succeeded in including a provision in the report that called for reinforcing the Philippines garrison by two groups of bombers, two groups of attack aircraft, two groups of pursuit planes, and one group of reconnaissance aircraft. Vandenberg maintained this radical fivefold increase in the army's

Philippines air strength would be implemented as soon "as the present expansion program makes the airplanes available."[6]

In the memo he was preparing for Spaatz's signature, Vandenberg proposed even heavier reinforcements than he had included in the AWC report. He now specified two *heavy* bomb groups and three *medium* bomb groups to go along with the two groups of pursuit aircraft. Including the supporting reconnaissance planes, the total worked out to 393 aircraft.[7]

Vandenberg's defense plan was visionary, but incapable of being implemented in 1939 or even 1940. Against his requirement for sixty-eight of the new B-17 heavy bombers, there were only *fifteen* in the entire Air Corps at the time, and it would be a year before the last of the next batch of B-17s off the assembly line—seventy-seven B and C models—was delivered. To obtain the 160 fighter planes needed to fill the two pursuit groups would have required the transfer of three-fifths of the available P-35s and P-36s in the Air Corps's arsenal.[8]

Moreover, the young staff officer's plan was not based solely on defensive considerations. For the first time, an Air Corps planner put forward a proposal for using the Philippines as a base for strategically *offensive* operations. His defense plan was only the first step in building up an offensive force capable of striking industrial targets on the Japanese home islands from Luzon in the northern Philippines, the focus of his unprecedented proposal. By his reasoning, the threat of bombing attacks from the Philippines would force Japan to acquiesce to U.S. national policies in the western Pacific, which was the political objective of his plan.

Like most of his Air Corps superiors, including Arnold, Frank Andrews, and Ira Eaker, Vandenberg was a disciple of the strategic offensive use of airpower—through employment of bombardment aircraft—rather than its use primarily in defense or in support of army ground operations, roles favored in the traditional thinking of most War Department officers that still influenced WPD decisions.[9] In recognition of this soon-to-be accepted view, the 1939 Air Board report had included as one of army aviation's major missions "offensive strikes" carried out at great distances from their bases.

Vandenberg's plan for offensive operations called for the transfer to the Philippines "upon the threat or outbreak of hostilities" of an additional six heavy bombardment groups and six supporting long-range reconnaissance squadrons to provide the striking power he estimated was needed to inflict adequate damage on targets in Japan. There was no specified timeframe in his plan, but he must have realized that his total requirements of B-17s (eight groups of 26 aircraft each, or a total of 208, plus 64 for long-range reconnaissance) to meet both the defensive and offensive needs of his plan would have completely outstripped expected production of B-17s through 1940.[10]

Vandenberg's plan for offensive operations was predicated on the availability of heavy bombers with an effective operating radius of two thousand miles in order to reach industrial targets in southern Japan from a base on Luzon and return. However, the latest model long-range heavy bomber available to the Army Air Corps in late 1939—the Boeing B-17C—lacked the range to meet Vandenberg's requirements. With a twenty-five-hundred-pound bomb load, the B-17C could not reach targets beyond 750 miles.[11] However, given the rapid technological changes occurring in the aviation industry at the time, Vandenberg undoubtedly anticipated the maximum range of the army's long-range bombers would soon be extended. Yet, even including the Consolidated XB-24, which was then on the drawing board, this assumption would prove unrealistic: no subsequent B-17 or B-24 models carrying an adequate bomb load ever attained an operating radius of two thousand miles.[12]

Arnold submitted the Vandenberg plan to the War Department along with four other secret studies in October, 1939, but it was relegated to the WPD's files. It languished there until late February, 1940, when the WPD resuscitated its aerial defense component. Over Marshall's objections in a meeting of the Joint Army-Navy Board on February 21, navy members had argued for even a minor increase in air reinforcements to deter Japan from attacking the Philippines, thus obliging Marshall to look further into the question. The army chief of staff asked the WPD to prepare a new study on the subject, which led to the resurrection of Vandenberg's 1939 plan.[13]

Two days after the board meeting, the WPD proposed the deployment of 441 aircraft to the Philippines, a number exceeding Vandenberg's ambitious total of 393. Following Vandenberg's thinking, the WPD included B-17s in the defense plan for the first time—although only one group of the heavy bombers rather than the two Vandenberg had sought. But it would cost $22.9 million to upgrade Luzon's airfields adequately to accommodate the proposed air force, $3.8 million to transport the aircraft to the Philippines, and $99.3 million to replace the wing in the United States from which the aircraft would be drawn. Due to the heavy cost, the WPD recommended that Marshall inform the navy it would be "impracticable" to increase army aviation strength in the Philippines unless national policy required the reinforcement of the islands on a scale as required and indicated in the WPD proposal. At a time when Congress was cutting War Department budget requests, Marshall decided to drop the proposal and so informed his counterpart, Adm. Harold R. Stark.[14]

In rejecting the WPD's proposal for reinforcing army aviation in the Philippines, Marshall had in effect finally taken action, albeit only partial, on the WPD's August, 1939, memo on military policy toward the Philippines. Option 3—modernization and augmentation of the Philippines defenses—was rejected due to cost considerations. However, he made no formal decision on the other two options presented to him: maintain the status quo or withdraw American forces from the Philippines and establish a defense line along the 180th meridian.

On May 6, 1940, Marshall stamped on the 1939 memo that it had been noted, but he took no further action. By not making a decision on the two remaining options, he was maintaining the status quo by default. He was preoccupied with far graver matters than the Philippines' defenses, though. Just one month earlier, German troops had invaded Denmark and Norway. The so-called phony war in Europe was once again a shooting war.

It was still morning on Saturday, July 27, 1940, but Prime Minister Fumimaro Konoe was already beginning to sweat in his heavy frock coat as he stood rigidly facing the chair in front of the gold screen at the far end of the vast room. Three days earlier, the temperature in Tokyo had hit 97.5 degrees Fahrenheit, breaking the all-time heat record set in 1886. Then, as the clock in the Imperial Palace's twenty-four-*tsubo* Room One–East indicated 10 A.M., Konoe and eleven other formally attired men bowed deeply toward the emperor's empty chair and took their assigned seats.[15]

Occupying the two raised upper chairs in the long room, resplendent in their bemedaled uniforms, were two royal princes, Field Marshal Kotohito Kan'in and Adm. Hiroyasu Fushimi, the chiefs of staff of the army and navy sections of Imperial General Headquarters (IGHQ), respectively.[16] Next to them were their principal assistants: Lt. Gen. Shigeru Sawada and Vice Adm. Nobutake Kondō, the vice chiefs of staff.

On the government side, the forty-nine-year-old Konoe had been accompanied to the meeting by Foreign Minister Yōsuke Matsuoka; Teruoki Hoshino, minister without portfolio and director of cabinet planning; and the war and navy ministers, Lt. Gen. Hideki Tōjō and Vice Adm. Zengo Yoshida. Of the nine participants, six were from the military. The remaining three persons present were secretaries: two military officers and a civilian. In their frock coats, Prince Konoe and the other three civilians contrasted sharply with the eight military officers dressed in formal uniforms.

Premier Konoe—a distant relative of the emperor—had convened this "Imperial Headquarters–Government Liaison Conference" five days after being appointed a second time to form a cabinet following the fall of his predecessor, Adm. Mitsumasa Yonai. The new Konoe government and the military supreme command were meeting to seek formal agreement on a matter of grave national importance: the future direction of Japan's foreign policy.[17]

Three days earlier, Konoe and his key cabinet members had agreed amongst themselves on a more active orientation for the empire's foreign policy, focused on a "new order" for East Asia. The IGHQ came to the conference prepared to present a paper spelling out what the military wanted in the way of action to give substance to the general parameters developed by Konoe's cabinet. Similarly, the government had prepared a parallel paper detailing domestic policies it proposed to follow for which it would be seeking IGHQ's endorsement. The IGHQ's policy paper, entitled "Outline of Main Principles for Coping with the Changing World Situation," was to be presented first. It represented the joint position of the army and navy sections of IGHQ. The army's draft version had been discussed and approved in meetings between the two sections the previous week.[18]

In an extremely solemn atmosphere, seventy-five-year-old Prince Kan'in started the proceedings by presenting the supreme command's paper. The army chief of staff was fully conversant with its contents, but he had merely endorsed it when the General Staff's First Bureau (Operations) submitted it to him. The paper was prepared by a nucleus of middle-grade officers in the department's Operations Section working in collaboration with the staff of the War Ministry's Military Affairs Bureau. The Operations Section group was the decision-making cadre of the army General Staff, and typically originated and pushed forward military strategies and policies the chief of staff invariably endorsed.[19]

As spelled out in the document, Japan was to take advantage of the opportunity presented to it by the sudden shift in the war situation in Europe. Faced with the possibility of German influence expanding rapidly in the area south of Japan following the Third Reich's defeat of France and the Netherlands and the probable fall of Great Britain, Japan needed to take decisive action to ensure the availability of the natural resources there for its own needs. The Dutch, British, and French colonies all looked ripe for the picking. "Never in our history has there been a time like the present," an army draft of the document circulated on July 4 maintained. On June 25, former army minister Shunroku Hata had exhorted his staff members to "seize this golden opportunity! Don't let anything stand in the way!"[20]

The policy paper under discussion provided that Japan would "cope with the changing international situation" by "expediting the settlement of the China incident" (which had been dragging on since 1937) and "solving the Southern Area problem when a favorable opportunity is presented." Specifically, if the situation in China remained unsettled, Japan would push the implementation of the new policy up to the point of "engaging in hostilities with a third power." On the other hand, if world developments were favorable (and China subjugated), "force of arms" could straightaway be used to solve the Southern Area "problem."[21]

After Prince Kan'in's presentation and explanation of the "Outline of Main Principles," a frank exchange of views between the government and IGHQ representatives took place. The army and navy chiefs of staff argued that Japan should sever itself from its economic dependence on Britain and the United States and become self-sufficient in natural resources by incorporating all of the southern area east of India and north of Australia and New Zealand into a "Greater East Asia Co-Prosperity Sphere." "It would be exceedingly difficult to find another opportunity like today's to accomplish this objective," they maintained at the meeting. Diplomatic efforts to attain this goal would be tried first, but if they failed, Japan would use force. To reinforce Japan's international position for this purpose, "we must strengthen our ties with Germany and Italy and readjust our relations with the Soviet Union," they asserted.[22]

Despite the risk of war with the United States and Great Britain that such a policy ran, Konoe did not offer any objections. Shy and effete in appearance, self-restrained and refined in manner, he listened to all sides of a question, but when he made a decision, he stuck tenaciously to it. Moreover, he had already made up his mind in this case following an earlier briefing on the content of the IGHQ proposal. Prince Konoe was opposed to war, but he had committed himself earlier to a "new order for East Asia" and the supreme command's proposed actions fitted such a foreign policy strategy. In actuality, the convening of this liaison conference was just a formality, since all parties concerned were familiar with the content of the proposed policy change and basically agreed with it.[23]

The meeting adjourned at 11:30 after the conferees reached complete agreement on the policies described in both papers. The "general prescription" for a southern advance would soon gain the approval of the emperor, who would subsequently need to endorse decisions derived from the guidelines spelled out in the "Outline of Main Principles." Chief among them were the incorporation of the Dutch East Indies, British Malaya, and other "resources-rich" areas in Southeast Asia into the "New Order," and the development of formal ties with Germany and Italy.[24]

When Lt. Tamotsu Yokoyama reported in at the Yokosuka Naval Air Station, seventy miles south of Tokyo, on Friday, June 29, 1940, he sensed immediately that his assignment there was going to be something special. The thirty-year-old crack pilot, a three-year veteran of the air war over China, had received orders to go to Yokosuka the day before, but had been left completely in the dark about the nature of his new duties.

Upon landing at Yokosuka, he had noticed strange new planes on the airfield. Shortly after Yokoyama's arrival, Lt. Manbei Shimokawa briefed him on the situation. It turned out that Shimokawa, who graduated from the Etajima Naval Academy and flying school a year ahead of Yokoyama, was the flying leader of the twelve mysterious aircraft Yokoyama had seen on the field. Six of them were to be turned over to Yokoyama for transfer to the China front, and the other six entrusted to another China veteran, Lt. Saburō Shindō. Shimokawa explained that the new plane, designated the twelve *shi* experimental carrier fighter, was still in the test stage and that there was no literature available on how to handle it. Nonetheless, it was to be placed into operational use as quickly as possible. Shimokawa would help Yokoyama familiarize himself with his new steed prior to departure for China.[25]

When Yokoyama went out to the field to look over this highly secret machine for the first time, he was immediately struck by its appearance. He was particularly impressed with its retractable landing gear and long, closed canopy over the cockpit, as well as its streamlined fuselage. It bore little resemblance to its antecedent, the Type 96 carrier fighter he had been flying over China. The Type 96 was a mid-1930s design featuring fixed landing gear and an open cockpit. The new fighter also packed a wallop: a 20-mm cannon in each wing, and two 7.7-mm machine guns in the engine cowling, as compared to the Type 96's two 7.7-mm machine guns.

The grandson of a samurai warrior, Yokoyama was excited to know that he would be the *first* to fly the new weapon operationally. He immediately devoted all his efforts to learning the handling characteristics of the new fighter. Taking it up into the sky over Yokosuka, he soon discovered that it had a phenomenal rate of climb, could do 330 miles per hour compared to the Type 96's 270, and was fantastically maneuverable.

Yokoyama also discussed with Shimokawa the organization of the unit he would lead to China. He was given his pick of the pilots assigned to the Yokosuka flying group (*kōkūtai*) to form his section of six pilots, plus supporting ground crew.

Yokoyama and his new charges daily practiced all kinds of aerial exercises until they reached a level of familiarity with the new fighter sufficient to take it into combat operations. Then Yokoyama received orders to lead his six-plane formation to the Japanese Naval Air Force's base at Hankow, China, with stops at Ōmura on southwestern Kyushu and Shanghai.

On Monday, July 15, Yokoyama elatedly headed his ship down the runway at Yokosuka, the other five pilots trailing in a line behind him. After takeoff, they linked up with a Mitsubishi G3M twin-engine bomber that would lead them as far as Shanghai on the long flight to Hankow.[26] The Mitsubishi Type 0 Carrier Fighter, Model 11, was at last operational—with all the portents that development would carry for Japan's southern operations. Eighteen hundred miles to the south, U.S. Army pilots based on the island of Luzon in the Philippines, felt no similar elation regarding the equipment *they* were flying. It was common knowledge that the 4th Composite Group was the dumping ground for aircraft that had reached the end of their combat usefulness in the continental United States and Hawaii. Some of the group's planes were so obsolete that they even carried the prefix "Z" in their designation, including the Thomas-Morse ZO-19E observa-tion biplane dating from 1931 and the Keystone ZB-3A bomber of 1930 vintage.

It was not just the antiquity of the aircraft assigned to him that both-ered the 4th Composite Group's commanding officer, Col. Lawrence Churchill, but also the personnel situation. The group's three tactical squadrons were grossly understrength in flying officers due to a net loss of pilots following recent personnel transfers between the United States and the Philippines. On top of that, too many of the pilots being sent to the group lacked adequate flying experience. As Churchill's predecessor had argued a year earlier, the Philippines was *not* a good place to train students just out of flying school. They needed a year or so of tactical flying state-side before going overseas. Flying was difficult enough in the Philippines, where airfields were few and primitive, and the weather was subject to rapid, frequent, and violent changes—all of which contributed to a high risk of accidents involving inexperienced pilots.[27]

And then there was the feeling of isolation. The Philippines were over seven thousand miles across the Pacific from the United States, with the means of travel—except for exceptional trips on Pan American's China Clipper flying boat—surface transports that slowly carried personnel back and forth on just four voyages a year.

"We are out of the world here and spend our time watching our friends to the north," Churchill's predecessor wrote Air Corps headquar-ters in Washington in August, 1939.[28] It was a description that summed up the feelings not only of army air officers assigned there but all of the U.S. Army personnel in the Philippine Department at a time when the Japa-nese were rampaging in China, creating apprehension among their neigh-bors about their intentions.

To Colonel Churchill, who had arrived only five month's earlier to assume command of all Army Air Corps operations in the Philippines, the needs of the 4th Composite Group—the only aerial defense force that stood between Japan and the Philippines—were being neglected by Washington. "Please don't forget we still belong to the Air Corps," he felt obliged to remind his superiors there in March, 1940.[29]

Dissatisfaction with the state of aerial defenses in the Philippines in 1940 was not limited to Churchill and his 4th Composite Group pilots. The commanding general of the Philippine Department was equally dis-mayed with conditions and intended to do something about the situation.

Like his predecessors, Maj. Gen. George Grunert did not feel constrained by long-standing War Department policy not to upgrade defense capabilities or to adhere to War Department plans for the islands.[30]

Grunert was fifty-nine years old when he assumed command on May 31, 1940, but he did not regard his new assignment as the capstone of his long army career, as did so many other senior officers assigned to the Philippine Department as they neared retirement. He had come up through the ranks as an enlisted man and knew the Philippines well from two earlier tours there as an officer. He impressed Francis Sayre, the U.S. high commissioner to the Philippines, with his work habits. "He takes his coat off and gets right down to the problems at hand and is a hard and constant worker," Sayre wrote to General Marshall in Washington. Furthermore, "He has good judgment and a lot of sound common sense."[31]

Scarcely a month after assuming his new responsibilities, Grunert began bombarding Marshall and the army adjutant general in Washington with requests for materiel and men with which to make his command a real deterrent to any Japanese who might have aspirations for the islands. In July alone, he wrote the War Department five times and Marshall twice regarding his needs. Two communications specifically addressed the air defense situation.

In a letter dated July 10, Grunert painted a dismal picture of his anti-aircraft defenses. "We are dependent, except for a few pursuit planes, upon ground installations for defense against aircraft," he informed the War Department. Nevertheless, the means available "are wholly inadequate, materiel is obsolescent in design, hopelessly antiquated and outmoded, and no match for the speed and maneuverability of modern aircraft." He concluded with a request that "steps be taken immediately to correct the deplorable condition" of the islands' antiaircraft defenses.[32]

The "few pursuit planes" to which Grunert referred were twenty-eight Boeing P-26A Peashooters, the survivors of thirty-four shipped to the Philippines in 1937–40 from Selfridge, Barksdale, and Wheeler Fields, where they had entered service in 1933. His other "combat" planes consisted of seventeen 1934-vintage Martin B-10B twin-engine bombers passed on to the Philippine Department in 1937–39 from March, Hamilton, Mitchel, and Langley Fields, where they were no longer wanted. Grunert also had fifteen observation planes, including ten Douglas O-46As, dating from 1935, and five Thomas-Morse O-19Es—redesignated as ZO-19Es. The latter were antiquated biplanes that had entered service in 1931 and were particularly scorned by army pilots in the Philippines. Supplementing this "force" of sixty combat aircraft were three noncombat types used for transport, messenger, and rescue duties: a former bomber, the Keystone ZB-3A, a 1930-vintage Douglas OA-4 amphibian, and a newer (1938) OA-9 amphibian.[33]

On July 22, Grunert wrote that he "considered it his duty" to describe to the War Department the aircraft and air personnel situation—which Colonel Churchill had first drawn to the attention of Air Corps headquarters in March. He then requested that his obsolete pursuit, bomber, and observation aircraft be replaced with "modern type aircraft" and that he be provided an additional ten light bombers particularly adapted to attack missions. If it were not possible to furnish all of the modern aircraft requested, he wanted a minimum of three each of the new pursuit, bombardment, observation, and light bombers being added to the Air Corps's inventory so that he could at least "acquaint" his pilots with them. Grunert pointed out that the three tactical squadrons of his 4th Composite Group were grossly short of flying personnel. The 3d Pursuit Squadron had 9 of its 21 authorized pilots, the 28th Bomb Squadron 7 of 14, and the 2d Observation Squadron 10 of 15. He asked the War Department to provide him the 39 additional Air Corps officers he needed to meet the minimum required for air operations.[34]

By the end of August, Grunert had received no reply to any of his missives to Washington. Impatient for a response, he fired off another letter to Marshall on September 1, this time drawing the chief of staff's attention to the atmosphere of "fear and defeatism" that pervaded the islands. Although he was doing his best to bolster morale, he wrote, "the lack of an announced policy, backed by visual evidence of defense means and measures, works against me."[35]

In Washington, the absence of any response to Grunert's pleas did not reflect sloth on the part of the War Department, but rather its need to analyze his requests in detail and check against availabilities before making a formal reply. On July 29, the WPD completed a study on Grunert's request for upgrading his antiaircraft defenses and recommended to Marshall that the Philippines be provided "as rapidly as possible modern weapons . . . to enable it to conduct a reasonable defense." Marshall accepted the recommendation on August 5, but Grunert was not immediately informed of the favorable decision.[36]

Nevertheless, Grunert's request for modern aircraft and more pilots met with the disapproval of the Army Air Corps chief, General Arnold, to whom it had been referred by the WPD on August 5. No modern aircraft should be sent as replacements, he argued, although three B-18s and four O-49s would be added to Grunert's force by July 1, 1941, which in effect partly responded to his minimum request for a handful of recent-model planes with which to familiarize his bomber and observation pilots. Grunert's most critical need—modern fighters with which to replace his antique P-26As—was turned down flat, with no consideration for even a few for pilot familiarization. Finally, Arnold informed the WPD in his August 8 response that no additional Air Corps personnel could be assigned to the Philippine Department without "depleting tactical units being formed or by taking them from pilot training activities." He concluded by recommending "no change in policy" with regard to aviation in the Philippine Department.[37]

Accepting Arnold's position, the War Department on September 12 returned Grunert's July 22 communication to him with an indorsement stating that his request for modern aircraft and additional pilots "had not been favorably considered."

Concerned about Grunert's likely reaction to this rejection and non-response to his other requests, Marshall himself wrote the Philippine Department commanding general on September 20. While expressing his understanding of Grunert's difficulties, he pointed out the problems he faced in meeting the needs of all bases in a time of rapid expansion and lagging materiel production. He wanted Grunert to know that he was "alert to your dilemma" and would do "my very best in every way to help you out." Indeed, with regard to Grunert's problem of an obsolete pursuit force, Marshall was considering ways he could get around the aircraft availability problem that was the basis for Arnold's rejection of Grunert's request. "I am going into the matter of planes very carefully with General Arnold to see whether we might get you some modern pursuit at an earlier date than planned," he informed Grunert in his September 20 reply.[38]

Eleven days before Marshall's response to Grunert, the War Department received yet another request from the Philippine Department commander, this one by radiogram. Grunert informed Washington that he had set up a "makeshift aircraft warning service" using available army and navy personnel plus Philippine Army and constabulary men, but that he really needed "a fully-equipped aircraft warning service company, including the newly developed aircraft detectors." He wanted to know the War Department's policy and plans for providing an air warning service, which he realized was the third essential component—along with an interceptor pursuit force and antiaircraft weapons—for conducting an effective aerial defense of the Philippines. The radiogram was passed to the WPD for action the same day it was received.[39]

Meanwhile, the Japanese army and navy General Staffs had been engaged in heated discussions following the approval of the new southern-oriented foreign policy at the July 27 liaison conference. Each had different views on how to proceed with preparations for a southern advance. For the army, totally involved with the war in China and preparations for defending against the Soviet Union to the north, planning for southern operations meant a complete shifting of gears. However, the new direction posed no problem for navy's planners, who as early as 1936 had initiated planning for just such a contingency. Indeed, some high-ranking naval officers resented the army's preemption of their own long-established ideas along those lines.[40]

Meetings between the top officials of the War and Navy Ministries and the army and navy General Staffs had skirted the important areas of difference. Unlike the army's, the navy's thinking went beyond what was stated in the army-inspired "Outline of Main Principles." Its great preoccupation was the likelihood of war with the United States if Japan stationed troops in French Indochina as the first step in implementing the southern advance. If the United States responded by introducing a more rigid embargo against Japan than was then in effect, Japan would need to seize the Dutch East Indies to secure its oil needs and accept the risk of war with the Americans as a consequence. Under such a scenario, carrying out the southern operation would lead to the basic issue "whether we like it or not," of "survival of the Empire."

Occupation of the Dutch East Indies—coveted for its rich oil resources, the life blood of the navy's ships—had been included in Japanese naval plans much earlier, before any chain of events leading to such a step had been contemplated. At section chief conferences of the naval General Staff in April, 1940, following Germany's invasion of Norway and Denmark, the chiefs had argued that "the time has come to occupy the Dutch East Indies." Planning accelerated after Hitler's invasion of the Benelux countries and France the following month, and the Fourth Fleet was ordered to move to Palau preparatory for an invasion of the Dutch East Indies. In mid-May the Navy Ministry carried out extensive map exercises for southern operations. Even though the exercises led to the conclusion that invading the Dutch East Indies would lead to war with the United States and Great Britain and Japan's defeat if such a conflict lasted more than a year, the Navy Ministry—except for Minister Yoshida—and the naval General Staff endorsed the plan. When Britain, France, and Germany failed to take advantage of the fall of the Netherlands to violate the Dutch East Indies' neutrality, the navy lost its excuse for sending its Fourth and Second China Fleets to occupy the islands for Japan. Nevertheless, the navy secretly continued to develop its plan. The main concerns now were time and the acquisition of the resources needed to complete preparations for war with Great Britain and the United States.[41]

During this period, the army was less concerned with the implications of the southern operation for war with the United States than with planning for the implementation of the first step for that operation as visualized in the "Outline of Main Principles": the acquisition of bases and stationing of troops in French Indochina. It had the backing of the navy, which favored such a move because it would provide a "great strategic advantage" in a war against the United States and Great Britain. The emperor, after a briefing by Army Minister Tōjō, authorized the plan as a step in implementing the southern advance policy, while accepting that the policy risked war with the British and Americans.[42]

On August 27, Maj. Gen. Kyoji Tominaga, chief of the army General Staff's First Bureau (Operations), accompanied by midlevel officers, left Tokyo for Hanoi with a draft agreement for the Vichy French authorities in Indochina. Two months earlier, Tominaga had insisted on invading French Indochina and now he was looking for a pretext to use military force, although IGHQ and the government had decided to employ diplomacy to gain their objectives. Following France's surrender on June 17, the foreign minister began seeking an agreement with French authorities on Japan's demand for a halt to transiting war materiel to Chiang Kai-shek's forces through Indochina, but now the army General Staff also wanted the right of passage for Japanese troops headed to the China front and permission to establish air bases in the region.

Threats from Tominaga when Governor General Jean Decoux refused to negotiate in the absence of instructions from the Vichy regime failed to intimidate the French official, who finally commenced negotiations when he received the information he sought from his government. On September 3, the governor general presented Tominaga a draft pact that the Japanese government and IGHQ accepted the following day. It provided for the stationing of a maximum of twenty-five thousand Japanese troops in northern Indochina and the use of three air bases there.[43]

The Japanese "Outline"-prompted efforts to speed up resolution of the "China incident" through diplomacy and military threats in early September, 1940, were meeting with equal success on the military front. The navy's newly operational Zero fighter was striking such terror in the hearts of Chinese pilots that they declined to engage in combat with the speedy, nimble aircraft, even as Chiang's capital of Chungking was being bombed to ruin.

Then, on September 13, frustrated by their inability to lure Chinese fighters out of hiding, the two commanders of thirteen Zeros escorting twin-engine Mitsubishi G3M bombers on yet another raid on the undefended Chinese city attempted a ruse. After departing with the bombers following the 2 P.M. raid, Lt. Saburō Shindō and Lt. (j.g.) Aya-o Shirane turned and led the new carrier fighters back to Chungking, where they found twenty-seven Russian-built Polikarpov I-15 and I-16 fighters that had taken to the sky after the raid. Diving down on their unsuspecting prey, the thirteen Japanese shot twenty-two of the hapless Chinese down in flames. Two others crashed into mountains trying to escape the Zeros, and three others bailed out in terror before being attacked. Within just thirty minutes, the entire Chinese force had been destroyed without the loss of a single Japanese plane.[44]

In Tokyo the following day, the Japanese engineer who designed the Zero fighter attended a ceremony at the Navy Ministry. Standing behind Mitsubishi Heavy Industry Company executives in the red-carpeted room, Jirō Horikoshi felt deep pride as a commendation signed by Vice Adm. Teijirō Toyoda, chief of the Naval Bureau of Aeronautics, was read to those present. After citing the unprecedented September 13 victory, Toyoda expressed the navy's gratitude for Mitsubishi's "meritorious work" in completing "this excellent fighter" in such a short development period.[45]

Wiping their sweaty brows in the unseasonable heat, the thirty-seven-year-old design chief and his Mitsubishi colleagues extended congratulations to each other. It was the first that Horikoshi had heard of his brainchild's performance over China. The existence of the new fighter was being kept secret from the Japanese public and the outside world.

Also secret were the proceedings of another Imperial Headquarters–Government Liaison Conference held on September 19 at the Imperial Palace. Unlike the July 27 conference, however, this one had been convened in the emperor's presence and thus was termed an Imperial Conference (*gozen kaigi*). At these special meetings called and presided over by the emperor, final decisions made at the liaison conferences were formally presented to allow him, as a constitutional monarch, to sanction them but not have to bear responsibility for them. As noted in the emperor's definitive biography, it was a legal device for transforming "the will of the emperor" into "the will of the state."[46]

With Emperor Hirohito seated before the gold screen mounted on a dais at the far end of the room, listening but making no comment as the formality of the proceedings indicated, Foreign Minister Matsuoka began presenting his proposal for a Tripartite Pact between Japan, Germany, and Italy. Seated with him on the government side were Prime Minister Konoe, Finance Minister Isao Kawada, Planning Bureau Director Hoshino, War Minister Tōjō, and Navy Minister Koshirō Oikawa, who had replaced Zengo Yoshida on September 5 due to Yoshida's illness and associated opposition to the proposed pact. Princes Kan'in and Fushimi, joined by their vice chiefs, again represented IGHQ.

Not only Yoshida, but also the commander in chief of the Combined Fleet, Adm. Isoroku Yamamoto, and former premier Mitsumasa Yonai, along with a number of other high-ranking naval officers, were against Japan joining the proposed military alliance with Germany and Italy. The new navy minister was no great supporter, either, but he was hesitant to speak up. However, other midlevel naval staff officers, as well as the naval General Staff, supported Matsuoka's proposal, as did the army and the prime minister himself. During the conference, Matsuoka acknowledged that Japan would automatically be obliged to enter the European war on the German and Italian side if the United States also took part. He argued that signing the pact would deter the Americans from encircling Japan and entering the war, as it would show Japan's firm stand. He had earlier secured German and Italian acknowledgment of Japan's sphere of influence in establishing the "new order" in Greater East Asia, including Manchukuo and China at the core, plus the former German mandates in the Pacific, French Indochina, French Pacific islands, Thailand, Malaya, Borneo, the Dutch East Indies, Burma, and India.[47]

Yoshimichi Hara, the president of the Privy Council, remained skeptical. In his view, signing the pact would have an opposite effect on the United States from that asserted by Matsuoka. The Americans would not feel intimidated, but rather would react by increasing their economic pressure on Japan by tightening the embargo and stepping up aid to China. Prince Fushimi, the navy chief of staff, also expressed reservations. He agreed to go along with the proposed alliance only if "every conceivable measure" was taken to avoid war with the United States and the southern advance was "carried out by peaceful means."[48]

However, when Hara—apparently speaking on behalf of the emperor—gave his reluctant approval to the pact as necessary for a continuation of the China incident and in view of the changing international situation, full agreement at last was reached. Hara concluded by expressing hope that the Japanese and Americans would not clash in the near future.

The Japanese government signed the Tripartite Pact on September 27, and Hirohito issued an imperial rescript to the nation that same day: "The great principle of the eight corners of the world under one roof (*hakkō ichiu*) is the teaching of our Imperial ancestors. We think about it day and night. Today, however, the world is deeply troubled everywhere and disorder seems endless. As the disasters that humankind may suffer are immeasurable, we sincerely hope to bring about a cessation of hostilities and a restoration of peace, and have therefore ordered the government to ally with Germany and Italy, nations which share the same intentions as ourselves."[49]

The previous afternoon, Japanese troops had landed on the coast of French Indochina and advanced unopposed to Haiphong, preparatory to taking up their new station in the north. The final pact between the governor general and the Japanese government signed on September 22 provided the Japanese four air bases in northern Indochina and the right to deploy six thousand troops to guard them, and authorized up to twenty-five thousand troops to be stationed in the same province while awaiting passage to the China front.[50]

With the occupation of northern Indochina and the backing of all-conquering Germany and its Italian ally under the Tripartite Pact, conditions for continuing the southern advance looked promising for Japan. The big question concerning the president of the Privy Council and many high-level naval officers was how the Americans would react to these hostile actions.

PART I

"By God, It Is Destiny That Brings Me Here!"

Washington, Tokyo, Manila, and Singapore:
September, 1940–June, 1941

REACTING TO THE JAPANESE INCURSION into north-

ern French Indochina, Secretary of State Cordell Hull called a press conference on September 23, 1940. In understated diplomatic language, Hull
indicated the State Department's "disapproval" of the upsetting of the status
quo in Indochina, which he alleged had been accomplished "under duress."
Three days later, President Roosevelt retaliated by ordering a complete
embargo—effective October 16—on the export of scrap iron and steel
except to Great Britain and Latin America, a step viewed as the strongest
sanction to date against Japan, which was almost totally dependent on the
United States for such material for its war machine.[1]

Although senior War Department officers were equally concerned
about the threat posed by the newly signed Tripartite Pact linking Japan
with Germany and Italy and the Japanese occupation of northern Indochina, they did not view such developments as necessitating a revision of
long-standing War Department policy toward defense of the Philippines.
On October 10, the War Plans Division chief addressed a memo to Chief
of Staff George C. Marshall recommending that the United States adopt
the second of three alternatives regarding defense of the Philippines: withdrawing American forces from the islands as soon as possible and establishing a new defense line along the 180th meridian, just west of Midway
Island. The three options in the policy paper were the same as those put
forward on August 21, 1939, that Marshall had failed to act upon.[2]

Secretary of War Henry L. Stimson met with Marshall in mid-October
to discuss the question of the defense of the Philippines. The seventy-
three-year-old Stimson, who in 1927–29 served as governor general of the
Philippines, had only recently been appointed to his new post, and thus
was a newcomer to War Department policy toward the islands. However,

his views on the subject were similar to those of his naval counterpart, Navy Secretary Frank Knox, with whom he had discussed the Far East situation on October 2. Stimson and Knox agreed that "soft methods would be no good at this time" for dealing with Japan. Abandoning the Philippines ran counter to their views on the Far East situation. Knox and his Navy Department were particularly concerned about the weak defenses for the naval base at Manila, where the Asiatic Fleet would be stationed beginning in mid-October after shifting from Shanghai.[3]

As early as February, 1940, the navy had argued—in opposition to the War Department position—that "even a minor increase" in army aviation strength in the Philippines would suffice to deter Japan from attacking the islands. Under pressure from both the navy and Maj. Gen. George Grunert in the Philippines to provide some of the modern fighter planes Marshall had promised the Philippine Department commander in early October, Marshall and Stimson developed a plan to take over a shipment of sixty Seversky EP-1 pursuits that had been contracted for Sweden and send forty-eight of them to the Philippines instead. On October 18, Stimson secured the president's approval of the plan, despite the fact that the decision ran counter to national policy not to reinforce the Philippine garrison.[4]

But who would fly the aircraft, which had been redesignated Republic P-35As, a modification of the ships currently assigned to the Army Air Corps? In October, 1940, there were only nine pursuit pilots stationed in the Philippines. The Army Air Corps chief, Maj. Gen. "Hap" Arnold, initially resisted Marshall's call for two of his few stateside-based pursuit squadrons to be transferred to the Philippines, but on October 16 reluctantly directed his own Plans Division to prepare a plan for assigning pilots from two pursuit squadrons in the General Headquarters Air Force (GHQAF) to the Philippine Department. Arnold in turn asked Marshall to authorize a compensatory increase in GHQAF strength. Two days later, the 1st Pursuit Group's 17th Pursuit Squadron, based at Selfridge Field, Michigan, and the 35th Pursuit Group's 20th Pursuit Squadron, based at Hamilton Field, California, were ordered to depart for Philippines duty.[5]

On October 24, the New York Times gave the precedent-breaking decision to send aerial reinforcements to the Philippines front-page billing. Two squadrons of planes and "about 320" officers and men were cited as being transferred. That same day, the Washington Post reported that Navy Secretary Knox, in response to the question of whether the Philippines could be defended, had snapped, "We can defend anything!"[6]

To Hanson W. Baldwin, the New York Times's respected military correspondent, the decision to send aerial reinforcements to the Philippines represented a major shift in American military strategy toward Japan. He surmised that the government wanted to send a signal to Japan in response to its alignment with the Axis powers that America did not intend to remain militarily weak in the Philippines.[7]

Unknown to Baldwin and the public, however, the action was more a one-shot operation than a sign of a policy shift regarding the defense of the Philippines. Navy planners that month had begun drawing up a study on U.S. military strategy that concluded the United States must prepare for land operations across the Atlantic and remain "on a strict defense" in the Pacific. The War Department accepted the navy's argument on November 13, and it became known as "Plan Dog."[8]

In Tokyo, Japanese naval planners met on October 1 to discuss preparations for mobilization for war with the United States. As far back as 1936, the navy had been planning for an advance to the south and had resolved to wage the war it concluded would eventuate should Japan take such an action, anticipating a U.S. embargo that would lead to a Japanese invasion of the Dutch East Indies to fulfill the nation's oil needs. Following completion of the mobilization plan, the naval General Staff secured the approval of Navy Minister Koshirō Oikawa to commence preparing for war, setting the end of March as the target date for completion of the mobilization effort.

But Adm. Isoroku Yamamoto, commander in chief of the Combined Fleet, was alarmed by the headstrong decision of the Navy Ministry and the navy's General Staff. Although he had no planning responsibilities, the strong-willed Yamamoto insisted that map exercises be held for southern operations and, when the General Staff hesitated, he took it upon himself to assemble officers from the staff and the Naval War College to conduct them. On November 30, Yamamoto presented the results to the navy chief of staff: the seizure of the Indies would trigger a war with the United States and Great Britain as well as with the Dutch East Indies. It was the same finding reached by a similar map exercise conducted by the Navy Ministry six months earlier.

Yamamoto concluded that since Japan had no chance to defeat the United States, it should abandon all plans to attack the Dutch East Indies. His argument was to no avail: the naval General Staff intended to push ahead with its preparations for war with the Americans and British, including procuring the materials it would need, requisitioning ships, and equipping airfields and ports.[9]

Although he was not privy to such secret moves, Adm. Thomas Hart, the commander in chief of the U.S. Asiatic Fleet, now based in Manila, proved to be a good judge of Japanese intentions, drawing on his long experience dealing with the Japanese military during his previous tour in China. On November 13, Hart wrote the chief of naval operations, Adm. Harold Stark, in Washington that "there seems no doubt Japan is resolved on a southward movement—employing force if necessary. Her most important early objective is the oil supply from the East Indies."[10]

Over at his office at Number 1, Calle Victoria, in the old walled city of Manila, retired general Douglas MacArthur also anticipated a southern move by the Japanese that would result in war with the United States. A former U.S. Army chief of staff, MacArthur had—since October, 1935—been serving as military adviser to Philippine president Manuel Quezon. However, as he implied in an interview on December 17, 1940, with the chief of *Time*'s China Bureau, he was holding himself in readiness to command the American expeditionary force when war broke out and he was called to assume that responsibility by the War Department. He told Theodore H. White that he was "building a new Philippine Army for President Quezon and if he had enough time, he could make it into a fighting force." More than 125,000 Filipinos already had received six months' training under MacArthur's direction. They had, MacArthur maintained, "changed the entire strategic plan in this part of the world." In a less formal meeting with White at MacArthur's penthouse in the Manila Hotel later that day, the general, carried away by his own perceived role in history, exclaimed, "By God, it is destiny that brings me here!"[11]

Unknown to the young and impressionable *Time* bureau chief, MacArthur's credibility with the person who most counted—President Quezon—had been falling during the past year. Quezon was becoming increasingly skeptical of MacArthur's grandiose plans for developing a Philippine Army and defense of the Philippines. He felt his sixty-year-old military adviser had duped him into spending too much money on a defense plan of dubious effectiveness and was seeking a means to send the general back home if possible. MacArthur's objective, as suggested in his *Time* interview, apparently was to saddle the United States with permanent responsibility for the Philippines' defense, despite the fact that such a position was contradictory to U.S. national policy toward the island country.[12]

Also impervious to MacArthur's rhetoric, stemming from a forty-year acquaintance with his family, Admiral Hart took exception to MacArthur's claim that the Philippine Army "would soon be prepared for anything the Japanese could throw against them." So did General Grunert, on whose shoulders rested the U.S. Army's responsibility for the defense of the Philippines. Grunert had written to Marshall on November 2, 1940, informing the chief of staff of the true situation of the Philippine Army. It was, he wrote, "capable only of defensive operations involving little or no maneuvering," and then only if "closely supervised by U.S. Army officers." Half of the Filipino officers lacked any active duty training, and almost 15 percent had no training whatsoever. In mid-November, the

WPD concluded that the Philippine Army "would be inadequate" in the event of war.[13]

Rebuffed by the Navy Ministry and the naval General Staff in his argument against precipitating war with the United States by invading the Dutch East Indies, Admiral Yamamoto in mid-December, 1940, urged full preparation for the apparently inevitable clash. In any such planning, he maintained, "it would be best to decide on war with America from the beginning and to begin by taking the Philippines, thereby reducing the line of operations and assuring sound execution of operations."[14]

To support the main objective of seizing resources in the southern area, Yamamoto had begun to plan for an audacious operation: a surprise attack on the U.S. Navy's Pacific Fleet at Pearl Harbor in the Hawaiian Islands. Simultaneously with the attack on Pearl Harbor, he urged that the navy should carry out "a forestalling and surprise attack on enemy air forces in the Philippines and Singapore." In early January he warned that if the navy declined to attack Pearl Harbor on the grounds that it would be "too risky," Japan faced the possibility that the Americans "would dare to launch an attack upon our homeland to burn down our capital and other cities." His views proved to be prescient, as discussions in Washington between Roosevelt and his top military planners only days later would show.

Nonetheless, the naval General Staff opposed Yamamoto's Hawaii operation, seeing it as a drain on scarce resources needed for carrying out the planned southern operations. He was regarded as overstepping his responsibilities, which were the conduct of operations, not war planning. His Combined Fleet was expected to carry out missions planned and approved by the naval General Staff.[15]

Not only the navy, but also the army had begun preparing for southern operations. In October, the army General Staff ordered the South China Army to begin training three of its divisions for tropical combat, particularly the conduct of an amphibious landing. In mid-December it established the secret Formosa Army Research Department at Taipei, and charged it with carrying out research and surveys deemed essential for landing operations in the south, including combat methods for tropical warfare. The geographic compass of the investigative work was to include the Dutch East Indies, British Malaya and Borneo, Guam, French Indochina, Thailand, Burma—and the Philippines.[16]

In Tokyo, the army General Staff's Operations Section was deep in planning for military operations in the south. Its activist chief on December 4 had urged the chiefs of other sections to be ready to conduct southern operations by the spring of 1941, but the War Ministry disagreed, arguing that it was "impossible to decide definitely on southern operations," and that only *preparations* for such possible operations should be advanced by that time.[17]

In Washington, President Roosevelt was concerned about the possibility of "sudden and simultaneous action by Germany and Japan against the United States," in the words of Army Chief of Staff George C. Marshall. Roosevelt had called upon Marshall to participate in a conference on January 16 with himself, Secretary of State Hull, Secretary of War Stimson, Navy Secretary Knox, and Chief of Naval Operations Stark. During the meeting, Roosevelt focused on the Far East situation and "our attitude towards Japan." He wanted priority given to the continued supply of materiel to Great Britain, but due to the constrained U.S. supply situation that meant little would be left over for a conflict with Japan. Therefore, the president directed, "we should stand on the defensive in the Pacific." With the Philippines in mind, Roosevelt noted that the army "should not be committed to any aggressive action until it was fully prepared to undertake it." The navy, meanwhile, should consider "the possibility of bombing attacks against Japanese cities."[18]

Roosevelt had called his top military planners together in order to develop an agreed-upon position on a global strategy prior to engaging in secret talks with a high-level British military delegation that would arrive in Washington later that month. He expected that the British would be pressing for assistance not only for the home islands but also for their Far East colonies, now threatened by Japanese operations pushing southward. However, in conformity with the president's global position, Marshall directed that the War Department would initiate no operation "which might tend toward committing us to a major effort in the Pacific."[19]

In talks with the British delegation that began on January 29 and lasted for two months, the two sides agreed that the overarching objective should be to defeat Germany and Italy first, then Japan. However, as anticipated, the British also wanted the Americans to underwrite the defense of their main Far East base in Singapore to ensure the security of the British Commonwealth. However, the U.S. Army members participating in the discussions believed that acceptance of this position was contrary to their instructions and would constitute "a strategic error of incalculable magnitude." The common basis of American strategy was security of the North Atlantic and the British Isles. It was England's responsibility to take care of its own interests elsewhere.[20]

While the "Germany first" policy served as the cornerstone of America's military strategy, defense of the Philippines was not to be totally downplayed. On February 25, Marshall decided to send thirty-one Curtiss P-40Bs—the most modern pursuit aircraft in the Air Corps's arsenal—to the Philippines in an effort to modernize Grunert's interceptor force, along with a squadron of B-18 medium bombers. The decision followed his statement to his staff officers that "if we had a single squadron of modern planes in the Philippines, it would at least give the Japanese something to think about." While not mentioning his decision in a meeting the next day with Roosevelt, Marshall must have had it in mind when he suggested to the president "the possible desirability of our following a more active course in the Philippines in the way of military preparations which would be impressive to the Japanese military authorities."[21]

On March 28, Marshall was the guest of honor at a dinner at the Mayflower Hotel hosted by Air Chief Marshal Hugh Dowding, the celebrated architect of the Battle of Britain. Detached from Royal Air Force (RAF) command on November 17, 1940, Dowding arrived in Washington on January 5 as a member of the visiting British Purchasing Commission. However, it soon transpired that the War Department had additional secret plans for him: evaluating arrangements for the aerial defense of the United States and making recommendations for improvement.[22]

Unlike most of his War Department staff, Marshall had developed an understanding of airpower's potential as a crucial weapon of war beginning in August, 1938, when he was head of the WPD. His appreciation of airpower's role expanded through his close association with Brig. Gen. Frank Andrews, the assistant chief of staff for operations and training (G3), following Andrews's appointment to the post in August, 1939. In late June, 1940, while proposing changes in the 1939 Air Board report, Marshall maintained that "air power must be free of geographic restrictions, not tethered for use as a fixed defense of the continental U.S." Four months later, following the Battle of Britain, he called for additional changes to the report so it would reflect that "the most effective strategic defense was a systematic aerial offense against the enemy's territory and its air power."[23]

Yet, while Marshall espoused the concept of airpower as a strategic offensive weapon, he was not yet prepared to project airpower in the defense of American interests in the Far East. Thus, in February, acting on the WPD's recommendations, he rejected General Arnold's request to develop facilities on Pacific islands "to meet a possible future requirement for the movement of long range bombardment aviation across the Pacific" on the grounds that neither the War Department nor the Navy Department had any plans for operations that would require the movement of army bombers to the Far East.[24]

While offensive airpower was being ruled out for the Philippines, the order to transfer modern P-40s to the islands suggested that limited improvements in aerial defensive capabilities were being condoned as an exception to the long-standing War Department policy of no reinforcement for the Philippines. Furthermore, in response to his request of March 6, Grunert was to have his 4th Composite Group upgraded to an air force, with Brig. Gen. Henry B. Clagett assigned as its commander.[25]

On the afternoon of April 2, the commander in chief of British land and air forces in the Far East, Air Chief Marshal Sir Robert Brooke-Popham, arrived unexpectedly by flying boat at Cavite Naval Base just outside Manila from his headquarters in Singapore. The purpose of his trip to the Philippines was to follow up at field commander level the just-concluded ABC-1 talks in Washington. However, he had not made any previous arrangements for the visit with the U.S. commanders in Manila. His meetings with Grunert, MacArthur, and Hart represented the first contact between British and American forces in the Far East. During the three days of discussions, all of the Philippines defense plans were explained to him, and the question of the U.S. Navy's use of Singapore as a base was raised.[26]

Following Brooke-Popham's visit, a delegation of U.S. army and naval staff officers traveled from the Philippines to Singapore in an attempt to reach an agreement with British and Dutch commanders on an operational plan covering the use of their forces in the theater in the event of war with Japan. At the conclusion of the discussions, which extended from April 21–27, a secret draft agreement was drawn up. The agreement recognized that while the global objective would be the defeat of Germany and its allies, the goal in the Far East would be to sustain economic pressure on Japan until the Associated Powers (America, Britain, and the Netherlands) could assume the offensive. The main interest in the Far East would be the "security of sea communications" and "the security of Singapore." An "important subsidiary interest" was to be able to operate air forces from bases in Luzon.

The draft agreement recognized that, given the lack of valuable economic resources in the Philippines, a Japanese attack on the islands would be solely for strategic reasons, that is, to eliminate the U.S. naval and air force threat to Japan's southward movement. Opting for a unified command with regard to air forces, it recommended that Brooke-Popham in Singapore assume strategic direction of all air forces in the Far East in order to "extract full strategic advantage" from airpower in the theater, including the mounting of air operations "against Japanese-occupied territory and Japan herself." By virtue of its offensive possibilities, the "defense of Luzon should be strengthened," including through "maintenance of a bombing force."[27]

When Grunert first heard of the conference recommendations, he felt that defense of the Philippines had received short shrift. Furthermore, in forwarding the conference report to Washington, he noted that building up Philippines defenses, including airpower, in order to mount offensive actions against the Japanese was contrary to his present mission. His views were similar to those reached by army and navy planners in Washington, who subsequently informed the British military mission that the United States intended to continue its policy of not reinforcing the Philippines "except in minor particulars."

On April 30, a draft of the new Rainbow 5 War Plan was submitted to the Joint Board for approval. Based on the ABC-1 talks with the British concluded on March 29 in Washington, its stated objective was the defeat of Germany and its allies, with policies aimed at ensuring the security of the Western Hemisphere and the United Kingdom, and the "ultimate security" of the British Commonwealth. With regard to the tasks of U.S. forces in the Far East, the army would defend the Philippine coastal frontier, but no army reinforcements would be sent there. The navy would provide support to the land and air forces defending British and Dutch territories in the Far East, raid Japanese sea communications, and destroy Japanese forces. The Manila-based Asiatic Fleet would support the defense of the Philippines as long as that defense continued, then that of the Malay Barrier, but there were no plans for its reinforcement either. On May 14, Rainbow 5 was approved by the Joint Board and forwarded to President Roosevelt for his endorsement.[28]

In Tokyo, indications of growing cooperation between American, British, and Dutch East Indies commanders were being reflected in Japanese military planning in mid-April. On April 17, the navy and army sections of Imperial General Headquarters formally approved plans to establish the Greater East Asia Co-Prosperity Sphere as a means of strengthening national defense. Diplomatic means would be used to attain this objective, but force would be applied if Japan's existence were threatened by a British-Dutch-American embargo or the Americans—acting alone or with the British, Dutch, and Chinese—strengthened their encirclement of Japan to the extent it was "no longer bearable for self-defense."[29]

The Japanese evidently were privy to the highly secret talks conducted in Singapore during April between the Americans, Dutch, and British. On the first day of the talks, Japanese newspapers reported that the United States, Great Britain, China, British India, Australia, and the Netherlands Indies had concluded a military pact to strengthen their defenses in the Far East and to oppose Japan's southward advance. Agreement was allegedly reached for Brooke-Popham to assume command of combined land and air forces, while Admiral Hart would command naval forces, with the headquarters of both in Singapore.[30]

In Manila, indications of Japan's Far East intentions reinforced MacArthur's conviction that the Japanese were preparing to move south. He proposed that the War Department establish a new American military command to oversee all army operations in the Far East, and that he be appointed to lead it, citing the example of Brooke-Popham's responsibility for all British land and air forces in the Far East.

The head of the WPD, Brig. Gen. Leonard T. Gerow, informed the army chief of MacArthur's proposal, but recommended against creating such a command on the grounds that the British example was not comparable to their own, the forces of the former being "scattered in the Far East," whereas U.S. forces were concentrated in the Philippines. Instead, he recommended that MacArthur be given command of the Philippine Department if he were recalled to active service.[31]

Marshall, however, rejected Gerow's recommendation. In a letter to MacArthur on June 20, he indicated that both he and Stimson were concerned about the situation in the Far East and that some three months earlier they had decided MacArthur was the "logical selection" to head a Far East army command "should the situation approach a crisis." While the time for such a decision had not yet arrived, Marshall wrote that Stimson had authorized him to inform MacArthur that the secretary of war would recommend his appointment to such a post "at the proper time."[32]

CHAPTER 1

"They Have Really Ripped the 17th All to Hell"

Sweat was already seeping through Maj. Kirtley J. Gregg's khaki chino shirt on a humid Manila morning in early December, 1940, as he limped over to the line of stubby fighters in front of Hangar 2 at Nichols Field. Accompanied by his youthful pilots, the commanding officer of the 17th Pursuit Squadron was going to inspect the eight Boeing P-26As turned over to the squadron following its arrival from the United States the previous week.

"Those look like the P-26As we had in Panama and Hawaii," he remarked to 2d Lt. George Armstrong. Then he discovered that one of them was the *same* bird he had flown in 1934–35 while serving with the 17th Pursuit Group at March Field in California: it had his initials painted on the inside left panel! His former steed no longer sported the brown, blue, and yellow color scheme of his old 95th Squadron and its kicking-mule emblem on the fuselage, but its brightly painted dark blue body and yellow wings were still striking.[1]

To Gregg, the situation was ludicrous. He had come seven thousand miles to the Philippines as commander of the renowned 17th Pursuit Squadron with nineteen newly assigned pilots, and they were being given the same pursuit ships that had been flown at March and Barksdale Fields in the mid-1930s. Back then they had been fresh-from-the-factory, top-of-the-line aircraft—the Army Air Corps's first all-metal, low-wing fighter. Now they were totally obsolete relics of the past, dumped on the Philippine Department after having outlived their usefulness stateside and in Hawaii. But it was just a temporary situation, Gregg reasoned, until the new Republic P-35As that had come with them on the USAT *Etolin* were uncrated and assembled.

GROUND CREWMEN RECONDITION A P-26A AT NICHOLS FIELD FOLLOWING ITS TRANSFER
FROM THE 3D TO THE 17TH PURSUIT SQUADRON CA. JANUARY, 1941. NOTE THE RECENTLY
ASSEMBLED P-35AS IN THE BACKGROUND. PHOTO COURTESY GEORGE H. ARMSTRONG.

The Philippine Department workday ended at 11:30. Gregg headed
back to the tent that served as the 17th Pursuit Squadron's headquarters. It
was pitched near rows of other tents in which his enlisted men were now
relaxing after the day's exertions. "Tent City" had been set up at Nichols
just before the squadron's arrival on December 5 to accommodate its 157
enlisted men. The airfield's only vacant barracks had been assigned to the
men of the 20th Pursuit Squadron following their arrival in Manila on
November 23, twelve days ahead of the 17th. It was a raw deal for his men,
but at least it was the dry season. Gregg knew that when the rains arrived
in a few months the nearby Paranaque River would overflow its banks and
flood the low-lying area occupied by his men.[2]

With no matters remaining to take care of, Gregg left his headquarters
tent and made his way to the main gate. There he hailed a taxi and
instructed the driver to take him to the Army and Navy Club, just a few
minutes' drive away. Entering his cramped inside room, he plopped down
on the bed. He did not like living at the club, but he had little other option
apart from sharing a house or quarters with another midgrade officer,

which appealed to him even less. The 17th had been ordered to travel to the Philippines without dependents, so he had been obliged to leave his wife Katherine and their two children behind.[3]

Lighting up a cigarette and fixing it in its holder, Gregg sank into solitary thought. Here he was, back in the Philippines again after nine years. He found that little had changed since the early 1930s, when he was a second lieutenant at Clark Field with the 3d Pursuit Squadron serving a standard two-year tour of duty. The easy working hours, the debilitating heat and humidity, and the general torpor that permeated all activity still character-ized an assignment to the Philippine Department. However, there was a big difference at the personal level between 1931 and 1940. He had not walked with a bad limp then. It was

MAJOR KIRTLEY J. GREGG, COMMANDER OF THE 17TH PURSUIT SQUADRON, ON ARRIVAL IN MANILA, DECEMBER 5, 1940. PHOTO COURTESY JAMES HIGHT.

the price he had paid for a foolish decision he made late one evening in October, 1932: A guard had shot him in the hip as he tried to sneak back into his quarters at Hensley Field, Texas, through a back window.[4]

Gregg would not turn thirty-nine until Christmas Day, but he felt much older. When writing to Katherine, he referred to his body as "that crippled carcass." He worried that he was eating and drinking too much. An uncharacteristic layer of fat was developing around the midsection of his slender frame as his weight pushed past its normal 163 pounds, the legacy of three weeks' idleness and heavy meals during the Pacific cross-ing. His teeth were bothering him, too. They were looser than ever, and he dreaded the thought of the annual physical exam for which he was sched-uled the next month. For sure, they were going to insist on yanking at least eight of them. He was also suffering from his usual "cigarette cough," and, since arriving in the Philippines, he had developed loose bowels.[5]

However, it was not his health but rather the situation of his squadron that bothered him the most. The 17th was an elite outfit with a distin-guished history going back to the World War. The Philippine Department seemed to care little about that. Even before they arrived—while still on the high seas—Gregg was ordered to select five of his nineteen pilots for reassignment to other 4th Composite Group squadrons based there. The reasoning was that the group's three tactical squadrons—the 2d Observation, 3d Pursuit, and 28th Bomb—were grossly understrength and needed an infusion of pilots from the Philippines-bound 17th and 20th Pursuit Squadrons. When they arrived on December 5, Gregg lost three more pilots to his former outfit, the 3d Pursuit. It was painful to see his squadron torn apart, even if it was to serve a larger purpose.[6]

Gregg pulled himself up from his bed, showered, changed clothes, and headed down the corridor to the bachelors' dining room for a solitary meal before it closed at 2 P.M. He preferred to eat alone. It was not that he was unsociable. He liked the other officers staying at the club, but to kill time with them meant going to the bar, drinking too much, and rolling for the drinks—all of which could prove to be very expensive on his limited budget.[7]

The sixteen bachelors among the nineteen flying officers Gregg brought with him to the Philippines did not face his solitude problem. They joined together in groups of three and four and rented houses. Although Gregg was self-controlled and quiet by nature, one of his pilots, Grant Mahony, was the other extreme: extroverted, outgoing, uninhibited, and highly observant of human and physical nature. The twenty-four-year-old graduate of the University of California with a B.A. in forestry spent his free time taking in the sights and sounds of his new Asian home that his assignment afforded him.

Barely off the *Etolin* and temporarily accommodated by a group of bachelor officers at Nichols Field, Mahony and fellow flying school Class 40-A classmate Gerald "Bo" McCallum, a Louisiana native, ventured into Manila town to buy bicycles. Mori Bicycle Shop was offering American bikes for $45 and up, Japanese for $20 and down. They opted for Japanese models, but made Mori, a Japanese, install New Departure wheels and brakes and American seats on the frames.[8]

The next day, after duty hours, Mahony climbed on his new steed and maneuvered out to the main road, where he turned right and joined the traffic on the left side, heading south. Riding on the left side of the road instead of on the right was going to be tricky, he figured, but after three weeks of inactivity on the *Etolin,* he was determined to get in some strenuous exercise. It was even harder than he had thought it would be. Vying for position on the road and oblivious to order were slow-moving water buffalo pulling carts laden with produce, sweating Filipino ponies hitched to two-wheeled covered carts and proceeding at a fast trot, little five-passenger Austin and Fiat buses, taxis with their horns blaring constantly, and private cars—a mixed bag of Lincolns, Packards, and Buicks, as well as smaller European models. The motorized vehicles all seemed intent on forcing Mahony off the road. As soon as Mahony cleared Manila, however, the heavy traffic thinned. Filipinos walking along the country road greeted him by yelling, "Hello Joe," which Mahony assumed was the only English they knew. But just short of the town of Cavite, drenched in sweat, Mahony decided to turn around and retrace the five-mile route to his temporary Manila residence.

The next day was Saturday, and Mahony was back at Nichols Field. But he was no longer one of Gregg's boys, having opted on the day of his arrival to transfer with Gerry Keenan and Bob Hanson to the 3d Pursuit Squadron, also based at Nichols. The decision had been forced on him: the alternative was to be assigned to the 28th Bomb Squadron at Clark Field in view of his multiengine time, and he did not want that.

Mahony was watching the men at the air depot break open shipping crates and extract the fuselages of their new aircraft, which had been redesignated P-35As. They still had the big Swedish national emblem— three yellow crowns on a blue background within a circle—painted on their fuselages, confirmation that they had indeed been made for Sweden before being commandeered by the Army Air Corps. Ever curious, the Irish-American from Vallejo, California, climbed inside the cockpit of one of the extricated fuselages deposited on the field and checked out the instrumentation. It was all in Swedish and calibrated in metric. The speedometer measured airspeed in kilometers rather than miles per hour, and the altimeter displayed meters above sea level instead of feet. One instrument was marked *upp* and *ned* for up and down. A caution note read *"lyft här"* instead of "lift here." He could not make out the Swedish word for "bank and turn." Was it *"glidenstragen"* or something like that?

At day's end, Mahony bicycled out the gate onto the narrow gravel road in the marshland that extended along Nichols Field's entire river side, then crossed the wooden bridge over the stinking Paranaque River and continued through the Baclaran barrio, passing flimsy shacks and open-fronted frame-and-bamboo shops before finally reaching the arterial road that would take him north to Manila and his hosts' house.

The next day, Mahony reached a decision about his accommodations. His hosts wanted him to stay with them, but he had found a house only three-fourths of a mile from Nichols Field that three of his 40-A classmates had agreed to share with him. Two were fellow forestry graduates: Bob Hanson from the University of California like Mahony, and Raymond "Lou" Gehrig from Syracuse University. His third housemate, Walt Coss, had an engineering degree from Carnegie Tech. The house was a large, traditional Spanish building located at 3984 Taft Avenue Extension, in the borough of Pasay. Huge paneled doors, instead of windows, were kept open all the time to let in light and air. The landlord had installed heavy iron bars over all the openings to keep out thieves.[9]

Resting that afternoon after moving in, the four new housemates stretched out on the chairs on the front porch and took in the sights and sounds of their new neighborhood. Naked children strolled by on the road, which they used as a sidewalk, as did old women smoking cigars, the lit end inexplicably kept in their mouths. The incessant sound of the hooves of cart-pulling ponies reverberating on Taft Avenue's hard surface reminded them of the ocean pounding against the shore, except when it was mixed with the honking of horns.[10]

This first experience outside their homeland promised to be an exotic one for the four young Air Corps officers.

ROOM 3018, MUNITIONS BUILDING
WAR DEPARTMENT, WASHINGTON, D.C.
LATE DECEMBER, 1940

Major Hoyt S. Vandenberg hurried down the corridor of the War Department's Munitions Building following a staff meeting to his office in Room 3018 of the Plans Division, Office of the Chief of the Air Corps. Stepping briskly through the door, he startled his young aide with a bit of hot news. "We are joining the British in the war," he announced to 1st Lt. William R. Burt. Vandenberg then told Burt to prepare a complete list of all Army Air Corps units in the United States and overseas for Air Commodore George C. Pirie, the air attaché at the British Embassy.[11]

The recent news that another, higher-level, British air officer would be coming to Washington the next month for discussions with the War Department General Staff was of even greater interest to Vandenberg and Burt than secret cooperation with Great Britain in its struggle against Nazi Germany. Former air chief marshal Sir Hugh Dowding, the celebrated architect of Britain's aerial defense against the Luftwaffe, had been asked by Lord Beaverbrook—Britain's aircraft production minister—to undertake a mission to the United States to attempt to coordinate America's aircraft production with Britain's needs. He would also discuss the implications of the Battle of Britain for the air defense of the United States and its overseas territories. Vandenberg hoped to meet Dowding and obtain his views on a plan for the aerial defense of the Philippines that Vandenberg was preparing.[12]

The forty-one-year-old Vandenberg, a 1923 West Point graduate who had chosen assignment to the Air Service, had been brought into Brig. Gen. Carl "Tooey" Spaatz's Plans Division in June, 1939, at the express request of

Spaatz himself. The two had become close friends while attending the army's Command and General Staff School at Fort Leavenworth, Kansas, together in 1935. Unlike the other Plans Division staffers, Vandenberg's aide, Lieutenant Burt, was a non-flying reserve officer picked by Vandenberg to assist him with the division's heavy workload. A 1936 Yale graduate with a strong interest in aviation, the twenty-six-year-old Burt seized the opportunity to work with the officer who had so impressed him with his vitality and personality when they had first met in July, 1940, during Burt's interview at the War Department for the job. At Vandenberg's request, the Plans Division had requisitioned a Reserve Officer Training Corps (ROTC) alumnus from Yale, and Burt was the right man at the right time.[13]

Major Hoyt S. Vandenberg in 1940 while serving under Col. Don Wilson in Plans Division's Section III in the Office of the Chief of the Air Corps in Washington. Photo courtesy Maj. Gen. Hoyt S. Vandenberg Jr., USAF, (Ret.).

When Burt reported for duty on October 18, 1940, a study requested by Maj. Gen. Henry H. "Hap" Arnold, the Air Corps chief—on air defense problems based on the experience of the RAF's Fighter Command in the defense of Britain—was under way. Completed on October 30 and submitted to Arnold, it recommended that the United States adopt a form of air defense organization similar to Great Britain's and that the Air Corps be designated as the War Department agency responsible for operating the command. Of particular interest to Vandenberg and Burt was the board's recommendation calling for the introduction of a similar air defense system for each of America's insular possessions: the Philippines, Hawaii, and the Panama Canal Zone. The board proposed that immediate steps be taken to provide for the establishments and technical equipment required for each location.[14]

The question of defending the Philippines against air attack had been a preoccupation for Vandenberg ever since he attended the Army War College's War Plans Course, where he served on the committee to study and make recommendations for a military policy to support defense of the Philippines. When Vandenberg completed his AWC tour of duty in July,

1939, and was assigned to the Plans Division, Spaatz gave him the task of preparing a thorough study "to determine the size, composition, and general method of employment of army aviation for strategic offensive operations in the Far East." The resultant memorandum that Spaatz signed on September 1, 1939, and submitted to Arnold proposed an offensive aerial force based on Luzon in the Philippines that would serve as a threat to the Japanese mainland.[15]

Vandenberg's plan reflected the views of his Air Corps superiors—Frank Andrews, Hap Arnold, Ira Eaker, and Carl Spaatz, as well as his immediate chief in the Plans Division, Col. Don Wilson—in support of the doctrine of strategic airpower. The army's airpower should not just serve in support of ground troops, but be utilized as an offensive force independent of ground operations. Although Army Chief of Staff George C. Marshall had made his support of a strategic role for army aviation known to the Air Corps and War Department, Vandenberg and other Air Corps officers found that most of Marshall's staff officers still viewed airpower as a ground-support arm. Since all Air Corps proposals had to be cleared and approved by the War Department General Staff, the efforts of Spaatz's Plans Division to have an expanded role for airpower translated into War Department policy were persistently stymied.

The Army Air Corps's failure to secure War Department approval of his 1939 Philippines' plan had not deterred Vandenberg from continuing to press for an aerial buildup in that distant possession, but he was now focusing on the islands' defense rather than their use as a springboard for offensive operations. When Dowding arrived, he hoped to gain insights from the master planner of the Battle of Britain that might cause the War Department to assume a more favorable stance toward defense of the Philippines. Specifically, Vandenberg was looking forward to obtaining Dowding's reaction to the detailed plan for a Battle of Britain–type aerial defense of the Philippines that he and Burt had been discussing for the past few months.[16]

At 10 A.M. on Monday, January 13, 1941, a group of Air Corps officers assembled at the AWC at Fort Humphreys—directly across the river from Bolling Field—to hear their celebrated visitor's views for the first time. All eyes were on their English guest, a slender man with a toothbrush mustache, attired in a suit rather than his RAF uniform. For that matter, his listeners were out of uniform, too. The War Department preferred for officers on staff assignments in Washington to wear civilian clothes during this period of antiwar sentiment in the United States.[17]

After being introduced by his host, General Arnold, Dowding began his presentation on the lessons of the Battle of Britain. He first apologized for the superficiality of his introductory statement that the main objective of fighters in aerial defense was to bring bombers down, not tangle with other fighters. Then, in the dry style that had earned him the nickname "Stuffy" in the RAF, Dowding proceeded to discuss fighter tactics and air defense organization as developed during the Battle of Britain. Major Vandenberg, who had pronounced opinions about the effective use of fighters stemming from his time as head of pursuit instruction at the Air Corps Tactical School, listened intently.[18]

At the conclusion of his speech, Dowding most likely met informally with the Air Corps officers attending the meeting before departing with Arnold at 12:10. Vandenberg was apparently introduced to Dowding and discussed his plan for a Battle of Britain–type aerial defense of the Philippines that he and Burt had been formulating. Dowding assured Vandenberg that an aerial defense of Luzon as Vandenberg outlined to him was viable.[19]

Vandenberg's plan called for an interceptor force of three groups of P-40Es—each with four squadrons of twenty-five planes each—in the Philippine Department. The two officers thought a force that size should be adequate to deter a Japanese invasion of the islands provided it was properly based, supplied, and supported by bombers to attack shipping. Vandenberg estimated that six months would be required to establish such an aerial defense force. One group of P-40Es would be deployed on northern Luzon and the Batan Islands to the north, a second to defend the Manila area, and the third sent to Mindanao to the south to provide control of the air to the east and south and protect supply convoys. The five hundred pilots assigned to the three groups ostensibly would train the Philippine Army Air Corps to prepare it for assuming responsibility for the defense of the Philippines when the islands attained their independence in 1946.

Vandenberg reasoned that an interceptor force half the size of the RAF's Fighter Command in the summer of 1940 would be sufficient because Japan's air force (including carrier-based fighters) would not amount to more than 50 percent of the force the Luftwaffe employed during the Battle of Britain. His plan was based on his original 1939 proposal, but provided for an increase in the number of fighters (to reflect the importance of a strong fighter force as shown by the Battle of Britain experience) and focused exclusively on defensive operations.[20]

After returning to the Munitions Building following the AWC meeting, Vandenberg reported back to Room 3018 and sat at his desk in the U-shaped arrangement of desks. Colonel Wilson sat at the head, with the other four staff officers in the room seated at the two desks extending down each side from their section chief. Vandenberg whispered to his aide to meet him in the corridor. He wanted to brief Burt on the meeting with Dowding that morning, but talking in the cramped area distracted Wilson from his paperwork, so private conversations had to be held outside the room. Vandenberg actually preferred this arrangement. It allowed him to discuss matters informally with other staffers before taking them up with Wilson or staff officers in the other Plans Division sections.[21]

Rather than discuss Dowding's speech in the hall, however, Vandenberg and Burt headed down the corridor to the washroom, where they could talk without being overheard by others. Once inside, they checked to make sure no one was using the toilets. Vandenberg did not wish to share private discussions with his aide with other Air Corps officers. This was especially true with regard to his idea of establishing a Philippines air defense command with Dowding serving as adviser. The exposed pipes in the bathroom, seized by the U.S. government from Germany after World War I and marked "Krupp," were a constant reminder that the entire Munitions Building was a relic of that conflict.[22]

Vandenberg and Burt were both optimistic that the meetings Dowding had been having with the War Department staff would have an impact on their thinking about the possibility for the aerial defense of the Philippines and not just for the continental United States. But three days later, any such hopes were dashed with the word that President Roosevelt had informed General Marshall of his opposition to any operations in the Far East that would tend to commit the United States to a major effort in the Pacific. The long-standing policy of refraining from any reinforcement of the Philippines was still in effect.[23]

The implications for Vandenberg, Burt, and the rest of the Air Corps chief's Plans Division were clear: No memoranda were to go forward from the OCAC to the War Department calling for any action not in accord with the president's position regarding a Philippines buildup.[24]

NICHOLS FIELD, LUZON
WEDNESDAY, JANUARY 1, 1941

All decked out in their locally made white formal uniforms as convention required, the young flying officers of the 4th Composite Group walked up the steps of Quarters 18 at Nichols Field at midday to pay the traditional New Year's Day call on the group commander. Colonel and Mrs. Lawrence Churchill received them on the porch one by one and then directed them to the punch "bowl." Actually, it was a three-foot-square block of ice that had been hollowed out to hold the punch. Fifteen minutes after the reception started, William "Red" Sheppard and the others noticed that the hot punch had melted a hole right through the ice block and was pouring onto the tile floor. But no one seemed to mind.[25]

The 17th Pursuit Squadron's commanding officer was there, too, milling around with the others on the porch that completely encircled the large wooden building. Two days before, he had lost yet another of the nineteen original pilots from his squadron when "Lou" Gehrig was assigned to Churchill's Headquarters Squadron. Although he politely paid his respects to Churchill, it rankled Major Gregg that the group commander's latest incursion into his squadron strength left him with just ten pilots plus himself from the original twenty. "They have really ripped the 17th all to hell!" he complained in a letter to his wife.[26]

One week later, Gehrig paid the price for being transferred to a non-tactical squadron. All three of his housemates were hurriedly collecting their gear on the morning of Wednesday January 8 to go on a three-day field maneuver. Walt Coss was going with Gregg and the 17th Pursuit to Batangas to the southwest, while Grant Mahony and Bob Hanson were off to Iba to the northwest with the 3d Pursuit. Gehrig would be remaining at Nichols Field and have to look after the house alone.[27]

Mahony and Hanson grabbed a taxi on Taft Avenue and headed to Nichols Field. When they arrived, Capt. W. A. R. "Robbie" Robertson, the 3d Pursuit's personable commander, briefed them and the others on the Iba Field arrangements, then joined his pilots as they climbed up on the roughened black strip on the left wing of their aircraft to the small hinged flap on the side of the fuselage. After lowering the flaps, they positioned themselves inside the open cockpits and strapped themselves in for the ninety-mile hop. Standing on each ship's left wing, a crew chief cranked the inertia starter just behind the cowling, stopped after several turns, jerked the handle out, and jumped off as the engine caught with a high-pitched whine. The pilots then pumped their wobble pump, turned the magneto switch, gave the throttle several pumps, and pulled the starter engage handle. Up and down the line, engines crackled and belched blue smoke, then settled down, producing a racket not unlike that of a host of outboard motors.

After waiting about thirty seconds, Mahony and the others taxied onto the Nichols Field runway and applied full throttle, lifting off the field at eighty miles per hour in a steep climb. Once they were aloft, the stubby little ships responded to the lightest touch on the controls. With the wind blowing in his face and the wings' bracing wires producing a delightful singing sound, Mahony flew low over Luzon's brilliantly green fields with the others, then through the pass in the Zambales Mountains just to the east of Iba. Ahead he could see the vast South China Sea, glimmering in the intense morning sunlight.[28]

One after the other, the fun-loving young airmen brought their Peashooters down on the short, grassy strip just to the west of the Iba barrio and taxied over to one end of the field. Mahony picked up his musette bag, into which he had crammed a change of clothing and toilet articles, and sauntered over to the long, two-story building just off the field. It was the barracks of the Philippine Army contingent based there and would be their home during their three-day visit to the primitive field.

Mahony discovered that the 2d Observation Squadron was there for maneuvers, too. He spotted another 40-A classmate from Kelly Field, Ray MacInnis, who had been reassigned to the 2d Observation when they arrived on the *Etolin*. MacInnis was preparing to take Iba's mayor up in his two-seat, high-winged Douglas O-46A observation ship for a spin. It was an exciting prospect for the Filipino, who had never been in an airplane before. Not immediately scheduled to fly for the rest of the morning, Mahony and his remaining squadron mates headed out to the sandy beach and the beckoning ocean. It was their first dip in Philippine waters. Later that day, the 3d Pursuiters were back over the field in their P-26As, going through their practice maneuvers.

When the day's flying concluded, Mahony followed Robertson down to land and hit the end of the field, consciously going lightly on the brakes. He knew that with its narrow landing gear and short body, too much brake pressure could cause the stubby little fighter to nose over. However, before Mahony realized what was happening, his ship tilted sharply forward, throwing him against the instrument panel. The radio microphone swung back and hit him his face, cutting his nose and giving him a black eye. After unfastening his safety belt and jumping out, Mahony grasped what had happened: he had hit a soft spot on the field that had caused the plane to nose over. The others around him laughed at his predicament. No one seemed to mind that he had bent a $2,000 propeller. The obsolete P-26A belonged in a scrap heap anyway. Still, Mahony felt sheepish about the accident. He regarded himself and his buddy Bob Hanson as the best pursuit pilots in the Philippines, yet here he was, the first of the *Etolin* pilots to wreck a plane since their arrival.[29]

ARMY AND NAVY CLUB, MANILA
LATE JANUARY, 1941

Back in Manila, after participating in the simultaneous maneuvers of his 17th Pursuit Squadron at Batangas, Maj. Kirtley J. Gregg felt as lonesome as ever. He had shifted to a freshly painted room at the Army and Navy Club overlooking Manila Bay and was spending too much time there. He continued to pass up invitations to go to the club's bar for nightly drinking sessions. By late January, however, his lifestyle was becoming so monotonous that he began joining fellow officers for nights out on the town.

During working hours, Gregg was preoccupied with writing a highly classified report. The 4th Composite Group commander did not have a staff to which he could assign such a task, so Colonel Churchill passed it to the one Air Corps officer he regarded as capable of undertaking it. Gregg was to submit it to a board chaired by Churchill. Gregg fretted over the exercise. He was feeling punk, lacking his usual drive. Preparing a plan for "The Minimum Air Force Required for an Effective Defense of the Manila Area," as the report was to be entitled, was a heavy responsibility. Finally, on the morning of Thursday, January 23, he finished the draft and dictated it in the form required. Despite all the handicaps of inadequate information, he felt pleased with his effort. So did Churchill and the other board members, who approved it later that morning without any reservations.

A little over two weeks later, some variety was introduced into Gregg's routine-dominated life. On Monday, February 10, he went to Pier 7 in Manila to greet the USAT *Etolin*. The old army transport had just docked, and there was much fanfare, as was typical on such an occasion. Crowds of military personnel based in the Philippines were pressing around him. As the passengers disembarked, the newcomers and greeters loudly exchanged salutations over the sounds of the army band playing on the pier.

The morning before, Gregg had conducted his own welcoming cere- mony, leading an eighteen-ship formation over the Alaska cannery veteran in Verde Island Channel as it approached the Philippines. It was the first time the 4th Composite Group had managed to get more than eight pur- suit planes in formation since his arrival two months earlier on the *Etolin*.

That evening, Colonel Churchill put on the usual "Buena Venida" party at the Nichols Field officers' club—commonly referred to as the Carabao Club—for the wives and members of the new contingent of Air Corps arrivals: twenty-four flying school graduates of Class 40-H. Gregg warmly welcomed the four men assigned to his squadron. It seemed the War Department was finally beginning to beef up the Philippines' pilot strength, although the number of newcomers was woefully short of what Gregg had recommended in his board report.[30]

Despite the happy occasion, Gregg was feeling blue at the party. Of the five married pilots who had come to the Philippines on the *Etolin*'s earlier voyage, only he and George Armstrong were unaccompanied, and Eloise Armstrong was due in on the next boat, the USAT *Grant,* scheduled to arrive on February 21. Concerned about the situation in the Far East, Gregg had delayed until only two weeks before to put in a request that his wife and children be sent over too, but it was too late for Katherine to connect with any transport arriving before May. At 12:30, still feeling slightly "stiff," he excused himself from the festivities and took a taxi back to the Army and Navy Club.

Two days later, at noon, Gregg was getting out of a taxi in front of Robbie Robertson's Nichols Field quarters after having shared a beer with him at the Carabao Club, when the base adjutant rushed over to tell them that he had been calling all over for them. Colonel Churchill wanted all of the squadron commanders back for a meeting in his office at 1:30. Gregg and Robertson wondered what was up: Churchill had dismissed them only an hour before from an earlier meeting.

The 4th Composite Group commander looked agitated as he welcomed them back to his office, apologizing for any inconvenience he may have caused. He had just returned from a meeting with General Grunert to discuss two War Department radiograms that had just been received. Sixty of the ninety Philippine Department officers scheduled to return to the states on the next three army transports following the expiration of their two-year tours of duty would *not* be making the trip. Their tours were being extended to three years. No Air Corps officers were among the thirty who would be returning home. The substance of the second radiogram wounded Gregg personally: All dependents of army officers were to be evacuated back to the United States as fast as transportation could be made available. Gregg's hopes for a family reunion appeared dashed.[31]

Confirmation of the widely disseminated rumor that the War Department was seeking to extend the tours of Philippine Department officers immediately triggered a morale problem among the pilots of Churchill's 4th Composite Group. The War Department decision was particularly unnerving for Grant Mahony. He was trying to *shorten* his two-year tour, not extend it.

After exploring the islands in his P-26A on every possible occasion during the past two months, the free-spirited, regulation-flouting Californian had become bored. He wanted to leave the Army Air Corps before his one-year tour of duty after commissioning as a reserve officer expired on March 23. He was anxious to return to California to join Pan American Airways, as his best friend and Class 40-A classmate Ernie Hummel had done. In his letters to Mahony, Hummel painted an exciting picture of flying Pan American's South America routes.

When pilots flying the China Clipper into Manila told Mahony in late January that Pan Am was being allowed to hire twenty-five more army pilots, he began trying any ruse to shorten his tour of duty, which would otherwise be automatically extended for an additional year. Mahony was trying to find out from the Philippine Department adjutant general exactly how long he was bound by his orders to remain in the Philippines. But the War Department radiogram put a damper on his efforts. It was beginning to look like he would not even be able to get out on March 24, let alone earlier than that.[32]

THIS MARTIN B-10B BOMBER OF THE 20TH AIR BASE SQUADRON WAS PHOTOGRAPHED
WHILE FLYING OVER SOUTHERN LUZON ON DECEMBER 30, 1940. U.S. ARMY AIR CORPS
PHOTO NO. 21793 AC, COURTESY NATIONAL AIR AND SPACE MUSEUM, WASHINGTON, D.C.

Although the rumor about a tour extension had not bothered Gregg,
another one that Churchill shared with him during the meeting did.
Churchill told him that he had "authentic dope" that the three pursuit
squadrons were to be withdrawn from his 4th Composite Group and
formed into a new pursuit group with Gregg as commander. Gregg was
not particularly keen about the idea, although it represented a big step up
for him in his Air Corps career. The pursuit squadrons in the Philippines
had "practically no experienced officers, just a bunch of green youngsters,"
he confided to his wife. Yet, if the secret tip were true, he assured her, "we
will whip up a workable outfit somehow."[33]

While Gregg was concerned about the number and qualifications
of the pursuit pilots he might soon be commanding, Maj. Gen. George
Grunert over in the Philippine Department headquarters at Fort Santiago
was preoccupied with his air force's *equipment* situation. Except for the
P-35As that were being assembled, all of his aircraft were obsolete—Air
Corps rejects that had been dumped on the Philippine Department. The
3d, 17th, and 20th Pursuit Squadrons were flying the twenty-four antiquated P-26As currently in commission. The 28th Bomb Squadron at
Clark Field had just twelve aircraft, all Martin B-10B bombers of 1935

vintage, and he considered the 2d Observation Squadron's ten 0-46As and two O-19Es museum pieces.[34]

Grunert was reading a letter dated February 8 that he had just received from General Marshall. It appeared that the Japanese had developed a fighter that could run circles around the P-35As Marshall had sent Grunert to replace his antiquated P-26As. According to Marshall, the new Japanese carrier-based fighter was rated at 322 miles per hour, had a very rapid rate of climb, was equipped with self-sealing fuel tanks and armor, and mounted two 20-mm cannon and two .30-caliber machine guns. The army chief of staff promised to try to send sufficient numbers of the newest army pursuit ship, the Curtiss P-40B, for Grunert to equip at least one of his pursuit squadrons. He implied that its top speed of 360 miles an hour, self-sealing fuel tanks and armor, and two .50-caliber and four .30-caliber machine guns would make it more than a match for the new Japanese fighter.[35]

CHAPTER 2

"A Troop of Boy Scouts Flying Kites Could Take These Damned Islands"

On a cold mid–February, 1941, day in Washington, Maj. Hoyt Vandenberg's aide, 1st Lt. William Burt, descended the stairway to the second floor of the Munitions Building and headed over to Room 2103, which was shared by two high-ranking Air Corps officers assigned to staff duties in the War Department's War Plans Division. Burt was following up on a February 11 memorandum from Maj. Gen. George H. Brett in the Office of the Chief of the Air Corps to Brig. Gen. Leonard T. Gerow, the influential head of the WPD. Vandenberg thought it would not be advisable for him to be seen discussing his Battle of Britain–style plan for the defense of the Philippines with the War Department General Staff and was therefore using Burt as a liaison with the WPD for any such discussions.[1]

Brett's memorandum formally recommended that the War Department authorize the creation of an air force command in the Philippines composed of a "striking force echelon and an air defense echelon" and that plans and estimates be prepared for the command, should the War Department decide to reinforce the Philippine Department. Brett wanted at least one long-range bombardment wing as the striking force and a pursuit wing for the air defense component, each to consist of three or more groups, plus additional ground and air components to create a balanced force.[2]

Brett's proposal—minus the bombardment force—clearly originated in the plan Vandenberg and Burt had designed during the preceding two months and were still hoping would gain War Department approval. As Burt described their plan in some detail, both Col. Joseph T. McNarney and Lt. Col. Charles C. Chauncey seemed to agree on its logic. They had been assigned to the WPD in order to reflect Air Corps input at the War Department staff level, but both had been too busy to study the lessons of the Battle of Britain for ideas applicable to the aerial defense of the United States and its overseas territories. Although Vandenberg's and Burt's plan had the support of their fellow Air Corps officers, they all knew the War Department would have to take the initiative in introducing it, and that Gerow would have to be won over first. At present, the War Department was still opposed to a buildup of defensive strength in the Philippines.[3]

Despite the War Department's unwillingness to support the establishment of an effective air defense force in the Philippines, it did not oppose a proposal from General Grunert that his staff "study the possibility of formation of an air defense command" for the islands. In response to Grunert's radiogram requesting "available data" to assist in preparing such a study, Gerow had authorized sending Grunert the report and recommendations of Brig. Gen. James E. Chaney—commander of the Air Defense Command at Mitchel Field, New York—on Chaney's October–November, 1940, visit to England as an "observer."[4]

As members of the General Staff, McNarney and Chauncey were also privy to information that the War Department was easing up slightly on its policy against reinforcement of the Philippines. Toward the end of February, Gerow would have informed them that General Marshall had authorized the shipment of "modern" P-40B pursuit planes and a squadron of B-18 twin-engine bombers to the islands, and that the president had approved the chief of staff's suggestion that airfields there be expanded to accommodate a larger force.[5]

On both qualitative and quantitative grounds, Vandenberg was quite unimpressed with the decision to send a squadron of P-40Bs to the Philippines. Three weeks earlier, he had written a note for Spaatz's signature advising Gerow that the P-40B's two .50-caliber and four .30-caliber machine guns provided inadequate firepower. He argued that six .50-caliber guns were needed to assure success against modern all-metal aircraft. Vandenberg considered the P-40B unsuitable "for operations against a first-class airpower." Moreover, even if it were, he would have felt that assigning a single squadron of such ships was a pitiful response to the real needs of an air defense force for the Philippines when compared to the twelve squadrons he wanted allocated to meet those needs.[6]

Vandenberg's detailed argument on the inferiority of the P-40B as an interceptor fell on deaf ears. The aircraft was still considered a "modern" pursuit ship and an improvement over the P-35As that were currently being flown in the Philippines.

NICHOLS FIELD, LUZON
FRIDAY, MARCH 7, 1941

R ed Sheppard and Russ Church could already feel the temperature at
Nichols Field building up toward another ninety-degree day as they
headed for the line of P-35As on the grass in front of Hangar 4 early in
the morning on Friday, March 7. When they located the two 17th Pursuit
Squadron ships with their names painted on the side of the fuselage, they
climbed up on the wings and into the cockpits. With the sixteen "newies"
of the Class 40-H contingent of pilots off the *Etolin* still confined to flying P-26As and the number of P-35As assembled and in commission now
exceeding thirty, Sheppard, Church, and the rest of the twenty-four "oldies" in the three pursuit squadrons each had their own P-35A.[7]

After using up only four hundred feet of runway, the nimble fighters
were aloft. Cruising along at two hundred miles per hour at three-fourth's
throttle, the pilots were enjoying flying the responsive new ships. They
were also roomier and much more comfortable than the old P-26As.[8]

The two 17th Pursuiters were scheduled for a little practice flying on a
cross-Luzon trip that would take them north over Cabanatuan to Bagabog,
then northeast to Ilagan and Aparri. On the return trip they would pass
over Laoag and land at Vigan, then continue south over Clark Field before
coming back to Manila. It was a fun trip for the Class 40-A classmates from
Kelly Field, a chance to see the real Philippines.[9]

Curious natives greeted them on the primitive grass field at Bagabog, where they made their first scheduled landing. The excited Filipinos
told their unexpected visitors the village would arrange a feast day for
them anytime the pilots wanted to come up for the day. The Americans
expressed their appreciation for the offer, but they had no intention of
accepting. There was nothing at the village but a rice field.

After landing at Aparri, the northernmost airfield on Luzon, Sheppard
and Church looked for someone with whom they could make arrangements to refuel their planes for the 270-mile flight back to Nichols. Only
the radio station operator spoke English. He directed them to a stack of
five-gallon tins of aviation gasoline. An audience of some two hundred
locals stood quietly nearby and watched the two pilots pour gas from
each can through a funnel and chamois filter into their P-35As' fuel tanks.
None of the Filipinos said more than two words during the several hours
it took the pair to fill their tanks. "But they sure do watch, though," Sheppard thought.

While Sheppard, Church, and the other oldies were experiencing the
pleasure of flying their P-35As in early March, the Class 40-H newies,

fresh from flying school, were required to undergo orientation and practice in the venerable P-26As before being allowed to move up to the new
pursuit ships. By the beginning of the month, Andy Krieger, who had
been assigned to the 3d Pursuit, had already put in some twenty hours in
the Peashooter.

On the morning of March 4, one of the squadron's senior pilots took
Krieger up to put him through the wringer. Within minutes, Krieger was
following his leader as he whipped his ship into slow rolls, half rolls, loops,
and Immelmanns. Only when the veteran pilot threw his ship into a steep
spiral straight down at full throttle did he succeed in shaking Krieger.

That afternoon, Krieger took his ship up again, but this time he was
with George Ellstrom, a fellow 40-H classmate and best friend from Sell-
ersville, Pennsylvania. In practices aimed at shaking the other pilot off
one's tail, a securely strapped-in Krieger spent as much time upside down
as right side up while flying at speeds ranging from three hundred miles an
hour to stalling speed. At cruising speed, he would be too easy a target. But
neither Krieger nor Ellstrom could shake the other off his tail. For Krieger,
the ground, sky, clouds, and ocean were swirling around so kaleidoscopi-
cally that he never knew for sure where he was, but he never lost sight of
Ellstrom.

After the day's practice, the exhilarated newie was sure he had made
the right choice upon graduation from Kelly Field: "Pursuit is the only
thing for me," he wrote to his father that evening.[10]

Squadron mate Grant Mahony did not share Krieger's enthusiasm for
a career in the Army Air Corps. He wanted to resign his commission as
soon as possible and return to the United States where he hoped to join
his buddy and Class 40-A classmate Ernie Hummel, who was flying with
Pan American–Grace Airways in Latin America. The possibility of exploring all of South America and taking classes in navigation, meteorology, and
advanced instrument flying was far more attractive to the adventurous
Irish-American than remaining in the Philippines and continuing to lead
the uninspiring lifestyle he shared with his fellow Air Corps pilots.

By early March, Mahony's request to resign his commission had cleared
all of the colonels in the Philippine Department, but General Grunert
returned it to Mahony rather than forward it to Air Corps headquarters in
Washington. Adding insult to injury, all of Mahony's efforts to see Grunert
personally on the matter were being blocked. Mahony had not discussed
his request with Col. Lawrence Churchill, commander of the 4th Composite Group. Mahony was interested only in its legality, so why discuss
it with the man? The fifty-year-old Churchill was an old fuddy-duddy in
Mahony's book; he was not known for showing sympathy for the personal
concerns of his young charges.[11]

CLARK FIELD, LUZON
FEBRUARY, 1941

The command situation was quite different at Clark Field, forty-five miles north of Nichols. Major Lester Maitland, the forty-two-year-old base commander, mixed easily with the officers assigned to Clark. In 1927, the same year Charles Lindbergh made his world-acclaimed solo flight from New York to Paris, Maitland gained recognition by making the first nonstop flight from California to Hawaii in Air Corps history—a feat that earned him the respect of all those serving under him at Clark. When he arrived in the Philippines on July 20, 1940, Maitland was given command of not only Clark Field, where he was the senior Air Corps officer present, but also of the only tactical squadron based there at the time, the 28th Bomb Squadron, whose Philippine service dated back to September, 1922.[12]

To Ted Fisch of the 28th Bomb Squadron and his new bride, Mimi, the red-haired, disheveled Maitland was putting on a performance that humid February evening unrelated to his Air Corps responsibilities. He was up on the porch of their married officers' quarters at adjoining Fort Stotsenburg with his wife Kathleen—called "Kay" by the other wives—paying yet another social visit on the officers based at Clark Field under his command. After sliding open the shutters that served as the entrance to their comfortable wood and plaster board house and inviting the Maitlands into the living room, Mimi slipped into the kitchen and asked her houseboy, Resurrection, if the bottle of scotch whiskey that was making the rounds of officers' row in sync with the Maitlands as they proceeded from house to house had arrived. As usual, Kay had arranged for the houseboys to take the bottle to the next house after each visit. Maitland and his wife knew that the young officers could not afford to buy whisky on their meager pay, so they provided their own bottle to satisfy the major's needs during each call.[13]

While Maitland's heavy drinking was not exceptional among the more senior officers in the Philippine Department, it was considered an unusual means of bonding with the junior officers under his command. Much more unorthodox was the extension of such behavior to include the enlisted men. He did not maintain the customary distance between officers and enlisted men, which made him highly popular with them. However, one drinking incident gave rise to an unflattering, albeit comic, nickname for Maitland that stuck during his Clark Field command days.

As was his habit on weekends, one Saturday afternoon while horseback riding around the base, Maitland stopped off at the 28th Squadron's PX to have a few beers with the men in the adjacent beer garden. A huge man— about six feet, four inches tall and weighing over 250 pounds—with a capacity for alcohol that matched his size, Maitland proceeded to down more than ten bottles of San Miguel beer, went briefly outside for a break, then returned and drank an equal number, which finally put him in an unstable state. Staggering out of the beer garden, he tried to mount his horse, but without success. Corporal Reid Brock and the other enlisted men present noticed his predicament and several of them accompanied Brock over to assist their commanding officer. With four men on one side of the horse and four on the other, they pushed Maitland up onto its back, but each time he fell down the other side.

The men finally decided it was a losing battle. They would need some other means to get Maitland back to his quarters, which was about a hundred yards from the squadron's barracks. Returning to the beer garden, they approached his chauffeur, Pvt. William Biggs, who was drinking with his mates. They told Biggs of Maitland's predicament and asked him to get the commander's car, which was parked right outside the beer garden, and bring it to where Maitland lay sprawled out on the ground.

After much pushing and pulling, the men managed to get Maitland stretched out on the automobile's backseat. Biggs slid into the front seat to drive to the CO's quarters and the others left to go meet him there to unload Maitland. After reaching the quarters on foot at about the same time Biggs arrived in the car, the men opened the back door and pulled Maitland out. After carrying him up on the porch, one of the men knocked on the door. When Mrs. Maitland opened it, Brock announced, "The Major is indisposed."

Kathleen Maitland looked Brock straight in the eye. "Throw the big pig under the house with the rest of them!" she declared, then slammed the door. The men knew she was referring to the Filipino custom of keeping their pigs under the house, but they had no intention of doing such a thing. Instead, they laid Maitland out on a bench on the porch and "high-tailed it out of there." They did not want to be around when their commanding officer sobered up and his wife jumped on him for getting drunk with the men. Social drinking as a married couple while visiting the officers under his command was one thing, but for her husband to get loaded by himself while drinking with the enlisted men was unacceptable behavior in Kathleen Maitland's book. Word soon got around Clark Field about Maitland's performance that afternoon and his wife's reaction. From that day on, the enlisted men jokingly referred to Maitland as "the Big Pig."

Some days later, following Maitland's promotion to lieutenant colonel, the Clark Field adjutant asked him if he knew what the enlisted men called him. "It doesn't make any difference, they are entitled to call me anything they want," Maitland replied. "They call you the 'Big Pig,'" the adjutant informed him. Unruffled, Maitland answered, "That's quite all right, but I'd better not hear an *officer* call me that!"[14]

HEADQUARTERS, PHILIPPINE DEPARTMENT
FORT SANTIAGO, MANILA
THURSDAY MARCH 6, 1941

If the commanding general of the Philippine Department had heard of Maitland's drinking and the nickname he had acquired as a result of it, he showed no signs of concern. Major General George Grunert thought that Maitland was doing "a superior job at Clark Field" and had so informed General Marshall in Washington when he recommended him for promotion to lieutenant colonel. However, as he dictated his secret letter to Marshall in his office at Fort Santiago in Manila on March 6, Grunert expressed dissatisfaction with the performance of his three highest-ranking air officers.

At the same time he asked Marshall for a general officer to command his expanding Air Corps element in order to weld it into a "confident, fighting force," Grunert asserted that "neither Richards, Churchill, or Savage are considered as capable of filling the job." His air officer, Col. Harrison H. C. Richards, the most senior of the Air Corps officers assigned to the islands, "is a hard worker [but] entirely too verbose, capable in a measure but apparently unable to get necessary cooperation." Grunert was particularly disturbed by "the constant bickering and working at cross-purposes between Richards and Churchill," who, Grunert added, "barely gets by." Grunert sensed that "the youngsters in the Air Corps . . . have no confidence" in their senior commanders. Although he wanted both Richards and Churchill sent back to the states ahead of the October 31 expiration date of their Philippine tours, he added that he would need replacements for them before he could let them go. Grunert also asked Marshall to send him another general officer to organize the Philippine Department's air defenses. He emphasized that he needed both generals as soon as possible.

In addition to the Air Corps command situation, Grunert wanted to fill Marshall in on the status of his air defense arrangements. He figured that an invader's first move would "probably be a series of bombing attacks and attempts to establish one or more bases for land aviation." To counter such a threat, he wanted to integrate all active and passive air defense measures. His present Air Warning Service (AWS), which was supervised by the department G2 rather than established as a command function, was a "make-shift" operation at best. He added that with the arrival of an Air Warning Company and its equipment the following month, he would be able to expand the AWS.[15]

ARMY AND NAVY CLUB, MANILA
THURSDAY, MARCH 18, 1941

Grunert's "insider" source of information on the Air Corps command situation in the Philippine Department was Maj. Kirtley Gregg. Frustrated in his attempts to get approval on necessary matters for which he was responsible, Gregg had decided to "go through the back door" and bring them personally to Grunert's attention. Unlike the department commander, Gregg did not have a low opinion of Churchill's capabilities. His immediate commander was "smart and a good C.O." in his view, but unable to gain Colonel Richards's cooperation. Although Gregg liked Richards personally, he told his wife the department's senior aviation officer was a bore "if you get stuck with him alone and had to listen to him for long." However, at the professional level, Gregg regarded Richards as "a good olde English Phart," a "died [*sic*] in the wool Cavalry man." He confided to his wife that Richards's "antiquated ideas of 'Air Service,' lack of any conception of today's Air Force, refusal to accept advice and admit facts when presented to him, and above all his personal animosity for Colonel Churchill and deliberate attempts to sabotage anything the Group CO tried to do (and withholding information from him)" were behind Grunert's request that an Air Corps general officer be sent to take command of all air units in the islands.[16]

At 6:10 A.M. on Tuesday, March 18, Gregg was listening to the local news station in his room at the Army and Navy Club before leaving for Nichols Field for the day when the announcer reported an item that caused him to drop any half-hearted aspiration to command the rumored new pursuit group in the Philippines. His former commanding officer at Selfridge Field, Brig. Gen. Henry B. Clagett, was being ordered to the Philippine Department! Only half-jokingly, Gregg informed his wife that when the news got around the department, the Air Corps officers "were discussing the possibilities for retirement for age, physical disability or insanity, or getting orders to China or Timbuctoo." Gregg was familiar enough with the fifty-six-year-old "Sue" Clagett to know that once he arrived, all hell would break loose. In Gregg's estimation, Clagett would not bother to find out the "what and why" behind the mess in the Air Corps command. "He will crack down, raise hell, and issue his usual specific orders before he finds out or anyone can tell him what the Big Picture is all about," he wrote his wife. "He is going to really be bad news" and "make matters worse rather than help in straightening out the present mess," Gregg concluded.

With the news of Clagett's appointment, Gregg had no idea what the Air Corps setup in the Philippines would be like. He had assumed the rumored new pursuit group would be made up of the 3d, 17th, and

20th Squadrons, but there were newspaper reports of two more pursuit squadrons en route to the islands. He had planned to turn the 17th Pursuit over to "Buzz" Wagner, his most senior pilot, if Churchill appointed him to command the new group. But with Clagett coming to head up air operations, Gregg no longer was interested in being a group commander. Besides, he figured the "old devil" would not want him on his staff.

That afternoon and evening, after finishing his squadron commander duties and other administrative tasks for the day, Gregg buried himself in concluding a major responsibility that had been passed on to him two months earlier. Through channels, General Grunert had personally asked Gregg for a complete report on the "Minimum Air Force Required to Ensure Air Supremacy for the Defense of the Philippine Archipelago," as it was to be entitled. To Gregg, it appeared that his first report, on the air defense of the Manila area, apparently was *too* well received, so now he was stuck with this new request for a plan that would provide broader coverage.

It seemed ridiculous to him that one individual should be asked to prepare such a report alone. Hell, "the War College, the War Plans Division of the War Department, and the General Staff in the Philippine Department have all been working on such a plan for at least 15 years, and with the G-2 information and technical assistance they had available!" he complained to his wife. Now he was being tasked to accomplish the job in two months, and to do so with only whatever information he had at hand. Earlier, Grunert had given him a single report from the War Department outlining lessons learned from the Battle of Britain. The report, written by an Army Air Corps observer in England, was all the general had received in response to his request that the adjutant general provide information for Gregg's study.[17] Anyway, it was just a "silly damned board report that does not mean a thing and that no one will pay any attention to," Gregg wrote to his wife while in a pessimistic mood. In his estimation, "A troop of Boy Scouts flying kites could take these damned Islands and not have a shot fired at them."[18]

Nevertheless, when he turned his report in on March 20, Gregg was convinced his final effort was "more practical and workable" than anything he had seen in the Philippine Department's files. In it, he proposed a Philippines air force composed of one long-range reconnaissance squadron, one bomb group consisting of one heavy and two medium squadrons, two pursuit groups of interceptors, and one pursuit group of fighters.[19] Although Gregg was unaware of Vandenberg's efforts in Washington to develop a plan for the Philippines' air defense, his conclusion that three pursuit groups were required exactly matched that of his counterpart at Air Corps headquarters.

CHAPTER 3

"They Will Be Shot Down as Fast as They Are Put in the Air"

arly in the afternoon on Friday, April 4, Brig. Gen. Henry B. Clagett eased his corpulent frame into a chair as Air Vice Marshal Hugh Dowding prepared to address a group of sixty-three officers assembled in a large room at the newly established Air Defense School at Mitchel Field, Long Island. It was Clagett's tenth day at the special course on air defense arranged by the General Headquarters (GHQ) Air Force to indoctrinate Air Corps, Signal Corps, and Coast Artillery officers in the latest thinking on the subject. All of the officers attending the three-week course, which had begun on March 25, were to be assigned to the various army zones in the continental United States and overseas territories upon its completion.[1]

Clagett was being prepared to assume his new position as air commander in the Philippine Department. General Arnold had personally picked the Selfridge Field commander for the job in response to General Grunert's request for a general officer to take over his growing Philippines air force. Clagett would also be responsible for setting up the islands' aerial defenses, which explains why he had been detailed to attend this course.[2]

After Dowding spoke briefly on the aerial defense lessons of the Battle of Britain, a committee of students responsible for drawing up an air defense plan for the Hawaiian Islands presented its report to Dowding for his reaction. The team of four Air Corps, Signal Corps, and Coast Artillery officers explained its plan in front of all the other attendees. It covered the integrated use of Signal Corps radar units, the interceptor force of pursuit aircraft, and radio communications.[3]

As in the case of the Hawaiian Department, committees covering other defense areas in the United States and overseas had prepared air defense plans for the areas to which they were assigned, with the exception of the

Philippine Department committee. The course's organizers had decided there was not enough time to bring in Philippine Department staff to attend the course and develop a plan. Those selected for the Philippines committee came from continental U.S. commands and were earmarked for assignment to the islands.[4]

Dowding must have been disappointed that no aerial defense plan for the Philippines had been prepared for his review, and certainly Clagett no less. But at least Lt. Col. Willis Taylor, the chairman of the Philippines committee, was being assigned to the islands from his previous staff position with Clagett at Selfridge Field. Taylor was considered highly competent and would be able to advise Clagett on his air defense command duties, the other part of the double duty, which included command of the new Philippine Department Air Force (PDAF).[5]

In addition to Taylor, only one of the other four officers on the Philippines Committee was actually going there after the course—Maj. Sam Lamb, Signal Corps. The other Air Corps officer on the committee—Capt. Joseph Lee—would be remaining at Mitchel Field, with Capt. Charles Sprague, attending the course from Hamilton Field, assigned in his stead. Meanwhile, Clagett had picked highly regarded Col. Harold H. George, commander of the 31st Pursuit Group at Selfridge and a World War I ace, to serve as his executive officer. George, however, was not attending the Mitchel Field course.[6]

A few days before, Clagett was informed of an additional task being given him. Marshall and Arnold had picked him to carry out Secretary of War Stimson's promise to Chiang Kai-shek to send an Air Corps general officer on a mission to China. Clagett's mission had three objectives: to determine the Chinese air force's capability to work in cooperation with the United States in the event of war, to assess the adequacy of new airfields being constructed, and to familiarize himself with the tactics and characteristics of the Japanese air force. Marshall underlined that the mission would have an important psychological effect on the Chinese, showing them that "we were considering them as potential allies, not beggars at the rich man's table."[7]

Clagett was ordered to report to Washington immediately after finishing the course for a briefing on his additional assignment, thus delaying his original April 15 departure date for the Philippines. The State Department had already issued him a passport as "Assistant Military Attaché at the American Embassy, Chungking," and arrangements were being made for Chinese, British, and Dutch visas, the last two covering possible visits to Hong Kong and the Dutch East Indies.[8]

Meanwhile, General Grunert anxiously awaited Clagett's arrival in Manila. He was looking forward to his new air commander assessing the

72   Part I

Philippine Department's aerial defense needs and "making the best use of what we have." Grunert, however, had not been informed of Clagett's China mission and of the concomitant delay of his arrival in the islands.[9]

PAN AMERICAN AIRWAYS TERMINAL
CAVITE, MANILA
SUNDAY MORNING, MAY 4, 1941

The army's top brass were at the Pan American terminal at Cavite, south of Manila, to welcome the silver Boeing 314 Clipper that had just landed on Canacao Bay. On board the gleaming amphibian were General Clagett and his executive officer, Colonel George, who were finally arriving to assume their new posts in the department. It had taken thirteen days following their departure from California on April 21 to reach the Philippines.[10]

Colonels Harrison Richards and Lawrence Churchill were there to greet the new arrivals as they debarked from the Clipper, but not Major Gregg and other second-echelon officers. Not having been invited to the official reception party, Gregg had decided to head down to the Taal Vista Inn at Tagaytay, on the rim of the crater around Lake Taal, south of Manila, to spend his day off with Maj. Robbie Robertson, the commander of the 3d Pursuit Squadron. At any rate, he had earlier arranged for the Clipper to be "escorted" in by an eighteen-ship formation of P-26As, which clustered around the immense flying boat like flies. He was later informed that the pursuit pilots had put on a show that pleased Clagett and George.[11]

Gregg and Robertson arrived back at the Army and Navy Club from their Tagaytay excursion at 10 P.M. and ate dinner there together. Hal George roamed in about midnight, while Gregg and Robertson were having a nightcap. Reunited after such a long time since their days at Selfridge together, Gregg and George sat around reminiscing and discussing the Philippine Department Air Corps setup and problems until 4:15 A.M. before turning in.[12]

After only two hours' sleep, Gregg was up again and down at Nichols Field to take care of essentials, then he went back to the club and over to Pier 7 on Manila Bay opposite the club to see off the USAT *Republic* at noon. Philippine Department dependents with East Coast destinations were being repatriated, and Gregg was there to say good-bye to the wives of Air Corps personnel who were shipping out. No 17th Pursuit officers' wives were leaving, just those of the squadron's noncommissioned officers (NCOs). The outwardly reserved Gregg felt awkward as the Air Corps officers and men spent their last emotional moments with their spouses. Les and Kay Maitland "both bawled like babies" for half an hour before

Brigadier General Henry B. Clagett (*LEFT*), newly assigned commanding
general of the Philippine Department Air Force, and his aide, Col. Harold H.
George (*LEFT REAR*), pose for an official photo with Maj. Gen. George Grunert
(*RIGHT*), commanding general of the Philippine Department, and his aide, Capt.
George R. Grunert (*RIGHT REAR*), at Fort Santiago in Manila on May 7, 1941.
U.S. Army Signal Corps photo no. 1249621 courtesy U.S. Army Military History
Institute, Carlisle Barracks, Pennsylvania.

P-35As of the 17th Pursuit Squadron fly low over the USAT *Washington* upon its arrival in Manila on May 8, 1941. Photo courtesy Walter Hinkle via Clyde Childress.

the *Republic* pulled out. After the ship's departure, Gregg joined the new "grass widowers" back at the Army and Navy Club, where all proceeded to drown their sorrows.

Breaking away from the crowd in the Blue Room later that afternoon, a sleep-deprived Gregg started toward the stairs to his room in anticipation of a shower and a long siesta. It was not to be: he bumped into "Sue" Clagett in the lobby. The newly arrived general cordially greeted his former 17th Pursuit commander at Selfridge and the two then proceeded to the Men's Bar for a Sholl Cup and what Gregg hoped would be a short chat. No such luck! The "Old Man" was in a garrulous mood and kept firing questions at Gregg. Even though five other Air Corps officers who had served with Clagett soon joined the twosome, most of the conversation was directed at Gregg. Clagett finally excused himself at 5:30, and Gregg at last headed up to his room.

At nine o'clock on Thursday morning, May 8, Gregg was down at Pier 7 again as another army transport arrived, this one with a load of additional Philippine Department officers, including thirty-nine Class 41-B graduates, fresh out of flying school. Eight of them were being assigned to Gregg's 17th Pursuit to help bring the squadron up to its authorized strength. An equal number were assigned to Grover's 20th Pursuit and Robertson's 3d Pursuit.[13]

Disembarking from the USAT *Washington* to cheers and band music, the latest batch of Air Corps officers was taken to the Army and Navy Club, where an all-day-long reception was being put on for them and for the officers' wives who would be departing on the *Washington* in six days with other dependents headed for U.S. West Coast destinations. As a Filipino orchestra blared out tunes, the new arrivals congregated in the ballroom and passed down the reception line welcoming them. Clagett and George were at the front of the line to meet the young and impressionable pilots. They clustered around the general, who was in his best sociable mood. Although standing straight and tall, his creased face, nearly bald head, and pronounced paunch made Clagett appear older than his fifty-six years. The commanding general of the newly designated Philippine Department Air Force nearly dwarfed the small, dark, forty-eight-year-old officer standing beside him. However, "Pursuit" George's quick smile and warm personality immediately endeared him to his new charges.[14]

In addition to the Class 41-B pilots, the *Washington* had brought over three of Clagett's new staff officers. Major Sam Lamb, whom Clagett had first met at the Mitchel Field course, was being assigned as signal officer, while Capt. Charles Sprague would serve as the operations officer (S3), although he had not been ordered to the Philippines as a member of Clagett's staff. Clagett envisioned him in the post only as a temporary arrangement; he wanted Air Corps headquarters to send him someone more experienced for that critical position. Sprague had, however, attended the Mitchel Field course—which was a significant plus factor. Finally, there was thirty-nine-year-old 1st Lt. Allison Ind, a reserve officer who had served as Clagett's intelligence officer at Selfridge Field and was now assigned as the PDAF's S2 and the general's nonflying aide-de-camp.[15]

Much to Clagett's disappointment, another officer earmarked for the PDAF staff would not be coming to the Philippines: Lt. Col. Willis Taylor, who had chaired the Philippine committee at the Mitchel Field course and was originally scheduled to serve as Clagett's S3, had instead been selected to lead the newly established 5th Interceptor Command at Fort Lawton, Washington. Curiously enough, Clagett had not confided in Gregg about his China mission, although Gregg had heard rumors about it. Nevertheless, Hal George told Ind that George and Clagett had been ordered there on a secret mission for the secretary of state and would be carrying diplomatic passports.[16]

When Ind reported the next day to his new office at PDAF headquarters in Fort Santiago, on the outskirts of Manila, he was immediately dismayed by conditions there. In this "relic of a bygone century," "pot-bellied and moss-green," its "stout sloping walls" leaning inward, he found an atmosphere of "old age retirement" permeating the one-time Spanish fort. To Ind, the Philippine Department headquarters, including its air force element, was "soft." A "flaccidity, a torpidity, an all-pervading lack of movement or resolution was fearfully widespread."[17]

In Ind's view, the Philippine Department had long been considered by the War Department and army officers nearing retirement as "an ideal place to polish off a career." One could take it easy in the Philippines, with work limited to the five hours between 8 A.M. and 1 P.M. People generally stayed inside until 4 P.M. due to the heat and humidity of the "continuous Turkish bath," which sapped will and strength.

HEADQUARTERS, PHILIPPINE DEPARTMENT AIR FORCE
FORT SANTIAGO, MANILA
FRIDAY MORNING, MAY 9, 1941

General Clagett issued sweeping orders that set in motion command changes throughout the tactical air units in the Philippines. Colonel Churchill was relieved of command of the 4th Composite Group by written order, and a verbal order made Gregg his successor as CO of the group—minus the 28th Bomb and 2d Observation Squadrons. Major Orrin Grover was appointed to serve as the group operations officer that same day.[18]

First Lieutenant Boyd "Buzz" Wagner, the senior ranking pilot in the squadron, was picked to replace Gregg as CO of the 17th Pursuit. At twenty-four, he was about the same age or only a little older than his pilots. Grover's replacement as CO of the 20th Pursuit was that squadron's senior officer, 1st Lt. Joseph H. Moore, a twenty-seven-year-old Class 38-B Kelly Field flying school graduate from Spartanburg, South Carolina. To complete the wholesale changes in command of the three pursuit squadrons, Maj. William H. Maverick was selected to lead the 3d Pursuit Squadron, replacing Robbie Robertson, who was scheduled to leave May 14 on the USAT *Washington* for stateside duty.

Although Clagett had originally told Gregg he could have any officer he wanted for his staff, he subsequently vetoed Gregg's selection of Maverick as his group operations officer—much to the relief of Maverick, who did not relish the idea of having "to tell people how to do it rather than to do it myself." Maverick had accepted a transfer to the Philippines from a staff job at Brooks Field based on the understanding that he would have a flying job there. However, when he arrived on November 1, 1940, as a captain, he was assigned to serve as executive officer of the 20th Air Base Group—a staff position with a nontactical unit. He was glad that Clagett had at last rescued him from yet another staff job.[19]

In addition to inheriting Robertson's squadron, Maverick also was given his quarters at Nichols Field. Gregg would be moving out of his room in the Army and Navy Club to share the quarters with Maverick. With the departure of all of the Philippine Department's dependents, officers were expected to double up with each other in the previously family-occupied quarters. A private person by nature, Gregg was not sure how he would manage sharing living accommodations with Maverick. The only Air Corps officer with whom he was fully compatible was Robertson, and now he was leaving. The thirty-four-year-old Maverick was from a well-known and politically influential Texas family, and although Gregg considered him "a good egg" and liked the Texan, he was not sure what the close living arrangement would do to their friendship—particularly since they did not share similar tastes.[20]

Ever the careful administrator, Gregg was upset that Clagett would be leaving on his China mission with Colonel George in five days without providing him with details of what was expected or having anyone attend to all the little matters necessary to make the general's verbal orders to Gregg workable. He was expected to train 110 brand-new pilots—including sixty-three Class 41-C and -D flying school graduates due in the following month—before Clagett and George returned. By then, he was supposed to have produced a full-strength pursuit combat group. He was expected to provide gunnery training, too—and there was not even a place to practice firing! Gregg felt very much on the spot.

However, the following day an unexpected visitor to the Philippines provided a diversion from Gregg's official worries. Ernest Hemingway was a special guest at a *despedida* beer party for Robertson arranged by his squadron's enlisted men at their mess hall at 1 P.M. to which Gregg had been invited. The celebrated writer had looked up Robertson's British girlfriend, Jill Feltham, who had known Hemingway for several years, following his arrival in Manila on May 6 aboard the Clipper from China, where he had been on a special six-week assignment for *PM* newspaper. Robertson had invited the author to the party being thrown for the homeward-bound squadron commander.[21]

As they downed their San Miguels, Hemingway explained to Gregg and the others that he had stopped off in Manila to write up his notes in order to avoid the censors in China. The editor of *PM,* a tabloid highbrow journal of current affairs, had contracted with him to write six articles on China's strategic, economic, and political situation and assess how the Sino-Japanese war was affecting U.S. commercial and military interests in the Orient. Hemingway had concluded that Japan might well go to war with America. It had not been a challenging assignment for the now-famous author of *For Whom the Bell Tolls.* He had no real interest in China and never actually saw the war during his visit there.[22]

Robertson arranged for Hemingway to meet with the Philippine Department's G2 and air officer on Monday, May 12, to share information on the military situation. Gregg picked the author up in midmorning and took him first to see Colonel Richards at the Philippine Department Air Office, and then Col. Joseph O'Hare, the department's intelligence officer. After having spent a "ghastly" evening at a dinner party given by the Philippine Writers' Association the night before, where he was so bored that he drank too much, Hemingway was happy to spend the day talking to military professionals about the air war in China. Gregg and Maverick then arranged to spend much of their free time with Hemingway until his scheduled departure for the United States on the May 15 Clipper. Hemingway told Maverick that he remembered Maverick's father from the last war and that he hoped to see him in San Antonio. Gregg regretted not having a copy of *For Whom the Bell Tolls* for Hemingway to sign. Gregg found the author to be "quite an interesting chap," and Maverick considered him "a marvelous fellow . . . a real genius" with a "striking personality."[23]

The day Hemingway flew out of Manila, Gregg was again fully occupied with the responsibilities of his new position as commander of the 4th Composite Group. At 10 A.M. he proceeded down to Nichols after a stopover at Philippine Department headquarters to convene his first meeting with his staff and squadron commanders. As first lieutenants, Buzz Wagner and Joe Moore were very junior to be assigned as COs, but Gregg had earlier suggested them to Hal George to command their squadrons, based on their demonstrated capabilities. On the other hand, as a major, Billy Maverick was quite senior to be in command of the 3d Pursuit. Gregg figured Clagett had given him the job because he wanted "someone with some rank to remain as senior Pursuit commander."

After the conference, Gregg went back to his room at the Army and Navy Club and began the tedious job of packing and weeding out papers for his move to the Nichols Field quarters. By 2 P.M. the next day he was settled in his new home. Both he and Maverick were happy to have the set of quarters to themselves instead of having to share it with a third officer, which was the usual arrangement following the dependents' departure. But Gregg, after living in relative comfort at the club, thought the quarters "were not so hot." There was just some GI furniture and Maverick's personal items to fill the rooms. Gregg, meanwhile, had "nothing but my bed, books, and a 35 peso electric fan" he had bought that day at the PX for the front bedroom and front-porch room that adjoined it. He was not feeling well: his teeth were still bothering him. He really needed to find a good time to have them pulled out.[24]

CLARK FIELD, LUZON
MID-MAY, 1941

At Clark Field, Ted Fisch was also going through a period of adjust-ment following his wife Mimi's departure on the USAT *Washington*. The day before Gregg and Maverick shifted to Nichols Field quarters, Fisch moved out of his married officers' quarters at Fort Stotsenburg and into officers' quarters he would be sharing with his 28th Bomb Squadron mate and close friend Perry Franks, who had arrived with Fisch in July, 1939, and had originally been assigned with him to the 3d Pursuit Squad-ron at Nichols Field. Fisch felt comfortable in his new bedroom: a nice breeze blew through it.

The departure of his wife of only one year was particularly depressing for the young officer from Oregon, however. The 28th's pilots had flown their B-10s out over Manila Bay to see the *Washington* off, but Fisch did not go along. He did not want to feel any worse than he already did.

A few days later, two more 28th Bomb Squadron pilots moved in with Fisch and Franks: 1st Lt. Roland "Barney" Barnick and Capt. Erickson S. Nichols. Like Fisch and Franks, Barney had come over in 1939 and served initially with the 3d Pursuit, too. A blueblood graduate of Princeton Uni-versity from a stockbroker family, Nichols—called "Nick" by his house-mates—had been assigned to the 28th Bomb Squadron upon his arrival in the Philippines on November 1, 1940, as its second-ranking officer. Following the promotion of the squadron CO, Maj. Lester Maitland, to lieutenant colonel on March 13, Nichols had moved up to take the com-mand of the 28th, while Maitland remained in charge solely of Clark Field.[25]

On May 20, Fisch and Barnick checked out the first B-18 delivered to the Philippines. It had been assigned to the 27th Materiel Squadron at Nichols. "They fly like an old lumber wagon, but at least you can get up and walk around," he wrote to Mimi. It was a definite improvement over the old B-10Bs with which they were still equipped. While Fisch was look-ing forward to having a whole squadron of the bombers as soon as they could be assembled at the Nichols air depot and turned over to them, Andy Krieger of the 3d Pursuit was less impressed with the new twin-engine bombers allocated to the Philippines. As he watched the first B-18s being uncrated and assembled at the depot, he wondered why the War Depart-ment had assigned them such patently inferior, underarmed equipment at a time when the risk of war was clearly increasing. Krieger wrote to his father that if Japan decided to attack the Philippines, these "great, lumber-ing, poky ships will be shot down as fast as they are put in the air."[26]

Unknown to Krieger, the Air Corps shared his assessment. In a May, 1941, evaluation of the type of aircraft assigned to the GHQ Air Force in the continental United States, the B-18 and B-18A were judged "very slow, obsolete." They lacked adequate defensive armament and had no self-sealing fuel tanks, the report indicated. Yet, the War Department in April had radioed Grunert of its decision to send eighteen B-18s and thirty-one P-40Bs to the Philippine Department. Earlier, Grunert had asked the War Department to replace his B-10Bs with B-23 bombers as part of his effort to replace his obsolete equipment with modern aircraft. Only a few B-23s had been produced, however, and it was decided to transfer B-18s based in Hawaii with the 5th Bomb Group instead because they were the only medium bombers available in quantity at the time.[27]

The Air Corps evaluation report also classified the P-35 as obsolete. The aircraft simply was "not suitable for combat." Nonetheless, the ancient P-26As in the Philippine Department's three pursuit squadrons were being replaced with P-35As. But as Allison Ind was happy to witness during a visit to the Nichols Field depot, thirty-one modern Curtiss P-40Bs were being uncrated and made operational at the rate of two or three a week. While Ind watched, the depot commander, Maj. William N. "Pinky" Amis, explained to him that the aircraft would not be operational for some time. They had arrived in the Philippines without Prestone coolant, and Amis pointed out that "to run those engines up, even for a few seconds, without Prestone, would ruin them beyond repair."

During an earlier visit to Nichols with Clagett and George before the PDAF commander and his executive departed for their China mission, Ind noted the row of sleek P-35As belonging to the 3d, 17th, and 20th Pursuit Squadrons lined up on the field in front of the hangars. The color of their noses indicated to which squadron they were assigned: red for the 3d, white for the 17th, and blue for the 20th. All fifty-six of the P-35s shipped to the Philippines were now operational. The gleaming aluminum bodies radiated heat as they sat in the blazing Luzon sun. In front of the 4th Composite Group's operations office, off-duty crew chiefs and armorers huddled in the shade of the corrugated iron porch. Inside, office personnel were milling around, hot and perspiring.[28]

Over at the 3d Pursuit's operations area at Nichols, Billy Maverick was deeply involved in the intensive training of his charges, particularly the eight new Class 41-B pilots assigned to him off the *Washington*. He had scheduled flying the P-35As from 5:45 in the morning to six in the evening, with half an hour off for lunch. The emphasis of their training would be on aerial gunnery practice. He then introduced additional flying from six in the evening until 9:30 at night, three times a week. He even had his pilots fly all day on Sunday, May 18, which "did not make for friendly smiles" among his pilots. However, as he explained in a letter to his mother, "I have an active combat unit in the position of a boxer with gloves, which he can better learn to use, and I intend to perfect the use of the arm, come what may." Maverick was happy to again be flying himself and to have the opportunity to teach some of the air-to-air gunnery techniques he had learned in Panama and at March Field and that had resulted in his setting the Army Air Corps record for hits scored on a sleeve target.[29]

Gregg was pleased with the progress that Maverick and the other two pursuit squadron COs were making in the training program. He also had arranged for air-to-ground gunnery practice for the pursuiters at the Philippine constabulary base at Iba, on Luzon's west coast in Zambales Province. However, he still feared that the Philippine Department, the Philippine government, the Philippine Army or constabulary, or local authorities would throw a "monkey wrench" into things before the move and upset his carefully considered plan. His efforts to get his new command functioning well had already been obstructed by various Philippine Department—including air force—brass, and he was exhausted from his exertions of the previous two weeks.

The biggest job Gregg faced was separating the various departments in the old "Headquarters Nichols Field and 4th Composite Group" setup that Churchill had commanded until the two organizations were split on May 9. The project required considerable detail work and readjustment. He had established his new headquarters at Nichols Field on May 19 and was satisfied with Grover as operations officer and with the rest of his staff. Churchill, who now commanded Nichols Field only, left most of the details to his subordinates and cooperated with Gregg on policy matters under the new arrangement, despite being sensitive over his demotion by Clagett.[30]

Gregg's living arrangements with Billy Maverick also were working out well. Although it was "quite a temptation," the 4th Composite Group CO and the 3d Pursuit Squadron CO refrained from discussing official matters in their quarters, despite the many problems they shared in their official capacities. Maverick made it a point never to mention "happenings at the post" that may not have come to Gregg's attention officially, unless it was "something that is being done against the best interests of the 4th Composite Group by parties not connected with it." And, as Gregg was experiencing, there were enough instances of that to thwart his efforts.[31]

On Wednesday evening, May 21, the 17th Pursuit Squadron invited Gregg to the squadron mess for a "farewell dinner." All of the squadron's current officers, as well as those who had come over with Gregg and were now dispersed among other squadrons—except those now stationed at Clark Field—were at the dinner, as well as the senior noncoms and enlisted men who had come from Selfridge with Gregg. The mess tent was too small to seat all of them at once, so the squadron arranged for two sittings.

Gregg's successor, Buzz Wagner, gave a very good and touching speech. He then presented Gregg with an engraved metal plaque with pilots' wings in the center, the inscription above and the 17th's snow owl insignia below, mounted on a wooden back in a sharkskin case. Although Gregg had not prepared for the occasion and had been too busy even to think of anything to say, he managed a speech of acceptance and *au revoir*. He was so moved by the situation that he felt like "weeping in my beer." Gregg's association with the 17th went back to his first assignment to the squadron fresh out of flying school in 1925 as mess and supply officer, and now he was saying good-bye as its CO.

"I like to think and really believe that the officers and men really were sincere in being sorry to see me leave," he wrote to his wife afterward. It clearly hurt Gregg to be leaving them, even though they were still indirectly under his command. "They have really been a grand and loyal bunch of men under rather adverse circumstances during the past year"—quartered in a "none-too-good tent camp" in the Philippines, having to send their families home, with lots of expenses and heart aches—but through it all they had carried on, done their jobs well, and stood by him.[32]

HEADQUARTERS, PHILIPPINE DEPARTMENT AIR FORCE
FORT SANTIAGO, MANILA
TUESDAY EVENING, JUNE 3, 1941

The evening air was steaming as the squadron commanders and higher-ranking Air Corps officers based in the Manila area assembled in the PDAF office at Fort Santiago, squirming in the suffocating heat and humidity that permeated the room. They had been called together by Colonel Richards, the ranking Air Corps officer in the Philippines while General Clagett was in China, to hear the assessment of an RAF officer who had just completed a tour of Air Corps activities in the Philippines.[33]

Group Captain Lawrence Darvall, the air officer on the staff of Sir Robert Brooke-Popham, commander in chief of British army forces in the Far East, had arrived in Manila via Clipper from Singapore on May 29, accompanied by Maj. Jacobus Wegner of the Dutch army and Lt. Col. F. G. Brink, the U.S. military observer in Singapore. During their unofficial visit, they met with General Grunert and Admiral Hart and visited several of the posts and airfields on Luzon.[34]

The forty-two-year-old British air officer's opening remarks electrified the gathering. "You will understand, I am sure, if I say that it is my belief that a sudden determined enemy attack would reduce the effectiveness of your present air force practically to zero." To Allison Ind, who was serving as the PDAF's intelligence officer, Darvall's words "seemed to snap home like machine gun bullets" among the attendees. Sitting in front of Ind, Major Gregg appeared deep in thought as he tapped the ashes off his cigarette in its inevitable holder, but showed no sign of emotional reaction to Darvall's assessment. Major Richard A. Grussendorf, CO of the 19th Air Base Squadron at Nichols, had his head down, his eyes fixed on the office's concrete floor as he drew deeply from his cigarette. Colonel Churchill's face was immobile. Major Grover seemed to be taking in Darvall's words and digesting them.

"You must have more airfields," Darvall asserted. There were only two fields from which bombers could operate and only two that could handle modern fighters, including Nichols. "You must have alternative airfields to which harassed airplanes can run for servicing and get out into the air again," their British visitor maintained. In Darvall's view, one heavy bombing attack on Nichols could cripple the PDAF's entire repair facility capacity, since all of the depot's equipment was centered in hangars, which made perfect targets from the air.[35]

His audience knew that Darvall was speaking the truth. Nothing that he stated was unknown to them. However, in the oppressive conditions of the crowded office that night, they were more concerned that he finish up his oral assessment and let them escape to their cooler quarters. Their British visitor would be sending them a written report of his visit that would provide a detailed statement on Luzon's aerial defense problems that they could study at their leisure.[36]

No one knew better than Gregg the weaknesses of the setup in the Philippines that Darvall had pointed out. One month earlier, in the Air Corps annex to the Philippine Defense Project document (1940 revision) that he had helped to prepare, a total of fourteen airfields was deemed necessary for central Luzon in addition to those at Clark and Nichols to allow for proper dispersion of the 4th Composite Group's aircraft. All should be at some distance from the coast so as to avoid being caught by a surprise attack from the sea. Thirteen suitably located airdromes were already in existence, but most of them required considerable work and enlargement to make them suitable for bombardment aircraft. A major item was the extension and improvement of Nichols Field by paving and draining the east–west runway, which at present was usable only during the dry season; grading a new northeast–southwest runway; and improving the existing north–south runway by filling in the low area. Clark Field was to have its east–west runway extended two thousand feet and its north–south runway six hundred feet. The annex recognized that the Nichols Field facilities offered "an excellent target for air attack," but did not include any proposals to alleviate the situation.[37]

According to the air defense plan included in the document, in the event of hostilities the 108 aircraft of the 4th Composite Group's five tactical squadrons would operate from widely dispersed and frequently changed landing fields and carry out continuous reconnaissance in an effort to locate enemy land, naval, and air expeditions. When conditions were favorable, they would attack targets of opportunity and, as coordinated with the navy, patrol the entire coast of Luzon and Mindoro at least once a day. The Philippine Army Air Corps's assets would be mobilized as part of this force.

Darvall had not brought the subject up during his presentation, but the Philippine Department was also concerned about the lack of antiaircraft protection afforded its airdromes. During his visit to Nichols Field in May, Ind saw no evidence of airdrome defense whatsoever for the second most important airfield in the Philippines—not even a machine gun, to say nothing of antiaircraft artillery. In response to Grunert's pleas, the War Department in January had approved the shipment of twenty 3-inch antiaircraft guns in addition to four that had been shipped in October, 1940, but they were not scheduled for shipment until April 1.[38]

Three days after the meeting with Darvall, Grunert received a radiogram from the War Department in response to his March 14 request for two additional pursuit squadrons and one additional bomb squadron as his "most urgent needs" to beef up his inadequate air force. On May 10, he had informed the War Department that he would soon have adequate landing fields to accommodate such an increase in his air strength. Now, however, the War Department informed him that "as the situation appears at present, it will not be possible to assign additional air units to the Philippine Department in the near future." He would have to make do with the squadrons on hand. One month earlier, in a radiogram sent April 15, the War Department had indicated that no additional aircraft would be assigned beyond the P-40Bs and "B-18As [*sic*]" already under shipment order, except for ten Curtiss 0-52 "Owl" observation planes scheduled for later shipment.[39]

Plans Division, Office of the Chief of the Air Corps
Munitions Building, Washington, D.C.
Thursday, June 5, 1941

Back in Washington, Maj. Hoyt Vandenberg in the Air Corps's Plans Division no longer was pushing his views on the aerial defense of the Philippines, unwanted as they were by the War Department. Dowding had returned to the United Kingdom in early May without ever having been approached on the possibility of serving as an adviser to the Philippine government on air defense buildup, as favored by Vandenberg and his aide, Lieutenant Burt.[40]

Although the War Plans Division never solicited Vandenberg's views, he noted the decisions the War Department made in response to Grunert's continuous requests for materiel and personnel reinforcements to build up his air defenses. Not surprisingly, he thought they were totally inadequate. Then, on June 5, he came down hard on a WPD-prepared study entitled "Air Force Requirements" on which the Air Corps had not been consulted. In a memo to the WPD that he prepared for General Brett's signature that day, he repeated the general Air Corps lament that it was not afforded the opportunity to study war plans drafted by the WPD that served as the basis for estimating the accuracy of any objective. Specifically, he wanted to know what basis the WPD had used to determine the size of the air force required to gain "decisive superiority" over the Japanese, as outlined in the WPD study covering air requirements for the Far East theater. Clearly, Vandenberg was still galled at being excluded from any planning for the Philippine Department's aerial defense, a subject he had specialized on since his War College days in 1939. Continuing, Vandenberg took up the Air Corps' long-standing criticism of the outdated War Department thinking regarding the proper use of airpower. Wars could only be won through "offensive action," which meant "adequate bombardment aviation" was essential, he asserted. "Defense pursuit interceptor operations are vitally necessary when we are in no position to wage an offensive air war." However, if America were committed to winning a war rather than just staving off defeat, "no plan should be predicated on building up a defensive arm at the expense of an offensive arm," he concluded.[41]

While Vandenberg's views represented the Air Corps's position on the use of airpower in general, they also formed the basis of his 1939 plan for a combined offensive/defensive air strategy for the Philippines. If the Japanese attacked the islands, he reasoned, they should not only expect to be engaged in American defensive operations over and approaching Philippines territory, but also should expect being bombarded on their own soil. On this position, he clearly retained the support of Air Corps decision makers.

PIER 7, MANILA HARBOR
TUESDAY MORNING, JUNE 10, 1941

On the morning of Tuesday, June 10, Colonel Richards and Allison Ind were down at Pier 7 to meet the *President Coolidge,* just in from Hong Kong on its eastern swing through the Pacific. As General Clagett and Colonel George disembarked from the two-funneled American

President Line transport in the withering heat, Richards and Ind came forward to greet them. Ind was shocked by Clagett's appearance. Skin hung loosely about his creased, sallow face. "His eyes looked tired and worn, sunk with innumerable skin folds above, beside, and beneath them." He was sweating profusely. Both Clagett and George had fallen ill during their trip to China, though Hal George less seriously.[42]

Major Gregg was surprised to see them back so soon, ahead of schedule and unannounced. They were not expected back from their China mission until about June 25, but they had terminated their work on June 6 due to Clagett's illness and secured return passage on the *Coolidge*.[43]

Clagett turned himself in at Sternberg Hospital for treatment. Ind regretted this turn of events because "a pile of work" had accumulated at PDAF headquarters during their absence. However, within two days, Clagett—with the help of Colonel George, Ind, a naval officer, and a Chungking attaché—produced an eleven-page report for Chief of Staff Marshall in Washington, to be sent via General Grunert, detailing the findings of his May 17–June 6 mission.[44]

Of particular interest to the Philippine Department were the sections dealing with Japanese aircraft and aerial tactics over China. Clagett's report indicated that the latest Japanese "Zero type" pursuit aircraft had a reported top speed of about 340 miles per hour and carried "belly tanks" that gave it a range of at least eight hundred miles. The Zero was armed with two 20-mm automatic cannon that used explosive, incendiary, tracer, and solid ammunition, and two 7.9-mm machine guns. According to Chinese reports, the aircraft did not have a small turning circle and was not very maneuverable.

Regarding tactics, Chinese pilots reported that the Japanese Zero pilots would not engage in a turning duel, but preferred to make a diving attack followed by a steep climb. The Chinese air force's Russian-made pursuit ships could not follow the Zero in a climb, and if they fell off, or if the Japanese otherwise got a good altitude advantage, he would kick his plane over in another dive on the Chinese aircraft, which would be nearly stalled at that point.

Based on reports they received and from air raids they personally observed, Clagett and George concluded that Japanese bomber pilots "have not indicated much ability in precision bombing." That assessment would come back to haunt them six months later.

Although neither Clagett nor George were "in harness" their first few days back from China, Gregg felt that his 4th Composite Group had not been doing too badly while they were gone. Moreover, this was despite a breakdown in cooperation with the Air Corps colonels over him—Churchill and Charlie Savage, and, to a lesser degree, Richards. All three were unhappy about the new command arrangements following Clagett's arrival, and in Gregg's view had been very busy "fixing things" so that the blame for any failure by the new group would fall squarely on Gregg. The group's CO was especially disappointed by Churchill's recent behavior. Gregg had told Clagett and George that he was sure Churchill would cooperate with the new arrangement despite taking his relief as a "slap in the face." Now Gregg had to admit that he was wrong in his decision to "play ball" with Churchill, who had "surely let me down," he wrote his wife.

The arrangement whereby Gregg was given command only of the group's pursuit units was working out all right. Les Maitland, as the CO of Clark Field, was, in effect, in command of the rest of the group: the 28th Bomb and 2d Observation Squadrons. In Gregg's judgment, Maitland, if rumors proved correct, would be given command of any bomb group organized in the Philippines. The other 4th Group officer who outranked Gregg was Lt. Col. Charlie Backes, but he was still assigned outside the group as air adviser to the Philippine Army, in effect acting as chief of the Philippine Army Air Corps.[45]

While progress had been made in organizing the PDAF into a more effective combat force, the other task Marshall had given Clagett—develop an air defense organization—was lagging behind. This was particularly true in the case of the Air Warning Service (AWS). Prior to May 4, the "Warning Service" served under the assistant chief of staff, G2, in the Philippine Department's Military Intelligence Division. However, with the establishment of the PDAF on that date, the operation and its three-officer staff, headed by Lt. Col. Alexander H. Campbell, a Coast Artillery officer, was shifted to Clagett's command, also located in Fort Santiago, and renamed the AWS, but with no change in its modus operandi.[46]

As described in the Philippine Defense Project report, revised in May, the AWS maintained a central Information and Operation Center manned by three officers and eleven enlisted men that was set up to receive messages from 509 observation centers manned by 860 local observers throughout the islands, using five radio, two telegraph, and ten telephone networks. The U.S. Army, Navy, and Coast Guard; Bureau of Posts and Aeronautics; Philippine Army and constabulary; and Philippine long-distance and provincial telephone company staffs manned the organization's stations and nets.[47]

Although it might have seemed impressive on paper, Allison Ind regarded the system as inadequate during a visit to the AWS at Fort Santiago in May. The test reports that were coming in were "halting and unreliable" and the AWS was "poorly prepared to coordinate them into a system," in his estimation. The hundreds of Filipino watchers who made up the backbone of the observer network were "not well trained" and were unable to identify aircraft accurately. The tasks of relaying telephone calls over great distances and ensuring that the interpreters at the Fort Santiago message center could understand the faint messages coming over the lines and relay them properly to the Information and Operations Center were really beyond the system's capacity, in Ind's view. The only piece of equipment Ind found in the AWS room was a big, electrically lighted map of the Philippines used as a plotting board, with "twinkling lights" indicating the origin of warning messages.[48]

Grunert was understandably dissatisfied with this primitive arrangement, and in September, 1940, had asked the War Department to install a more modern system. On January 9, 1941, the Philippine Department commanding general informed the War Department by memo of his top-priority requirement for a complete, mobile AWS, with sufficient equipment and personnel for five detector stations. In mid-January, the War Plans Division indicated to Marshall that a complete AWS for the Philippines would require eight fixed and two mobile detector stations plus an information center. It called for a minimum of one fixed and two mobile detector stations and an information center to be provided Grunert at once, and that $500,000 be allocated to the Philippine Department in Fiscal Year 1941 for that purpose.[49]

By early June Grunert still had not received the promised new equipment. Now, however, a new problem was beginning to cause him headaches. His command was suffering from an intense morale problem that he had informed Marshall on June 2 was probably greater than in any other army command. It had been triggered the month before by the repatriation of officers' families, Grunert explained. The Philippine Department commander was taking a tough stance toward the situation, which he thought involved mostly young reserve officers. "With a few month's education and a bit of discipline, [they] will shake themselves into harness," he argued. "Work, and plenty of it, together with a bit of sympathy, seems to be the best cure."[50]

CLARK FIELD, LUZON
MID-JUNE 1941

At Clark Field, the morale problem was particularly bad and was becoming even more intense because the two-year tour of duty requirement for overseas assignments was being extended to three years. Ted Fisch and his roommates Roland Barnick and Perry Franks were spending most of their off-duty time "bitching and figuring out ways and means of leaving the islands." Fisch had written his father-in-law inquiring if there was any way he knew of to get him out of "this hellhole."[51]

Concerned about the morale in his command, Clark Field commander Les Maitland had accepted a suggestion submitted by Capt. Maurice "Moe" Daly in early May that Maitland order all the enlisted men and officers at Clark to grow beards to inject some humor into the situation at the base. By mid-June, the beards were beginning to show up in all shapes, sizes, and colors. Fisch regarded his as one of the best on the post.[52]

Just as Grunert had expected, added work was keeping officers such as Fisch and his 28th Bomb Squadron colleagues too busy to dwell on their personal situations—although only during duty hours. Sixteen of the B-18s had been delivered to the squadron, and Fisch was busy checking out the younger pilots in them. He still regarded the bombers as "regular old lumber wagons," but they were excellent for twin-engine flight training. The rumor that some of the B-18s were going to make a trip to Singapore after the rainy season and that he might also get to go bolstered his spirits.[53]

PART II

"If We Make Our Attack Now, the War is Not Hopeless"

Tokyo, Washington, and Manila:
June–October, 1941

GERMANY'S UNEXPECTED INVASION of the Soviet Union

on June 22, 1941, emboldened the Japanese Navy Ministry and the naval General Staff in their planning for southern operations. On June 23, they decided to set up bases and airfields in southern Indochina even if that action "risked war with Britain and the United States." The newly appointed (from April 10, 1941) chief of the naval General Staff, Adm. Osami Nagano, asserted that the establishment of military bases in French Indochina and Thailand was necessary. Two days later, a liaison conference approved the decision and the emperor gave his imperial sanction.[1]

On July 2, an Imperial conference called by Premier Konoe endorsed the establishment of the Greater East Asia Co-prosperity Sphere and a southward advance. The "Outline of the Empire's National Policies in View of the Changing Situation" for the first time used the expression "war with Britain and the United States" in a formal policy statement, although the conference concluded that moving troops and aircraft into southern Indochina would not provoke the United States into "coming out against Japan." At any rate, the operation was considered worth the risk, in the view of the participants. Emperor Hirohito approved the policy document, but hoped to avoid a war with either the United States or the Soviet Union. The justification given for the southern advance was "self-defense and self-preservation."[2]

A move into southern Indochina and the subsequent establishment of bases for the navy's land-based bombers there would reduce the need for carriers in support of southern operations. All of the navy's land-based airpower had been centralized six months earlier under a single strategic command with the establishment of the Eleventh Air Fleet on January 15,

1941, and Vice Adm. Takajirō Ōnishi began preparing its pilots in April for
an attack on the Philippines.[3]

Following negotiations with Vichy France, more than forty thousand
Japanese troops began entering and occupying southern French Indochina without incident on July 25. Four days earlier, Admiral Nagano
proclaimed at a liaison conference that if war began immediately with the
United States because of such a move, the Japanese "would have a chance
of achieving victory" because they were far ahead of the Americans in
their war preparations, although he acknowledged that the advantage
would decline if such a war dragged out. Nagano also argued for seizure
of the Philippines to make it easier for the navy to carry on the war. His
statements displeased Hirohito; the emperor knew that the navy's preparations were by no means sufficiently advanced to take on the United States
at that time.[4]

In immediate response to the Japanese move, President Roosevelt on
July 26 issued an executive order freezing Japanese assets in the United
States, thus halting all trade with Japan. It was correctly regarded as an
"oil embargo" by the press, and was followed by similar embargoes by the
British and Dutch. To the *New York Times,* it was "the most drastic blow
short of war." Prior to Roosevelt's decision, the army and navy chiefs had
recommended against such an action. General Marshall and Admiral Stark
both were convinced an embargo would force the Japanese either to drop
their long-term strategic objectives or to meet their oil needs by seizing
the Dutch East Indies—a move that would surely lead to war.[5]

Marshall was planning a less dramatic and unpublicized response to
the preparations Japanese were making for their southern movement. On
July 16, he informed the Air Corps chief, General Arnold, that he had
decided the Philippines were to be given "great strategic importance,"
and thus was reversing the War Department's long-standing position on
defense of the islands. The naval and air bases in the Philippines were
now seen as constituting a threat to the "immediate flank of the Japanese
southern movement."[6]

Signaling the beginning of the change in the Philippines' role in War
Department strategy, Roosevelt on July 26 created a new army command
in the islands—U.S. Army Forces in the Far East (USAFFE)—and recalled
Gen. Douglas MacArthur to active duty from his retirement position as
military adviser to the Philippine Commonwealth to serve as its commanding general with the rank of lieutenant general. The president's decision did not come as a surprise to Marshall. A month earlier the army
chief of staff and Secretary of War Stimson had decided that MacArthur
should head such a new command should the Far East situation "approach

a crisis," and had so informed MacArthur. The Indochina incursion was just such a crisis.[7]

In Tokyo, the imposition of the de facto embargo on petroleum imports caused the Konoe government to "panic." It was estimated that the navy would be entirely disabled within two years and Japanese industries dependent on oil "would be paralyzed in less than a year." The options open to the Japanese appeared to be two: either "capitulate" under the economic pressure of the embargo or "take some other course to end, neutralize, or escape the pressure."[8]

In Manila, MacArthur saw the parallel reaction to the Japanese occupation of southern Indochina of calling him up to head the new USAFFE command as meaning that the United States "intends to maintain at any cost its full rights in the Far East." In a statement to the press on July 27, MacArthur asserted that "it is quite evident that [the American government's] determination is immutable, its will indomitable." In his new position of authority, MacArthur intended to put into practice his "oft-expressed conviction that he could save the Philippines." He was not going to be satisfied with the long-standing mandate under War Plan Orange Three to defend only Manila Bay. Rather, he intended to expand it to cover the entire Philippine archipelago.[9]

Following Emperor Hirohito's ratification of the southern advance at the Imperial Conference on July 2, liaison conferences were held on several occasions. Such meetings now fully usurped the cabinet's decision-making function. After each meeting, Konoe and the army and navy chiefs of staff briefed the emperor on the latest developments in the crisis.[10]

In August, Hirohito became very familiar with the navy's argument that the embargo was gradually weakening Japan's military strength and that it was desirable to opt for an early commencement of hostilities. Rear Admiral Sōkichi Takagi, a navy leader with particularly close ties to the palace, convincingly expounded this view. On August 8, he told a palace representative:"if Japan lets the time pass while under pressure from lack of materials [due to the oil embargo], we will be giving up without a fight. If we make our attack now, the war is militarily calculable and not hopeless. But if we vacillate, the situation will become increasingly disadvantageous for us."[11]

Hirohito had begun to believe that military considerations should determine whether the decision should be made to undertake a new war and was relying on the army and navy high commands to provide the details necessary for him to make such a decision. The army's General Staff was completing a master plan toward the end of August that it had begun working on in April in close cooperation with operations officers of the navy General Staff. The staff officers had decided to drop the idea of an offensive to the north in 1941 and were now concentrating their planning efforts on southern operations. At the beginning of August, the navy General Staff's Operations Section was instructed to start preparing for hostilities, and by the end of the month had finished a draft strategic plan in cooperation with army General Staff operations officers.[12]

The navy General Staff's plan did not include what was now being referred to as the "Hawaii operation": the proposed attack on Pearl Harbor that was being insisted on by Admiral Yamamoto. Yamamoto's staff had recently completed its own strategic plan for the Combined Fleet that prominently featured the Hawaii operation. It called for an attack on Pearl Harbor by part of the Combined Fleet, while most of the fleet remained committed to southern operations. However, the navy General Staff—responsible for planning for naval operations—regarded Yamamoto's Hawaii operation as dangerous and having little hope of success. It wanted to reserve all of the Combined Fleet's carriers for southern operations, not split them between the two.[13]

The War Department initially viewed the establishment of USAFFE as a purely defensive move. However, by August the rationale was "changing radically" and it was being touted as a deterrent to any further Japanese southern expansion. Both Marshall and MacArthur believed the Philippines could play a large role in thwarting such Japanese ambitions.[14]

When Prime Minister Winston Churchill and President Roosevelt met at the Argentia Conference, the decision was made on August 7 to give MacArthur aerial weapons with which to conduct offensive operations from the Philippines. Agreement within the War Department had been reached in July on this policy change, and late that month the Army Air Forces had begun making arrangements for ferrying B-17 heavy bombers to the Far East. In August, the Joint Board approved a project that would establish a ferry route across the Pacific for heavy bombers, which the War Department had turned down when General Arnold first broached the subject in February.[15]

The decision to base heavy bombers in the Philippines was also reflected in the Air Annex (AWPD/1) to the so-called Victory Program being prepared in August by the War Department in response to the president's July 9 request for an estimate of the munitions requirements needed to defeat America's enemies. Arnold's planning officers included the provision of four groups of heavy bombers (a total of 272 B-17s and B-24s) in AWPD/1 in order to maintain "a strategic defense in Asia and for the protection of American interests in the Philippines."[16]

ARMY CHIEF OF STAFF GEN. GEORGE C. MARSHALL POINTS OUT A STRATEGIC CONSID-
ERATION ON A MAP FOR SECRETARY OF WAR HENRY STIMSON DURING A JANUARY 16,
1942, MEETING. PHOTO NO. 1050 COURTESY THE GEORGE C. MARSHALL LIBRARY AND
ARCHIVES, VIRGINIA MILITARY INSTITUTE, LEXINGTON, VIRGINIA.

Based on the aircrafts' performance characteristics as explained to them
by Arnold's air planners, both Stimson and Marshall had become enthusi-
astic believers in the potential of heavy bombers to deter Japan from any
further movement south. With the safe arrival of the first nine B-17s in
the Philippines on September 12, Stimson recorded in his diary that the
B-17 "has completely changed the strategy of the Pacific and lets American power get back into the [Philippine] Islands in a way which it has not
been able to do for twenty years."[17]

At the Joint Board meeting on September 19, Marshall maintained that the B-17 buildup in the Philippines "would have a profound strategic effect and it might be the decisive element in deterring Japan from undertaking a Pacific War." A week earlier he had informed his navy counterpart, Chief of Naval Operations Harold Stark, that the B-24s being transferred to the Philippines "can reach Osaka with a full load [fourteen thousand pounds of bombs] and Tokyo with a partial load."[18]

Although no one was acknowledging it, War Department policy now embraced the approach proposed by Capt. Hoyt Vandenberg and endorsed by Air Staff Chief Carl Spaatz in September, 1939, regarding the use of offensive airpower in the Philippines to deter Japan's southern ambitions.

In early September, Tokyo introduced a time element into the government's strategic thinking. A national policy document was submitted and adopted at the September 3 liaison conference. It provided that the empire "for its existence and self-defense shall complete war preparations by about the latter part of October, with the resolve not to hesitate to go to war with the U.S., Great Britain, and the Netherlands." Furthermore, if "by early October" there was no prospect for achieving the government's demands through diplomatic negotiations, "we shall immediately decide to initiate war with the U.S., Great Britain and the Netherlands."

At the Imperial Conference held three days later, Hirohito was presented the decision made at the liaison conference. In the "most important decision of Hirohito's life," the emperor gave his sanction to the "Outline to Carry Out the National Policies of the Empire" generated at the liaison conference. Moreover, he did so "with misgivings, without an optimistic prospect of victory or even any notion of the course a protracted war might take."[19]

As provided for by the "Outline," all of the participants at the Imperial Conference had to complete their war preparations by the last ten days of October. If by early October there appeared to be no possibility of achieving their demands through the negotiations in Washington that began on August 6, they would be obliged to make the decision to enter into war with the United States, Great Britain, and the Netherlands.[20]

Premier Konoe was becoming "increasingly despondent" over the course of events. He continued to hope for a diplomatic breakthrough to resolve the crisis. Admiral Yamamoto, seeking to ease Konoe's anguish, assured him during a visit on September 12 that if there was to be a war, he would do "everything he could to force an early, decisive battle" in which he would commit the entire Combined Fleet. If he won such a battle, "a long war of attrition might be avoided" or the war even won.[21]

Following the Imperial Conference, the army General Staff began preparing in earnest for southern operations. Earlier operational plans had to be recast: men and materiel originally earmarked for China and the Soviet Union would have to be reassigned to support southern operations. On September 9, General Sugiyama, the chief of the army General Staff, presented a detailed report to the emperor on the army's plans for southern operations. By the end of the month, following a full study by operations officers, the plans were virtually complete.[22]

Five days before the Imperial Conference, the navy General Staff had placed the entire sea service on a war footing. At the Imperial Navy Staff College, war games were held from September 11–20 at which both the southern and the Hawaii operations were studied. In the southern operations war games, discussions were held on how the Philippines, Malaya, and the Dutch East Indies could be seized by March, 1942. For the Hawaii operation, the Combined Fleet staff wanted all its carriers assigned to the Pearl Harbor attack, but the navy General Staff refused the request. By the end of the war games, the naval staff remained strongly opposed to the Hawaii operation.[23]

The war games did not generate full confidence among the participants, and at least one key player thought they were entirely too theoretical. Admiral Nishizo Tsukahara, the commander of the Eleventh Air Fleet, whose land-based bombers and fighters would play a key role in the southern operations, thought the games seemed "unrealistic and confusing." At a September 29 meeting of senior staff officers from the First and Eleventh Air Fleets, Tsukahara expressed concern that he was not being allocated adequate fighter protection for his bombers and argued for strong carrier-based support from the First Air Fleet, whose aircraft were being earmarked by Yamamoto and his staff for the Pearl Harbor attack.[24]

In Manila, Adm. Thomas Hart, the commander in chief of the Asiatic Fleet, succeeded in arranging a meeting with General MacArthur on September 22 at which Hart wanted to discuss the coordination of USAFFE and Asiatic Fleet plans. MacArthur seemed uninterested in Hart's plans and wanted to hold forth on his own instead. With a land force growing to two hundred thousand troops by April, 1942, and an air force of "600 planes" promised to him, he told Hart he planned to hold all of the Philippines except Mindanao.[25]

On October 1, MacArthur wrote to the adjutant general in Washington to seek a change in his defense responsibilities along the lines he had discussed with Hart. His "strategic mission" of defending only the entrance to Manila Bay by employing "a citadel type defense" should be "broadened to include the defense of the Philippine Islands." Due to the "wide scope of enemy operations, especially aviation," he believed it was "imperative" to

Air Chief Marshal Sir Robert Brooke-Popham, commander of British Forces in the Far East, confers with USAFFE Commanding General Douglas MacArthur during Brooke-Popham's visit from Singapore, October 3–5, 1941. Acme photo courtesy the Library of Congress.

broaden "the concept of Philippine defense." He believed his forces were "sufficient to accomplish such a mission."[26]

Meanwhile, the War Department was thinking of an even wider role for MacArthur than defense of the Philippines alone. In a radiogram to the USAFFE commander on October 3, Marshall expressed interest in the air defense of Australia, the Dutch East Indies, and Singapore, as well as of the Philippines, and the need for cooperation with British authorities in the Far East to promote such a wider approach. Specifically, he wanted MacArthur to contact the British in Singapore "at once" to gain permission for the use of airfields at Singapore, Darwin, Rabaul, and Port Moresby by his B-17s. MacArthur was also asked to contact the Dutch for "emergency use" of their airfields in the East Indies.[27]

There was no need for MacArthur to take the initiative on the matter, though. That same day, Brooke-Popham, the British commander in the Far East, and three of his staff officers arrived at Sangley Point just south of Manila from Singapore to resume conversations on regional defense plans with MacArthur, Hart, and Philippines president Quezon. Brooke-Popham focused his attention on MacArthur, who he knew was no longer just Quezon's military adviser, but commander of all U.S. Army forces in the Philippines.[28]

Brooke-Popham brought with him a copy of his "Most Secret Memo" of September 19 and gave it to MacArthur. The document covered Brooke-Popham's plans for defeating Japan. His strategy was to "confine Japan to her own islands and sever its sea communications" while launching aerial attacks from Luzon and Vladivostok in the Soviet Union to "destroy . . . Japan's war industries." He also discussed with MacArthur his proposal to base "an American Expeditionary Force in the area, where it would be more easily conveyed and supplied than if it were taken across the Atlantic." Brooke-Popham was pleased to find in his discussions with the USAFFE commander that MacArthur "is not thinking merely of local defence." However, he failed to make much of an impression on Admiral Hart, who, as Hart's biographer concluded, had no respect for Brooke-Popham's "strategic vision," found little to discuss with him, and thought there was "slight reason to worry how to work with the British."[29]

On October 13, just a week after Brooke-Popham left the Philippines to return to Singapore, it was the Dutch's turn to discuss the coordination of defensive plans following the arrival that day of Maj. Gen. Hein ter Poorten, the chief of staff of the Netherlands East Indies army. However, ter Poorten was forced to abort his scheduled three-day visit when summoned back to Batavia the next day due to the death in an aircraft accident of his chief, Lt. Gen. G. J. Berenschot, on the day ter Poorten arrived in the Philippines.[30]

In Washington in October, the War Department was caught up in developing and expounding its new strategy for deterring Japanese southern expansion by threatening to attack the Japanese home islands with heavy bombers being sent to the Philippines if Japan did not cease such operations. Marshall's planning chief, Brig. Gen. Leonard Gerow, and his air commander, General Arnold, were providing Secretary of War Stimson with information Stimson wanted in order to impress Secretary of State Cordell Hull and President Roosevelt with the rationale behind the strategy and the need for sending as many heavy bombers to the Philippines as possible to execute the plan.

On October 4, Stimson sent Hull a map of the Far East that used concentric circles to depict the radii of operation of B-17s and B-24s based in the Philippines, as well as operating from Vladivostok, Singapore, Darwin, and Rockhampton. The B-24s could fly to Tokyo from northern Luzon and land in Vladivostok. "Tremendous changes" were being introduced "by the new establishment of heavy bombers in the Philippines," he informed Hull in a covering note.[31]

In a memorandum to Stimson on October 8, Gerow maintained that "air and ground units now available or scheduled for despatch to the Philippine Islands in the immediate future have changed the entire picture in the Asiatic Area" and "may well be the determining factor in Japan's eventual decision [to move south]." That same day, Arnold informed Stimson that ninety-five of the 128 B-17s and thirty-five of the ninety-five B-24s expected off the production lines by end of February, 1942, were earmarked for the Philippines. In arguing that more B-24s should be sent to the Philippines than to the British, Arnold informed the secretary of war that the bomber's range made it possible "to reach the interior of Japan, while the range of the B-17 brings only the southern tip of Japan within our bombing range."[32]

In response to Roosevelt's query regarding the "proper strategic distribution" for the new four-engine bombers, Stimson, in a letter dated October 21, argued against diverting production of the bombers away from the needs of the Army Air Forces (AAF). The heavy bombers were the key to a "strategic opportunity of the utmost importance that has suddenly arisen in the southwestern Pacific." Stimson maintained that from a previous impotency to influence events in the area, "we suddenly find ourselves vested with the possibility of great effective power." The threat of bombing attacks on the Japanese homeland by heavy bombers based in the Philippines and using Vladivostok to refuel before proceeding "to safety in the north," would serve to "protect against aggression of Japan" as well as to "preserve the defensive power of Russia in Europe."[33]

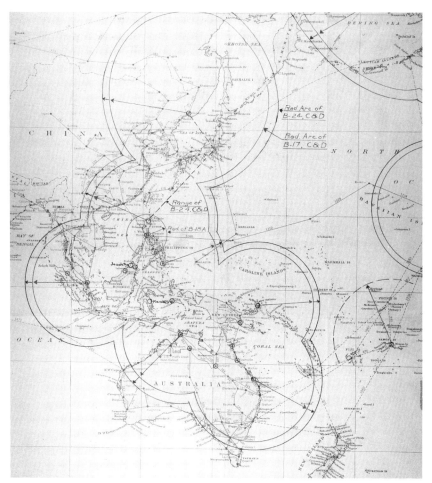

MAP PREPARED FOR SECRETARY OF WAR STIMSON IN EARLY OCTOBER, 1941, SHOWING IN
CONCENTRIC CIRCLES THE RADII OF OPERATION OF B-17S, B-18S, AND B-24S FROM BASES
IN THE PHILIPPINES. COURTESY THE NATIONAL ARCHIVES AND RECORDS
ADMINISTRATION, RG 107

However, Stimson recognized that such a strategy required time to
become effective. The heavy bomber force needed to implement it would
not be fully deployed in the Philippines until March, 1942. For that reason, it was imperative that a war in the Far East and Pacific be postponed
until at least that time. On October 6, Stimson asked Hull to continue
negotiating with Japan "for three months" to "secure our position." Three
weeks later, he reconfirmed his request to Hull, adding that in support
of such diplomatic efforts he would "avoid any boasting about what we
are doing or any flamboyant announcements" about the movement of

heavy bombers to the Philippines. He told Hull his policy harkened back to Theodore Roosevelt, who advocated that one "Speak softly but carry a big stick."[34]

The War Department's new strategy for the Philippines as enthusiastically adopted by Stimson was conveyed to MacArthur in the form of Gerow's "Strategic Concept of the Philippines" memorandum to the secretary of war on October 8. On October 18, in response to MacArthur's October 1 letter requesting that his mission be broadened, General Marshall sent a memorandum to the USAFFE commander informing him that a revision had been drafted and was awaiting action by the Joint Board, "with approval expected in the next ten days." Under the revised Rainbow 5 plan, USAFFE would defend not only Manila Bay but the rest of the Philippine archipelago, too, just as MacArthur had requested. However, in keeping with the new heavy-bomber oriented deterrent strategy, he was to "conduct air raids against Japanese forces and installations within tactical operating radius of available bases." In addition, reflecting the growing defense relationship with the British and Dutch, the revised plan called for USAFFE to "cooperate with the Associated Powers in defense of the territories of these powers in accordance with approved policies and agreements."[35]

Lacking authority over the army and navy high commands, and with the emperor leaning increasingly toward war, Prince Fumimaro Konoe turned in his resignation as premier on October 16. According to Hirohito's biographer, Konoe was "a victim of the time element in the national policy document he himself had helped to craft." He was convinced that the emperor "no longer had confidence in him," that Germany was going to lose the war, and that Japan had no chance to win a war.

Hirohito accepted Konoe's resignation and gave his support to Army Minister Hideki Tōjō, who was appointed premier on October 17 and promoted to full general the following day. Tōjō was adamantly opposed to yielding to U.S. demands and was the army's strongest advocate for war. The emperor supported his views, believing that war was by then unavoidable.[36]

Meanwhile, the Imperial Army conducted tabletop maneuvers from October 1–5 at the Army War College in which the General Staff and staff officers of the field armies slated to participate in southern operations studied various scenarios for the planned invasions. By the end of the month, agreement was reached on an operations plan.[37]

The navy's Combined Fleet also held tabletop maneuvers for southern operations, extending from October 9–11 on Yamamoto's flagship *Nagato,* and followed on October 13 by an exercise for the Hawaii operation. For the latter, only three carriers participated, with the other three earmarked for the southern operation. A particular concern was how to synchronize the two operations so as to ensure that the Pearl Harbor attack occurred *before* the southern operations forces heading for the attacks were discovered.[38]

The navy General Staff remained opposed to including the Hawaii operation in its operational plan. Matters came to a head on October 18 when Admiral Yamamoto threatened to resign as commander in chief of the Combined Fleet if the operation were not accepted. Faced with Yamamoto's "thunderbolt," Navy Chief of Staff Nagano backed down and agreed to incorporate the Hawaii operation in the navy's plan, provided it did not interfere with southern operations in any way or weaken naval air strength in their support. Yamamoto was given all six of the carriers that he had sought for the Pearl Harbor attack. On October 20, Admiral Nagano formally approved the navy's operations plan, which now included the Hawaii operation.[39]

During the tabletop exercises on the *Nagato,* the Combined Fleet planners aimed for December 8 as the target date for starting the war. Six factors were behind the selection of that date: (1) "the U.S. was growing stronger day by day in the Pacific, especially in the Philippines," (2) winter weather conditions in the northern Pacific would foreclose January and February as possibilities for the Hawaii operation, (3) the navy's oil stocks were dwindling rapidly, (4) the phase of the moon had to be right so there would be maximum moonlight for the Pearl Harbor task force's night operations, (5) the army wanted to move as quickly as possible "to avoid the worst of the monsoon season," and (6) intelligence indicated that most of the U.S. Pacific Fleet would be in port on a Sunday.[40]

CHAPTER 4

"Why Send Over These Ninety-Day Wonders?"

O n the morning of Tuesday, June 24, 1941, Maj. Kirtley Gregg was surprised to learn that the USAT *President Pierce* was at Pier 7 in Manila Bay with a load of pilots being assigned to the Philippine Department Air Force. He was expecting the pilots' arrival about June 27 or 28, but no one in the Philippine Department had been informed of the exact date. The *Pierce* had maintained radio silence during its entire voyage from San Francisco due to security precautions imposed on it by the War Department. Gregg hurriedly made his way to the pier to greet the newcomers. He was being assigned 63 of them for his three pursuit squadrons, with the other 33 being allocated to the 2d Observation Squadron and the 28th Bomb Squadron. Of the 96 pilots disembarking, 68 had graduated from flying school the month before in Class 41-C, and 28 in Class 41-D—just one week prior to departure for the Philippines.

Despite the lack of preparation, the newies were taken immediately to the Army and Navy Club for an impromptu welcoming party given by the squadrons to which they were being assigned. Of the squadrons under Gregg's command, Billy Maverick's 3d Pursuit was given twenty-two of the brand-new pilots, Buzz Wagner's 17th received twenty-one of them, and Joe Moore's 20th Pursuit had twenty allocated to it. In one stroke, the pilot strength of each of the group's pursuit squadrons had been doubled.[1]

At the reception, Gregg explained to the new arrivals that all of them were going to be transferred to Clark Field in four days because a major construction program was to be started at Nichols and the squadrons sent out. Due to Nichols's boggy terrain and the submergence of its single runway during the rainy season, pilots were often grounded and training curtailed. To overcome this obstacle, Gregg, supported by Maverick and Grover, had proposed closing the airfield for repairs upon the arrival of the next batch of pilots and shifting to Clark Field for the necessary extended training. Nichols's oft-flooded landing strip would be drained and lengthened; a concrete runway would be built; more hangars, maintenance, and shop facilities constructed; additional storage areas for bombs, ammunition, and gasoline created; and barracks and officers quarters erected.[2]

Gregg told his new charges that as soon as the party ended they would board trucks for the fifty-five-mile journey north to Clark and adjoining Fort Stotsenburg, where they would be accommodated. The oldies, with the exception of those in the 17th Pursuit, would join them on June 28. The 17th's pilots were headed for the gunnery camp at Iba Field in Zambales.[3]

After the reception, Gregg went back to making final arrangements for the move. He had been fighting for this plan for the past few months, but with the PDAF commander and executive officer away in China since mid-May, had not been able to get it approved in the face of the opposition of Colonels Richards and Churchill. However, on June 18—a week after Clagett and George returned—Gregg dropped "a bug in the ear" of five different persons that nothing had been done about his plan. His complaint quickly made it to Colonel George's attention and on the following morning his strategy paid off. Colonel George called at 8:30 to inform Gregg that the entire 4th Composite Group would be shifting to Clark by the twenty-seventh and would remain in the field until the sixty-three pilots being assigned to Gregg completed their advanced training. He had also been given the option of sending one of his Clark-bound squadrons to Iba Field in Zambales, on Luzon's west coast, for air-to-ground gunnery practice if he so desired.

Gregg was elated. The Nichols Field command had "not done one damned thing towards functioning as a Base—but they are going to produce now, or else!" he asserted in a letter to his wife. Gregg felt that he had "almost earned my last 16 years' pay in the last 48 hours."

Two days after the newies left for Clark, however, it was the elements' turn to conspire to thwart his plan. "One of the worst storms that I have ever seen over here" began to slam into the Manila area. The enlisted men were flooded out of their tents at Nichols and obliged to move into their squadron's hangars. Yet Gregg, anxious to get in his mandatory four hours' flying time for the month, went out that afternoon for the first time in June and stayed out an hour longer than he had planned, "playing tag" with the forerunner of the typhoon headed their way. His housemate, Billy Maverick, thought "he looked like a drowned cat when he came in."[4]

At noon on June 27, with torrential rain and winds up to forty miles an hour wreaking havoc, the PDAF canceled the move scheduled for the next day. The roads were in such bad shape that trucks would be unable to get supplies and equipment to Clark. Concerned about the effect the

PILOTS OF THE 17TH PURSUIT SQUADRON PASS TIME CHATTING WHILE WAITING TO FLY FROM NICHOLS FIELD TO IBA ON JULY 3, 1941. *LEFT TO RIGHT:* GEORGE ARMSTRONG, RED SHEPPARD (*BACK TO CAMERA*), ED KISER (*PARTLY OBSCURED*), BILL FEALLOCK, DAVE OBERT, AND LARRY LODIN (*HAND TO FACE AT RIGHT*). PHOTO COURTESY WILLIAM M. ROWE.

high winds would have on the pursuit ships, Gregg and Maverick planned to remove their propellers, let the aircraft down on their bellies, tie them down firmly, and weight them with sandbags.

Taking advantage of the delay in implementing Gregg's plan, Colonel Richards, acting in his capacity as Philippine Department air officer, ordered a detail including all of the experienced pilots in Maverick's 3d Pursuit to act as liaison officers for the Asiatic Fleet's ships for the next month! Furious, Gregg called Colonel George, who told General Grunert, who immediately called off the liaison detail. After receiving a stinging rebuke, Richards telephoned Gregg, shouted, "This time you win, Major Gregg!" and slammed down the receiver.

For his part, Colonel Churchill was refusing to designate storage places at Nichols for equipment belonging to the 17th Pursuit, bound for Iba. Despite the typhoon, Gregg ordered 1st Lt. Red Sheppard, the 17th's assistant operations officer, to load a convoy of seven trucks that evening with all of the squadron's maneuver equipment and head for Iba at five in the morning before anyone at Nichols Field could stop him. Sheppard was pleased to carry out his instructions. Like Gregg, he was irritated with the "sit down strike" tactics of the faction of old-time Air Corps colonels whom he regarded as being in the Philippines on "vacation." Their refusal to make decisions was affecting operations all the way down to his squadron's level.[5]

With the obstructionist tactics of Colonels Churchill and Richards becoming increasingly apparent to General Clagett and Colonel George, renewed efforts were made to replace them. Following General Grunert's March 6 request to the War Department for replacements for Churchill and Richards on efficiency grounds, Clagett wrote to General Brett at Air Corps headquarters in Washington on July 7, asking him to send a replacement for Churchill, although the Nichols Field commander's two-year tour (like Richards's) did not end until October.[6]

Although Clagett was out of the hospital, where he had been sent immediately following his return from China, in Gregg's view he was still not his old self. Colonel George had picked up the slack at PDAF headquarters, and in Gregg's estimation was "doing a damned good job," he wrote to his wife. "Between Colonel George and myself, we can get the business end of the Philippine Air Force working."[7]

BETWEEN NICHOLS AND CLARK FIELDS, LUZON
TUESDAY MORNING, JULY 2, 1941

The typhoon that had hit Luzon finally subsided and the order to move was at last executed. Billy Maverick led off from Nichols with his squadron's entire complement of serviceable aircraft, 12 P-35As and 7 P-26As. Joe Moore was obliged to ferry his squadron's 14 P-35As and 6 P-26As in two shifts, as the 20th Pursuit's commander did not have enough experienced pilots to do the job in one trip. The shortage of such pilots in the 17th Pursuit forced Wagner to employ the same method to get his squadron's 13 P-35As and 7 P-26As to Iba.

As Maverick arrived over Clark, he formed his pilots up for single plane landings. He came in and made a "really perfect landing" with his P-35A, but after rolling only about thirty yards, his left wheel drag strut snapped. With nothing to hold the wheel down, it folded up into the wing nacelle. As his left wing started dragging the ground, he could feel the plane trying to nose over, "so I kicked full left rudder to throw the plane sideways into the direction of the landing." Still going over eighty miles per hour, he knew a cartwheel would result in a complete washout of both plane and pilot. Maverick skidded completely sideways, dragging the tip of his left wing, thus limiting the damage to bent propeller tips and a slightly damaged wing tip. Disengaging himself from the cockpit, "mad as a hornet" over his first crack-up in over five thousand hours of flying, he found himself talking about the accident a few minutes later to Lt. Col.

Les Maitland, the Clark Field commander. Maitland had been watching Maverick's approach and landing. "Forget about it," he said. He believed that by kicking the plane around sideways at that speed, Maverick had averted a more serious accident.[8]

Just two days earlier, an order had been received from the Materiel Division at Wright Field, Ohio, to triple the tensile strength of the drag strut on all P-35As. Earlier, all of the P-35As' struts had been removed and tested at the Nichols Field air depot following several failures. The conclusion was that they had to be strengthened immediately. Unfortunately, Maverick mused, it was "Too late to do me any good." On a more pleasant note, he was glad to learn that Gregg wanted to continue sharing quarters with him at their new posting. Gregg's operations officer, Maj. Orrin Grover, would be joining them in their field-grade officers' quarters. The oldies in the Headquarters, 3d, and 20th Pursuit Squadrons were assigned in groups of four to the other officers' quarters, joining the newies who had arrived a week earlier. The latter were unimpressed with their first living accommodations in the Philippines, which were "dusty, dirty, and virtually without furniture."[9]

However, they were better off than the group's enlisted men. With no barracks available for them, they were assigned to three of the old, 1919-vintage hangars at Clark and issued bedrolls, knapsacks, and tin mess kits that had to be washed in cold water after each meal, there being a complete lack of hot water for any purpose. Row on row of canvas field cots were set up on the cement hangar floors, with aisles dividing the privates from the noncoms.[10]

Gregg quickly set up a training schedule for the newies in the 3d and 20th squadrons. They would start out with three–four hours in the two-seater A-27, then move up to the P-26A—in which they would spend about twelve hours—and finally move on to the P-35A. In his effort to keep all available aircraft "going every minute that the weather is flyable," Gregg had the pilots starting off at first light—5:30 A.M.—and working straight through the day, ending up with night flying at 11:30 or midnight. Not the same pilots continuously, of course.[11]

The 20th Pursuit's oldies, having completed their required fifty hours on the P-35A, were anxiously waiting to start transition training on the squadron's twenty-five brand-new P-40Bs. Prestone coolant had finally arrived, and the ships were being ferried up to Clark Field from the depot after being tested. Each oldie was being assigned his personal aircraft, with his name painted below the cockpit. It appeared they would be one short for a while, however: 1st Lt. Ozzie Lunde, testing the first ship assembled at the depot on July 8, ended up making a forced landing in Manila Bay. Fortunately, there was little damage to him or the plane. Meanwhile, the

Ozzie Lunde discusses tactics with Bob Duncan (*wearing headset*), Marshall Anderson (*hand on neck*), and two unidentified 20th Pursuit Squadron pilots at Clark Field in the summer of 1941. Photo courtesy Lloyd Stinson.

20th Pursuit's pilots told the 3d Pursuiters that Lunde had washed out one of the two aircraft earmarked for their squadron, an assertion that was received cynically at 3d Pursuit operations.[12]

In the 28th Bomb Squadron's operations area, Ted Fisch and the other senior pilots were grumbling about the transfer of the two pursuit squadrons to Clark. For one thing, "the goddamn pursuiters fly over the house with their motors tuning up and it is enough to rock the teeth out of your head as they take off over Officers' Row." Moreover, the traffic around the field "is awful." Upon his return from a practice bombing mission on July 9, Fisch was forced to circle the field for forty-five minutes before being cleared to land.

Fisch simply could not understand why the War Department was sending out so many additional pilots when there were already more in the Philippines "than anyone knows what to do with." If the Philippine Department needed pilots as badly as Secretary of War Stimson claimed it did, "why send over these 90-day wonders?" Fisch complained in a letter to his wife, Mimi. "The damn dopes" his squadron had received "don't even make good co-pilots. All they do is get drunk and crack up airplanes."[13]

Maverick agreed with Fisch's assessment. He had to train twenty-two additional "wet behind the ears" newies who "know absolutely nothing about the Army, not even having had the rudiments of drill or military bearing and customs, in addition to knowing little more about flying." His work with them would have to include "every imaginable phase of the Air Corps, from the very beginning."[14]

IBA FIELD, ZAMBALES, LUZON
THURSDAY, JULY 3, 1941

Over at Iba, thirty-seven miles due west of Clark Field, the arrival of the 17th Pursuit's twenty-one newies by bus from Clark on July 3 had made the squadron officers' accommodations situation similar to that of the enlisted men at Clark. Some forty-five bodies were jammed into a large, one-room, run-down and leaking Philippine Army barracks, where they slept on old army cots. But at least they were better off than the outfit's 157 enlisted men, who were obliged to live in tents. It was Nichols Field all over again for them.

On July 8, the newies were finally able to start their training program, split up into three flights of seven pilots each under the direction of the squadron's senior flying officers. At twenty-seven years of age, Forrest Hobrecht, an ex-actor from Dallas, Texas, and the oldest of the twenty-one pilots just assigned to the 17th, found that he was going to have to unlearn a lot of the flying habits he had picked up at Stockton Field. Flying as a trainee in the squadron's two-seat A-27, an attack version of the AT-6 Texan trainer, Hobrecht was told to forget all the safety precautions he had learned in flying school, since he was supposed to know all the rudiments of flying now. By the time he made his second hop in the A-27, his initial nervousness had disappeared, though he had to "think and act very fast" in an aircraft much more powerful than the one he had flown in flying school.[15]

Outside of flying when the weather permitted, there was not much to do at the isolated post. They could swim in the China Sea if they wished, but most of the men found the water rough and dirty, and there was a dangerous undertow. Except for an occasional late-night poker game, the pilots were turning in at eight every night.[16]

On the morning of Friday, July 25, all the pilots were in a good mood. They were going to spend the weekend in Manila, a welcome break from the deadly monotony of camp life. There would be a big party for them Saturday night at the Iniet Birdman's Association house. A couple of bombers would pick them up that afternoon for the hop down to Manila, then fly them back to Iba on Sunday morning. At noon, however, the plans fell through. A wire from PDAF headquarters directed that all flying stop, that the squadron's P-35As' machine guns be bore sighted and ammunition loaded, and that all leaves be canceled.[17]

Buzz Wagner flew to Manila to find out what was happening. When he returned, he brought alarming news: navy PBY patrol planes on a regular reconnaissance patrol had spotted a large Japanese convoy headed south on the China Sea. Although they were most likely en route to French Indochina, no one could be sure they would not turn east and head for Luzon instead. All forces on the island were alerted and instructed to follow blackout rules. One flight from each pursuit squadron was to stand by for immediate takeoff at all times of the day and night. In accordance with subsequent orders, Wagner instructed that all aircraft be camouflaged after they had been combat-loaded and then made ready for action. The planes were to be dispersed around the short, narrow field at night so they would not be in a straight line in the event of an attack.[18]

Over at Clark Field, the 3d and 20th Pursuit Squadrons were also hurriedly carrying out the orders. Maverick had his men apply camouflage paint to their P-35As in the afternoon, then combat load the two .30-caliber and two .50-caliber machine guns in each of the 3d Pursuit's twenty-two P-35As. Bomb racks also were installed. That evening, the ships were dispersed around the edges of the field, none in a straight line, and readied to take off within one and a half minutes of the order being issued.[19]

Joe Moore's 20th Pursuit followed the same procedures. He gave the dispersion job to 2d Lt. Carl Parker Gies. A civil engineer by training, Gies was concerned that the field was too small for adequate dispersal. In his view, it was really only large enough for the 28th Bomb Squadron to operate from, but now, in addition to the 2d Observation Squadron, it had to accommodate two of the 4th Group's three pursuit squadrons. Working all night in the rain on July 25, Gies and another pilot built a "quick bridge" over which they were able to clear all of the 20th Pursuit's aircraft from the landing area into another field. Gies was particularly worried that the 3d Pursuit and the other squadrons had been obliged to disperse their planes around the edge of the field, many of them at the end of the "already too short" runways. He warned the 3d Pursuit's leaders that they were tempting fate by putting planes there, because they ran the risk of being rammed by any pilot who overshot the field when landing and ran off the edge. Five days later, Gies's worst fears were realized. Although word came down on July 27 that the Japanese ships had gone into Indochina as expected, the Luzon pilots were kept on alert and their aircraft dispersed because there was always the possibility of a night attack from Indochina, only eight hundred miles to the west.

The morning of July 30, Gies's roommate, John Geer, landed too far down the runway in his P-40B and had just begun giving it the gun to go around again when he smacked head-on into one of the 3d Pursuit's P-26As, which had been dispersed at the north end of the runway. The heavy P-40B completely demolished the little P-26A, pinning one of the 3d's crew chiefs—who had been standing behind the wing of the smaller aircraft filling out a report—between the two wrecks. Geer received only a few bruises, but the crew chief died in the hospital an hour later, never having regained consciousness and "chewed almost to bits."[20]

Overhead, Billy Maverick was coming in from a flight and spotted the demolished P-26A bearing his squadron's red nose paint. Wreckage was strewn all over the place. As soon as he landed, he taxied up the line to find out what had happened. He then rushed over to the hospital, but the sergeant was already dead. While Maverick expressed no bitterness toward Geer, Gregg was less charitable. "I would like to wring his neck," he wrote his wife. To Gregg, the crash "was the dumbest and most inexcusable accident that I have ever witnessed or heard of." At the time, he did not know of Gies's warning to the 3d Pursuit that its dispersal scheme was ill conceived.[21]

Geer was already suffering more remorse than any harsh judgment by Gregg could have inflicted on him. He was in extreme shock and had to be given sedatives to calm him down. Yet, even when his roommate Gies tried to rationalize with him that it was better that the man had died than spend the rest of his life a helpless cripple, Geer, who was conscientious by nature, "almost went crazy."[22]

Concerned about the effect the accident would have on his men, Maverick ordered the squadron to report to the mess hall at 6:30 P.M. He instructed the officers to wear their dress whites and the men to wear their inspection uniforms. After each of the officers and men had been issued a bottle of beer, Maverick tried to express some of the thoughts that were on everyone's mind. "We're all here together to say farewell and to wish happy landings to one of us who went away today," he began. "We will all miss him individually as the Third Pursuit Squadron will miss him." Then he proposed a toast "which expresses his spirit as well as the spirit of our squadron: Keep 'em Flying!"[23]

CLARK FIELD, LUZON
LATE JULY, 1941

During the Indochina scare, Maj. Moe Daly, commander of the 28th Bomb Squadron, called off all flying the afternoon of the alert and ordered that his B-18s be concealed under the overhanging trees along the airfield's perimeter. The following day, all of the squadron's aircraft were painted in camouflage colors and the pilots were restricted to base.

First Lieutenant Ted Fisch in the cockpit of B-18 serial no. 36-434 at Clark Field in September, 1941. Photo courtesy Miriam Pachacki.

Daly had replaced Capt. Erickson Nichols as CO of the 28th Squadron after Nichols's July 10 transfer to PDAF headquarters to serve as S4 and as General Clagett's flying aide-de-camp. While Ted Fisch and his other housemates were sorry to see "Nick" go, but happy for him in his new assignment, Maverick had a low opinion of his character. He thought that the Princeton-educated, ambitious Nichols had "finally shined enough boots to be made Clagett's aide and is he ever the proud little bantam rooster these days."

Fisch savored his role as one of the squadron's most senior pilots assigned to train the newies. He spent most of July "carting around" the "poor, dumb brand-new 2nd Lts" so that they could get in the eight hours of flying time needed to collect flying pay. On one training mission he let his two copilots fly the B-18. He briefly considered going into the back of the ship to get some sleep to "while away the weary hours," but then reasoned that it was not such a good idea. They were constantly getting off course because of the pilots' failure to watch the instruments, and if they were not gaining altitude, they were losing it. But Fisch did not blame his charges: after all, none of them had over five hours in a B-18.[24]

A P-40B over the Clark Field area in July, 1941. Photo courtesy Fred Roberts.

Unlike the pursuit squadrons, the 28th Bomb had not suffered any accidents. Fisch had a low opinion of the pursuit pilots. "Almost every day, someone ties up and ground loops or stands one on its nose," he wrote to Mimi. "The place is full of bunged-up pea-shooters."[25]

Major Gregg could not have agreed more with Fisch's assessment. The pursuiters "have been driving me nuts the way they are cracking up airplanes," he complained. While the fatal accident caused by Geer was uppermost in his mind, a spate of other accidents reduced the stock of pursuit aircraft during the month of July—both at Clark and at Iba. In addition to Geer's P-40B, the 20th Pursuit wrecked another P-40B, two P-35As, and two P-26As. The 3d Pursuit managed to crack up five ships, all P-35As, plus the loss of the P-26A in Geer's accident. Wagner's pilots at Iba had the fewest accidents: one P-26A lost nosing up, one of the squadron's two A-27s damaged in a wheels-up landing, a P-35A rammed by another P-35A, and another P-35A ground looped.[26]

The headaches Gregg suffered as a result of his pilots' crack ups were in addition to those he experienced as temporary commander of Clark Field, including handling the alert initiated during the Indochina scare. Les Maitland had turned over his Clark Field job to Gregg on the morning of July 21 when he drove down to Manila. Along with Clagett and Clagett's S2, Allison Ind, Grunert had ordered Maitland to undertake a mission to Singapore, Malaya, and the Dutch East Indies beginning July 22, with the first leg being a flight on the Anzac Clipper departing at 6 A.M. from

Cavite for Singapore. Clagett was deemed sufficiently recovered from the yellow fever he had contracted in China to lead the new mission. Maitland told Gregg that he expected to be back by August 6. Before leaving Clark on the twenty-first, one of Maitland's last actions was to relax his May order calling for all of the officers and men on the base to grow beards by making them optional. The reaction was mixed: a majority of the men maintained full foliage or at least kept a mustache as a memento.[27]

The July 26 announcement that General MacArthur, since 1935 the military adviser to Philippines president Manuel Quezon, was being recalled to active duty and assuming command of all U.S. Army forces in the islands—which were given the name U.S. Army Forces in the Far East—did not have much of an impact on Major Gregg at Clark Field. To him, it was just a change in names and commanding generals. He would now be reporting to Headquarters, Air Force, USAFFE, instead of to Headquarters, Philippine Department Air Force, following the shift of air units from the Philippine Department to USAFFE.[28]

LIEUTENANT GENERAL DOUGLAS MACARTHUR PAYS A FORMAL CALL ON FRANCIS B. SAYRE, U.S. HIGH COMMISSIONER FOR THE PHILIPPINES, ON JULY 30, 1941, FOLLOWING MACARTHUR'S APPOINTMENT AS COMMANDER OF ALL U.S. ARMY FORCES IN THE FAR EAST FOUR DAYS EARLIER. PHOTO COURTESY AP/WIDE WORLD PHOTOS.

On August 4, USAFFE General Orders 4 confirmed the change in name and command of the former PDAF. MacArthur had reappointed Clagett as commanding general of the newly designated Air Force, USAFFE. Although there was no order to so confirm, Colonel George would continue to serve as Clagett's executive officer, and the rest of Clagett's old staff remained in their positions. Away in Singapore and Malaya with Maitland and Ind, Clagett knew nothing of the changes that had occurred in the Philippine command structure during his absence.[29]

MacArthur received a radiogram from the War Department on July 31 stating that it was planning to send him a squadron of B-17s from Hawaii as soon as the availability of fields to accommodate them was assured. The message was the first indication the USAFFE commander had that plans were afoot in the War Department to reinforce the Philippines and upgrade his bomber and pursuit forces. Twelve days later he received another War Department radiogram informing him that fifty new P-40Es were to be shipped to him in early September.[30]

The USAFFE commander suddenly decided that his newly inherited air force needed a plan to cover all aspects of the expanded operations the War Department evidently had in mind for it. With Clagett away, the USAFFE commander called in Clagett's executive officer, Colonel George, and directed him to prepare a study—for Clagett's approval upon his return—to determine air force requirements for the Philippines from USAFFE's point of view. The study was to indicate the number of current aircraft types needed, plus equipment, organization, and ground installations for the force's maintenance and operation.[31]

In typical fashion, George plunged immediately into his new task. In the past, he had worked closely with Gregg on any plans that were being formulated for the 4th Composite Group, but with Gregg up at Clark and overworked in his dual role as acting Clark Field CO and group commander, George decided to work alone on this exercise. He regarded it as a golden opportunity to present his own thinking about the airpower requirements for an adequate defense of the Philippines. He would not be bound by past War Department policies, which, in the event, seemed to be changing anyway, or by constraints on the availability of combat aircraft as dictated by U.S. production possibilities. MacArthur had given him broad terms of reference and imposed no limitations on what he might request.

After two weeks of intensive thought and writing, George came up with a draft plan that corresponded to his ambitions for MacArthur's air arm. To carry out its defensive mission, George included an offensive capability to nullify Japanese forces within striking distance of the Philippines and to serve as a deterrent to Japanese expansion to the south and southwest: strikes against Formosa, Indochina, and the small Japanese islands south of Japan proper, but not on any of the major home islands.

What forces did George believe were required to fulfill this mission? In this respect, he was not going to be timid. To give him the interceptor capability he wanted, he asked for three pursuit wings with a total of nine groups consisting of twenty-seven tactical squadrons plus headquarters squadrons for each group, which added up to 729 pursuit aircraft.

He was no less modest in his demand for the offensive capability he envisaged under his plan. He said he would need three heavy bomber wings consisting of ten groups, plus supporting reconnaissance units, giving a total of 320 heavy bombers. George also wanted two light bombardment/dive-bomber wings in order to allow him to carry out short-range missions against Japanese landing forces. The total number of aircraft envisaged for the two wings was 294.

Next was the question of how many airfields this gigantic force would require. George's plan indicated a need for a total of fifty-six, each capable of accommodating heavy bombers. He estimated the construction cost of these fields to be $83 million, including $5 million already received for upgrading or building six fields, including Clark, Nichols, Bataan, and O'Donnell on Luzon and Malabang and Zamboanga on Mindanao.[32]

While George was drafting his ambitious plan, the War Department queried MacArthur on the capacity of his airfields. In a radiogram to USAFFE on August 12, Washington asked how many additional pursuit and heavy and medium bomb squadrons could be operated from existing airfields, as well as the numbers and types of additional squadrons that could be accommodated by mid-November, 1941, and by mid-February, 1942. A week later, based on Colonel George's information, MacArthur radioed Washington that his existing fields could immediately accommodate an additional ten pursuit squadrons, seven medium bomb squadrons, and three heavy bomb squadrons. By mid-November he believed he could handle three more heavy bomb squadrons, and by mid-February three more pursuit and two more medium and four more heavy bomb squadrons.[33]

In the plan he developed for MacArthur, Colonel George was clearly asking for combat aircraft in excess of the Philippines' capacity to accommodate them even by February, 1942—which he himself had indicated to the USAAFE commander. While MacArthur reported to the War Department that his air force could manage thirteen pursuit squadrons by that date, George was calling for a total of twenty-seven. For medium and dive-bombers, George wanted eighteen squadrons, nine more than he had acknowledged was the maximum his airfields could accommodate in February, 1942. Most dramatically, George's plan stipulated a requirement for thirty heavy bomb squadrons, whereas Philippine airfields would be capable of handling only ten such squadrons within six months.[34]

Moreover, MacArthur's less ambitious totals hinged on the immediate availability of funds and equipment from the War Department for the construction of an additional four airfields to accommodate two pursuit squadrons and seven heavy bomb squadrons. The equipment must be at hand within two months, MacArthur's response indicated.

MacArthur concluded his radiogram by noting that the four proposed airfields were part of a "comprehensive defense plan" currently being prepared by USAFFE headquarters that would be submitted to the War Department "in the near future." He evidently was referring to the plan on which Colonel George was currently engaged.

While Colonel George was preparing the air plan, the Air Warning Service chief was finalizing a proposal for modernizing the AWS for submission to MacArthur and subsequent transmission to the War Department. Radar units were needed to serve as the basis for detecting enemy aircraft to replace the "observer" system currently in operation.[35]

In response to General Grunert's earlier pleas to the War Department for modernizing his antiquated air warning system, the Air Warning Company, Philippine Department, had just arrived on an army transport from San Francisco. When the company's 194 men—under the command of 1st Lt. Robert H. Arnold, Signal Corps—disembarked from the USAT *President Coolidge* on the morning of Friday, August 1, at Pier 7, they were immediately trucked south to an open area just outside the gate of Fort McKinley and told to pitch tents. For the next several days, while awaiting the arrival of their two SCR-271 fixed-location radar units, Lieutenant Arnold put them through general military training that they had missed before being hurriedly dispatched from the United States.[36]

OPERATIONS HANGAR, 4TH COMPOSITE GROUP
CLARK FIELD, LUZON
MID-AUGUST, 1941

Meanwhile, at Clark Field, the interception capability of Clagett's command had been enhanced by the installation of an interceptor control system linked to the primitive AWS at PDAF headquarters at Fort Santiago. Following the transfer of the pursuit squadrons under Major Gregg's command to Clark Field on July 2, Gregg and his operations officer, Major Grover, saw the obvious need to arrange for receiving warning messages at the 4th Composite Group's operations hangar at Clark from the AWS at Fort Santiago and to vector his pursuit force to intercept any approaching Japanese aircraft. Previously, with no interception capability at Clark, there had been no need for such a system there.

Private Arvid Seeborg of the 4th Group's Headquarters Squadron, regarded by all as a "tough Finn," was proud to have been selected to help operate the interception system, under the direction of Gregg and Grover, who were working "shoulder to shoulder" with Seeborg and the other four Headquarters Squadron men assigned to it in the group operations hangar. As early as July 10, during Manila's first practice blackout, they had practiced with it as B-18s staged mock raids on Manila.

Seeborg wrote to his brother in early July:

> We have a big circular plotting table on which huge maps of the islands are spread. When enemy planes are on their way to attack and bomb our fields or Manila, they can be spotted along their entire route by a system of civilian observation posts who immediately radio to us the number of ships, type, direction headed in, etc. When we receive the flash, we immediately mark the spot where it came from with a pin and after several of these pins are put down, we can determine within seconds the average speed and how long it would take to get to such and such a place. It takes a bit of fast figuring to do it the way it's supposed to be done, because nowadays a couple of minutes lost on the plotting table means many miles covered by modern planes.

Then, when the intruders "get close to a point of interception, the signal is given to our pilots to get into the air in a helluva hurry," he later amplified.[37]

Based on such calculations, Gregg and Grover would be able to order the group's pursuit pilots aloft to intercept the incoming forces at a particular place and time. Already the 28th Bomb Squadron's B-18s had conducted mock raids on Manila, including the July 10 night attack, starting from several hundred miles away, to test the system. Working closely with a buddy from Headquarters Squadron, Seeborg had been practicing on the side by asking each other to figure the attackers' average speed by only the miles given and memorizing a scale. One of the other men stuck pins in the map they used, another recorded the flashes, a third sat at the phone and took down the messages as they came in, and Seeborg and his pal used the speed scales to determine the average speed and how long it would take the attackers to get to such-and-such a point.[38]

WAR ROOM, WAR DEPARTMENT
MUNITIONS BUILDING, WASHINGTON, D.C.
1:30 P.M., SUNDAY, AUGUST 10, 1941

Major Hoyt Vandenberg joined other midgrade Air Corps officers in the War Room on the penthouse level of the War Department building in Washington for a meeting of the utmost importance. Although

Westinghouse oscillating fans were blowing full blast to cool the top-floor room, they only slightly reduced the heat and humidity that made the officers' working conditions difficult at best. Vandenberg had been asked to attend as a member of a select group of Air Corps officers tasked with preparing the air annex to a War Department plan called for by President Roosevelt on July 9 to determine the munitions and personnel required by mid-1943 to defeat the Axis powers in the event the United States entered the European war on the side of the Allies. The group's work was virtually completed, and Lt. Col. Harold George, in charge of the air annex exercise, had asked each of the participants to bring his final compilation of the number of combat aircraft required under his subcomponent of the plan.[39]

For the first time, Vandenberg was being given the opportunity to participate in the preparation of a war plan involving the use of airpower, a goal he had been pursuing for two years—ever since his assignment to Air Corps headquarters—but one which the War Department had kept him and other staff officers in the Plans Division from achieving. Ironically, since June 15 he had not even been assigned a planning function on the newly created Air Staff. Following the Army Air Corps's redesignation as the U.S. Army Air Forces (USAAF) on that date, he was transferred from the Air Corps Plans Division to the USAAF A3 Operations Section as the second-ranking officer in the unit.[40]

Lieutenant Colonel George headed the newly created Air War Plans Division (AWPD), which was the successor to the Plans Division. He was known as "Bomber" George to differentiate him from the other Harold George in the Army Air Forces: "Pursuit" George in the Philippines. As his nickname implied, he was an advocate of the key role of bombardment aircraft in the application of airpower, as was his deputy in the AWPD, Lt. Col. Kenneth Walker. Along with another bomber enthusiast, Maj. Laurence S. Kuter, serving at the time in the War Department G2 but borrowed for this exercise, they constituted the nucleus of the team that was drawing up the plan. The threesome were old friends and supporters of each other's thinking on the use of strategic bombardment as expressed at the Air Corps Tactical School at Maxwell Field in the 1930s.[41]

Colonel George emphasized to his team the absolute necessity of completing the air annex by 1:30 P.M. on August 12, ready for presentation the next day. He said they should start putting the report together immediately after the meeting. It was the first time that Air Corps officers had been allowed to prepare an airpower strategy for the country, and he was anxious that they not muff the unprecedented opportunity given to them.[42]

Vandenberg already knew exactly what he was going to include in the tab to the annex covering pursuit aviation required for the strategic defense of Asia. He was not surprised that Colonel George had given him the responsibility, along with two other Air Corps officers, to draw up this part of the plan. He was well known as an advocate of pursuit aviation in airpower strategy and as a fervent supporter of building up the Philippines' air defenses.[43]

Specifically, Vandenberg and the other two members of his group were proposing the assignment of two pursuit groups to the Philippines: one for the defense of Manila, naval forces, and vital establishments in the vicinity, and the other to protect advanced bomber bases on northern Luzon. They further determined that the two groups would require 210 daylight interceptors and fifty night interceptors. Vandenberg and the others concluded that two groups were "all that are justified in the Far East."[44]

Vandenberg had either scaled down his earlier estimates of pursuit needs for conducting a Battle of Britain–type defense of the islands that he had been ardently advocating since the beginning of the year, or had been overruled by the officer in charge of his team, Lt. Col. Reuben C. Moffat. In January, he and his aide, Lt. Bill Burt, had argued for *three* groups equipped with three hundred P-40Es, with one group sited at forward bases on northern Luzon, a second in the Manila area, and a third to defend the central and southern Philippines. His team did not include a third such group in the A-WPD/1 annex.

Walker and Kuter were responsible for determining the number of heavy bombers to be included in the tab covering bombardment needs for the Philippines. They considered a strong force of long-range heavy bombers the key to the strategic defense of the Far East. For this purpose, the two bomber proponents advocated sending the Philippines four groups totaling 272 B-17s and B-24s, with an operating range of fifteen hundred miles carrying two thousand pounds of bombs, as the means to "seriously threaten the northern approaches to the China Sea" and "provide a strong defense to any overseas operation directed against the Philippines."[45]

Ideally, if the availability of heavy bombers permitted it, "a satisfactory strategic defense against Japan could be most effectively accomplished by a vigorous air offensive against the sources of Japan's military and civil strength," Walker and Kuter maintained. However, "actualities force the modification of that concept to the creation of a striking force designed to deter Japanese aggression and expansion in Asia." Eventually, they hoped to base 136 of the newly conceived B-29s or B-32s in Alaska or the Philippines. Those aircraft would have the four-thousand-mile range needed to carry twenty-five hundred pounds of bombs each to Japan's heartland.[46]

Another team of USAAF officers working on the annex had identified the aviation needs required to support ground forces in the Philippines as two squadrons of dive-bombers and two squadrons of light bombers (A-20 type). Finally, the planners determined the proposed air force for the Philippines would require an observation squadron.[47]

With one notable exception, all of the USAAF officers were in agreement with each other's assessments of aircraft needs for the Far East and for Europe by mid-1943, the target date set by the War Department plan, which soon was referred to as the "Victory Program." The dissenting voice was that of the forty-five-year-old senior aviation officer serving in Gerow's War Plans Division, who from the outset had been associated—though not directly involved—with the preparation of the air annex: Lt. Col. Clayton L. Bissell. In particular, Bissell questioned including the extra-long-range B-29s and B-32s in the plan while they were still on the drawing board. "I can go along on the 4,000 mile bomber as an experimental development *only* at this time," he argued. "When we find there is a good chance we can get such a ship, we should set up a production objective for it. To do so now is unsound." Bissell also maintained that the number of interceptor planes advocated by Vandenberg and his colleagues was "insufficient" to protect the four bomb groups Walker and Kuter projected for the Philippines under the plan. He estimated that the number of pursuit groups should be doubled to four and, taking into consideration likely replacement needs, there should be an aircraft reserve of 50 percent. This meant that Bissell was calling for a total of 780 pursuit ships to be based in the Philippines, including 260 in reserve.[48]

When Maj. Gen. Hap Arnold returned from his Argentia mission on August 19, he evidenced no great interest in the AWPD's pioneering efforts in producing the first strategic air plan ever incorporated into a War Department plan. His subordinates were not surprised by this feeble reaction. As Kuter well knew, "Arnold was just not keyed to long-range plans and policy. He wanted something done tomorrow." Moreover, the USAAF's commanding general was preoccupied with the top-level political decision made at Argentia to build up airpower in the Philippines for both defensive and offensive operations *right now*. On August 19, in a conference with the Air Staff, he instructed the AWPD to prepare a plan as soon as possible to bolster the Philippines with a group of B-17s and a group of P-40s. Actually, the chief of the Air Staff, Brig. Gen. Carl Spaatz, had anticipated Arnold's request three weeks earlier when he directed the AWPD on July 26 to study the requirements for reinforcing the Philippines with heavy bombers "in the shortest possible time."[49]

The job fell to Lt. Col. Orvil Anderson, a forty-six-year-old Mormon from Utah who had been assigned to the AWPD at the time of its formation. Anderson had played a relatively minor role in the preparation of the Victory Program's air annex: determining pursuit aviation needs to support ground forces. However, following completion of the annex, when the AWPD was broken down into geographic areas of coverage, Anderson ended up with the Far East as his responsibility.[50]

Anderson finished his new task on August 30, and, in a memo to Spaatz from the AWPD on that date, spelled out the details of the action plan he had worked up. He asked that MacArthur also be informed, assuming his recommendations were approved. To meet the needs for one heavy bomber group, the 19th Bomb Group (Heavy)—less one squadron—currently based at Albuquerque, New Mexico, with fourteen B-17s, would be assigned to the Philippines and augmented with twelve more B-17s from other sources.[51]

Since there already were three pursuit squadrons in the Philippines, Anderson indicated no need for additional tactical units to form a pursuit group, but he specified that an interceptor control squadron was needed. However, Anderson was forced to acknowledge there was no such organization in the USAAF! He thus provided Spaatz a table of organization for such a unit and recommended it be constituted and activated without delay and assigned to the envisaged pursuit group in the Philippines.

Similarly, a headquarters squadron for the interceptor command, as well as a Signal Corps headquarters company for the Air Warning Service of that command, "are absolute essentials to the conduct of efficient Pursuit operations in air defense," he maintained. Considering that no such units outside the four organized air defense commands in the continental United States were available for such an assignment, Anderson recommended that they, too, be constituted and activated as soon as possible, as they would require a minimum four months training before being ready for assignment to the Philippines.

Six days later, Spaatz approved Anderson's plan and forwarded it to Arnold for necessary action. The first organizational steps in building up an effective air defense capability in the Philippines had at last been taken.[52]

OPERATIONS HANGAR, 4TH COMPOSITE GROUP
CLARK FIELD, LUZON
NOON, SUNDAY, AUGUST 17, 1941

Major Gregg was occupied in the 4th Composite Group's operations hangar at Clark Field when his phone rang. It was Col. "Pursuit" George in Manila informing him that General Clagett was due to land at Clark in fifteen minutes. However, by the time Gregg left the hangar and reached the field, a twin-engine Lockheed sporting the distinctive orange and black triangle insignia of the Netherlands East Indies Air Force on its fuselage had already landed. Gregg was surprised to find only Colonels Richards and Maitland on board. They told Gregg that Clagett had been extremely sick on Java on the last leg of their three-country inspection trip, down with tertiary malaria this time, and hospitalized. Richards had flown down to substitute for him at the time of his indisposition. Clagett was on his way back aboard a steamer with his aide, Allison Ind.[53]

Gregg talked with Richards and Maitland and the two Dutch officers for a few minutes while they waited for lunch at the Clark Field mess before Richards and the Dutch officers continued on to Nielson Field in Manila. However, he could not get much information out of Richards and Maitland as to what had happened on Java.

At any rate, Gregg was relieved to turn Clark Field back over to Maitland and devote his efforts solely to his 4th Composite Group responsibilities. It had been a longer-than-expected wait for Maitland's return. Gregg believed that either job was enough "to keep anyone busy as hell." Furthermore, in his view, it was "impossible to do justice to either." It did not help that "No one seems to do what they are supposed to do," Gregg complained in a letter to his wife.[54]

Perhaps Gregg was thinking about the unmilitary behavior of the commander of his old 17th Pursuit Squadron and some of his senior pilots. When Richards and Maitland had arrived back at Clark Field at midday on the seventeenth, Buzz Wagner and twelve of his oldies were into the third day of a continuous party at the Clark officers' club, waiting for an improvement in the weather so they could fly back to Iba after having been summoned from Iba five days earlier to attend a speech by the Fort Stotsenburg commander, Brig. Gen. Edward P. King. Then, in the afternoon, there was a phone call for Wagner at the club, right in the middle of one of the singing and drinking sessions. The 17th Pursuit was cleared for return to Iba—the weather was clearing.[55]

Wagner sauntered over to the table occupied by Bill Rowe and the others and, not exactly sober, announced in the loud voice he used at the time of takeoffs: "Let's go, 17th Pursuit Squadron!" Without waiting for anyone else, the CO took off immediately in his P-35A and circled above Clark while waiting for his wingman—which meant whoever happened to be next off the ground—to catch up. This time it was Rowe.[56]

Wagner led his squadron mates in two-ship formations down through the buildings of adjoining Fort Stotsenburg and then around and down again ten feet off the deck, giving the brass there a good buzzing. Then they climbed and headed west, passing through the ravine in the Zambales Mountains. In the middle of the pass, Wagner did a slow roll in place as only a hotshot pilot could do with ease. The others knew the rule: whatever the CO did in flight, everyone else had to follow suit. Adjusting their ailerons, elevators, and rudders in an effort to maintain the position of the noses of their P-35As and prevent turning, the other pilots nevertheless fell out of formation one by one, ending up scattered all over the pass. On rejoining Wagner's wing, Rowe and the others continued on to Iba and landed without incident, although some stalled out ten feet in the air and others dove their ships onto the runway and bounced. "Needless to say, our depth perception was off," Rowe recalled forty-two years later. Despite—or perhaps due to—his antics, Wagner was extremely popular with his charges. They were pleased to have such a youthful and competent pilot as their commanding officer.

The same could not be said of the CO of the 28th Bombardment Squadron. In Ted Fisch's estimation, "the 28th Bombardment has certainly turned into a lousy outfit" following Nichols's replacement by Moe Daly. "The ranking officers are a bunch of tits and they don't know a goddamned thing about bombardment tactics and seem to care less," he complained to Mimi.[57]

PIER 7, MANILA HARBOR
WEDNESDAY, AUGUST 20, 1941

When the Dutch steamer *Tjinigara* pulled into Manila Bay on Wednesday, August 20, a noticeably weakened Clagett disembarked with his aide, Allison Ind, and headed for his quarters at 7 Military Plaza. Yet, despite the fact he was still suffering from the malaria that had laid him low on Java, Clagett refused to reenter Sternberg Hospital, maintaining that he had fully recovered from his illness. Later in the day, doctors at Sternberg concurred that it was not necessary for Clagett to be hospitalized again.[58]

The day after his return, Clagett called on his new commander, Lt. Gen. Douglas MacArthur, and briefed him on his trip to Singapore, Malaya, and the Netherlands East Indies. Two days later, Clagett was back at MacArthur's headquarters in Intramuros, this time to introduce his staff and pay their formal respects to MacArthur.[59]

While trying to catch up on the backlog of work that had piled up in his absence, Clagett reserved his evenings for reviewing the air plan for MacArthur that George had drafted in his absence. For several nights running, he invited his executive officer to his Military Plaza quarters for dinner and discussions on George's draft plan. Clagett was strongly opposed to the proposed size of the air force for which George was arguing, and before and after—but never during—dinner, Clagett ripped into his chief aide. "You want ten groups of this, eight groups of that, and six of something else," Clagett growled. "Young man, you more than amaze me, you render me quite uncomprehending—that you, an experienced army man and Air Force officer, should even entertain the thought of demanding such preposterous totals," he exclaimed. He demanded to know just where George intended to obtain so many groups of aircraft. George's reply was simple: "Ask for them! We'll certainly not get 'em if we don't."

In his weakened condition, day and night work proved to be too much for Clagett. He became ill again and once more turned himself in to Sternberg Hospital, where he was given his old room. The final decision on what to do about MacArthur's air plan would have to await his release.[60]

With Clagett disabled again, "Pursuit" George was once more in charge of MacArthur's air force, and he refused to shy away from making bold decisions. However, even before Clagett went back into the hospital, George had called Gregg down from Clark Field to meet with him at air force headquarters in Manila to discuss supply problems, which Gregg thought had worsened. He explained to George what he had been doing and what he thought headquarters needed to do "to straighten out the mess and fix things up." George approved all of Gregg's recommendations, and then, at the end of the meeting, dropped a bombshell on the group commander: George and Clagett were considering moving Gregg to air force headquarters to serve as the S4 (logistics) officer. "I screamed and tore my hair," Gregg wrote his wife that night. He did not want to give up command of the 4th Composite Group for a staff job. He felt he was "just getting the outfit whipped into shape where I would have a real Group instead of a Flying School." But George insisted that his services were more badly needed at headquarters as S4 than as the 4th Group commander. "If it is ordered, I guess there is nothing to do but make the best of it and do the best I can," Gregg resignedly informed his wife.[61]

Back at Clark Field on August 25, Gregg received confirmation of the bad news by radio from George. He was to report to air force headquarters in two days and assume his new duties as S4. Major Orrin Grover, Gregg's operations officer and housemate, was being given command of the 4th Group. Replacing Grover as group operations officer would be his other housemate, Billy Maverick, who would relinquish command of the 3d Pursuit to 1st Lt. Benny Putnam, CO of the 4th Composite Group's Headquarters Squadron.

On the evening of August 26, Gregg's pursuit commanders threw a farewell party for him. The 17th Pursuit's officers flew over from Iba in B-18s so that they could honor him along with their comrades from the Clark-based 3d and 20th Pursuit Squadrons.

HEADQUARTERS, AIR FORCE, USAFFE
NIELSON FIELD, MANILA
12:45 P.M., WEDNESDAY, AUGUST 27, 1941

After arriving in Manila, Gregg stopped for lunch at the Army and Navy Club, then headed straight for his new headquarters, located in a large, V-shaped building just off Nielson Field. It was the first time he set foot in it. Although it was not fully ready for occupancy, Colonel George had arranged for the USAFFE air force headquarters staff to move from the Philippine Department headquarters at Fort Santiago to this building—formerly occupied by the American Far Eastern School of Aviation—in mid-August. However, the headquarters was practically closed when Gregg reported in, so he proceeded to his former quarters at Nichols, unpacked, and turned in early.

Gregg was up early the next morning and went over to Nielson Field at 8:30, where he promptly "started to dig in." By the end of the day, he had begun to understand why Colonel George had shifted him into the new job. Although he still "felt like hell losing the Group," he now appreciated that "this is bigger and more important," and he hoped he could handle his new responsibilities. Aided by 1st Lt. Bernard Anderson, the assistant S4, Gregg was charged with supervising the requisition of all of the air force's supplies, planning for the transport of supplies and personnel, and determining the location of suitable sites for air bases.

In the headquarters building's other wing, Pvt. John "Pete" Legg—a twenty year old assigned to the Air Warning Company—was becoming proficient in Teletype operations and radio work in the communications room of the AWS, which had been shifted to Nielson Field with the rest of the air force headquarters on August 16. He was now a rated Teletype operator and was hoping to get some extra pay for his specialty rating. After work each day he reported back to Fort McKinley, outside of which the men of the Air Warning Company were still living in tents. The young man from Tioga, West Virginia, was still suffering from Manila's heat, and living in tents seemed to make it hotter.

Up at Clark Field, Billy Maverick was hoping for the best for his friend and ex-housemate. "K. J. is badly needed in his new position," he wrote to his wife, "where he will be able to straighten out some of the many kinks which have existed in the supply job he will do." Maverick regarded his own move to the group operations officer position "definitely as a promotion." Although it entailed a great deal of office work and responsibility, he was still glad to have the opportunity. He would continue serving as the 3d Pursuit Squadron CO for the next few days in order to change over all of the unit's financial and property accounts.[62]

CHAPTER 5

"The Creation of the Five-Engine Bomber Has Completely Changed the Strategy in the Pacific"

n early September, while still in Manila's Sternberg Hospital being treated for tertiary malaria, Brig. Gen. Henry Clagett called his executive officer at air force headquarters at Nielson Field. He demanded to be shown the finished product of Colonel George's efforts to prepare the plan on air force requirements for MacArthur that he and George had wrangled over in late August just before he turned himself in for treatment at Sternberg.

After George dropped his version of the plan off at the hospital, Clagett went through the draft document and began rejecting sections specifying the amounts of fuel and bombs required to attack particular targets that Clagett argued were not of military value but George claimed were of potential military significance. Forced by Clagett to revise the plan, George and his S2, Allison Ind, found that such an alteration made only a slight difference in the total amounts of bombs and fuel needed to carry out the plan. George then turned the revised version over to Clagett, who began to rewrite it entirely—despite his acknowledged weaknesses in literary expression. Later, as George and Ind were going over the abbreviated "hybrid" that Clagett had produced, they felt that "all the strength, conviction, and raison d'être had disappeared." Clagett had reluctantly retained the "terrific totals" of aircraft that George had worked to preserve, but had largely deleted the supporting rationale needed to justify them. To his staff officers, neither MacArthur nor the War Department would be convinced of the need for such a large increase in airpower for the "aggressive defense" of the Philippines in the absence of any articulated arguments in favor of them.

Upon release from the hospital several days later, Clagett reported to MacArthur's headquarters with the revised version of the plan in hand. Seated behind his richly carved desk, MacArthur perused the document, which Clagett had entitled "Study of Air Force for United States Army Forces in the Far East." He did not like the presentation and announced that he wanted to see the plan as George had originally prepared it.

A few days after having absorbed the put-down by MacArthur, Clagett called his executive officer to his office at Nielson Field headquarters. "Hal, I'm licked!" he acknowledged to Colonel George. "They like your way of putting it more than mine." Clagett asked George to give him a copy of the original version to submit to MacArthur. On September 11, Clagett sent the document to MacArthur's headquarters.[1]

Just three days earlier, MacArthur had forwarded to the War Department a study Clagett had submitted to him on August 28 that had been prepared by his Air Warning Service chief, Col. Alexander H. Campbell, and was considered complementary to the plan Clagett and George had come up with for expanded airpower for USAFFE. Clagett had asked MacArthur to assign the study, entitled "Emergency Aircraft Warning Service Project to Air Defense Plan, USAFFE," a high priority. In his covering indorsement dated September 8, MacArthur recommended the War Department approve the project and requested funds for its early commencement.

In the study, Campbell asked for sufficient modern detection equipment and personnel to conduct round-the-clock operations. Specifically, he wanted two SCR-270B mobile radar units and eleven SCR-271 fixed-location units for the operation of the AWS, six of which were understood to be en route to the Philippines already. Campbell estimated a need for thirty-three officers and 882 enlisted men to operate the system, as opposed to the 194 that had arrived on August 1 assigned as the Air Warning Company, Philippine Department.[2]

As MacArthur's request winged its way to Washington, it crossed paths with a report prepared by the Air Defense Board airmailed to MacArthur on September 2 by the War Department that was to be considered standard doctrine on the organization of air defense for the continental United States and its overseas territories. Although it had not yet received War Department approval, in view of the critical situation in the Far East, it was being sent to MacArthur with a request for USAFFE to submit a recommendation outlining its AWS requirements based on the tables of organization included in the Air Board report, but taking into consideration USAFFE's particular situation.

Upon receipt by MacArthur's headquarters in mid-September, the seventeen-page report was immediately passed to Clagett for transmission to

Colonel Campbell. The AWS chief was impressed. For the first time, the USAAF had worked out a basic air defense doctrine, followed by detailed requirements for organizing air defense units, differentiating between the needs of continental U.S.-based organizations and those overseas.

In his office at air force headquarters at Nielson Field, Campbell, a forty-eight-year-old West Point graduate and Coast Artillery officer who had arrived in the Philippines in October, 1939, skimmed the document to pick up what had been recommended for the Philippines. The three pursuit squadrons should be formally removed from the 4th Composite Group and formed into a pursuit group, with a new headquarters squadron assigned to command it in its interception role. An interceptor control squadron should also be assigned to the pursuit group to install and operate radio equipment for interception purposes. MacArthur's USAFFE headquarters was instructed to report the "definite requirements" of the Philippines AWS to the War Department. In this respect, the report envisaged upgrading the Philippines AWS from a company to a battalion and providing it one SCR-270 and nine SCR-271 radar units.

Campbell must have been pleased to see that his earlier AWS request had anticipated the increased personnel strength proposed in the Air Defense Board report. His equipment request exceeded the board's by one SCR-270 and two SCR-271s. Curiously enough, Marshall had informed MacArthur by telegram just days earlier—on September 9—that one SCR-270 and two SCR-271s had earlier been shipped to USAFFE. Three additional SCR-270s would be shipped after October 1. Meanwhile, Campbell had set up an improvised information and communications center in the AWS area of the air force headquarters building at Nielson Field that would have to suffice until permanent underground facilities could be built at Fort McKinley.[3]

Oblivious to all of the brass' plans affecting their future, Pvt. John "Pete" Legg and the Air Warning Company's other enlisted men were still living in tents at Fort McKinley a month after their arrival in the Philippines. The young West Virginian was suffering from the heat, and living in a tent made it even hotter for him. During the day, when he was not taking morning classes on radio operations, he was over at the AWS information and communications center at Nielson doing Teletype and radio operations work, "hoping to get a rating out of it."[4]

At Clark Field, Pvt. Arvid Seeborg also hoped to get a specialist rating—and the extra pay that went with it—as a reward for his work on the plotting board in the 4th Composite Group Headquarters Squadron's operations hangar. He had been performing well, plotting mock raids on Manila by 28th Bomb Squadron B-18s to test the effectiveness of the system that Majors Gregg and Grover had set up.[5]

Meanwhile, 1st Lt. Herb Ellis and five other senior 3d Pursuit Squadron pilots participating in a September exercise thought the operation was a total flop. The plan was for B-18s to fly north of their Clark Field base, Filipino watchers to be alerted and to call AWS operators at Nielson Field when they spotted the bombers heading south, and for Nielson to relay the warning to Seeborg's operation at Clark. The six 3d Pursuiters, lined up in echelon ready for takeoff in their P-35As, and another six pilots from the 20th Pursuit, also on standby near their P-40Bs on the other side of Clark's turf runway, would then be ordered to intercept the B-18s as they headed south to "attack" Manila, based on calculations provided by Seeborg and the rest of the team.[6]

Minutes ticked by with no takeoff order from group operations. As the twelve pursuit pilots fidgeted, takeoff was delayed past the planned interception time. Finally, almost an hour after the intended interception time, Major Maverick, who had been impatiently awaiting the call from Nielson, signaled the two flights to scramble. The AWS had obviously failed, but the pilots might as well make a practice interception to avoid having the exercise written off as a total waste.

Following takeoff, Ellis and the others proceeded as previously directed to a position north of Clark at an altitude between ten thousand and twelve thousand feet and began patrolling. Flying an east–west course north of the field, perpendicular to the anticipated bomber route, they could find no trace of the "enemy," nor did they receive any information by radio from group operations. Finally, running low on fuel, they were ordered to return to base. The B-18s must have passed through unnoticed by the pursuiters.

Ellis was particularly annoyed with the futility of the exercise. Why was it, he wondered, that the USAAF had no ground-controlled interception system a year after the RAF had developed a highly successful one and used it to great effect against the Germans in the Battle of Britain?[7]

MUNITIONS BUILDING, WASHINGTON, D.C.
FRIDAY MORNING, SEPTEMBER 12, 1941

Colonels Harold George and Ken Walker and Maj. Larry Kuter, carrying an armload of maps and charts, headed down the main east–west hallway in the Munitions Building to Room 2033. It was a big day for them. They were to formally present A-WPD/1 to the secretary of war. Chief of Staff Marshall had been favorably impressed with the air plan when the airmen had briefed him on it on August 30, and he wanted Stimson to be fully informed on it, too.

The air planners waited only a few minutes in the waiting room near the secretary's office. At 10:30 sharp, they were ushered into Room 2036. Familiar with the layout of Stimson's office, Colonel George led his colleagues through a side door into a large carpeted room with curtained windows, where the seventy-three-year-old statesman welcomed them, then sat down behind his heavy wooden desk, prepared for the presentation his visitors were about to make. Assistant Secretary of War John J. McCloy then joined Stimson for the presentation.[8]

The previous afternoon, Stimson had called them down from the AWPD for an informal discussion of the air plan, questioning them for an hour and thirty-five minutes. Stimson had cross-examined the three officers in considerable detail on the methods they had used to identify vulnerable targets in Germany and the methods for demolishing those targets and was satisfied with their responses. It was the first time the three senior Air Corps officers had ever met with the secretary of war.[9]

Their style finely honed after the many presentations they had made during the past month, the air planners went smoothly through their Friday morning exposition. During the discussion following the presentation, Stimson showed particular interest in the relative cheapness of heavy bombers in terms of tons of bombs delivered compared to medium bombers. As the secretary hesitated and paused in developing his views, the airmen politely waited for Stimson to make his points. In response to this indication of Stimson's interest, Colonel George promised to send him an informal paper on the subject.[10]

When the air planners left shortly after noon, fresh ideas began shooting through Stimson's mind. The heavy bomber that the air officers had described to him over the past two days could be the means by which "to let American power back into the Philippines in a way it has not been able to do for 20 years." Ever since his service as governor general of the Philippines in 1927–29, Stimson had been preoccupied with the islands' unsatisfactory defense situation. Now it looked like a means had been found to deter Japanese aggression against the commonwealth. "It has just come home to us that the creation of the five-engine bomber has completely changed the strategy in the Pacific," he recorded in his diary that evening. Moreover, he had heard earlier in the day that nine B-17s had just arrived in the Philippines, proof positive of the USAAF's ability to transfer them all the way across the Pacific.[11]

Upon returning to his office after the morning session with Stimson, Colonel George prepared a memo in response to Stimson's request for more information on the utility of the "big bomber" versus the "little bomber." In it, George compared the cost effectiveness of operating B-17s or B-24s as opposed to B-25s or B-26s in one example, and B-29s compared to B-17s ad B-24s in another. A third comparison pitted a hypothetical bomber with a four-thousand-mile range against the B-29. The AWPD chief offered seventeen reasons why big bombers were superior to small ones.

Stirred up by this potential strategy shift in the Far East that A-WPD/1 appeared to make possible, Stimson called Col. Robert W. Crawford of the War Plans Division into his office on the morning of September 16 and discussed the Philippines situation with him. They repaired to the "secret map room" that the War Department G2 had fixed up for the secretary earlier that morning to go over the maps of the Far East that had been provided him.[12]

Later that afternoon, Stimson summoned Brig. Gen. Carl Spaatz and the USAAF G3, Col. Earl Naiden, to go over the Far East maps with him again. Stimson wanted to be sure he knew exactly how far the heavy bombers could reach from the Philippines and "what could be done to protect them" there. He called in the WPD chief at the end of the discussions and told Gerow that he wanted to be kept up to date on the progress being made on Philippines rearmament. He also asked Gerow to make a special study on the general strategic situation in the Far East and instructed Spaatz to produce a document detailing airpower's role in such a strategy, both from the offensive and defensive points of view.[13]

Returning to his office in Room 2007, not far down the hall from Stimson's, Spaatz summoned his senior Air Staff officers for their daily meeting. The main topic was his and Naiden's meeting with Stimson. Spaatz ordered Colonel George to have the AWPD prepare the study Stimson had requested. He said he wanted it to include a thorough analysis that considered such aspects as Japanese capabilities, types and numbers of aircraft, and ranges of the aircraft from the Philippines to Formosa, supported by maps. Spaatz would take care of informing Arnold of the request.

In the Air Staff meeting on September 19, Spaatz instructed George to make sure a copy of the memorandum he had prepared for Stimson was sent to Arnold. Spaatz did not want his boss to be caught flatfooted if Stimson asked Arnold about it.[14]

OVER THE SOUTHERN PHILIPPINES
FRIDAY MORNING, SEPTEMBER 12, 1941

High over the southern Philippines, heading north toward Luzon, Maj. Emmett "Rosie" O'Donnell in his lead B-17D was receiving instructions from air force headquarters at Nielson Field before dawn on the morning of September 12. "Go back to Del Monte," the voice on the radio ordered. Manila and Clark Field to the north were being struck by a typhoon, and there was no visibility because of the torrential downpour. Del Monte? O'Donnell had never heard or seen the name before, except on a can of peaches. The only maps O'Donnell and the pilots of the other eight B-17Ds had been given were naval charts. "We are coming in, I don't know where Del Monte is," he replied. They already knew about the bad weather to the north anyway. They had been receiving regular calls from the Clark Field weather office about the typhoon conditions since 2 A.M. Unfortunately, they had no choice but to land at Clark Field—regardless of the situation.[15]

When they reached Negros in the central Philippines, the weather closed in on them. O'Donnell ordered the pilots to break formation, go on instruments, and make their way north individually. Over Mindoro, just south of Luzon, they dropped down through the heavy rain to within a hundred feet of the water and headed for Manila Bay. Near Corregidor they found "a dome of good visibility" and circled over the area as O'Donnell dispatched one plane every three minutes to head to Clark Field. Hedgehopping their four-engine bombers and buffeted by the high winds, each pilot continued north at treetop level until he located the airfield through an opening in the overcast and pouring rain. As Ed Teats began his final descent, the control tower and hangars "suddenly leaped from the fog and rain directly in front of me." Pulling up sharply, he barely missed them. On which runway were they supposed to land? Unable to contact the tower for landing instructions because his radio had failed earlier, Capt. Bill Fisher in the second of the nine ships chose a strip in the poor visibility that, unknown to him, was under construction. As he taxied after landing, Fisher failed to notice a B-18 on the edge of the field and hooked it in the nose, ripping up his B-17's tail section.[16]

Gathered around the landing area, Clark Field personnel who had braved the torrential rain to watch the arrival of the nine B-17s wondered if the big ships could possibly get down without mishap under such weather conditions. They were pleasantly surprised to see only one succumb to an accident, and that not serious.

After climbing out of his lead ship, Rosie O'Donnell was warmly congratulated by the Clark Field CO, Les Maitland, for successfully completing the unprecedented eighty-five-hundred-mile trip, zigzagging across the Pacific via Midway, Wake, Port Moresby, and Darwin from Hickam Field, Hawaii. The West Pointer's face fell, however, when Maitland informed him that General Clagett wanted to court-martial O'Donnell for disobeying the order to return to Del Monte. Considering that the thirty-five-year-old commander of the 14th Bomb Squadron had just successfully transferred his B-17s in one week all the way across the Pacific, Maitland told O'Donnell that such an action would be stupid on Clagett's part.[17]

PRIVATE FIRST CLASS ROBERT S. ALTMAN, A MEMBER OF CAPT. COLIN P. KELLY'S 14TH
BOMB SQUADRON CREW, LEANS AGAINST A PROPELLER BLADE ON HIS B-17D (40-3095)
FLANKED BY FIFTY-FIVE–GALLON DRUMS OF GASOLINE FOR REFUELING AFTER FLYING NON-
STOP FROM HAWAII TO MIDWAY ISLAND ON SEPTEMBER 5, 1941. PHOTO BY WILLARD L.
MONEY; COURTESY EUGENE EISENBERG.

If Ted Fisch of the long-resident 28th Bomb Squadron had thought
two months earlier that landing at Clark Field was becoming a problem
due to aircraft congestion, what did he think now, with the assignment of
a squadron of big bombers to Clark? Two additional landing strips were
being constructed to ease the situation, including the one on which Fisher
had inadvertently landed, whose intended seven-thousand-foot length was
half-completed. The third runway, which was three thousand feet long by
August, was being extended to five thousand feet.[18]

Less successful was the construction effort at Nichols Field. Two
runways had been put in by mid-September, but they were "just like
real spongy swamps," as far as the 17th Pursuit's George Armstrong was
concerned. Engineers were scheduled to tear both of them up and relay them with heavier foundations. It would be some time before the 4th
Composite Group's pursuit squadrons would be returning to their home
field—except that they were no longer part of the 4th Composite Group.
On September 16, the three pursuit squadrons were reassigned to the
newly constituted 24th Pursuit Group (Interceptor), along with a newly

AERIAL VIEW OF CLARK FIELD IN AUGUST, 1941, BEFORE THE RUNWAYS WERE EXTENDED.
FOLLOWING THE ACTIVATION OF THE 24TH PURSUIT GROUP IN SEPTEMBER, THE OPERA-
TIONS SECTION WAS HOUSED IN THE LOWER HANGAR IN THE BACKGROUND ON THE RIGHT.
CLARK FIELD OPERATIONS WAS LOCATED IN THE SMALL BUILDING BETWEEN THE HANGARS
ON THE LEFT. PHOTO COURTESY VARIAN K. WHITE VIA DOROTHY W. TILFORTH.

formed Headquarters and Headquarters Squadron. MacArthur had acted
on the recommendation in the Air Defense Board report he had received
that week from the War Department, as well as on the authorization he
received in a War Department letter dated August 16.[19]

Not surprisingly, General Clagett reassigned the 4th Composite Group
CO as commander of the 24th and allowed Major Grover to bring along his
operations officer, Billy Maverick, to serve in the same position in the new
group. Meanwhile, at air force headquarters at Nielson, the activation of the
24th Pursuit Group reminded Major Gregg that he was originally intended
for the command job when it was first rumored back in March that a pursuit group was to be organized. If he had not been shifted to the S4 job on
Clagett's staff, he would certainly have been first in line. Although he was
officially the number three man in the air force headquarters setup, which
meant he was in charge whenever Clagett and George were both away, it
meant nothing to him. He did not like his new job. "I work all-out," he
complained to his wife. But with his "hands tied" the way they were, he was
able to "get nothing really done." He sorely missed operational activities.[20]

Under Grover's supervision, Maverick assumed responsibility for training the pursuiters, which previously had been Gregg's concern. He had

high hopes that he could mold the dominant newies into good pilots. "They are young and foolish enough to make fine Pursuit pilots in time of trouble," he reasoned. "And it's my job to see that they do."

The oldies also were under pressure to improve their flying abilities. When Maverick relinquished command of the 3d Pursuit Squadron to Benny Putnam on August 27, Grover had told Putnam he thought the 3d Pursuiters "flew like a bunch of old ladies," an evaluation that would certainly have offended Maverick had he gotten wind of it, given his pride in the abilities of his former charges. Putnam decided that he was going to prove Grover's judgment correct.[21]

CLARK FIELD, LUZON
THURSDAY MORNING, OCTOBER 2, 1941

Just before daybreak, Putnam went down to the 3d Pursuit's flight line and told his operations officer, Herb Ellis, to line up nine P-35As. He was going to take the squadron over to Iba and wake up the 17th Pursuit. Just six days earlier, two of the 17th Pursuit's ships had buzzed their 3d and 20th Pursuit counterparts, and Putnam was intent on repaying them. To Ellis, it was clear that the new CO intended to put his pilots through the ringer.[22]

Flying as tightly as possible, the eight veteran pursuit pilots maintained a stepped-down three-ship formation behind Putnam at sixteen thousand feet as they approached Iba. Then their CO pushed over and headed straight down, both his wingmen hanging with him, maintaining their wings level with the horizon, followed by the six others. The planes' engines screamed loudly as the diving P-35As picked up speed. Putnam inadvertently let up on his left rudder, however, and the others followed suit in order to maintain position. The sudden relaxation of pressure caused all of the ships to yaw to the right, creating a vacuum on the right side of the aircraft that caused the Plexiglas cockpit panels on that side to pop out of their frames. Pulling out of the dive, they leveled off and headed west out over the China Sea, then back to Clark. After they landed, Putnam left the line without a word to his pilots. An inspection of the planes indicated that four of the P-35As had lost their canopies and several others suffered cuts in the metal skin when struck by the others' canopies. Most of the aircraft had to be grounded, but Ellis and the others were more concerned about their reputations. They had proven to Putnam (and Grover) that they did not fly like "little old ladies."

Major Grover intercepted Putnam as he left the line. He told the 3d Pursuit CO he was being offered a transfer to the newly formed Headquarters Squadron in Grover's 24th Pursuit Group or a court-martial, and that he had to decide on the spot. Putnam accepted the assignment to Headquarters Squadron and would not fly again until after the fall of Bataan in April, 1942. Taking over from Putnam was Capt. William K. "Hoot" Horrigan, a twenty-eight-year-old West Pointer who had flown with the 3d Pursuit in 1939, but was currently serving as a staff officer at Air Force, USAFFE.[23]

The heavy demand put on the 3d Pursuit's twenty-three P-35As to meet the flying needs of the squadron's twenty oldies and twenty-one newies, as well as accidents—climaxed by the October 2 incident—combined to put most of the ships out of commission. Their engines were wearing out prematurely. Although engine changes ordinarily were not due until the ships had accumulated four hundred hours, many needed replacement at only 250 hours.[24]

TAKAO NAVAL AIR BASE, FORMOSA
EARLY SEPTEMBER, 1941

Five hundred miles due north of Clark Field—at the Japanese navy's Takao air base on the southern tip of the island of Formosa—Sea1c. (Ittō Hikōhei) Masa-aki Shimakawa was feeling apprehensive. Veteran Zero pilots from the China front were expected any day, to be incorporated with Shimakawa and other junior pilots in a new land-based carrier fighter unit, the Tainan Kōkūtai (air group). Shimakawa, a nineteen-year-old farm boy from a small mountain village on the island of Shikoku, did not know anyone at the Takao base, not even Hancho, the contingent leader who had led them in their eighteen open-cockpit Type 96 carrier fighters from Kanoya to Formosa via Okinawa in early September to take up their new assignments.[25]

When FPO1c. (Ittō Hikō Heisō) Saburō Sakai landed at Takao several days later with a group of more than twenty China veterans in their Mitsubishi A6M2 Zero fighters after flying six hundred miles nonstop over the East China Sea from Shanghai, he was returning to his old base, having been released from temporary duty with the 12th Kōkūtai. To all of the Takao Kōkūtai members, the order to return to their home base meant they were heading into a new war to the south. Many of them, including Sakai, were slated to join the new Tainan Kōkūtai as soon as it was formed because their old Takao Kōkūtai was being converted to a land-based attack bomber unit.

Shortly after his arrival, toward evening, Sakai called for all of the novice pilots being assigned to the new air group to attend a meeting behind its hangar to receive instructions. Shimakawa was awestruck at the thought of meeting a pilot of such considerable combat experience: he himself had totally missed engaging in air combat during his tour flying the Type 96 fighter at Hankow. Meanwhile, his fellow pilots were whispering: "It seems that the man called Sakai is a horrible person. We must be careful or we'll get in trouble."

But Sakai was not as frightening as his reputation suggested. He and the other China veterans were even allowing the novices to climb into their fabled Zeros down at the airfield. Climbing into the cockpit of one of them, Shimakawa later recalled feeling "out of the world." He was particularly impressed with the retractable landing gear, the fully enclosed cockpit, and the streamlined fuselage, all features missing on his old Type 96. And what firepower: 20-mm cannons in the wings![26]

Shimakawa and the other novice pilots had not yet met the Tainan Kōkūtai's designated flying commander *(hikōtaichō)*. Lieutenant (Tai-i) Hideki Shingō had arrived at Takao earlier, on September 10, and was sorely disappointed to find only a few veteran pilots and the two *chūtai* (nine-plane units) of outdated Type 96 fighters flown in by Shimakawa's contingent. There was not even any maintenance staff at the base, and the new air group's commander had not yet arrived.

Shingō, Sakai, Shimakawa, and the others slated for assignment to the new air group would be waiting until October 1 for the formal transfer to take place and assignments to specific *chūtai* and *shōtai* (three-ship elements) made. During the interim period, the newies were meeting the China veterans. In addition to Sakai, an enlisted man, there was the China war ace, FPO2c. (Nitō Hikō Heisō) Kuniyoshi Tanaka, being assigned from the Kanoya Kōkūtai; CFPO (Hikō Heisōchō) Gitarō Miyazaki, transferred from the old 12th Kōkūtai; and Lt. Masao Asai, who had flown earlier from the carrier *Akagi*. Of the forty-five first-line pilots assigned to the air group, twenty-one had China experience. The nine in Shingō's 1st Chūtai each had over a thousand hours' flying time. Having just left the Hankow base, they were all tanned, and their flight suits had the smell of the battleground.[27]

Although construction work at their Tainan base, located thirty miles up the west coast from Takao, was still incomplete, the new *kōkūtai* was ordered to shift there and start training immediately. Shimakawa and the other novice pilots flew their Type 96 fighters on the short hop north, joined by the China veterans in their Zeros.

To put on a suitable event for the occasion, it had been decided that a *chūtai* made up of Type 96 fighters would stage an acrobatic show when it arrived at their new Tainan base. When Shimakawa's *chūtai* descended to land, the nine pilots participating in the show had just completed their acrobatics. Standing outside the Tainan Kōkūtai's operations shack, Shimakawa and his *chūtai* mates spotted a Type 96 stopped in the middle of the field. They clambered onto a truck and drove out to the aircraft. As they neared the Type 96, they could see that the right aileron was almost sheared off and the pilot was blue-faced. He evidently had stalled at the top of his acrobatic maneuver and then collided with two of the other pilots. A 1940 flying school classmate of Shimakawa's, Shinkō Itō, assigned to the 1st Shōtai, had been forced to bail out of his damaged aircraft. The accident was blamed on the *chūtai* leader, who had made a mistake in calculating the speed they needed to be at before they started the maneuver.

The spectators on the ground had watched in awe. As Itō descended in his parachute, someone yelled, "My God, they really do spectacular acrobatics!" Everyone applauded.

The accident upset Shimakawa and his *chūtai* mates. Their Tainan Kōkūtai was starting off on the wrong foot![28]

Such accidents would not be tolerated by their new flying leader, as the China veterans who had served with him before knew all too well. To China veterans and novice pilots alike, Hideki Shingō's slender cheeks and narrow, sharp eyes were physical manifestations of his strong willpower and the strict discipline he would be introducing. Already he was commencing a very severe training program, despite the fact that construction work at the base was still going on, even at the far ends of the landing field.

Flight Petty Officer 2d Class Kuniyoshi Tanaka was dismayed to learn that he was being assigned as Shingō's second wingman. Shingō had a reputation as an inflexible, frightful man. At the San Seto base, Shingō once had landed on the strip and continued taxiing right toward a group of ground crewmen who were moving just-landed Zeros by traversing directly across the strip instead of using the taxiways. It was his dramatic way of warning the men not to use such a shortcut again. It was very dangerous, risking fatal accidents, and could disturb the Zeros' landing pattern as they came in one right after the other.[29]

Now the Tainan base's pilots and men were humming a tune that went: "San Seto island more fearful than the land of the ogre, because you hear the voice of Shingō"—but not within earshot of their flying CO!

ROOM 2017, OFFICE OF THE COMMANDING GENERAL,
ARMY AIR FORCES
MUNITIONS BUILDING, WASHINGTON, D.C.
8:45 A.M., MONDAY, OCTOBER 6, 1941

Major General Lewis H. Brereton, the Third Air Force commander, was heading down the long second-floor corridor of the Munitions Building for Room 2017. The previous Friday he had received a call in Tampa, Florida, from Air Staff chief Carl Spaatz to come to Washington immediately. The chief of the Army Air Forces (AAF), Lt. Gen. Hap Arnold, wanted to confer with him about a permanent change of station. Brereton wondered what it was all about. Was he going to be relieved of command of the Third Air Force?[30]

Entering Arnold's office, he was warmly greeted by the AAF chief and a gaggle of senior Air Corps officers Arnold had invited to the meeting: Delos Emmons, Spaatz, Ken Walker, and Ira Eaker. As they sat down around the table, Brereton's anxiety diminished when he was informed that he was not being relieved due to any shortcomings on his part during the problem-ridden Louisiana maneuvers in which he had been involved, but because General MacArthur wanted him to assume command of his rapidly expanding Philippines air force. MacArthur had chosen Brereton on October 2 from among three candidates proposed to him by General Marshall. It appeared to Brereton that he had been selected because the air force buildup in the Philippines would initially focus on preparing services and facilities, which was his long suit.[31]

For the next forty-five minutes, Arnold and his aides gave Brereton an overview of the Philippines' situation and current War Department strategy. He would be getting more detailed information from Spaatz's staff during his Washington stay, as well as from other AAF officers, the WPD, and Marshall himself. However, Arnold was anxious to get him out to his new station as soon as possible.

Arnold and the others next informed Brereton of the status of the air-power buildup that had been taking place for the past month in the Philippines following the change in strategy based on President Roosevelt's decision in late July to get tough with the Japanese. Twenty-six B-17s from the 19th Bomb Group at Albuquerque would leave the United States about October 20 and follow the same trans-Pacific route flown by the nine 14th Bomb Squadron B-17s already based in the islands. The thirty-five B-17s would fill out the envisaged heavy bomb group, with protection provided by a group of P-40s that was already in place, to be augmented with two more pursuit squadrons. A dive-bomber group would also be sent soon.[32]

Those were the reinforcements envisaged for the near future. But longer-term plans for the reinforcement of the Philippines approved in A-WPD/1 called for a total of 272 B-17s and B-24s in four groups and 260 interceptor pursuits in two groups, in addition to the fifty-two dive-bombers, and associated air and ground units, including AWS personnel and equipment. The additional bomb squadrons would be dispatched in the immediate future, but it would be some months before the additional pursuit group and the interceptor command supporting units could be sent.[33]

After being briefed on the planned air reinforcements for the Philippines, Brereton expressed his objections to the arrangements being made. "I told General Arnold I considered it extremely hazardous to place bomber forces in any sensitive area without first having provided the necessary fighter cover and air warning service," he later recalled. Brereton urged the need for providing air warning services and fighters *before* sending bombers to a location so vulnerable to surprise attack as the Philippines. He feared that the presence of a large force of unprotected heavy bombers might be "a decisive factor to incite an aggressive enemy to attack."[34]

Arnold and his staff told Brereton that they recognized the hazards involved. However, the AWPD had only in late August learned that much additional time would be required to constitute and train personnel for the interceptor command and expanded AWS based on modern equipment that were envisaged for the Philippines air defense. They thus had decided to proceed with the planned heavy bomber reinforcements. The other units would be sent as soon as they were organized and initial training completed.[35]

ROOM 2000, OFFICE OF THE CHIEF OF THE
WAR PLANS DIVISION
MUNITIONS BUILDING, WASHINGTON, D.C.
MONDAY, OCTOBER 6, 1941

While Brereton was conferring with his AAF superior and his senior staff officers on the decisions made that had such momentous implications for the success—or lack of it—of his new command, just down the hall, the WPD chief was personally finalizing the study Stimson had requested three weeks earlier that represented the War Department's new strategic thinking regarding the Philippines' role in the Far East theater. Two days later, Gerow forwarded his memorandum to the secretary of war. He had entitled it "Strategic Concept of the Philippine Islands." The text amounted to only three pages, plus a one-page annex covering the strengths of Japanese forces and American forces based in the Philippines at present or expected by October, 1942, and a map indicating the arc of potential operations of B-17s and B-24s from Philippines and other bases.[36]

In his memorandum, Gerow argued for the strengthening of deterrents to discourage the Japanese from moving south through "the provision of strong offensive air forces in the Philippines prepared to operate from bases in British possessions to the south and from eastern Russia," as shown on the attached theater map. If the Japanese tried to bypass the Philippines to the west or east of the islands, Philippine-based bomber and naval forces would threaten them. In addition, a direct attack on the Philippines to remove the islands as an obstacle to Japan's southward expansion "would be a hazardous military operation," in Gerow's view, if opposed by the "strong aviation forces" of the U.S. and associated powers. Any air attack on the Philippines would necessarily "rely on carrier-based aviation and . . . long-range aircraft based on Taiwan," the costs of which would be so great that "Japan will hesitate to make the effort except as a last resort."

Gerow noted that the aviation strength in the Philippines would be raised to a total of 170 heavy bombers, eighty-six light (including dive-) bombers, and 195 pursuit ships by October, 1942. Curiously enough, these totals were lower than those given to Brereton and included in A–WPD/1. On the attached map depicting the heavy bombers' radii of operation, B-24s operating from Aparri at Luzon's northern extremity were shown to be capable of striking Tokyo, provided they could land at Vladivostok, whereas B-17s operating from Luzon did not have the range to bomb the Japanese home islands and return.

To facilitate the operation of American heavy bombers in such an enlarged theater, Gerow indicated to Stimson that MacArthur was being directed to confer with British and Dutch military representatives to obtain permission to store ammunition, bombs, and gasoline at selected Dutch and British airfields for use by American aircraft "should such action become necessary."

In conclusion, Gerow maintained that the air and ground reinforcements currently in, or being sent to, the Philippines "have changed the entire picture in the Asiatic Area." Indeed, the War Department's action "may well be the determining factor in Japan's eventual decision and, consequently have a vital bearing on the course of the war as a whole."[37]

HEADQUARTERS, AIR FORCE, USAFFE
NIELSON FIELD, MANILA
EARLY OCTOBER, 1941

Back in Manila, General Clagett knew nothing of the command change that had just been arranged by Arnold, Marshall, and MacArthur. Nor did MacArthur inform Clagett directly himself. The Philippines air force commander was busy tending to responsibilities MacArthur had given him in response to the radiogram the USAFFE commanding general had received from the War Department September 30 asking MacArthur to confer immediately with the British commander in the Far East to obtain authority for American heavy bombers and reconnaissance planes to use airfields in British possessions. In particular, the War Department wanted the use of a field between Singapore and the Philippines capable of handling B-17s, and proposed that one be developed in British North Borneo. It also wanted the use of an advanced depot at Rockhampton in Australia. Similarly, MacArthur was instructed to discuss the emergency use of airfields in the Netherlands East Indies with Dutch authorities.[38]

MacArthur had already informed Air Chief Marshal Brooke-Popham in Singapore about the War Department's request. Ever keen to obtain U.S. military support for his vulnerable Singapore base, the commander in chief of British forces in the Far East made himself instantly available. During a heavy rainsquall on the afternoon of Friday, October 3, he arrived aboard an Empire flying boat at the Pan American Airways base at Cavite, just below Manila, accompanied by his air operations officer, Group Captain Lawrence Darvall, and two other air officers. Two hours later, he was conferring with MacArthur in the USAFFE chief's Manila Hotel penthouse.[39]

MacArthur would rely on Clagett to obtain responses to the matters posed in the War Department request from the British visitors during their three-day visit. But first the usual diplomatic protocols needed to be observed. Thus it was that just after 8 A.M. on October 4, Clagett found himself taking Brooke-Popham and Darvall on a three-hour survey of the vital sectors of Philippines air defense. At Clark Field, Brooke-Popham said he was impressed to see "nine real long distance heavy bombers in this part of the world." Offered a ride in one of them, joined by two other B-17s, he was "silently pleased" that the formation leader did "a bit of showing off in the air, maneuvering his flight rather as if it were fighters." After his return to Manila at the conclusion of the tour, Brooke-Popham was taken to MacArthur's 1 Calle Victoria office for a meeting with the USAFFE commander and Brig. Gen. John Magruder, the head of Roosevelt's military mission to Chungking, China, who also was visiting Manila at the time. The three general officers surveyed and exchanged views on the Far Eastern strategic situation.[40]

Getting down to the substance of the War Department request, Clagett the following day took up the specific matters addressed in the radiogram. In discussions with Darvall, he obtained agreement for the use of British or Australian airfields in Malaya (including Singapore), Darwin, Rabaul, Port Moresby, and Rockhampton. MacArthur was also given permission to store munitions and base defense forces at these bases, if he so wished. However, Darvall told Clagett that no suitable location for an airfield was available in northern Borneo at the present time. Clagett informed MacArthur of the results of his meeting with the British air officer that same afternoon. Major Gregg, Clagett's S4, was also involved in the discussions. With the start of direct collaboration with the British involving a U.S. role in a wider theater defense, "the fireworks have really started," he confided to his wife.[41]

A few days later, Clagett was preoccupied with a matter that was more important to him than collaboration with likely Allied nations in the region. At three in the morning on October 9, he was awakened by an overseas call from his wife Mary in Washington. She had somehow gotten wind of Marshall's decision to replace him as McArthur's air commander! Mary Clagett was as worked up as her husband—if not more so—and had asked Marshall's secretary for a personal meeting with the chief of staff. In the event, she was foisted off on Marshall's deputy, Maj. Gen. William Bryden.[42]

Clagett was dumbfounded by the news. Just three months earlier he had pushed Air Corps chief George Brett for a second star for himself. Ironically, he had argued that a promotion to major general "would work well in contacts with the British and Dutch." Without informing his staff of the War Department's decision, Clagett began making changes in his command that Gregg and other staff members "could not figure out." Adding to Clagett's woes, the casting on his swivel chair fractured and gave way under his bulk while he was sitting at his desk one day. The portly general struck the concrete floor hard, causing serious damage to his arthritic back.[43]

Finally, in mid-October he informed each member of the staff individually of the decision to replace him with Brereton, but without offering any reason for the switch. His S2, Allison Ind, was certain it was due to his repeated health problems. To Gregg, Colonel George implied that Clagett's replacement had "something to do" with their trip to China in May and June, but declined to be more explicit.[44]

Gregg felt sorry for his boss, but the decision was "probably the best thing for him and the Air Force." In Gregg's view, Clagett's health was such that "he probably would not have lived long under the strain," he wrote his wife. Never having believed in the value of a staff and wanting to "do it all himself," Clagett had, in Gregg's view, been "slowing things down by not using his staff or letting them function as they should," despite the much bigger workload he now had compared to his earlier commands. Nonetheless, Gregg was happy to note that the "Old Devil" was "taking it with his chin up" and continuing on as best he could in his duties until Brereton arrived.[45]

At Fort McKinley on the afternoon of Monday, October 13, Clagett received Maj. Gen. Hein ter Poorten, chief of staff of the Netherlands East Indies Army, who had hosted him during his ill-fated Java visit two months earlier. The next morning, he flew ter Poorten and other Dutch air officers to Clark Field in his C-39 transport. Arriving at 8:30, they were given a chance "to look the place over," guided by the Fort Stotsenburg commander, Brig. Gen. Edward King. After returning to Clark Field an hour later, ter Poorten went for a ride in one of the new B-17Ds.

VICE ADMIRAL NISHIZO TSUKAHARA, WHO
COMMANDED THE ELEVENTH AIR FLEET AT
TAKAO, FORMOSA, IN 1941. U.S. NAVY PHOTO
NO. NH 63366 COURTESY NATIONAL ARCHIVES
AND RECORDS ADMINISTRATION.

Instead of returning to Clark, however, the bomber took him back to Manila: his trip to the Philippines was being cut short by an order to return to the Dutch East Indies immediately to take command of Dutch forces because their commander in chief, Lt. Gen. G. J. Berenschot, had just been killed in an airplane accident. At 11:30, Clagett transported the Dutch officers who had been left behind at Clark back to Manila in his C-39 to join their chief.[46]

HEADQUARTERS, ELEVENTH AIR FLEET KANOYA, KYUSHU, JAPAN FRIDAY, OCTOBER 3, 1941

In the headquarters building of the Japanese navy's Eleventh Air Fleet at Kanoya, on the southern tip of Kyushu, one of Japan's home islands, a breeze from the sea was passing through the open windows as the fleet commander, Vice Adm. Nishizo Tsukahara, and his chief of staff, Rear Adm. Takijirō Ōnishi, met with the staff. On this third day of October, 1941, the land-based Eleventh Air Fleet's headquarters staff and senior staff officers from its tactical units were in the midst of conducting a three-day chart exercise in connection with the air fleet's key role in the planned southern operations against Malaya and the Philippines.[47]

While the navy General Staff in Tokyo had days before supported Ōnishi's insistent demands for the allocation of carrier-based Zero fighters from the First Air Fleet as essential to the success of his Philippines' attack operations by transferring the large carriers *Akagi, Sōryū,* and *Hiryū* to him, there were still serious doubts as to how operations from these carriers could be coordinated with the Eleventh Air Fleet's land-based bombers on Formosa.[48]

Use of carriers to position the fighters within operational range of American air bases on north Luzon was a critical component of Ōnishi's operations plan, dating back to the time when only the three small carriers *Zuihō, Ryūjō,* and *Taiyō* were available to him. His land-based Zeros simply did not have the range to make the eleven-hundred-mile trip from their southern Formosa bases to central Luzon and back, even discounting combat time over the American air-fields.[49]

As the discussions continued throughout the day, nagging doubts about the feasibility of using big carriers in the Philippines operation remained. Would it really be possible to link up the carrier-based Zeros and land-based *rikkō* at the right moment? What would happen if enemy fighters attacked while the land- and carrier-based planes were trying to link up? What if the carriers were spotted and subsequently attacked by U.S. submarines based in the Philippines before the carriers reached the Zeros' fly-off point? And what if the Zeros were unable to take off at the agreed time due to bad weather? Were there any other possibilities that could be considered, the staff participants wondered. At this point, a representative of

VICE ADMIRAL TAKIJIRŌ ŌNISHI, CHIEF OF STAFF OF THE ELEVENTH AIR FLEET AT TAKAO, FORMOSA, IN 1941. U.S. NAVY PHOTO NO. NH 73093 COURTESY NATIONAL ARCHIVES AND RECORDS ADMINISTRATION.

the 3d Kōkūtai offered a suggestion. Commander *(Chusa)* Takeo Shibata, the flying group's executive officer *(hikōchō),* was highly regarded in the Imperial Japanese Navy as an outstanding tactician as well as an eminent fighter pilot. Three years earlier, as the navy's chief fighter test pilot, he had successfully insisted that the project that led to the creation of the Zero fighter should emphasize speed and range over dogfighting performance.[50]

Now, the thirty-seven-year-old Shibata, a 1924 graduate of the prestigious Etajima Naval Academy, stood up and declared that in China, the 12th Kōkūtai's Zeros were able to cover the 430 nautical miles (495 statute miles) from their Hankow base to attack Chengtu and return. Furthermore, he stated that Lt. Tamotsu Yokoyama, the 3d Kōkūtai's flying leader, had told him that the 3d Kū made a 1,000-nautical-mile (1,150 statute miles) round-trip when it attacked Chungking. Shibata's point was that since the straight-line distance from Takao to Clark Field was about 450 nautical miles, and to Manila and Nichols Field 480 and 510 nautical miles, respectively, "it should therefore be possible to attack Luzon directly from

LIEUTENANT COMMANDER TAKEO SHIBATA IN MARCH, 1941, JUST PRIOR TO BEING ASSIGNED AS EXECUTIVE OFFICER OF THE 3D KŌKŪTAI. PHOTO COURTESY NAOMI SHIBATA.

Formosa, provided that strict fuel consumption were observed."[51]

The conference room fell silent. None of the officers listening to Shibata had imagined such a proposal could be possible. No other contemporary fighter plane in the world could fly 500 nautical miles, engage in dogfighting, and safely return to base. Chief of Staff Ōnishi brought the conference participants back to earth. He asserted in his usual severe way that Shibata's proposal was not based on practical experience and was not supported by precise data sufficient to warrant changing the operational plan based on use of carriers. Facing Shibata, Ōnishi forced a smile and sarcastically declared: "what you have said would be useful only as data for the flying experiment department of the Kugisho Naval Air technology center." The fifty-year-old Ōnishi was known for his penchant for deliberately aggravating younger officers. Publicly rebuked by his superior, Shibata straightened bolt upright in his seat.[52]

Not having been invited to participate in the planning debate, 3d Kōkūtai flying leader Tamotsu Yokoyama was busy in the air group's operations area at Kanoya Field, putting his new charges through an intensive training program. Originally formed in April as a land attack bomber *(rikkō)* unit, the 3d Kōkūtai had been reorganized in September as a fighter outfit, with China veteran Yokoyama assigned as its *hikōtaichō*. At the beginning of October, it was equipped with forty-one Zeros, nine Type 96 fighters, and nine Type 98 reconnaissance planes. Compared to its sister unit, the Tainan Kōkūtai—the only other Zero organization in the Eleventh Air Fleet—the 3d Ku's ratio of senior, experienced pilots was high, many having transferred in from the old 12th Kōkūtai, which had introduced the Zero to the world in air combat over China in September, 1940. Even the unit's less-senior pilots had some one thousand hours of flying time to their credit.[53]

Yokoyama was giving priority to formation flying instruction, the first need when a new group was formed. During this first month following its establishment as a Zero unit, he had taught his pilots a formation that allowed them to make quick movements for an attack. The conduct of mock dogfights between two individual planes was also emphasized. Aerial gunnery practice from all angles was another important component of Yokoyama's training program. Night flying training was also included and gradually extended from dusk takeoffs and landings to pitch-dark night operations.[54]

From October 1, Carrier Division 4, built around the light carrier *Ryūjō*, was assigned to the Eleventh Air Fleet for training and operations. After its arrival in Kagoshima Bay, facing the Kanoya base, shipboard landing and takeoff drills from October 11–19 were scheduled for those pilots in Yokoyama's *kōkūtai* who lacked such experience. Yokoyama was opposed to such training. The majority of his pilots lacked the experience aboard aircraft carriers he and some of the others had. To Yokoyama, it would not be easy to train these inexperienced pilots in carrier landings and takeoffs, but he was forced to acquiesce to the wishes of Eleventh Air Fleet headquarters, which argued that since the 3d Kōkūtai would be operating from carriers as provided for in the operations plan, such training was essential.[55]

A B-17D of the 14th Bomb Squadron on a visit to Iba Field in late September or early October, 1941. Photo courtesy William R. Wright.

CLARK FIELD, LUZON
EARLY OCTOBER, 1941

While the Japanese naval aviators to the north were in disagreement on how best to use their Zeros against the Americans' Luzon air bases, the subjects of their planned attacks disagreed as to where the air force squadrons based at Clark Field should be moved to make room—including housing accommodations—for the impending arrival of the 19th Bomb Group's three squadrons. On one hand, Clagett and his staff wanted to base such decisions on Clark Field housing availability considerations, but on the other, his field commanders and the affected pilots were mainly concerned about relative living conditions.

"I sure hate all this indecision on somebody's part," George Armstrong of the 17th Pursuit complained at Iba. While Clagett was arranging for the 17th to be transferred back to Nichols Field base in mid-October after the completion of construction there, Major Grover was trying to block that move and have his old 20th Pursuit Squadron, with which he maintained strong personal connections, transferred to that favored base instead. Clagett wanted to shift the 20th to the dispersal field at Rosales and was being opposed by Grover, who did not want "his boys" sent to the boondocks. Similarly, Lieutenant Colonel Maitland and the pilots of the 28th Bomb Squadron were "bucking" a move by Clagett to transfer the squadron from the relative comforts of Clark to nearly completed Cabanatuan Field and its primitive conditions.

Armstrong felt that the 17th Pursuit had already served enough time in the field with its three months at Iba and was due for a return to civilization. "I hope that somebody makes up his mind and puts us someplace where we aren't living like the natives all the time," he wrote his wife. With rumors flying left and right and the higher ups locked in dissension, Armstrong judged the handling of the matter to be "a bunch of Damn Foolishment!"[56]

In any event, a compromise was worked out that satisfied all concerned. The 17th would indeed return to Nichols Field, and the 20th would not go to Rosales but remain at Clark instead, as would the 28th Bomb. To allow the 20th Pursuit and 28th Bomb to stay at Clark, Clagett ordered the 2d Observation Squadron shifted from Clark to Nichols and the 3d Pursuit at Clark to move to Iba for its turn to conduct three months' worth of air-to-ground gunnery practice. The dispersal fields at Rosales and Cabanatuan would remain unoccupied.[57]

CHAPTER 6

"Feasibility of Direct Attack on Luzon in the Philippines"

A t 9:45 on the morning of Wednesday, October 15, 1941, General Brereton was back in Hap Arnold's office as a follow-up to his initial meeting with the AAF chief on October 6. During the preceding week he had gone back to Tampa to make arrangements for winding up his duties as the Third Air Force commander.[1] This time Arnold had called Brig. Gen. Oliver P. Echols, Maj. James A. Doolittle, and Spaatz to join him for discussions with the newly designated—as of October 7—commander of the USAFFE air force in the Philippines.[2] It was intended to be only a very brief meeting, however, and after fifteen minutes Brereton and Spaatz walked down the hall to the War Room for the main briefing item of the day: a presentation of the new A-WPD/1 plan.

This time "Bomber" George and his team were not trying to convince an outsider of the merit of their plan, but simply providing information on it to Brereton and his designated chief of staff, Col. Francis Brady, and his intended G3, Maj. Charles Caldwell, whom he had brought to Washington from Tampa for briefings on their Philippines assignments.[3] After the briefing, George informed Brereton that the Air War Plans Division staff was trying to get everything together they possibly could by the end of the day that would be of help to him in his new assignment.

That afternoon, Brereton met with Marshall for the first time, as arranged earlier in the day by the chief of the War Plans Division, Brigadier General Gerow. The chief of staff spoke frankly to Brereton: building up airpower in the Philippines had been given top priority.[4] Marshall gave Brereton detailed instructions on his mission and emphasized the islands' increased importance in War Department strategy.

As he had with Arnold, Brereton responded frankly to the chief of staff. If the situation were indeed critical in the Far East, the basing of a vulnerable force of B-17s in the Philippines ran the risk of a Japanese air attack to neutralize it before units arrived to protect it. Brereton's concern was shared by another of Marshall's top-ranking officers. Major General Joseph A. Green, chief of the Coast Artillery branch, who three weeks after Marshall's meeting with Brereton warned the chief of staff that "almost surely the enemy, in an effort to neutralize these [bombardment] forces, will undertake at any cost air raids against [their] bases." Viewing the antiaircraft forces in the Philippines as "totally inadequate," Green recommended that Marshall send antiaircraft regiments "now trained in the U.S." to the Philippines as soon as possible to protect the B-17s from enemy air attack. But Marshall replied in much the same language Arnold had used nine days earlier. It was a calculated risk that he was willing to take. The Japanese were unlikely to take any hostile action before April 1, 1942, and by then all of the Philippines' air reinforcements should be in place, including for air defense.[5]

"When can you leave for the Philippines?" Marshall asked.

"As soon as my instructions are complete and transportation can be provided," Brereton replied.[6]

He had one more day's worth of briefings to attend, after which he was scheduled to fly to San Francisco to pick up the Pan American Clipper to Manila. Colonel Brady would be remaining in the WPD until Saturday, October 18, to collect a final batch of documents that Hal George's staff was preparing for him to take to the Philippines.[7]

The following day, Arnold and his senior staff officers met with Brereton in the War Room for a final briefing. The AAF chief wanted to elaborate further on the Far East situation and decide exactly what was needed to ensure Brereton's new command would operate efficiently. They agreed that Brereton would receive an Air Warning Service battalion (less the company already in the Philippines) from Fort Lawton, Washington, giving him a total of 1,174 AWS personnel. A battalion of aviation engineers would also be sent to speed up the construction of airfields. Signal and ordnance companies would be dispatched to improve the Philippines air force's communications and logistics posture.[8]

Arnold said that Brereton's new command would cease to be known as the Air Force, USAFFE, and would instead be called the Far East Air Force (FEAF). It would consist of a Bomber Command and a Far East Air Service Command. The rump 4th Composite Group would be disbanded and its personnel assigned to the FEAF and Bomber Command. Arnold also wanted to share with Brereton recent changes in War Department thinking regarding his command's role in Far East strategy. Two days earlier, Arnold had sent a secret letter to MacArthur outlining his plans with regard to air operations from the Philippines in a larger theater of operations. As he now explained to Brereton, those plans envisaged Brereton's B-17 and B-24 force operating out of Singapore, Darwin, Rockhampton, Rabaul, Davao, and Aparri to cover sea routes between Japan and Singapore, and Japan and the Netherlands East Indies.[9]

However, Arnold—and the War Department—were not thinking exclusively in terms of defensive operations in the event of a Japanese offensive. As he had written to MacArthur, "B-24s operating out of Aparri [at the northern tip of Luzon] can cover the south sector of the Japanese islands as far north as Nagasaki." Furthermore, if arrangements could be made for the use of airfields in the Vladivostok region of the Soviet Union, "operations from that point can cover most of the Japanese islands."[10] The next day, a memo to Arnold from the AWPD called for augmenting the defensive firepower of B-17s and B-24s "as soon as possible," or providing them with fighter escorts if they were to be employed in attacks against the Japanese home islands, as the bombers could expect "serious resistance from defending fighters."[11]

Arnold was not developing a scheme for an air offensive against Japan, just merely pointing out the possibility for strikes against the Japanese homeland afforded by the greater range of the B-24C and -D Model Liberator bombers that would be sent out in the coming months. However, Arnold told Brereton he would also be giving him studies prepared by Spaatz's Air Staff on Japan's steel and petroleum industries and electric power establishments before Brereton left for the Philippines.[12]

HAMILTON FIELD, CALIFORNIA
FRIDAY EVENING, OCTOBER 17, 1941

Across the United States at Hamilton Field, just north of San Francisco, the crews of twenty-six B-17s from the 19th Bombardment Group were anxiously awaiting the order to take off. It was early in the evening, and they were bound for the Philippines, seventy-five hundred miles across the Pacific, but eleven thousand miles for them, as they would be flying the same zigzag route from Hawaii as the pioneering 14th Bombardment Squadron had taken the previous month.

Just before dark, the B-17 crews were assembled in the Hamilton operations tower as Maj. Gen. Jake Fickel, CO of the Fourth Air Force headquartered at March Field, was giving them a pep talk. They and their B-17s were to be America's "big stick" in the Philippines, the proof that the United States meant business when it was talking to the Japanese emissaries in Washington, Fickel told them. But 2d Lt. Carey Law O'Bryan, a West Point graduate and copilot in the 93d Bomb Squadron, did not feel like a potent big stick at the time. Like the others, the Earlsboro, Oklahoma,

EUGENE L. EUBANK AS A MAJOR COMMAND-
ING THE 32D BOMB SQUADRON, 19TH BOMB
GROUP (HEAVY), AT MARCH FIELD, CALI-
FORNIA, JUNE 30, 1938. PHOTO NO. 342-FH-
4A8023-146569 COURTESY THE NATIONAL
ARCHIVES AND RECORDS ADMINISTRATION.

native was anxious about the long flight ahead of him.[13]

Fickel also swore in the 19th Group CO, forty-eight-year-old Eugene Eubank, with the permanent rank of lieutenant colonel in a "short and impressive ceremony" that nevertheless irked Eubank since it took up too much time in his view. Then Eubank's chief aide, Maj. Birrell Walsh, "had everyone in a quandary with all the detailed information they were jotting down—radio frequencies, altitudes, power settings, reports, courses, weights, and caution in setting of turbos." Fortunately, the crews each later received a large folder with all the necessary information enclosed. Nine of the twenty-six first pilots were to return to the United States immediately after the trip because senior B-17-qualified pilots were in drastically short supply stateside.

Finally, at 8:13 P.M. sharp, Eubank piloted the first B-17 down the cement runway and lifted off for Hickam Field on Oahu in the Hawaiian Islands, the first stop on their trip across the Pacific. The others followed at three-minute intervals. Eighth in line for takeoff, 1st Lt. Bill Bohnaker and his copilot, 2d Lt. Ed Jacquet, waited anxiously for their turn in B-17D serial 40-3073, "the tension almost reaching the breaking point." Together they had reviewed several times the motions and signals they were to make. They had never carried such a heavy load in a B-17 before: nine crewmembers, two bomb bays full of gas, armor plating, and machine guns—but no ammunition. They estimated the total weight at about 55,500 pounds before takeoff.

When the sweep hand on Jacquet's Hamilton watch reached the sixty-second mark, Bohnaker shoved the throttles forward and they roared down the runway. Jacquet was concentrating on keeping the manifold pressure and engine rpm correct, while Bohnaker checked the instruments and tried to keep the green lights at the end of the runway in the right position on the windshield. After taking the whole length of the runway, the ship lifted off "very beautifully," relieving Bohnaker and Jacquet of their anxiety. Having gained altitude, they turned gently toward the Golden Gate Bridge, their first and last checkpoint until they reached Hickam, three thousand miles away. Within minutes they were all alone in the black night, the other eleven ships already out of sight.[14]

Unknown to Bohnaker and Jacquet, the weather at Hamilton Field deteriorated rapidly after the first twelve B-17s were airborne. It was decided to hold the other fourteen on the ground. It was three days before the balance of the group was cleared to depart. One aircraft had to be left behind due to mechanical trouble.[15]

OFFICERS QUARTERS
FORT STOTSENBURG, LUZON
FRIDAY AFTERNOON, OCTOBER 17, 1941

Late in the afternoon on Friday, October 17, Ted Fisch retired to his quarters at Fort Stotsenburg. He was totally pooped out. Since early morning, he had been ferrying 3d Pursuit Squadron newies and senior noncoms, as well as the squadron's equipment, from Clark Field to Iba in his B-18. After dumping his cargo at Iba, he loaded up with newies and noncoms from the 17th Pursuit Squadron and their gear and flew them to Nichols Field, then continued on to Clark to repeat the cycle. It took him all morning to cover the circular route, and he had repeated it in the afternoon. "Today I feel as though I earned the $8 that the government pays me," he mused in a letter to his wife Mimi. That afternoon, flying through the pass in the Zambales Mountains on the way from Clark to Iba, Fisch gazed at the sun reflecting off the China Sea. "Twas very brilliant through the haze and way off at sea on the horizon were cumulus clouds billowing up almost out of sight. I thought someday I'll fly out of there and never come back."[16]

While Fisch and other B-18 pilots were engaged in ferrying junior pilots from the 3d and 17th Pursuit Squadrons to their new duty stations and trucks transported the squadrons' enlisted men, the oldies were flying their P-35As to their new airfields. With the opening of Nichols Field the day before, the 17th Pursuit was returning home after finishing more than three months of aerial gunnery at Iba, the 3d Pursuit was replacing them. The 17th Pursuiters were excited at the prospect of checking out the squadron's new P-40Es that were being uncrated and assembled at the Nichols depot. The SS *American Press* had docked in Manila on September 29 carrying the long-awaited shipment of fifty of them. The 17th Pursuit was scheduled to receive half of the new ships, with the other half earmarked for the 3d Pursuit.[17]

On October 18, oldie George Armstrong climbed into a half-assembled

A DOUGLAS B-18 FERRYING 17TH PURSUIT SQUADRON PILOTS FROM IBA TO NICHOLS FIELD, OCTOBER 17, 1941. PHOTO COURTESY R. LAMAR GILLETT.

ship to see how it differed from the P-35As they had been flying. "They're certainly small inside the cockpit," he wrote his wife. "I have trouble with my knees and feet, because the gadgets are all in the way." Although the oldies were to have first shot at flying the new ships, it would be several days before they would be ready.[18]

FORT McKINLEY, MANILA
SATURDAY MORNING, OCTOBER 18, 1941

Equally excited by the new developments taking place in mid-October were thirty men from the Air Warning Company at Fort McKinley. Lieutenant Arnold was ordered to take a detachment to Iba on Luzon's west coast with the first tested of the four SCR-270B mobile radar units that had been received and set up it up. He designated 2d Lt. Charlton J. Wimer to command the detachment made up of the thirty men selected for the job.[19]

That Saturday morning, Arnold, Wimer, and the men of the detachment climbed into their trucks and set out for Iba, accompanied by a Filipino engineering unit. In the convoy were the operations truck carrying the oscilloscope and other radar equipment, the prime-mover truck pulling the trailer on which the antenna array was mounted, the stake-body truck hauling antenna parts, and, bringing up the rear, the heaviest truck in the convoy, the fourteen-ton power van. Corporal Lou Vasey was driving the power van, with Pfc. Melvin Thomas as his "copilot." After proceeding north to San Fernando, then west to Olongapo, they headed north up Luzon's west coast, stopping for a lunch break high up in the Zambales Mountains. After lunch, as Vasey and Thomas proceeded down the mountains, they lost their brakes and went shooting across a bridge at the bottom with only six inches' clearance on either side. The van's weight caused the bridge to sink several inches before the truck slowed down. Finally, as night descended, after having crossed a gorge and another bridge, the convoy reached the Iba area. Vasey and the other drivers turned west off the paved road onto a dirt road that crossed the runway and brought them to the base.[20]

The base at Iba was in the process of being taken over by the 3d Pursuit Squadron, which had arrived the day before from Clark Field to begin gunnery practice. Vasey, Thomas, and the others climbed out of their trucks and began to set up tents in the open area behind the former Philippine Army barracks in which the 3d Pursuit pilots had settled. The next morning, the men of the Iba detachment positioned their equipment and began preparing it for operation. Although Lieutenant Arnold explained the setup to the 3d Pursuit's CO, 1st Lt. Hoot Horrigan, the other pilots and men in the squadron were kept in the dark about its function. The detachment's men simply told any inquisitive 3d Pursuit visitor that it was a "hush-hush" operation.[21]

OVER THE FORMOSA STRAITS
MID-OCTOBER, 1941

High over the Formosa Straits in his Zero fighter, Masa-aki Shimakawa strained to find the carrier *Zuihō* somewhere down below him. Then, from an altitude of three thousand meters, he spotted it. To the novice Tainan Kū pilot, the deck looked small, "like a leaf of a tree." He wondered if he would be able to successfully complete his first-ever attempt to land on an aircraft carrier.[22]

Since early October, Shimakawa and other pilots in the Tainan Kū who lacked carrier experience had been going through trials designed to prepare them to make actual carrier takeoffs and landings. At first they had practiced on a section of land marked out in the dimensions of a carrier's flight deck. Veteran pilots stood at the location where the novices were to land and guided them through their landing patterns. After each landing, the veterans commented on the pilot's technique.

FLIGHT SEAMAN FIRST CLASS MASA-AKI SHIMAKAWA OF THE TAINAN KŌKUTAI'S 3D CHŪTAI IN 1941. PHOTO COURTESY MASA-AKI SHIMAKAWA.

With the arrival of the light carrier *Zuihō* off the coast of Takao on October 14 to provide ten days of carrier landing practice for the Tainan Kū pilots, the second phase of training commenced.[23] Shimakawa and the others had been flying out from their Tainan base to the carrier's announced location and practicing simulated landings on it. As they descended toward the deck, they would apply power and go around again, a technique similar to the "touch-and-go" landings made on land.

Now, as Shimakawa descended and approached the *Zuihō* for his first actual landing, he was comforted to know that his arrestor hook was down and he would not risk going off the far end of the deck. The landing officer waved his flag, signaling him to cut his engine and come on in, and Shimakawa made a good landing. Nearby, the Tainan Kū flying leader, Lt. Hideki Shingō, was evaluating Shimakawa's performance. With the initials of each pilot's name written in white chalk next to the large red *hinomaru* insignia on the fuselage, there was no problem identifying them.

A few days after his first successful landing, Shimakawa was attending the usual evaluation of the day's exercises given by Shingō at the Tainan Kū commander's headquarters. He was particularly pleased with his performance this day.

Suddenly, Shingō barked in a loud voice, "During the practice today, some of you didn't notice the red flag not to land. If you believe you were one who ignored the red flag, step forward!"

"My God," Shimakawa thought as he looked into Shingō's face, "I wonder what fool made such a mistake."

"Shimakawa, come forward! How come you didn't see the red flag?"

Wondering why the Tainan Kū commander had called on him, Shimakawa stepped forward. Shingō slapped him twice on his jaw. Now Shimakawa felt really bad. He had landed safely, but evidently had failed to notice that the landing officer was waving a red flag. Now he realized that he must have been watching the Zero in front of him too intently as it was waved off to go around for a third time and had not noticed the red flag indicating he should not attempt to land either.

KANOYA NAVAL AIR BASE
KYUSHU, JAPAN
LATE OCTOBER, 1941

Nine hundred miles to the northeast, at the Kanoya naval air base on the extreme southern tip of the Japanese home islands, the 3d Kū's ten-day carrier landing exercises in Kagoshima Bay on the carrier *Ryūjō* ended on October 19. Yokoyama could now lead his pilots to Formosa and their new base at Takao. The Eleventh Air Fleet's headquarters also was moving to Takao, as was the Takao Kōkūtai, which flew twin-engine *rikkō* (land-based medium attack bombers) and was returning to its home base.[24]

Yokoyama was quite pleased with the results of the training he had supervised during the past month and a half at Kanoya. The fighters' carrier landing drills also had been successful, although he had been opposed to them—just as he was to the Eleventh Air Fleet's plan to put the Zeros slated to support the Philippines attack on carriers. Shortly before their day of departure, Yokoyama gathered all the members of the Flying Group together for a brief speech:

> I thank you all, pilots and mechanics alike, for your cooperation in bearing the severe and continuous training according to my wishes. I believe that we have reached a level of skill that can enable us to meet any situation with full confidence.
>
> Our 3d Kōkūtai will soon be moving to Takao on Formosa, but it is planned that we will continue our training there. As no one knows what will happen after our move to Formosa, I would advise each of you not to leave anything undone of a personal nature that you might regret later. Since from now on we will be moving by air, you should try to minimize the belongings you carry. Furthermore, I say this only for your own good—if you have any debts, you should settle them now.[25]

On Thursday, October 23, Yokoyama led his pilots on a nonstop flight nine hundred miles southwest across the East China Sea to Takao. It was the first time Zero pilots had flown such a distance over water, and all forty-one of the fighters landed at their new base without any problem, a performance Yokoyama attributed to the excellent maintenance of their ships by the *kōkūtai's* mechanics.

The pilots were impressed by the size of the airfield at Takao. They realized that it had been constructed extrawide in order to be able to accommodate the Takao Kōkūtai's twin-engine *rikkō,* which would be sharing the field with their Zeros. Arrangements already had been made for the Takao Kōkūtai to make available part of its hangar space for maintenance work on the 3d Kū's Zeros.

On arrival, the pilots were assigned to prefabricated barracks that had been put up rapidly to provide them with living quarters. Surrounded as they were by coconut, papaya, and banana trees, the pilots felt like they were living on a South Seas island. Mid-October in Takao was still warm, compared to the cool weather at Kanoya, so they were able to dress in short-sleeve shirts and shorts. Takao definitely had the feel of a forward base.[26]

NICHOLS FIELD, LUZON
LATE OCTOBER, 1941

At Nichols Field, 550 miles south of Takao, the pilots of the U.S. 17th Pursuit Squadron were enjoying new conditions, too. They were glad to be back at their old base after three months in the boondocks. The squadron's oldies were trying out their new steeds, the Curtiss P-40Es that were being turned over to them as fast as they could be assembled. George Armstrong found that flying a P-40E was much more complicated than operating a P-35A. The hydraulically operated landing gear was different than the P-35A's electrically run gear; it had an electric motor for changing the prop blade angle, as opposed to the P-35A's motor run by oil pressure; a chemically cooled engine compared to the P-35A's air-cooled power plant; "and the blamed cockpit is too small for my long legs!"[27]

Although Armstrong had test-hopped his P-40E without incident, not all of the oldies taking P-40Es up on their initial flights were so fortunate. On October 23, on a flight between Clark and Nichols Field, the Allison engine on Bud Powell's ship failed. Too far away from Clark to turn back, and with neither the altitude nor range to reach an emergency field, the twenty-two-year-old Missouri native decided to set his plane down on Highway 3, which looked like a narrow black ribbon down below. Avoiding power lines, Powell glided his P-40E down to an empty stretch of the road just north of Calumpit. Rolling along the highway at a fast clip, he spotted a big bus heading right for him and closing fast. He instinctively kicked the left rudder hard, gunned the engine, and hurtled off the road in a ground loop. Powell climbed out of the cockpit with hardly a scratch on him and walked down the road to the nearest phone, leaving his ship behind, a total wreck with just 5.6 hours on it.[28]

The day of Powell's accident, the army transport *Tasker H. Bliss* pulled into Pier 7 in Manila Bay with another load of pilots fresh out of flying school. Among the graduates of flying school Class 41-G from Luke Field, Arizona, were ten pilots who had received training in single-engine operations and were to be assigned to pursuit squadrons. "Why in hell send them here?" Armstrong wondered. Refusing to assign them to the 24th Group's three tactical squadrons, as had been the practice with earlier newies fresh off the boat, Grover ordered them attached to Headquarters Squadron for initial training. Not until after they had been trained and acclimated would they go to the pursuit squadrons.[29]

At the 28th Bomb Squadron hangar near the Headquarters Squadron hangar, Ted Fisch and the squadron's other senior pilots were still training the batch of Class 41-C and Class 41-D pilots that had been assigned to them earlier. Fisch thought of his outfit as "more of a training squadron than anything else." He complained to his wife: "We have an ungodly amount of these 90-day wonders to train and are they poor fliers!" Although he enjoyed the work when he saw that he was getting results, it was really wearing him down. "You have to know what the damn fools are going to do and you have to be right on the edge of your seat all the time."[30]

Fisch and his fellow pilots would now be required to train six of the latest bunch of newies that descended on Clark Field toward the end of October. These were the fifteen Class 41-G pilots who had gone through twin-engine training at Stockton Field and come over to the Philippines on the *Tasker H. Bliss* with the Class 41-G grads who had gone through single-engine training. After a few days in Manila, they were transported to Clark Field for assignment. In addition to the six assigned to the 28th Bomb, three were sent to the 14th Squadron and three each earmarked for the 30th and 93d Squadrons, whose flying crews were due in shortly.[31]

Earlier, on the evening of October 23, a convoy carrying 548 ground officers and men of the 19th Bomb Group who had crossed the Pacific on the *Holbrook* and arrived at Pier 7 earlier that day with the *Tasker H. Bliss* reached Clark Field near midnight after a three-hour bus ride from Manila. They had left San Francisco on October 4. They were quartered in recently erected *nipa* barracks located behind the hangars.[32]

Clark Field was literally jammed to the rafters with personnel, including those of non–Air Corps units, mainly the 200th Coast Artillery Regiment and the 194th Tank Battalion, both of which had arrived in the Philippines in late September and were immediately moved to the Clark-Stotsenburg area. Colonel George was pressing MacArthur's newly appointed engineer, Hugh Casey, to provide housing at the other airfields under construction to allow dispersal for some of the Clark units and to meet the needs of other FEAF units that were being sent to the Philippines. In priority order, as indicated in his October 17 request to Casey, he wanted the construction of housing and messing for one group each at Del Carmen, Cabanatuan, Lipa, O'Donnell, and Rosales Fields, each group consisting of a headquarters squadron and four combat squadrons. Housing at Del Carmen was top priority, for MacArthur had been informed that the personnel of the 27th Bomb Group (Light) were scheduled to sail from San Francisco for the Philippines on November 1. Six days later, MacArthur requested an additional $5 million in funds to carry out the construction program.[33]

On October 29, Colonel George increased his request. He now wanted MacArthur's engineering officer to devise plans as soon as possible for the construction of facilities at Del Monte Field on Mindanao, including housing for 339 officers and 2,743 enlisted men. Formerly planned as an emergency field, Del Monte was to be upgraded to an active field. MacArthur indorsed George's request and directed Casey to start construction as soon as the $5 million requested from the War Department on October 23 was made available. In any event, housing construction was not to begin later than January 1, 1942.[34]

Why did MacArthur support such an ambitious housing program for Del Monte? What air force units did Colonel George and MacArthur envisage as occupying quarters on such a vast scale at the Mindanao base? Eight days earlier, MacArthur was advised by the War Department that in addition to the 26 heavy bombers en route to the Philippines, he would be receiving 33 more in the month of December, 51 in January, and 46 in February, according to current projections. "Will your airdromes accommodate this schedule of deliveries?" MacArthur was queried. The War Department also wanted to know where the bombers were going to be based. Spaatz in Washington was worried about USAFFE's ability to disperse and operate the large numbers of heavy bombers being sent to MacArthur.[35]

With Del Monte the only field in the Philippines capable of operating four-engine bombers besides Clark, Colonel George was evidently planning to base the increment of heavy bombers being sent by the War Department at that field. The 7th Bomb Group was to ferry the first thirty-five B-17s scheduled to leave the United States in December and January as planned by Arnold and the War Department; orders for its forty-eight ground officers and 852 enlisted men to travel by sea had already gone out to its Fort Douglas, Utah, base on October 27.[36] The large number of quarters George wanted for Del Monte Field suggests he was planning to base not only the 7th Bomb Group there, but a pursuit group to protect the bombers, an air base group to service the bombers, and other supporting ground units, such as ordnance companies.

The deployment of a total of 165 heavy bombers by March 1, 1942, would fulfill the War Department's target for the buildup of B-17 and B-24 strength in the Philippines. MacArthur was keen to have them, even if he knew that the pace of the airfield construction program was too slow to accommodate the aircraft and personnel being sent to him. Ever the optimist, he wrote Marshall on October 28 that "we are prepared to take care of the contemplated additional units as rapidly as they can be sent out."[37]

HEADQUARTERS, ELEVENTH AIR FLEET
TAKAO, FORMOSA
LATE OCTOBER, 1941

Lieutenant Hideki Shingō stared at the writing on the big chalkboard in the center of the room and was shocked. The large letters used were similar in style to those in documents from government agencies: "Feasibility of direct attack on Luzon in the Philippines." Just below this subject of discussion appeared the list of those scheduled to speak at the meeting. Shingō headed the list: "1. Flying leader of the Tainan Kōkūtai."

"What does this mean?" Shingō wondered. "What direct attack? Is war with the Americans that close?" In a state of shock, he looked around the room for a clue. Nearby, the Tainan Kōkūtai's commander, Capt. Masahisa Saitō, caught Shingō's perplexed glance toward him, but did not react.[38]

Shingō had been summoned from Tainan during the last week of October to attend this "study meeting" at Takao called for by Eleventh Air Fleet headquarters, which had shifted to its new Formosa base from Kanoya just days earlier, on October 21.[39] No one had informed him of the subject to be discussed at the meeting. Entering the room, he had wordlessly greeted the senior officers present: one-armed Vice Adm. Nishizo Tsukahara, the Eleventh Air Fleet commander, and his abrasive chief of staff, Adm. Takijirō Ōnishi. The top officers of the Eleventh Air Fleet's two Zero squadrons, Capt. Yoshio Kamei of the 3d Kū and Capt. Masahisa Saitō of the Tainan Kū, were there too, along with the 3d Kū's *hikōchō*, Comdr. Takeo Shibata, and the *hikōtaichō*, Lt. Tamotsu Yokoyama.

Ōnishi, who was moderating the meeting, called on Shingō to offer his opinion on the subject of discussion: Would it be possible to fly nonstop to attack the American air bases on Luzon? Deeply irritated, Shingō cried out, "I don't know! How could one be expected to reply immediately to such a question? The Tainan Kū was only formed at the beginning of this month and is still in the process of training. It would take a month before we could say whether we could carry out a direct attack from Formosa on the Philippines or not." No one had ever discussed with him a plan to attack the Philippines with Zeros flying round-trip from Formosa. In

LIEUTENANT HIDEKI SHINGŌ, FLYING LEADER OF THE TAINAN KŌKŪTAI IN SEPTEMBER, 1941, WHILE BASED AT HAINAN IN 1939. PHOTO COURTESY HIDEKI SHINGŌ.

fact, since he had arrived on Formosa the previous month, he had not been consulted at all about the details of the proposed southern operations and had not even been informed about the chart exercises held earlier in the month at the Kanoya base. Even though his Tainan Kū was still undergoing carrier-landing drills, he had not been told the reason for such practice.

Shingō turned to face his 3d Kū counterpart, Yokoyama, who was seated next to Shibata. Yokoyama did not change his expression at all. Unlike Shingō, he seemed to be familiar with the subject. As Shingō extended his glance to the others sitting at the table, he felt increasingly angry. It appeared to him that he was the only one left completely in the dark about the meeting's agenda.[40]

Do they really expect me to go out and die without knowing anything? he wondered. Here I am, the flying leader of the Tainan Kōkūtai, with whom any secret should be shared, and with the likelihood of war in a few months' time.

"Flying leader Shingō," Ōnishi said harshly. "You said that you don't know about the direct attack plan because you don't want to go, isn't that so?"

"No," Shingō replied sharply. "I simply said that I don't know because I don't know. No position on this subject can be taken in less than a month."

"You are afraid to go, aren't you? Tell us if you are afraid," Ōnishi fired back.

Shingō remained silent. He was determined not to compromise his position in the face of Ōnishi's direct challenge. He was not going to let himself be publicly cowed by the chief of staff. He knew that if he told Ōnishi in anger that he *would* go on the direct attack, Ōnishi would have smiled and said, "That's what I wanted you to say."[41]

The rest of the morning, the participants expressed conflicting points of view about the proposed plan. With the naval General Staff's withdrawal on October 19 from southern operations of the First Air Fleet's carriers *Akagi, Sōryū,* and *Hiryū* for employment in the Pearl Harbor operation, some members of the Eleventh Air Fleet staff supported a plan to use the three small carriers *Zuihō, Ryūjō,* and *Taiyō* for the Philippines attack. However, others leaned toward the new idea of relying exclusively on Zeros making a direct attack. The direct attack adherents doubted whether Zero pilots lacking operational carrier experience—the majority in both *kōkūtai*—could become sufficiently skilled in such very difficult techniques in the short time allotted them. Furthermore, a total of only eighty-six Zeros could operate from the three small carriers, and the loss of pilots and aircraft in takeoffs and landings was a likelihood. Moreover, this did not take into consideration the problems of departure time, including the influence of weather, and protection of the twin-engine *rikkō* on their way back to Formosa. Also remaining was the basic problem of coordination between the carrier-based Zeros and the land-based *rikkō* they were to protect. On the other hand, the supporters of carrier operations argued that flying over a thousand miles round-trip to Luzon and engaging in combat over the target was just not possible in the Zero, given fuel limitations. When the meeting broke up, there still was no consensus on which course of action to follow.[42]

But the 3d Kū's *hikōchō* was still convinced that a direct attack was possible. Undaunted by Ōnishi's criticism at the Kanoya meeting in early October, Takeo Shibata was still working on his direct-attack plan. His anxiety was gradually being overcome by the support he was receiving from Yokoyama, who also ardently believed that direct attack, not the use of carriers, was the only feasible way to go. The 3d Kū's *hikōtaichō* on his arrival in Takao with his pilots and the Eleventh Air Fleet Headquarters staff was continuing the training program he had initiated in early October at Kanoya, which aimed to reduce the Zero's fuel consumption by 10 percent, from 125 liters per hour to 115. Even allowing for the heavy fuel use that would be required in combat over the Luzon airfields, Yokoyama felt that his pilots could extend the range of their Zeros by 10 percent through such fuel savings, or enough to carry out the direct attack plan.

On October 30, Shibata was ready to put his final proposal before his 3d Kū comrades for approval to transmit it to Eleventh Air Fleet headquarters. Captain Kamei had invited Shibata, Yokoyama, each of the 3d Kū's five *buntaichō* (nine-plane unit leaders) and the engineering staff to hear final arguments on Shibata's views in the 3d Kū commander's office. As the officers entered the flimsy, prefabricated structure made of wood panels, the floor squeaked under their feet. The barracks-like office even lacked adequate furniture. It reminded them that they were operating under the crude conditions of a forward base, not those of a base in Japan anymore. Kamei directed his officers to take any seat they wished. There would be no formality at this meeting. He himself sat down in the middle of the room. Then, in his usual courteous style, he asked his thirty-seven-year-old *hikōchō* to lead off the discussion.

"Today we would like to reach our conclusions regarding the question of direct attack by Zeros on the Philippines, which so far we have insisted on," Shibata began. He then opened the floor for the views of the participants.

Requesting permission to speak, Lieutenant Yokoyama then rose. "Following my instructions to each *buntaichō* to extend the range of their Zeros for a thousand nautical mile (1,150 statute mile) round-trip to Luzon plus allow for one-half hour combat time, we have succeeded in reaching an almost satisfactory level after a month's training," he announced. "I therefore conclude that this plan will be possible to carry out with sufficient margin." The three small carriers would not be needed for the Philippine operation and could be deployed for other purposes, he asserted. One by one, his five *buntaichō* —Lts. Takeo Kurosawa, Ichirō Mukai, Takaichi Hasuo, and Zenjirō Miyano, and Ensign (shō-i) Tsuneo Nakahara—took the floor and backed up Yokoyama in reporting the results of their training to date.

As the two-hour meeting progressed, Captain Kamei's anxiety eased. Not a demonstrative man by nature, the 3d Kū CO even laughed occasionally during the course of the discussion. Ironically, he was the second officer in the Japanese navy to successfully land on an aircraft carrier—in 1925—but he was now commander of a unit opposed to the use of carriers in a critical operation. At the end of the meeting, he announced that he would be submitting the 3d Kū's proposal to Eleventh Air Fleet headquarters. "Shibata, would you put it in written form?" he asked his *hikōchō*.

One by one, the participants rose and left the room. All except Shibata, who began writing up a summary of the discussion that had taken place. The importance of his task made him feel tense. Not only did he have to prepare a document showing the rationale for a direct attack on the Philippines as opposed to the use of carriers instead, but he also had to make it convincing enough to stand up against the opposition of the Eleventh Air Fleet headquarters staff. On top of it, he knew that he lacked skill in preparing memoranda. After all, he was a fighter pilot, not a writer! As he was about to leave the room, he suddenly thought of Ōnishi's cold and ridiculing eyes, which he would have to face the next morning, and made up his mind: "I won't be defeated," he told himself.

Back in his room in the barracks at the base, Shibata gazed out the window as night descended on Takao City in the distance. The coconut palms and papaya trees outside the barracks gradually disappeared from view in the encroaching darkness. Pen in hand, he started writing in a careful and painstaking manner, making dark characters. Although his penmanship was not good, his forceful strokes indicated a strong personality. "One: the most important elements of our fighting force in the forthcoming operation."

Shibata started off by enumerating the disadvantages of employing aircraft carriers for the Philippines operation. The arguments against their use were now well known, and he recorded them all. Next, he presented in great detail the conclusions he had derived from the results of training to date for an attack on a target at a distance of 450 nautical miles (518 statute miles), based on the oral presentation Yokoyama had made at the meeting.[43]

1. It is possible to extend the range of our Zeros for a round trip by about 100 nautical miles (115 statute miles) if we limit our combat time to 20 minutes or less.
2. We can extend the round trip range by about 10 per cent by using the 320 liters of fuel in the drop tank on the outward leg of the mission and returning on the fuel in the fuselage and wing tanks.[44] The saving in weight of about 320 kg of the full drop tank on the return trip plus the reduced air resistance following jettisoning the drop tank make this range extension possible.
3. The reduction in cruising speed to that of the *rikkō* group that the Zeros will be escorting on the outward leg means that the fuel in the drop tank should be adequate for the needs of the outward trip.
4. Constant employment of optimum air mixture control—except during the combat period—and reducing cruising speed wherever appropriate to save fuel will help further in extending the range.
5. By utilizing the nine-plane *chūtai* formation of three three-plane *shōtai* and giving each *buntaichō* the freedom to make appropriate engine power adjustments for his nine Zeros, fuel consumption will be much less than when flying in "show" formation typically giving rise to greater fuel requirements.

Synthesizing his arguments, Shibata concluded that "it is possible to carry out the attack operation covering a 450 nautical mile range with a safety margin of about 20 percent, providing that the weather is fine."

However, anticipating the likely opposition that the Eleventh Air Fleet headquarters staff officers could be expected to put up to his proposal, Shibata also acknowledged the weaknesses in his plan: (1) in the event of a deterioration of the weather, there was a risk of forced landings due to additional fuel requirement, and (2) considering the need to strike the Luzon targets at daybreak, there was also a risk of accidents during night takeoffs in formation from Formosan airfields and in assembling overhead after night takeoffs. However, in response to these two risks, he proposed situating picket boats in the water between Formosa and Luzon to pick up the pilots of any ditched Zeros and honing the pilots' skills with intensive night training, respectively. Continuing to develop his argument, Shibata noted that the Eleventh Air Fleet staff's argument that the necessary range would be much less if they utilized the carriers was not really valid. Once the Zeros from the carriers entered into combat over the target, they would have to jettison their drop tanks and thus would have to return to Formosa on only whatever fuel remained in their main tanks—the same situation faced by the Zeros under the direct-attack option. Furthermore, he argued, in the event of bad weather, the operational difficulties affecting carrier-based Zeros would be even greater than under the direct-attack alternative.[45]

The sky outside Shibata's room began to lighten as dawn approached. His intense all-night effort was drawing to a close. "The conviction of the 3d Kū of sure victory," Shibata wrote in conclusion, "is based on intensive training and on the premise that we take off from our base on Formosa, not from carriers." With that, he put his pen down.

At 8 A.M. on the morning of Friday, October 31, Shibata entered his commander's office, eyes blood-shot from the night's exertions. Captain Kamei, already behind his desk, looked up and welcomed his *hikōchō*. Immediately taking Shibata's draft from his hands, he went through it, item by item. Not a talkative man, Kamei reacted by only saying "good." Then together they went to the office of Rear Adm. Ryūzu Takenaka, commander of the 23d Kōkūsentai (Air Flotilla) to which the 3d Kōkūtai was assigned.

"It would be better that you explain this proposal directly to the chief of staff," Takenaka told Kamei. He then went out of his office to invite Admiral Ōnishi to join the discussion.

"About this proposal of ours," Kamei led off after Ōnishi had seated himself in Takenaka's office. He got no further. "Who has written this?" Ōnishi demanded to know as he looked at the document given him. When Kamei replied that it was Shibata who had drafted it, the chief of staff switched his attention to Shibata. His piercing eyes fixed on the *hikōchō*, he thundered, "Okay, Shibata, then *you* should do the explaining."[46]

Shibata felt his body flush with heat. He knew that his every effort of the past month hung in the balance. Thinking of the days of intense effort that Yokoyama and his pilots had put into their training program, Shibata felt a heavy weight on his chest. "It's now or never," he thought. Using his copy of the document, Shibata went over his reasons for the proposal, emphasizing every word and phrase. In front of him, his back ramrod straight, the unusually physically fit man of fifty years followed along with Shibata from his copy, nodding as each item was presented and muttering, "uh huh, uh huh" in approval. Finally, Shibata finished his presentation. A smile spread across Ōnishi's face. Then, in a loud and forceful voice, he announced: "Okay, I am going at once to see Admiral Yamamoto and have him accept this proposal. The 23d Kōkūsentai should immediately suspend training for carrier landings and make every effort to improve its skills for air combat." He then ordered Takenaka to implement a training program for night takeoffs and for making a long-distance attack.[47]

Looking at the back of the chief of staff's big body as Ōnishi abruptly left the room, Shibata felt the strength draining from his body. His ordeal over, Shibata was left wondering how Ōnishi could issue such orders without first obtaining Admiral Tsukahara's approval. He surmised that the Eleventh Air Fleet commander must have given his chief of staff the authority to make decisions on military strategy, leaving Tsukahara to handle administrative matters.

But it was also a reflection of the different personalities of the two men. Tsukahara, who had lost his left arm in a 1939 attack by Chinese bombers, was known for his eloquence and quiet, warm demeanor. He appeared always to defer modestly to Ōnishi, a nonconformist military planner whose naval career, focused single-mindedly on the establishment of a naval air force, had been marked by strongly expressed views on the merits of aircraft carriers over battleships in naval warfare.[48]

In any event, Ōnishi did not personally go from Takao to see Yamamoto on his flagship *Nagato,* anchored in Saeki Bay, but sent his senior staff officer instead. Arriving at Saeki Bay in early November on a Type 96 *rikkō,* Capt. Chihaya Takahashi reported the results of Shibata's research and requested the Combined Fleet staff's approval for the proposed change in the plan. Approving the change, Yamamoto confirmed the decision in a November 5 radio message to Tsukahara. The Eleventh Air Fleet's scheduled operations for the attack on Luzon with Carrier Division 3 *(Zuihō)* and Carrier Division 4 *(Ryūjō* and *Taiyō),* as well as its training exercises with the two divisions, were ordered canceled.[49]

CLARK FIELD, LUZON
MONDAY MORNING, NOVEMBER 3, 1941

Just after daylight, 2d Lt. Ed Jacquet anxiously looked out the copilot's window as first pilot Bill Bohnaker began his approach to Clark Field. Jacquet wanted to catch a glimpse of his home for the next three years. As B-17D serial 40-3073 descended and the air base came into closer view, Jacquet was disappointed to see that it was a small, sandy field crowded with airplanes. It "looked like a mess" from the air, and on landing his assessment proved correct.[50]

As the 15 B-17Cs and -Ds landed one by one, the crews did not give much thought to the fact that they were completing the greatest mass flight in aviation history. The group's twenty-six ships had begun departing Hamilton Field seventeen days earlier and, after hopping base by base across the Pacific, they had finally reached their destination. All except two, that is: Bill

McDonald's B-17D was still at Darwin, having limped in from Port Moresby on two engines, and Pinky Hoevet's B-17D also required an engine change at Darwin. Nine others had arrived earlier, eight on October 31, and one (Kenny Kreps of Headquarters Squadron) on November 2.[51]

As he greeted the 19th Group's commander, Eugene Eubank, and congratulated him on his record-setting flight, Les Maitland knew that his tenure as commanding officer of Clark Field would be coming to an abrupt end. Both of them were lieutenant colonels, but Eubank—whose serial number was 0-10580, whereas Maitland's was 0-11043—was 463 files senior. With Eubank remaining at Clark in command of the B-17s and outranking Maitland, he was slated to take over the base commander position.[52] But such questions involving the brass did not enter the heads of the newly arrived pilots and flight crews. They wanted to know where they would be staying at the crowded base.

After taxiing their B-17D into one of the few open spaces left on the field, Bill Bohnaker and Ed Jacquet, like the other officers, were "more or less left to ourselves to find barracks." About all they could find was a *sawali* hut with a few empty bunks, no doors, and which "was covered half-way up the side with grass mats, the rest left open." This certainly was not Albuquerque! They were told that *sawali* officers' quarters offering less primitive conditions were under construction for them, but it would be some ten days before they would be ready for occupancy. Some of the other new arrivals were more fortunate. Second Lieutenant C. L. Moseley Jr. and other officers were accommodated in the large, old wooden family quarters at Fort Stotsenburg, housed six to eight per set of quarters, including on cots on the porch and in the living room. Mel McKenzie of Headquarters Squadron, who had flown as copilot to Kenny Kreps and arrived a day earlier, ended up in a schoolhouse. However, most of the Stotsenberg quarters were already occupied by officers from the 14th and 28th Bomb and 20th Pursuit Squadrons. A rumor was making the rounds that Eubank would be moving the 28th Bomb officers out of their relatively comfortable housing, sending shock waves through the squadron. In such an event, Ted Fisch intended to "move every last stick and dish out of the house and let the other boys start from scratch." As he wrote to his wife, "Tis not very charitable, but the Colonel isn't being that way either."[53]

With the arrival of the 19th Group's flight crews, and earlier its ground crews, living conditions at Clark were deteriorating fast. "There is such a shortage of electricity that we can't even keep lights on in our dry closets," Fisch complained to his wife. Even worse, "the water is turned off from 8 to 11 every morning, from 1 to 4 each afternoon, and from 9 P.M. to 4 A.M. each night. What a rat's nest and would I like to get out of here." With the rumor that the 28th Bomb would be going down to Del Monte on

Mindanao, it looked like Fisch's wish to leave Clark might materialize. He hoped so: "I would like it down there with its cool weather, swimming pool, golf course, and good library."[54]

Kenny Kreps and eight of the other first pilots who had made the flight did not expect to be staying at Clark long, either. Their orders instructed them to ferry their B-17s to the Philippines and then return to the United States because of the shortage of senior pilots qualified on four-engine bombers there. Four of the pilots—Clyde Box, Jim Connally, Fred Crimmins, and Morris Shedd—were from the 93d Squadron, three—Kreps, Pat McIntyre, and Arthur Schmitt—from Headquarters Squadron, and Lee Coats and Ray Schwanbeck from the 30th Squadron.[55]

MANILA
TUESDAY AFTERNOON, NOVEMBER 4, 1941

Thousands of Manila's inhabitants craned their necks and stared skyward as forty-two P-40s and P-35As from MacArthur's command roared low—in V formations of three ships each—over the city, then headed east to carry out their mission, as reported in the press: They were to intercept the Pan American flying boat bringing in the new USAFFE air force commander, Maj. Gen. Lewis H. Brereton. The Clipper was finally coming in after having been held up for eleven days in Hawaii, Wake Island, and Guam due to bad weather and other factors.[56]

Over the Polillo Islands, seventy-five miles east of Manila, Andy Krieger of the 3d Pursuit spotted the flying boat above him at ten thousand feet after first missing it due to the overcast. Then, along with the other Pursuiters, he put on a show, performing upside-down rolls and disporting himself immensely as he tried to scare the Clipper pilots. But afterward, Krieger and the others were left with the mind-numbing task of "escorting" the ship to Manila. They had to hold their formation speed down to the flying boat's one hundred miles per hour, which was near the stalling point for their pursuit ships.[57]

The Clipper finally arrived over Cavite at three o'clock and headed for the Pan American terminal in Canacao Bay. Waiting to welcome Brereton, Colonel Brady, Major Caldwell, and Brereton's aide-de-camp, Capt. Norman Lewellyn, at the landing stage as they disembarked were the USAFFE Air Force's top-ranking brass: General Clagett and his executive officer, Colonel George, as well as his aide, Captain Nichols; the Philippine Department air officer, Colonel Richards; and the Nichols Field commander, Colonel Churchill. The Philippine press was waiting for Brereton, too. The reporters wanted to know about American plans for expansion of U.S. air strength in the Philippines. "None that I know of," he replied, not exactly candidly.[58]

Having disposed of the press, the air force brass repaired to the Manila Hotel, where reservations had been made for Brereton and his staff. After checking into a large, air-conditioned apartment at the hotel, Brereton spent the next hour talking about the Philippines situation with Clagett, whom he was now replacing. Clagett also undoubtedly wanted to know where he would fit in the new setup under Brereton and perhaps whether he should ask for a stateside assignment. Following Clagett's departure to return to his Nielson Field headquarters, Brereton phoned MacArthur in his penthouse apartment atop the Manila Hotel.

"Where are you, Lewis?" MacArthur asked. "Here in the hotel, sir," Brereton replied. "Come up immediately," MacArthur urged.[59]

When MacArthur opened the door to receive Brereton, he was clad only in his West Point bathrobe. Brereton had evidently fished him out of his bath. Nonetheless, the USAFFE commander general warmly received his new air force commander. He even recalled last seeing Brereton in the spring of 1918, when Brereton had commanded the 12th Aero Squadron in France. Brereton's squadron had flown missions in support of the 42d Division, in which MacArthur had served as chief of staff.

"Eager as a small boy to hear all the news," MacArthur slapped Brereton on the back and threw his arm over his shoulder. "Well, Lewis, I have been waiting for you. I knew you were coming and I am damned glad to see you. You have been the subject of considerable conversation between myself, George Marshall and Hap Arnold. What have you brought for me?"

Brereton explained to MacArthur that his papers, including a secret letter from Marshall, were in his briefcase, which had been taken to USAFFE headquarters for safekeeping upon his arrival. However, during the next twenty–thirty minutes, Brereton informally outlined the War Department's plans for air and ground reinforcements for the Philippines. MacArthur was so interested in Brereton's information that he almost decided to send for the papers and ask his chief of staff, Brig. Gen. Richard Sutherland, to join them. But he decided instead to wait until the next morning and asked Brereton to come in then.[60]

HEADQUARTERS, USAFFE
1 CALLE VICTORIA, MANILA
10 A.M., WEDNESDAY, NOVEMBER 5, 1941

General Brereton, accompanied by his chief of staff, Colonel Brady, reported to his new commander on a more formal basis at MacArthur's headquarters at 1 Calle Victoria in the walled city. When Brereton turned over the secret package he had brought "for eyes of General

MacArthur only," the USAFFE commander immediately opened it and scanned its contents. It was a memorandum from Marshall dated October 18, assigning MacArthur the broader mission he had asked for on October 1 and which had required that revisions be made to the Rainbow 5 war plan. Marshall indicated in the memorandum that the War Department had approved the revisions and was awaiting formal approval by the Joint Army-Navy Board, which was expected within ten days.[61]

MacArthur became elated as he read the new responsibilities assigned to USAFFE. Jumping up from behind his ornate desk and throwing his arms around Brereton, he blurted out, "Lewis, you are as welcome as the flowers in May!" He then turned to his chief of staff and exclaimed, "Dick, they are going to give us everything we asked for!"[62] Instead of being restricted to a defense of the Manila Bay installations, the draft revision now called for:

1. Defense of the whole Philippine coastal frontier.
2. Supporting naval raids on Japanese sea communications and destroying Axis forces.
3. Conducting air raids against Japanese forces and installations within the tactical operating radius of available bases.
4. Cooperation with the Associated Powers in the defense of their territories as agreed upon in approved policies.

The amplified role his air force had been given particularly pleased MacArthur. The heavy bomber reinforcements being sent to the islands indicated that the War Department was switching from a purely defensive posture in the Philippines to one that included "offensive air operations in furtherance of the strategic defense."[63]

Brereton next briefed MacArthur in detail on the air and ground reinforcements USAFFE would be receiving shortly, based on the information Marshall had provided him in Washington three weeks earlier. He also outlined the new organizational structure of the Air Force, USAFFE, Arnold had agreed upon, as well as what Arnold expected of him in his new command.[64]

Now it was MacArthur's turn to provide information. The USAFFE commander outlined the policy that would guide Brereton in developing his new command and what preparations MacArthur wanted to see Brereton make. He also gave Brereton his own estimate of the current situation in the Far East. In MacArthur's opinion, Japan was unlikely to take hostile action before April 1, 1942. The pace of USAFFE's reinforcement and the mobilization and training of the Philippine Army, which had been called into U.S. service on August 15, were based on that assumption.

Brereton asked his chief for a week to inspect his air force installations and recommend what he deemed was needed. He also wanted necessary construction begun as soon as possible. MacArthur agreed and asked Brereton to meet with Sutherland and the USAFFE G4, quartermaster, and engineer to work out a continuing construction program. If there were any difficulties, Brereton should alert MacArthur.

HEADQUARTERS, AIR FORCE, USAFFE
NIELSON FIELD, MANILA
WEDNESDAY AFTERNOON, NOVEMBER 5, 1941

Following his meeting with MacArthur, Brereton and his staff paid a visit to Air Force, USAFFE, headquarters at Nielson Field. He was not impressed with its location: a "former civilian flying school building." Clagett led them on a tour of the offices and introduced them to his staff. As he entered Allison Ind's S2 room, the new commander extended his hand and said crisply, "I'm Brereton." Speaking in "clipped sentences," he told Ind: "I hear you've been doing some good work here. I hope you'll feel free to pitch right into it just as before and give it all you've got."[65]

However, Brereton's impressions of the staff setup and the qualifications of the rest of Clagett's personnel were generally unfavorable. In his view, the number of officers and enlisted men assigned was "entirely inadequate" and, except for one or two officers, the staff was "inexperienced and not organized to carry on the functions of an Air Force Headquarters." Among other things, "No officer of G.S. qualifications" was assigned, there was "no G-1 Section, no G-4, no Quartermaster, no Medical Officer, no Communications Section or a qualified Weather Officer."

The next day, Brereton had Clagett's entire officer staff assemble in Colonel George's office, together with members of the adjutant general's office and those of associated services, including the AWS. Speaking in his usual terse, clipped speech, and controlling his energy by supreme effort of will, Brereton briefed the gathered personnel on the current situation of negotiations with the Japanese in Washington. He took a pessimistic view on the likely outcome. The United States must be put on a war footing, in his view, and that meant his command in the Philippines, too. Then Brereton turned the floor over to his chief of staff, Col. Francis Brady, a man known throughout the Air Corps for his abrasive personality. True to form, Brady informed the air force headquarters staff "in loud terms that some changes were to be made. And if they didn't bring the desired results, further changes would follow."[66]

The changes that Brereton and Brady had in mind were announced later in the day with the issuance of General Order 6 indicating that the Air Force, USAFFE, headquarters henceforth would have a G rather than an

S staff. Brereton was formally identified as the commanding general, Air Force USAFFE, and Brady as chief of staff. Major Charles Caldwell was assigned as the G3 (operations officer) and acting G2 (intelligence officer).

To what positions would Clagett's current staff be assigned? Most significantly, Colonel George became Brereton's G4 (supply officer). Clagett's S2, Allison Ind, was assigned as the assistant G2. Captain Horace Greeley was made assistant G3 rather than Bud Sprague, the S3 on Clagett's staff. Major Kirtley Gregg, who had lost his supply officer post to Colonel George, became George's assistant. Clagett's S1 (personnel officer), Captain Nichols, was replaced by Capt. John Spigler as acting G1, and Nichols was to devote all of his time to serving as Clagett's flying aide.[67]

Curiously enough, Clagett himself was not assigned any duty in the reorganized headquarters.[68] He was being left in limbo, perhaps to consider a possible request on his part to be reassigned stateside or to await War Department orders transferring him out of the Philippines to some other overseas post. His S4, Major Gregg, expected that Clagett "would be ordered home soon." Facing a similar situation, Clagett's former commander, General Grunert, had been relieved of command of the Philippine Department on October 21 and ordered back to the states, with MacArthur absorbing that position as part of his USAFFE responsibilities.[69]

Colonel George regarded his assignment as Brereton's G4 as "temporary." To George, it was a logical decision at the present time, as he was particularly familiar with the supply problems and airfield construction questions. "Being G-4 will give me the authority I need to deal with all of them," he explained to Ind. One month earlier, Gregg had anticipated that *he* would be named G4 under the awaited new setup, rather than assigned as George's assistant.

Gregg, however, had finally taken action on the long-standing dental problem that had made him feel "so lousy for the last few months." He had four teeth pulled on November 1, and another four on November 3, leaving his head feeling like "it had been hit by a sledge hammer." On the morning of November 7, he reported to the Nichols Field hospital, whose dental staff tried to put him in Sternberg General Hospital. Gregg managed to talk them out of that and was assigned to "Quarters" instead. In an effort "to drag around and keep my fingers on what was going on," Gregg met later in the day with "Louie," who told him to "take it easy and "turn in" until the teeth were fixed up. Meanwhile, Brereton informed Gregg that he was temporarily assigning George as his G4, and that Gregg would officially be listed as the assistant G4. Gregg expected that Brereton would later reassign George to a pursuit command and hoped that the air force commander would send Gregg with him. His worst fear was that "I may be stuck with the G-4 job when I get back on duty status."[70] His fears would not prove unfounded.

"The Inability of an Enemy to Launch his Air Attack on These Islands Is Our Greatest Security"

Tokyo, Washington, Manila, and Takao:
November–December 7, 1941

AT THE IMPERIAL CONFERENCE HELD NOVEMBER 5,

Emperor Hirohito made his near-final decision for war by sanctioning the completion of "preparations for operations" and approving the midnight December 1 deadline set at the November 1 liaison conference for terminating negotiations with the United States. The emperor was no longer "agonized" over the deadlocked negotiations and had become committed to war. Now he would pursue a strategy "to string Washington along" until the time when he and his military commanders were ready for the "showdown" with America.

Later that day, Admiral Nagano met with Hirohito to discuss the navy's war plan in detail. Entitled "Imperial Navy Operations Plan for War Against the United States, Britain, and the Netherlands," it had been drafted by Admiral Yamamoto's Combined Fleet staff and subsequently submitted and approved by Nagano's navy general headquarters. At this meeting, the emperor gave his final approval for the Hawaii operation that Yamamoto had finally succeeded in having included in the navy's plan.[1]

On November 6, Army Chief of Staff Sugiyama activated the Southern Army and designated sixty-two-year-old Field Marshal Hisaichi Terauchi as its commander. Terauchi was ordered to make immediate preparations for an invasion of the southern strategic area. He was provided with "The Outline of Operations for the Southern Army" and the "Army-Navy Central Agreement Covering Southern Operations," on which to base his own operations plan. He met with Admiral Yamamoto in Tokyo between November 8 and 10 in order to make the necessary arrangements with the Combined Fleet. He then summoned all of his field army commanders to Imperial GHQ/Army on November 10 and gave them detailed instructions regarding the preparations that needed to be made.

On the naval side, Imperial GHQ/Navy Order 1 issued on November 5 announced the decision to open hostilities against the United States, Great Britain, and the Netherlands. The Combined Fleet was ordered to make the necessary preparations for war operations and to advance its forces to specified assembly points before the commencement of operations. In response, Yamamoto issued Combined Fleet Operations Order 1 the same day, detailing the plan his staff had worked out earlier in secret discussions with Imperial GHQ/Navy.[2]

In Washington, Army Chief of Staff George C. Marshall and his navy counterpart, Chief of Naval Operations Harold R. Stark, met with President Roosevelt on November 5 to discuss a memo they had written for him regarding strategy in the event of war. They both argued for a Germany-first approach, with no corresponding unlimited Allied offensive to be launched against Japan. With regard to the Pacific, they told the president that if they could continue the Philippines buildup until mid-December, any Japanese forces operating south of Formosa could be threatened. However, if they had until February or March, 1942—by which time Philippines air strength would have been built up to its planned level—such airpower might constitute "a deciding factor in deterring Japan in operations south and west of the Philippines." They stressed that war with Japan must be avoided during the buildup. In this connection, they advised the president not to seek a declaration of war in the Pacific if the Japanese attacked Kunming in China, Russia, or most of Thailand. They recommended that America go to war only if Japan attacked or directly threatened territories "whose security to the U.S. is of very great importance," which meant all U.S. possessions, the British Commonwealth, the Dutch East Indies, and some parts of Thailand. The strategy under such circumstances would be to remain on the defensive, hold territory, and seek to weaken Japan's economy.

Roosevelt concurred with his service chiefs' views. The following day, he told Secretary of War Stimson that he was "trying to find something that would give us further time." However, when Roosevelt suggested a six months' truce during which there would be no troop movements, Stimson objected that it would halt the ongoing buildup of forces in the Philippines. Roosevelt immediately dropped the idea.[3]

Stimson's current preoccupation was the safe arrival in the Philippines of the twenty-six B-17s that had departed San Francisco on October 17. Since October 20 he had been asking for almost daily reports on the trans-Pacific progress of the heavy bombers on which he was basing his Far Eastern strategy. He was relieved to learn in the November 5 update from Arnold that twenty-four of the aircraft had arrived in the Philippines, with two remaining behind at Darwin, Australia, awaiting repairs.[4]

Back in Tokyo, Emperor Hirohito was given the completed war plan on November 15. A week earlier he had been briefed on the controversial Hawaii operation, which was described in the war plan as "extremely bold" and "largely dependent on the luck of the battle." The war plan was predicated on success in the first stage of the offensive, which would provide the conditions for economic self-sufficiency required for engaging in a protracted war. However, there was no "long-term, concrete plan" for a lengthy war.

On November 14, Imperial GHQ/Army issued orders to the Southern Army to attack the southern strategic areas. No time was given for commencing the invasion, just the mission of the operational forces: "to destroy the main bases of the U.S., Britain, and the Netherlands in East Asia and to occupy the strategic points in the Southern Areas." The area to be seized was vast—covering the Philippines, Malaya, and the Dutch East Indies, extending more than two thousand miles from east to west and two thousand miles from north to south—and its scale unprecedented.[5]

In order to coordinate army and navy operations for each component of the southern operations, Field Marshal Terauchi called for a three-day meeting, November 14–16, at Iwakuni (at the west end of the Inland Sea on Honshu island) of all the assigned commanders and senior staff officers from both services. A few days earlier, Admiral Yamamoto and the commanders in chief and senior staff officers of his fleets had arrived at Iwakuni Naval Air Station to participate in a conference on Combined Fleet operations, based on Combined Fleet Operations Order 1 issued on November 5.[6]

Detailed operational agreements were worked out between the army and navy commanders. With regard to the allocation of aircraft, the army agreed to commit significant air strength to the southern operations. The 3d Hikōshidan (Air Division) with 450 aircraft was being transferred to French Indochina and the 5th Hikōshidan with 190 planes was ordered to move to southern Formosa. The chief of the navy General Staff's Operations Section, Capt. Sadatoshi Tomioka, was relieved to learn of this heavy allocation of army aircraft, for by not draining off the navy's limited availability of planes for the Malaya operation, the navy for the Philippines attack would enjoy at least a two-to-one superiority over the Americans.

For the Philippines operation, the commanders of the navy's Third Fleet and Eleventh Air Fleet and the army's Fourteenth Army and 5th Hikōshidan conferred to reach an operational agreement. The strategy they finally adopted called for destroying U.S. air forces on Luzon first, then quickly occupying their airfields. The 5th Hikōshidan would be responsible for the sector of Luzon north of the 16th Parallel and the Eleventh Air Fleet for the areas south of it. The navy would cooperate in the initial air attacks and support ground operations. The main Fourteenth Army invasion force would land at Lingayen on Luzon's west coast fifteen days after X-day for the opening attack on the Philippines, and a smaller element would come ashore at Lamon Bay in southeastern Luzon, with the two forces converging to capture Manila. Details on the dates and places of the attack operation were spelled out in the formal army-navy agreement reached on November 16.[7]

After the conference, Vice Adm. Ibo Takahashi, commander of the Third Fleet, which would carry the invasion force, felt that the joint navy-army air force would overwhelm the Americans: they had twice as many aircraft in the operation than did the Americans, and he believed that Japanese pilots and other aircrew were better trained. Lieutenant General Masaharu Homma, the Fourteenth Army commander, was less optimistic regarding the ground operations for which he was responsible: he wondered how anyone could expect him to seize Manila in just fifty days with only two divisions of troops.[8]

In Washington, progress was being made in early November on American-British military cooperation in the Far East in the event of war. On November 11, Marshall and Stark had informed the British Joint Staff Mission that the United States concurred with the British decision to send more warships to Singapore, specifically a "capital ship force" as earlier proposed by the British. They also urged the British to send air reinforcements to Singapore as soon as possible to serve "as a powerful deterrent against a possible Japanese move to the South." Marshall and Stark further recommended that new conferences be held in Manila between Admiral Hart, MacArthur, and Vice Adm. Sir Tom S.V. Phillips, commander in chief of the British Eastern Fleet.[9]

General Marshall arranged for a conference of another kind on the morning of November 15. He had invited seven Washington correspondents to the War Department to hear about the top-secret plans and preparations the War Department was making for an offensive war against Japan. He confided to the participants, who were sworn to secrecy, that the United States was building up its strength in the Philippines for that purpose "to a level far higher than the Japanese imagine." While he did not want a war with the Japanese that would divide American military strength, if it should come, "we'll fight mercilessly," he declared. Referring to the ongoing buildup of B-17s in the Philippines, Marshall asserted that in the event of war, "Flying fortresses will be dispatched immediately to set the paper cities of Japan on fire," with "no hesitation about bombing civilians." While they did not have the range for a round-trip to Japan, the B-17s could reach Vladivostok in the Soviet Union, which he illustrated by pointing to a large map of the Far East, where they could refuel and rearm for the return trip to their home bases. The B-24s coming off the assembly lines and being sent to the Philippines would not need Soviet airfields— they had the range to bomb Japan and return without an intermediate stop.

Marshall told the correspondents that he wanted them to know of this strategy so that their interpretations of recent events "did not upset key military strategy of the United States." He also wanted American preparations for an offensive war with Japan to leak from the White House or the State Department "directly to Japanese officials" in hopes such a threat to their cities would cause them to think twice before attempting to achieve their ambitions in Asia. However, he warned the reporters, there must be no leak to the Japanese public, which would provide a reason for "the Army fanatics" to demand a war immediately, before the Philippines could be sufficiently fortified. For that reason, he concluded, "nothing that I am telling you today is publishable, even in hinted form."[10]

To President Roosevelt, the likelihood that the United States would be attacked by the Japanese appeared to be growing daily. At a meeting with Stimson, Hull, Knox, Marshall, and Stark on November 25, the president focused the discussion on relations with the Japanese. Roosevelt said that in his view, "we were likely to be attacked perhaps next Monday [December 1], for the Japanese are notorious for making an attack without warning." To Roosevelt, the question was "how we should maneuver them into the position of firing the first shot without allowing too much damage to ourselves."[11]

In a meeting with his senior staff officers the following day, Marshall disclosed that Roosevelt and the secretary of state thought the Japanese were dissatisfied with the ongoing negotiations in Washington "and will soon cut loose." The president and Secretary Hull "anticipate a possible assault on the Philippines" by the Japanese. Marshall indicated that he did not subscribe to that view "because the hazards would be too great for the Japanese." Brigadier General Leonard Gerow, the War Plans Division chief, thought it was more likely that the Japanese would go into Thailand, but avoid the area where the U.S. government would consider its interests imperiled. Gerow proposed informing MacArthur that negotiations were bogged down and that if war could not be avoided, the United States should at least not commit the first overt act. However, MacArthur should not be constrained from acting, "particularly as to reconnaissance," if the Philippines were in danger. The participants agreed that the message to MacArthur should "direct" that "prior to a state of war," and in cooperation with the navy, he should "take such reconnaissance and other measures you deem necessary." As to whether such reconnaissance should include flying over Japanese territory, the decision would be left

GENERAL GEORGE C. MARSHALL MEETS WITH MEMBERS OF THE WAR DEPARTMENT GEN-
ERAL STAFF IN HIS OFFICE, ROOM 2030 OF THE MUNITIONS BUILDING, IN WASHINGTON,
NOVEMBER, 1941. *LEFT TO RIGHT:* BRIG. GEN. LEONARD T. GEROW, BRIG. GEN. R. A.
WHEELER, BRIG. GEN. SHERMAN MILES, MAJ. GEN. HENRY H. ARNOLD, MARSHALL
(*SEATED*), BRIG. GEN. W. H. HAISLIP, BRIG. GEN. HARRY L. TWADDLE, AND MAJ. GEN.
WILLIAM BRYDEN (*SEATED*). PHOTO NO. 1054 COURTESY THE GEORGE C. MARSHALL
LIBRARY AND ARCHIVES, VIRGINIA MILITARY INSTITUTE, LEXINGTON, VIRGINIA.

to MacArthur. In the case of hostilities, MacArthur should carry out the
tasks assigned in the revised Rainbow 5 war plan that Brereton had given
him.[12]

While the War Department was preoccupied with the distinct possibility of a Japanese attack, Secretary of State Hull was drafting a note on the
conditions the United States required for an end to the crisis with Japan.
Frustrated with the lack of progress in negotiations with the Japanese, he
did not consult either Stimson or Marshall. Hull's ten-point program—
communicated to Ambassador Nomura and his special assistant, Saburō
Kurusu, on November 26—required Japan to withdraw its military forces
from Indochina and China and to recognize Chiang Kai-shek's government in exchange for unfreezing Japanese assets and signing a liberal

trade agreement with Japan. Realizing the conditions were certain to be rejected, Hull told Stimson the same day: "I have washed my hands of it and it is now in the hands of you and Knox—the Army and the Navy."[13]

In Tokyo, the receipt of the so-called Hull note on November 27 provoked a sharp reaction from Premier Tōjō, who misrepresented it as an "ultimatum to Japan" when it was really only a "tentative" proposal and did not impose a time limit for acceptance or rejection. By regarding it otherwise, the Tōjō government could maintain that the "hard-line" American position had "forced" the Japanese "to opt for war in self-defense," absolving them of moral responsibility for their actions. Meanwhile, at dawn the morning before, a huge Japanese task force built around six aircraft carriers weighed anchor in Hitokappu Bay in the southern Kurile Islands. Its destination was Pearl Harbor.[14]

On November 29, Tōjō called a conference of Japan's senior statesmen to advise them of the government's policy and the likelihood of war with the United States. Admirals Okada and Yonai opposed the direction in which Tōjō was headed and urged him to refrain from war even if negotiations failed. "If this war were for self-existence," the two former navy ministers argued, "then we must be prepared to wage war, even if we foresaw eventual defeat, but it might prove dangerous if we resorted to war simply to uphold the Greater East Asia Co-prosperity Plan."

At the Imperial Conference held on December 1, Privy Council president Yoshimichi Hara voiced disagreement with the admirals' line of reasoning. In his view, war was preferable to accepting Hull's proposal, since that would mean giving up "the fruits of the Sino-Japanese War" as well as those of the "Manchurian Incident," he declared. "The existence of our Empire is threatened." Hirohito nodded in agreement with each explanation made by participants who supported the war option.[15]

During the conference, Navy Chief of Staff Nagano stated that both the navy and the army sections of IGHQ had completed their preparations for operations and were in a position to begin as soon as they received Imperial sanction to resort to force. Although the United States, Great Britain, and the Netherlands had strengthened their defenses, they "will present no hindrance to our launching military and naval operations," he maintained. At the conclusion of the proceedings, Hirohito indicated his approval of Nagano's request.[16]

On Formosa, General Homma received his final instructions from Field Marshal Terauchi that same day. Terauchi informed him that the Pearl Harbor attack would be made early in the morning of Sunday, December 7, and that his own Philippines invasion operations must commence soon afterward.[17]

That night, Admiral Yamamoto's chief of staff, Rear Adm. Matome Ugaki, received a confidential telegram from the vice chief of the navy General Staff. It instructed him to open the top-secret message sent several days earlier. The communication explained that the decision had been made to commence operations against the United States, Great Britain, and the Netherlands some time during the first ten days of December. The exact time and date would be communicated later.[18]

On November 27, General Marshall dispatched the "war warning" message that he and his staff had agreed on the day before to MacArthur in the Philippines. The cable read:

NEGOTIATIONS WITH JAPAN APPEAR TO BE TERMINATED TO ALL
PRACTICAL PURPOSES WITH ONLY BAREST POSSIBILITIES THAT JAPA-
NESE GOVERNMENT MIGHT COME BACK AND OFFER TO CONTINUE
PERIOD JAPANESE FUTURE ACTION UNPREDICTABLE BUT HOSTILE
ACTION POSSIBLE AT ANY MOMENT PERIOD IF HOSTILITIES CANNOT
COMMA REPEAT CANNOT COMMA BE AVOIDED THE UNITED STATES
DESIRES THAT JAPAN COMMIT THE FIRST OVERT ACT PERIOD THIS
POLICY SHOULD NOT COMMA REPEAT NOT COMMA BE CONSTRUED
AS RESTRICTING YOU TO A COURSE OF ACTION THAT MIGHT JEOP-
ARDIZE THE SUCCESSFUL DEFENSE OF THE PHILIPPINES PERIOD
PRIOR TO HOSTILE JAPANESE ACTION YOU ARE DIRECTED TO TAKE
SUCH RECONNAISSANCE AND OTHER MEASURES AS YOU DEEM
NECESSARY PERIOD REPORT MEASURES TAKEN PERIOD SHOULD
HOSTILITIES OCCUR YOU WILL CARRY OUT THE TASKS ASSIGNED
IN REVISED RAINBOW FIVE WHICH WAS DELIVERED TO YOU BY
GENERAL BRERETON PERIOD CHIEF OF NAVAL OPERATIONS CONCURS
AND REQUEST YOU NOTIFY HART

MARSHALL[19]

Marshall met with Stark later that day and drafted a memorandum for Roosevelt on the Far Eastern situation that covered the issues Marshall and his staff had discussed the day before. In the memorandum, they recommended several courses of action that depended on what the Japanese did following the breakdown of negotiations. Marshall and Stark underlined the importance of gaining time until all of the Philippines reinforcements were in place. Should the Japanese enter Thailand, they should be warned that advancing beyond certain lines "may lead to war." Finally, Marshall and Stark recommended that agreements be reached with the British and Dutch as soon as possible on the issuance of a Thailand-incursion warning.[20]

As far as Secretary of War Stimson was concerned, November 27 had been "a very tense day." He had received news of the southward movement of a large Japanese expeditionary force from Shanghai toward Indochina. It also might be headed for the Philippines or Burma or the Dutch East Indies, but the more likely consideration was that the concentration was moving into Thailand to occupy a position from which the Japanese could attack Singapore "when the moment arrives."

When Stimson received a response the next morning on his request to the G2 for information on the movement of the Japanese force, "it amounted to such a formidable statement of dangerous possibilities" that he took it to Roosevelt before the president had arisen rather than wait for the noon meeting Roosevelt had scheduled for his "War Cabinet"—Hull, Knox, Stark, Marshall, and himself. Stimson gave the intelligence report, which dealt primarily with where the Japanese expeditionary force might be headed, to Roosevelt to read before the meeting. The president saw three alternatives open to him: do nothing, issue an ultimatum indicating a point beyond which the United States would fight, or "fight at once." Only the last two seemed feasible to Stimson, and Roosevelt concurred.[21]

Later in the day, an important assumption in the heavy bomber deterrent strategy that Stimson, Marshall, and Arnold had adopted seemed to have slipped. The secretary of war's "forebodings about the difficulty we are going to have in dealing with Russia" were confirmed in a meeting with the U.S. ambassador to the Soviet Union. He now worried that "we shall be unable to get the use of any airplane bases from her on the coast of Siberia." His fear that heavy-bomber landing fields at Vladivostok would not be available was not unfounded, as events would soon show.

Although the possibility of cooperation with the Soviet Union in the event of war with Japan was beginning to seem remote, the War Department went ahead with plans for joint operations with two more amenable allies, the British and the Dutch. Following up on the agreement reached in Washington on November 11, the War Plans Division on November 28 drafted instructions for MacArthur to "proceed with preliminary conferences" with British and Dutch military leaders in the Far East. When the secret communication was cabled to the USAFFE commander the following day, it informed MacArthur of the position Marshall and Stark had taken with regard to proposed British steps to strengthen their Far East defenses (as seen in the November 11 U.S. response to the British Joint Staff Mission in Washington). In the secret telegram, Marshall and Stark indicated their support for the British proposal to increase their naval forces in the Far East to six battleships and eight destroyers by early 1942, but hoped the fleet would be further augmented by at least one aircraft carrier and several cruisers. With regard to British air strength, they had advised the British that the "strategic situation elsewhere warrants reinforcement of the British air force, Malaya, by fighters and long-range bombers" and recommended that such aircraft "be sent without delay." The American chiefs of staff also proposed "broader tasks for land and air forces in the Far East and Australia/New Zealand areas" than were spelled out in the ABC-1 agreement. They did not support using Manila—"at least initially"—as the base for the British Far Eastern Fleet, but agreed that Manila and other Philippine harbors could be used "as advanced operating bases."[22]

The instruction to MacArthur indicated that the question of the British Fleet using Manila should be a subject for discussion between MacArthur and the other "supreme commanders" when they convened to make major military decisions, and that detailed operations plans should be developed based on such decisions. Coordination between naval, army, and air units should be accomplished "as found desirable." The first conference between British and U.S. authorities should be held in Manila, followed by conferences of staff officers "whenever desirable." It was proposed that Admirals Hart and Sir Tom Phillips, the British Far Eastern Fleet commander, meet and agree on an outline of a joint naval operations plan, then invite Dutch naval authorities to join in developing a three-navy joint plan. MacArthur was instructed to collaborate in a similar manner with British and Dutch army and air commanders in preparing a joint land and air operations plan. The coordination of naval, land, and air operations "would be by cooperation except when unity of command for particular task forces is agreed upon by ... commanders on the spot."

Marshall and Stark concluded by asking MacArthur and Hart to hold "preliminary conferences" and follow up with other conferences with the British and Dutch in line with the program they had outlined. In this connection, Admiral Phillips was expected to arrive in Singapore on December 6.[23]

The proposed plans for joint action with the British and Dutch pre-supposed agreement between MacArthur and Hart on command questions involving cooperation between them in operations. However loath MacArthur might be about giving Hart command of any of his units, Marshall instructed him in a cable dispatched November 29 that "in matters of sea patrolling and action not directly concerned with immediate threats against the Philippine Islands, you will ... provide the desired air support for naval operations" and "place Army forces under naval unity of command for such specific tasks." Marshall concluded by saying that he and Stark "hope very much that you and Admiral Hart can find a genuinely amicable basis for the conduct of affairs in the Far East," which they saw as a particularly important matter "in view of the complications inevitably involved in possible joint action with the British, Australians, and Dutch."[24]

Immediately after the December 1 conference, Emperor Hirohito began to finalize the text of his imperial rescript declaring war on the United States and the "British Empire." Over the previous months, Foreign Ministry officials had been engaged in preparing the initial drafts, but with Hirohito playing an active role in composing and checking the text at all stages. Since the whole southern operation involved the violation of international law, no references were made to it as in previous rescripts. Nor was any reference made to the Greater East Asia Co-prosperity Sphere as an official war aim, since it was decided not to pretend that the war was to be a racial struggle. Instead, the Japanese Empire was obliged to fight "for its existence and self-defense."[25]

On December 2, the date for commencing hostilities was confirmed as December 8. IGHQ had earlier based its war preparations on that date, but now it was formally agreed upon. At five that afternoon, Admiral Ugaki received a telegram from the navy General Staff authorizing him to open Imperial Naval Order 12. The order authorized the Combined Fleet to attack any time after midnight on December 7 (Japan time). Based on this order, Ugaki sent a wireless communication to the Combined Fleet at 5:30 "with one of the briefest but most historical messages in the annals of naval warfare": *"Niitaka yama nobore ichi-ni-rei-ya"* (Climb Mount Niitaka, 1208).[26]

That same afternoon, Field Marshal Terauchi sent telegrams to his field commanders to launch their Malaya and Philippines invasions, as directed earlier that day by Army GHQ. Terauchi's coded message read "Adopt Kotabuki Ko no. 5 Yamagata." When Lt. Gen. Tomayuki Yamashita, who would lead the Twenty-fifth Army in the occupation of Malaya, and Lt. Gen. Masaharu Homma, whose Fourteenth Army was charged with seizing the Philippines, followed Terauchi's instructions and opened sealed IGHQ Order 569 that had been sent to them earlier, they found that they were being ordered to initiate operations on December 8.

At 4:30 P.M. on December 4, a convoy of transports carrying General Yamashita's Twenty-fifth Army left the island of Hainan off China's southern coast escorted by the Malay Force of twenty-four cruisers and destroyers and headed due south.[27] Unlike for the Philippines invasion operation, there would be no preliminary effort to knock out British airpower in Malaya and Singapore to ensure the safety of the invasion operation. Southern operations planners did not consider British air strength in the area as formidable as that in the Philippines.

While the Japanese high command respected the *defensive* capabilities of MacArthur's Luzon-based air force against a Philippines invasion, it did not take seriously the rumored *offensive* threat it posed, contrary to Marshall's hopes as expressed in his November 15 secret press conference.

Thus, on December 3, a retired Japanese rear admiral serving as a spokesman for the military informed a Tokyo newspaper reporter that there was
"no cause for apprehension" among the Japanese people that the "ABCD
camp" could threaten Japan proper. The "twenty" B-17s sent to the Philippines were the "old B and C types" with a range "insufficient to enable
them to carry out effective bombing raids from Manila and back." Even
the twenty-some "Consolidated PBY-28 heavy bombers" with reportedly
"the greatest flying capacity in the world at present" are not able to "per-
form what is expected of them," he maintained.[28]

In Manila, General MacArthur had received the army chief of staff's "war
warning" message of November 27 in the small hours of the following
day (Manila time) and immediately fired off a response advising the War
Department of the measures he had taken: "Air reconnaissance has been
extended and intensified in conjunction with the Navy" and "ground
security measures have been taken." He assured Marshall that "everything
is in readiness for the conduct of a successful defense."[29]

The day before the war warning message was received, MacArthur
discussed the tense situation in a series of meetings with President Quezon, High Commissioner Sayre, Admiral Hart, and General Brereton. At
a meeting in Sayre's office, the high commissioner recorded that MacArthur "paced back and forth, back and forth over my office floor, smoking a black cigar and assuring Admiral Hart and myself . . . it would be
impossible for the Japanese to attack the Philippines before the following
April." MacArthur conferred the next day with Rear Admiral W. R. Purnell, Hart's chief of staff in Hart's absence, on Corregidor. On both days,
"important dispatches were received from Washington," MacArthur's aide
recorded in the USAFFE commander's office diary.[30]

The vexed question of command relations between MacArthur and
Hart was still unresolved on the eve of impending discussions with the
British on strategic plans for conducting joint operations. In response to
Marshall's November 29 cable urging MacArthur to support naval operations "not directly concerned with immediate threats against the Philippine Islands" by placing his forces under naval command, the USAFFE
commander replied on December 2 that his support of naval operations
"was never at issue," but "unity of command under the Navy"—particularly opposed by Brereton with regard to his Far East Air Force units—
would yield less effective results than a "coordination of mission." MacArthur informed Marshall "Admiral Hart has apparently now accepted this
position."[31]

Early on December 5, Vice Adm. Tom Phillips, commander in chief
of the newly established British Far Eastern Fleet in Singapore, arrived in

Manila with two staff officers to meet with Admiral Hart to begin drafting of a plan for joint naval operations in the Far East theater. Three days earlier, his six-ship fleet had arrived in Singapore, led by the battleship *Prince of Wales* and battle cruiser *Repulse,* the centerpieces in the British naval buildup in the area.[32] Hart had invited MacArthur and his chief of staff, Sutherland, to participate in the discussions at the initial meeting between the two admirals on December 5. MacArthur informed the two fleet commanders that he would support Hart's naval operations through "coordination" of his army air forces, but that "Army air will be under Army control," implying that the navy would in no circumstances exercise command over army air operations. However, MacArthur reassured the participants, this arrangement with Hart would not pose a problem, for "he and I operate in the closest coordination" and "are the oldest and dearest of friends." Reacting to this hilarious evaluation of MacArthur's relations with his navy counterpart, Hart's staff at the meeting "had trouble keeping their composure."

MacArthur was asked to brief Phillips about the security aspects—with regard to possible air or ground attacks—of Manila Bay as a base for naval operations, a particular concern of the British admiral. While acknowledging that antiaircraft defense potential was "low," MacArthur was upbeat about his air defense capabilities, citing the ongoing buildup of his aviation assets, particularly the thirty-five B-17 bombers that made up his "ace unit." When Phillips pointed out that "the defense of this place so much depends on the ability to operate fighters in any area," MacArthur replied that he "practically" had that ability now. In fact, the USAFFE commander maintained, "The inability of an enemy to launch his air attack on these islands is our greatest security," which "leaves me with a sense of complete security." However, he acknowledged that his assertion did not mean that a "heavy bomber attack" might not get through to attack a fleet anchored in Manila Bay, but the bombers "would be punished severely." In concluding his assessment of the air defense question, MacArthur told Phillips that "nothing would please me better than if they would give me three months and then attack here" for "that would deliver the enemy into our hands."[33]

After MacArthur left the meeting, Hart and Phillips began discussing plans. The main subject was the proposal that Phillips's fleet join with Hart's in Manila, as it was considered that Manila "would make a suitable base for combined *offensive* operations in the event of war against Japan." They recognized, however, that such a joining of their fleets "would have to remain a long-term plan dependent on more British aircraft being sent to replace the Navy and protect Singapore."[34]

Near midnight, MacArthur cabled the War Department in response to its cable of November 28 requested by Arnold and instructing MacArthur to take all precautions against subversive activities and to report actions taken to Arnold by December 5. MacArthur replied that "all Air Corps stations here on alert status . . . airplanes dispersed and each under guard, all airdrome defense stations manned, guards on installations increased," and FEAF headquarters was organizing countersubversion activities.[35]

During the second day of meetings between Phillips and Hart, the discussion was interrupted by "an American officer" who brought a dramatic message: a convoy of "no less than" twenty-five Japanese merchant ships escorted by a battleship, cruisers, and destroyers had been spotted by an Australian Hudson aircraft as the convoy steamed on a westerly course south of Saigon in French Indochina. It appeared that the ships were making for Thailand or Malaya. Within an hour, Phillips was flying back to Singapore.[36]

Very early in the morning on Sunday, December 7, MacArthur sent a message to Marshall advising him of the agreement that had been reached between MacArthur, Hart, and Phillips. With regard to air operations, they had agreed that in the event of an attack on the Philippines, the British and Dutch would move their air units forward in their territories to provide protection for lines of communication directly south of the Philippines. If British or Dutch territories were attacked, MacArthur's FEAF would operate from Philippines bases against the Japanese lines of advance. MacArthur also indicated that if Phillips's request to use Manila "or Mariveles" (at the southern tip of Bataan) as an advanced naval base "to wage offensive war" were approved, he would need an increase in antiaircraft and pursuit protection.[37]

In Washington, Marshall and Stark had been following the movements of the Japanese expeditionary force down the China coast and Indochina that now clearly appeared to be heading into the Gulf of Siam bound for Thailand's Kra Isthmus and Malaya. If the Japanese went into the Gulf of Siam, "that meant that they were on the back door of Singapore and could have . . . only a direct hostile motive," Marshall later recalled. Unknown to Marshall and Stimson, on December 4 President Roosevelt had told the British ambassador to the United States, Lord Halifax, that if the Japanese mounted a direct attack on the British or Dutch in the Far East, "We should obviously all be together." In addition, America would come to Britain's aid if it undertook a defense of the Kra Isthmus leading into British Malaya. Both commitments exceeded Roosevelt's constitutional powers, but he "left no doubt" that if war broke out in the Far East, the United States would back Britain.

During the first week of December, Stimson and Marshall, as well as Gerow and Brig. Gen. Sherman Miles of Marshall's staff, were preoccupied with the delivery of supplies to the Philippines and the additional "big bombers which we are trying to fly over there." Thirteen B-17s were

ready to depart from California on Saturday, December 6, but the transfer
of an additional thirty-three scheduled to depart for the Philippines the
same day was running behind schedule. Arnold was sending reports to the
WPD almost daily for transmission to Stimson. In them was information
detailing when AAF personnel and small aircraft were sailing and when
heavy bombers were departing for the Philippines.[38]

Also on Saturday, Marshall instructed members of the WPD to collect materials on the Far East and Southwest Pacific that the chief of staff
wanted for a conference with the president scheduled for 3 P.M. the next
day. The studies and documents were waiting on Marshall's desk Sunday morning. However, before he had the opportunity to go over them,
another development came to his attention: The War Department had
learned via an intercepted Japanese radio message that Japan would be
presenting a note to the U.S. government later in the day that would put
an end to further negotiations.[39]

On the evening of December 7, troop-laden Japanese transports in a protective convoy were approaching the Thai towns of Singora and Patani on
the Kra Isthmus, while to the south others were heading for Kota Bharu at
the northern tip of British Malaya. The twenty-eight transports carrying the
Twenty-fifth Army troops embarked at Hainan and Saigon had rendezvoused
at 9:05 that morning at a point in the middle of the Gulf of Siam and split
into three groups for the landings. They soon would begin debarking the
troops, thus initiating the southern operations to start the Pacific War.[40]

That evening, two smaller groups of troops, each on six transports
escorted by a cruiser and destroyers, were heading south in the South
China Sea from Mako in the Pescadores, thirty miles off Formosa's west
coast. They were carrying advance-force troops scheduled to land on
December 10 at Vigan and Aparri on northern Luzon, where they would
seize the small airfields at each location to provide air support for the
Fourteenth Army's main landings. Also proceeding south that night, traversing the Luzon Strait between southern Formosa and northern Luzon,
was a small naval landing unit headed for Batan Island, located halfway
between Formosa and Luzon. Its objective was to occupy the small airfield
at Basco, needed to provide air cover for the Aparri and Vigan landing
forces and to serve as a staging base for initial army fighter operations on
northern Luzon.[41]

On Formosa, army and navy air units scheduled to lead the air attacks
on Luzon at sunrise the next morning were making final preparations for
their long flights south. Of the 192 aircraft of the army's 5th Hikōshidan
arrayed on the southern Formosa fields at Heito, Koshun, Choshu, and
Kato, only the 8th Sentai's twin-engine light bombers at Kato and the

14th Sentai's twin-engine medium bombers at Choshu would be participating in the opening day's operations. They were slated to bomb Baguio and Tuguegarao, both of which were north of the 16th Parallel on Luzon.

That evening, at the large navy airfield at Takao base on southern Formosa, eighty-one twin-engine attack bombers of the Takao and Kanoya Kōkūtai and fifty-four Zero fighters of the 3d and Tainan Kōkūtai were being checked out by their ground crews preparatory to their scheduled predawn takeoff for the initial strikes on Nichols and Clark Fields on Luzon. To the north, similar preparations were being made that night for the 1st Kōkūtai's twenty-seven twin-engine bombers and the Tainan Kōkūtai's thirty-six Zeros, which would be leaving Tainan air base during the same small hours of the morning for their attack on Clark Field.[42]

Staff officers at the Eleventh Air Fleet headquarters at Takao were worried that their bomber and fighter force might not be adequate for the task. The number of twin-engine attack bombers had been reduced on December 4 from 135 to 108 with the transfer of half of the Kanoya Kōkūtai's aircraft to Saigon in response to the appearance of the British Far Eastern Fleet in Singapore's waters. Earlier, on November 26 and 27, they had lost twenty-seven Zeros from the Tainan and 3d Kōkūtai when they were also transferred to support the Malaya operation.

Against their force of 108 bombers and 90 fighters, the Eleventh Air Fleet staff estimated that MacArthur's FEAF would be sending up 110 fighters based on different fields on Luzon. It was believed that there were about 30 P-35s at Clark Field, 30 P-35s at Nichols Field, about 25 P-40s at Del Carmen, and about 25 P-35s and P-36s at Iba. They thus expected to be slightly outnumbered in fighter aircraft. However, three-fourths of the U.S. interceptors were believed to be "relatively old type" P-35s. On the other hand, the P-40s were considered "very good fighters." The rest of the American airpower on Luzon was believed to consist of 30–35 B-17s at Clark—the main target of the Japanese attack—and 7–10 B-17s and B-18s at Nichols Field. The B-17D model they would meet was considered to be "a very good bomber" because of its "maneuverability and attack capability."[43]

The navy General Staff officer with primary responsibility for planning the naval operations commencing the Pacific War was spending another sleepless night at his desk at IGHQ in Tokyo. Captain Sadatoshi Tomioka and his Operations Section staff had been working all night every night since November 26, consumed by the risk being run in sending out the huge carrier force to attack Pearl Harbor thousands of miles from its base in Japan. He kept a .38-caliber revolver in his desk drawer. If his decision to approve the Pearl Harbor operation—albeit under unbearable pressure from Admiral Yamamoto—led to failure, he would shoot himself.[44]

CHAPTER 7

"We Are Going Much Too Far on the Offensive Side"

The new commanding general of the air force units assigned to U.S. Army Forces in the Far East was checking out the situation at the Nichols Field air depot and did not like what he found. "Completely inadequate," he told his staff and the officer in charge of the depot as they went through the depot's hangar one day during the second week of his assignment (November 10–15). He found no spare parts available for the fifty P-40Es that the depot had assembled weeks before or for the P-40Bs operational since July. Nor was there "so much as an extra washer or nut" for the Clark-based B-17s. There also was not a single spare motor for the P-40s, B-17s, or outmoded P-35As. Even more damning, the depot had few tools of any kind with which to undertake "even rudimentary repair and maintenance" of Nichols-based aircraft. He was informed of the plans for expanding depot operations to cater to the huge buildup of aircraft under his command, but the project memorandum covering the expansion had just been referred back to USAFFE by the War Department for modification and a revised estimate of funding. Such delays only exasperated Maj. Gen. Lewis Brereton, who was a man of action, not words.[1]

At Clark Field, Brereton was somewhat more encouraged. He was impressed with the "enthusiasm and efficiency" with which his pursuit and bomber personnel—including the recently arrived 19th Bomb Group (Heavy) aircrews—were carrying out their training. They were all handicapped by the lack of equipment, but they were taking steps to prepare their units for all eventualities. However, Brereton noted that none of the aircraft had been camouflage painted and that no blast pens had been built to protect them. Nor had the field's antiaircraft artillery defenses been emplaced.[2]

Brereton also paid a visit to Del Monte Field on the northern end of Mindanao. He thought the field was adequate for conducting basic air operations, but it completely lacked support facilities. He knew that, as elsewhere, a project memorandum had been submitted to the War Department for developing the field into a full-fledged operational facility, but the timing depended on how fast the War Department approved the project and made funds available to complete it.

Brereton's general impression following his inspections was that work hours, training schedules, and operating procedures in his command were based "on the good old days of peace conditions in the tropics." The general's aide, Capt. Norman J. Lewellyn, wrote his wife "We found that few people work here." Those who had been serving under Clagett must have wondered what Brereton would have thought had he observed conditions before May, 1941. Certainly there had had been improvements since then, although as late as October slack conditions were still in effect at Clark, at least among engineering personnel. However, with the October 23 arrival of the 7th Materiel Squadron, charged with engineering support for the 19th Bomb Group, three shifts began operating, providing round-the-clock maintenance for the B-17s. Prior to the squadron's arrival, shop personnel had been coming to work fifteen minutes to half an hour late each morning, "puttering around for a couple of hours," taking one-hour coffee breaks, then knocking off for the day at 11:30, according to a 7th Materiel Squadron man.[3]

In response to the conditions he judged unsatisfactory, Brereton issued new orders. Work hours devoted to training "were increased to the maximum" and at least 40 percent of all flight training was to be devoted to night operations. Aircraft maintenance was to be carried out day and night until completed. No aircraft were to be taken out of commission during flying hours for routine checks or for the scheduled twenty- and forty-hour inspections. The Nichols Field air depot was put on a two-shift, sixteen-hour workday.[4]

These and other orders issued by Brereton did not always sit well with the officers and men affected by them, including Lt. George Armstrong. On Tuesday, November 11, Armstrong found himself spending the day and night confined to his house near Nichols Field as the 17th Pursuit's "Alert Officer" for twenty-four hours. Under the "Preparation for Emergency" orders that Brereton issued the day before, he had to stay either at home or in the 17th's Operations Office at Nichols, ready to receive instructions from the Nichols Field alert officer and pass them on to the three pilots from his squadron standing by for immediate takeoff in their P-40Es, ready to intercept attacking enemy aircraft. The same orders pertained to the 3d and 20th Pursuit Squadrons as well as the bomber squadrons at Clark. Armstrong was peeved because November 11 was Armistice Day, a holiday in the Philippines as well as in the United States.[5]

Brereton also sought to obtain additional qualified officers to staff his new headquarters. On November 12 he radioed the War Department, through MacArthur, requesting that assistant chiefs of staff for G1 (personnel), G2 (intelligence) and G4 (supply) be sent from the United States. He also wanted the additional officers and enlisted personnel needed to form the headquarters and headquarters squadrons for his Far East Air Force, 5th Bomber Command, and Far East Air Service Command—all units General Arnold had previously agreed would be established in the Philippines. Brereton clearly did not believe that the personnel released when the 4th Composite Group were disbanded would be adequate to fill the headquarters and bomber command needs planned for during his October 16 discussions with Arnold in Washington. Curiously enough, there was no mention of a 5th Interceptor Command. "Any attempt to draw personnel from combat units will seriously jeopardize combat efficiency," he warned the War Department.

Following up on his boss's request days later, Brereton's chief of staff, Colonel Brady, wrote directly to General Spaatz in Washington with the same plea. Brady argued that only by having an organization such as Brereton had in the Third Air Force in Florida could "this place be put on an efficient operating basis within the short period allowed." He upped the ante by asking Spaatz to send a complete air force headquarters and headquarters squadron in addition to sufficient experienced personnel for setting up the bomber and service commands, plus additional engineer troops.[6]

But Brereton's and Brady's hopes for new assistant chiefs of staff for their headquarters were dashed on November 15. The War Department notified MacArthur by telegram on that date that the G1, G2, and G4 officers for his air force's headquarters should "be selected from officers now on duty in your Department." There was an "extreme shortage" of such officers in other combat units. At any rate, in the War Department's view, there was "an excess of experienced Air Corps officers" in Brereton's command "especially suitable as Assistant Chiefs of Staff."[7]

At Clark and Nichols Fields, Brereton's orders stepping up training operations, including night flight training, were being put into effect by the 24th Pursuit Group's commander, Maj. Orrin Grover, beginning in mid-November. The Clark-based 20th Pursuit Squadron was practicing night flying in formation, their P-40Bs only showing little blue formation lights. "You cannot imagine the thrills one gets doing half rolls in twelve-plane formations at night," 2d Lt. Max Louk wrote his parents. At Nichols Field, the 17th Pursuit was regularly practicing night flying from 4:30 to

6 A.M., then flying in formation from 7:30 to noon, trying to find out as much as possible about their new P-40Es' formation flying capabilities. For Forrest Hobrecht, it was "quite an experience" to watch the sun rise from an altitude of twelve thousand feet after having completed the night practice.[8]

Mock interceptions of Clark Field's B-17s were also being staged as a means of testing the air warning system and interception capabilities of 20th Pursuit Squadron pilots in their P-40Bs. During November, the 93d Bomb Squadron twice simulated attacks on Manila by way of Clark Field, a point out in Lingayen Gulf, Iba, Subic, Olongapo, San Marcelino, and San Fernando. On the morning of November 17, twelve P-40Bs took off and climbed to thirty thousand feet to intercept the bombers, the 20th Pursuit pilots encumbered with oxygen masks, headsets, throat mikes, life vests, parachutes, sunglasses, and flying caps. But while the 20th Pursuiters were able to get their ships up to the altitude of the high-flying B-17s, their Allison engines performed so sluggishly that the faster B-17s simply flew away from them. The 20th Pursuit pilots were sorely disappointed with the ineffective performance of their P-40Bs as interceptors. Max Louk complained bitterly to his sister that while the brass maintained that "we are getting the latest equipment, we who are here flying it know that it is no good. Our planes—the latest P-40s—are not good enough to fight with!"[9]

The pilots were also concerned about the lack of gunnery practice. None had yet fired their P-40Bs' four .30- and two .50-caliber machine guns. Their CO, Joe Moore, had repeatedly called attention to the fact that the ships' guns had never been fired, but was told that the squadron would have to wait for gunnery practice until the 3d Pursuit finished its training at Iba in early December. In the meantime, in response to his expressed concern as to whether the nose fifties would fire properly between the three-bladed propeller, he was given permission to test-fire fifty rounds of ammunition on one P-40B—but no more, because the supply of .50-caliber ammo was so low.[10]

HEADQUARTERS, 11TH AIR FLEET
TAKAO, FORMOSA
EARLY NOVEMBER, 1941

Eleventh Air Fleet Headquarters was becoming concerned about the possibility of reconnaissance over its bases on Formosa by American aircraft based in the Philippines. Already, on October 13, a PBY had been spotted circling the island twice at an altitude of fifteen hundred meters before disappearing to the southeast. Admiral Tsukahara on November 3 ordered all aircraft in the Taiwan Channel and the South China Sea to be

A PBY-4 OF VP-101 ON PATROL IN LATE 1941. THE AIRCRAFT SPORTS A MOTTLED GREEN AND BROWN CAMOUFLAGE PAINT SCHEME. PHOTO COURTESY GORDON EBBE VIA THE U.S. NAVAL INSTITUTE.

on the lookout for enemy planes or submarines and to immediately report any sightings. On November 5, the Navy Ministry ordered the Eleventh Air Fleet to carry out secret air defense drills for a month and to prevent any leaks about them to the Formosan public. Earlier, the Navy Ministry had instructed the Eleventh Air Fleet to build a bombproof emergency command center, additional air-raid shelters, and aircraft revetments at its Takao base, and air-raid shelters at its Tainan base.[11]

Intruding PBYs continued to be spotted from time to time in November over southern Formosa. According to the Tainan Kū's Saburō Sakai, they would come in on cloudy days, flying at low altitude over the air bases. On November 27, the Japanese government filed a formal protest with the U.S. State Department about an intrusion at 12:30 P.M. on November 20 over Garampi on the southernmost tip of Formosa, fifty-eight miles south-southeast of Takao base. The single aircraft allegedly circled at two thousand meters for fifteen minutes before heading back south, according to the Japanese naval source.[12]

When the air-raid alarm went off following an intrusion by a PBY, attempts were made to intercept it, but proved unsuccessful. The Eleventh Air

Fleet and other Combined Fleet units had been authorized on November 21 "to use force in self-defense" in case they were challenged by "American, British, or Dutch forces." On December 2, the Japanese army air force unit on Formosa was more specifically ordered to shoot down—"even before D-Day"—any plane "which is sighted [over Formosan territory] and recognized as hostile."

Following the Combined Fleet's November 5 order to abandon the carrier-based plan for the attack on the Philippines, Sakai and the Tainan Kū's other pilots were conducting intensive training on how to stretch their Zeros' range for a direct attack on Luzon under the direction of their *hikōtaichō*, Hideki Shingō. Test flights were conducted with six selected planes to measure airspeed and fuel consumption per hour employing different cruising altitudes, different power and RPM settings, and different fuel densities. The test results indicated that the optimum cruising altitude was four thousand meters, and the optimum cruising speed was 115 knots (132 miles) per hour, which was close to that of the Type 1 *rikkō* they would be escorting. The mixture control was set at a point just before the Zero's 950 horsepower Sakae 12 engine would start to malfunction.

The fuel-saving exercises were nerve-wracking for Sakai and the others, causing great anxiety. The training proved to be even more intensive than that for dogfighting. It was calculated that the maximum acceptable fuel consumption rate would be 90 liters (23.8 gallons) per hour, with an average of 80–85 liters (21.1–22.5 gallons) estimated. Sakai himself would eventually manage to get his down to 67 liters (17.7 gallons), which set the record for the *kōkūtai*.[13]

At Takao, the 3d Kōkūtai pilots had benefited from an earlier start in fuel-saving training, thanks to the early conviction of *hikōtaichō* Yokoyama that the Zero's range could be extended to reach central Luzon and return to Takao, nonstop. At the end of their training—directed by each *buntaichō* —every one of the 3d Kū's pilots proved himself capable of flying for ten hours and reducing his fuel consumption to 70 liters (18.5 gallons) per hour. Some were even able to get it down to 67 liters, as had Sakai at the Tainan base.

Yokoyama had been working his pilots every day of the week, or, as they said in the navy, "Monday, Monday, Tuesday, Wednesday, Thursday, Friday, Friday." Now, after three weeks of intensive training since their arrival at Takao, he decided to give them a day off to spend in Takao city. After enjoying the city's good sake, beer, and fish, they prepared for "night training outside the base." Yokoyama had organized a banquet for them at one of the best restaurants in the city. After the pilots took their places in the restaurant, the designated spokesman stood up and delivered the following greeting:

In accordance with the order given by our *hikōtaichō,* we now begin night training outside the base. Activities of the training are drinking and singing. Those who cannot handle alcohol are allowed to drink cider instead. Each *chūtai* should make a formation flight after the first part of the training—no solo flying is permitted. There will be no saving on fuel consumption this evening. You are permitted to continue your flight as long as your fuel lasts. Landing time at Takao base should not be later than midnight. Every formation leader is requested to make sure that no one needs to make an emergency landing.[14]

CLARK FIELD, LUZON
3:00 A.M., SUNDAY NOVEMBER 16, 1941

The roar of the four Wright Cyclone engines revving up broke the night stillness as the party of six officers prepared to board B-17D number sixty-seven of Headquarters Squadron, 19th Bomb Group. Earlier that evening, General Brereton, accompanied by his G3, Colonel Caldwell; his aide, Captain Lewellyn; his engineering officer, Capt. Harold "Lefty" Eads; and Captain Ind, the assistant G2, had driven up from Manila to make the rendezvous with the bomber that would be taking them to Australia. The 19th Group CO, Colonel Eubank, was waiting for them at the airfield and would be joining the party. Several days earlier, MacArthur had ordered Brereton to go to Australia and establish working relations with Australian officials. Specifically, he was to survey the trans-Pacific air ferry route from Australia to the Philippines and Java, including its extension to Singapore and China, in addition to making arrangements for the establishment of bases in northern Australia and throughout the Malay Barrier from which American bombers could operate in the event it became necessary to withdraw them from the Philippines. When the Australian government approved the War Department's plan to construct and operate air bases in Australia, MacArthur issued orders on October 24 for Colonel George to undertake the mission, but subsequently decided to postpone the trip and send Brereton instead after he arrived in the Philippines.[15]

At exactly three o'clock, the big bomber roared down the sod field with its high-ranking passengers and climbed into the pitch-black night sky. The forty-nine-year-old Eubank was at the first-pilot controls, with 2d Lt. Melvin McKenzie of Headquarters Squadron serving as copilot and doubling as navigator. Brereton, Caldwell, and Lewellyn took places forward, with Eades and Ind behind.[16]

204 PART III

B-17D 40-3067 at Archer Field in Queensland, Australia, November 20–24, 1941. The bomber ferried Maj. Gen. Lewis H. Brereton and his party on a mission to Australia. Photo courtesy Mrs. Reita Jackson.

Just before Brereton's departure, MacArthur's staff took care of a bit of unfinished business. Effective November 16, Air Force, USAFFE was redesignated Far East Air Force, the name agreed upon during Brereton's Washington briefing the month before. At the same time, the 5th Bomber Command and a Far East Air Service Command were activated, again as agreed earlier. The 4th Composite Group was disbanded and its Headquarters and Headquarters Squadron personnel reassigned to the bomber and air service commands. Finally, the 28th Bomb Squadron (Medium) was redesignated the 28th Bomb Squadron (Heavy) and assigned to the 19th Bomb Group.[17]

But what about the 5th Interceptor Command, also included in the War Department's October 28 letter to USAFFE authorizing the new commands? It was not officially activated on November 16, although the Manila newspapers had reported its establishment as far back as November 7.[18] The FEAF issued no official orders designating the commanding officers of the new units, but Brereton had decided on the appointments before his departure and they were reported in the Manila press. Colonel Eubank was to head the 5th Bomber Command, Colonel Churchill was put in charge of the Far East Air Service Command, and General Clagett was to become commanding general of the 5th Interceptor Command. Displaced earlier as CO of Clark Field, Lt. Col. Les Maitland was assigned to serve as Colonel Churchill's executive officer in the service command. Major Bill Fisher, the 14th Bomb Squadron's operations officer, would be taking command of the 28th Bomb Squadron on its November 16 conversion to a heavy bomber outfit and assignment to the 19th Bomb Group. He supplanted Maj. William "Hoot" Horrigan, its interim commander, who had replaced Maj. "Moe" Daly when Daly took command of Clark Field.[19]

Billy Maverick would be moving, too. On November 16 he was relieved as operations officer of the 24th Pursuit Group and ordered to report to FEAF headquarters for a new assignment. "I hate to leave the Pursuit Group, but this appears to be something big," he wrote his wife that evening. When Maverick checked in the next day, Colonel Brady informed him that he was taking command of the newly established 20th Air Base Group at Nichols, where he would also serve as executive officer to the base commander, Col. Charley Savage, who was replacing Churchill. Savage, however, was awaiting orders to return stateside, at which time Maverick was told he would take over Nichols Field.[20]

Effective November 19, Colonel Richards was relieved as air officer of the irrelevant Philippine Department and assigned to the FEAF, but without an official position. Maverick understood that Richards was being given the job of "Air Corps Inspector" with the FEAF, a meaningless function. While Army Air Force headquarters in Washington had deemed him suitable for an A1 (Personnel) position if reassigned to the states, Brereton had not considered him for the vacant G1 position on his own FEAF staff.[21]

In Brereton's absence, Brady was busy not only with the organizational and command changes in the FEAF, but also with efforts to speed up the airfield construction program. "The general picture here is quite discouraging," he wrote Spaatz on November 13. Airdrome construction was lagging due to a lack of engineering personnel, equipment, and the "inability to secure competent civilian assistance from any Filipino or local contractors," Brady explained.

Brady visited Del Carmen Field, just south of Clark, on November 16 to see for himself what construction conditions were like. He found a single company of aviation engineers there, consisting of "about 190 men" and working with "very limited equipment." A single landing strip measuring 300 by 3,600 feet had been leveled, but the remaining 2,000 feet for the proposed runway was still a cane field. Brady figured that on the pulverized loam surface of the field, "warming up and taking off in a B-17 would raise dust clouds that wouldn't dissipate or blow away for a lengthy period." Yet no plans had been made nor material secured to stabilize the surface. Equally damning, there was no water at the site. It was being hauled seven miles in tank trucks.

The conditions at Del Carmen particularly disturbed Brady, for the field had to be ready "no later than December 1" for occupancy by heavy bombers from either the 19th Group or the 7th Group. The latter had already been assigned for transfer to the Philippines starting in December. Brereton's chief of staff felt that additional engineer troops, "supplemented by Filipino labor and possible use of an American construction firm," offered the only solution. While Brereton had been promised more such troops during his briefing in Washington, "I understand that [the order] has been suspended because MacArthur didn't consider it wise to have additional colored troops in the islands," Brady confided to Spaatz.[22]

MacArthur and the FEAF were also under pressure from Marshall to develop a field at Aparri, at Luzon's northern tip. It was the only location in the Philippines deemed close enough to Japan to be reached by the B-24s scheduled for assignment to the FEAF in December and January. On November 13, Marshall instructed Arnold to draft a radiogram to MacArthur "that will secure for us some explanation of why there is no airfield in the vicinity of Aparri." Based on Brady's response to this query, MacArthur replied by radio five days later that while an airdrome near Aparri "is projected," construction of an airfield in that remote location would be "difficult" due to "a lack of communication and transportation facilities." Nevertheless, MacArthur assured Marshall, "every endeavor is being made to facilitate action."[23]

Construction of air warning facilities also fell within Brady's purview following the assignment of the Air Warning Service to FEAF's 5th Interceptor Command in mid-November. However, by November 15, plans and specifications for eight of the ten out-of-the-way air warning stations, each to house an SCR-271 fixed-location radar unit, were but 5 percent complete. Of even greater concern to Lt. Col. Alexander H. Campbell, the AWS commander, was the slow pace of construction of the underground chamber at Fort McKinley, from which Campbell's headquarters was to operate after shifting from its present temporary location in the FEAF's headquarters at Nielson Field. The ambitious tunneling work required, not even begun until October 15, was running behind schedule.[24]

Meanwhile, at Clark Field, one construction project of great importance—at least in the view of those directly affected—had been completed. On November 13, the *sawali* officer quarters that had been under construction since mid-October were finally ready for occupancy. Each *sawali* hut had two rooms, one for each of the assigned 19th Group officers. Second Lieutenant Ed Jacquet and his close friend 2d Lt. Owen "Tuffy" Graham of the 93d Squadron decided to share one room as the bedroom and use the other as a sitting room, where they also parked their new Japanese bicycle, their only means for getting around the base.[25]

Far East Air Force officers at Clark Field who were captain or higher were given two-room suites for two officers in the wooden bachelor officers' quarters (BOQ) a short distance from the *sawali* quarters. The E-shaped BOQ building had a mess hall in the center appendage.[26]

Jacquet's squadron mates and fellow lieutenants Clyde Box, Jim Connally, Fred Crimmins, and Morris Shedd moved into the primitive *sawali* quarters, too, although the four first pilots were awaiting confirmation of their orders to return to the states, along with five first pilots from Headquarters and 30th Squadrons. Six days later, however, General MacArthur received a radio from AAF headquarters in Washington allowing him to retain all nine pilots. But Arnold's decision was just a pacifier for what was to follow. Unknown to MacArthur and the FEAF, the AAF commander, badly in need of qualified heavy bomber pilots to train others in the United States, was developing a plan calling for all experienced officers piloting heavy bombers to the Philippines from December to return stateside after they trained the junior officers accompanying them overseas to take over first pilot duties on their aircraft in the Philippines. But novice pilots were exactly what Brereton did *not* want sent from the United States. Three days after his arrival on Luzon, he sent a request to Arnold asking for only those pilots "who are capable of flying service aircraft and need no transition training." He proposed that Arnold send "trainee" pilots coming out of flying school to stateside units "temporarily" and ship him pilots who already had some operational experience. In Brereton's view, it was "uneconomical" to send aircraft to the Philippines in the face of such difficulties and then subject them to "high attrition" due to training accidents caused by inexperienced pilots, especially at a time when he lacked the repair facilities to handle the damage caused by even minor crashes. Brereton argued that bomber pilots sent to him "should have at least bi-motor training, and should in large proportion be second pilots, 4 motor." As for pursuit pilots, he asked that those assigned to the Philippines have operational experience in tactical flying *before* arrival. "We can't stand losses and bring pursuit to even a minimum service status, which they are not at present," Brereton concluded.[27]

Senior pursuit and bomber pilots serving in Brereton's command could not have agreed more with their chief's request to Arnold. Assigned by 24th Pursuit commander Grover to Headquarters Squadron to help train the latest batch of newies—fresh graduates out of flying school Class 41-G at Luke Field—17th Pursuit oldie Russel Church tried unsuccessfully to have Grover release him back to his squadron. He was fed up with the "carelessness" and "undeveloped flying abilities" of the ten newies, which had led to the loss of three P-35As on November 11 and 12, all due to "pilot error."[28]

Ted Fisch in the 28th Bomb Squadron was even more upset with the six 41-G graduates supposedly trained on bi-motors who had been assigned to the squadron at the end of October. Struggling to contain himself while providing instruction to one of the two brand-new 28th Squadron copilots on November 21, he complained in a letter to his wife that "the damned co-pilot I have is bouncing the ship all over the sky. The fool doesn't seem to realize he should be flying the ship, not the ship flying him."[29]

ROOM 2427, WAR DEPARTMENT
MUNITIONS BUILDING, WASHINGTON, D.C.
FRIDAY AFTERNOON, NOVEMBER 21, 1941

In his office adjacent to that of his chief—Col. Walter Bedell Smith, secretary of the War Department General Staff—Maj. Larry Kuter was completing a draft of a secret memorandum for Smith's attention. Only seventeen days earlier, Kuter had been appointed to his new position as one of the assistant secretaries at the instigation of the army chief of staff, Gen. George C. Marshall, who had been impressed by the thirty-six-year-old AAF officer's performance while presenting the Victory Program's air annex to Marshall on August 30. In recognition of Kuter's acknowledged intelligence, drive, and influence in the War Department, AAF headquarters and other War Department officers handling matters related to the AAF had always checked with Kuter before taking action, even though he was the War Department G3 Division's most junior officer.[30]

Now, in the large office he shared with the other assistant secretaries, Kuter was preparing a response to Marshall's request, two days earlier in an informal meeting, for the secretary of the General Staff (SGS) to provide him information regarding a possible air offensive against the Japanese Empire. Kuter apparently knew of Marshall's secret press conference on November 15 in which the army chief of staff had referred to "general incendiary attacks to burn up the wood and paper structure of the densely populated Japanese cities."

Marshall wanted Kuter to provide him with answers to four questions:

(1) what General MacArthur would attack in Japan (from bases in the Vladivostok area) if war were declared December 1, 1941,
(2) what data we have assembled in Washington on this subject,
(3) what appears to us to be profitable systems of objectives, and
(4) how much of our data was presented to and was taken to the Philippines by General Brereton.[31]

In his memorandum, Kuter noted that prior to Brereton's departure for the Philippines, all discussions with him were based on the employment of his air force "on the strategic defensive." Considering the small offensive force projected for the Philippines, "a sustained air offensive against the Japanese Empire was never discussed." Objectives envisaged for Brereton were limited to shipping in the northern approaches to the Philippines, although Japanese naval bases in the islands off Formosa and on the mandated islands (based on operations from New Britain) had also been discussed. However, Kuter noted, Brereton did take with him "separate Air Staff studies on the steel and petroleum industries and on the electric power establishment in Japan." Furthermore, after Brereton's arrival in the Philippines, the War Department G2 received cable requests from USAFFE for data on objectives in Japan. In reply, the War Department had sent MacArthur "a series of maps showing the location of approximately 600 industrial objectives in Japan proper." He was also informed that objectives folders supporting the maps were being prepared and would be sent to him as soon as possible. A third of the folders could be completed and sent to MacArthur by December 15.

Kuter regarded the steel industry as the highest priority target in Japan "due to its extreme degree of concentration." However, burning down Japanese cities was not a suitable course of action. In his view, their inflammability "has been considerably over-estimated" and any such attacks would "serve more to warn and train the population than toward any military end."

In a personal comment appended to the memorandum, Kuter expressed his belief that "we are going much too far on the offensive side." The 160 to 170 heavy bombers being sent to the Philippines were "far from [being] a strong air force." The use of such a relatively small force in a major air offensive would be "a strategic blunder," Kuter argued. Considering that the Victory Program's Air Annex established a requirement of eight thousand bombers to destroy 154 industrial objectives in Germany, it was unrealistic to expect much of Brereton's envisaged heavy bomber force against six hundred industrial targets in Japan.

Marshall's reaction to Kuter's carefully reasoned argument is unknown. Ironically, it was Kuter's, George's, and Walker's enthusiasm for the offensive employment of heavy bombers as expressed in their August A/WPD-1 plan that had rubbed off on Gerow, Marshall, and Stimson and led to the exaggerated significance these airpower neophytes had given the bombers in Far Eastern strategy that Kuter was now trying to tone down.

HEADQUARTERS, FAR EAST AIR FORCE
NIELSON FIELD, MANILA
FRIDAY, NOVEMBER 21, 1941

Brereton's top staff officers were busy putting the final touches on a plan covering the facilities and installations deemed necessary for FEAF operations and appropriate locations for them throughout the islands. Before Brereton's departure on his Australia mission, MacArthur had verbally instructed him to prepare such a plan—an assignment Brereton had passed on to Brady and his G4, Colonel George, just before departing.[32]

For Colonel George, this new request from USAFFE headquarters came just two months after his earlier effort to develop a similar plan for MacArthur, but focused on the size of the air force required for the defense of the Philippines. However, MacArthur had put George's September 11 plan aside after receiving a radiogram from Marshall on September 9 informing him of additional air reinforcements to be sent—two squadrons of B-17s, two more squadrons of pursuit aircraft, and a group of light bombers—as soon as the construction of his airfields was sufficiently advanced to accommodate them. Then, on October 21, the War Department had radioed MacArthur that 130 more heavy bombers were planned for delivery to him during December, January, and February. George's concern now was *where* this massive force should be based—in terms of FEAF's mission and considering the likelihood of Japanese air attack—and what facilities were required to support its operations.[33]

Based on the premise that Japanese bombers would not be able to attack farther south than Luzon due to their range limitations, Brady and George argued in favor of basing "the mass of heavy Bombardment aviation" FEAF was projected to receive on *Mindanao.* This represented an important change in the current plan to concentrate the majority of FEAF's airpower in *central Luzon,* where they believed it risked significant losses should the Japanese launch surprise attacks. From northern Mindanao, they estimated that B-17s with a half-load of bombs could mount direct attacks against Japanese bases on Formosa and return to central Luzon, while longer-range B-24s could carry full bomb loads from anywhere on Mindanao to Formosa and return. In fact, B-24s operating from northern Luzon could bomb the Japanese home islands and return to their home bases, according to AAF headquarters. Clark Field and other suitable airfields on central Luzon would be used as advanced operational fields for the shorter-ranged B-17s during Formosa strike missions, with subsequent return to Mindanao.[34]

In conclusion, Brady and George recommended that MacArthur take action "without delay" to provide the facilities required for basing the heavy bombers on Mindanao as proposed, as well as a supporting pursuit group. This would require additional air bases and auxiliary units on Mindanao, including a "sub air depot or mobile depot" at Del Monte Field's main airdrome area. While the main depot facilities would remain at Nichols Field, a subdepot would be established at Cabanatuan in central Luzon in addition to the one at Del Monte.[35]

To support operations as well as to permit dispersion, facilitate ferrying operations, and accommodate the awaited aircraft reinforcements, Brady and George identified locations in central and northern Luzon as well as the Visayan Islands in the central Philippines to be developed as airdromes. These were in addition to the already-established air bases in the Nichols Field, Clark Field, and northern Luzon area, which would support operations from Luzon. From Mindanao, the heavy bombers and pursuits would operate from three airdromes in the Del Monte area, plus four auxiliary fields elsewhere on the island.[36]

Finally, the two senior FEAF staff officers proposed that FEAF headquarters and its commands be moved from their "temporary" locations at Nielson Field. Far East Air Force headquarters should be moved to a permanent site at Fort McKinley, as should the 5th Interceptor Command and Far East Air Service Command. The advance echelon of the 5th Bomber Command headquarters would remain at Nielson Field, but its rear echelon would be located at Del Monte with its main force of heavy bombers.[37]

Shortly after Brady submitted the FEAF plan to MacArthur on November 21, General Sutherland called upon him to attend a meeting at USAFFE headquarters. MacArthur's chief of staff had read it and was not happy with its main point. "The war plan for the Philippines does not provide for any ground forces for the defense of Mindanao," he asserted. For that reason, the FEAF "could not base any aircraft in Mindanao in the event of hostilities"—they should "be operated from facilities in Cebu or islands north, including Luzon," Sutherland argued. After considerable discussion with Sutherland, Brady succeeded in reaching a compromise. Sutherland agreed that part of the B-17 force could be located temporarily at Del Monte to relieve the congestion at Clark Field. Del Monte Field would be used as an auxiliary base "until facilities could be completed on Luzon, Cebu, and other islands to the north." Sutherland agreed to authorize Brady to send the Headquarters and Headquarters Squadron, 5th Air Base Group—which had just arrived in the Philippines—and other necessary (Clark Field–based) support units to Mindanao to construct facilities at Del Monte.[38]

Several days later, MacArthur, in a letter to Marshall that used strategic planning terminology, somewhat altered the arrangement worked out between Sutherland and Brady by downplaying the construction of fields on Luzon and focusing exclusively on the development of bases in the central Philippines. While he agreed that the bombers needed to be based beyond the range of potential Japanese air attacks, he wanted them in the Visayan Islands, not on Mindanao, as proposed by the Brady-George plan. "The definitive location of the Bomber Command base in Mindanao is not acceptable because that island is strategically a salient and its defense a difficult problem," MacArthur maintained. Bases in the Visayans would offer equal security from Japanese attacks and would be well-protected with coast artillery defenses and available troops. However, until suitable fields could be constructed on those central Philippines islands, MacArthur was allowing the bomber command to be based in the Del Monte area. Placing his bomber force there would "give immediate relief from the congested conditions on Luzon." The Del Monte airfields would serve as auxiliary airdromes to the Visayan bases when ready for operations, he informed Marshall. In MacArthur's strategy, 5th Bomber Command would execute its shorter-range attack missions nonstop from the Visayans, and would refuel and bomb up at fields in central or northern Luzon for longer-range attacks.[39]

Brady and George had included Cebu and Tacloban in the Visayan Islands as the proposed sites of auxiliary airdromes in their plan, but they knew that the development of fields there capable of handling B-17s and B-24s was a longer-term proposition. Even MacArthur acknowledged that airdromes in the Visayans would be difficult to build due to the need for hard-surface runways for the heavy bombers, such as those in use at Del Monte. He was unable to identify suitable sites in the Visayans to develop as airfields for the heavies in his letter to Marshall.

After securing the agreement with USAFFE headquarters covering short-term needs, Brady and George were anxious to move on to more immediate problems. They had to finalize the preparation of airfields, housing, and other facilities for the personnel and equipment of the pursuit and light bomber squadrons that had just arrived, as well as for the B-17 crews of the 7th Bomb Group expected to arrive soon. Brady informed MacArthur he wanted priority accorded to the completion of runway work, development of water supplies, and housing at San Marcelino, Del Monte, and Del Carmen Fields—in that order. If construction capabilities were inadequate to accomplish the full program of airdrome construction the FEAF wanted, then the projects at O'Donnell, Clark, and Nichols Fields should be curtailed.

Finishing work at San Marcelino and Del Carmen was particularly urgent. The 27th Bomb Group arrived at Pier 7 in Manila aboard the *President Coolidge* on November 20, but their assigned base at San Marcelino—just south of Iba on Luzon's west coast—was not ready to receive them. There was no water supply, no housing for personnel, and no facilities capable of providing even the most basic maintenance for their aircraft. Its four squadrons—Headquarters, 16th, 17th, and 91st—were temporarily assigned to Fort McKinley pending their permanent move to San Marcelino. At any rate, Brady did not need to move the 27th Group's pilots to any particular field at the present time—their fifty-two A-24 dive-bombers had been shipped separately, and their arrival date was unknown.[40]

Del Carmen Field was scheduled to be ready for occupancy by the 7th or 19th Bomb Group's B-17s by December 1, but construction work was running behind schedule. At twenty-six hundred feet, its single landing strip was still too short to accommodate heavy bombers, and the dust conditions were intolerable. Brady wanted it upgraded to support operations by B-17s and B-24s as soon as possible, but in the meantime he assigned the newly arrived 34th Pursuit Squadron to the unfinished field.

The 34th Pursuit, along with its sister squadron, the 21st Pursuit, had arrived on November 20 aboard the same ship as the 27th Bomb Group and the following day had been assigned to Nichols Field. Like the 27th Group, the two 35th Pursuit Group squadrons had been shipped without their aircraft. In addition, they were at half their authorized pilot strength. The rest of their pilots were scheduled to sail from San Francisco on November 21.

The commanding officers of the two squadrons—1st Lts. William "Ed" Dyess of the 21st and Sam Marett of the 34th—were displeased to find that the fifty P-40Es they had been promised would be ready for them when they arrived were still at sea. Pending receipt of the P-40Es, they were being given the 24th Pursuit Group's P-35A—a ship they had never flown before—discards. On the afternoon of November 27, the 34th Pursuiters flew fifteen well-worn P-35As from Nichols to their new field at Del Carmen. Six of them ground looped on landing. Their more fortunate sister 21st Pursuit Squadron was remaining at Nichols, expecting delivery soon of twenty-four P-40Es that had arrived on November 25—the first of the fifty ships expected—and were in the process of being uncrated and assembled.

Like those in the 34th Pursuit Squadron, the 27th Group pilots were also in a sour mood over their situation:"Where in the hell are our planes?" No one seemed to know when their aircraft would arrive. The men were living in tents and the officers in vacated quarters at Fort McKinley.[41]

HEADQUARTERS, 11TH AIR FLEET
TAKAO, FORMOSA
MID-NOVEMBER, 1941

Capt. Chihaya Takahashi, the senior staff officer in Eleventh Air Fleet headquarters, was concerned about the lack of accurate information on the buildup of U.S. airpower on Luzon. On November 1, the Japanese consul in Manila had sent an alarming message to the Foreign Office in Tokyo that reported 1,283 army aircraft in the Philippines, including twenty-nine large bombers and 819 pursuit aircraft. Since the consul had failed to confirm these numbers despite the Foreign Office's request to do so, Eleventh Air Fleet headquarters decided to obtain firsthand information instead and mount reconnaissance flights from Formosa. It had been more than six months since the Eleventh Air Fleet had flown reconnaissance missions over the Philippines using modified Type 96 twin-engine *rikkō* equipped with cameras, and the information they had provided was now totally out of date.[42]

Given the responsibility for conducting the initial reconnaissance missions were the commander of the Tainan Kōkūtai's six-plane reconnaissance unit, Lt. Masami Miza, and Lt. Tetsutaro Suzuki of the 3d Kōkūtai. Each was to serve as an observer in the rear seat of one of their flying group's six Mitsubishi C5M2 single-engine reconnaissance aircraft capable of reaching an altitude of 31,430 feet.

TAINAN NAVAL AIR BASE, FORMOSA
FRIDAY MORNING, NOVEMBER 21, 1941

At 8:30 on the morning of November 21, Masami Miza and his pilot, FPO1c Mitsuru Ōhara, prepared to board their two-seat plane in front of the aviation shed at Tainan base, where it was ready for takeoff. The aircraft was a curious sight: its *hinomaru* national insignia had been painted over. Miza had also been instructed to remove the lieutenant insignia from his uniform. He suddenly felt that this would be the last time he would see his comrades.

Miza's orders were to carry out a photoreconnaissance of Iba and Clark Fields and the PBY base at Olongapo at an altitude between seven thousand and eight thousand meters (twenty-three thousand and twenty-six thousand feet). One of the other C5M2s was to reconnoiter the Mariveles coast at the southern tip of Luzon, while the third aircraft was to cover the Philippine Army Air Corps field at Batangas and the Asiatic Fleet base at Cavite. The outward trip over the sea should be flown fifty miles from the coastline, keeping a strict lookout.

Miza was not happy with another condition of his flight: If he was discovered and chased by an enemy pursuit plane, he was to escape to the islands south of the Philippines. However, it was obvious that he did not have enough fuel for such a course of action. Nor did his C5M2 have a single machine gun with which to defend itself; its 7.7-mm gun had been removed from the rear cockpit to save weight in an effort to exceed its normal top speed of 303 MPH.[43]

About an hour and a half after taking off from Tainan—halfway to his destination— Ōhara climbed to eight thousand meters. Miza planned to go to Olongapo first, then Clark Field, and finally Iba. But at 10:30 A.M. (Formosa/Philippines time), Miza and Ōhara found they were ahead of schedule, so they killed twenty minutes, rambling over the eastern part of the South China Sea, before approaching Olongapo. From eighty-five hundred meters (twenty-eight thousand feet), they could not see any flying boats at Olongapo as they flew over the base at 10:50. Arriving over Clark Field, they did not spot any fighters in the sky, and Miza figured the pilots were at lunch. On the field below, he confirmed the presence of three large planes and twenty-two small ones. However, to make sure, Miza had Ōhara reverse course and fly back over the field to take a second set of photos. Ōhara suddenly yelled, "Two enemy fighters to the rear on the left!" and applied full power and headed west to the East China Sea. Traveling at its maximum speed of 368 MPH, the C5M2 easily outdistanced the pursuing P-40s, which were unable to exceed 320 MPH, and after ten minutes the Americans gave up the chase.[44] Ōhara cautiously proceeded on to Iba, on Luzon's west coast, where Miza spotted sixteen small planes on the field and three flying at low altitude. The American pilots apparently did not notice their reconnaissance ship far above them.

Back at Tainan, Miza reported the results of his reconnaissance. When the reports of all three planes had been tallied, including Lieutenant Suzuki's C5M2 from the 3d Kū out of Takao, the number of American planes observed by the pilots totaled only three hundred—one-fourth the number in the Japanese consul's exaggerated report three weeks earlier.[45]

While the Tainan Kū's reconnaissance unit was occupied with clandestine flights over the Philippines in late November, the fighter echelon was improving its gunnery capabilities. On this day, its flying commander had organized a ground strafing competition between the Tainan Kū's *shōtaichō*. To test the skill level they had attained in air-to-ground gunnery training, Shingō had arranged for the three pilots of each *shōtai* to fire at a cloth the size of a Zero that had been placed flat on the beach.

Saburō Sakai was determined that his *shōtai*—made up of NCOs only—would not be beaten by any officer's *shōtai*. "I will surely obtain 50 percent hits and you two should get the other 50 percent," he told

FLIGHT PETTY OFFICER FIRST CLASS SABURŌ
SAKAI, ONE OF THE THREE *SHŌTAICHŌ* OF THE
TAINAN KŌKŪTAI'S 1ST CHŪTAI. PHOTO COUR-
TESY SABURŌ SAKAI.

his second wingman, FPO2c Kazuo
Yokokawa and third wingman, FPO3c
Toshiaki Honda, patting each on the
shoulder.[46] Sakai saw that there was a
westerly wind of seven kilometers an
hour blowing across the field as the
first *shōtai* took off and made a men-
tal note of it. He and his two wingmen patiently waited for their turn:
they were the last of the fifteen *shōtai*
scheduled to participate.[47]

Sakai, Yokokawa, and Honda finally
climbed into their Zeros, taxied down
the field, and took off. Climbing to
five hundred meters altitude, they
turned left and formed a line with
Sakai in the lead. One by one they
began diving at an angle of 30 degrees.
When they had dropped to the minimum fifty-meter altitude limit they
fixed the white target fully in their
electric gun sights and pressed the
trigger. Sixty shells sprayed out of their
two 7.7-mm machine guns.

Forming up over the target after completing their firing pass, Sakai
slid open his canopy and with his hand signaled, "How did you do?" to
Honda, who was approaching him. Honda merely shrugged his shoulders
in reply. Yokokawa, laughing, raised his right hand and seemed to be indicating, "Perfect!"

After landing back at the airfield, Sakai and his wingmen waited in
front of the Tainan Kū's operations building to hear the results of the
competition. It was taking a long time to count the number of bullet
holes according to the color of the mark left by the hits: each *shōtai*'s
shells had been dipped in a distinguishing color dye. Suddenly, smiling
and shouting in a loud voice, Shingō announced "The top *shōtai* is Saburō
Sakai's, with 27 hits!" Shingō continued on, but Sakai was too pleased
after hearing the results to pay attention to the rest of his commander's
announcement, including that his own *shōtai* had come in second. Later,
Sakai and his wingmen presented themselves to Shingō to accept their
prize. "You did it, didn't you?" Yokokawa and Honda exclaimed to their
leader in praise. Then they took possession of two-dozen bottles of beer,
their reward.[48]

Takao Naval Air Base, Formosa
Late November, 1941

The 3d Kū's Zero pilots were also finishing up their intensive training program with air-to-ground gunnery practice, likewise firing at a piece of cloth simulating a Zero that was placed on the ground just inland of the seashore. Their flying commander, Yokoyama, had not staged a competition for his pilots as an incentive to hone their strafing skills like Shingō, but he was so impressed with the results achieved by his senior *buntaichō,* Lt. Takeo Kurosawa, whose score was "head and shoulders above anybody else's," that he put Kurosawa in charge of the 3d Kū's strafing operations. During the last weeks of November, Yokoyama had also put his suntanned charges through exercises in night takeoffs and landings, air combat in formation, dogfighting tactics, and the use of radio communications.

Some of the 3d Kū pilots were logging over 100 hours of flying time a month due to the demands of training, compared to an average of 25–30 hours flown by pilots in other Japanese naval air force units. Such heavy use of their aircraft put a heavy burden on the 3d Kū's mechanics to keep their ships in perfect order. While the pilots took afternoon naps, the mechanics were busy carrying out repairs and servicing the Zeros to ensure they were ready for night training exercises. Top priority was given to the scheduled overhaul of aircraft after every 100 hours of flying time. To ensure that as many of the unit's forty-five Zeros would be available on D-Day as possible, training was carried out according to a timetable based on when the scheduled overhaul was due.[49]

On November 28, Yokoyama hurriedly penned a letter to his wife in Kanoya. It would be his last. Beginning the next day, all contact with the world outside the Takao base was banned. The only exception would be if someone had to leave the base on official business.[50]

Clark Field, Luzon
Wednesday afternoon, November 26, 1941

The sun was just setting when the lone B-17D overhead descended to land and came to a halt in front of the Clark Field headquarters building. There to greet General Brereton and his party returning from their Australia mission was a reception committee headed by the Clark Field CO, Maj. Moe Daly, and Maj. David Gibbs, CO of the 30th Bomb Squadron, who was serving as the 19th Bomb Group's acting CO in Lieutenant Colonel Eubank's absence. They had received a radio message from the bomber earlier that day giving Brereton's expected arrival time.

The FEAF commander was in no mood for exchanging pleasantries. In his typical machine-gun fashion, "his eyes snapping," Brereton fired off an unexpected arrival message: "Gentlemen, I have just seen this field from the air. Fortunately for you and all who depend on us, I was not leading a hostile bombing fleet. If I had been, I could have blasted the entire heavy bomber strength of the Philippines off the map in one smash."

"Do you call that dispersal?" he asked sarcastically, gesturing toward the field where the 19th Group's thirty-four other B-17s were parked in various groups, most of them neatly lined up. Packed even more closely together on the congested base were the 20th Pursuit Squadron's seventeen operational P-40Bs and the 28th Bomb Squadron eight airworthy B-18s. To Brereton, they constituted perfect targets for bombing and strafing attacks.

"It's wrong, completely wrong," he declared. "And wrong practices will have no place in the functioning of this field, or any other field under this command. You will rectify the condition at once. And you'll never permit it to occur again. Do we understand each other, gentlemen?"[51]

Standing next to Brereton as he lambasted the cowed "welcoming committee," Lieutenant Colonel Eubank was too tactful to question the validity of his chief's assessment of the situation. But the 5th Bomber Command CO knew that there was little room for properly dispersing heavy bombers around Clark Field. Most of the surrounding ground was too soft to support the weight of a B-17. However, he thought they could at least arrange the big bombers so that no more than two would be in a line. Eubank also apparently failed to mention to Brereton that Clark Field was now ringed by the 200th Coast Artillery's antiaircraft guns, which would provide a modicum of protection for his otherwise vulnerable B-17s. Three days earlier, all its batteries were emplaced in combat positions and a program initiated to provide training for the men under simulated war conditions.[52]

At 3:45 P.M. the next day, Brereton conferred with MacArthur at USAFFE headquarters on the results of his ten-day mission to Australia. The USAFFE commander was pleased with the plans that Brereton had developed with the Royal Australian Air Force's senior staff officers and approved them without change. He now asked Brereton to immediately undertake a similar mission to Singapore and the Dutch East Indies. The FEAF commander asked for a few days' delay so that he could inspect his units and ascertain the results of the training program he had introduced following his assumption of command.

Following his meeting with MacArthur, Brereton informed his aide, Capt. Norman Lewellyn, about his discussions with the USAFFE chief. He told Lewellyn to be prepared to leave with him on Monday, December 1, for another ten- to twelve-day trip "if war doesn't break out today or tomorrow."[53]

The next day, it *did* look like war might break out immediately. MacArthur told Brereton that he had received a secret priority cablegram from Marshall reporting that negotiations with the Japanese in Washington appeared to be broken off and that hostile action was possible at any moment. If hostilities could not be avoided, *Japan* should commit the first overt act. Marshall had directed him to conduct reconnaissance and take any other measures MacArthur deemed necessary.

Reacting to the gravity of the news imparted by his chief, Brereton recommended that the FEAF immediately be put on a war footing. MacArthur concurred and agreed that Brereton issue a twenty-four-hour alert order to all of his units. All personnel were to be confined to their bases. Under the circumstances, MacArthur also told Brereton to suspend his mission to Singapore and the Dutch East Indies.[54]

Brereton issued his alert order the same day. It was addressed to the commanding officers of the 5th Interceptor Command and Far East Air Service Command (FEASC) at Nielson Field, 5th Bomber Command at Clark Field, and 2d Observation Squadron at Nichols Field. The FEAF was now placed on "readiness" status, with each headquarters down to group level operating around the clock. All personnel were to be available at their duty stations within an hour's notice at all times. Passive defensive measures were to be implemented at each airdrome, including the dispersion of aircraft, with the most effective means to be determined by the FEASC, the 5th Bomber Command, and the 5th Interceptor Command. All combat aircraft on training flights were to be prepared for an emergency, including installation of armament and loading of ammunition.[55]

The order included additional instructions for the 5th Bomber Command CO. He was to make the necessary arrangements to provide for the movement of two squadrons with sixteen B-17s from Clark Field to Del Monte within twelve hours' notice. Tentage, food, and other items necessary for a seventy-two-hour detail, including ammunition for all the machine-gun positions on the B-17s, were to be provided. Brereton's intention was to relocate half of his heavy bomber force temporarily to the airfield on northern Mindanao on short notice, depending on developments in the Japanese threat. With no provisions available at Del Monte to sustain the aircraft and personnel, he needed to arrange for enough to sustain them for a three-day stay at least.[56]

On Saturday, November 29, Brereton followed up on his alert orders issued the day before by assembling key staff officers and base and air unit commanders at his headquarters at Nielson Field to elaborate on the actions he wanted them to take. Some of the staff had just received new appointments. Colonel George had been transferred to the 5th Interceptor Command to serve as General Clagett's chief of staff, his G4 post having been turned over to Major Gregg, who was back on duty after resolving his dental problems. Billy Maverick was there as CO of the newly established 20th Air Base Group, awaiting his appointment as Nichols Field commander. Major Reginald Vance, who had come over as commander of the 27th Bomb Group, was now the FEAF G2, just as Brereton had intended. While General Brereton held forth at the high-level meeting, the 5th Bomber Command CO, Lt. Col. Eugene Eubank, hurriedly scribbled notes on the points his chief was rapidly covering. After summarizing the "threatening" international conditions as described to him the day before by MacArthur, Brereton instructed his air commanders to assemble their officers and senior NCOs to explain the seriousness of the situation. All FEAF personnel were to be prepared for action at once. Ensure the greatest possible dispersal of aircraft. See to it that all command posts, communications and message centers, hospitals, and transportation facilities were ready to act. Blackout conditions were to be introduced at once: windows blackened, auxiliary lights and lanterns tested daily. Shelter pits were to be dug and sandbags filled. Introduce camouflage measures. Gas masks were to be checked and issued, and daily drills conducted with them. First-aid personnel were to be in place. The antiaircraft defenses were to be readied, with weapons manned in dispersed positions near the aircraft at all times. Alarm systems were to be checked and liaison established with ground forces for local airdrome defense. Bomb loading and fusing was to be practiced. All aircraft were to be prepared for immediate action, fully combat-loaded with ammunition. No nontactical missions were to be assigned. Absolute secrecy must prevail—there was to be no discussion of the situation outside of official meetings.[57]

That same day, Brereton issued new orders via USAFFE headquarters aimed at developing Del Monte field as the 5th Bomber Command's "temporary" rear operating base. The 19th Bomb Group's ground echelon (less one squadron), totaling sixty-one officers and 887 enlisted men, was to proceed with organizational equipment (except tentage) and ten days' rations from Clark Field to Del Monte "on or about December 8th," along with the ground echelons of the 3d and 17th Pursuit Squadrons. The 7th Materiel Squadron, the 701st and 440th Ordnance Companies, and other units needed to support 19th Group operations were to move to Del Monte four days earlier than the ground echelon. The day before, Headquarters and Headquarters Squadron, 5th Air Base Group, was ordered to depart from Fort McKinley for Del Monte "on or about November 29th" with ten days' rations and heavy tentage, as agreed upon by Brady and Sutherland several days earlier. Ordered to accompany the air base group was a detachment of one officer and twelve enlisted men from the 19th Group at Clark Field, which was to set up radio communications for the Del Monte base.[58]

NIELSON FIELD, MANILA
SATURDAY, NOVEMBER 29, 1941

Seemingly oblivious to all the goings-on of the high command in their headquarters building just off the field, newly promoted 1st Lt. Ted Fisch was in Manila from his base at Clark Field on temporary duty. Fisch and a few other 28th Bomb Squadron pilots had been detailed to fly four of their B-18s to Nielson Field and spend time taking up 27th Bomb Group pilots who did not yet have aircraft so that they could get their minimum four hours' flying time in for the month in order to qualify for flight pay. Fisch had gotten in about thirty hours himself since arriving on November 25, but on Saturday the twenty-ninth, FEAF headquarters had called a halt to the operation and ordered the 28th Bomb pilots back to Clark to go on alert with the rest of the squadron. Fisch was furious. He had planned to have a good time in Manila on the twenty-ninth. That Saturday night the annual Big Game Party was scheduled at the Army and Navy Club, featuring the all-night broadcast of the Army-Navy football game in Philadelphia.[59]

Unlike Fisch and his 19th Group mates confined to Clark by Brereton's alert orders, the 27th Group had no aircraft subject to the alert conditions and thus its pilots were free to attend the bash at the Army-Navy Club that evening. Looking forward to getting "tanked" to forget the realities of their new Philippines assignment, the exuberant pilots headed to the club from their Fort McKinley tent city that evening. After all, they had no planes, were still living in tents, and were slated for a bush assignment at the primitive, facility-less base at San Marcelino, which they had checked out in the B-18s they had been copiloting for the past few days with Fisch and the 28th Bomb's other first pilots. Except for the booze, they were in for another disappointment that evening. Everything had been arranged at the club for plotting the Army-Navy game on a big scoreboard on the lawn, with the play-by-play provided by the Philippine Long Distance Telephone Company. Their own Lt. Jim McAfee was a cheerleader for the Army side. However, due to static interference, the play-by-play was not possible. They later found out that Army lost.[60]

Meanwhile, at Nichols Field, George Armstrong and the rest of the 17th Pursuit Squadron entertained no thoughts about attending the Army-Navy game themselves. They were confined to the post around the clock. "No chance to do anything but just stand-by, which is nerve-wracking at best," he wrote his wife. Like the other pursuit pilots, Armstrong and his squadron mates were on an hour's notice to take off and intercept the enemy. Their P-40Es were fully loaded with ammunition, which added eighteen hundred pounds to a ship that already was considered too heavy as an interceptor. His buddy Johnny Brownewell had come into Nichols the other day with his combat-loaded P-40E and told Armstrong that "my knees are still shaking. The ship doesn't handle good at all, just barely gets off Nichols, to say nothing of how it climbs or maneuvers."

To add to their discontent, a rumor had been making the rounds that the 17th Pursuit was scheduled to be sent to Del Monte. "There's not much down there, and its 700 miles from Manila," Armstrong complained to his wife. Squadron mate "Red" Sheppard was not looking forward to "existing very uncomfortably out in the provinces again" either. After all, they had put in three months at Iba and only been back to the Manila area a little over a month. Armstrong was hoping that the alert order would result in the cancellation of plans to transfer them to the "sticks" again.[61]

CLARK FIELD, LUZON
SUNDAY, NOVEMBER 30, 1941

All of the 19th Bomb Group's officers were assembled out on the sunbaked lawn in front of the Clark Field BOQ. Their commanding officer, Lieutenant Colonel Eubank, was going to address them, following up immediately on Brereton's instructions to his station and unit commanders the day before. Properly attired in shirts and ties, the pilots listened as Eubank ticked off the points covered in Brereton's discourse: the imminence of war, the need for and purpose of dispersal, why slit trenches were being dug, the need for camouflaging their B-17s and B-18s, and that any flight thereafter would be fully armed. They knew that their CO was a perfectionist who insisted that things be done correctly the first time around.[62]

At the end of his statement, Eubank asked, "Any questions?" When 2d Lt. Eddie Oliver, a navigator with the 30th Squadron, piped up, "What about neckties?" Eubank replied, "You can take them off." From now on, he told the pilots, they were expected to be informally dressed. Next they were instructed to go to the 19th Group supply room and draw tin helmets, .45-caliber pistols, canteens, and gas masks, which were to be carried at all times.[63]

As they dispersed back to their squadron locations, 2d Lt. Francis Cappelletti, a 93d Squadron navigator, wondered how they were supposed to carry out the order to camouflage their B-17s when they did not have enough green paint to go around. He and the rest of the 93d had been flying simulated attack missions during November in support of the air

warning tests being staged by the 24th Pursuit Group, including one on
Manila and others on Iba, San Marcelino, and other bases. They also were
continuing their bombardment training. Second Lieutenant Art Hoffman—a navigator also trained as a bombardier—enjoyed unloading on
a reef off Luzon's west coast during practice runs in his B-17D. Now,
however, all bombing training in the 19th Group's B-17 squadrons was
suspended in accordance with Brereton's alert orders.[64]

Training continued in the 28th Bomb Squadron, however, as it had
been converted into a heavy bomber outfit just two weeks earlier and
assigned to the 19th Bomb Group. Five of the first pilots from the 14th,
30th, and 93d Squadrons had been transferred to the 28th to provide training for the squadron's senior pilots in operating the five B-17s shifted to
the squadron. The transfer of experienced B-17 pilots and bombers was
mainly intended to balance pilot capabilities and numbers of B-17s evenly
among the 19th Group's four tactical squadrons. In exchange for the influx
of first pilots, Capt. Bill Fisher—reassigned from his operations officer
position in the 14th Squadron to CO of the 28th when it converted to a
heavy bomber outfit—transferred many of the 28th's newies over to the
14th, 30th, and 93d Squadrons for B-17 training.[65]

The 93d Squadron's CO, Capt. Cecil Combs, objected to siphoning
off B-17s to the 28th Squadron. Given the tense international situation, he
thought it preferable to keep the thirty-five ships evenly distributed—at
ten each—among the original tactical squadrons and the remaining five
in Headquarters Squadron, and not shift crews around. However, Eubank
rejected his argument. The 19th Group CO wanted the 28th Squadron
brought up to heavy bomber operational capability as soon as possible.[66]

Second Lieutenant Bob Michie was pleased to be one of the 28th
Squadron's newies remaining with the squadron rather than being
switched to one of the B-17 outfits. A few days before the order assigning the 28th to the 19th Group was issued on November 16, Michie and
the squadron's nineteen other Class 41-C and -D pilots had undergone
a grueling flight evaluation at the hands of Ted Fisch and other oldies to
determine if they were qualified to be upgraded to first pilots on the B-18.
Michie was one of the 41-C pilots who passed with flying colors, along
with 41-Ds Oscar St. John Hillberg and Bill Ambrosius. Those who failed
the check ride were assigned to the 14th, 30th, and 93d squadrons, which
were equipped solely with B-17s.[67]

Although Ambrosius was happy to be rated as a B-18 first pilot, his
ambition was to fly B-17s. Qualifying in a four-motor plane would make
it easier for him to get a job with a commercial airline after the war, his
longer-term objective in life. However, he knew it would be a long time
before he would get the opportunity to be checked out in one of the

B-17s that had just been assigned to the 28th. The squadron's more senior pilots were first in line for such transition training, and Ambrosius figured it would take "a couple hundred hours [as] co-pilot on them" to get the first-pilot qualifications he would need with a commercial company.

Unlike Ambrosius, Ted Fisch was thinking more about the short-term situation. The 28th Squadron oldie was focusing his plans on getting through the current international crisis in one piece and eventually home to his new wife. "God alone knows when this deal with Japan is going to blow wide open and when it does, this is going to be a very nasty place," he had written her three weeks earlier. He was not keen on gaining B-17 qualification, and had tried to "stay out of those buggies." Aware of plans afoot to use the FEAF's B-17s in a wider regional defense strategy, Fisch wrote Mimi earlier: "if they put me in a B-17, God knows where I'll be sent."

Where they might be sent was currently a major topic of conversation among 28th Squadron personnel as they observed their alert-enforced confinement at Clark Field, along with the other FEAF officers and men assigned to the base. They had narrowly avoided being sent to Del Monte the month before as a means of easing the congested conditions at Clark, but with Eubank's dispersal concerns deriving from the deteriorating international situation, it appeared that they were going to be reassigned there for security reasons. Ambrosius had heard on November 28 that his squadron would be moving to Del Monte "in about a month unless we get into a war first."

The next day it looked like the *whole* 19th Group would be moved there. The Clark-based pilots had heard of USAFFE's just-issued Special Order 83 calling for the transfer of the 19th Group's ground echelon—minus those of an unidentified squadron—to Del Monte on December 8, a sure indication that the flying crews would be following soon afterward. To Ambrosius, "that means back to tents for us and no more conveniences of a post," he wrote his wife. But Fisch welcomed the likelihood of a move to the airfield on northern Mindanao: "I would like it down there with its cool weather, swimming pool, golf course, and good library." He was thinking of the facilities at the nearby Del Monte pineapple plantation and the likelihood they could be made available for use by the 28th Squadron's officers. Fisch knew that the base itself offered only primitive living conditions.[68]

IBA, ZAMBALES, LUZON
LATE NOVEMBER, 1941

To the west, at Iba Field, the 3d Pursuit Squadron in late November was also expecting to be transferred to Del Monte. Like its sister 17th Pursuit at Nichols, the 3d Pursuit was scheduled to move there to provide fighter protection for the B-17s to be based there. The ground echelon would be going first: it was due to move out of Iba for Del Monte "on or about December 8th," as directed by the November 29 USAFFE Special Order.

At the beginning of November, the squadron's oldies had checked out the twenty-five P-40Es the unit received several days earlier. Andy Krieger was favorably impressed with the new pursuit ship. "It is very fast and heavily armed, although it could handle easier," he informed his father. Herb Ellis, on the other hand, thought it was underpowered with its 1,150 horsepower Allison engine and would be ineffective as an interceptor. The new P-40Es would not be used for gunnery training due to the shortage of .50-caliber ammunition. The 3d Pursuiters would continue to employ their P-35As for strafing ground targets, using the ships' .30-caliber nose guns, until the older aircraft were turned over to the newly arrived 21st and 34th Pursuit Squadrons.[69]

The squadron had a new commanding officer, 1st Lt. Hank Thorne, who had taken over at the end of October when Capt. "Hoot" Horrigan was sent to the 28th Bomb Squadron. He was the 3d Pursuit's fifth CO in the past six months, a fact not lost on the squadron's wag, oldie Herb Ellis. The day Thorne showed up at Iba—transferred from his job at the Philippine Air Depot at Nichols—Ellis quipped that it was "Squadron Commander's Day" again and wondered out loud who would be replacing Thorne. The new CO was not amused.[70]

When he arrived to take over the squadron, Thorne met with Lt. Charlton J. Wimer, commander of the Air Warning Company detachment at Iba, and was briefed on the strange operation Wimer was secretly running near the 3d Pursuit's barracks. Wimer was keeping curious 3d Pursuiters away from the equipment that had been set up by his thirty-man detachment when it first arrived on October 18. On November 29, Lt. Col. Alexander H. Campbell, the AWS chief at Nielson Field, instructed Wimer to assume a twenty-four-hour alert status until further notice. Campbell had attended the meeting Brereton called that day and was following instructions to inform his officers and senior noncoms of the current critical international situation and of the alert the commanding general had ordered for all FEAF units, including the AWS.[71]

Wimer's small detachment was now working three eight-hour shifts. Under the supervision of the NCO shift chief, two scope operators, two plotters, two men working the power plant, and two radiomen operated the SCR-270B radar equipment. The radio equipment and oscilloscope were located in the K-30 operating truck, which was connected to the K-31 truck that provided power for it. The antenna array was mounted on the K-22B trailer, which was connected to the operating truck by forty feet of wire.[72]

THE CAMOUFLAGED ANTENNA AND TRAILER MOUNT OF AN SCR-270B RADAR UNIT OF
THE TYPE INSTALLED AT IBA. U.S. ARMY SIGNAL CORPS PHOTO NO. SWPA 44-15533
COURTESY NATIONAL ARCHIVES AND RECORDS ADMINISTRATION.

The equipment worked perfectly, thanks to the efforts of 1st Lt. Jack
Rogers, who had been sent to Iba earlier to make final adjustments in
order to get it into operating condition. Rogers had majored in electrical
engineering at the University of Arizona and had been assigned to the Air
Warning Company because of his professional qualifications. After checking
out the electrical connections and installations and ensuring that the tech-
nically complicated unit got on the air properly calibrated, he had reported
back to AWS headquarters at Nielson Field to await his next assignment.[73]

MEMBERS OF THE AIR WARNING COMPANY'S IBA DETACHMENT POSE FOR A UNIT PHOTO IN NOVEMBER, 1941. *FIRST ROW, FROM LEFT:* WILLIAM L. TODD, MELVIN E. THOMAS, CHARLES B. HEFFRON, WILLIAM A. SNYDER, 1ST LT. JACK ROGERS, 2D LT. CHARLTON J. WIMER, THOMAS J. HOSKINS, STEPHEN E. NOVOTNEY, EUGENE J. McDONOUGH, JAMES A. HOWELL. *SECOND ROW, FROM LEFT:* CLARENCE O. PERKINS, CARROLL HEATH, LEWIS E. RAYL, LOUIS P. VASEY, JAMES M. OFFIELD, DANIEL A. MAIDHOFF, EDWARD J. PAUL, RONDELLE J. McCAFFREY, JOHN N. HARLER, HAROLD W. KOOPMAN. *THIRD ROW, FROM LEFT:* JAMES S. RIEGEL, BYRON K. HARRIS, ROBERT D. RICHARDSON, HENRY BRODGINSKI, ROBERT A. CLARKE, JAMES C. SMALLWOOD, LAWRENCE N. BARNHOUSE, WADE S. NELMS, THOMAS J. LLOYD, EARL D. BLACKMON, LOUIS GOLDBRUM. PHOTO COURTESY MELVIN THOMAS.

Scope operator Henry Brodginski—one of the more dapper men in the detachment—enjoyed his work, which consisted of picking up planes as they left Clark Field ninety miles to the east and following them westward, out over the China Sea, to the SCR-270B's 150-mile tracking limit. The radiomen on his shift would then communicate the aircrafts' movements directly to AWS headquarters at Nielson. However, during the last two days of November, Brodginski and the other scope operators noted a sharp falloff in their pickups of aircraft taking off from Clark. They had not been informed that the 19th Group's practice flights had been suspended in compliance with Brereton's alert order.[74]

"Struck by Its Resemblance to a Railroad Timetable"

A t about eight o'clock one evening at the beginning of December, the air-raid alarm suddenly went off all over blacked-out Clark Field. Another practice alert! Reacting quickly, the 19th Bomb Group's B-17 and B-18 crews ran from their squadron operations areas to meet the trucks rushing to collect them and piled in for the quick trip to their waiting aircraft on the flight line.

After Capt. Bill McDonald and his navigator, 2d Lt Francis Cappelletti, had climbed into their 93d Squadron B-17D and taken their positions, they noted that all the crewmembers were on board, ready for takeoff, except for the crew chief, M.Sgt. Richard Olsen. As the precious minutes ticked by, McDonald and his crew wondered what had happened to Olsen. The 93d had been practicing alerts day and night since November 28 and he had never been late to one before. The crews of the 93d's other seven ships had already started their engines and taxied out to their takeoff positions, then turned off their motors, following the alert procedure.

Finally, at about 8:20, Olsen came running toward the ship, waving his arms and shouting, "Get the chocks from out of the wheels, come on, get those engines turned! Roll that plane out, come on, let's get going!" Then McDonald pointed out to his crew chief—who appeared slightly inebriated—that the alert was over and that he did not have to get so excited. There was a moment of silence. Then Olsen decided that the whole affair was not over. To make sure, he asked the flight engineer if the ship was fully gassed. Intimidated by the tough crew chief, the flight engineer replied truthfully that there were only fifteen hundred gallons aboard.

A short, stocky, slightly bald fellow, Olsen usually went around the base with a tough look in his eye, as though he were all set to fight the world. Never dressed in anything but coveralls with the sleeves rolled up, he spent most of his working hours around the plane. Olsen immediately went into a rambling, cursing rage, stimulated by the effect of yet another of his well-known alcoholic overindulgences, his only known weakness. "Why in the hell was there not seventeen hundred gallons in the wing tanks?" he shouted at the engineer. "Why did you not see to it that the ship was gassed up immediately upon landing? What in the hell were you doing in the meantime, putting in some sack time?"

The engineer, a meek man who was much too old to be serving as flight engineer, answered feebly that he could not get the gas truck.

"How much do you wanna bet I can get that damn gas truck right now?" Olsen thundered. "When this plane gets into the air, everything must be in perfect shape, every nut and bolt tightened. The pilot must know that the plane will not fail him. You ought to be proud of this ship, it has gone through more trouble than any other ship in the group and it still is here to take it. When it's in the air, she's the Queen of the Skies!" he roared.

McDonald and the others did not interfere with Olsen's tirade against the hapless engineer. He was well known for his devotion to 40-3074, his only apparent interest in life outside of the grape. It had been the last of the 19th Group's twenty-six B-17s to arrive at Clark, occasioned by the need for an engine change in Darwin after two failed on the way from Port Moresby.[1]

The introduction of practice alerts had given rise to keen competition within each 19th Group squadron for speediest execution of takeoff preparations. Invariably, the bombardier would be the last man to reach the aircraft—he had to go by the 19th Group vault to pick up the secret Norden bombsight. In the 30th Squadron, the contest one day was for fastest bomb loading and reporting in to operations. The crew of Olympic diving medallist Frank Kurtz won that particular squadron event.[2]

The only flight operations being conducted by the 19th Group were daily reconnaissance missions to the north by a single B-17. In response to the November 27 "war warning" message from Washington, MacArthur had the following day arranged with the navy to cooperate in intensified air reconnaissance to the north and northwest of Luzon. Brereton would take over the navy's missions toward Formosa, while Patrol Wing (PATWING) 10's PBYs would concentrate on flights to the west of Camranh Bay in Indochina and the approaches northwest of Luzon. Brereton, however, thought the agreement calling for his command to cover the area to the north to two-thirds of the distance between north Luzon and south Formosa was unsatisfactory. Although MacArthur gave permission for the B-17s to extend their reconnaissance flights to the international treaty line between the Philippines and Formosa, which would bring the bombers within sight of the Japanese-occupied island, Brereton was still dissatisfied. The B-17s still would not be able to approach Formosa closely enough to observe activities at Takao on the island's southwest corner, where they knew the Japanese naval air force was based.

In a conference at USAFFE headquarters, Brereton now asked for permission to conduct high-altitude photo missions over southern Formosa, mainly in the Takao area, but MacArthur rejected the request. He told Brereton that such missions over Japanese territory would be considered an overt act and would thus contradict the instructions in General Marshall's war warning message. Any overt act would have to originate from the Japanese side, as the message had made clear.[3]

MacArthur was not being candid with his air commander, however. He did not tell Brereton that the War Department had informed him the previous week that two B-24s equipped for high-altitude photography were being sent to him "for missions as you may direct." They would, in the meantime, photograph Japanese bases in Micronesia while en route— the main basis for the decision. Nor did MacArthur tell Brereton that he had responded to the War Department message by asking that the B-24s also photograph the Japanese-occupied Palau Islands east of Mindanao, an "overt act" that seemingly did not bother the USAFFE commander—perhaps because it would not be staged from Philippine territory.[4]

Tainan Naval Air Base, Formosa
Early December, 1941

At 11:36 on the morning of Tuesday, December 2, Lt. (j.g.) Yoshio Matsuda lifted off from Tainan air base in his C5M2 on yet another secret flight for the Tainan Kū's reconnaissance unit. He was headed for the Luzon Strait, between southern Formosa and northern Philippines. Matsuda's orders were to determine if there were any aircraft carriers cruising in the strait. He returned from his mission at 2:28 P.M. without having spotted any carriers.

Eleventh Air Fleet Headquarters, however, was not relying exclusively on reconnaissance flights made by the Tainan and 3d Air Groups for the intelligence information it wanted on the disposition of U.S. aircraft on Luzon. Since November 17, the Takao communications unit had been intercepting radio messages from airborne B-17s and navy PBYs to glean information on activities in the Luzon and Manila areas. Such radio conversations provided the Eleventh Air Fleet with detailed information about the 19th Group's daily bombing practice and patrol missions. On November 27, the communications unit monitored Jim Connally's B-17D (40-2062) as it carried out a bombing drill at 10 A.M. However, on December 3 it reported a drastic falloff in pickups from army planes after November 30, although the radio traffic from navy planes had increased.

To Masa-aki Shimakawa and the other Zero pilots, the atmosphere around the Tainan base was very abnormal during the first days of December. Their ships were on stand-by, combat-loaded, their fuselage, wing and drop tanks full, in readiness for immediate takeoff. The base had become very quiet, disturbed only by the sounds of their Sakae engines revving up from time to time. It appeared that war would soon break out with the Americans and that they would be attacking targets to the south—but exactly where? No one had informed them.[5]

On December 3, the Tainan Kū's commander, Capt. Masahisa Saito, called the pilots under his command to the operations shack. He made a brief statement, then turned to his deputy, Comdr. Yasuna Kozono, to speak. Kozono, well known by the pilots as an idealist, immediately electrified his audience with his words. "Japan is facing the most serious threat ever to its existence," he announced. "Our country is being encircled by the ABCD powers, led by the Americans and the British, who are cutting off our supply of raw materials. They don't allow even a drop of petroleum to our country, even though there is an abundant supply in the world. The shortage of petroleum is a matter of life or death for us." Then, with fierceness in his voice, he declared: "if they don't sell it to us, we must go and take it by force! And it is available to us, just one jump from Formosa. You pilots will be the spearhead of the forces to invade the petroleum areas to the south."

Kozono's speech left the Tainan Kū pilots feeling tense. Many of them, however, did not relate personally to the decision to go to war with America and its allies. Kuniyoshi Tanaka, for example, realized the momentous significance of the event, but he nevertheless felt detached, unable to place himself within the context of the situation as an individual. And, as the Tainan Kū pilots dispersed after Kozono's speech, they were left wondering about the one major question that was still on all of their minds: *When* would they be launching their attack?

The Eleventh Air Fleet bomber crews at Tainan, Takao, and Taichung were also informed of the decision to go to war that day. At Takao, Comdr. Yoshizo Suda, *hikōchō* of the Takao Kōkutai, had called together the crews of the fifty-four Mitsubishi G4M1 "Betty" land-based attack bombers under his command and briefed them on the planned operations to the south.[6]

The bombardier in Suda's lead Betty, Seiji Ozaki, was not surprised by the decision to attack. What he had expected to happen was about to take place. Ozaki was proud to be flying with the Takao Kū, one of the elite units in the Japanese naval air force. It had been chosen as the first land-based attack bomber unit to receive the G4M1 when it began coming off the production line in the spring of 1941. In its combat debut against the

Chinese on August 11, the Type 1's high performance had greatly pleased the Takao Kū crews. The cigar-shaped bomber had a top speed of 266 MPH and a maximum range of twenty-six hundred miles combat-loaded—characteristics that put it among the top-performing twin-engine bombers in the world. Crews also appreciated its relatively heavy armament: a 20-mm cannon in the tail and four 7.7-mm machine guns. Just fifteen days earlier, the Takao Kū crews had completed a week of special bombardment training at the Kanoya base against a moving target: the old battleship *Settsu.* Ozaki and the others were sure they were ready to fly their Type 1s against targets to the south.[7]

At the Taichung naval air base 125 miles north of Takao, the crews of the fifty-four Type 1s of the Kanoya Kōkūtai—based at the Formosa field since their transfer from Kanoya on November 22—had benefited from air attack practice against battleships and cruisers in October and again in November. However, the unit would lose half of its strength for the Philippines operation on December 4 when the 1st, 2d, and 3d Chūtai took their twenty-seven *rikkō* and flew to Saigon to join the land-based attack bomber force there. They were scheduled for deployment against the British battleships *Prince of Wales* and *Repulse,* which had arrived at Singapore on December 2. The remaining twenty-seven *rikkō* crews in the 4th, 5th, and 6th Chūtai had gotten the word on the southern attack plan from their flying group detachment leader, Lt. Comdr. Toshii Irisa.[8]

At the Tainan base, where the 1st Kōkūtai had been assigned since November 18, Lt. Comdr. Masami Matsumoto, the unit's *hikōchō,* briefed the crews of his twenty-seven Type 96 land-based attack bombers scheduled to participate in the southern operation. Introduced in 1936, and the mainstay of the Japanese navy's bombing operations in China since 1937, the Mitsubishi G3M was still the most numerous *rikkō* in service. The 1st Kū had participated with the Kanoya Kū in the mid-October and November bombing and torpedo attack practices against Japanese battleships and cruisers. A third of its crews were particularly well trained in night attacks.[9]

HEADQUARTERS, FAR EAST AIR FORCE
NIELSON FIELD, MANILA
EARLY DECEMBER, 1941

Major Kirtley Gregg was grappling with supply problems he had inherited following his appointment as G4 by General Brereton several days earlier. They were bigger than any he had faced earlier as the 4th Composite Group commander. First, the need to overhaul the engines of the greatly expanded number of aircraft was beyond the Philippine Air Depot's capacity. Overhaul requirements had escalated from two to one hundred engines a month. In consideration of the depot's limited overhaul facilities and lack of skilled personnel, Gregg, through his chief Brereton, had recommended in a memo to General Arnold in Washington that all aircraft engines requiring overhaul be shipped back stateside for such work until the depot was able to handle the task. He further suggested that Arnold arrange to ship to the Philippines engines to replace those being sent back to the states so as to ensure that no aircraft would be immobilized due to the unavailability of serviceable engines.

Of more immediate concern was the shortage of .50-caliber ammunition. It was so acute that the pursuit pilots had not been able to fire their fifties in gunnery practice. The six wing guns in the new P-40Es turned over to the 3d and 17th Pursuit Squadrons had been boresighted, but they had yet to be test fired. Nor had the twin nose fifties in the P-40Bs. There were only 3.75 million rounds on hand in the Philippines for all USAFFE needs, as against an FEAF requirement alone of 6 million rounds. Some 21.8 million rounds, intended to meet the total estimated needs of U.S. forces in the islands by December 20, would not be shipped from the United States before March 1, 1942, according to the A4 at AAF headquarters in Washington.[10]

The problem facing the 19th Bomb Group was bombs. Although an adequate supply of 500-pound demolition bombs had been received recently, there still was a shortage of 300-, 1,000-, and 2,000-pound bombs—which the War Department promised to send no later than March 10, 1942. The FEAF also needed more 100-pound bombs; twenty thousand of those were scheduled for shipment between December 5 and 10.

There was concern at FEAF headquarters that MacArthur's B-17s did not have an adequate supply of incendiary bombs on hand should the Japanese home islands become an eventual target. Gregg had just received a War Department cable via MacArthur and Brereton indicating how "improved alterations" could be made to the FEAF's stock of eight hundred thirty-pound white phosphorous incendiary bombs. This was just a stopgap measure, however. The first available fifty thousand newly designed four-pound incendiary bombs were to be shipped to the Philippines "as soon as manufactured, but not later than January 1."

Unknown to Gregg, there was also a problem with the bombing capabilities of the A-24 dive-bombers expected for the 27th Group in a few weeks' time. Army Air Forces headquarters had discovered that the aircraft had inadvertently been shipped to the Philippines without the trunnion bands required for carrying five-hundred- and one-thousand-pound bombs, and the suspension bands needed for one hundred pounders, including gas-filled incendiaries. The required bands would not be available to the FEAF until February.[11]

ROOM 2427, WAR DEPARTMENT
MUNITIONS BUILDING, WASHINGTON, D.C.
THURSDAY, DECEMBER 4, 1941

Major Larry Kuter was following up on his earlier efforts to provide information to MacArthur that the USAFFE commanding general would require in order to attack Japan with his heavy bomber force. Kuter's earlier negative position on the feasibility of such an operation had not resulted in a change in strategy by Marshall. On December 4, in a memo he was finalizing for the attention of his immediate chief, the secretary of the General Staff, Kuter reported on the status of maps, photos, and objective folders that were to be provided to MacArthur. Five hundred sets of 1:500,000 maps of Japan had been produced, half of which were already with USAFFE. A number of 1:150,000 scale maps "suitable for use in approaches to specific objectives" had been obtained from the Bureau of Naval Intelligence, from which 250 sets were being reproduced for mailing to MacArthur "in the immediate future." Kuter still lacked aerial photos of potential target areas in Japan, but he was having 250 sets of large-scale maps of principal Japanese cities that would "suffice in the absence of suitable aerial photos" reproduced for MacArthur. By December 15, he would be sending the USAFFE commander "much descriptive data on individual objectives" of the six hundred targets identified. Completion of the objective folders was proving to be a slow operation, however, because the data and photographs had to be extracted "from a set of secret Japanese books" and Kuter's office and AAF headquarters were short of Japanese-reading staff.[12]

Down the second-floor hall that same day, Colonel George told those present at General Spaatz's Air Staff meeting that the Air War Plans Division hoped to complete a "Far Eastern Plan" by Saturday, December 6, that would give "complete, up-to-date information" in loose-leaf form for the use of Spaatz, Arnold, the War Plans Division, and Marshall. Updating the document "would eliminate the [frequent] necessity of Marshall to call on the Air War Plans Division for [the latest] information," he explained. In preparing the plan, AWPD would need the assistance of some of the other Air Staff divisions.

Spaatz circulated a memo to the AWPD, A1, A2, A3, and A4 the next day, asking each division to make its contribution as quickly as possible to the "Strategical Estimate of the Far East" that Lt. Col. Orvil Anderson in the AWPD had been tasked to prepare. Each division's contribution should reach the AWPD by the morning of December 9, the day set as the deadline for completing the estimate.

Meanwhile, WPD chief Gerow's staff had brought him up to date on the status of aircraft shipments to the Philippines as of December 1. Forty-

<small>Major General Henry "Hap" Arnold checks over a map with members of his Army Air Forces staff in the fall of 1941. *From left:* Col. Edgar P. Sorensen, Lt. Col. Harold L. George, Brig. Gen. Carl Spaatz, Arnold, Maj. Haywood S. Hansell Jr., Brig. Gen. Martin F. Scanlon, and Lt. Col. Arthur W. Vanaman. U.S. Air Force photo courtesy the National Air and Space Museum, Washington, D.C.</small>

eight heavy bombers were scheduled to depart from the United States by December 15, including 19 on December 3, 8 on December 4, 6 on December 5, 11 on December 6, and 4 on December 10. En route by sea and due in Manila January 4 were the *Meigs* with fifty-two A-24s and *Blomfontein* with 18 P-40s, while the *Ludington,* with a cargo of 20 P-40s, was expected in Manila by January 10. An additional 9 P-40s and twenty-five P-39 Airacobras would be shipped on December 7 or 8 and arrive in the Philippines by January 15. Sixty-four more P-40s were to be shipped by Christmas Eve.[13]

Iba, Zambales, Luzon
Midnight, December 4–5, 1941

Lieutenant Charlton Wimer, in charge of the Iba radar detachment, woke up Lt. Hank Thorne, CO of the 3d Pursuit. As it had the previous night, his SCR-270B was picking up bogies. Thorne and Wimer hurried downstairs and out of the barracks to the site of the radar unit. After entering the operations van, they looked at the oscilloscope and could see dots about fifty miles offshore, heading south. The scope, however, could not show *how many* aircraft were approaching because it was unable to distinguish individual planes when they were within three miles of each other.

Thorne decided to check out the situation himself. After hurriedly making arrangements for the 3d Pursuit's radio crew to vector him, he climbed into his waiting P-40E, took off, and headed toward the China Sea. About twenty-five miles out, he lost radio contact with Iba and cumulus clouds restricted visibility. Unable to spot anything and ignorant of the altitude at which the intruders were flying, he returned to Iba after half an hour. Wimer informed him that the bogies had turned and headed back north.[14]

After only a few hours' sleep, Thorne was up again, this time to lead a six-ship flight to Clark. They were to participate in the night interception practices that Major Grover had introduced on December 2 for the 24th Pursuit Group's combat squadrons. To minimize the risk of accidents, they were scheduled to fly two hours before dawn so the pilots could land at first light. It was the 3d Pursuit's turn to make the 4–6 A.M. practice flight on December 5. Reaching Clark at about 4:30, Thorne contacted ground control and climbed with the others to ten thousand feet. At that altitude, Thorne and his squadron mates circled and waited for the B-18 acting as the bogey to show up from the north and be illuminated by searchlights. Twenty minutes later, Thorne noticed aircraft navigation lights below him and to the east, near Mount Arayat. He called 2d Lt. Bob Hanson, leading the third two-ship element of P-40Es, to go down and check out the mystery ship. But Hanson and his wingman could find no trace of it in the dark as the plane had turned off its navigation lights.

CLARK FIELD, LUZON
FRIDAY MORNING, DECEMBER 5, 1941

After Thorne and his men landed at Clark at daylight, they went over to the 24th Group's Headquarters Squadron mess for breakfast. When Grover joined them, they related the incident to him. The 24th Group's CO then told them of a similar incident he had experienced during the previous night's interception practice. This latest occurrence was enough for Grover. He called Colonel George at 5th Interceptor Command headquarters at Nielson Field. George was not surprised: the Iba detachment's radar unit had been calling in reports to his AWS the past few days about aircraft flying off Luzon's west coast. He decided to ask Sutherland for authority to intercept any bogies appearing over Philippine territory. After first checking with MacArthur, Sutherland issued an order for pilots to shoot down any intruders. Violating Philippine airspace was considered a hostile act, and USAFFE would respond accordingly.[15]

Equipped with the authority he needed, Grover ordered Buzz Wagner of the 17th Pursuit Squadron to fully arm his six P-40Es scheduled for the predawn practice on December 6 and intercept any bogies that showed up over Clark. Any unidentified aircraft encountered were to be forced down, or, if they tried to elude Wagner's pilots, shot down.[16]

After Thorne's interception practice flight landed at Clark Field early that morning, Capt. Colin Kelly and his 14th Bomb Squadron B-17C crew began preparing for the 19th Bomb Group's daily reconnaissance mission toward Formosa. However, as Kelly confidentially briefed his crew, this time they would fly over the southern tip of the island to observe and take photos of shipping concentrations in Takao harbor and the airfield at Takao base. They were to carry live ammunition for their four .50- and single .30-caliber machine guns.[17]

After an uneventful three-hour flight northward, Kelly's B-17C approached the southern tip of Formosa in midafternoon. As it proceeded on at the usual reconnaissance altitude of about twenty thousand feet, the crew spotted a single-engine floatplane climbing up, headed straight for their ship. When waist gunner Jim Halkyard fired at the Japanese aircraft as it approached the B-17, the floatplane pilot broke off the engagement.[18]

Upon landing back at Clark Field at dark after completing their photorecon mission, Kelly would have briefed Lieutenant Colonel Eubank on the mission's results and the floatplane interception. Eubank wanted his pilots to fly such missions over Formosa, but higher-ups constantly frustrated him. He had gone to Manila earlier in the day to get General Brereton's permission to send a B-17 over Formosa at altitude and take photos. Constrained by MacArthur's dictum, Brereton turned down Eubank's request. However, Eubank may have implied that if individual pilots took it upon themselves to fly such missions without formally securing his permission, he would not make a fuss.[19]

The 19th Group's officers and enlisted men knew about the Japanese incursions into Luzon's airspace, and they were angry about the formal ban against flying their own recon missions over Formosa. Lieutenant Ed Jacquet of the 93d Squadron felt they were merely "guinea pigs," obliged to let the other side "strike first" in order to avoid an international incident that would brand the United States as an aggressor nation.[20]

After returning to Clark following their recon of southern Formosa, Kelly and his crew hurried to prepare their ship for another trip. This time they were going south, to Del Monte. Eubank had ordered the sixteen B-17s of the 14th and 93d Squadrons to leave that evening for temporary operations at the north Mindanao airfield in accordance with the November 28 order stipulating that move. At 6:07 P.M., Colonel Churchill, as head of the FEASC at Nielson Field, radioed the commanding officer at Del Monte, instructing him to be prepared to receive and feed sixty-four officers and eighty enlisted men from the 19th Bomb Group beginning Saturday morning, December 6. Major Ray Elsmore's 5th Air Base Group's headquarters squadron had arrived there on the interisland ship SS *Legaspi* with personnel and equipment and set up the bare necessities to support operations by the two squadrons. The 19th Bomb Group's headquarters detachment, led by Lieutenant Heald, had brought an SCR-197 radio set for communications between Clark Field and Mindanao and Mindanao and Australia that was now operational. Major Elsmore had flown down in one of the two B-18s that had been assigned him from the twelve belonging to the 28th Squadron at Clark Field.[21]

Earlier plans to shift the entire 19th Group to Del Monte, along with supporting units and the 3d and 17th Pursuit Squadrons, were canceled by USAFFE on December 2. With the 7th Bomb Group's heavy bombers due in soon—followed by its ground personnel, who were en route by sea—and with Del Carmen Field on Luzon still in no condition to accommodate them, Eubank had advised Brereton to base the new group at Del Monte instead. Under such conditions, the field would be too crowded to handle more than two of the 19th Group's squadrons, and those on a temporary basis only.[22]

As Jacquet and the rest of his 93d Squadron crew loaded their B-17D with tents, cots, blankets, field kitchen equipment, and rations for their stay at Del Monte, he wondered why his squadron had been picked to go on this unwanted trip. But then "the 93d always received the worst details, always got it in the neck," he reasoned. For Jacquet, "it was terrible to look forward to field conditions for [what he believed would be] an indefinite time."

It was about 10 P.M. when the first of the 93d Squadron's eight B-17s and the eight from the 14th Squadron lifted off from Clark Field for the estimated three and one-half to four-hour flight south to Del Monte. The ships were flying individually rather than in formation and were to stay aloft until dawn, at which time they would be cleared to land.

After B-17D 40-3074 cleared Clark, at first heading east, its navigator, 2d Lt. Francis Cappelletti, worked out a drift correction problem, gave the pilot, 1st Lt. Elmer "Pappy" Parsel, a heading, and then just sat back. After having navigated his ship all the way from the United States to the Philippines seven weeks ago, he felt sure of his skills. He did not bother to take celestial shots, because he planned to watch the coastline and get a ground speed check. After reaching their turning point, Parsel headed south and was over Iloilo, Panay, within a couple of hours. From there it was a matter of eating up time until dawn. Parsel flew a square pattern around the area, spending twenty minutes on each leg, before finally heading for Del Monte. When they were southwest of their destination, Parsel flew a course that took them due east and, in about half an hour—at 6:30 A.M.—arrived over Del Monte. As they came in to land, Parsel and his crew found that the landing field was just an open stretch of ground, all grass, sloping gently toward a canyon. Upon disembarking from their ship, they could see no permanent buildings anywhere around. On hand to greet the new arrivals were personnel from the 5th Air Base Group who had been sent down earlier to set up the new base. Their commanding officer, Maj. Ray Elsmore, was surprised to find that all of the B-17s were silver, making them visible for miles on the airfield's grassy plain. None had been painted in camouflage colors at Clark. He intended to rectify that potentially risky act of omission as soon as possible.[23]

TAINAN NAVAL AIR BASE, FORMOSA
SATURDAY, DECEMBER 6, 1941

Gathered in front of the operations shack, each of the Tainan Air Group's four *buntaichō* and their eight *shōtaichō* were handed a thick mimeographed document. It looked like all the others they had received in the past, except that this one had a white cover on it. Saburō Sakai wondered if the difference had any significance as he accepted his copy. His eyes were drawn to the letters at the very top of the cover: "The great Japanese empire has decided to open the war against the U.S., Great Britain, and the Netherlands at 00:00 on 00 day of 00 month." There was a notation that the date and time would be provided later. Skimming through the thick volume, Sakai saw that it provided information about the enemy situation and a detailed attack plan. He felt his body tensing up. He knew that he and the others all had experienced combat in China, but this was still a momentous time. Sakai again told himself that he would do his best, come what may.[24]

The Tainan Kū was to attack Clark Field after it was bombed by twenty-seven Type 96 *rikkō* of the 1st Kū from Tainan and twenty-seven Type 1 *rikkō* of the Takao Kū. The 3d Kū's Zero-sen taking off from Takao would hit Nichols Field after it was bombed by the Kanoya Kū detachment and the other half of the Takao Kū's Type 1 *rikkō,* both flying from Takao.

The reactions among the other eleven Tainan Kū leaders leafing through the document were mixed. Some were highly pleased and animated, unable to remain still. Others were smiling in a fatalistic way, accepting the facts of the situation. Some had no expression at all that Sakai could detect. A few appeared nervous and tense.

Masa-aki Shimakawa and the other wingmen of the *shotai* leaders had not been asked to attend the meeting. They were junior pilots and most lacked any combat experience. At nineteen, the youngest of the Tainan Kū's pilots, Shimakawa was uneasy about the prospect of flying five hundred miles over the ocean, engaging in combat, then flying all the way back to base. Another factor added to his anxiety: although he had successfully completed his training, the former village boy lacked confidence in his ability to maneuver his Zero.

One of the Tainan Kū's *buntai* leaders and his two *shōtaichō* were not at the gathering. Lieutenant Yukio Maki and the other eight Zero pilots of his *buntai* had been detached and sent to Takao to serve with the 3d Kōkūtai during the first day's attack operations. That left the Tainan Kū with just thirty-six Zeros following the earlier loss of one *buntai* to the planned Malaya operations.[25]

Lieutenant Masami Miza had also been given a copy of the attack plan at the briefing in his capacity as *buntaichō* of the Tainan Kū's six-ship reconnaissance unit. The previous morning, his *shōtaichō*, Lt. Wataru Furukawa, with FPO2c Yohinori Kamibeppu in the pilot's seat, had taken his Type 98 reconnaissance plane south on another Philippines reconnaissance mission. They passed over Iba field at eight, Philippines time, then over Clark Field at 8:20. Upon landing back at Tainan Field at noon, Tainan time, Furukawa reported to Captain Saito that they had observed twenty-three enemy fighters on Iba Field and thirty-two large planes and seventy-one fighters at Clark. At Takao, the 3d Kū's FPO1c Shinichi Shimada landed in his Type 98 at 10:10 A.M. after a six-hour reconnaissance flight to Olongapo and Del Carmen. He had seen nine flying boats in the harbor at Olongapo and, at Del Carmen, nine aircraft in the air and about twenty-five small aircraft on the field. It was the first news that the Americans had a new operational field just south of Clark Field.[26]

OFFICERS CLUB
FORT STOTSENBURG, LUZON
SATURDAY, DECEMBER 6, 1941

With Colonel George mincing no words as he described the situation to them, the 3d, 20th, and 34th Pursuit Squadron pilots assembled at the Fort Stotsenburg officers club near Clark Field were becoming increasingly anxious. Only recently transferred from his G4 desk job at FEAF headquarters to serve as Clagett's chief of staff in the 5th Interceptor Command, Colonel George had come up from his Nielson Field headquarters late in the morning to tell the pilots under his command in no uncertain terms what they were up against. He had given the same message earlier that morning to pilots in the 17th and 21st Pursuit Squadrons at Nichols. The young men listened tensely as Colonel George informed them that a great fleet of Japanese ships was moving slowly south through the South China Sea, destination unknown. He told them to make out their wills and deposit them in their squadrons' safes during the next few days. Electrifying the atmosphere as he concluded his briefing, Colonel George declared: "You are not necessarily a suicide squadron, but you are Goddamn near it!"

Back at their assigned fields after hearing George's disturbing assessment, the pursuit pilots discussed the situation among themselves. Although they knew Formosa-based bombers could reach them, they were certain fighters based there lacked the range to stage an attack and return nonstop. But what if the Japanese pilots flew from carriers? They had no information on the possibility that carriers might be used in an attack. Most were not overly concerned that they would be heavily outnumbered in combat. After all, the Japanese fighter pilots would be flying aged navy Type 96 and army Type 97 open-cockpit jobs with fixed landing gear and light armament, as described in War Department Field Manual 30-38, *Identification of Japanese Aircraft,* which they had all seen. The bombers would be twin-engine navy Type 96 and army Type 97 ships, both of which were slow, weakly armed veterans of the China war. True, there was a new Japanese fighter cited in the manual as "Fighter 100," also known as the Zero type, but the unillustrated description of it included ridiculous performance characteristics that must have been based on a report of a sake-soused, Tokyo-based American military attaché, one pilot surmised. Moreover, they considered themselves superior pilots to those the Japanese would send. They had all heard stories that the Japanese were not emotionally or physically suited for combat flying, that they were nearsighted, and that their nervous systems were not up to the violent maneuvers of air combat. While such reasoning relieved most of the pursuit pilots, some lacked confidence in their equipment. The P-40E might be the most modern pursuit ship in the arsenal, but its slow rate of climb when combat loaded threw into question its interception capabilities. And even if it did catch up with an attacking force, it performed poorly above eighteen thousand feet, as interception practices had shown. Finally, who knew if the ship's guns would work? Except for those on one or two P-40Es, none had yet been tested. At any rate, they were all tired of waiting. If the Japanese were going to attack, let them do it now! Anything was better than the constant state of alert they had been maintaining for the past ten days.[27]

General Brereton was also at Clark Field to speak to FEAF officers on December 6. Unlike Colonel George, he intended his speech to be more of a "pep talk." General Honeycutt Theater was crammed with officers of the 19th Bomb Group and its supporting units as the FEAF commander described "the delicate situation" and his "plans in the event of attack." During his Clark Field visit, Brereton also talked to Eubank on procedures for a bombing mission by his B-17s if hostilities should break out. Brereton told Eubank he had no information on the location of the main enemy forces, but Eubank and he agreed that any Japanese aerial attack would come from the west or the north. Despite the lack of up-to-date photographs of the Formosa bases, they selected Takao Harbor as the "juiciest target" to bomb in the event of hostilities.

Southwest of Clark, the 27th Bomb Group's medical officer was visiting San Marcelino Field to check out the situation of the unit's intended airbase. He and a few other group officers had driven there from Fort McKinley, where they were still housed in tents. Captain Bill Marocco found that all of the buildings planned for the base had been erected and were ready to be occupied. However, there was no water supply for them. Nor were there any facilities for maintaining their A-24s, which were expected to arrive soon. Although the 27th Group was assigned to Lieutenant Colonel Eubank's 5th Bomber Command, he had not included it in any of his plans covering the expected imminent outbreak of hostilities. Its fifty-two A-24 dive-bombers were intended for attacks on Japanese landing forces offshore, not considered likely as part of the initial attack on the Philippines. At any rate, without aircraft, the group could not play a role in his tactical plans.[28]

At Iba, twenty-seven miles north of San Marcelino, an AWS detachment had passed through earlier in the day to pick up a scope operator and a few other men from the Iba detachment and then continued north to their destination: Cape Bojeador on Luzon's northwestern tip. At 8 A.M. on December 5, Air Warning Service chief Colonel Campbell had ordered Lieutenant Arnold to take his last SCR-270B mobile radar unit and thirty men at McKinley to that distant location and begin operating immediately after arrival. Sergeant Bill Snyder—a scope operator and the most experienced man on the SCR-270B at Iba—and some eleven others joined Arnold's detachment as it made its way slowly northward with its heavy equipment over poor roads.[29]

Campbell had sent out four detachments from his Air Warning Company since October, three during the past week. On December 3, Lt. Jack Rogers led thirty-seven men from the company out of McKinley in a southeasterly direction. He had been assigned to set up their SCR-270B equipment and begin operations at Paracale, on southeastern Luzon. At the same time, Lt. Willard Weden had drawn a damaged SCR-270B and taken his detachment to Tagaytay Ridge, forty-five miles due south of Manila, where Campbell hoped it could be put into operational order. A fifth SCR-270B had been turned over to the 4th Marines' Air Warning

Company and was operational at Nasugbu, Batangas, providing protection for the Cavite Navy Yard. Two fixed-location SCR-271s remained in storage, awaiting the preparation of sites and permanent towers on which they would be mounted.[30]

Hamilton Field, California
Saturday evening, December 6, 1941

Across the Pacific at Hamilton Field, California, Maj. Gen. Hap Arnold, the AAF commander, had assembled the officers of thirteen B-17s scheduled to fly out that evening for Hickam Field in Honolulu on the first leg of their flight to the Philippines. Arnold had flown in from Washington for a personal inspection of the preparations under way for the movement of eight B-17Es from the 7th Bomb Group's 88th Reconnaissance Squadron and the one B-17E and four B-17Cs from the 19th Group's 38th Reconnaissance Squadron. He was concerned that the transfer of the 7th Group's B-17s was running behind schedule. Thirty-three should already have left by December 6, according to information General Spaatz, the chief of the Air Staff, had passed to the War Department on December 1. Arnold was aware that "general confusion and lack of coordination" at the Sacramento Air Depot had caused delays in making depot modifications to the Philippines-bound B-17Es and disrupted the schedule for transferring them to MacArthur. Their factory-fresh fuselages required reinforcing for wartime conditions, and missing nose guns and twin tail guns needed to be installed.[31]

Arnold was frank in his briefing to the crews that evening just prior to their takeoff. They "would probably run into trouble somewhere along the line" out to the Philippines, he acknowledged. They might even have to use their guns. Arnold was thinking of the trouble they might encounter flying near the Japanese mandated islands of Ponape and heavily fortified Truk in the Carolines in the event war broke out between Japan and the U.S. by the time they started on that leg of their trip to the Philippines. He did not mention that he had sent two photorecon B-24s out of Hamilton Field two nights earlier that were to fly over those islands on purpose to photograph Japanese bases there. The officers were too polite to correct Arnold regarding his statement on the possible use of their machine guns. Due to the heavy load of fuel required for the flight to Hawaii, the B-17s would not be carrying any ammunition for them.

Shortly after Arnold's brief talk, the crews of Maj. Richard Carmichael's eight B-17Es and Maj. Truman Landon's single B-17E and four older B-17Cs boarded their ships for takeoff. They were due to land on Oahu early in the morning on Sunday, December 7.[32]

CLARK FIELD, LUZON
SUNDAY EVENING, DECEMBER 7, 1941

The situation at Clark Field was tense that Sunday evening. Half of the base's B-17s had been transferred to Mindanao and the crews of those that remained were expecting an attack on their field. When Major Gibbs, CO of the 30th Squadron, brought his ship back to Clark after dark following a reconnaissance "toward" Formosa, he reported flying over southern Formosa at two thousand feet and seeing landing fields stacked with bombers. The 19th Group personnel at Clark knew the bombers were intended for an attack on them, despite what MacArthur was saying (according to the grapevine): that the Japanese on southern Formosa were preparing for a strike on Indochina or Thailand, not the Philippines.[33]

To provide protection to personnel in the event of an attack, trenches and foxholes had been dug during the past several weeks around the hangars, barracks, and other structures. In some of the trenches, Lewis .30-caliber machine guns had been set up for protection against low-flying aircraft. The field was also ringed with antiaircraft weapons belonging to the 200th Coast Artillery Regiment, which had been on alert status since November 29. These included twenty-two 37-mm guns, twelve 3-inch guns, and one battery of twenty-four .50-caliber machine guns. However, due to the shortage of ammunition, none had been test fired. M3 Stuart light tanks of the 192d and 194th Provisional Tank Battalions were also dispersed around Clark to oppose paratroop landings.[34]

Headquarters Company, 803d Aviation Engineers, was still busy extending the runways for the B-17s at Clark with bulldozers. Off to the sides of the runways in open areas, fifteen-foot-high U-shaped earth revetments were being built to shelter the group's B-17s; two had been completed so far. Little could be done in the way of dispersal except to ensure that no more than two of the bombers were parked in line. To protect the men around the bombers, empty fifty-five gallon gasoline cans had been filled with sand and stacked two high in an L-shaped configuration near the B-17s to serve as a wall against the fire from strafing enemy aircraft.[35]

At the back end of the 24th Pursuit Group's operations hangar, a Teletype machine had been set up, protected by sandbags all around and across the top. An integral component of the Clark Field communications center located in the 24th Group's hangar, it was connected with the Air Warning Service at Nielson Field. Any Teletype messages from Nielson on sightings of intruding Japanese aircraft would be passed to Private Seeborg and others in his small group of interceptor control men for tracking on the plotting board—a map of the Clark Field area mounted on a table—at the other end of the hangar.

Before dawn, Buzz Wagner had flown his six-ship flight of P-40Es up to Clark from Nichols for the sixth searchlight interception practice with B-18s and to encounter any Japanese intruders that might show up. The practice ended without any bogie sightings, and the 17th Pursuit Squadron pilots flew back to their home field.[36]

Based at Clark Field was Joe Moore's 20th Pursuit Squadron, with twenty-three P-40Bs in commission. All but Moore's ship were sheltered in newly constructed V-shaped revetments built up from empty fifty-five gallon gasoline drums filled with sand and stacked two high and facing in different directions. Moore's personal aircraft was positioned across the road from the squadron's operations shack so that Moore could reach it quickly in the event of a takeoff order. Major Grover's P-40B was parked near Moore's.[37]

With the departure of the aircraft and flight crews of the 19th Bombardment Group's 14th and 93d Squadrons to Del Monte, only the group's Headquarters Squadron, the 28th and 30th Bomb Squadrons, and ground crews of the other two squadrons remained at Clark. In the 28th Squadron, B-17 transition training for the squadron's senior pilots had been going slowly due to the restrictions on flight operations, and none were yet qualified on B-17s. Only the five senior pilots transferred to the 28th Squadron from the 14th, 30th, and 93d Squadrons were assigned to the five B-17s the 28th had received from the other squadrons. The 28th's obsolete B-18s had been withdrawn from tactical operations and were to serve as transport and training aircraft only. Most were in the process of reassignment to the Philippine Army Air Corps.[38]

IBA FIELD, ZAMBALES, LUZON
SUNDAY EVENING, DECEMBER 7, 1941

To the west, Hank Thorne had positioned eighteen of his twenty-four P-40Es on the Iba Field flight line in tactical readiness. Due to a shortage of sandbags, they were not in revetments, as at Clark, nor could they be dispersed in the confined area. The six .50-caliber machine guns had been installed in the wings of each ship and the guns of the last four P-40Es were being bore sighted, but none had been test fired. In compliance with a Wright Field order, the squadron's armorers had plugged the valves of the cockpit-controlled hydraulic gun charging mechanism of each ship, limiting the pilots to manual charging of the guns while the aircraft were on the ground. They would not be able to fly above fifteen thousand feet for more than a few minutes, as the squadron lacked the adaptors needed to transfer oxygen from the high-pressure tanks they were given to the P-40E's low pressure system. As antiaircraft protection for the field, the squadron had only twelve World War I–vintage .30-caliber Lewis guns mounted in gun pits at its disposal.

Oldie Herb Ellis and other senior pilots in the 3d Pursuit Squadron were concerned that they had not been given enough time during the past month for training in combat tactics with their new P-40Es. The pilots had required too much time in November to make the transition from the P-35A to the P-40E. In particular, they needed more practice intercepting bombers, as shown by the number of failed interceptions they had made while flying P-35As in September and October.

NICHOLS FIELD, LUZON
SUNDAY EVENING, DECEMBER 7, 1941

"Red" Sheppard and many other senior pilots in the 17th Pursuit at Nichols Field shared the worries of Ellis and the other 3d Pursuiters. They, too, had spent most of November learning to handle the troublesome P-40Es and to fly them in formation. No interception practice was conducted. Indeed, even while at Iba with their P-35As earlier, the squadron had not once practiced intercepting real or simulated bombers. Beginning November 28, all training was suspended—except for the senior pilots who participated in the special night interception practice missions flown against B-18s at Clark.[39]

Thanks to accidents occurring after the delivery of the squadron's twenty-five P-40Es at the end of October, the 17th Pursuit had only twenty-one ships in commission, or only three more than the eighteen needed for daily availability for its three flights. The P-40Es' .50-caliber wing guns had been installed and bore sighted, but none had been test fired yet. Like their 3d Pursuit counterparts, the 17th Pursuit's armorers had deactivated the hydraulic charging mechanism on each of the squadron's ships. Nevertheless, they were not convinced of the need to do so following tests of their own which showed that operating the system did not rupture the rubber hoses leading to the guns, contrary to what the Wright Field order maintained. Despite concern that the pilots would not be able to recharge their guns should they jam while they were in combat, the armorers were obliged to maintain the crude manual charging procedures while waiting for Wright Field's approval to rescind the order.

At the other end of Nichols Field, the 21st Pursuit Squadron had received its first ten P-40Es on December 4, followed by another ten on December 6, with two more scheduled for delivery on December 8. On the evening of December 7, Ed Dyess had dispersed the twenty ships in the woods at the edge of the field, ready for combat on a moment's notice. None had more than two hours' flying time on their engines. Guns had been installed in all the aircraft after being taken from their packing crates and cleaned of the thick coat of Cosmoline in which they were packed, a filthy job for the armorers. Bore sighting consumed a few of the scarce rounds of .50–caliber ammunition supplied to the squadron. As in the other P-40Es in the 24th Group, the squadron's hydraulic charging systems had been rendered inoperative.[40]

To bring the 21st Pursuit up to authorized pilot strength, arrangements had been made to transfer in pilots from the other pursuit squadrons. By December 7, the 3d and 17th Squadrons had provided six pilots to augment the 21st's original thirteen. Ten of the thirteen who had come over to the Philippines on November 20 were very junior—from flying school Classes 41-C, -D, -E, and -F—but they did have some experience flying earlier P-40 models while at Hamilton Field, unlike the graduates who had come over at the end of June.

Del Carmen Field, Luzon
Sunday evening, December 7, 1941

The 34th Pursuit at primitive Del Carmen Field south of Clark had also experienced a pilot infusion to bring it up to strength from its original complement of fifteen pilots. In preparation for the awaited attack by the Japanese, the 34th Pursuiters had been flying daily patrols of sixty miles, covering the area between Clark and Nichols Fields. Takeoffs from Del Carmen and landings there during the current dry season were difficult because the thick dust clouds on the field obscured vision. The squadron now had twenty-two P-35As at the field after the 21st Pursuit turned over its P-35As on December 4. The pilots were most dissatisfied with their equipment, however. The P-35As' engines were long overdue for a change, having been subjected to heavy use during the training of the group's newies since July. The squadron's mechanics had a job on their hands trying to keep the worn-out planes airworthy, and the pervasive dust on the field did not help.[41]

Manila Hotel
Sunday evening, December 7, 1941

At least the 34th's pilots had planes to fly. That was not so for the pilots of the 27th Bombardment Group (Light), who were still awaiting their scheduled transfer from the Fort McKinley area to San Marcelino—which had been postponed pending the arrival of their fifty-two A-24s in

FROM LEFT: LIEUTENANTS GLEN MILLER, OLLIE LANCASTER, AND CARL MANGO (MEDI-CAL CORPS) OF THE 27TH BOMB GROUP CHECK OUT THE SIGHTS IN MANILA ON DECEMBER 1, 1941. PHOTO COURTESY DAMON GAUSE.

Manila. Unlike the personnel in the other FEAF tactical squadrons, they were not subject to confinement to their base as dictated by the November 28 alert order. Following a spirited softball game at the Manila Polo Club—which they lost by a score of 19-2 to the Polo Club—the group's officers repaired to the club's bar, where they proceeded to loosen up in preparation for the dinner the 27th Group was throwing that evening at the Manila Hotel in honor of General Brereton. He had been their CO when the group was part of the 17th Bombardment Wing he commanded at Savannah Air Force Base, Georgia, in 1940–41.

The young pilots were already fueled by the time the dinner for Brereton started at the Manila Hotel, and they manifested no inhibitions around the FEAF commander. Second Lieutenants Jim Mangan and Ed Townsend kept making faces at their squadron CO, 1st Lt Herman Lowery, who was sitting at the head of the table with Brereton. Zeke Summers of the 16th Squadron was giving his CO, Capt. Bill Hipps, hell at the other end of the table. To the pilots, Brereton seemed to be "keeping his eyes on the floor from disciplining the lot." Brereton was not known as a "party pooper" himself. As the party progressed, the participants regarded it as "the best entertainment this side of Minskys." During a competition between the fifty-one-year-old Brereton and a pilot—not from the 27th Group—for the attention of a White Russian girl attending the party, Brereton cut the presumptuous subordinate's tie. Unfazed, and emboldened by one glass to many, the younger man retaliated and cut the FEAF commander's tie, too. A telephone call somewhat after 11:30 P.M. abruptly ended Brereton's participation in the festivities, however. The AWS at Nielson Field wanted him to know that Iba's radar had picked up unidentified planes to the north. The FEAF commander immediately extended his apologies and headed over to the AWS section at his Nielson Field headquarters. There, Brereton watched the AWS men tracking the intruders' movements. The radio operator was taking calls from the Iba detachment on the southern progression of the bogies and calling the information over to the plotters.[42]

It was beginning to look serious; Brereton summoned his staff to headquarters immediately. At the meeting, Colonel Brady was instructed to notify all airfields and all commanders that they were to go on "combat alert" at first light. Brereton called off the "extensive field exercises" that he had planned for the 19th Bomb Group's squadrons. The 14th and 93d Squadrons would thus remain at Del Monte.[43]

TAINAN NAVAL AIR BASE, FORMOSA
SUNDAY EVENING, DECEMBER 7, 1941

It was early Sunday evening when Masa-aki Shimakawa and the other Zero pilots of the Tainan Air Group were ordered to report to the commander's office immediately! Shimakawa did not know what it was about, but he guessed that the big day had arrived. Upon entering Captain Saito's room, Shimakawa and the other thirty-five pilots bowed to the picture of the emperor, then listed buoyantly to Saito's words:

> Early tomorrow morning, at 6:30, our Air Group will attack the enemy air force at Clark Field. It is the day we have all been waiting for. All our training, day after day, was meant for this day. I ask you all to fight courageously with the skills you have developed during your intensive training to destroy the enemy's air force.
>
> I am also thinking that not all you 36 pilots who are in this room will be gathered here tomorrow night. Therefore I ask you to look each other in the face now.[44]

Saito's concluding words left the young pilots in a pensive mood as Shimakawa and the others turned to face their comrades, wondering whom they were seeing for the last time. The Tainan Kū pilots then took leave of their commander and walked to the dining room for their last evening meal before the momentous day. A special meal of red colored rice *(seki han)* and a small amount of sake was served to each pilot. Then they retired to their barracks.

Instead of turning in for the night, Shimakawa and a few others began outlining their flight route from Tainan to Clark Field on a pad. Shimakawa marked every thirty and sixty nautical miles on the five hundred nautical mile course and calculated the time needed to reach each thirty- and sixty-mile point, based on a cruising speed of 140 knots for his Zero on the route. If there was a good landmark on the way, he marked that on the chart, too. He would need to keep this chart before him. He knew that in a single-seat plane like the Zero, he would not be able to open up a map to check his direction and progress.

He next occupied himself by cleaning the Browning pistols belonging to his *shōtaichō,* CFPO Gitarō Miyazaki, and his *chūtaichō,* Lt. Masao Asai. Then he cleaned his own pistol. Each pilot had been given a pistol. In the event of an emergency landing in enemy territory, a pilot was expected to kill as many of the enemy as possible, but to save the last bullet for himself. Ever since Shimakawa had joined the navy, it had been drummed into his head that being captured alive is the greatest shame a fighting man can experience.

Shimakawa busied himself with other final practical matters. He checked all his personal belongings and put them in his duffel bag, to be given to his family in the event of his death. Finally, he began writing his will. He started writing it in the traditional way, stating that he did not deserve his parents and asking forgiveness for dying before them. Thoughts streamed through his mind, and he told himself that dying for the emperor relieved him of the impiety of dying before his parents.

It was after 10 P.M. when Shimakawa finally climbed into his hammock. He began thinking of the significance of the occasion. Here he was, a young farm boy of nineteen years who had never before even seen the ocean, who now had 490 hours of flying time and was poised to participate in the opening of the Pacific War! When he finally shut his eyes, he thought of his mother and father, his brothers and sisters, and of all the familiar faces of childhood friends, as well as other enjoyable moments. Then, without realizing it, he fell into a deep sleep.[45]

TAKAO NAVAL AIR BASE, FORMOSA
SUNDAY EVENING, DECEMBER 7, 1941

A t Takao, the flying commander, rather than the commanding officer, conducted the 3d Air Group's final meeting of pilots prior to dinner. Lieutenant Yokoyama emphasized the importance of their mission

against Nichols Field the next day and the expected benefits of the intensive training he had put them through. He also made sure that each of
his fifty-three pilots—including Lt. Yukio Maki and his *chūtai* borrowed
from the Tainan Kū—fully understood the battle plan. They would take off
immediately after the eighty-one *rikkō* of the Takao and Kanoya Kū had
cleared the field for their attacks on Clark and Nichols Fields, the *rikkō*
takeoff commencing at 2:30 A.M. After the Kanoya Kū's twenty-seven *rikkō*
and the Takao Kū's twenty-seven-plane detachment had bombed Nichols,
Yokoyama's pilots would strafe the field and other targets in the Manila
area after having cleared the sky of any American interceptors. As he
talked, Yokoyama began to realize that he risked putting his charges under
undue strain. He did not want them to become nervous on the eve of
their unprecedented air operation covering over a thousand nautical miles
of nonstop flying. He thus concluded his briefing by telling them to rest
and go to bed early after their dinner and bath.

After dinner, Yokoyama went out to the field to check his fifty-three
Zeros, which had already been lined up so they could take off according
to *chūtai*. After returning to the barracks, he climbed into his hammock,
but found he could not sleep, keyed up as he was. "I had insisted that my
young pilots get to sleep quickly, but I found that I myself could not fall
asleep," he wrote years later in his memoir.[46]

Lieutenant Takeo Kurosawa was also worked up and feeling anxious. The
3d Kū's senior *buntaichō* fully expected that two-thirds of the 3d Kū's pilots
would be killed the next day in combat against the Americans. At the other
end of Takao Field, the Takao and Kanoya Air Groups' *rikkō* were also ready
for the next day's action. Lieutenant Commander Irisa's twenty-seven type
1s had been shifted south to Takao from Taichung that day and now joined
the Takao Kū's fifty-four Type 1s. The transfer of half of the Kanoya Kū's
land-based attack bombers on December 4 had reduced the Eleventh Air
Fleet's total *rikkō* attack force from 135 to 108. Irisa had been informed that
his force would be taking off at 2:30 in the morning to attack Nichols Field,
as would half of the Takao Kū under Commander Suda. The Takao Kū's
other twenty-seven *rikkō*, under Lt. Comdr. Taro Nonaka, would be heading
for Clark Field instead. They would be joined by the 1st Kū's twenty-seven
G3Ms based at Tainan under Lt. Comdr. Takeo Ozaki. The slower Type 96
rikkō would take off at 1:30, an hour ahead of the others, to allow them time
to rendezvous with Nonaka's G4M1s for the attack on Clark.[47]

At the Eleventh Air Fleet's Takao headquarters, Lt. Comdr. Koichi
Shimada, a staff officer, was suffering from anxiety. When he had first seen
the plan for the intricately designed first-phase air operation against the
Philippines, he was "struck by its resemblance to a railroad timetable" and
wondered "if a war could really be fought in this manner, so completely

LIEUTENANT TAMOTSU YOKOYAMA, FLYING LEADER OF THE 3D KŌKŪTAI, BRIEFS HIS PILOTS
ON THE PLAN OF ATTACK ON IBA AND CLARK FIELDS FLYING FROM FORMOSA, DECEM-
BER 8, 1941. PHOTO COURTESY ZENJIRŌ MIYANO VIA YOSHIO IKARI.

at the will of one side." His doubts had eased somewhat since then, but
now, with the execution time just hours away, "I was once again assailed by
apprehension that our grandiose plan of conquest might just be a castle in
the air." At 10:30, however, Shimada's anxiety gave way to a pressing operational task. He was ordered by headquarters to fly as an observer on one of
two 2d Weather Reconnaissance Unit G3Ms being sent out to check the
weather in the area between Formosa and Luzon. Two hours earlier, two
other G3Ms of the 1st Weather Reconnaissance Unit had been dispatched
for the same purpose. Since the Formosa attack groups were scheduled to
take off beginning at 1:30 and fly virtually all the outbound trip in darkness to be able to hit Clark and Nichols shortly after dawn, headquarters
had deemed it important to secure all possible information about weather
conditions along the flight route.[48]

ABOARD THE CARRIER RYŪJŌ
SUNDAY EVENING, DECEMBER 7, 1941

Fourteen hundred miles southeast of Formosa, twenty-nine-year-old
Lt. Takahide Aioi was feeling uneasy as the light carrier *Ryūjō* made its

way west through rough seas toward Mindanao, some six hundred miles away. The flying group leader of the *Ryūjō's* twelve Type 96 fighters had doubts about his mission: to lead the out-of-date fighters in support of the strike on Davao Field by the *Ryūjō's* thirteen Nakajima Type 97 carrier attack planes. The Davao attack was an integral component of the initial operations against the Philippines scheduled for the next morning. Not only were Aioi's planes obsolete, their pilots had not had adequate time to train for the operation.

Earlier that day, Aioi had been shown the cable sent by Rear Adm. Kakaji Kakuda, commander of the 4th Carrier Division, to the *Ryūjō's* captain: "Air raid on Davao at dawn on December 8. Each group should fight courageously according to the already-established plan." The *Ryūjō's* aircraft were scheduled to take off for the Davao attack when the carrier reached a point 140 miles to the east, which was expected to be at about five in the morning.

A veteran carrier pilot, Aioi had been assigned his new command in November just before the *Ryūjō* left Saeki—on November 28—for Palau. No longer wanted as part of the Eleventh Air Fleet's attack mission against U.S. air bases on Luzon following the November 5 decision to drop the three light carriers from the mission plan, the *Ryūjō* was assigned to the Davao strike operation.[49]

On November 11, Aioi had inherited twelve A5M Type 96 carrier pilots—six each transferred from the land-based Tainan and 3d Air Groups—and needed to provide training for them before the carrier's departure from Saeki for Palau. That same day, the 4th Carrier Division's *Taiyō* (formerly the *Kasuga Maru*)—another light carrier originally scheduled for the attack on Luzon—left Sasebo after taking aboard eighteen Type 96 fighters earmarked for Aioi's unit for the Davao attack. When they arrived at Palau on December 6, twelve of the Type 96 fighters (later code-named "Claude" by the Americans) were flown from the *Taiyō* to the *Ryūjō,* which had reached Palau the day before. The remaining six fighters were transferred to Palau to defend the base there. Later on the sixth, the *Ryūjō* departed Palau on its strike mission.

Aioi felt that he had been given the Tainan and 3d Air Groups' least qualified pilots and the unwanted remnants of the navy's old Type 96 fighters. All the Zeros had been skimmed off for the Pearl Harbor and Luzon attacks. With the navy so pinched for modern fighters due to slowness of Zero production, Aioi wondered how long Japan could be expected to fight against the Americans with their much superior production capacity.[50]

SCR-270B OPERATIONS VAN
IBA, ZAMBALES, LUZON
11:45 P.M., SUNDAY DECEMBER 7, 1941

In the Philippines, at Iba on Luzon's west coast, the scope operator on duty until midnight in the SCR-270B operations van was still tracking the unidentified southward-heading aircraft he had first picked up shortly after 11:30 P.M. He could not determine the number of aircraft or their altitude due to the radar set's limitations. Meanwhile, the Iba detachment's radioman was maintaining continuous communication with the AWS at Nielson Field regarding the bogies' course. Sleeping near the radar set, five of Hank Thorne's alert flight pilots were ready to take off on a moment's notice and intercept any intruders.[51]

PART IV

"I Shall Die Only for the Emperor, I Shall Never Look Back"

Washington, Pearl Harbor, Tokyo, Manila, Iba,
and Clark Field: December 7–8, 1941

IN WASHINGTON ON THE MORNING of Sunday, December 7,

1941, Navy and War Department officers were fretting about a Japanese message that had just been intercepted. The Foreign Ministry was instructing Ambassador Nomura to submit to Secretary of State Hull the fourteen-part message received earlier "at 1:00 P.M. on the 7th your time." The officers feared that a Japanese attack was imminent and wanted to send a warning immediately to all field commanders in the Pacific. When Chief of Staff Marshall finally arrived at his office at about 11:25, he read the strange message and concurred with his anxious staff that it must mean the Japanese would be striking American bases somewhere in the Pacific on or just after 1 P.M. Washington time. But where? Some thought it would be in the Philippines, others felt it might be Pearl Harbor. It was decided to send a warning message to the army commanders of all four major Pacific installations: the Philippines, Hawaii, the Canal Zone, and San Francisco.[1]

At 12:05 the first of the top-priority secret messages went out of the War Department Message Center Code Room to the USAFFE commander in the Philippines.[2] Radiogram 733 informed MacArthur that

JAPANESE ARE PRESENTING AT ONE P.M. EASTERN STANDARD TIME
TODAY WHAT AMOUNTS TO AN ULTIMATUM ALSO THEY ARE UNDER
ORDERS TO DESTROY THEIR CODE MACHINE IMMEDIATELY STOP
JUST WHAT SIGNIFICANCE THE HOUR SET MAY HAVE WE DO NOT
KNOW BUT BE ON ALERT ACCORDINGLY STOP INFORM NAVAL
AUTHORITIES OF THIS COMMUNICATION

MARSHALL

One hour and eighteen minutes after the warning message left Washington for MacArthur, 183 Imperial Japanese Navy torpedo bombers, dive-bombers, and carrier fighters were flying low over different coastal entry points on the island of Oahu in the Hawaiian Islands. Elated that they had achieved complete surprise, Comdr. Mitsuo Fuchida—the leader of the strike group—told his radioman at 7:53 A.M. local time to tap out the signal: "Tora, Tora, Tora." Those code words informed Vice Adm. Chuichi Nagumo, commander of the Pearl Harbor Striking Force aboard his flagship *Akagi,* that Fuchida's first wave had caught the U.S. Pacific Fleet at Pearl Harbor unawares.

Minutes later, the chief code officer aboard the Combined Fleet flagship, anchored off Hashirajima in Japan's Inland Sea, excitedly shouted over the voice tube, "We have succeeded in surprise attack!" Thanks to a "skip" caused by atmospheric conditions, he had picked up Fuchida's signal, too. The Combined Fleet staff officers all shook hands, "bursting with elation and relief after their prolonged anxiety." To an emotional Yamamoto, his insistence on the need for the surprise attack had been vindicated. Sake and dried squid were brought out to celebrate, followed by the exchange of numerous toasts.[3]

In Tokyo, a relay of Fuchida's "Tora, Tora, Tora" message was picked up by the code officer in the message room at Imperial GHQ/Navy just after Fuchida sent it at 3:23 A.M. December 8 Tokyo time. As elsewhere, it occasioned wild jubilation among the staff officers. The news was particularly welcome to the chief of the Planning Section, Capt. Sadatoshi Tomioka. He would not need the revolver in his desk drawer after all.

But what about the Malaya landings? Their timing was to be synchronized with that of the Pearl Harbor attack, originally set for 5:45 A.M. Hawaii time but pushed back two hours at the last minute because many of Nagumo's pilots were worried about the hazards posed by a pitch-dark takeoff. Unfortunately, the Malaya force commander was not informed of the timetable change for the Hawaii operation and thus continued to plan his landings for 1:15 A.M. local time.

It was early dawn when Imperial GHQ/Army received a priority telegram from the commander of the Malay force's 2d Landing Group that provided the anxiously awaited information. It informed the army staff officers that the spearhead group of the Twenty-fifth Army's Malaya assault force had gone ashore at Kota Bharu at the northern tip of Malaya at 1:30. Contrary to plans, the Pacific War had commenced two hours before bombs began falling on Pearl Harbor.

Now IGHQ had a new worry: Would the British forces in Malaya report the landings to the Americans in time to alert Pearl Harbor?

Fuchida's relayed message to Imperial GHQ/Navy two hours later dispelled their anxieties.[4]

In Washington, Navy Secretary Frank Knox was talking to Chief of Naval Operations Harold Stark and his war plans chief, Rear Adm. Richmond Kelly Turner, in the office of Knox's confidential assistant, John Dillon. It was sometime after 2 P.M. when their discussions were interrupted by the arrival of a navy officer with a dispatch in his hands. The terse message announced that Pearl Harbor was under attack and that "this is no drill." Knox grabbed the message and read it. "My God, this can't be true, this must mean the Philippines!" he exclaimed. But it was clear the message had come from the office of the commander in chief, Pacific Fleet, and was thus authentic. "No, Sir, this is Pearl," Stark replied to Knox.

When Secretary of War Stimson received word of the Pearl Harbor attack, his mind turned immediately to his preoccupation of the past months, the Philippines. He directed that a secret coded cablegram, "priority above all other messages," be sent to MacArthur immediately. At 3:22 P.M., less than one and one-half hours after the attack on Hawaii commenced, cablegram 736 was sent to the USAFFE commander from the War Department Message Center. It read:

> HOSTILITIES BETWEEN JAPAN AND THE UNITED STATES COMMA
> BRITISH COMMONWEALTH COMMA AND DUTCH HAVE COMMENCED
> STOP JAPANESE MADE AIR RAID ON PEARL HARBOR THIS MORNING
> DECEMBER SEVENTH STOP CARRY OUT TASKS ASSIGNED IN RAINBOW
> FIVE SO FAR AS THEY PERTAIN TO JAPAN STOP IN ADDITION COOP-
> ERATE WITH THE BRITISH AND DUTCH TO THE UTMOST WITHOUT
> JEOPARDIZING THE ACCOMPLISHMENT OF YOUR PRIMARY MISSION
> OF DEFENSE OF THE PHILIPPINES STOP YOU ARE AUTHORIZED TO
> DISPATCH AIR UNITS TO OPERATE TEMPORARILY FROM SUITABLE
> BASES IN COOPERATION WITH THE BRITISH OR DUTCH STOP REPORT
> DAILY MAJOR DISPOSITIONS AND ALL OPERATIONS STOP YOU HAVE
> THE COMPLETE CONFIDENCE OF THE WAR DEPARTMENT AND WE
> ASSURE YOU OF EVERY POSSIBLE ASSISTANCE AND SUPPORT WITHIN
> OUR POWER
>
> MARSHALL

As the hours passed that afternoon with no response from MacArthur to either cables 733 or 736, Stimson and Marshall became increasingly impatient. They wanted to know if the Japanese had attacked the Philippines, too. Late in the afternoon, Stimson requested that another message be sent to MacArthur, this one asking for confirmation of the receipt of

Marshall's earlier cablegrams and whether there had been an attack on the Philippines. Radiogram 737 instructed MacArthur to "reply immediately."[5]

In Manila, MacArthur was awakened in his penthouse apartment in the Manila Hotel at 3:30 A.M. by a call from his chief of staff, Brig. Gen. Richard Sutherland. The USAFFE Signal Corps chief had just informed Sutherland of the attack on Pearl Harbor. "Pearl Harbor!" MacArthur exclaimed. "It should be our strongest point." Twenty-five minutes later he received confirmation of the attack through Admiral Hart.

At 4:30 A.M., as he prepared to go to his office at 1 Calle Victoria in the walled city, he was handed a radiogram from Marshall that had been received at USAFFE headquarters. It was the one Marshall had sent alerting him about the 1 P.M. Washington time message breaking off negotiations.

After arriving at his headquarters, MacArthur assembled his staff at five to inform them of the situation and to set in motion necessary actions in response. Then, at 5:30, he was given "an unnumbered RCA message of 3:22 P.M." from Marshall informing him of the Pearl Harbor attack and the opening of hostilities with Japan. He was instructed to immediately initiate the Rainbow 5 war plan.[6]

Two hours later, at 7:55 A.M. Philippines time, MacArthur picked up his phone for a long-distance call from Washington. Marshall's War Plans chief, Brig. Gen. Leonard Gerow, was on the line. It was 6:55 in the evening in Washington and Marshall still had not received a response to the three cables sent to MacArthur that afternoon. Marshall had evidently asked Gerow to get on the phone to the USAFFE commander and find out what was going on in the Philippines. MacArthur acknowledged in response to Gerow's query that he had indeed received the two War Department messages about the 1:00 P.M. ultimatum and the attack on Hawaii, the former "about 4:00 o'clock Philippines time" and the latter "about fifteen minutes" later. MacArthur did not, however, offer any excuses for failing to respond to either message or the reminder that had followed later.[7]

"Have you been attacked?" Gerow asked. "No attack at all," MacArthur replied. However, he said that radar operators had reported "a Japanese bombing squadron" the previous night "between 11:30 and 12:00 P.M.," but it had turned back thirty miles short of the coast. Then, "in the last half hour," radar had picked up planes "about 30 miles off the coast." MacArthur paused and added, "We have taken off to meet them."[8]

MacArthur agreed to Gerow's request to confirm their conversation by radio "as quickly as possible," and to report on his situation. He also would make a report on the receipt of the two War Department messages and on the two Japanese air incursions he had mentioned to Gerow.

Gerow then asked MacArthur to "keep us informed by radio at all times of anything that happens and we will telephone you or try to get a telephone connection to you every day." He added that the USAFFE commander should immediately report any Japanese operations or indications of operations. "I wouldn't be surprised if you got an attack there in the near future," Gerow said, then repeated his words for emphasis.

MacArthur concluded the conversation by asking Gerow to "tell General Marshall that 'our tails are up in the air.'"

At about 8:30, MacArthur partially responded to Gerow's requests. He did not refer to his conversation with Gerow in his radiogram to Marshall, but he did acknowledge receipt of Marshall's two messages. His "interceptor pursuit" was now reported to be in contact "with about 13 enemy planes north of Clark Field." He also indicated that Davao had been bombed and that he had just received word of a "bombing attack on Camp John Hay" in Baguio.[9]

In Tokyo, anxious Japanese citizens were listening to their radios on the morning of December 8 for any news of the rumored commencement of war. Then, at 11:40 A.M., they heard the solemn notes of the national anthem. They knew it meant that an important announcement was about to be broadcast. Moments later, Premier Tōjō began reading an Imperial rescript:

> We by grace of heaven, Emperor of Japan . . . hereby declare war on the United States of America and the British Empire. The men and officers of Our army and navy shall do their utmost in prosecuting the war . . . the entire nation with a united will shall mobilize their total strength so that nothing will miscarry in the attainment of our war aims.
>
> It has been truly unavoidable and far from Our wishes that Our Empire has now been brought to cross swords with America and Britain . . . these two Powers, inducing other countries to follow suit, increased military preparations on all sides of Our Empire to challenge us. They have obstructed by every means our peaceful commerce and finally resorted to a direct severance of economic relations, menacing gravely the existence of Our Empire . . . they have intensified economic and military pressure to compel thereby Our Empire to submission. This trend of affairs would, if left unchecked, not only nullify Our Empire's efforts of many years for the sake of stabilization of East Asia but also endanger the very existence of Our nation. . . . Our Empire for its existence and self-defense has no other recourse but to appeal to arms and to crush every obstacle in its path.

The hallowed spirits of Our Imperial Ancestors guiding Us from above, We rely upon the loyalty and courage of Our subjects in Our confident expectation that the task bequeathed by Our Forefathers will be carried forward and that the sources of evil will be speedily eradicated and an enduring peace immutably established in East Asia, preserving thereby the glory of Our Empire.[10]

The stunned and silent populace then listened to the strains of the martial song *Umi Yukaba,* played immediately following the reading of the rescript:

> Across the sea, Corpses in the water;
> Across the mountain, Corpses heaped upon the field;
> I shall die only for the Emperor,
> I shall never look back.[11]

It was 12:35 P.M. at Clark Field, forty-five miles north of Manila, when officers and men of MacArthur's Far East Air Force looked up in the sky in response to the drone of many aircraft engines. During the next fifty minutes, fifty-three twin-engine Japanese navy medium attack bombers and thirty-four Zero fighters, followed by fifty-three Zeros joining them after attacking Iba Field to the west, bombed and strafed to destruction the FEAF's B-17s and P-40B interceptors they had caught on the ground. In one blow, MacArthur's vaunted B-17 force—on which the War Department's deterrent strategy against Japan was posited—was cut in half. In Manila, news of the disaster reached the FEAF commander at one, and MacArthur ten minutes later.[12] Over the next several hours, the extent of the human and material losses suffered at Clark and Iba Fields became known to USAFFE in reports sent in by the commanders of units that had undergone the ordeal and shock of crushing defeat in their first experience of warfare.

Early that evening in Manila, MacArthur received another secret radiogram from Marshall, this one with a terse, one-line message: "Request report on operations and results."[13] Although it was some six hours or more since the attack on Clark and Iba Fields, MacArthur had still not sent a report on the attack to Washington, which remained unaware of the disaster that had befallen the FEAF. Also ignorant of the attack, General Arnold shortly afterward radioed his own message to MacArthur:

REPORTS OF JAPANESE ATTACKS ALL SHOW THAT NUMBERS OF OUR PLANES HAVE BEEN DESTROYED ON THE GROUND PERIOD TAKE ALL POSSIBLE STEPS AT ONCE TO AVOID SUCH LOSSES IN YOUR AREA INCLUDING DISPERSION TO MAXIMUM POSSIBLE EXTENT COMMA CONSTRUCTION OF PARAPETS AND PROMPT TAKE OFF ON WARNING PERIOD[14]

Late that night, MacArthur sent a radiogram to the War Department—apparently in response to Marshall's request for information, though not citing it in his message. In it he reported that Clark Field

EXPERIENCED HEAVY ATTACK BY FIFTY TWO TWO ENGINED BOMB-
ERS AT HIGH ALTITUDE COORDINATED WITH FORTY DIVE BOMB-
ERS STOP DAMAGE HEAVY AND CASUALTIES REPORTED AT ABOUT
TWENTY THREE DEAD TWO HUNDRED WOUNDED STOP OUR AIR
LOSSES HEAVY AND ENEMY AIR LOSSES MEDIUM STOP NOW HAVE
AVAILABLE SEVENTEEN HEAVY BOMBERS COMMA FIFTY TO FIFTY
FIVE N DASH FORTY AND FIFTEEN P DASH THIRTY FIVES . . . AM
LAUNCHING A HEAVY BOMBARDMENT COUNTER ATTACK TOMOR-
ROW MORNING ON ENEMY AIRDROMES IN SOUTHERN FORMOSA[15]

MacArthur waited two days before responding to Arnold's warning message. In seeking to explain how his air force could have been caught on the ground at Clark Field as had happened to the AAF's Hawaiian units on airfields on Oahu ten hours earlier, MacArthur maintained that "every possible precaution within the limited means and time available" had been taken by the FEAF, whose losses "were due entirely to the overwhelming superiority of enemy force." His pilots "have been hopelessly outnumbered from the start" and "no item of loss can be properly attributed to neglect or lack of care. . . . They fought from fields not yet developed and under improvised conditions of every sort which placed them under the severest handicap as regards to an enemy fully prepared in every way."

Nothing in MacArthur's defense of his airmen addressed the basic question of how it was possible that an air force on full alert, notified of the attack on Pearl Harbor, and forewarned of a force of enemy aircraft approaching could have been caught with its planes on the ground when the attack began. This was not a surprise attack, as was the case at Pearl Harbor. Arnold went to his grave without ever receiving an adequate answer to this question.[16]

CHAPTER 9

"What a Fog!"

Shortly after midnight on December 7–8, 1941, Pvt. Henry Brodginski was in the Iba operations truck manipulating the oscilloscope of the SCR-270B radar set. Generally considered the Air Warning Company's best scope operator, he had reported for duty on the midnight to 8 A.M. shift. He immediately began following blips on the screen, moving south, that had first been picked up at about 11:30 by the earlier shift. From the dial on the scope, Brodginski read their location to be about 115 miles north of Iba.[1]

While the radar detachment's radio operator continued to communicate Brodginski's reports of the bogies' southward progress to the Air Warning Service at Nielson Field, the detachment commander, 2d Lt. Charlton Wimer, left the operations van and rushed over to the 3d Pursuit area to wake up 1st Lt. Hank Thorne. Roused out of bed, the 3d Pursuit's CO told the bugler to wake up the squadron's personnel, including the five pilots of Thorne's alert flight, who were sleeping near the radar unit, ready to take off on a moment's notice. Meanwhile, FEAF headquarters had grounded the other pursuit squadrons that evening so as to avoid confusion if an order to intercept bogies were issued.

After entering the operations van, Wimer and Thorne stood behind Brodginski and followed the bogies' movement on the oscilloscope. The blips had already passed Iba and were moving southeast toward Corregidor. Leaving the van, Thorne headed over to the landing strip and ordered the five pilots in the alert flight to join him in an attempt to intercept the bogies. Their orders were to shoot down any intruders. Minutes later, their engines warmed up earlier by the crew chiefs, six P-40Es tore down the strip and climbed into the night sky.[2]

Crowded into the operations van, the twelve pilots of Thorne's other two combat flights followed the bogies' course on the scope. Nearby, in the 3d Pursuit's operations area, 1st Lt. Jim Donegan radioed the bogies' course and compass headings to Thorne's third element leader, 1st Lt. Gerry Keenan, as they were fed over the phone to Donegan by the radar unit. Donegan was transmitting in Morse code on a long-range high-frequency channel because voice transmissions had proved inadequate three nights earlier. Keenan knew Morse code better than the other 3d Pursuit pilots, so Thorne had selected him to receive any Morse calls radioed to the alert flight.

Flying conditions were not ideal that evening. There were rainsqualls around the Iba area, and visibility was poor, but Thorne's flight broke out into bright moonlight at four thousand feet as the pilots continued to climb, then headed south on a course that Donegan told them should bring the P-40s into contact with the bogies. At nine thousand feet, however, Keenan began having difficulty receiving the Morse code messages and soon afterward could no longer pick them up at all. Reduced to searching blind for the Japanese, Thorne ordered the other pilots to fly in pairs at staggered altitudes in the hope of making an interception at whatever altitude the intruders were operating.[3]

In the 3d Pursuit's radio shack, Donegan was no longer receiving any acknowledgments from Keenan regarding the Morse code messages he had radioed to him. In the radar operations van, the 3d Pursuit's pilots were excitedly watching the two sets of blips converging: the bogies flying southeast and the P-40s heading due south. Then, at a point about four miles west of Corregidor, the tracks merged and one of the pilots yelled, "Contact enemy!" The pilots' elation turned to disappointment, however, when about a minute later the bogies emerged from the confused mass of blips and reversed course, heading back out to the South China Sea.[4]

With no radio calls to guide them, Thorne gave up on his flight's fruitless search for the intruders and gave orders to turn north and head back to Iba. As the pilots approached the field, they were happy to see it outlined in the darkness by the headlights of all the squadron's cars and trucks, which had been lined up along the edges of the landing strip. The six P-40Es landed easily with the aid of such excellent illumination. It was the first time the 3d's pilots had ever made a night landing at Iba.

Back in the squadron's operations area, Thorne explained to his disappointed squadron mates that they never saw the bogies—not even at the point where the two sets of blips had converged on the oscilloscope. Apparently all three of his two-ship elements had passed below the Japanese, despite flying at staggered levels. The debriefing over, Thorne and the rest of the pilots in his flight, exhausted from their nocturnal ordeal, turned in for what little sleep they could get before daylight.[5]

To the east, at Clark Field, all of the pilots in Joe Moore's 20th Pursuit Squadron had assembled at about 1:15 A.M. in the operations shack after being roused out of bed by a call from Moore. The CO of the 24th Pursuit Group, Maj. Orrin Grover, was there to explain what was up. He had received a message from the AWS at Nielson Field relaying the information the Iba detachment had radioed to Nielson regarding the radar pickup of bogies proceeding down Luzon's west coast and believed headed for Manila. Grover had ordered Moore to have all thirty-six pilots in his two sections report to the line, ready to make a night interception. However, after waiting by their planes from 1:30–2:00 A.M. with no call, the eighteen pilots in Moore's own 1st Section were allowed to go back to their quarters to sleep while 1st Lt. Charley Sneed's 2d Section remained on alert.[6]

HEADQUARTERS, ELEVENTH AIR FLEET
TAKAO, FORMOSA
11 P.M., SUNDAY DECEMBER 7, 1941

Over five hundred miles to the north—at Takao on southern Formosa—Capt. Chihaya Takahashi and the other staff members of the Eleventh Air Fleet's headquarters and its component 23d Kōkūsentai (Air Flotilla) were suffering extreme anxiety. It was after 11 P.M. local time and they had yet to receive any reports from the four Type 96 bombers sent out earlier that night, at 8:35 and 10:35, to check on the weather conditions between Formosa and Luzon. They had an urgent need for weather information because any deterioration of conditions over the attack force's route would seriously affect the 2:30 A.M. takeoff time of the main group of attack bombers leaving Formosa, which had been coordinated with that of the first group of slower *rikkō,* set for 1:30.

Looking at the bright side of the situation, one of the staff officers commented, "The weather must be good." The weather reconnaissance pilots had been ordered not to use their radios if at all possible if the skies between Formosa and central Luzon were normal, as the Japanese were anxious not to alert the Americans of their activity. The fact that Eleventh Air Fleet headquarters had not received any reports was an indication that the weather was indeed satisfactory.[7]

A little later, a messenger arrived from the Takao naval communications unit, which was monitoring U.S. radio communications on Luzon with its high-powered equipment. "We have picked up American radio conversations," the messenger informed Takahashi and the others in the headquarters building. They had been informed earlier that a message stating that Clark and Iba Fields were on a fifteen-minute standby alert had been intercepted, but this time the news was more serious: six American fighters had taken off at midnight from Iba to attack unidentified planes approaching the base.[8]

Commander Takeo Yasunobu, the 23d Air Flotilla's senior staff member, shook his head skeptically as he looked at Lt. Comdr. Ryōsuke Nomura, the flotilla's staff officer in charge of air operations, and asked, "How could the Americans have detected our reconnaissance planes on such a dark night?"

The likelihood of hostile actions between the American interceptors and the weather reconnaissance planes created a new anxiety on the part of the staff officers. Such a development would jeopardize the Hawaii attack operation. The attack force aboard the six carriers approaching Hawaii had not yet taken off on their Pearl Harbor mission, and its success depended on the avoidance of any hostile acts prior to the Pearl Harbor attack scheduled for 2:30 A.M. Formosa/Philippines time.[9] Tensions eased with the receipt of a new message from the communications unit stating that American fighters had searched for the Japanese intruders but, after failing to find them, had gone back to land at Iba.[10]

However, just when the Eleventh Air Fleet headquarters staff officers were beginning to feel relieved that the American interception attempt had failed, another unexpected report came in, this one bearing bad news. The Tainan base, twenty-four miles to the north, was covered with a thick fog! It would be too dangerous to send off the Tainan attack groups in such conditions.

"No good!" muttered the Eleventh Air Fleet chief of staff, Admiral Ōnishi, frowning and crossing his arms. "We will have to modify the operational attack plan." Staff officer Nomura was ordered to drive to the Tainan base and convey a change of orders: the departure of the Tainan attack groups is to be delayed. Ōnishi was taking no chances that a telephone message to Tainan on this critical subject would be picked up by the Americans.

Tainan Naval Air Base, Formosa
Early morning, Monday, December 8, 1941

When Nomura reached the Tainan base shortly after 12:30 A.M., he gave the leaders of the two attack groups assembled there a simple message: only the Takao attack groups would take off as scheduled. "What a fog!" he exclaimed as he returned to Eleventh Air Fleet headquarters. "We can't even see one meter ahead of us in the light of the headlights of the car." Flying is completely impossible under such conditions, he thought.[11]

The Zero pilots at the Tainan base took the bad news stoically. To Saburō Sakai, the fog "was really an unexpected mischief of God." He had been awakened earlier after an unexpectedly sound sleep, changed into brand-new underwear, washed up, and headed for the operations area with his comrades. At that hour, the sky was full of stars and there was almost no wind. Sakai noticed the movement of light beams from flashlights in the darkness and the sound of tense voices as the mechanics checked the Tainan Kū's thirty-six Zeros. The mechanics had been working all night, Sakai surmised.

By the time that Masa-aki Shimakawa left the barracks and approached his plane parked on the apron out front, fog was already covering the area. He gave the aircraft an affectionate pat on the fuselage and asked it to do its best. His life depended on this small machine, particularly the engine, on such a long-distance mission. Shimakawa felt grateful to the mechanics who had gotten up so early to ready his plane for the flight. Nevertheless, he gave it his own personal check before proceeding to the mess hall for an early breakfast, again of *sekihan*. He was so anxious that he could get only half his meal down.

After breakfast, Shimakawa prepared the items that he and his *shōtaichō* would be taking with them, including the lunch of vinegar rice in a pouch of fried bean curd. He went back to his V-135 and put the items in the cockpit, then walked over to his *shōtaichō's* plane for the same purpose. After returning to his own aircraft, Shimakawa climbed into the cockpit and sat for a while, waiting in vain for the fog to dissipate. He could not even see the tips of the Zero's wings. Suddenly, the stillness of the night was shattered by an announcement over the loudspeaker system ordering the Tainan Kū pilots to report immediately to the operations area. In a state of excitement, Shimakawa joined his mates and hurried to the meeting, fully expecting to receive the order to take off, fog or not.

When all thirty-six pilots were assembled before him according to *chūtai*, Flying Commander Hideki Shingō began to give them a final and detailed briefing on their mission. They would be up against a stronger adversary than the Chinese this time; they must steel themselves for combat with the Americans. He emphasized the importance of their role in defending the 1st Kū *rikkō* they would be escorting, but they also were to clear the sky over Clark of any enemy fighters. Only when all aerial opposition had been eliminated were they to strafe the planes and base facilities at Clark. Shingō reminded his pilots that they would have only ten minutes for combat over the airfield. If there were still enemy planes in the air after ten minutes, they should break contact to avoid consuming precious fuel needed for the return flight to Formosa.[12]

After completing their attack on Clark Field, they were to assemble in the vicinity of Mount Pinatuba north of Manila ("smaller than Fuji," Shingō explained) at an altitude of four thousand meters for the homeward journey. The flying commander instructed pilots needing to ditch to head for Aparri at Luzon's northernmost tip and crash-land there. Concluding the briefing, he declared, "As soon as the fog dissipates, we'll take off."

Shimakawa now turned his attention to the large chart that Shingō had set up to indicate each *chūtai*'s composition. He noted that he would indeed be flying in Lieutenant Asai's *chūtai*. Asai now called his eight pilots together for his own briefing. Shimakawa was pleased to have the Etajima Naval Academy graduate as his leader. Asai had a warm personality, and it seemed to Shimakawa that he came from a good family.

Asai again emphasized the importance of protecting the Type 96 *rikkō* so that they could carry out their objective of bombing the airfield. Afterward, his *chūtai* would strafe any aircraft or facilities that the bombers missed. They were to commence strafing when he gave the signal to do so.

When Asai completed his short briefing, his pilots met with their *shōtaichō* for further instructions. Shimakawa and FPO2c Toshio Ōta listened to the words of *hisōchō* Gitarō Miyazaki, then walked back to their aircraft, along with the others of the flying group. Some of the Tainan Kū pilots climbed into their cockpits, while others sat under the wings, waiting for the fog to lift. Unfortunately, it just seemed to be getting thicker and thicker. Nervously, they kept checking their watches.[13]

Just after 2:30 A.M., the tension on the flight line was broken by a message passed to the pilots from the operations staff. Takao base headquarters had just received word that the Hawaii task force had succeeded in conducting a surprise attack on Pearl Harbor! Anxiety now gave way to shouts and cries. This was exciting news! However, Saburō Sakai, for one, felt resentment that the navy had given the Hawaii task force and not them the honor of being the spearhead to open the war. Similarly, Shimakawa felt that their's was a lesser glory on this historic day. He also worried that the lengthening postponement of their takeoff was giving the enemy in the Philippines more time to prepare their defenses. Damn this fog![14]

HEADQUARTERS, ELEVENTH AIR FLEET
TAKAO, FORMOSA
1:30 A.M., MONDAY, DECEMBER 8, 1941

Upon his return from Tainan, Eleventh Air Fleet headquarters staff officer Nomura was upset to find that the hated fog had also enveloped Takao. Admiral Ōnishi was thus obliged to postpone the takeoff time for the three attack groups at Takao, too. At 1:30 A.M., he reset their departure hour to four. The time of the commencement of their attack on the Americans' Luzon bases—originally scheduled for 6:30, twenty-one minutes after sunrise—would now be one and one-half hours later.

The change in time followed a change of targets. Admiral Tsukahara had called a meeting of his Eleventh Air Fleet headquarters staff at 1 A.M. to discuss changes in the operations plan occasioned by the near-interception of the photoreconnaissance planes. Instead of Nichols Field, they would hit Iba. The radio intercepts had shown that Iba was an important P-40 base. If they stuck with the original plan to attack Clark and Nichols, the P-40s—alerted by the weather reconnaissance aircraft incident—would be ready for them and could strike the flanks of the attack forces as they flew down to Luzon and again during their return to Formosa. The downside of this changed plan was that all of the heavy bombers based at Nichols would be spared.[15]

The revised plan now provided that the Zero-sen of Yokoyama's 3d Kū would be attacking Iba Field instead of Nichols and other targets in the Manila area, as originally scheduled. With small Iba Field considered a relatively limited target, it was decided that the 3d Kū should proceed to Clark Field after Iba to finish off the Tainan Kū's attack, releasing Shingō's pilots to proceed to Del Carmen, fifteen miles farther south, to engage pursuit ships based there and strafe the field after their attack on Clark.[16]

The fog began to thin out at about 3:20 A.M. A little later, as conditions began to appear satisfactory for takeoff, Tsukahara once again decided to revise the attack plan. The Kanoya Kōkūtai's twenty-seven *rikkō* would take off ahead of the other groups and proceed to the vicinity of Iba, where they would maneuver close to the field in order to draw off the P-40s based there. They would attempt to keep a safe distance from the would-be interceptors for two hours and then rejoin the rest of the strike force in all-out attacks on Iba and Clark Fields just as the Iba P-40s landed to refuel. The fog began to thicken again at about 5 A.M., however, and the feint by the Kanoya *rikkō* was dropped. Eleventh Air Fleet headquarters reasoned that the additional two-hour takeoff delay of the balance of the attack force that the deception required would increase the likelihood of the entire attack force not returning to its bases on Formosa until after dark—which was a strong possibility given the additional delay for the Kanoya *rikkō*'s takeoff occasioned by the returning fog.[17]

With the Takao base and the attack groups' aircraft once again covered with a thick layer of fog extending an estimated one hundred meters up from the ground, the Zero pilots were beginning to show signs of acute irritation. Some of them were looking up into the dark winter sky as if praying. Meanwhile, at the Takao base operations shack, Admiral Ōnishi was standing next to Admiral Tsukahara. "No good!" Ōnishi muttered. "It has become difficult, hasn't it?" Tsukahara nodded in agreement.

The entire operations plan for the attack on the Philippines was based on seizing the initiative, but now, with each passing hour, Tsukahara and Ōnishi knew the risk was increasing that the Americans would strike first. They knew from an intercepted radio message that the U.S. Asiatic Fleet in Manila had received word of the Pearl Harbor attack. It was only natural to expect the Americans to send their B-17 force in the Philippines to attack the airfields on Formosa. The B-17s could be expected to arrive anytime from 7 A.M. onward, bombing through the fog layer that covered the bases and held the Eleventh Air Fleet's planes on the ground. The fuel- and bomb-laden aircraft would go up in flames, along with the surprise attack plans.

As a consequence of the Eleventh Air Fleet's single-minded focus on offensive operations, little preparation had been made for the defense of the Formosa airfields. Adequate antiaircraft defenses were lacking, and no air-raid shelters had been built. The air-raid warning system was totally inadequate. Furthermore, there was little air strength left on the island: all first-line aircraft had been committed to the offensive or to provide support for the convoys that had left the day before for the landings planned at Aparri and Vigan on December 10. Only twenty-four obsolete Type 96 carrier fighters were left on Formosa for local defense, twelve each from the 3d and Tainan Air Groups, plus some equally obsolete army Type 97 fighters.[18]

At 6 A.M., the weather reconnaissance plane carrying Lt. Comdr. Koichi Shimada that had left at 10:30 P.M. arrived back over Takao. As he looked down, Shimada was dismayed to see that the base was completely shrouded by fog. The pilot was obliged to continue all the way north to Taichu in north-central Formosa to get beyond the thick blanket of mist covering all of the southern part of the island in order to land. The fog finally began to clear at 7:50 A.M., and Admiral Tsukahara issued a revised takeoff timetable. The 1st Kōkūtai with its twenty-seven slow Type 96 *rikkō* would lead off at 8:15 from the Tainan base, with the other attack groups departing at 9:15. After linking up over Luzon, they would launch coordinated attacks on Iba and Clark at 12:30 P.M. Much to the relief of the Eleventh Air Fleet personnel, no B-17s had yet made an appearance over the Formosa bases.

A greatly delayed takeoff had one advantage: the *rikkō* and Zero-sen would not need to waste time positioning themselves in the night formations they had rehearsed earlier or to cruise at a lower speed in order to avert midair collisions in the dark. The total time for the aircraft to reach their targets after takeoff would thus be considerably reduced from the four to five hours originally scheduled.[19]

CHOSHU ARMY AIR BASE, FORMOSA
4 A.M., MONDAY, DECEMBER 8, 1941

At Choshu Army Air Force Base, twenty miles southeast of Takao, 1st Lt. Yoshiaki Kubo was preparing to board the Mitsubishi Ki-21-IIA bomber to which he had been assigned as observer/commander for the

morning's scheduled mission. The eighteen Type 97 twin-engine aircraft
would be leading off the AAF's initial attacks on northern Luzon, as per
the army-navy agreement. Kubo had graduated just nine months earlier
from the Rikūgun Kōkū Shikan Gakko (Army Air Academy) and had
been posted to the 14th Sentai (Army Air Regiment), a heavy bomber
unit. That morning he would be flying in the second aircraft of the 3d
Chūtai, which, like the other two *chūtai,* was operating only six Type 97s
for the mission.

As at Takao and Tainan, fog had begun to build up at Choshu as Kubo
and the others prepared for their mission in the predawn hours. At the
scheduled 4 A.M. takeoff time, the bombers were being held on the ground
because of the poor visibility occasioned by the fog. However, after an
hour's delay, it was decided that the fog was not thick enough to impede
takeoff operations. At 5:21, the eighteen bombers began thundering down
the field, led by the formation leader, Capt. Ryōsuke Motomura, leader of
the 2d Chūtai. Each Type 97 bomber was loaded with ten one-hundred-
kilogram (220-pound) bombs.[20]

KATO ARMY AIR BASE, FORMOSA
5:30 A.M., MONDAY, DECEMBER 8, 1941

At the newly constructed army airfield at Kato, some ten miles south
of Choshu, the 8th Sentai, which operated Kawasaki Ki-48-Ib
twin-engine light bombers, had also been scheduled to take off at four
in the initial Japanese Army Air Force raid on northern Luzon. Twenty-
five of the Type 99 bombers were to attack the airfield at Tuguegarao in
northeastern Luzon. Although fog did not prevent an on-time takeoff
at Kato, another factor did. Staff officers of the 5th Hikōshidan (Army
Air Division) at Heito to the north were worried that American pursuit
ships would be ready and waiting to attack an early morning Japanese
strike on northern Luzon following receipt in the Philippines of news
of the Japanese attack on Pearl Harbor. Consequently, after receiving
confirmation at 2:19 A.M. of the attack on Hawaii, they had ordered
the 8th Sentai to send one of its reconnaissance planes over northeastern Luzon to determine if American planes were patrolling in the area.
When the Mitsubishi Ki-15-II reconnaissance plane of the 8th Sentai's
1st Chūtai returned from its surveillance mission, the pilot reported that
he had not met any enemy aircraft in the sky over the area. Relieved,
5th Hikōshidan headquarters decided that they could go ahead with the
unescorted strike as planned.[21]

As Capt. Kyosato Gotō, leader of the 3d Chūtai, was about to board his
ship for the delayed takeoff, he saw the 8th Sentai's adjutant running out

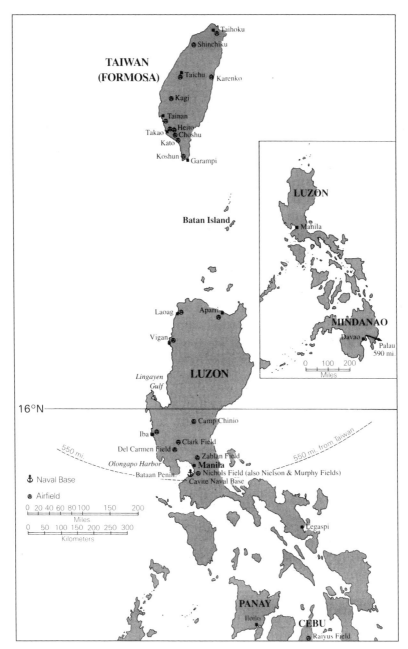

MAP SHOWING THE LOCATION OF JAPANESE ARMY AND NAVY AIR BASES ON FOR-
MOSA IN RELATION TO TARGETS ON LUZON. MAP FROM *THE JAPANESE NAVY IN
WORLD WAR II,* DAVID C. EVANS, ED. COPYRIGHT 1969 AND 1986 BY THE U.S.
NAVAL INSTITUTE, ANNAPOLIS, MARYLAND.

A KAWASAKI KI-48IB TYPE 99 LIGHT BOMBER OF THE 8TH SENTAI OVER THE NORTHERN PHILIPPINES AT THE BEGINNING OF THE PHILIPPINES CAMPAIGN. PHOTO COURTESY SEKAI NO TSUBASA (1942) VIA DICK SEELY.

from the headquarters building toward the 8th's commanding officer with a piece of paper in his hand. After talking to the CO, the adjutant came around to Gotō and the other *chūtai* leaders, showing them the text of the message just received from 5th Hikōshidan headquarters: "In the predawn hours today, the Imperial Navy succeeded in a surprise attack on Hawaii."

In full formation by *chūtai*, the twenty-five Ki-48s began taking off. Behind the last ship of the 2d Chūtai, Gotō led off his 3d Chūtai. It was still so dark that he could see only his immediate wingman as his light bomber began its climb to altitude and headed south. Despite the reassuring report of their reconnaissance plane, Gotō and the others were uneasy. Certainly with the news of the attack on Pearl Harbor, the Americans would be waiting for them over northern Luzon. Some twenty minutes later, as the formation reached Bashi Channel after passing over Garampi on Formosa's southern tip, the eastern horizon began to grow pale. Gotō could now see the aircraft of the 2d Chūtai ahead of him and those of the 4th Chūtai behind him.[22]

Sunrise had also greeted Kubo and the others in the 14th Sentai's Ki-21-IIAs as they flew over Bashi Channel on a heading of 180 degrees due south. After passing Luzon's northern tip, they continued on their southerly course along the island's west coast. They had, however, become nervous when they noticed a succession of fires being lit in the coastal mountains. Were these signal fires being set by the Filipinos to alert the Americans of the attack? They expected to be intercepted at any moment by American pursuit ships.[23]

Aboard the carrier *Ryūjō*
4 a.m., Monday, December 8, 1941

The light carrier *Ryūjō* was experiencing rough weather some 140 miles east of Davao, Mindanao. The ocean waves were high and the sky was covered with thick clouds. The *Ryūjō's* deck was awash with sea spray, and the accompanying destroyer *Shiokaze* seemed almost to sink into the rough sea as the carrier prepared to launch its strike force of Type 96 fighters and Type 97 attack bombers.

It was 4 a.m. when CFPO Mutsuo Sagara lifted off the deck in his open-cockpit fighter at the head of his three-ship *shōtai,* his destination the airfield at Davao and the ships in the neighboring Gulf of Davao. Forty-five minutes later, Lt. Takahide Aioi—the flying leader of the *Ryūjō's* fighter group—led the six remaining fighters of the two other *shōtai* off the carrier and headed for the same targets. Immediately after the last Type 96 fighter cleared the deck, the *Ryūjō* began launching its thirteen single-engine attack bombers.

Aioi was focused on reaching the Davao area through the bad weather. The flying was bumpy through the occasional squalls and visibility was poor. Aioi knew that he could expect difficulty returning to the *Ryūjō* in such poor weather conditions, but it was comforting to know that the cruiser *Jintsū* and the destroyers *Amatsukaze* and *Hatsukaze* would be in position on the line of the return journey to indicate the way back to the carrier.[24]

Message Center, Headquarters, Far East Air Force
Nielson Field, Manila
2:30 a.m., Monday, December 8, 1941

In the cryptographic section of the FEAF's Nielson Field message center, Pvt. Norman Tant—the 409th Signal (Aviation) Company man on duty that night—pulled a coded message off the Teletype machine and began decoding it. Noting that it was from the Hawaiian Department, he was shocked as he read its text: "Attention all commanders. Japan has begun hostilities. Conduct yourselves accordingly." Tant hurriedly distributed copies of the decoded message to the 5th Interceptor Command and the FEAF G2 and G3 sections. He also put a copy on General Brereton's desk.[25]

Shortly before 4:15 a.m., the phone rang in Quarters 43 at Fort McKinley, which Colonel George shared with the FEAF engineering officer, Capt. Harold "Lefty" Eads, and the FEAF assistant G2, Capt. Allison Ind. Quickest to the phone, guided in the darkness by the light of the closet bulb, Eads announced, "I'll take it." It was Bud Sprague, the 5th Interceptor

Command operations officer, on the line. He told Eads that Pearl Harbor had been hit. Eads called Colonel George to the phone. "Jesus Christ!" George exclaimed when Sprague repeated the message he had received. "All right, thanks, Bud," the 5th Interceptor Command chief of staff said as he replaced the receiver. Turning to Eads and Ind, he declared, "Japan has commenced hostilities."[26]

About fifteen minutes earlier, a telephone call had also awakened General Brereton in the quarters he shared with his chief of staff, Col. Francis Brady, and his G3, just-promoted Lt. Col. Charles Caldwell. Caldwell answered the phone. "What is it, Charley?" Brereton called out. "General, Pearl Harbor's been bombed," Caldwell replied. "Sutherland is on the phone and wants to talk to you."

After being informed of the Pearl Harbor attack, Brereton dressed in a hurry while instructing Brady and Caldwell to inform all FEAF units of the attack and order them to prepare for action. He also asked them to call Lieutenant Colonel Eubank at Clark Field and have him come down to FEAF headquarters at Nielson Field at once. Brereton was expecting an attack by the Japanese "any time after daylight." He himself was going over to MacArthur's headquarters to ask the USAFFE commanding general's permission to launch an attack on the Japanese bases on Formosa "immediately after daylight."[27]

At Fort Stotsenburg, adjoining Clark Field, the telephone rang in Eubank's quarters shortly after four. Major William Kennard—the FEAF flight surgeon, who shared the quarters with Eubank and Majs. Dave Gibbs and Lee Johnson—answered, and then passed the phone to Eubank. It was Brereton himself calling. After putting the phone down following the brief call, Eubank exclaimed to the others: "Well, boys, here it is. It's what we've been waiting for."

Eubank immediately telephoned his operations officer, Maj. Birrell "Mike" Walsh, with the Pearl Harbor news, which Walsh in turn shared with the four 19th Group senior pilots who shared his quarters: Capts. Ed Broadhurst and Bill McDonald, and 1st Lts. Jim Connally and Sam Maddux. Eubank told Walsh that Brereton had told him to report to FEAF headquarters. Eubank wanted Walsh to join him.[28]

HEADQUARTERS, USAFFE
1 CALLE VICTORIA, MANILA
5 A.M., MONDAY, DECEMBER 8, 1941

It was still dark in Manila when Brereton's staff car entered Intramuros through an archway in the thick, thirty-five-foot-high wall and continued past Fort Santiago along the narrow street leading to USAFFE headquarters. After negotiating a fifty-yard passageway flanked by plaster walls,

Brereton's driver pulled up in front of 1 Calle Victoria. The general got out and mounted the stone steps to a rambling wood building sitting atop the Old Wall that housed USAFFE headquarters, expecting to see MacArthur and discuss his request to bomb Japanese bases on Formosa with the USAFFE commanding general. He was met by Sutherland, however, who informed him that MacArthur was in conference and unable to see him. Brereton informed MacArthur's chief of staff that he wanted "to mount all his available B-17s at Clark for missions previously assigned" against Formosa and to prepare the B-17s at Del Monte for movement to Clark, where they would be refueled and bombed up for the same purpose.[29]

Sutherland agreed with Brereton's plans and told him to go ahead with preparations, but that he would need MacArthur's approval before he mounted any attacks. Sutherland added that he himself "would obtain General MacArthur's authority for the daylight attacks." Unable to take any action until MacArthur had passed judgment on his request, Brereton left USAFFE and returned to his quarters, intending to return later for MacArthur's decision.[30]

19TH BOMB GROUP OPERATIONS
CLARK FIELD, LUZON
5:30 A.M., MONDAY DECEMBER 8, 1941

Major Mike Walsh at Clark Field was on the phone with 1st Lt. John Carpenter, acting CO of the 93d Bomb Squadron following the squadron's move to Del Monte on December 5 because his B-17's generator had been acting up and thus had not flown down to Mindanao with the others. The 19th Group operations officer told Carpenter he wanted the COs of all the group's squadrons to meet with him at group headquarters immediately. Standing in front of the big wooden building just before daylight, Walsh told Carpenter, O'Donnell of the 14th Squadron, Gibbs of the 30th, and Fisher of the 28th that they should get their pilots together and tell them they were at war now that the Japanese had attacked Pearl Harbor.

As the brief meeting broke up, Walsh headed for the B-18 on the field that would take him and Eubank to FEAF headquarters at Nielson Field. The first rays of dawn were spreading over Clark when the obsolete bomber, now relegated to transport work, lifted off the field. Before Eubank departed, he instructed Gibbs to take charge of the group in his absence.

Many of the 19th Group pilots were in the mess hall for an early, predawn breakfast while their COs were being briefed, but they already knew about the attack. They were excitedly discussing what was likely to happen next after having been informed that they should stand by for orders. Most expected that they would be sent to bomb Formosa.[31]

After daylight, another gaggle of 19th Group pilots entered the mess hall for breakfast, including 2d Lt. Ray Teborek of the 30th squadron, 1st Lt. Hewitt T. "Shorty" Wheless's copilot. The night before, Wheless and Teborek had been told they were to fly a reconnaissance mission the next morning and to report for a briefing at 19th Group operations at seven. While they were eating, they listened on the radio to Don Bell in Manila as he reported the news about Pearl Harbor. It was the first public announcement of the surprise attack.

When they had finished eating, 1st Lt. Frank Kurtz and the other pilots in the 30th Bomb Squadron hurried over to the squadron's operations tent. Following up on Walsh's instructions, their CO, Dave Gibbs, was waiting to brief them on the situation. Facing his flying officers, the boyish-looking Gibbs told them: "If they have hit Hawaii, they can't miss hitting us. I can't tell you when it will come, but it will come. However, I *can* tell you where it will come from." Raising the tent's canvas flap, Gibbs pointed to the north. They all understood that he meant Formosa. As the pilots left, Gibbs announced that they were on stand-by and that orders would be coming through all morning.

Wheless and Teborek were not at the meeting. They had left the mess hall and headed to group operations for the briefing on their morning recon mission. They were again told that they were to fly north and patrol the waters from Luzon to Formosa, hitting any targets of opportunity in the event they spotted Japanese ships headed for the Philippines. Their B-17 was to be loaded with one-hundred-pound bombs. Wheless and Teborek wondered why they were going to carry such light bombs: What damage would they do to ships?[32]

Over at the 20th Pursuit Squadron's operations area, the early morning hours had been characterized by excitement, confusion, and, particularly for the pilots in Charley Sneed's 2d Section, strain. Sneed and his pilots had been waiting in their P-40Bs for orders ever since reporting to the line at 1:30 in response to Iba radar's report of bogies. Their CO, Joe Moore, had told them the news of the Pearl Harbor attack at about 4:30 and was keeping them on the line for that reason. He had also ordered the eighteen pilots of his own 1st Section to report to the line.

3D PURSUIT SQUADRON MESS HALL
IBA FIELD, ZAMBALES, LUZON
6 A.M., DECEMBER 8, 1941

The 3d Pursuit's pilots were in the mess hall at six for breakfast, drowsy from the ordeal of the squadron's attempt to intercept the bogies in the early morning hours, when someone with a radio picked up Don Bell's announcement about the attack on Pearl Harbor. Following receipt of orders from 24th Group headquarters at Clark, their CO, Hank Thorne, instructed Andy Krieger, the assistant operations officer, to assign the squadron's eighteen ranking pilots to the eighteen P-40Es on the line. Thorne then led the pilots of his A Flight to the south end of the field, while 1st Lt. Ed Woolery took the pilots of his B Flight to the north end, and Herb Ellis sited his C Flight pilots just off the center of the strip, where they awaited takeoff orders in their combat-loaded ships.[33]

NICHOLS FIELD, LUZON
6 A.M., DECEMBER 8, 1941

At Nichols Field, just south of Manila, eighteen 17th Pursuit Squadron pilots had taxied their P-40Es to the east end of the runway in the darkness. An hour later, they were still waiting for takeoff orders after having been ordered to report in following the news of the Pearl Harbor attack. At the other end of the field, eighteen 21st Pursuit pilots—including five borrowed from other squadrons—had also taxied their P-40Es into takeoff position, then waited for the word to go from their CO, Ed Dyess. None of their ships had more than three hours' flying time on their engines.[34]

OVER DAVAO AIRFIELD, MINDANAO
6 A.M., MONDAY DECEMBER 8, 1941

Lieutenant Takahide Aioi arrived over Davao, Mindanao, at the head of his formation of six Type 96 carrier fighters just as the thirteen Type 97 attack bombers off the carrier *Ryūjō* were dropping their 132-pound bombs on the undefended airfield. After the bombers left the scene of destruction, Aioi led his fighters down in a strafing attack on targets of opportunity, each firing their two nose-mounted 7.7-mm machine guns. With the bombers, they managed to damage the field's hangar, petroleum tanks, and radio station, but they struck no aircraft because there were none on the strip.

Aioi was angry. "Absurd!" he mumbled to himself. "Why did the war start like this?" Disappointed by the lack of opposition in his first combat experience of the war, Aioi headed southwest to Malalag Bay, thirty-five miles southwest of Davao. Two days earlier, a "Bristol class" seaplane tender had been reported at anchor there. When Aioi's group arrived over Malalag Bay at 7:05 A.M., they found the seaplane tender anchored offshore, as expected. Searching for other possible targets, they spotted two PBY-4 flying boats moored to buoys near the shore opposite the seaplane tender.

Aioi ignored the tender and led his men down under a low overcast in a strafing attack on the hapless flying boats. As the six fighters roared past, both PBYs exploded and burned in pools of their own gasoline.

While making a wild dash to get out of Malalag Bay into the wider waters of the Gulf of Davao, the seaplane tender was set upon by seven of the *Ryūjō's* attack bombers that had also proceeded south from Davao in search of targets. For nearly half an hour, the tender—a former destroyer— maneuvered to avoid their bombs. All of them fell into the sea, some dangerously close, raising columns of water a hundred feet high. Disappointed by their lack of success and out of bombs, the bomber pilots headed back to the *Ryūjō*.[35]

In the meantime, Lieutenant Sugara's second *shōtai* of three Type 96 carrier fighters, joined by two of the Type 97 attack bombers, was searching for targets elsewhere in Davao Gulf. The fighters located and strafed a merchant ship and an oil tanker, but FPO2c Hiroshi Kawanishi's plane was hit by antiaircraft fire during the action and made an emergency landing. Fearing capture, and in the true Bushido spirit, Kawanishi burned his aircraft and committed suicide.

Back aboard the *Ryūjō,* results and losses were tallied. In addition to Kawanishi and his aircraft, Aioi reported the loss of two other fighters. In addition, one of the attack bombers had ditched in the sea due to engine trouble, but the destroyer *Kuroshio* rescued its three-man crew.[36]

HEADQUARTERS, FAR EAST AIR FORCE
NIELSON FIELD, MANILA
7 A.M., MONDAY, DECEMBER 8, 1941

Lieutenant Colonel Eubank landed at Nielson Field on the southern outskirts of Manila at about 6:30 A.M. He and his operations officer climbed out of the B-18 and headed over to the V-shaped building on the field that housed the offices of Brereton's FEAF headquarters. The building and the nearby hangar struck them as a tempting target for an aerial attack. There was no natural cover and the roof of the hangar retained its civilian pattern of black and yellow squares. In anticipation of an attack, sandbags had been piled up against the wall of the headquarters building.[37]

Gathered in Brereton's office were the senior staff members of both his headquarters and the 5th Interceptor Command. In Brereton's absence, Colonel Brady, the chief of staff, was conducting the meeting. Captain Ind recalled that Brady was standing beside Brereton's chair, casting "swift, hostile, inclusive glances about the room and out into the corridor." Of the FEAF staff, Lieutenant Colonel Caldwell was there, as were Lieutenant Colonel Campbell of the AWS; Major Lamb, the signal officer; and Captain Eads, the engineering officer. Colonel George, Captain Sprague, and Captain Ind represented the 5th Interceptor Command. Their chief, General Clagett, was in and out, reflecting his marginalized status following Brereton's arrival.

Eubank was pacing around the room when someone asked him about his B-17 force at Clark Field. Irritated, he barked: "Sure they're ready. They've been ready since before daylight. What're we going to do with 'em? That's what I want to know."

Brady finally called the meeting to order. He told everyone that Brereton was still at USAFFE, "but we'll have a plan ready for him when he comes." The objective was to decide on what course of action the FEAF should follow now that the Japanese had struck at Pearl Harbor. A "great deal of arguing back and forth" ensued before a unanimous agreement was reached that the B-17s should be sent to attack Takao Harbor on Formosa without delay. Colonel Caldwell asked Ind if the objective folders he was preparing for targets on Formosa were ready. When Ind answered in the affirmative, Brereton's G3 told him: "Go check them over. Be absolutely sure. We're playing for keeps now. And it looks we'll be dealing out a hand any minute."

Ind was exultant when he later repeated Caldwell's request to his G2 staff. They had spent many weeks preparing the folders, using data compiled in Manila and Washington. While the folders were not up the standard of the RAF or Luftwaffe, Ind thought they were complete enough for mounting an effective bombing mission on southern Formosa.[38]

HEADQUARTERS, USAFFE
1 CALLE VICTORIA, MANILA
7:15 A.M., MONDAY, DECEMBER 8, 1941

Across town, at MacArthur's USAFFE headquarters in Intramuros, it was 7:15 when Brereton returned for his second visit of the morning. Again he entered Sutherland's office, anxious to know of MacArthur's decision. Sutherland told him that the commanding general had not responded to his request. Irritated, Brereton told Sutherland that he wanted to discuss the matter directly with MacArthur. While acknowledging that his chief was alone, Sutherland would not allow Brereton to enter. "I'll ask the General," he told Brereton, then slipped into MacArthur's office. He was back a moment later. "The General says no," he informed Brereton. "Don't make the first overt act."[39] Incensed, Brereton argued with Sutherland that bombing Pearl Harbor *was* an overt act! But Sutherland, in his usual cool and aloof manner, refused to budge from his chief's alleged position on the matter. Sutherland also expressed the belief that Brereton lacked sufficient information on targets on Formosa to justify offensive operations, and instructed the FEAF commander to maintain a defensive stance while awaiting further orders.[40]

Brereton stormed angrily out of Sutherland's office and climbed into his staff car, telling the driver to go directly to FEAF headquarters. He knew his staff officers were waiting there for him, expecting to hear of MacArthur's approval to bomb Formosa.

HEADQUARTERS, FAR EAST AIR FORCE
NIELSON FIELD, MANILA
8 A.M., DECEMBER 8, 1941

General Brereton strode down the corridor in the FEAF headquarters building, "his face pale, his jaw hard," as he passed Ind, who had just left the meeting. Taking over from Brady, he asked what the staff had decided on as a course of action and was told that all had opted for an immediate bombing attack on Formosa. Grimly, Brereton responded, "No, we can't attack until we're fired on." He told his staff about his discussions with Sutherland. The B-17s were to be prepared for action, but they would remain on standby until USAFFE headquarters issued the order to attack.[41]

To everyone attending the meeting, the position taken by MacArthur and his chief of staff was at once shocking and incomprehensible. Did not the attack on Pearl Harbor constitute an overt act of war, freeing them from their enforced defensive posture? Faced with the restrictions imposed on him by USAFFE headquarters, Brereton discussed with his staff what actions they should take. It was eventually decided to complete earlier plans for an attack on Takao Bay, targeting Japanese transports and warships. In order to obtain detailed target information, the FEAF would also prepare to send three B-17s on a photoreconnaissance of southern Formosa "without delay." Specifically, the reconnaissance would be aimed at determining the location and strength of Japanese airdromes in particular, with highest priority to those at Takao and Reigarzo, Koshun, Okayama, and Laito, as well as other airfields and port facilities below 23 degrees, 10 minutes north latitude. All precautions were to be taken to avoid combat with hostile pursuit aircraft. The rest of 5th Bomber Command would remain on alert, along with 5th Interceptor Command.[42]

While Brereton was issuing the order to carry out the photoreconnaissance mission, he was informed that he had a phone call from Washington. It was General Arnold, concerned about the surprise attack on Pearl

Harbor and the destruction of his Hawaiian Air Force there. The Army Air Forces chief did not want to hear of a repetition of such a disaster in the Philippines. Brereton assured him that he was taking all precautions to guard against that possibility.[43]

As the meeting broke up, Eubank was mentioning to Brady the possible need to get his Clark-based B-17s in the air if necessary when Colonel George interrupted them. He informed Eubank that "just a while ago" a "large force" was reported to be heading in from Lingayen and that Clark Field had been notified. Eubank, irritated, replied, "we can't be taking off for every alarm," but after a moment's reconsideration headed for the telephone to put through an emergency call to Clark. Colonel George grimly headed for his office and called Major Grover at Clark to get his pursuit squadrons in the air to meet the threat coming in from the north.[44]

Back in his own office, Brereton placed a call to USAFFE headquarters. He wanted to find out if MacArthur and Sutherland had changed their stance on bombing Formosa. At 8:50 A.M., Sutherland called back. MacArthur's chief of staff told Brereton to "hold off bombing of Formosa for the present."[45]

BURGOS, CAPE BOJEADOR, LUZON
7:50 A.M. DECEMBER 8, 1941

At the extreme northwest tip of Luzon—Burgos, Cape Bojeador—the men of the Air Warning Company detachment ordered there on December 5 were trying to get their SCR-270B radar unit operational. They had arrived at the distant location at 2 A.M. on December 7 after driving more than twenty-fours from Iba over poor roads and weak bridges in their trucks with the heavy equipment, accompanied by Philippine Army engineers. It was shortly before eight and they were still having trouble setting up the azimuth settings on the set's antenna mount. Suddenly, they heard the roar of airplanes and looked up. A flight of twin-engine aircraft was passing overhead, heading south. They did not need a radar set to pick up those intruders![46]

First Lieutenant Robert Arnold, the detachment commander, hurried over to the operations van to radio the sighting to FEAF headquarters at Nielson. However, much to his frustration, he could not get through: the AWS was not listening on the agreed channel. Unknown to Arnold, the SCR-197 radio trailer at FEAF headquarters had been removed that morning for use at MacArthur's command post and the radio set substituting for it was operating on a different frequency.[47]

CLARK FIELD, LUZON
8:30 A.M., DECEMBER 8, 1941

By 8:30, a chaotic situation prevailed at Clark Field. In response to the report he would have received from the AWS at Nielson and Colonel George's call, Maj. Orrin Grover at 24th Group headquarters had ordered the 2d Section of Joe Moore's 20th Pursuit Squadron to take off in their eighteen P-40Bs and head north to the Tarlac area to be ready to intercept the Japanese planes reported heading down northern Luzon. He had also contacted Buzz Wagner at Nichols Field and directed him to have his 17th Pursuit Squadron take off and patrol the area west of the 20th Pursuit's position. Finally, 1st Lt. Sam Marett's 34th Pursuit Squadron at Del Carmen, fifteen miles due south of Clark, was ordered to take off and cover Clark Field.[48]

At 8:45, Major Gibbs, the acting commander of the 19th Bomb Group in Eubank's absence, was also ordering all the group's flyable B-17s and B-18s off the field in response to the AWS message he had received via Maj. Moe Daly, the Clark Field CO. The bombers were to stay clear of the Clark area and patrol within control tower range of the field until ordered to land.[49]

There was no coordination between the 24th Pursuit Group headquarters and the 19th Bomb Group on takeoff procedures. The 20th Pursuit's P-40s; the B-17s of Headquarters, 28th, and 30th Squadrons; and the 28th Squadron's B-18s were roaring down the sod strips of Clark Field in all directions—upwind, downwind, and crosswind—in many cases crossing each other's paths dangerously. In the rush to get airborne, 1st Lt. Ed Green of Headquarters Squadron had taken off in his B-17 without first warming up and on three engines only, not starting the fourth until he was already airborne. Second Lieutenants Dick Carlisle and Francis Thompson, his copilot, ran over to an out-of-service B-17 and took off on three engines, too—the fourth was disabled. By nine, however, all aircraft at Clark Field that had been ordered to take off had taken to the air without mishap and were clear of the area.

The flight crew of Shorty Wheless's B-17 was still being briefed on its recon mission when they were told to forget about loading the bombs and get off the field as quickly as possible to avoid being caught in an air raid. They still were to carry out their patrol assignment.[50]

A number of other B-17s were left on the ground. Two were in Hangar 3 and one in Hangar 4, being painted in olive drab camouflage. As ordered earlier that morning, 2d Lt. Austin Stitt, a bombardier with the 30th Squadron, and Major Gibbs' ground crew, were going at the major's ship, serial number 40-3075, with spray guns and brushes in Hangar 4. Two other B-17s were out of service. John Carpenter's B-17D, which had been left behind when his 93d Bomb Squadron went down to Del Monte on December 5, had a problem with generators constantly burning out and was still undergoing repairs. Over on the far end of the field, B-17D serial number 40-3093, which the 14th Bomb Squadron had flown over in September, was still inoperative with a damaged tail.[51]

Over at the 20th Pursuit Squadron operations area, the eighteen pilots of Charley Sneed's 2d Section saw the red flag being run up the flagpole at the squadron's operations shack. Instantly reacting to the long-awaited takeoff signal, they taxied their P-40Bs out to the sod runway and began going into their takeoff rolls. They barely missed ramming B-17s that were also trying to get airborne as quickly as possible. After they reached fifteen thousand feet in their slow-climbing ships, they picked up a radio call from group headquarters telling them to patrol in the vicinity of Tarlac—just twenty miles due north—and intercept a flight of Japanese aircraft reported headed toward Clark.

NICHOLS FIELD, LUZON
7:45 A.M., DECEMBER 8, 1941

Eighteen combat-loaded 17th Pursuit Squadron P-40Es roared down the Nichols Field runway and began their climb to the north. In third position, just behind Wagner and his wingman, Cy Blanton, 2d Lt. Dave Obert was not feeling optimistic about their chances for a successful interception. He was thinking of the failures they had experienced while attempting bomber interceptions in their P-40Es during practice missions the previous month.[52]

DEL MONTE FIELD, MINDANAO
9:45 A.M., DECEMBER 8, 1941

Some five hundred miles south of Manila, 2d Lt. Earl Tash took off in his fully armed B-17D, climbed above the overcast, and headed north in the direction of Luzon. His 93d Squadron ship was in need of repairs that could not be carried out under the primitive conditions at Del Monte Field. The ranking officer among the flying crews of the 14th and 93d Squadrons on their temporary detachment to Del Monte, Maj. Emmett "Rosie" O'Donnell, had ordered Tash to take his bomber back to Clark for the needed repairs. He wanted every one of the sixteen B-17s there under his command ready for the combat missions they could face at any time. O'Donnell had learned of the Pearl Harbor attack in a radio call from Eubank at 6:05 that morning.[53]

Tainan Naval Air Base, Formosa
7:50 a.m., December 8, 1941

The fog finally lifted at 7:50 A.M., and the pilots of the Tainan and 1st Kōkūtai were relieved that no B-17s had been reported approaching their base. By that late hour, they certainly should have arrived if they were coming at all, they reasoned.[54]

Final arrangements for the takeoff of both flying groups were now made. At 8:18, the pilots of the Tainan Kū watched from the side as the 1st Kū's twenty-seven old Type 96 land-based attack bombers taxied into position for takeoff. As the lead bomber made a slow turn over the apron of the field, the Zero pilots could make out the white scarf of Lt. Comdr. Takeo Ozaki, the leader of this bomber attack force, who was sitting in the pilot's seat. They also saw the 1st Kū's ground crews lined up along the apron, waving their caps to say good-bye to the flying crews as they headed out on this momentous mission. As the *rikkō* stopped and waited at the takeoff point, the thundering sound of their engines permeated the air. Each of the twin-engine bombers was heavily loaded with twelve 132-pound bombs and fuel for the long round-trip to Clark Field and would need every foot of runway in order to get off in the almost complete absence of any wind over the field.

The *rikkō* slowly began their takeoff rolls, one by one. However, as the pilot of the bomber in the seventh position accelerated its engines for the takeoff—still some several hundred meters from the takeoff point—the bomber's landing gear suddenly collapsed. The ship veered to the right and the right wing touched the runway. Shocked by the scene, Sakai noticed a little fire on the ship that seemed to touch the gas tank. Burning gasoline spread over the fuselage. As members of the crew jumped out of the stricken bomber, Sakai heard what sounded like machine-gun fire, followed by explosions, and finally a tremendous explosion. The bomber was blown to bits before the Zero pilots' incredulous eyes. Fire engines had approached the burning aircraft, but they were too late.[55]

"What a bad omen for our departure on this historical occasion!" Sakai murmured under his breath. This moment should be a source of celebration, he reflected. Instead, the takeoff process was interrupted as ground crews hurriedly cleaned up the debris of the luckless bomber and removed the bodies of the five crewmembers killed in the accident. Within minutes, the runway was clear and the 1st Kū's remaining twenty *rikkō* resumed taking off.[56]

NEAR BAGUIO, LUZON
8:15 A.M., DECEMBER 8, 1941

Approaching Baguio after flying 145 miles due south along Luzon's mountainous west coast, 1st Lt. Yoshiaki Kubo, flying as observer/ commander in the eighth position in the formation of seventeen Ki-21-IIAs, was relieved that they had met no opposition. Earlier, one of their eighteen Type 97 heavy bombers had dropped out and returned to Choshu after becoming separated from the others. Aside from that, everything had thus far gone according to mission plan.

It was about 8:25 A.M. when the *rikko* passed over Camp John Hay in Baguio at thirteen thousand feet (four thousand meters) and on the signal of Capt. Ryōsuke Motomura in the lead ship began unloading their 220-pound bombs on the barracks and installations. The pilots hoped that General MacArthur was at the USAFFE summer retreat. They had been told prior to the mission that their attack on the camp was predicated on that assumption. After completing their bomb run, the Ki-21-IIAs made a wide right turn and headed west toward Lingayen Gulf, then began following the Luzon coastline north over the same route they had followed during the outward journey. None of the bombers had suffered any damage during the attack.[57]

OVER TUGUEGARAO AIRFIELD, LUZON
8:25 A.M., DECEMBER 8, 1941

At about the same time that the 14th Sentai bombers hit Baguio, the 8th Sentai's twenty-five Ki-48s were approaching their target: the airfield at Tuguegarao, sixty miles inland from Luzon's north coast. Captain Kiyosato Gotō and the other pilots had kept a sharp eye out for the enemy pursuit ships they feared would intercept them at any time. Much to their relief, none had been seen. Looking down on their target, they were disappointed to discover that the field had no installations whatsoever and there were no planes on the ground. There were just two runways connected in an L-shape, one longer than the other. It was about 8: 30 when the three *chūtai* of twin-engine bombers began their bomb run. Gotō watched as the lead 2d Chūtai bombs hit midway along the longer runway. Following behind, his own *chūtai* dropped its bombs on the angle of the L. The bombs of the 4th Chūtai, bringing up the rear, detonated about the same place as those of the 2d Chūtai. Their bombing mission completed, the 8th Sentai ships wheeled and headed back for Kato, 460 miles to the north.[58]

TAINAN NAVAL AIR BASE, FORMOSA
9:40 A.M., DECEMBER 8, 1941

The pilots of the Tainan Kū climbed into their Zero-sen and prepared for takeoff following the departure of the rest of the 1st Kū's *rikkō*. Although the twenty G3M2s had taken off without incident almost an hour earlier following the temporary aborting of the takeoff, the Tainan Kū pilots were still preoccupied with the terrible accident they had witnessed at 8:25. Masa-aki Shimakawa reflected on how loaded down his plane—like the G3M2 *rikkō*—was. The two 190-liter wing tanks, the 145-liter fuselage tank, and the 330-liter belly tank were full of gasoline for the long mission. Each of the two 20-mm cannon in the wings was loaded with sixty rounds of ammunition, and there were six hundred rounds of 7.7-mm ammunition for the two nose guns. But at least he had saved the twenty-kilogram (forty-four pounds) weight of the radio—Shingō had ordered them taken out.

Shimakawa put his pistol against his chest, holding it in position with the straps of his jacket. He then placed the flight chart beside his left foot. Ordinarily, he would have put on his parachute harness—he was sitting on the chute—but today he did not. He noticed that the other pilots were not taking their harnesses to attach to their parachutes, either. No one wanted to run the risk of being captured in the event of a bail-out over enemy territory. Shimakawa felt uneasy leaving his parachute harness behind, but the sound of his wheels squealing in protest as his Zero, "V-135" painted on its tail to identify it as a Tainan Kū fighter, was being held back with the throttle wide open reminded him that everything had already been decided. He was now in the hands of fate.[59]

Lieutenant Hideki Shingō began leading the eight pilots of his 1st Chūtai down the field for takeoff at 9:45 A.M. They needed to give the 1st Kū's slow Type 96 *rikkō* a considerable head start so that they—as well as the Takao Kū's faster Type 1 *rikkō*—could link up with the 1st Kū's bombers over northern Luzon for the run to Clark Field. As they passed over the part of the field where the accident had occurred, they were worried about the risk of puncturing their tires on scattered pieces of the wrecked bomber that had not been picked up.

Following behind Shingō's *chūtai* were the nine Zeros of Lt. Masuzō Setō's 2d Chūtai. Then came Lt. Masao Asai's 3d Chūtai. Shimakawa was in twenty-fourth position for takeoff—in Asai's *chūtai* as second wingman to Gitarō Miyazaki. Bringing up the rear were the nine pilots of Lt. Akira Wakao's 4th Chūtai.

After Shimakawa retracted his ship's landing gear, he set his engine for eighteen hundred rpm to save fuel. Using the manual pump, he then

Mᴀᴛsᴜʙɪsʜɪ A6M2 Zᴇʀᴏs ᴏғ ᴛʜᴇ 3ᴅ Kōᴋūᴛᴀɪ ʟɪɴᴇᴅ ᴜᴘ ᴏɴ Tᴀᴋᴀᴏ Fɪᴇʟᴅ ᴘʀɪᴏʀ ᴛᴏ
ᴛᴀᴋᴇᴏғғ ᴏɴ Dᴇᴄᴇᴍʙᴇʀ 8, 1941, ғᴏʀ ᴛʜᴇ ᴀᴛᴛᴀᴄᴋs ᴏɴ Iʙᴀ ᴀɴᴅ Cʟᴀʀᴋ Fɪᴇʟᴅs. Pʜᴏᴛᴏ
ᴄᴏᴜʀᴛᴇsʏ Tᴀᴍᴏᴛsᴜ Yᴏᴋᴏʏᴀᴍᴀ.

switched to the belly tank. They had been told to use the fuel from the
belly tank first so that they would not be encumbered with it when they
entered into combat. He knew he was not supposed to switch tanks at
such low altitude, but like the more experienced pilots, he did it anyway.
Climbing to three thousand meters (ten thousand feet), Shimakawa joined
the others circling at that altitude to form up before heading south. He
now adjusted his distance from the other ships by increasing his engine
rpm. Pessimistic thoughts flashed through his head. He expected that 80 to
90 percent of his fellow Tainan Kū pilots would not be coming back.[60]

Leading his three-ship *shōtai* in the Tainan Kū's seventh position, Saburō
Sakai looked up from his seat as he passed over southern Formosa, heading
south in his Zero with the recognition code "V-107" painted on its tail.
Above him was a huge formation of G4M1 Type 1 bombers, also moving
south in a V of Vs pattern. Must be the *rikkō* that took off from Takao to
the south, he thought.

At Takao, the Takao Kōkūtai's twenty-seven Type 1 *rikkō*, had begun
taking off at 9:30 A.M., led by Lt. Comdr. Taro Nonaka—fifteen minutes
ahead of the Tainan Kū's Zeros to the north. They were the first of the
three *rikkō* groups at Takao to get airborne. Their destination was Clark
Field. Eight minutes later, Comdr. Yoshizō Suda led his twenty-seven Type 1
bombers—the other half of the Takao Kū—into the air. Their target
was Iba Field. The last group of *rikkō* to leave the base—beginning at

9:55—was led by Comdr. Toshii Irisa, who was taking his twenty-seven Type 1 bombers of the Kanoya Kū to Iba Field, too.

Just after the Kanoya Kū's *rikkō* headed down the field in their take-off roll, Lt. Tamotsu Yokoyama began leading his group of 53 Zeros from the 3d Kū to the takeoff point according to the prearranged positions of each aircraft. Yokoyama's command *chūtai* of six aircraft was in the lead. Right behind was the 1st Daitai with 12 Zeros led by Lt. Takeo Kurasawa, followed by Lt. Ichirō Mukai's 2d Daitai, also with 12 Zeros. Lieutenant Zenjirō Miyano was at the head of the 3d Daitai's 17 Zeros behind Mukai, which included 9 under Lt. Yukio Maki, who had been borrowed from the Tainan Kū for this mission. Finally, in the trail position, were the six Zeros of Lt. Takaichi Hasuo's rear-defense *chūtai*.[61]

The five units that made up Yokoyama's attack force formed up perfectly after takeoff and headed south. The six Zeros of Yokoyama's *chūtai* were to serve as the spearhead of the attack, with Kurosawa's fighters directly behind them. Mukai's group was off on the right and Miyano's large *daitai* on the left. Hasuo's men brought up the rear behind Kurosawa's group. Way off to their right, the 3d Kū pilots could see Irisa's twenty-seven *rikkō* formed up in a beautiful V of Vs.[62]

A sense of immense pride swept through Yokoyama. Never before in his long flying career had he led fifty-three fighters into combat. He felt that life could hold nothing greater in store for him now.

CHAPTER 10

"Go Get 'Em!"

A s his P-40E circled over the Tarlac area in central Luzon at between
twelve thousand and fifteen thousand feet, Dave Obert wondered
where the Japanese intruders were that had been reported coming
in from the north. He and the rest of Buzz Wagner's 17th Pursuit
Squadron had reached the assigned position at about 8:45, but there
was no sight of the enemy. Suddenly, Obert's radio crackled: "prepare to
attack!" In response to his CO's order, he went into a sharp diving turn,
in third position behind Wagner and his wingman, Cy Blanton. But when
Blanton became separated from Wagner during the turn, Obert found
himself in second position in the six-ship flight. For a split second, his
heart in his throat, "pounding like a sledgehammer," Obert was tempted to
get lost on purpose. Suffering from the extreme tension of first combat, his
mouth was so dry that he was nearly choking. But he managed to control
his nerves and continued on down with the others.[1]

As soon as he drew close enough to make out his two adversaries,
Obert was shocked to see they were American B-17s, not Japanese bombers! Obert and his squadron mates had not been informed that the B-17s
had been ordered off of Clark Field for protective purposes at the time the
Japanese were reported headed toward the airfield. Reacting to the anti-
climactic turn of events, Obert felt deep disappointment that he was being
deprived of his first combat experience. He felt like letting off some steam.
"I'll test fire the guns," he thought. Like the others in the 17th Pursuit, he
had never tested his P-40E's six .50-caliber guns. Pulling the trigger, he
was taken aback by the tremendous recoil effect firing the six guns in uni-
son had on his ship.

After rejoining the others, Obert returned to his assigned patrol altitude. There they continued to circle the Tarlac area, but there was still no
sign of Japanese aircraft. Soon it was two and one-half hours after their
takeoff from Nichols and they were getting low on gas. Wagner radioed

them to head back to Clark field and land. Evidently the Japanese had changed their plans about bombing the field.[2]

Farther to the east, Charley Sneed's section of eighteen P-40Es had not spotted any Japanese during its patrol, either. Earlier, the 20th Pursuiters had been informed over their radios that the enemy was approaching. They, like the 17th Pursuit, now headed back to Clark Field.

While the 17th and 20th Pursuits circled near Tarlac on their fruitless interception mission, the pilots of the 3d Pursuit at Iba Field to the west were also a frustrated lot, sitting in their cockpits and waiting for orders that never came. They were becoming increasingly bored. For want of anything else to do, 1st Lt. Frank Neri and some of the others started playing with the receivers of their radio sets. Running across the different frequencies, Neri stopped at one and was startled to hear what was being reported. Baguio was being bombed, Aparri was also under attack, and Tuguegarao had been hit! The others also heard the reports. Yet they were still waiting for orders to take off![3]

The story was the same at Nichols Field. First Lieutenant Ed Dyess and the other twelve pilots of his 21st Pursuit Squadron, plus the five pilots attached to his squadron from the 3d and 17th Pursuit, sat under the wings of their P-40Es waiting for orders to take off that did not come. They were a tired lot, having twice that night been roused out of bed to report to 21st Squadron operations ready to take off. Then, at about 11 A.M., Dyess called them into the operations tent for Coca-Colas and sandwiches. Unlike the 3d Pursuiters, they had heard no reports of bombing attacks to the north.[4]

HEADQUARTERS, FAR EAST AIR FORCE
NIELSON FIELD, MANILA
10 A.M., DECEMBER 8, 1941

Lieutenant Colonel Eugene Eubank was meeting with his chief, Maj. Gen. Lewis Brereton, in Brereton's office in the FEAF headquarters building. Brereton had put another call through to MacArthur's chief of staff, Brig. Gen. Richard Sutherland at USAFFE headquarters. Brereton was urging offensive action by his 19th Group B-17s, but Sutherland continued to insist that USAFFE was still in a defensive posture. Sutherland's position was incomprehensible to Brereton, who had received a report more than half an hour before that Tarlac and Tuguegarao north of Clark Field were being bombed. Incensed, he warned Sutherland that if Clark Field were taken out by an attack, the FEAF would not be able to operate offensively. Moreover, to make sure that his position was on the record, Brereton instructed his chief of staff, Col. Francis Brady, to make a note of his conversation with Sutherland.

After his telephone exchange with Sutherland, Brereton told Eubank to get the 19th Bomb Group ready for a mission to Formosa and, in anticipation of eventual approval of a strike on the Japanese, prescribed the bomb load to be carried. Eubank, however, did not think it would be wise to load the bombs just yet. A change might be needed, he pointed out, which would require unloading and reloading. He added that it would also be dangerous to have fully loaded bombers on the ground in the event the Japanese attacked before they departed. Brereton agreed with his bomber chief's arguments and dropped his bombing-up instructions. Eubank should focus on preparations for the photorecon mission over southern Formosa, which Sutherland had just told Brereton MacArthur now approved.[5]

As Eubank took off in his B-18 at 10:10 and headed for Clark Field to take charge of bomber operations, most of his ships were milling around over central Luzon after being ordered aloft by Maj. Dave Gibbs, whom Eubank had left in command when he headed down to Nielson earlier that morning. The pilots had been told to keep their radios tuned to the Clark Field tower frequency for eventual orders to return, which meant they had to fly around central Luzon, keeping within the control tower's limited radio range.[6]

Six of the 19th Group's ships in the air were obsolete B-18s remaining with the 28th Bomb Squadron, "the bastard child of the Group," in the view of one of the original pilots, 1st. Lt. Thomas H. "Speed" Hubbard. Piloting one of them, 1st Lt. Tom Christian and his crew were flying continuously round and around Mount Arayat, to the east of the field, waiting for the recall order. Meanwhile, 1st Lt. Jim Bruce and his copilot, 2d. Lt. Dick Haney, were flying over Lake Taal, eighty-five miles south of Clark and well out of control tower range. Their B-18 was circling inside the rim of the well-known volcanic lake: up the fifteen-mile length, then across the ten-mile width, then down the length and over the width again, killing time while waiting for the radio call to return to Clark.

One of the B-17s was farther north than the others, on an armed patrol mission covering the waters between Formosa and Luzon. First Lieutenant Shorty Wheless and his crew in the 30th Squadron's 40-3070 had been ordered to take off with the other bombers during the 8:30 A.M. alert at Clark and then fly the prearranged patrol, looking for any sign of Japanese invasion forces on their way to the Philippines. By 10:30 they still had not spotted any Japanese forces in the waters north of Luzon.[7]

It was 10:30 before 1st Lt. John Carpenter was able to take off on his recon mission up Luzon's east coast. The generator on his 93d Squadron B-17D had finally been repaired. Meanwhile, at about the same time Carpenter took off, the Clark Field control tower radioed the other B-17s and

B-18s flying around over central Luzon that it was safe for them to land. Out of range of the control tower's radio, Wheless, who was far to the north, received an all-clear message from 19th Group's communications section and told his radio operator to find out if they were supposed to report back, too. They were instructed to continue their mission.[8]

OVER GARAMPI POINT, FORMOSA
10:15 A.M., DECEMBER 8, 1941

A t the head of a formation of thirty-five Zeros heading south at three thousand meters (9,840 feet) in loose formation, Lt. Hideki Shingō was just passing Garampi Point on Formosa's extreme southern tip when he noticed a formation of large aircraft below and ahead of him, heading north over the water toward Formosa. From his position in the sixth aircraft behind Shingō, FPO1c Saburō Sakai saw them, too. He immediately surmised that they were Americans, coming to attack the bases on Formosa as expected. He smiled as a strong fighting spirit surged through his body. "They will find an empty nest," he thought. All the bombers and fighters of the Philippine attack force had already left their bases.[9]

Sakai knew what he and eight other Tainan Kū pilots had to do in this situation. Prior to their departure from Tainan, Shingō had designated them to split off from the main group and attack any enemy planes they might encounter heading north from the Philippines to bomb their bases. They should keep their attack on the intruders brief and rejoin the main force as soon as possible. With strict fuel discipline in effect for this critical mission, no one could afford to be diverted from the objective of attacking Clark Field.

Plunging down, Sakai approached the enemy bombers. However, just as he was about to fire, he noticed that the aircraft had the Japanese *hino-maru* on their wings! "They are Army bombers!" he blurted out to himself. A feeling of relief gave way to anger. "At this moment when the destiny of Japan hangs in the balance, what are these Army planes doing here?" he wondered. "And what if we nine had dropped our belly tanks in preparation for attack? How could we have participated in the attack on the Philippines then?"[10] Sakai and the others immediately broke off their attack and began climbing to rejoin their formation, which looked like dots in the sky above and ahead of them.

But one of them would not be rejoining the group. Flight Petty Officer Third Class Shizuo Ishii, who had been slow to identify the intruders below, had needed more time to get into interception position. When he finally broke off his attack, he was unable to find the others. Alone, he had no alternative but to turn around and head back to Tainan base on Formosa. That left Ishii's *shōtai* leader, FPO1c Yoshimichi Saeki, all alone. Saeki had lost his other wingman, FPO2c Yoshimi Hidaka, soon after taking off from Tainan when Hidaka was unable to retract his landing gear. Now he was without his second wingman! Saeki slid into position fifty meters above and behind his *chūtai* leader, Lt. Masuzō Setō, determined to do his best to protect him.[11]

As he left Garampi behind and entered the Luzon Strait, Masa-aki Shimakawa watched the white caps of the waves below to estimate the direction and velocity of the wind. There seemed to be an extremely strong westerly wind. He entered this information into the logbook that he had started soon after takeoff. He was flying by compass, which was important in such a loose formation, out of sight of the others. Shimakawa and the eight others in Lieutenant Asai's *chūtai* were responsible for protecting the 1st Kōkūtai's twenty-six Type 96 *rikkō*, which were way ahead of them. They expected to catch up with the slow bombers over central Luzon and escort them for the last ten minutes of the outward flight, just before arriving over Clark Field. Shingō, with another twenty Zeros, was leading the group assigned responsibility for maintaining air control over the target, while the remaining pilots would escort the Takao Kōkūtai's twenty-seven Type 1 *rikkō* in the Clark Field attack force. One lone C5M2 from the Tainan Kū, commanded by Lt. Masami Miza, was also in their group, charged with observing the results of the attack.

Due to lack of sleep the night before, as well as the sun reflecting off the ocean below, Shimakawa began to feel very drowsy as he continued southward over the monotonous expanse of water. He took out some natural energy food to put in his mouth and tried to chew it, but was too sleepy even to do that, or even to reflect on whether this mission would be his last. Suddenly he realized he had moved up and was approaching too close to his *shōtaichō's* plane, almost ramming it! He could see Gitarō Miyazaki looking back at him, his fist pressed against the canopy as a warning. "If I ever return alive from this mission, I'll be reprimanded," Shimakawa thought.[12]

Ahead of Shimakawa, FPO1c Kuniyoshi Tanaka, flying as Shingō's main wingman, was not feeling sleepy, but he was bored, cooped up as he was in the Zero's small cockpit on the long flight. To break the monotony and also to provide some energy, he reached into a bag on the cockpit floor and extracted several bananas he had brought with him. He had packed two bags of them, one to eat on the way to the Philippines and one on the way back. Shingō turned to his left inside his cramped cockpit and saw his wingman moving his mouth, a banana in his left hand. Smiling weakly, he mumbled to himself, "He, too, is bored." Unseen by Shingō, others in the formation were chewing caramels or drinking cider. It was indeed a long and boring flight.

Two months earlier, upon being promoted to flight petty officer first class and transferred to the Tainan Kū, Tanaka had expected to be made a *shōtaichō*, a position to which his new rank and long experience entitled him. Instead, Shingō had designated him as his lead wingman. Initially angry, Tanaka later realized it was more important to protect the flying commander than to have his own *shōtai*. Anyway, he figured, Shingō was "a bit old" and would let him fly *shōtai* lead in combat.[13]

HEADQUARTERS, FAR EAST AIR FORCE
NIELSON FIELD, MANILA
10:14 A.M., DECEMBER 8, 1941

The telephone in General Brereton's office rang. When he picked it up, he found to his surprise that General MacArthur himself was on the line. It was the first time that day the USAAFE commander had made direct contact with his air force commander. Brereton informed him that the Japanese aircraft earlier believed to be heading for Clark Field had not bombed his base after all and that his bomber force remained intact. Accordingly, he had ordered Eubank to mount a photoreconnaissance mission over southern Formosa and was holding his B-17s in readiness until the recon reports were received. However, even in the absence of such reports, he wanted to attack Formosa late that afternoon. MacArthur told Brereton the decision on offensive action was his to make. The FEAF commander was relieved. The USAFFE commander had finally decided to allow him to take action. Sutherland's order to abstain from offensive operations, issued just fourteen minutes earlier, had just been countermanded by his chief.

Given the authority he needed, Brereton called his staff in for a meeting to decide on a course of action. After briefing them on his phone conversation with MacArthur, Brereton told them to develop a plan of attack against known airdromes in southern Formosa. The plan was completed by 10:45, and Brereton approved it. Two squadrons of B-17s loaded with one-hundred- and three-hundred-pound bombs would attack airfields on southern Formosa south of 23 degrees, 10 minutes north latitude "immediately before darkness" to neutralize Japanese airpower on the island. Meanwhile, the two B-17 squadrons at Del Monte would be moved up to San Marcelino airdrome on Luzon's west coast "at the earliest practicable moment," then would shift to Clark Field after dark and prepare for operations at daybreak on December 9.[14]

CLARK FIELD, LUZON
11 A.M., DECEMBER 8, 1941

Lieutenant Colonel Eubank and his operations officer, Major Walsh, landed in their B-18 at about 11 A.M. following their meeting with Brereton and his staff at FEAF headquarters in Manila. The 5th Bomber Command chief found that there had been an alert in their absence and that Major Gibbs had "very properly" ordered all of the 19th Group's planes into the air. Eubank and Walsh were informed that an "all clear" had been issued at Clark and radio calls made to the bombers circling in the area to return to base.

When 1st Lt. Kenny Kreps, 19th Group Officer of the Day, walked into 19th Group operations building shortly after Eubank's return, he found Eubank and Walsh in discussion there. Eubank looked at Kreps and said: "We've got our mission. It's a photographic mission to Formosa. The other planes are just to stand by." Eubank had received FEAF Field Order 1 to mount the photographic mission over southern Formosa, which had been Teletyped to him at Clark at 11:20 by FEAF headquarters.[15]

Except for those flown by Wheless and Carpenter, which were still patrolling, all of Eubank's B-17s had returned to Clark, as had some of his B-18s. They taxied over to dispersal positions around the field, including horseshoe-shaped revetments made of dirt heaped fifteen feet high. Gas trucks were sent out to refuel them as the crews walked to the mess hall for lunch.[16]

When he landed at about eleven after his section's fruitless patrol over the Tarlac area, Charley Sneed led the 20th Pursuit's P-40B pilots back to their usual perimeter location in their revetted positions for refueling. Upon landing, the 17th Pursuit's pilots, on the other hand, had taxied their P-40Es over to Hangars 1 and 2, where they parked their ships out front, wingtip to wingtip, for refueling. As visitors to the field, they had no pre-pared dispersal positions.[17]

The pilots of the two pursuit squadrons headed over to 24th Group operations to report on their Tarlac patrol. In the group's operations hangar, Major Grover informed them that while they had been circling around the area to which they had been ordered, Baguio and Tuguegarao to the north had been bombed by two flights of Japanese planes. Shocked, the airmen tried to figure out what had happened. Dave Obert thought that the bombers that hit Baguio must have spotted the P-40s waiting for them seventy miles to the south and decided to switch their original target of Clark to Camp John Hay in the summer capital city. Carl Gies in the 20th Pursuit had a more ominous explanation for the assumed aborted mission of the Japanese: He suspected that fifth columnists operating secret radio stations on Luzon had alerted both groups of Japanese bombers that P-40s were waiting for them to the south.[18]

Masa-aki Shimakawa looked down from his high-flying Zero and saw blackness ahead of him instead of the water over which he had been cruising for the past hour. Trying to make out what he observed, he realized that it was actually *land,* greenish-black rain forest. "We are finally arriving over enemy territory," he thought, his adrenalin pumping. The excitement caused him to feel the need to urinate. Taking out the receptacle for this purpose next to his seat, he relieved himself with difficulty in the cramped cockpit. Then he slid back the canopy and threw the full container out, taking care not to hit the fuselage. As it passed out of sight, he mused, "My first bullet of the war!"[19]

Shimakawa realized that Clark Field was still a long way from Luzon's north shore (225 miles to be exact), but he began to look closely around him for any sign of enemy planes. There were none. He would not have sighted the Takao Kōkūtai's twenty-seven Type 1 *rikkō*—on their southward mission a few minutes ahead of the Tainan Kū pilots—and he was much too late to have spotted the 1st Kōkūtai's twenty-six slower Type 96 *rikkō,* which they would eventually escort to Clark, and which would have passed over Luzon's northern tip at about 10:45.[20]

Unknown to Shimakawa and the others in the attack force, they were being picked up by radar as they proceeded in their different formations down Luzon's central valley after reaching a point about 150 miles short of Clark Field, the outer range of Iba's SCR-270B set. To their right, off Luzon's western shore, the Kanoya Kōkūtai's twenty-seven *rikkō* and the other twenty-seven of the split Takao Kōkūtai, with fifty-three 3d Kū Zeros under Yokoyama following behind, were also being picked up by the Iba radar as they entered the range of its set, too.[21]

Private Tom Lloyd was working the oscilloscope after going on duty in the SCR-270B operations van at Iba at ten that morning. After staring at a blank screen for more than an hour and a quarter, he began picking up bogies at about 11:20. One group was headed south, coming toward Iba from the west, 129 miles out. Seven minutes later he reported that it was farther south, about seventy miles west of the Lingayen Gulf. A second group was also producing many echoes as it headed south over Luzon toward Clark Field. The SCR-270B's limitations did not allow him to determine the exact number of aircraft or their altitude, but the strength of the echoes indicated to Lloyd that the formations were large. One of the operations van men excitedly telephoned the information to Sgt. Wade Nelms in the detachment's radio tent. Following established procedures, Nelms then radioed the sightings to the AWS at FEAF headquarters at Nielson Field. Private Maurice Chartoff, an AWS radio operator, received the report, which gave the tracks of the planes heading toward Clark and Iba according to range and azimuth, and passed it to the officers in the AWS room.[22]

The duty crew inside the operations van was frantically busy as new flights appeared on the oscilloscope before old ones were out of sight. Each sighting was telephoned to Nelms, who radioed it to the AWS at Nielson Field. Lloyd estimated that the group heading toward Iba was forty-seven miles out when he turned his position over to Pvt. Henry Brodginski at noon. However, as the other group headed down Lingayen Valley to the east in the direction of Clark Field, interference from the echoes produced by mountains between Iba and the valley made further aircraft tracking impossible.[23]

Air Warning Service Operations
FEAF Headquarters, Nielson Field, Manila
11:30 a.m., December 8, 1941

In the AWS's big operations room, which shared one wing of the FEAF headquarters building with the 5th Interceptor Command, Lt. Col. Alexander Campbell and his executive officer, Maj. Harold Coyle, and Capt. Sam Lamb, CO of the FEAF communications section, watched excitedly as their operations men plotted the sightings on a horizontal, electrically lighted, table-mounted map of the Philippines measuring about fifteen feet square as the radioed reports from Iba were being received. They were also receiving telephone calls from numerous watchers on Luzon reporting sightings of aircraft heading south in groups of varying numbers. By then, Colonel George; his operations officer, Bud Sprague; and intelligence officer, Allison Ind, had joined them, as had General Brereton himself.

At about 11:30, and again at 11:45, after watching the progress of the flights—one headed toward Iba and the other on a line to Clark—Campbell had warning messages sent out to all FEAF units by radio and by Teletype, where available. They were Teletyped to the Clark Field communications center, located in the 24th Pursuit Group's operations hangar.[24]

After absorbing the information radioed to the AWS by the Iba radar detachment, Brereton walked back to his office in the other wing of the FEAF headquarters building. Then at 11:55, Sutherland was on the telephone to him again. He informed Brereton that MacArthur wanted to be brought up to date on air operations developments since his call to Brereton at 10:14. Brereton briefed Sutherland on the Iba radar reports. The Japanese were operating in two groups, with from fifteen to twenty-four planes in each group. Thus far there had been no actual contact with them. Brereton then informed Sutherland of his plans to strike the Formosa bases late in the afternoon and that he would be shifting his two squadrons of B-17s at Del Monte to San Marcelino, ready for offensive operations out of Clark after daybreak on December 9.[25]

24TH PURSUIT GROUP OPERATIONS
CLARK FIELD, LUZON
LATE MORNING, DECEMBER 8, 1941

The Teletype machine in the rear of the 24th Group's operations hangar at Clark Field was clicking away late in the morning as messages were being received by its operator, Pfc. Sam Litchfield. To protect it during a bombing attack, the headquarters men a few days earlier had put sandbags all around and across the top of the brown, civilian-issue machine. Major Grover had already gone into the sandbagged area several times to pick up Teletype messages.

In addition to the radar sightings, reports by Filipino civilian spotters were flooding into group operations from the AWS, including via its big SCR-197 radio communications van just outside the hangar as well as over the Teletype machine. From about eleven on, 1st Lt. George Armstrong—detailed from the 17th Pursuit a week earlier to provide Grover with an experienced communications officer—and the 24th Group headquarters communications men struggled to identify bona fide messages from among all those of various sources the AWS was sending them so that they could indicate on the big plotting board at their end of the hangar the positions of the enemy flights heading southward over Luzon and the South China Sea.[26]

At about 11:30, Grover received a Teletype report from the AWS of a large formation of bombers over the China Sea, which he believed was headed for Manila. Fifteen minutes later, he received another Teletype report, this one of a bomber formation headed south over the Lingayen Gulf. The 11:30 report prompted Grover to order the 3d Pursuit Squadron at Iba to attempt to intercept the bombers heading in from the China Sea.

The SCR-197 radio operator was instructed to transmit orders to Thorne at Iba to get his eighteen P-40Es airborne immediately and to wait over Iba at fifteen thousand feet for the incoming Japanese.[27]

Grover apparently realized that the 11:45 message meant the Japanese planes might be headed for Clark Field. However, neither his Clark-based 20th Pursuit nor the visiting 17th Pursuit had been completely refueled and rearmed. That left him the 34th Pursuit at nearby Del Carmen, with its eighteen P-35As, and the 21st Pursuit at Nichols, with eighteen brand-new P-40Es. The 34th was ordered to patrol over Manila. Just after receiving the 11:45 message, Grover radioed orders over the SCR-197 instructing the 21st Squadron to take off and cover Clark Field.[28]

IBA FIELD, ZAMBALES, LUZON
11:45 A.M., DECEMBER 8, 1941

The 3d Pursuit Squadron's radio operator handed a message to his CO, 1st Lt. Hank Thorne. It was from Major Grover at Clark and tersely stated, "Point Iba, 15,000 feet." Thorne passed the instructions to his three flight leaders, who had been impatiently waiting since early morning for takeoff orders, then ran to where his P-40E was parked at the south end of the field. By the time the last of the six aircraft in Thorne's A Flight had lifted off, a giant cloud of dust heavily obscured the field. With his visibility limited, B Flight leader Ed Woolery opted to take off from his position at the north end of the field instead of taxiing to the south end for takeoff, as originally agreed. From his midfield position, Herb Ellis found on taxiing to the south end that the other five planes in his C Flight had not joined him. With his engine beginning to overheat, Ellis decided to take off alone and pick up the rest of his flight over the field.

Minutes later, circling over Iba Field at a thousand feet, Ellis waited for the others in his flight to join him. He had watched them taking off, but was unable to spot them afterward in the sky over Iba. For some reason, they apparently were not going to link up with their leader, he figured. After a few more minutes, Ellis gave up and started to climb to his assigned altitude of fifteen thousand feet.[29]

Unseen by Ellis, four of the pilots from his C Flight were also climbing and had run into the six P-40Es of Ed Woolery's B Flight as they were ascending. Ellis's orphans joined up with Woolery's group. A few minutes later, several of the pilots picked up a radio call from 24th Group operations at Clark Field, ordering them to head to Manila instead of patrolling over Iba. Aborting his climb at six thousand feet, Woolery turned southeastward to lead his ten-ship group to the capital city. However, out of sight of Woolery's contingent, Hank Thorne and the rest of his A Flight continued their climb to fifteen thousand feet over Iba. They had not picked up the radio call changing the squadron's instructions.[30]

21ST PURSUIT SQUADRON OPERATIONS
NICHOLS FIELD, LUZON
11:45 A.M., DECEMBER 8, 1941

Ed Dyess was in the operations tent with his pilots, having an early lunch of sandwiches and Coca-Cola, when the phone rang. It was a takeoff order from 24th Group operations: "Tally Ho, Clark Field." Responding instantly, the 21st Pursuit Squadron's pilots ran to their P-40Es lined up at one end of the field and began taxiing to the runway. Minutes later, Dyess, climbing for altitude at the head of the twelve ships of both A and B Flights, got on the radio and advised group operations that he was taking the squadron up to twenty-four thousand feet and heading for Clark Field as ordered.

Second Lieutenant Bob Clark's C Flight was not with him, however. Clark and several others were having trouble with the Allison engines of their brand-new P-40Es, which had been assembled only a few days earlier. When C Flight finally did get airborne five minutes later, the pilots were unable to locate the rest of their squadron. There was no message from Dyess over their radios, either, so Clark, in the absence of orders, decided to take the opportunity to test their guns for the first time and led the others southwest to Laguna de Bay, the huge lake five miles south of Nichols Field, for that purpose. As soon as they were over the lake they fired their six .50-caliber wing guns in short bursts into the water below.[31]

Just north of Manila, Dyess received a radio call from group operations as he led his twelve-ship formation north toward Clark Field. He was to turn around and take his squadron back to the Manila area, to a point over Manila Bay between Corregidor and Cavite. There they were to await incoming Japanese bombers, apparently coming in from the west to attack Manila.

After testing their guns over Laguna de Bay at low altitude, C Flight leader Bob Clark and his wingman, 2d Lt. Jimmy May, were again having problems with their brand-new ships, whose engines had not yet finished being slow timed. The Allisons were throwing oil on their windshields, obstructing their vision. Clark radioed the others that he and May would have to abort the mission and return to Nichols Field.[32]

Second Lieutenant Sam Grashio, a Class 41-C flying school graduate from Spokane, Washington, took over the rump flight. Neither Grashio nor the three others had picked up the radio call from group operations.

With 2d Lt. Gus Williams on his wing, and 2d Lts. Joe Cole and Johnny McCown (Cole's wingman), Grashio headed north to Clark in a steep climb, unaware of the squadron's changed orders.[33]

19TH BOMB GROUP HEADQUARTERS
CLARK FIELD, LUZON
11:30 A.M., DECEMBER 8, 1941

Some forty senior 19th Bomb Group flying officers were assembled in the wooden, two-story group headquarters building at the west end of Clark Field, summoned to meet there by their commanding officer, Lieutenant Colonel Eubank. All but two of them were members of the group Eubank had brought with him from the states in October. The exceptions were Capt. Bill Fisher and 2d Lt. Richard Carlisle, who had come over with the 14th Bomb Squadron in September from Hawaii. Most were assigned to the 30th Bomb Squadron, with several others coming from Headquarters Squadron and five from the 28th Bomb Squadron, who had recently been transferred in from the 14th (Fisher, Carlisle), 30th (1st Lt. Al Mueller), and 93d Squadrons (1st Lts. Clyde Box and Fred Crimmins) to provide the 28th Squadron with B-17 capability. Many had eaten an early lunch before reporting for the meeting.

Eubank had received two orders from FEAF headquarters to execute missions over southern Formosa that he wanted to inform them about. The earlier order had been sent via Teletype from Nielson at 11:20, and the other, received just minutes before the meeting, had been passed to him by Capt. Charles Miller of his headquarters. The 11:20 order confirmed the oral instructions Eubank received from Brereton at FEAF headquarters to mount a photoreconnaissance mission over southern Formosa, focusing on the location and numbers of aircraft on airdromes. The second order was the one they had been waiting to hear all morning: They were to strike Japanese airfields on southern Formosa with sixteen B-17s before dusk.[34]

Eubank gave three 30th Squadron pilots the photorecon mission. First Lieutenant Ed Broadhurst, the squadron operations officer, would lead the mission, joined by 1st Lts. Sig Young and Ray Schwanbeck. Eubank released them for a quick lunch, but instructed them to report back at noon with their flight crews for a briefing on the mission. Since their B-17s did not have cameras, Eubank ordered that a B-18 be sent up from Nichols Field with the K-7 cameras they were to use to take the photographs.[35]

Eubank next discussed plans for the bombing attack with the remaining officers. He told them to arrange to have their B-17s gassed and bombed up with fourteen three-hundred-pound bombs each, ready to take off at about 2 P.M. so as to be able to hit Japanese airfields on Formosa south of 23 degrees, 10 minutes before darkness fell. The order called for sixteen ships to stage the mission, but Eubank had only thirteen available. Of the 19 B-17s at Clark, 2 were out flying on patrol, 1 was still out of commission (40-3093), and 3 were assigned to the photorecon mission.[36]

Broadhurst, Schwanbeck, and Young showed up at group headquarters with their flight crews shortly after noon, and Eubank accompanied them to the briefing room on the ground floor of the wooden building. Their B-17s had been prepared for the mission and were ready to go, except that the cameras due up from Nichols had not yet arrived. Eubank turned the briefing session over to his operations officer, Major Walsh, who was using a chalkboard in front of the crews. Out of the corner of his eye, Cpl. Douglas Logan, a 30th Squadron gunner and armorer selected to go on the mission as a cameraman, noticed Eubank on his left, alternately standing and sitting.[37]

Some of the pilots slated for the attack mission were still discussing plans elsewhere in group headquarters, while others were leaving for lunch or to make arrangements with their crews for servicing and bombing up their ships before sending them off for lunch. As Dick Carlisle headed for his quarters to eat, he paused momentarily as a squadron of P-40s roared off the field. Squadron mate Fred Crimmins had left the building to check out his B-17D (40-2067) in its revetment. He was pleased to find that the crew had already loaded it with the three-hundred-pound bombs. It was 12:25.[38]

In another room in the group headquarters building, Melvin McKenzie was delaying going to lunch so that he could complete a special task: tracing a classified sketch of Japanese airfields on southern Formosa and making copies of it for the navigators going on the photorecon and strike missions. Ed Whitcomb, in charge of the maps and general navigation equipment for the group's squadrons, had just received some new maps of Formosa and fellow navigator Hal McAuliff was helping him make mimeograph copies of them. The photorecon mission puzzled Whitcomb, who wondered, "What do they want to know that they don't already know?"[39]

Just behind Whitcomb's office, in the SCR-197 communications van next to the 19th Group's little communications building, 2d Lt. Stancill Nanney was just leaving for lunch. Working in 1st Lt. Warner Croxton's group communications section on loan from the 93d Squadron, Nanney had been kept busy that morning sending and receiving radio messages, including in code, to and from the radio operators on Carpenter's and Wheless's patrolling B-17Ds. Just before leaving the van, he radioed Carpenter instructions to return. However, Nanney had received no radio messages from the AWS at Nielson regarding Japanese aircraft heading toward Clark, nor had 24th Pursuit Group's operations called on the telephone to relay any such messages, as called for in FEAF standard operating procedures.[40]

OVER CENTRAL LUZON
12:15 P.M., DECEMBER 8, 1941

At three thousand meters over central Luzon and about sixty-five miles due north of Clark Field, the Tainan Kōkūtai's thirty-four pilots began their final attack preparations. In another twenty minutes they would be over the enemy air base. Shōtai leader Saburō Sakai reached for his oxygen mask and put it on, preparatory for a gradual climb to seven thousand meters (22,966 feet). As Sakai and the others began ascending in their Zeros, they tightened up their loose formation, first according to *chūtai,* then by *shōtai,* so as to be in the best position in the event they were attacked by enemy fighters.

In Masao Asai's *chūtai,* Masa-aki Shimakawa was paying close attention to his front, back, left, right, up, and down as he moved closer to his *shōtai* leader to assume his fighting position. He did not want to miss even the smallest objects in the sky. He did not like wearing his oxygen mask because it restricted neck movement so much. However, he knew that if he did not use oxygen at the altitude he was headed for, both his eyesight and thinking ability would be adversely affected. They had almost caught up with the slow-moving Type 96 bombers they were to escort on the last leg of the flight to Clark Field. Shimakawa could make them out, ahead of him, off to his right, heading south. There were no enemy planes in the air. Everything seemed so peaceful. It was hard for him to believe that a war would soon be starting.[41]

Behind and to the right of Shimakawa and the rest of the Tainan Kū, Lt. Masami Miza in his Type 98 reconnaissance plane was surprised to find no east–west line of enemy fighters across northern Luzon, waiting to intercept them. Why were the Americans not patrolling? Turning and bending forward, Miza yelled to the pilot, "Ōhara, we will reconnoiter the fighting over Clark and then head to Iba and Del Carmen."[42]

SCR-270B OPERATIONS VAN
IBA, ZAMBALES, LUZON
11:55 A.M., DECEMBER 8, 1941

Some seventy miles to the southwest of Shimakawa's position, the atmosphere was tense inside the operations van housing Iba Field's SCR-270B radar set. Just before scope man Henry Brodginski was due to go back on duty at noon in relief of Tom Lloyd, the Iba AWS detachment commander, Lieutenant Wimer, told him that Lloyd had picked up two large groups of bogies half an hour earlier. One was headed toward Iba from the northwest and the other down Luzon in Clark Field's direction.

Wimer had been watching the progress of the flights with Lloyd. The huge echoes visible on the oscilloscope were an indicator of the two groups' large size. He told the men they were going to be bombed.

Taking his position in front of the oscilloscope, which was enclosed by a black curtain, Brodginski began manipulating the antenna array mounted on the trailer outside the van to rotate it back and forth through its 360-degree arc to reach the position where the echoes given off by the bogies reached their maximum amplitude. Fixing on the location of the Iba-bound group, he yelled "range, 37 miles!" to Pfc. Eugene McDonough, the plotter-teller on duty with him, who passed the information to Sergeant Nelms in the radio tent outside for transmission to the AWS at Nielson Field. Nelms had been constantly busy for the past forty-five minutes, radioing the flights' progress every additional twenty or thirty miles as the reports were given to him to pass on to Nielson.[43]

AIR WARNING SERVICE OPERATIONS
FEAF HEADQUARTERS, NIELSON FIELD
12:15 P.M., DECEMBER 8, 1941

Lieutenant Colonel Campbell was becoming increasingly anxious as he watched the reports radioed in from Iba being marked on the plotting table. Half an hour had passed since the 11:45 warning message about the Clark-bound radar sighting had been sent via Teletype to Clark Field and other FEAF units, but no further warnings had gone out. Particularly concerned about the group of bogies heading toward Clark Field, Campbell had been urging Colonel George and his operations officer, Capt. Bud Sprague, to send another message to the 24th Group. However, George and Sprague were waiting for the bogeys to reach a certain distance from Clark before acting. They assured Campbell that the pursuit group would be ready to intercept the attackers when ordered to do so. Then, at about 12:15, Sprague wrote out a message and showed it to Colonel George and Lieutenant Colonel Campbell. After reading the text, the AWS chief asked Sprague, "What does 'kickapoo' mean?" He replied: "Go get 'em!" Then Sprague took the message to the Teletype room for transmission to 24th Group operations.[44]

OVER CARIDAD, SOUTHWEST OF MANILA
12:15 P.M., DECEMBER 8, 1941

As the interception order to Major Grover at Clark Field was being routed via Teletype from FEAF headquarters at Nielson Field in Manila, Ed Woolery and the nine other pilots in the 3d Pursuit Squadron's

B and C Flights were flying six thousand feet above Caridad, headed northeast for Manila. They had been spotted and their presence reported to the 16th Naval District in Manila as "nationality unknown." Unseen by the 3d Pursuiters, twelve P-40Es from the 21st Pursuit led by Ed Dyess were beginning to patrol about twelve miles to the south, but ten thousand feet higher.[45]

On reaching Manila Bay minutes later, Woolery and the others decided to circle for a while, hoping to pick up a radio call with further orders. However, they were unable to pick up anything on their radios, which were tuned to the standard 4495-kilocycle frequency assigned to the 24th Group for all air-to-air and ground-to-air calls. At about 12:20, Andy Krieger heard a lot of yelling over his radio. The radio operator was excitedly calling "Tally Ho, Clark Field! All pursuit to Clark! Messerschmitts over Clark!" Krieger and the other 3d Pursuiters responded immediately, turning their aircraft northward.

Woolery's group heading to Clark was down to eight ships. Instead of circling Manila with the others, the two "tail-end Charlies" in the ten-ship group had continued to the east, past the capital city. Second Lieutenants Don Steele and Ship Daniel had not heard the call for help from Clark Field, but they did spot the others turning to go north. They pointed their P-40Es in the same direction, but not knowing the gravity of the message, dawdled behind the others and soon fell some thirty miles behind their squadron mates racing toward Clark.[46]

24TH PURSUIT GROUP OPERATIONS
CLARK FIELD, LUZON
12:05 P.M., DECEMBER 8, 1941

In the 24th Group's operations hangar at Clark, 1st Lt. Buzz Wagner of the 17th Pursuit and his two flight leaders anxiously awaited the order to take off, but Major Grover seemed unable to make up his mind on a course of action. Earlier, he had radioed the airborne 3d Pursuiters over Iba to cover the Manila area instead of trying to intercept the incoming Japanese over Iba. He then ordered Dyess's 21st Pursuit to switch its patrol area from Clark Field to Manila Bay. To Grover, the apparent target of the approaching Japanese force was Manila, the capital city. He had not received any other Teletype warning messages since the 11:45 one of aircraft over Lingayen heading toward Clark, which he distrusted. Meanwhile, the radio in the SCR-197 van crackled with AWS calls based on native spotters' sighting reports, but how reliable were they?[47]

Responding to the anxiety of 1st Lt. Buzz Wagner and his flight leaders, 1st Lts. William Feallock and John Brownewell, Grover finally ordered

COLONEL ORRIN L. GROVER, COMMANDER OF THE 24TH PURSUIT GROUP AT CLARK FIELD FROM SEPTEMBER–DECEMBER, 1941, POSES AT HIS DESK IN JULY, 1943. U.S. AIR FORCE PHOTO COURTESY NATIONAL AIR AND SPACE MUSEUM.

them to get the 17th Pursuit aloft at about 12:10. They were to patrol the Manila area at eighteen thousand feet and intercept any Japanese bombers approaching from the west. Grover apparently still considered Manila as the objective of both Japanese attack groups. As the trio raced from the building, Wagner yelled at the fifteen pilots waiting outside the hangar and they all ran to their ships, parked in a long row in front of Hangars 1 and 2, where they had been refueled and serviced. With the exception of B Flight leader Feallock and Dave Obert in A Flight—each delayed by engine trouble—the 17th Pursuiters roared off the field, led by Wagner, and climbed for altitude before heading south to the Manila area.[48]

Minutes later, another Teletype message came in over the group's machine. It was an order from Colonel George at 5th Interceptor Command instructing the 24th Group CO to intercept Japanese aircraft approaching Clark Field.[49] Grover, in response to the order, apparently directed his communications section to radio all airborne pursuit ships over its powerful SCR-197 transmitters to get back to Clark Field posthaste. The radio operator in the communications van repeatedly called out: "Tally Ho, Clark Field! Tally Ho, Clark Field!" over the group frequency. Inside the hangar, Sgt. James Madden and the others heard the order being given over the loudspeaker on the hangar wall, which amplified all radio traffic between the communications van and aircraft in flight.[50]

While other pursuit pilots were being ordered to Clark, Grover was holding his old 20th Pursuit Squadron on the ground. Sitting in their cockpits, the pilots of Joe Moore's 1st Section anxiously awaited takeoff orders while eating sandwiches sent out to them by their CO. The ground crews sought shelter from the searing midday sun under the wings of the eighteen P-40Bs. Moore himself was in the 20th's operations shack some two hundred yards from the group operations hangar, sticking close to the telephone in case Grover called. The 24th Group CO had earlier told him that as soon as the conflicting reports of Japanese aircraft sightings could be sorted out, he would order the squadron to take off.[51]

Over at the Clark Field headquarters building, the base adjutant general had just received a disturbing phone call from his counterpart at Fort Stotsenburg, a few thousands yards to the east. Captain Garry Anloff at Fort Stotsenburg had received a call from the postmaster at Tarlac, just twenty-one miles to the north, saying that about twenty-five unidentified planes had been spotted in the vicinity of Tarlac at 12:25 and were headed south toward Clark Field. Anloff was calling to pass the information on to the Clark Field adjutant, Maj. Lee Johnson, for action on his part. Unknown to Anloff and Johnson, the Tarlac postmaster had also called the report in to the AWS at Nielson in accordance with prescribed Air Warning procedures for spotters.[52]

Over Clark Field
12:30 p.m., December 8, 1941

Ed Woolery and his B Flight—minus Don Steele and Ship Daniel, but plus the four C Flight pilots—began flying in a circular pattern over Clark Field at about 12:30. The 3d Pursuiters had applied maximum rpm to reach Clark as soon as possible in response to the "Tally Ho" call they had picked up over Manila Bay some fifteen minutes earlier. But where were the Japanese planes they were supposed to intercept? Then Andy Krieger noticed two aircraft above him and pointed them out to Woolery. After Krieger and Woolery went into a climbing turn and chandelled onto the tails of the two planes, they realized they were P-40s, but no one could make out who was flying them. "False alarm," Krieger figured. However, with no radio messages coming in from 24th Group below them, Woolery decided to lead the eight-plane contingent back to their home base at Iba for refueling and new orders.[53]

Unseen by Woolery's pilots, four other P-40s appeared over Clark, but at a much higher altitude than that being flown by the 3d Pursuiters. Sam Grashio had led the remnant of the 21st Pursuit's C Flight up to Clark from Manila, still ignorant of the change of orders shifting the 21st's patrol area to Manila Bay. Everything seemed peaceful as they began circling in the cloudless sky. After a few minutes, the four 21st Pursuiters spotted a group of single-engine aircraft to the west of Clark Field, headed toward the China Sea. Grashio assumed they were the P-40Es that Dyess had led off from Nichols Field at 11:45, patrolling over Clark according to the orders Dyess had received from 24th Group operations prior to takeoff. Happy to be able to link up with the rest of the pilots in his squadron, Grashio led the three others after them. As they gained on the other aircraft, Grashio could identify them as P-40s, but he was puzzled to see only six of them—half the number Dyess had led off from Nichols. Wondering which squadron they were from, the 21st Pursuiters closed in to try to identify the ships by their tail numbers, but were unsuccessful.

Ed Woolery and the five other 3d Pursuiters he was leading back to Iba did not notice the four P-40s approaching from the rear at their own altitude. Woolery's splintered 3d Pursuit group had become separated from Fred Roberts and Bill Powell while over Clark Field and was down to six ships. Roberts and Powell were also headed back to Iba, but they were still several miles behind Woolery's group as their watches indicated 12:35.[54]

CHAPTER 11

"Navy, Hell, It's the Japs!"

Joe Moore was still outside the 20th Pursuit Squadron operations shack at Clark Field at 12:35 P.M., waiting for orders from Major Grover at 24th Group operations to scramble his pilots for takeoff. Suddenly, one of the squadron's crew chiefs standing near the shack cried, "Good God Almighty, yonder they come!" The 20th Pursuit's CO looked up into the cloudless sky and saw a long line of planes flying very high in a V of Vs. They looked awfully small to Moore. Could they possibly be carrier fighters? Ready for just such a situation, Moore ordered the squadron's red flag run up the flagpole outside the operations shack as a signal to the pilots of his 1st Section, waiting in the cockpits of their aircraft near the flight line, to take off immediately. Running to his waiting P-40B, he yelled at his crew chief to "Wind her up!"

Behind Moore's ship, his wingman, 2d Lt. Randy Keator, was standing next to his P-40B, parked in the number-two position for takeoff. Second Lieutenant Edwin Gilmore was sitting in his cockpit in the number-three position, anxiously awaiting the order that was now received. Behind him, parked near the operations shack, were A Flight's other three P-40Bs. Spread out in the squadron's dispersal area, the pilots of B and C Flights also reacted to the signal to take off.[1]

Second Lieutenant Jack Gates of Charley Sneed's 2d Section came out of the operations shack and stood looking skyward at the formation of twin-engine planes. They were in perfect formation, coming from the northwest in two waves, which would carry them in a straight line over Clark. When the lead V of nine bombers was almost directly overhead, Gates began to count them. Behind the lead ships to each side were two other Vs of nine planes each, widening out the formation into a big V of Vs. As he saw bombs from the first nine ships begin to fall, the second big V came into sight, flying on the same northwest to southeast course but positioned a bit south of the first group. Gates counted fifty-four in all before running to a large

THE CLARK FIELD OPERATIONS BUILDING AS IT LOOKED IN SEPTEMBER, 1941. PHOTO
COURTESY JAMES H. COOKE VIA KATHLEEN COOKE.

L-shaped trench some thirty feet away and jumping in for cover. He was
joined by many of the other 2d Section pilots as well as enlisted men from
the squadron. Still others piled into another nearby trench.[2]

When Sgt. Bill King saw the high-flying Japanese, he fired his pistol
three times in the air as a warning before rushing into the 20th Pursuit's
operations shack to phone group operations. First Lieutenant Benny Putnam answered. King told him to sound the air-raid alarm because Japanese
planes were just about over the field. Putnam passed the message to his chief,
Major Grover, but the 24th Group CO questioned King's identification.
"How does he know they are Japanese planes?" Grover asked. Overhearing
the question King yelled, "We don't have so goddamn many!"

A few moments later, someone burst into the hangar and shouted that
there were bombers overhead. Putnam and 1st Lt. Bill Cummings, the
group operations officer, ran out the back door of the hangar just in time
to see bombs start tumbling down. As the air-raid siren wailed, the two
ran for the nearest slit trench and dived in, with George Armstrong just

behind them. But Grover elected to stay in the hangar, huddling in the sandbag area for protection.³

In the wooden Clark Field operations building in front of the 24th Group's hangar, Sgt. Leroy Cookingham, the senior NCO in the Weather Detachment quartered in the rear of the building, also heard the siren begin grinding. Wondering what was up, Cookingham and the detachment's radio operator checked with the base operations officer, the only person they found in the front of the building. "Wait a minute, I'll see," 1st Lt. Willie Strathern told them. He put through a call to 24th Group Operations and was informed that there was an alert. Cookingham and the radio operator immediately ran out the rear of the building and jumped into the L-shaped trench just outside. Strathern went the other direction, rushing out the front of the building and climbing the stairs of the hangar next to the base operations building. Once on the rooftop, he reached for the hand siren positioned there and began grinding away. As the klaxon began its "insistent, hoarse bleating," everyone in the hangar area ran for protection.⁴

19TH BOMB GROUP HEADQUARTERS
CLARK FIELD, LUZON
12:35 P.M., DECEMBER 8, 1941

Lieutenant Colonel Eubank heard the siren go off and interrupted his briefing for the B-17 crews slated for the armed reconnaissance of southern Formosa. "Just a second, I'll see what it is," he told the assembled men. He stepped out the front door of the wooden headquarters building just as the first bombs exploded on the nearby field. The 19th Group CO instinctively threw himself flat at the foot of the steps outside the building. He figured that trying to run to safety ran a high risk of being hit by bomb fragments. Meanwhile, Maj. Dave Gibbs, commander of the 30th Bomb Squadron, elected to jump behind a nearby tree. Ed Broadhurst remained in the building, seeking shelter under a desk. Ray Schwanbeck, who had been standing next to Broadhurst, ran outside and jumped into the trench about twenty feet outside the building.

In the back of the building, Ed Whitcomb moments earlier had dropped his map reproduction activity when 1st Lt. Pat McIntyre entered the back door and screamed, "Here they come!" and dashed out the rear for the trench, too. It seemed to Whitcomb that just about everyone else in and around the headquarters building had chosen the same ditch for protection. The trench was vastly overcrowded: it was only forty feet long, two and one-half feet wide, and three feet deep. Everyone was trying to get down as low as possible. As the bombs fell, Whitcomb struggled to get on his gas mask. The next thing he knew, one terrific explosion was followed immediately by another, and then another, and then another. The earth around the ditch shook and huge chunks of dirt fell into it, further terrifying the inhabitants. Whitcomb writhed at the bottom of the trench, his face buried in the dirt. Nearby, higher up in the ditch, Ray Schwanbeck was hit in the leg by a bomb fragment, bloodying his pants.

19TH BOMB GROUP MESS HALL
CLARK FIELD, LUZON
12:35 P.M., DECEMBER 8, 1941

Captain Bill Fairfield of the 7th Materiel Squadron had just finished lunch with his buddies and was standing around with several others on the porch outside the mess hall, still laughing about a ridiculous announcement they had just heard on the radio: Clark Field was being bombed! Suddenly, they noticed a large formation of planes coming in high over the hills. "Well, it must be the Navy," someone piped up. One of the officers took out his field glasses and turned them on the aircraft. "Navy, hell, it's the Japs!" he shouted.[5]

Just ahead of Fairfield as he ran for the slit trenches was 1st Lt. Bill Cocke of the 19th Group's Headquarters Squadron. He was followed by Maj. Clarence "Buck" Davis, commander of the 7th Materiel Squadron, and Capt. John Bergstrom, a ground officer in 19th Group headquarters. Then the bombs started exploding all around them, fragments flying in all directions. Fairfield saw Davis, on his immediate right, fall down and lie motionless. Bergstrom took a terrible hit in his lower back that eventually proved fatal. Sheltering behind a tree, Fairfield noticed that his buddy Bill Cocke had been hit. Yelling at him to hang on, he left the tree and ran toward Cocke, but was only halfway there when something hit him, knocking him down on his face. Only half conscious, Fairfield struggled to stand up, but his left leg gave way and down he went again.

28TH BOMB SQUADRON ENLISTED MEN'S BARRACKS
CLARK FIELD, LUZON
12:35 P.M., DECEMBER 8, 1941

In the 28th Bomb Squadron's wooden barracks buildings south of the BOQ, Cpl. Grant Adami of the Weather Detachment was listening on the day-room radio to Don Bell's 12:30–12:45 news report. He had just finished lunch. Adami burst into laughter when Bell announced that there were rumors Clark Field had been bombed. Then he heard men running outside the day room and, "smelling a rat," jumped up and ran outside to see what was happening. Looking northwestward, he saw a perfect flight of "ghost-like," silver-colored two-engine aircraft high up in the sky heading toward him and the others standing out in the open. He counted the twenty-seven ships in the lead formation and then ran pell-mell to the V-shaped trench just around the corner of the barracks. Jumping into the five-foot-deep trench, Adami landed on top of some of the 28th Bomb men who had preceded him. At that moment he and the others heard for the first time "the blood-curdling scream of falling bombs." The earth around them shook as if during an earthquake, and near hits caused the sand walls to cave in on them despite their having been lined with bamboo. As the noise of the explosions blasted his ears, the twenty-six-year-old former Texas cattle rancher trained as a weather observer experienced uncontrollable fear for the first time in his life.

Clark Field, Luzon
12:35 p.m., December 8, 1941

Sergeant Howard Harper, an instrument specialist in the 19th Group's Headquarters Squadron, was standing beside 1st Lt. Ed Green's B-17D (40-3068) waiting with other enlisted men for Green and the rest of the ship's officers to return from their mission briefing. Harper was going along as flight engineer, relieving the noncom who had performed that job on the morning evacuation from Clark Field. Hearing a noise high in the sky, Harper looked up and could make out a formation of aircraft approaching. He climbed inside the big bomber to get a pair of binoculars. Using the field glasses, he was able to make out a big V and began counting the ships, which he at first assumed belonged to the navy until it dawned on him that the navy did not have that many. The next thing he knew, bombs were detonating on the runway, about a half-mile away near the end of the hangar line. The explosions were marching in a line straight toward him. What to do? He saw one of the crewmen climb into the plane, evidently intending to man the guns. But that was not for him, even though he was slated to be the top turret gunner for the mission. Failing to find a hole to jump into, Harper ran to the rear of the big ship and lay down on the ground, pulling his helmet over his head.[6]

Private Jim Bibb had been sitting under the wings of the B-17 when the bombing started. Like Harper, unable to find a hole and too far from any of the trenches, the twenty-three-year-old country boy from Marmaduke, Arkansas, took refuge "behind a weed." He was less fortunate than Harper.

When a bomb exploded near him, the concussion threw him up in the air and fragments dug into both of his arms and legs. Particularly severe was a wound caused by a big piece in his right leg, between the knee and ankle. Looking around after he hit the ground, Bibb saw that he was luckier than Sgt. Russell Cornford, who had both of his arms and legs blown off by a bomb blast. He bled to death within minutes, screaming in agony.

19TH BOMB GROUP HANGAR AREA
CLARK FIELD, LUZON
12:35 P.M., DECEMBER 8, 1941

First Lieutenant Fred Crimmins of the 28th Squadron had just arrived with a waist gun from his B-17D (40-2067) to have it repaired at the shop in the rear of one of the hangars when he heard the fire alarm start its low-pitched, klaxonlike wailing. Crimmins and the sergeant who was working on the weapon ran outside the front of the hangar and looked up. Like so many of the others, the sergeant took them for navy planes, but not Crimmins. Running back through the hangar, they came out the backside and dove into the slit trench behind it, lying facedown in the dirt as the bombs started falling. As the explosions marched toward him, the enormous blasts causing the ground to tremble, a terrified Crimmins almost threw up.

In front of the 28th Bomb Squadron's hangar, 2d Lt. John Cox was standing around after lunch, talking to squadron mate 1st Lt. Clyde Box while waiting for the rest of the crew of Capt. Bill Fisher's B-17D to come into the hangar from the plane's location so that he, Fisher, and the others could replace them for the impending mission to be flown and they could go to lunch. A twenty-three-year-old navigator from the state of Washington, Cox had flown over with the 30th Squadron, but had been reassigned to the 28th in mid-November, where he joined the squadron commander's crew. As he gazed at the sky, Cox spotted two V-formations of planes approaching from the west and remarked to Box, a first pilot in the 28th Squadron, that it looked like the navy was coming to salute the field. Box, however, had noticed black spots coming from the bellies of the planes and yelled, "Navy, hell, it's the Japs! Air raid!" As they turned to run through the hangar, they heard the air-raid siren start to wail. Going out the rear, they kept running, passing the supply hangar behind their own, then crossed the road and jumped into a partially dug manhole in the new drainage and sewer system that was being introduced in the area. They hunkered down in the hole and watched as a stick of bombs hit the corner of their hangar where the bombsights were stored and another struck the supply hangar. Two other sticks of bombs straddled the hole in which they

cowered. On the other side of the road, bombs were falling on an open
storage area filled with fifty-five-gallon drums of gasoline. Fascinated, Cox
and Box watched the drums blowing up in ones, twos, and threes, their
tops flying around in the air, the explosions creating tall, black columns of
smoke that billowed skyward, capped with huge white blossoms, and cul-
minating with a *whoof!* A roaring fire consumed the gas dump, adding to
the heat and noise.[7]

Second Lieutenant Austin Stitt was supposed to have been in Hangar 4,
next to the one Crimmins was in, supervising the crew camouflage painting Gibbs's B-17D (40-3075), but he instead was over at the 30th Bomb
Squadron's operations tent with 2d Lt. George Berkowitz, listening to
announcer Don Bell on the radio. Just outside the tent, 2d Lt. Jim Colovin
was looking up in the sky. Suddenly, Colovin exclaimed, "What a beautiful Navy formation!" Stitt looked up, but it was too late. The bombs were
well on their way down. With Berkowitz behind him, Stitt ran as fast as
he could toward the big ditch behind the tent and Hangar 4. As he passed
by a fire truck near the hangar, he noticed a man on it begin cranking the
handle of the vehicle's siren, then he jumped into the ditch just as bombs
started hitting the field. Stitt and an army private first class hugged each
other as the earth reverberated and debris fell around them, including a
bloody, severed leg.

The 28th Bomb Squadron's Dick Carlisle was eating lunch with his
four housemates when a terrific explosion rocked Building 13 and ceiling
beams and rafters began crashing down on them. The next thing Carlisle
knew, he was in a bedroom, "curled up in a ball and calling upon Jesus
and Mary, Mother of God, to spare them." When the house stopped shaking after about a minute and a half, Carlisle pulled himself together and
searched through the ruins for his lunch companions. Two were dead, one
was wounded, and the other was unscathed. With the help of the uninjured
officer, Carlisle helped 2d Lt. Francis Thompson stop the bleeding from a
wound in his upper left arm by using a tie from his uniform.[8]

First Lieutenant Bill McDonald of the 19th Group's Headquarters
Squadron was trying to make it to the slit trenches behind his *sawali*
quarters when he heard the bombs swishing through the air. He threw
himself flat on the ground "and tried to hide under a blade of grass,"
more terrified than ever before in his short life. It seemed to the young
pilot as if his world had suddenly turned to smoke and flame. Planes,
houses, hangars, oil drums, and cars were all burning furiously, whipped
by a brisk east wind. Filipino *lavenderas* and houseboys rushed by, screaming, some frantically clutching bleeding arms, others groping around like
blind persons. The smoke and dust was so thick that McDonald could
scarcely see fifty feet.[9]

HIGH OVER CLARK FIELD
12:28 P.M., DECEMBER 8, 1941

Saburō Sakai arrived over Clark Field at 22,400 feet (seven thousand meters) in his A6M2 Zero V-107. Looking down from that altitude, he could not make out any planes on the wide airfield and wondered if they had all taken off. Then, looking down again, he spotted a number of large and small aircraft scattered around the field. "We've got them!" he murmured to himself. Sakai, however, was not concentrating exclusively on the target below. Although they had not encountered any interceptors yet, he kept scanning the sky above for planes that might dive down on them. Then, looking below and to his left, he saw them. One, two, three, four—five of them, small planes in dark-green camouflage paint, coming up at them from about seven thousand feet below. Sakai signaled to the others by banking his wings and then dropped his belly tank. His Zero lurched forward as the tank fell away, its weight reduced.

Up ahead, Kuniyoshi Tanaka had spotted the slowly climbing Americans before Sakai did. They were about twelve miles in front of them at about ninety-five hundred feet altitude. Tanaka signaled their presence to Tainan Kū CO Hideki Shingō by shooting ahead of him and flipping his wings. Shingō had also noticed them, but he shook his head, a signal to Tanaka not to attack. Following orders, Tanaka returned to his position off of Shingō's wing.[10]

Shingō thought the entire operation might become confused if his own *chūtai,* leading the top cover group of Zeros, got involved with a small number of the enemy. Their nine-ship group must stick to its instructions and leave any attack on the would-be interceptors to the other *chūtai.*

Saburō Sakai, in Shingō's 3d Shōtai, was uneasy about the situation, as he knew the bombers would be arriving in two or three minutes. However, following orders, he refrained from breaking formation to attack. He watched the belly tanks of his *shōtai* tumbling downward, leaving a white wake as the precious gasoline remaining in them spilled out. In the rear of the top cover group, CFPO Yoshimitsu Harada, a member of Lt. Akira Wakao's 4th Chūtai, noticed Sakai's *shōtai* jettisoning its belly tanks. Assuming that it was a sign they were going into combat, Harada and his two wingmen dropped their tanks, too.

While continuing to patrol in wide circles over the base, the Tainan Kū pilots flying top cover saw the huge formation of *rikkō* arriving in two groups below them, escorted by Asai's *chūtai.* Moments later, the Type 96 attack bombers of the first group appeared to be on their bombing run, but Sakai and the others could not be sure, as they were flying directly over the *rikkō* at that moment.[11]

CLARK FIELD DURING THE ATTACK OF THE 1ST AND TAKAO KŌKŪTAI 's *RIKKŌ* ON DECEM-
BER 8, 1941. THIS PICTURE WAS TAKEN FROM TWENTY THOUSAND FEET BY ONE OF THE
BOMBER CREWS JUST AFTER COMPLETION OF THE BOMB RUNS (ABOUT 12:38 P.M.). THE
TWO RUNS WERE MADE ON A MAGNETIC HEADING OF 110 DEGREES, OR NORTHWEST TO
SOUTHEAST AS INDICATED BY THE PATTERN OF BURSTS EXTENDING FROM LEFT TO RIGHT.
THE LOWER PATTERN OF BURSTS COVERS CLARK FIELD'S HANGAR AREA. THE 19TH BOMB
GROUP'S *SAWALI* QUARTERS VISIBLE AT THE BOTTOM OF THE PHOTO WERE NOT HIT.
THE TWO WHITE AREAS AT THE UPPER AND MIDDLE RIGHT ARE BELIEVED TO HAVE BEEN
FRESHLY BULLDOZED RUNWAY EXTENSIONS FOR THE B-17S. PHOTO FROM AUTHOR'S
COLLECTION.

From in front of the twenty-six high-flying Mitsubishi Type 96 bombers poking along at 132 miles per hour, Lt. Comdr. Takeo Ozaki looked down at Clark Field some twenty thousand feet (six thousand meters) below and was disappointed. The 1st Kōkutai's *hikōtaichō* saw neither antiaircraft fire nor any pursuit ships rising to intercept his group of twin-engine attack bombers as they prepared to pass overhead on their bombing run. As soon as he got the order, the bombardier began to release the *rikkō's* full load of twelve 132-pound bombs in train from its external racks. It was 12:35 P.M.[12]

To Sakai, the whole of Clark Field seemed suddenly to be covered by a brown carpet of bomb bursts. He closed his eyes. He wanted to capture this day and this moment in his consciousness forever. Overcome, he could not stop the tears streaming down his face. Sakai continued to watch as the Takao Kū's twenty-seven Type 1 *rikkō*, following immediately behind the 1st Kū's Type 96 *rikkō*, began dropping their loads of 132-pound bombs. He was impressed with their accuracy: their training seemed to have yielded excellent results. Clark Field appeared to be totally covered with black smoke that rose thousands of feet into the sky.[13]

20TH PURSUIT SQUADRON OPERATIONS
CLARK FIELD, LUZON
12:35 P.M., DECEMBER 8, 1941

Down below, Joe Moore taxied his P-40B out onto the grass runway and began his takeoff roll as the "Nell" bombers overhead neared their drop point. In his hurry, he had not even taken time to buckle on his parachute. His wingman, Randy Keator in the second position, was applying maximum rpm for takeoff, and the second element leader, Ed Gilmore, was right behind him. The three remaining pilots of Moore's A Flight—2d Lts. Dan Blass and Max Louk, and Louk's wingman—were ready for takeoff, too. At the north and west ends of the 20th Pursuit's dispersal area, the pilots of B and C flights started up their engines and began taxiing toward the runway. As Moore, Keator, and Gilmore became airborne, a train of bombs followed them down the field. As the first of them exploded on the ground, the turbulence shook Gilmore's ship. Applying maximum power as they struggled for altitude, Moore and Keator looked back and down at their home field. It was already covered with flames and smoke.

Still on the field, Dan Blass was almost airborne when his ship lurched to a halt, its tires shredded by bomb fragments. The Louisiana native climbed out of his immobilized ship and ran toward the trenches outside his squadron's operations shack, joining others who had minutes earlier jumped into the ditches. Max Louk was less fortunate. An incendiary bomb struck his ship seconds before it would have finished its takeoff roll.

Frantically trying to get out, Louk could not get his canopy to open. It was stuck, evidently from the bomb damage. Even the emergency release failed. Trapped inside his cockpit, the young Kansan died in flaming agony.

At the north end of the 20th Pursuit's dispersal area, 1st Lt. Fred Armstrong had taxied his P-40B out and was about to lead B Flight diagonally across the open field to get airborne as soon as possible. The next thing he knew, he was keeled over, head down by his knees, after having been momentarily knocked unconscious by a bomb that hit near the back of his ship. As flames swirled up from the cockpit floor, he climbed dazedly out and jumped onto the wing root, from which he slid down to the ground. Burning fuel streaming out of its gas tanks ringed the area around his aircraft. As he crawled over the blazing earth, flames seared his face, hands, and knees.

Two ships behind Armstrong, Carl Gies had just buckled his chute and started up his Allison when bombs struck twenty feet in front of him, riddling his aircraft. Gies instinctively shut down his engine, unbuckled his belt, and jumped out. He reached a trench fifty feet away just as the second wave of bombers began dropping their loads on the field.[14]

When 2d Lt. Jim Fossey saw the train of bombs exploding in a line across the field, he aborted his takeoff and taxied his P-40B away from the line of progression. His tactics failed when bombs started falling around him, rocking his ship violently. He then headed to the west, toward an area not subject to the bombing. His crew chief, however, was waving excitedly for him to get out. In a moment, he knew why: gasoline was pouring out of a hole in the fuselage right behind the cockpit. The Oklahoma boy threw himself on the ground. Then, realizing that the *cogan* grass around him was burning, he climbed back into his punctured ship, taxied it over to the west to a parking area, jumped out, and ran toward a trench near cars parked on the field.

Second Lieutenant Lowell Mulcahy was in position to take off directly behind Fossey. Only three months out of flying school and just married, the twenty-two-year-old Californian had, just moments before, taxied his ship out of its revetment to the runway. Then the shower of bombs began falling. One landed directly on his P-40B, blowing it and its occupant to pieces. Second Lieutenant Jesse Luker met exactly the same fate as he taxied his ship for takeoff.[15]

28TH BOMB SQUADRON OPERATIONS
CLARK FIELD, LUZON
12:35 P.M., DECEMBER 8, 1941

Over at the 28th Bomb Squadron's operations area, one of the squadron's young copilots was taxiing Ted Fisch's B-18 to a refueling pit when bombs started falling. With only his flight engineer and bombardier on board, the green pilot decided to make a run for it with the help of the bombardier, Sgt. Lloyd Leicester, in the copilot's seat. Ordered to handle the throttle and flaps, Leicester pushed in the throttle and started to pull up the old "lumber wagon's" wheels even before the ship had cleared the field. As soon as they were airborne, the flight engineer handed Leicester a crude map, which he pored over in search of Rosales, a small auxiliary field to the north. The copilot intended to fly the ship there to get it out of harm's way.[16]

WEST OF CLARK FIELD
12:35 P.M., DECEMBER 8, 1941

Overhead, 2d Lt. Sam Grashio and the three remaining 21st Pursuit pilots in his C Flight were just about to catch up with Ed Woolery's flight of six 3d Pursuiters, which was headed west toward Iba, their home field. Suddenly, a frantic voice broke in on Grashio's radio frequency: "All pursuit to Clark Field! All Pursuit to Clark Field. Enemy bombers overhead!" Grashio could hear the sound of explosions in the background as the caller continued to plead for assistance. Responding quickly, Grashio turned his flight around to go back to Clark Field. Meanwhile, the P-40 pilots in the other group—whose identity was still unknown to him—continued west, oblivious to the situation. Grashio figured that they had not picked up the frenzied call for help, evidently from 24th Group operations. Heading toward Clark at thirteen thousand feet, Grashio and the other 21st Pursuiters were shaken to see a massive pillar of smoke rising from the field. As they got closer, they could distinguish red fires at the base of the roiling cloud.

Thirty-seven miles to the west, 1st Lt. Hank Thorne was still circling over Iba when he, too, picked up the radio call from Clark Field. The radio operator was yelling: " Many bombers Clark Field! Many bombers Clark Field!" He then called out, "Go get 'em!" Thorne turned to the east, leading his A Flight over the Zambales Mountains and then in a gradual descent to twelve thousand feet the rest of the way to Clark. He was down to five ships now. Gerry Keenan had fallen out sometime earlier while patrolling with the others over Iba.

Some sixteen miles southwest of Clark, sluggards Don Steele and Ship Daniel in Woolery's original flight were heading for the field at about eight thousand feet altitude when they also heard the distress signal from 24th Group operations. After the radio operator yelled "Tally Ho!" another voice screamed that Clark Field was being blown up. Shaken out of their lax attitude by the gravity of the situation, the two 3d Pursuiters closed up and sped toward Clark.[17]

Heading toward Clark from the direction of Mount Arayat to the east, radio operator Arthur Norgaard, in 2d Lt. Earl Tash's B-17D flying up from Del Monte, was listening to a caller explain that the airfield was under attack and that all aircraft should approach the area with caution. Tash broke out his field glasses and searched through the overcast toward Clark but could see no enemy activity. Still sighting no Japanese as they approached the beleaguered airfield, Tash lowered his ship to five hundred feet and let down the wheels preparatory to landing. As they approached through the light overcast he could clearly make out the field. Suddenly, he saw the first of a train of bombs bursting on the ground in a perfectly straight pattern across the base. "Wheels up!" he yelled, then applied full throttle and began to climb out of there. When he reached four thousand feet, he circled the base while trying to decide what to do. After making some hasty calculations, they figured they had enough gas to circle around for another thirty-five minutes, with enough in reserve to make it back to Del Monte if necessary. They would wait until then before deciding what course of action to take.

Unseen by Tash, another B-17 was coming in to land from the north. First Lieutenant John Carpenter was returning from his patrol and had just begun letting down "when the field seemed to blow up right in my face, like a thunderstorm." Carpenter spotted the other B-17 coming in and decided to follow it in after it lowered its wheels. When the other ship aborted its landing and started climbing, however, Carpenter decided to follow suit and headed for a cloud. His radioman called the airfield for instructions and was told not to land but to head to Del Monte instead. Carpenter knew they did not have enough gas for the 550-mile run there, so he decided to keep out of harm's way behind Mount Arayat to the east until the attack was over.[18]

CLARK FIELD, LUZON
12:36 P.M., DECEMBER 8, 1941

When a bomb exploded near the trench in which 24th Group officers Benny Putnam and Bill Cummings were sheltered, the walls caved in on them. Blood from a decapitated enlisted man was spraying all over Putnam. Digging themselves out, they noticed the legs and rear end of someone protruding from the pile of dirt in the collapsed trench. Pulling the half-buried man out by his belt, they discovered it was George Armstrong, who had dived into the trench headfirst just before the bomb exploded. Collecting their wits, they spotted burning gasoline from a fuel truck about twenty feet away draining into their previous sanctuary. They raced toward another trench three hundred feet away and jumped in as the second wave of bombers began dumping their loads on the field.

In the nearby 20th Pursuit Squadron operations shack, 2d Lt. Lloyd Stinson rolled under a cot when he heard the bombs exploding on the airfield. Fragments from two bombs that straddled the shack tore through the flimsy structure, ripping holes in Stinson's trousers, and one of them penetrating his big toe. Just outside, a number of 20th Pursuit officers and men were jammed together at the bottom of two large, L-shaped trenches. Fragments from each explosion whizzed through the air, pieces striking the earth edges of the trenches, but not touching the huddled, terrified occupants. No one would ever call the trenches "Maitland's Folly" again in derision of the former Clark Field CO who had ordered them dug.[19]

As the two formations of Japanese bombers made their run over Clark Field, the handful of 200th Coast Artillery crews not at lunch were trying to get their newly positioned 3-inch antiaircraft weapons into operation against the high-flying aircraft from emplacements dug five feet into the ground. It was a frustrating experience. They had been supplied a meager stock of shells that morning and had not fired their guns in practice since arriving in the Philippines three months earlier. First Lieutenant Russell Hutchinson's gunners first had to clean off the green corrosion on the shell casings in order to get them to go into the breechblocks. They also had to break the frozen fuses with a wrench. To the dismay of Hutchinson's and the other 3-inch batteries, only one out of six shells was exploding at the correct altitude, but they still fell some two thousand to four thousand feet short of the high-flying bombers. Most of the shells proved to be duds. Even with good ammunition, the guns simply could not reach the height of the Japanese aircraft with the old powder-train fuses.[20]

After the first wave of twenty-six bombers finished its run and headed south, Sgt. Albert Allen, a twenty-one-year-old assigned to the 192d Tank Battalion, squirmed out from under an M3 Stuart tank in a state of shock and panic. Straightening up and preparing to dash for his motorcycle, he was halted by the gruff voice of Col. James Weaver, commander of the Pro-visional Tank Group, a National Guard outfit, who had been calmly taking home movies as the bombers flew overhead. "You're out of uniform, Ser-geant," he barked at Allen. The young NCO—who had on dirty fatigues, a dented steel helmet, gas mask, pistol, canteen, and web belt—could feel his knees shaking. He stopped short and responded with an angry and disgusted grunt, "Huh?" Weaver pointed at Allen's fatigue trousers and snapped, "Your ankle flaps are unbuttoned, Sergeant!" As Allen leaned over to button the flaps, he heard the second wave of bombers approaching. But the absurd order had caused his initial terror to dissipate. As Allen moved out to help guide C Company's tanks to defensive positions around the air-field, he heard Weaver yell after him, "Good luck, Soldier!"

In the two trenches near the 20th Pursuit's operations shack, Jack Gates and the other survivors climbed out and surveyed the situation. The air reeked of cordite and yellow-brown dust and smoke rising from the long *cogan* grass burning on the field restricted their visibility.

Getting up from his prone position on the ground as the bombers passed beyond the field, Bill McDonald of the 19th Group's Headquarters Squadron regained his composure and started running toward the BOQ to offer what help he could to those in need. He found many of the *sawali* structures burning. It looked like the mess hall had received a direct hit. "Some of my best friends were in there," he reflected. Swearing under his breath, McDonald then raced toward the flight line. As he passed by a bomb crater, he stopped—three officers were lying nearby, bleeding. McDonald gave them water from his canteen, then continued running toward the line. The agonized cries of the wounded filled his ears.[21]

When Ed Whitcomb was finally able to stand up in the trench in which he had taken refuge, he wiped the sand from his eyes and surveyed the situation. A pall of smoke from an oil storage dump to the east of where he stood was covering them "like a shroud," carried along by an easterly wind. It had so darkened the field that, looking through it, "the sun became like the moon" to Whitcomb. He headed over to the nearby 19th Group headquarters building to see what had been damaged. Across the field, he saw several B-17s burning, the blazes periodically punctuated by explosions.

As soon as the Japanese attackers had passed, Lieutenant Colonel Eubank got up from his prone position in front of the steps leading into his headquarters. He was unscathed by the bombs that had detonated in the adjacent field. Fortunately, none had hit the wooden structure. He now wanted to check out the damage to his precious four-engine bombers. Since his own staff car was not around, he took Major Gibbs's and drove around the field. To his extreme satisfaction, he found that only a few of his ships had been badly hit by the bombers.[22]

Near the 19th Group's hangars, Fred Crimmins and the sergeant who had taken shelter with him climbed out of their trench and watched as the Japanese bombers vanished to the south. Turning his attention to the condition of his own B-17D, Crimmins could make out its silhouette across the field. It was burning. Crimmins then recalled that he had passed another B-17 having a coat of camouflage paint applied at the front entrance to the hangar, where he had been at the time the bombing started. He decided to return to the hangar and try to get the big bomber out if it was still serviceable. The sergeant refused to join him, however. The hangar was on fire from a direct hit and ammunition stored in the back of it was cooking off. The air in the hangar reeked of cordite as Crimmins climbed into the cockpit of the relatively undamaged ship. After starting up the two outboard engines, he taxied the plane out to the edge of the runway. He then opened the left cockpit window so that he could see better to avoid the craters dotting the airfield. He was trying to get the big ship over to one of the bomber revetments, where it would be out of harm's way.

Austin Stitt had also climbed out of his ditch after the bombers finished their run. Troubled by a guilty conscience for not having been at his duty station in Hangar 4, he ran past the fire truck and an ambulance outside the hangar. Two orderlies lying on the ground next to the fire truck appeared to be dead, as did the lifeless man on top of it, one hand still clutching the siren crank. Entering the hangar, Stitt could see a fire burning in the rear. There were big holes in the hangar roof and boxed ammunition was exploding, but old '075 seemed undamaged. First Lieutenant Ray Cox—the 30th Squadron's engineering officer—rushed over to Stitt and together they threw ladders, paint cans, pails, and compressors "every which way" as they cleared a passage for getting the B-17D outside. Cox had at first planned to tow the ship outside with the help of T.Sgt. Floyd Deterding, but the only aircraft tug around was on fire. Although he was a bombardier and not a pilot, Stitt clambered aboard the B-17D and tried to start the engines. In his ignorance he attempted to start all four at once. Two of the engines caught just as Cox joined him in the cockpit and released the brakes. They taxied the big bomber outside the hangar, but had to stop because bomb craters surrounded them. Looking up, Stitt saw what he thought were P-40s flying "all over the place."[23]

OVER CLARK FIELD
12:38 P.M., DECEMBER 8, 1941

As the huge V-formation of fifty-three bombers completed its northwest–southeast bomb run over Clark Field, the aircraft wheeled in perfect order and began a large turn to the left for the return trip to their bases on Formosa. Not one had been touched by antiaircraft or aerial machine-gun fire. Saburō Sakai and the rest of the Tainan Kū pilots in Shingō's 1st Chūtai escorted the bombers northward for about ten minutes.

While the 1st Chūtai was escorting the *rikkō* out of the Clark Field area, Asai's 3d Chūtai remained high overhead as Setō's 2d and Wakao's 4th Chūtai went down to strafe. According to Shingō's plan, the two *chūtai* would make three strafing runs each while the 1st Chūtai escorted the bombers out and the 3d Chūtai flew top cover for the strafers. Then they would switch roles, with the 1st and 3d Chūtai making three strafing passes while being protected by the 2d and 4th Chūtai. Depending on the circumstances, each *shōtaichō* was given the discretion to deviate from the plan if he deemed it necessary. During the strafing attack, pilots would use both their 20-mm cannon and 7.7-mm machine guns. Total time over Clark was to be limited to thirty minutes.[24]

Leading off the strafing attack, Setō's 2d Chūtai began descending through the great pillar of black smoke rising from Clark Field, which reached up to 15,500 feet (forty-five hundred meters)—higher than their formation. Setō was down to seven ships, having lost Hidaka and Ishii at the beginning of the mission when they aborted. The two were Shōtaichō Yoshimichi Saeki's wingmen. He was now flying the tail-end-Charlie position in Setō's *chūtai*. Saeki was just about to put his finger on the trigger as he aimed at aircraft on the ground when he realized that bullets fired from above and behind were falling in front of him. To escape the enemy's fire, he slid his ship to the side, then looked to his rear and spotted three P-40s high above, ganged up on him. He yanked back on the stick, throwing his Zero into such a sharp climb that his tail almost hit the ground, and prepared to counterattack. One by one the three Americans fired at him as they passed by, but Saeki kept sliding to the side and below just as they reached the firing point, evading their bullets.

As the battle continued in this way, Saeki gradually climbed into a more advantageous position. Spotting a cloud, he twice entered and exited it, the second time finding himself in position to attack one of the P-40s flying at the same altitude. However, when Saeki got within firing range, the pilot plunged into a steep dive. Following him down, firing all the while, Saeki was obliged to break off the attack when he lost sight of the P-40 as it headed over a heavily wooded area. Diverted from his strafing mission by the combat with the P-40, the luckless Japanese began climbing, then headed north for his *chūtai's* rendezvous point.[25]

As Lt. Akira Wakao's 4th Chūtai descended behind Setō's flight, Sea1c. Haruo Fujibayashi in the sixth position and the other seven in the group followed suit when Wakao dropped his belly tank preparatory to strafing. Fujibayashi thought that Wakao had spotted enemy planes, as they had been told to keep their belly tanks even during the strafing attack. When they reached the assigned altitude for forming up for the strafing run, Fujibayashi and the others looked down and saw many planes burning on the ground after the bombardment by the *rikkō*. As Wakao led his nine-ship formation on its run after Setō's *chūtai* completed its pass, Fujibayashi spotted two or three B-17s that still were not burning. All the pilots concentrated their 20-mm cannon fire on these survivors as they made their circular strafing run. Much to their frustration, the B-17s would not burn despite their efforts to set them afire.

Flying top cover while the pilots of Setō's and Wakao's *chūtai* strafed below, the nine pilots in Lt. Masao Asai's 3d Chūtai searched the sky below for any Americans seeking to disrupt the strafing attack. Their view obstructed by the heavy black smoke billowing up, they had not seen the P-40s that dove on their comrades from medium altitude while they were strafing the field. Shimakawa, flying in the sixth position in Asai's *chūtai,* looked down and, through an opening in the smoke, noted that all but one of the B-17s he had earlier seen were now burning, the result of the strafing by Setō's and Wakao's *chūtai.*[26]

OVER CLARK FIELD
12:40 P.M., DECEMBER 8, 1941

Arriving over Clark Field from the west at about five thousand feet in response to the radio call for help, Sam Grashio and his wingman, Gus Williams, surveyed the disaster scene below them. It looked like single-engine planes were strafing, darting in and out of the smoke covering large areas of the field. Nearby, but no longer linked up with Grashio and Williams, Joe Cole and his wingman, Johnny McCown, also were sizing up the situation over the airfield. Hesitating to attack, Grashio and Williams were moved to action when one of the Japanese apparently completed his strafing run and started returning to a position about three thousand to four thousand feet below them. Diving down on the unsuspecting pilot, Grashio fired his six .50-caliber machine guns and the Japanese plane fell off to one side, smoking. Then Williams spotted nine other planes coming in their direction but about fifteen hundred feet below them, evidently about to begin a strafing run. As they passed underneath Williams, he tipped his P-40E to see what markings they carried. Williams froze: they had large red meatballs on their wings!

Grashio joined Williams in a tight, diving turn and Williams fired a few short bursts at the tail end of the Japanese formation. However, before the two 21st Pursuiters were able to complete their turn, the two lead Japanese ships completed a tight, climbing turn of their own and, from a distance of only three hundred feet—much to the Americans' surprise—began shooting at *them.* As tracers whizzed by on both sides of his fuselage, Williams yelled to his leader, "Let's get out of here!" Grashio, trying to elude his adversary, veered sharply to the left, but to no avail. A 20-mm explosive shell tore through his ship's left wing and ammunition cartridge can, causing the P-40E to shudder momentarily. Although he was already at low altitude, Grashio plunged into a steep dive through the smoke covering the airfield and pulled out just in time at treetop level to the west. Looking back, he was relieved to find that the two Zeros that had been chasing him were falling steadily behind, their fire wide of the mark.

Nearby, Williams employed the same survival tactic. Turning his ship upside down and pushing his throttle all the way forward, he dove straight for the ground, then pulled out over the treetops. He noted that his airspeed indicator was registering over five hundred miles per hour as he broke the dive. His Japanese pursuer had opted to break off at fifteen hundred feet, unable to match the heavy P-40E's diving speed and perhaps fearful of flying into the ground. Figuring he had little hope of climbing back to altitude for another diving attack on the strafers without being shot up by the nimble mystery pursuit ships, Williams decided to head south to Nichols Field instead.[27]

Cole and McCown had also attacked the nine strafers. As he came out of the smoke at the end of his dive, McCown found that he had entered the circle of the Japanese group. He decided to stay in their formation and closed up on the ship in front of him. When the Japanese pilot completed his pass and began turning, McCown had him fixed in his gun sight. Squeezing the trigger on the control stick, he watched as .50-caliber fire ripped into the Zero's tail, then proceeded up the fuselage and into the engine. It appeared to McCown that the tail of his adversary's plane fell off as it plunged steeply earthward. In reaction to the traumatic incident, McCown felt as if in a dream as he climbed to higher altitude, his leader Cole at his side. A stream of tracer fire passing just under his wing brought him back to reality: Japanese coming out of their strafing run were jumping them.

The high-rpm combat proved to be too much for Cole's brand-new Allison engine. It started throwing oil on the windscreen, impeding his vision. Like Williams, Cole decided to break off the combat and head back to Nichols, leaving his wingman McCown to continue the unequal contest alone. However, with his ammunition nearly exhausted, McCown opted to return to Nichols shortly afterward.[28]

OVER CLARK FIELD
12:48 P.M., DECEMBER 8, 1941

Arriving over Clark Field shortly after Grashio's group of 21st Pursuiters, 1st Lt. Fred Roberts and 2d Lt. Bill Powell of Woolery's original formation of ten 3d Pursuit ships also could see the Japanese strafers shooting up the field below them. About twelve minutes earlier, they had split off from Woolery's eight-ship formation heading back to Iba when Roberts happened to look behind him and saw a pillar of black smoke rising from Clark. He instantly decided to return to the beleaguered airfield. Roberts now led Powell in a diving attack on a line of five strafers that Powell figured they had "cold turkey." However, when Roberts depressed his gun trigger, he saw that only *one* of his six fifties was firing—and *none* of Powell's guns would fire! Entering into their angled Lufberry, a defensive maneuver dating back to World War I, the two hapless 3d Pursuiters were being shot at by the Japanese behind them as they pursued the tails of the ones in front. At that point, a terrified Powell broke out of the formation and pointed his ship in the direction of his home field at Iba. Roberts also decided to break off and head for home. The Japanese ship behind him had torn holes in his wings, shot out the control cables at his feet, and shredded his leg with metal fragments.

When they arrived over Clark Field from the southeast at eight thousand feet, fellow 3d Pursuiters Don Steele and Ship Daniel were appalled to see fires all over the base and huge columns of smoke rising to eighteen thousand feet. Above them, they noticed a huge formation of twin-engine bombers retiring to the north in an impressive formation. Looking down through the smoke on the airfield, they could make out single-engine planes diving down and then following one after another on strafing runs. When they headed down to intercept them, however, Steele and Daniel were cut off by six ships that had been flying top cover for the strafers, unseen by the two Americans.[29]

"They came at us, head-on," Steele recorded in his diary entry that day. "Golly, what a feeling! My throat got dry and my breath got short, but we tore into them, nevertheless." As one of the Japanese faced Steele, he fired his two wing cannons and 7.7-mm machine guns at point-blank range. Twenty-millimeter shells ripped into the P-40E's left wing, sounding to Steele like a sledgehammer pounding on his ship, while machine-gun fire punctured his fuselage. A piece of metal grazed his forearm, causing a six-inch-long gash. Steele was sure the two ships were going to collide, but at the last instant the Japanese turned to one side. Steele had fired, too, but with only one of his six fifties working, it appeared that only five or six rounds had hit his adversary. Much to his satisfaction, he saw that the Japanese pilot's aircraft was smoking as it passed by. Turning to follow it down, Steele saw it go into a spin at about three thousand feet. A few moments later it appeared to Steele that it crashed into the mountains. Following his apparent victory, Steele joined Daniel in a fruitless attempt to catch the rest of the Japanese fighters. Low on gas, however, they were forced to head back to Iba. It was about 12:56.[30]

At twelve thousand feet over Clark Field, Hank Thorne with four other 3d Pursuiters was circling after having led his A Flight east from Iba in response to the frenzied radio call from group operations. Huge pillars of thick black smoke reached almost up to their altitude, but they could make out no other aircraft in the sky. Their view obscured by the smoke, they did not notice the Japanese strafers far below. Suddenly, Thorne's radio crackled, "Many bombers, Iba!" The 3d Pursuit CO assumed the excitable call on his frequency was from one of his pilots flying over their home field. Turning his flight around, Thorne started to climb for the return to Iba. However, he quickly noticed that only two members of his flight were left with him. Vern Ireland and Gordon Benson had become separated and evidently were still over Clark.

Caught over Clark Field during the attack in his B-17D, John Carpenter managed to survive several passes made by from five to ten Japanese fighters. Dropping his ship down to five hundred feet, Carpenter had succeeded in discouraging further attention. He was now hiding behind Mount Arayat, ten miles due east of Clark, getting lower and lower on gas and anxious for the attack to end so that he could land. On the east side of the mountain, Earl Tash's B-17D was also waiting out the attack.[31]

OVER CLARK FIELD
12:50 P.M., DECEMBER 8, 1941

Lieutenant Shingō's 1st Chūtai reassembled at thirteen thousand feet over Clark Field after completing its *rikkō* escort duty. The nine pilots made final preparations for the ground strafing part of their attack mission. Lieutenant Asai's 3d Chūtai would join them. The airfield below was obscured by black smoke rising up to and beyond their altitude. They saw no enemy planes in the sky.[32]

As Shingō led his *chūtai* down for its first strafing run, FPO1c Kuniyoshi Tanaka, just behind him in second position, spotted a B-17 slowly coming out of a burning hangar. Shingō's wingman was surprised that it had remained undamaged in the heavy bombing the hangar area had suffered. "What a brave pilot to try to save the plane in the middle of an air raid," he thought. Suddenly, the B-17 caught fire, evidently hit by Shingō in front of him. As he passed over the bomber, Tanaka saw flames enveloping the big bomber and assumed it must have been loaded with fuel. Figuring the crew must have been burned alive in the plane, Tanaka momentarily shut his eyes, touched by the Americans' bravery.

Five ships behind Tanaka, FPO1c Saburō Sakai led his three-ship *shōtai* down for its first strafing run. Flying low over the field, he saw for the first time the renowned four-engine American bombers, many of them on fire from strafing runs by the Zero-sen from Setō's and Wakao's *chūtai*. However, he was having difficulty seeing through the thick black smoke covering the airfield. To add to the difficulty, the Americans were firing machine guns and heavier antiaircraft guns located around the base at them. Sakai dropped his nimble Zero down to 1,000 feet (three hundred meters) as he began his strafing run behind the others making the west–east sweep of the field. Signaling his intentions to his two wingmen, he continued losing altitude as he lined himself up with an undamaged B-17: 850 feet, 700 feet, 500 feet. The fuselage of the huge ship was already too big to fit in his gun sight. "Not yet, not yet," he told himself as he held back from firing. He had noticed that some of the less-experienced wingmen in the two *shōtai* in front of him had fired too soon, sending their shells into the ground in front of their targets.[33]

Sakai's altitude continued to drop: 100, then 70, then only 35 feet above the airfield. The B-17 loomed just 350 feet in front of him. Now! He pulled back on the firing lever of his 20-mm cannon as hard as possible. Pleased with the sound of the firing of the two cannon and the recoil reverberating throughout the fuselage of his Zero-sen, Sakai continued to hold the lever down as he came up and over the bomber, then skimmed past it, turning to the left. He turned around in his cockpit and looked down. The sight of a fire breaking out along the B-17's wing root rewarded him.

Behind Sakai, FPO2c Kazuo Yokokawa, one of his wingmen, had also succeeded in setting a B-17 on fire, using the same method as his *shōtaichō*. However, Sakai's second wingman, FPO3c Toshiaki Honda, had failed to start a fire on the B-17 he hit. Sakai figured that the bomber had been drained of gasoline before their strafing attack commenced.[34]

Minutes later, Shingo's *chūtai* commenced its second strafing run. As Sakai led his 3d Shōtai down to a thousand feet to get in position for a repeat performance, he instinctively checked to the rear to be on the safe side. His caution was rewarded. He could make out a few black dots coming down toward him, the sun behind them. Sakai realized immediately that the enemy had been waiting for the Zeros to descend for their strafing run before attacking them. He thought it was a smart move. Sakai signaled to Yokokawa and Honda to abort the strafing run. Deciding instantly on his tactic, Sakai "jerked the stick and rudder pedal and spiraled sharply to the left, then yanked back on the stick for a sudden climb." Evidently surprised by the maneuver, the pilots of the five P-40s "abruptly rolled back and scattered." It seemed to Sakai that four of them were trying to flee as they "arced up and over into the thick columns of black smoke." The fifth pilot, however, went into a sharp turn to the left, the wings of his ship going up and down during the strenuous movement. As Sakai climbed and approached the P-40E from below, the American "half rolled and began a high loop." With the six-hundred-foot altitude difference narrowed, Sakai framed his adversary's belly in his gun sight from just 120 feet back and pulled his gun triggers. The Zero-sen's 20-mm shells struck the wings and 7.7-mm fire sprayed the fuselage. The P-40E's canopy blew out and the ship staggered, then turned left before spinning through the scattered clouds. Sakai watched for a few moments as the ship headed toward the ground, but saw no smoke. Elated over what he assumed to be his first victory over an American, Sakai signaled his two wingmen to reassemble for the return trip to Tainan and headed for the Tainan Kū's designated assembly point thirty miles north at an altitude of 13,800 feet (four thousand meters).[35]

In Lieutenant Asai's 3d Chūtai, Masa-aki Shimakawa, flying in the sixth position, had switched his fuel cock to the main tank, set his engine for twenty-four hundred rpm, and turned on the gun sight as he descended with the others for their turn at strafing the American planes on Clark Field. Their uneventful top cover duty was over. They passed through five thousand feet, Shimakawa following behind his *shōtaichō,* Gitarō Miyazaki, and Miyazaki's other wingman, Toshio Ōta, as they continued their descent and made a ninety-degree turn to the left to get into position for their strafing run with the rest of the ships in Asai's *chūtai.* It was their turn now, Shingō's *chūtai* having completed its strafing pass.

As Miyazaki and Ōta in front of him lined up to fire on the parked B-17s, Shimakawa noticed a dark-colored single-engine ship he recognized as a P-40 rapidly climbing about three thousand feet ahead of him. He hesitated for a moment before dropping his belly tank in anticipation of combat, reluctant to lose the remaining fuel in it, which he knew he might need to get back to Formosa. After breaking off his preparations for strafing, Shimakawa checked to make sure there were no enemy planes behind him, then fixed the P-40 in his gun sight. He felt the distance was too great, but in his excitement he depressed the gun triggers anyway. His 20-mm cannons did not work, but both 7.7-mm machine guns scored hits. Continuing to fire as the P-40 went into a dive, Shimakawa saw white smoke coming from the underside of its left wing. Suddenly, the smoke turned black and the stricken American veered to the left, and headed toward the ground in a tight spiral. "I did it!" he shouted. He did not see the P-40 crash, however. Black smoke coming up from the field obstructed his view just as the American would have hit the ground. He decided to report it as an uncertain victory.

Breaking off his gaze, Shimakawa checked all around his position, which was now somewhat north of Clark Field. He was alone, separated from the rest of his *shōtai.* There were no enemy pursuits around, either, but black smoke puffs followed his ship. He did not realize until later that they were caused by antiaircraft fire from guns on the airfield. No longer in formation with the others, Shimakawa decided to head north to the rendezvous point and link up with any others there. Applying maximum power, he started climbing to the agreed altitude for reassembly. On the way, at about ten thousand feet, he spotted Lieutenant Asai and his wingman, also heading north for the return trip.[36]

19TH BOMB GROUP HANGAR AREA
CLARK FIELD, LUZON
12:40 P.M., DECEMBER 8, 1941

Ray Cox and Austin Stitt looked out the cockpit windows of the B-17D they had just taxied out of Hangar 4 and tried to identify the pursuit ships they saw flying all over the field. When they spotted the red meatball insignia on them, the two 30th Squadron officers knew they were sitting ducks. Jumping out of the bomber, Cox headed in one direction and Stitt ran into a nearby ammo tent and picked up a box of ammunition and a machine gun before heading toward the ditch near the hangar where he had earlier taken cover. As he was about to jump into the ditch, he discovered that he had grabbed .50-caliber ammo for the .30-caliber gun he was carrying. Disgusted, he flung the ammo box and gun aside.

Then he spotted a B-17 nearby that seemed to be in good condition, but with some smoke coming out of the cockpit. Stitt ran over to a nearby truck and took out a tiny fire extinguisher, then went over to the big bomber and trained the spray on the cockpit in an effort to extinguish the flames. Moments later, fearful the fully gassed aircraft might explode, he aborted his effort, threw the extinguisher into the cockpit window, and ran as fast as he could toward the mountains to the east.

Out on the airfield past the tents, he approached an antiaircraft gun emplacement and decided to join the crew. One of the gunners was dead and the other was trying to work his 37-mm gun, but it was jammed. Stitt tried to help him fix it, but moments later the gunner concluded that the breech was broken. Although the emplacement was well protected with sandbags around the edge, it was also full of live ammo, which scared Stitt. He climbed out of the pit and this time ran toward the center of the field. As he ran, it suddenly dawned on Stitt that he was in the middle of a strafing attack. He watched for a few moments as the Japanese fighters made 180-degree turns and came back again, flying in "a pattern like knitting, north to south and south to north," as they sprayed everything in sight. Then he hid himself in some tall grass, lying flat on his back. Reaching for his .45-caliber sidearm, he fired two magazines of ammo at the strafers without result.

Just beyond the 19th Group's hangar, Fred Crimmins had been making progress taxiing a B-17D to the safety of a revetment when, out of the corner of his eye, he saw bad news coming: a single-engine plane just commencing its strafing run. Instinctively, Crimmins swung the big four-engine bomber around, bringing the tail between him and the Japanese strafer. It was too late. A 20-mm shell smashed through the cockpit window and exploded in the B-17's instrument panel, starting a fire, and 7.7-mm machine-gun bullets hit the armor plate outside. As Crimmins looked out the window, the Japanese pilot flashed by, followed by two more behind him. Two more shells smashed through the cockpit dome, one driving fragments into Crimmins's scalp and the other shattering his left wrist as he reached forward to turn off the two engines. As he cut the power, two more 7.7-mm bullets hit him in the right shoulder. Other shells tore through the fuselage and started a fire that Crimmins knew doomed the Flying Fortress. Crawling painfully through the plane, Crimmins managed to get out through the backdoor as metal fragments from more hits dug into his neck, head, legs, and arms.

Dropping to the ground near the center of the field, Crimmins crawled to a gun emplacement manned by three 200th Coast Artillery men with a 37-mm gun and a .50-caliber machine gun. Not having been supplied with any ammunition for the machine gun, they were able to fight back with only their 37-mm weapon, which traversed too slowly for the gunner to track the strafing aircraft roaring across the field. The men looked confused and frustrated to Crimmins, who, after sitting down in the back of the sandbagged emplacement, started giving them instructions on how to operate the gun. Noting that the strafers seemed to be following a rigid circular pattern as they crisscrossed over the airfield, Crimmins told the gunner to aim along the line of the planes' departure point and hold the gun there. "Crying like children" as they fired at the low-flying Japanese passing by, they scored a direct hit on the belly of one of the ships as it swept over their heads. Instantly bursting into flames, it hit the ground and exploded with a blinding flash.[37]

Elsewhere, other antiaircraft crews watched with anguished expressions as cannon and machine-gun fire streamed from the strafing aircraft and ripped apart B-17s, B-18s, and P-40s caught on the ground. Never having fired their 37-mm guns before, some men aimed at too low an angle and blasted holes through trucks, tents, and other airfield installations. Many of the shells they fired were duds, with only one in ten rounds bursting in some cases, much to the men's disgust.

First Sergeant Joe Smith of Battery F was having better luck in his emplacement. He had figured out the strafers' tactics. As each of the nine Japanese pilots approached his gun position, Smith and his crew would fire at the point where the plane commenced the dive for its strafing run. After a while, it seemed to the gunners that the Japanese would break off their attacks as they came within six hundred feet of their position, apparently hesitant to come within range of their 37-mm fire.

Anticipating a strafing attack after the bombing, Sgt. Zenon "Bud" Bardowski of B Company, 192d Tank Battalion, moved a Headquarters Company half-track into a clearing near some of the 200th Coast Artillery's gun emplacements so that he would have a good crack at any strafers passing near his position with the .50-caliber Browning on a swivel mount in the front of the armored vehicle. Firing at the diving ships as they passed by on his right, Bardowski used up about six hundred rounds of ammo without success. After reloading, he noticed that instead of passing to his right, one of the strafers had banked to the left, evidently trying to avoid his fire. The tank crewman hit the Zero with the first round fired from the new belt and continued to stitch the plane as he swung the barrel around to follow the Japanese pilot's undeviating line of flight. Bardowski saw the strafing aircraft catch fire and then crash some distance from his position.[38]

On the other side of the field from Bardowski, in the 20th Pursuit's dispersal area, Carl Gies was taxiing an undamaged P-40B into takeoff position when the ship's wheels fell into a bomb crater. At the same moment, the 20th Pursuiter from Oregon spotted low-flying aircraft shooting across the field. "Strafers!" he yelled as he cut the power switch, jumped out of his disabled ship, and ran back to the midfield trench he had occupied during the bombing run. Nearby, 2d Lt. Jim Drake had taxied another P-40B past the holes in the pockmarked field and was approaching the takeoff point on the grassy strip. That was as far as he got. A Zero pilot had Drake's ship lined up in his gun sight and was pouring cannon and machine-gun fire into it. The P-40B's fully loaded gas tanks burst into flames, immolating Drake, who was trapped in the cockpit.

Over in the two L-shaped trenches near their operations shack, 20th Pursuit officers and men were jammed together as the strafing Zeros fired all around them, splintering the boards lining the tops of the trenches. The cannon fire made a popping sound, whereas the 7.7 machine-gun fire sounded like firecrackers. Dense black smoke blew across the trenches, emanating from Major Grover's P-40B, burning fiercely from bomb damage, and Lloyd Stinson's car, which had been set on fire by the strafers.

To the right of the 20th Pursuit's operations shack, strafers fired their cannons and machine guns at the big SCR-197 communications van parked outside the 24th Group's hangar. One 20-mm shell entered one end of the van, passed by the head of Pvt. Bernard Pothier, and went clear through the transmitter, missing all the tubes and not exploding. Although fire from other strafers heavily damaged the van's transmitting and receiving equipment, it continued to operate until about 12:47. Then, in an effort to prevent any further damage to the vitally important radio unit, its crew disconnected all of the lines while one of the pursuit pilots hitched a truck to the van. As the pilot towed it out to the road behind the hangar, strafing aircraft kept firing at him and the van. Minutes later, he pulled into the adjoining jungle and left the van under a grove of trees, about a mile from its original location and out of sight of the Japanese.[39]

Hunkered down in the trench near the 19th Group's headquarters building, Ed Whitcomb was surprised to see his CO, Lieutenant Colonel Eubank, standing nearby with his back to the trench, hands on hips, as the Japanese made pass after pass on their strafing runs. A few minutes before the strafing attack, Eubank had checked out his B-17 force and found it in relatively good condition. Now, "standing right out in the open like a damn fool," Eubank silently watched as the low-flying Zeros destroyed his bombers. Anxious for Eubank's safety, Whitcomb called out, "You'd better take cover, Sir," but the distraught group commander did not respond.

In another ditch near the 30th Squadron's operations tent, 1st Lts. Frank Kurtz and Glenn Rice watched as single-engine ships flying at about two thousand to three thousand feet approached them "in a long string like geese" from the direction of Mount Arayat to the east. Then they made a 270-degree turn and peeled off singly, dropping down to only fifteen feet altitude, and then making a beeline for their target: a B-17 parked snugly in a U-shaped sandbag revetment near the ditch. One by one they lined up on the bomber, each starting off with 7.7-mm tracer fire, then following up with 20-mm shells, setting the hapless B-17D ablaze.

Near 2d Lt. Bill Railing's B-17D, T.Sgt. John Fleming and S.Sgt. Tom Crumley had jumped into a pit near their ship when the bombs started falling and began firing a .30-caliber Browning machine gun mounted there at Zeros approaching the Flying Fortress. Struggling with the old type canvas ammo belts, Fleming and Crumley were nevertheless having success in diverting the efforts of the strafers to destroy what the bombers had missed, very few hits being scored on their ship.[40]

Meanwhile, T.Sgt. Anthony Holub was alone inside a Headquarters Squadron B-17D, firing the paired .50-caliber dorsal guns at strafers approaching his ship. During the bombing run, Holub had run to the plane from the supply hangar, where he had been looking for parts needed to install a new engine in the ship. When he finally reached the B-17, he found that the rest of the crew was gone. It was too far to the foxholes now, though, and he "didn't even think" of getting behind the fifty-five-gallon drums placed near the ship, so he climbed into the radio compartment, intending to bring down some of the Japanese strafers. When his ammo supply ran out, Holub climbed out of the bomber and braved heavy fire from the strafing Zeros to reach Ed Green's nearby B-17, from which he removed as many ammo cans as he could carry and headed back to his ship. Behind his guns again, he continued loosing streams of .50-caliber shells at the strafers, distracting them as they made their firing runs. Despite poor visibility due to the heavy smoke enveloping the field, he managed to get in "a few good shots," although he was unsure if he had downed any of the Japanese.[41]

Over at Green's B-17D, Pvt. Greeley B. Williams was also inside his ship, firing at the Japanese from one of its machine guns as they made their strafing runs. The gun went silent when one of the strafers struck Williams's position with its 7.7-mm fire, killing him instantly. Like Holub, the men around Green's B-17 did not think of taking shelter behind the nearby fifty-five-gallon drums set up for their protection during strafing attacks. Private First Class Robert Menzie, one of the radio operators in the ship's crew, had run toward a foxhole not far from the bomber and jumped in, but was nevertheless hit and killed instantly by one of the strafers.

Sergeant Otto Wellman, like the other men around the ship, was lying prone on the ground. Less than ten feet away, Jim Bibb saw the back of Wellman's head blown off by one of the 20-mm shells hitting the ground at three- to four-foot intervals. Bibb, wounded in all his limbs during the bombing attack, kept moving around on the ground in order to face the strafers as they made their runs, the helmet on his head providing hoped-for protection. Sergeant Howard Harper's helmet failed to save him. A 20-mm shell hit him in the left leg, midway between his hip and knee, passing through without striking a bone or causing arterial bleeding.

Although Green's B-17 had escaped the bombing attack unscathed, the strafers were able to set it on fire. Realizing that its gas tanks were full for the intended mission to Formosa, Harper feared the bomber would explode. Unable to stand up, he began rolling himself through the burning *cogan* grass in an effort to get as far away from the ship as possible.[42]

Over where the 28th Squadron had positioned its newly acquired B-17Ds, Pfc. Joe McElroy was inside one of the ships filling in for the regular radioman, who had gone to lunch. He had stayed in the bomber during the bombing attack and was now firing the .50-caliber waist machine gun at the strafing Zeros. It appeared to him that he had scored hits on several of the Japanese planes, but when the strafers finally succeeded in setting the big ship on fire, McElroy was forced to evacuate. He managed to get through the ordeal without being hit.[43]

From his trench, 2d Lt. Owen "Tuffy" Graham of the 93d Squadron was amused to see that the strafing pilots were also pouring fire into the decoy B-17 models mounted on the flight line in front of the officers' quarters. There was a downside to this, however. The Zeros' heavy firepower was going through the wooden structures and hitting the *sawali* residences behind the dummy ships. Even more disturbing to Graham was the manner in which the strafers also methodically set fire to the rows of fully loaded gas trucks neatly lined up bumper to bumper as required under peacetime procedures.

In his partially caved-in trench near the 28th Bomb Squadron's barracks, Cpl. Grant Adami could see the Japanese passing just over the top of the barracks as they came in for each strafing run. At the beginning of the attack, Adami fired at them with one of the three World War I–vintage .30-caliber Lewis guns that had been set up in the trench, but the "awful thing" promptly jammed and he did not have "the slightest idea of how to start it going again." Then a "cursing habitual drunkard—now cold sober—of a Sergeant" took over the firing of another of the guns, "haphazardly" shooting at the low-flying strafers. That gun also jammed several times, but unlike Adami, the sergeant was able to "coax it back into working order."

There were two new additions to the men packed in the trench: Pvt. William Biggs (Maitland's former chauffeur), with a piece of shrapnel in his big stomach inflicted during the bombing attack, and another 28th Squadron man who had been hit in the leg below the knee, breaking the bone and causing a steady flow of blood. Although Biggs moaned a lot, he was not bleeding much.

No one in the trench said anything at the beginning of the attack. "But to look at their faces was not good—what you saw merely mirrored what you felt." During slight lulls in the raid, a second lieutenant "tried to do his duty" by giving "pep talks," but he sounded "so unnatural" to the dispirited men that "the effect was lost." The only man in the trench who "braced" Adami's spirits was the sergeant operating the Lewis gun. He was at least fighting back, even if ineffectually.

Near the 28th Bomb's barracks, Capt. Bill Fairfield of the 7th Materiel Squadron was lying on the ground next to the 19th Group's BOQ. His helmet had been blown off during the bombing attack, and bullets were "bouncing off the ground like rain off a puddle." One burst had hit him in the right leg. Fairfield noticed that the Link Trainer building alongside the BOQ was on fire and likely to fall on him. Unable to stand up, he unbuckled his belt and pulled his trousers off so he could bandage his leg wounds. Burning embers from the Link building began falling on him and started to set his uniform on fire, while overhead one of the Zeros prepared for another run over the open field where Fairfield lay sprawled, "fair game" for the Japanese. Then Fairfield spotted squadron mates 1st Lt. Harry Glenn and 2d Lt. Jack Kaster, as well as 1st Lt. Kenny Kreps from the 19th Group, standing alongside a nearby slit trench. In response to his call for help, they grabbed Fairfield by his hands, dragged him over the *cogan* grass, and deposited him roughly in the bottom of the trench, then joined him. Lying immobilized on his back, all Fairfield could do was look up and watch the strafers continue doing their "lazy eights."

Fairfield could see 19th Group medical officers Maj. Luther Heidger and 1st Lt. Roy Day walking around outside the trench in the midst of the hail of fire, minus their helmets. Going from one wounded man to another, they were doing their best to tend to their immediate medical needs.

Fairfield was impressed by their devotion to duty under fire. Minutes later, an ambulance pulled up alongside the trench, braving the strafing attack. The medics began lifting the wounded out of the trench and dumping them in the "goon car," as they used to call the vehicles. As Fairfield was assisted over to the ambulance, he saw Kaster, shot through the hip, sitting on the front seat. Second Lieutenant Jim Elder of the 93d Squadron, who had a gaping hole in his left thigh, was lying on the backseat. The medics heaved Fairfield onto the floor and tossed his gun and pistol belt in after him. He looked to see who was lying beside him and saw his close friend Capt. Bill Cocke of the 19th Group's Headquarters Squadron, his back and chest blown out. Trying to ease Cocke's agony as he rolled around on the ambulance floor, Fairfield put an arm around him and pressed Cocke's back up against his shirt, hoping to stem the flow of blood.[44]

MANILA BAY
12:50 P.M., DECEMBER 8, 1941

While the radio operator aboard the minesweeper *Lark* in Manila Bay was reporting to the 16th Naval District that the *Lark*'s crew had just sighted seventeen enemy planes over the harbor, pilots of the 17th Pursuit Squadron circled overhead, unaware of the attention they were attracting below. They were, after all, acting in accordance with the orders they had received from Major Grover at Clark Field when they took off forty minutes earlier. Contrary to Grover's expectations, they had not spotted any Japanese bombers heading for Manila.

About eight minutes before they reached the Manila area, the pilots lost contact with the 24th Group's communications van at Clark Field, which had earlier been directing them by voice transmission. This failure did not particularly bother Dave Obert, however. He knew from past experience that the van's radio operations often were sporadic due to breakdowns.[45]

Somewhat to the east of the 17th Pursuit Squadron, Ed Dyess was patrolling over the Cavite area with the twelve P-40Es of his A and B Flights. The navy had also mistaken his 21st Pursuiters as enemy planes, and Cavite's antiaircraft gunners fired at them as they passed over the naval base.[46]

CHAPTER 12

"Whatever You Do, Don't Get under the Damned Truck!"

Private Henry Brodginski was still behind the oscilloscope in the SCR-270B operations van at 12:40 P.M., excitedly monitoring the approaching Japanese bombers. His commanding officer, Lieutenant Wimer, had told him to stay on the scope until the first bombs hit. Except for the plotter and Brodginski, all of the other operations van crewmen had taken refuge in the trench just off Iba beach. Sergeant Wade Nelms was in the Air Warning Company detachment's nearby radio tent, preparing to leave his duty station for safety, accompanied by his assistant, Pfc. Orville Street and the telephone operator, Pvt. Jarriet Moore. Nelms and his men had kept busy all morning taking calls from the operations van on the Japanese pickups and radioing the information to the AWS at Nielson. Now he left the tent with the others, headed for the trench where the rest of the detachment's men had taken refuge.

Down on the beach, Pvt. Melvin Thomas was busy filling sandbags. Sergeant Thomas J. Hoskins had asked Thomas earlier in the morning to help the other off-duty men in the detachment to fill as many as possible after they received the news of the Pearl Harbor attack. As he passed by the big power truck connected to the operations van, Thomas ran into his two best friends in the company, Pfc. Bill Todd and Pvt. John Harler. Like to the others expecting an attack on Iba that day, Thomas told them, "Whatever you do, don't go under the damned truck!" Thomas knew that if his power truck with the big Leroy engine full of gasoline were hit, it would create an inferno. Seeking shelter under the big truck would be a ticket to disaster.[1]

At the north end of Iba Field, S.Sgt Woody McBride and his crew of nine men were eating sandwiches in their gun emplacement, prepared for the impending attack on their base. The 3d Pursuit men had dug pits on either side of the empty fifty-five-gallon gasoline drums around the emplacement. Corporal Eric Schramm was behind one of the two .30-caliber Lewis guns and Cpl. Claire Cross was in charge of the other. Meanwhile, Pfc. Orville Roland was becoming increasingly anxious as he busily added sandbags to another Lewis gun emplacement near the 3d Pursuit's communications tent. How were they going to defend this place against a Japanese bombing attack with the few World War I–vintage Lewis guns they had set up? They had no other antiaircraft weapons at their disposal.[2]

HIGH OVER IBA FIELD
ZAMBALES, LUZON
12:40 P.M., DECEMBER 8, 1941

Twenty thousand feet overhead, Lt. Tamotsu Yokoyama arrived over the Iba area leading a column of fifty-one Zeros. They flew in a large circle, searching for enemy planes in the sky protecting the base, and he was puzzled to find none. Surely the Americans had issued orders to prepare to repel an attack on Iba before the Japanese arrived. Still, after checking for several more minutes, he confirmed that for some unknown reason there were no American pursuit ships waiting to intercept them.[3]

Three thousand feet higher than Yokoyama's force ahead of him, Comdr. Yoshizo Suda was spreading out the Takao Kū's twenty-seven Type 1 land-based attack bombers under his command in preparation for their northwest–southeast bombing run over the airfield. His own *chūtai* consisting of nine of the *rikkō* under Lt. Jirō Adachi was in a perfect V formation, with the *chūtai* of Lts. Hirose Mine behind and on his left and Koshirō Yokomizo behind and on his right, also forming Vs. Each of the bombers was to unload its twelve 132-pound bombs at three-second intervals as it passed over the field so that the bombs would carpet the small base below. Seated in front of Suda at the controls of the lead *rikkō,* Lieutenant Adachi observed the target from on high as he prepared to lead his nine-ship formation over it. The Takao Kū's senior *buntaichō* and a veteran of many attacks on Chungking in earlier years, Adachi was piloting the lead bomber in his *chūtai's* first attack against Japan's new enemy, the Americans.[4]

Adachi's bombardier, Seiji Ozaki, was also looking down at the base. He was surprised to find many planes lined up on the field. Why had they not taken off yet? Then he figured they must have landed in order to refuel after patrolling the sky over Iba in expectation of the Japanese attack force's arrival. Flying as observer/commander in the lead *rikkō* of the second three-plane *shōtai* in Adachi's *chūtai,* Lt. (j.g.) Kokichi Nakahara was looking down at Iba base as they began their bomb run. He was unim-

THESE MITSUBISHI G4M1 TYPE 1 *RIKKŌ* ("BETTY") FROM THE KANOYA KŌKŪTAI'S 6TH CHŪTAI BOMBED IBA FIELD ON DECEMBER 8, 1941. PHOTO FROM AUTHOR'S COLLECTION.

pressed with the size of the field located so near the coast. At that moment, he spotted three planes flying around at very low altitude, apparently about to land. Then he shifted his eyes to Adachi's lead ship, waiting for it to start dropping bombs.

As Adachi's *chūtai* approached the northwest part of the airfield, Commander Suda gave the order to commence bombing. It was 12:44 when Ozaki began releasing the twelve 132-pound bombs from the open bomb-bay door. As he watched them tumble downward, he noticed what appeared to be a small plane coming in to make a landing on the field below. Still, none of the aircraft he saw on the ground were taking off. A minute later, the twenty-seven *rikkō* had completed their bombing run. Suda next ordered his formation to swing to the right, toward the China Sea, and drop down to sixteen thousand feet. They would cruise at that height during the return to Takao. He was pleasantly surprised by the absence of antiaircraft fire coming from the base below.[5]

Trailing immediately behind Suda's formation at 132 MPH in a similar V-of-Vs pattern, Comdr. Toshii Irisa's twenty-six Kanoya Kū *rikkō* began their bomb run a minute after Suda's. Each plane in the chain dropped a single eleven-hundred-pound bomb plus six 132-pound bombs. Iba Field was blanketed by explosions.[6]

CIRCLING OVER IBA FIELD
ZAMBALES, LUZON
12:44 P.M., DECEMBER 8, 1941

Some seventeen thousand feet below the Japanese bombers, 1st Lt. Herb Ellis had been slowly circling five thousand feet above Iba Field. Unable to find the other five C Flight pilots following their confused take-off earlier, he was trying to make up his mind what to do in his situation. When he noticed something flashing by, he figured it was "Just another tropical rain shower." Then he realized that there was not a single cloud in the sky. Looking up to check out the situation, he was stunned to find the largest aircraft formation he had ever seen. It was flying directly overhead, dropping bombs on all sides of his ship. He suddenly realized that the sun glinting off the bombs was what had caught his eye. Ellis was impressed by the beautiful formation. Moving slowly from north to south, the two great Vs of Vs looked like giant sets of corporal's chevrons. He estimated their altitude to be about twenty-five thousand feet.

Ellis continued to watch as the formation began a gentle turn to the southwest, its bombing run completed. He noted that the aircraft on the outside, located so far from the pivot point of the turn that they were unable to keep up, began to fall behind the others. But enough of watching! Ellis put his P-40E into a climb. He was going to try to intercept the bombers alone, despite the great difference in altitude and the known sluggishness of his ship's Allison engine.

Unnoticed by Ellis as he circled the field, squadron mate Andy Krieger was also circling at about five thousand feet while providing top cover for three other ships as they descended to land. Krieger had returned to Iba with the B Flight leader, 1st Lt. Ed Woolery, and four others from their 11:45 A.M. patrol, which had taken them to Manila and Clark Field. They were low on fuel. First Lieutenant Frank Neri and 2d Lt. Dana "Chubby" Allen remained high while Woolery, 1st Lt. Ray Gehrig, and 2d Lt. Richard "Hawk" Root approached the field and Krieger hovered overhead.

Woolery, in the lead ship, put his flaps down for the final approach, cleared the fence at the field's south end, and touched down in a three-point position. At that moment, however, he was startled to see bombs exploding at the far end of the field. As his P-40E continued to roll north on the runway, explosions progressed down the field toward him. Then a bomb hit right behind him, blowing the tail off his ship. That was enough for Woolery. His plane upended, its nose to the sky but propeller still turning, the terrified pilot jumped out of the cockpit, hit the ground, and ran to a nearby gun emplacement for safety.[7]

When the first stick of bombs hit the north end of the field, Ray Gehrig was leveling off behind Woolery preparatory to landing. Aborting the maneuver, Gehrig advanced his throttle to combat rpm and pulled away from the field in a steep climb. Reaching a safer altitude, he saw that the field was covered by a mass of smoke and fire as he circled overhead.

Approaching the field behind Gehrig was his wingman, Hawk Root. He, too, aborted his landing and applied power, but he was still low over the north end of the field when fragments from an explosion tore into his ship. Out of control, the P-40E crashed nearby, killing Root instantly.[8]

Frank Neri, flying overhead, radioed the Iba tower for landing instructions just before his squadron mates approached the field to land. The reply was terse: "Do not land, enemy planes overhead!" Neri and his wingman, Chubby Allen, turned and headed out a bit beyond the coast off of Iba to check out a small boat, then minutes later came in low over the water toward the field. As Neri approached the landing strip at very low altitude, it seemed like the whole field blew up before his eyes. Shocked, he flew through debris from their barracks blown skyward by exploding bombs. Moments after clearing the explosions on the field, Neri realized that he had lost his wingman. He decided to try to intercept the bombers alone. He put his P-40E into a slow climb for altitude in the hope of catching up with the bombers he saw heading southwest.

Andy Krieger was also climbing, having decided to attempt an interception after witnessing the hellacious pounding his home field took. However, after giving his Allison full combat rpm as he began his climb at five thousand feet, Krieger's engine overheated and he was obliged to level off at twelve thousand feet to let it cool off and shift to a reduced rpm setting. Looking up from his new altitude, he was disappointed to see that the Japanese bombers were still far above him.[9]

3D PURSUIT SQUADRON OPERATIONS
IBA FIELD, ZAMBALES, LUZON
12:44 P.M., DECEMBER 8, 1941

Second Lieutenant Glenn Cave had been standing near the SCR-270B radio tent with another pilot when they heard the drone of planes overhead. "Look at the pretty formation of B-17s!" his fellow 3d Pursuiter exclaimed. Looking up, Cave quickly came to a different conclusion: "You're crazy—there aren't that many B-17s in the Philippines," he yelled.

As the bombs started tumbling down, Cave ran toward the beach in search of shelter. Seeing saw one of the foxholes the squadron had dug earlier, he dove into it. But it was very shallow. His heart pounding, he tried to compress his body into as small an object as possible.

Over at the 3d Pursuit's sandbagged communications tent, WO John McBeath and S.Sgts. Kelly Davis and Floyd Grow were on duty with Cpl. Maxon "Skedee" Gillett, one of the squadron's trainee radio operators. Davis was taking a message from Manila on the SCR-191 radio when they heard bombs exploding in a train toward their position. Grow threw himself down just as one hit outside the tent. Still on the radio, Davis was picked up and thrown thirty feet by the blast. Dazed but uninjured, Davis stood up amidst debris from the tent and sandbags. Joined by McBeath and Grow, he ran toward the beach and crawled under a *nipa* shack.[10]

Private First Class Hardy Bradley and another radio trainee had left the communications tent some ten minutes earlier, headed for the squadron mess hall. On the way, they met up with another radio trainee, Pvt. Harry Terrill, and Cpl. Cecil Bird. When they heard planes overhead and saw objects fluttering down accompanied by a whistling sound, they started running toward a line of slit trenches some two hundred yards away. It was too late. A bomb exploded near Bradley, throwing him into the air and then slamming him facedown into the ground. Something hot and sharp hit his elbow. Jumping to his feet, he was flattened again by another blast. Crawling on his hands and knees, he reached the edge of a large bomb crater. Bradley eased into the hole and then dropped the six feet to the bottom, which was hot and sizzling with metal fragments. Moments later, a body fell on top of him. It was his buddy, Terrill, also unhurt, but as dirty and scared as Bradley.

Sergeant Herb Tyson was eating lunch with many of the other men from the squadron in the 3d Pursuit mess hall when someone yelled, "Get out of the mess hall, here they come!" Men leaped to their feet, grabbed their helmets from a table on which they were stacked, and ran out the door. Tyson looked up and saw the high-flying formation and the bombs glinting in the sun as they descended, then headed for his Lewis gun position. He made it only halfway before bombs started exploding on the airfield. Spotting a large garbage pit just across from the fence where he was standing, Tyson plunged into it. He fell on top of several other men from the squadron who had chosen the smelly shelter for safety.[11]

At Woody McBride's Lewis gun emplacement just off the north end of the field, three 3d Pursuit officers had pulled up in their 1941 Ford coupe to check out McBride's situation. Second Lieutenant Shelton Avant was making the rounds of the gun positions with 2d Lts. John "Casa" O'Connell and Bob Hinson in his capacity as the 3d Pursuit's ground defense officer. Avant and O'Connell got out of the car, leaving Hinson behind. As O'Connell walked toward the emplacement, he stopped momentarily and looked up. Like many others, he saw what he figured were navy planes high overhead, but when he made out the shapes of bombs falling in a north to south pattern, he raced toward the nearest gun emplacement. He did not make it. A piece of shrapnel from a bomb exploding nearby tore off the back of his head.

As soon as the bombers were gone, McBride and his men climbed out of their pit to come to the aid of O'Connell and Avant, who had also been hit by bomb fragments and was "bleeding like a sieve." He was still conscious when they pulled him into the gun emplacement. He called for first aid, but there was no place to take him for help. The only uninjured officer from the original trio was Hinson, who had put on his helmet and hunkered down on the seat as the Ford jumped up and down from near misses.[12]

AIR WARNING DETACHMENT AREA
IBA, ZAMBALES, LUZON
12:45 P.M., DECEMBER 8, 1941

Over in the SCR-270B operations van, Henry Brodginski had finally gotten free of his scope and was heading out the door when a bomb exploded nearby, partially destroying the van and sending metal fragments tearing through the walls. One piece of shrapnel hit him in the back, and two caught him on the back of his right leg—but plotter Eugene McDonough was unscathed. The AWS men in the detachment's radio tent had gotten out and headed for the ditch on the beach just before a bomb shredded it. Like many others, they did not make it to safety. Flying fragments from a bomb hit struck and killed Orville Street and wounded Jarriet Moore. Sergeant Nelms was badly wounded in both arms by bomb fragments. His comrades dragged Moore toward the ditch to safety as the bombers finished their run.[13]

Caught on the beach while filling sandbags, Mel Thomas was unable to get to a ditch in time before bombs began hitting nearby. The first explosions sent flying metal into his abdomen right under the rib cage, knocking him down and ripping a kidney open. The AWS man was unable to get up on his own, but the next bombs to hit threw him up in the air. When he landed on the beach, he found himself flat on his back, but with his legs hanging over a crater. He tried to get up, but could not. He was bleeding from his wounds and his kidney and bladder had leaked out all the water. Seeing Sgt. Charles Heffron running by as he fled the explosions, Thomas called out for help, but Heffron did not even look at Thomas as he raced past him.

Disregarding Thomas's warning that morning, Bill Todd and John Harler took refuge under the SCR-270B's big power truck. Prophetically, a direct hit on the gasoline-powered unit turned it into a blazing inferno. Thomas's two AWS buddies were incinerated.

Other bombs struck the barracks building and the kitchen at one end of the mess hall that the AWS detachment shared with the 3d Pursuit Squadron. In the resulting kitchen fire, the detachment's cook, Pfc. Wash Shaffron, burned to death, as did the 3d Pursuit's popular Filipino cook, who had taken refuge in the icebox. While trying to get the kitchen staff to safety, 2d Lt. Andy Webb—one of the 3d Pursuit's pilots—was killed when the bomb hit the kitchen.[14]

OVER IBA FIELD
ZAMBALES, LUZON
12:46 P.M., DECEMBER 8, 1941

Having assured himself that there were no American fighters in the sky over Iba, Lt. Tamotsu Yokoyama signaled for his pilots to begin strafing the airfield below. Prior to leaving Takao, he had instructed them to limit their total combat time over Iba—including for strafing—to fifteen minutes in order to have enough time left to attack Clark Field afterward. Yokoyama left one *chūtai* behind to fly top cover and began descending from twenty thousand feet with the others. As they reduced their altitude, they still could see no enemy planes in the air.

When they had descended sufficiently, they formed up into the nine-plane strings in which they would fly their strafing pattern. Chief Flight Petty Officer Chitoshi Isozaki of the Tainan Kū *chūtai* attached to the 3d Kū for this mission was at the head of his three-plane *shōtai* and, like the others, maintaining a distance of 660 to a thousand feet between ships as they commenced their strafing attack. They flew in their box formation at very low altitude, pouring fire into the remaining spare or out-of-service ships on the airfield and its structures, including fuel depots. Some were strafing so low that they picked up electric cables with their wings. With no American fighters around to harass them, the strafers were having an easy time shooting up the field. Suddenly, Isozaki was surprised to find that a P-40 had penetrated his formation and was firing on the others. He tried to attack the intruder while maintaining the strafing pattern, but without result. Turning around in his ship afterward, he wondered if there were any other P-40s that had broken into their strafing pattern, but he did not see any.[15]

After completing several strafing runs, Isozaki looked at his watch to check the time. It was about 12:55, fifteen minutes since they had arrived over Iba. He realized it was time to break off the attack. Isozaki immediately put his Zero in a climb to meet with the others at the rendezvous point to the east, from which they would swing over to Clark Field.[16]

Over Iba Field
Zambales, Luzon
12:47 p.m., December 8, 1941

Twelve thousand feet over Iba Field, and still undecided whether he should try to climb and intercept the withdrawing bombers, Krieger looked down on the smoking airfield and noticed what seemed to be P-35As circling around. He assumed they were trying to land, and wondered why the fools could not see that the field had been cratered by a bombing attack. Then the thought occurred to him that maybe they were not P-35As, but rather Japanese ships, although they did not resemble any of the aircraft that intelligence had told them to expect. Krieger decided to descend to try to identify the mystery ships. To his dismay, he was soon able to see that they were Japanese, and that they were circling the field and methodically strafing in a beautiful right-hand traffic pattern. They looked impressive to Krieger, painted light gray with big red *hinomaru* on their wings. The thought finally dawned on him that he was in a serious predicament: he was alone against nine deadly adversaries.

Krieger decided to call for help to even the odds. "All pursuit to Iba!" he yelled over his radio. But immediately afterward a call came booming through his receiver: "All pursuit to Clark!" Wondering what had happened at Clark Field, he looked over in that direction. What he saw shocked him: a huge pillar of smoke was rising from the base up to what appeared to him to be about twenty thousand feet. Figuring that Clark Field would soon be receiving enough response to its cry for help, Krieger again called on the radio, but this time he stipulated "All 3d Pursuit to Iba!"[17]

For the present, however, he decided to take on the strafers by himself, diving into the nine-ship formation. After accomplishing the maneuver he discovered he was unable to line up his gun sight on any of the Japanese when they were within firing range because they were flying too low to pass under them. He boldly elected to enter their traffic pattern. As he was firing his .50-caliber wing guns at the ship in front of him, tracers whizzed past his P-40E. He kept his gun sight on the enemy plane to his front and saw that he was scoring hits on the Japanese strafer. A moment later it began smoking. Looking to the rear to check the situation, he was startled to see that three of the mystery ships were "throwing everything at me but the kitchen sink." That was enough for the novice combat pilot. Krieger swung out of the strafing formation and applied power as he hauled back on the stick and pulled his P-40E into a vertical climb. When he looked down a few minutes later, he was relieved to find that the Japanese had continued their strafing run instead of breaking off and trying to rid themselves of the intruder.

"Now what?" Krieger wondered. He was low on gas and would need to put down somewhere—and soon. He decided to call for instructions. In response, he heard the voice of Hank Thorne, his commanding officer, who told him to head for Rosales, which had been designated as the 3d Pursuit's auxiliary field. It was fifty-eight miles to the northeast.

OVER THE SOUTH CHINA SEA
12:49 P.M., DECEMBER 8, 1941

To the west, out over the South China Sea heading toward the Zambales coast, Herb Ellis could see a gigantic pall of black smoke hanging over the Iba area. He had aborted his attempt to intercept the bombers responsible for the attack on his home field due to the absence of an oxygen supply in his ship and the P-40E's notoriously sluggish performance at the seventeen-thousand-foot altitude he had reached while trying to close the gap with the Japanese. He was also worried about running out of fuel over water.

Approaching closer to Iba from the south at fifteen thousand feet, Ellis could make out low-flying aircraft in a right-hand traffic pattern around the field. That made no sense to him. The 3d Pursuit Squadron always used a left-hand pattern—regardless of whether they were preparing to land from the north or the south. As he drew nearer, however, he was able to make out the large red-orange *hinomaru* on the tops of their wings. They were Japanese, not Americans! He also realized why they had set up a right-hand traffic pattern: they were flying north off the coast, parallel to the landing strip, and then making a 180-degree turn to the south, making their strafing passes on the north-to-south run.

Despite the odds, Ellis decided to take on the Japanese. After first rechecking that his guns were loaded and then turning on the firing switch, he plunged down in a long, steep dive, planning to join the Japanese in the offshore leg of their traffic pattern—but in a left-hand pattern just outside their right-hand pattern. At the end of his dive, Ellis came in just over the top of one of the Zeros, closing rapidly. He leveled out as the other one approached to within about five hundred feet distance. Preparing to open fire, he hesitated for a moment when he remembered being told that a pilot's usual tendency when going into combat for the first time was to start firing too soon. Holding off until he was about a hundred yards short of the onrushing Japanese, Ellis fired his six .50-caliber wing guns in short bursts. He could see tracers going down both sides of his opponent's fuselage and ricocheting off the wing roots. At the last second, with the Zero looming in his windscreen, he pitched his P-40E underneath it, barely avoiding a collision. As soon as he was clear, Ellis began climbing to the left in a chandelle and positioned himself for a second run on the strafers.

On his second pass, the speed differential with the selected Japanese was not as great. Once again, he pitched under the Zero after firing, preventing the following Zeros from getting a fix on his belly, which they would have if he had pulled up instead. Fewer of his guns were working this time around, but his fire appeared effective, as the pilot did not try to take evasive action.[18]

While making his third run, Ellis found that only two of his six fifties were firing, and nothing happened at all when he pulled the gun trigger on his fourth pass. At that point, he decided to break off his attack. Climbing out of the Japanese formation in a circular pattern, he looked below to see if any of the Zeros were going to try to intercept him. To his relief, they all appeared to be continuing their systematic strafing of the airfield. Ellis wondered why none of the Japanese had fired on him or broken out of the pattern to give chase. He also noticed that five Japanese aircraft appeared to be lying in the shallow water just offshore.

While he was climbing, Ellis repeatedly pulled the gun chargers in an effort to recharge the six fifties and tested to see if the guns would fire, but without success. He was sure that he had not expended all of his ammunition, so he concluded that the firing mechanism had jammed.

What next? Attempting to land on what remained of Iba base appeared out of the question, so Ellis decided to head for Clark, hoping his remaining fuel would get him there. As he zigzagged through the mountain pass east of Iba, keeping an eye out for other Japanese, Ellis realized he had never felt so alone or scared in his whole life.[19]

Unnoticed by Ellis on his way to Clark Field, two pilots from his splintered C Flight were headed in the opposite direction over the same route, trying to get back to Iba after their terrifying experiences over Clark several minutes earlier. As Bill Powell flew through the pass in the Zambales Mountains, he noticed another P-40E to one side and below, proceeding in the same direction. Powell recognized the plane as Fred Roberts's. Arriving over the Iba area a few minutes later, Roberts was shocked to find his home field covered with flames and smoke. He would not be able to land his badly damaged ship there, and it looked like enemy aircraft were still over the airfield strafing ground targets.

Despite his harrowing experience against strafers at Clark Field, and with most of his guns still inoperative, Roberts plunged down in a diving attack on the string of Zeros. Getting behind one of them, he started firing on its tail, but only two of his .50-caliber guns were working. As the nimble fighter took evasive action, Roberts tried to stay in the tight turn with him. At the same time, another Zero right behind him was scoring hits on his ship. The P-40E caught fire, and with only ten gallons of fuel left in its tanks, Roberts decided to head for the South China Sea and try to beach his ship close to shore off of Iba. Descending at 120 MPH, he came in too high on his approach and nosed down when he hit the water about 150 yards offshore.[20]

Meanwhile, Powell had been circling overhead, watching the activity below. None of his guns were working, so he saw no point in joining Roberts in taking on the Japanese strafers. Then he spotted a Zero climbing rapidly from offshore, evidently with him in mind as its next victim. Unfamiliar with the climbing capabilities of the P-40E compared to those of the ship coming up after him, Powell switched his Allison engine to a military power setting in an effort to out-run the Japanese to higher altitude. However, after turning 180 degrees to get himself headed toward the north and his intended destination—Lingayen Field, fifty-eight miles away—he had leveled out and looked back to check his rear. Much to his surprise, "that bird was right on my tail!" In a near panic, Powell "opened her wide-open, to the firewall." A few minutes after attaining an indicated airspeed of three hundred MPH, he was relieved to find that he was gradually putting distance between himself and his pursuer. Nonetheless, the Japanese had managed to put a few more holes in his ship.

Shortly after Roberts and Powell reached Iba, Hank Thorne and the two remaining pilots of his A Flight were approaching Iba from the south at fifteen thousand feet after leaving Clark Field. The sight of their home field covered with smoke and flames and cratered by the Japanese bombing dismayed them. They began to search the sky above for signs of the Japanese bombers they had heard reported on their radios as being over Iba. Thorne was the first to spot them: two waves flying on a northerly course over the field. They appeared to be at about twenty-three thousand feet. Although they were some eight thousand feet above Thorne's altitude, the 3d Pursuit CO decided to attempt an interception and began a power climb with his two wingmen.[21]

After about nine minutes, the slow-climbing P-40Es had succeeded in reaching twenty-one thousand feet, but they were still some two thousand feet below the bombers, and their Allison engines were behaving sluggishly in the rarified air. Lack of oxygen had given Thorne a headache. He was concerned that the other two pilots might pass out from anoxia. Furthermore, their fuel was running low, rapidly being consumed in the power climb. Considering the circumstances, Thorne decided to break off the interception attempt. They were about twenty miles north of Iba and just over the South China Sea. Thorne led the others in a turn to the northeast and reduced his altitude. In an effort to reassemble all his scattered squadron mates and get them to a secure airfield, he flicked on his radio and called for all 3d Pursuit pilots to head to Rosales.[22]

Thorne was taken aback by a sudden response to his call that was shouted into his earphones: "Go to hell, you Japanese bastards!" He recognized the angry voice as Chubby Allen's. It was clear he believed that what he had picked up on his radio was a decoy call from one of the Japanese pilots. Allen had become separated from his flight leader Frank Neri during the bombing of Iba Field. In the meantime, Neri had managed to get up to about eighteen thousand feet in his attempt at a solo interception of the bombers withdrawing to the southwest after completing their attack on Iba. Like Thorne, Neri, running low on fuel and unable to continue at that altitude without oxygen, gave up on the chase and began a steep descent.[23]

3D PURSUIT SQUADRON OPERATIONS
IBA FIELD, ZAMBALES, LUZON
12:46 P.M., DECEMBER 8, 1941

As the Japanese strafers began their low-level attack on the remaining targets at Iba Field after the bombers finished making their run, Cpl. Claire Cross in Woody McBride's Lewis gun emplacement was ready for them. Positioned in one of the two pits, Cross began to pour a steady stream of .30-caliber fire into the line of Zeros after they turned right at the north end of the field and began their north–south strafing run over the field. McBride, who was in the next pit, saw a piece of one of the Zeros fly off when Cross fired on it.

After exhausting the first ammunition drum, Cross switched to a second one. Much to his frustration, the World War I–vintage machine gun would fire only a couple of rounds at a time after that. It was jamming from the sand and dust the bombing had kicked up and which got into it when he switched ammo drums. Cross and the others were trying to clear the jams manually after each round or two fired. The Japanese were so low as they passed over the emplacement that McBride's men felt like they could have gotten better results throwing rocks at them instead.

In the emplacement's other gun pit, McBride was hunkered down beside the empty gas drums with a badly wounded Lieutenant Avant when he suddenly hollered in pain. He had been hit in the left hip and the superheated metal fragment "burned like fury." When McBride screamed, Cpl. Eric Schramm, who was manning the Lewis gun in the pit, yelled, "My God, they've got Mac!"[24]

Near McBride's emplacement, Lt. Bob Hinson opened the door of Avant's 1941 Ford as soon as the strafing ended, intending to walk over to the gun pits. He took one step and fell flat on his face with a broken left leg. Bomb fragments earlier had penetrated his leg, right thigh, and the

arch of his foot. Sprawled on the ground, he groped for his helmet, which
had fallen off. It had a hole in it, punched from the inside out. Unknown
to him, a shell fragment had pierced it between the liner band and the
edge while he was wearing it in the car. Corporal Bob Doolan, a member
of McBride's crew, tried to help Hinson stand up to get him over to the
comparative safety of the emplacement, but Hinson resisted. He was anxious to get away from the airfield in anticipation of another bombing run.
Complying with Hinson's wishes, Doolan supported him as they headed
for a coconut grove across the road from the base.

Others in McBride's gun crew put Lieutenant Avant on a cot to carry
him off the field. He was in bad shape. Blood was oozing out of "what
looked like a thousand holes." Lieutenant Ed Woolery then joined them.
He had headed over to McBride's emplacement after getting out of his
wrecked P-40E uninjured. Together, the group carried the mortally
wounded Avant over to the coconut grove.[25]

Not far from the 3d Pursuit's mess hall, Pfc. Hardy Bradley and
those who were with him had scrambled out of the shallow bomb crater in which they had taken refuge. They had not gone fifty feet before
machine-gun fire from the strafing Zeros began whizzing by them. Suddenly, Bradley's helmet flew off, grazed by a bullet, but sufficient for the
concussion to knock him flat on the ground. Momentarily stunned, the
young soldier got up and ran with his buddy Harry Terrill to a double row
of fifty-five-gallon gasoline drums. Halfway down the line of drums, he
heard machine-gun fire thudding into them, followed immediately by a
loud explosion that blew the drums sky high and knocked the twosome
flat on the ground. Getting up once more, they ran flat-out toward the
trenches and the nearby Lewis gun position. Safely inside the emplacement, Bradley was stunned to see Pfc. George Jones holding his wrist,
which was connected to his hand by only a single tendon after being
severed by a machine-gun bullet. Another 3d Pursuit man was holding his
shoulder, his shirt soaked with blood.

Blown off his feet during the bombing attack, 2d Lt. Bart Passanante
lay on the ground in a shallow crater near the 3d Pursuit Squadron's burning radio tent. Blood oozed through the pants covering his broken right
leg. Hearing the sound of machine-gun fire, he turned his head and saw
the strafers coming right toward where he lay immobile. With a Herculean
effort, Passanante dragged himself over to a nearby cistern and propped himself up against the side of the concrete structure opposite to the direction
of the strafing Zeros. When the low-flying Japanese finally left, he lay down
on his back to ease the pain in his leg. Moments later, he called out to two
enlisted men who were approaching and asked them for help. They stopped
and stared at Passanante, then ran off, saying they would be right back. Later

Passanante found out that the two men thought the top of his head had been blown off. It seems he had smeared blood from his trousers all over his bald pate while trying to rub sweat from his head under the hot sun.[26]

Over on the beach, Mel Thomas of the AWS detachment was also on his back as the strafers began their first pass. Like Passanante, he was unable to get up because of wounds he had sustained during the bombing run. He watched the Japanese as they came down low and banked to get around the AWS antenna array and then proceeded down the field. However, they did not seem to have picked him out as a target, although their fire was hitting close to him.

Jarriet Moore, another member of the AWS detachment, was less fortunate. After being wounded in the bombing attack, he was being dragged toward a ditch but was hit and killed by the strafers before he reached the shelter. Meanwhile, Lieutenant Wimer told his men in the ditch to stay down. He had the high-powered .30-caliber rifle that he had brought to the Philippines with him all the way from his Texas home. During each of the three passes the strafers made on their SCR-270B equipment, Wimer drew a bead on the lead plane and fired at point-blank range as the Japanese skimmed low overhead. Wimer believed he hit the pilot on the third pass. He watched the Zero break off from the rest of the string of strafers and head out to sea alone.[27]

From the sanctuary of his foxhole on the beach, Lt. Glenn Cave was also looking up at the strafers flying in their rectangular pattern. He had at first thought they were P-35As, but when he saw red lights blinking on their noses and bullets kicking up sand near him, he immediately revised his initial identification. Hunkered down, the terrified 3d Pursuiter watched transfixed as the lines of nine ships passed by so low that he could almost count the rivets on the bottoms of their fuselages. When it appeared that the Japanese had finally finished shooting up the base, Cave checked his watch. It was 1:05 P.M.[28]

SOUTHEAST OF IBA
ZAMBALES, LUZON
12:57 P.M., DECEMBER 8, 1941

Flying at an altitude of about eight thousand feet southeast of the Iba area, Frank Neri was alone and undecided on his next course of action after having broken off his attempt to intercept the bombers. Unknown to him, he had also missed out on the strafing attack on Iba Field.

"Anyone around?" he called on the 3d Pursuit's radio frequency. He immediately picked up a response: it was the voice of his best friend, 1st Lt. Gerry Keenan. Unknown to Neri, Keenan had become separated from

Thorne's A Flight while patrolling over Iba at fifteen thousand feet. "Where are you?" Keenan asked. "I'm over Pinatuba at eight thousand feet," Neri replied, adding that he would wait for Keenan to join up with him there. Keenan informed his buddy that he would be coming from the south.[29]

As Neri circled over Mount Pinatuba at five thousand feet waiting for Keenan to join him, he noticed that his P-40E seemed to be vibrating. He checked for possible sticking valves, but found his engine to be in fine condition. A quick glance at the gun switches confirmed they were all off. He wondered what was causing the vibrations. Then Neri spotted three aircraft approaching him and called out on his radio, "Hey, Gerry, is that you?" When Keenan replied, "Yeh," Neri asked, "But who are you with?" Keenan's response was, "Nobody." To which Neri yelled, "Oops, you've got two Nips on your tail!"

Then the thought occurred to Neri that if his buddy had Japanese chasing him without his knowing it, perhaps he did, too. He looked back and, sure enough, a Zero was sitting on his own tail, red lights blinking on the top of its fuselage. That explained the vibrations: he was taking hits. Neri shoved the stick forward, sending his heavy ship into a sudden dive, heading straight down. After eating up several thousand feet, he pulled out and started into a climbing turn that would allow him to size up the situation. However, after coming only a fourth of the way up the oblique loop, he shot a glance back and was shocked to see the Japanese pilot cutting way inside of him! The desperate 3d Pursuiter immediately headed for some low-lying clouds and plunged into them. When he finally came out, he was relieved to note that he had eluded his pursuer. Unfortunately, he was heading right at another Zero. Neri cut loose with his six fifties, but his quarry eluded him by disappearing into another cloud formation. After scanning the skies around him for other Japanese and finding none, Neri looked for Keenan's ship, but he was nowhere to be seen either. Alone again, Neri decided to head east to Clark Field to see what the situation was like there.[30]

APPROACHING IBA FIELD
ZAMBALES, LUZON
1:05 P.M., DECEMBER 8, 1941

Alone, shot-up P-40E coming from the east appeared over Iba Field. Piloting it was 2d Lt. Don Steele, hoping to land at his home field after his earlier intimidating experience with the Japanese over Clark. Much to his chagrin, the entire base area was shrouded by smoke punctuated with flames. He could not make out any aircraft below, and the landing strip appeared to be pocked with bomb craters. Moreover, it looked like a destroyer was lying offshore shelling the field. Concluding that Iba was "strictly an unhealthy place to be," Steele, his fuel supply rapidly dwindling, realized he had to put his ship down somewhere soon. But where? He decided to check out San Marcelino thirty miles down the Zambales coast.[31]

Not far behind Steele as he approached Iba was his wingman, Ship Daniel, who was looking for a place to land his own P-40E. All six of his .50-caliber machine guns were jammed, and he was too low on gas to consider heading for the 3d Pursuit's auxiliary field at Rosales. Despite the airfield's pockmarked condition, he figured it was Iba or nothing. As Daniel touched down on the strip, he maneuvered to avoid the bomb craters and brought his ship to a halt without damaging it. Squadron mate Glenn Cave rushed up to greet him and congratulate him on his successful landing.

Another 3d Pursuit pilot had made it back to what remained of Iba, too, but not in his plane. When Fred Roberts crash-landed offshore, S.Sgt Al Bland and two other men from the squadron ran down to the shoreline and plunged into the sea. After swimming for a few minutes, they reached Roberts's ship. Climbing up on the wings, the three enlisted men reached down into the open cockpit and unfastened the dazed pilot's seatbelt. Once Bland and his two assistants managed to extricate him from the cockpit, they helped Roberts make his way through the shallow water to the shore, none the worse for his experience.[32]

CHAPTER 13

"All We've Got Left Is the Key to the Airplane"

At about 1 P.M., three of the Tainan Kū's *chūtai* broke off their devastating strafing attack on Clark Field and, according to plan, headed south for the airfield at Del Carmen, fifteen miles due south. They were going to shoot up the landing strip and thirty-four or so pursuit ships that were reported to be based there by a 3d Kū reconnaissance pilot on December 5.[1] However, barely outside Clark Field, led by Lt. Hideki Shingō's 1st Chūtai, Lt. Masuzō Setō's 2d Chūtai, and Lt. Akira Wakao's 4th Chūtai ran into what they identified as P-35As, evidently coming up from Del Carmen. In Wakao's *chūtai* Haruo Fujibayashi first thought the four he spotted in two two-plane formations were friendlies, but soon realized his error when they started shooting at the planes in his *chūtai* as they crossed in front of the Americans while they were climbing. When the *chūtai* had an altitude advantage of between seventeen hundred and two thousand feet, it began its attack. The P-35As did not counterattack, but despite firing at them three times, Fujibayashi and the others failed to score any hits.[2]

Wakao's *shōtai* fared badly. Both his wingmen—FPO2c Yasujirō Kawano and FPO3c Yoshio Aoki—were lost between 1:05 and 1:15 P.M. in the combat with the Americans. In Setō's 2d Chūtai, one of his *shōtaichō*, CFPO Ryōichi Nakamizo, was lost at 1:05 under similar circumstances.[3]

Just as the Tainan Kū's three *chūtai* started in the direction of Del Carmen, forty-two Zero-sen from the 3d Kū arrived over Clark after having departed Iba at about 12:50. Looking down, they spotted more than ten planes, which looked like a mix of P-40s and P-35s, apparently guarding the sky over the airfield at about fourteen thousand feet. Leading the formation, and highly excited by the prospect of engaging in combat with the Americans for the first time, Lieutenant Tamotsu Yokoyama raced ahead of the others. As he did, he realized that if they rushed into combat from three different *chūtai* positions, their excess speed would keep them from firing effectively. Yokoyama signaled for his pilots to maintain an appropriate distance and approach the enemy from above. Yokoyama's command *chūtai* of 6 Zero-sen, along with the 12 in Lt. Ichirō Mukai's 2d Daitai (consisting of two *chūtai* with 6 Zeros each) and the 6 remaining in Lt. Zenjirō Miyano's 1st Chūtai (3d Daitai), were to attack the Americans while Lt. Takeo Kurosawa's 1st Daitai with its 12 Zeros would fly top cover for them.[4]

Yokoyama caught up with the enemy's lead plane and engaged in a dogfight with it. Shells from his 20-mm cannon struck the American's wing and sent the plane in a plunge to earth when its wing blew off. The 3d Kū's flying commander exulted as he tore into other enemy ships: there was nothing he enjoyed more than dogfighting. It soon appeared to Yokoyama that most of the Americans had been shot down, with only two or three escaping.[5]

After confirming that there were no more enemy planes in the air, Yokoyama left Miyano's *chūtai* to fly top cover at fourteen thousand feet while the others descended for a strafing attack, passing through the black smoke rising up from the earlier attacks by the *rikkō* and the Tainan Kū's Zero-sen. Each *daitai* split into two six-plane *chūtai* to approach from different directions in a string formation, weaving through the heavy smoke obscuring the field and firing on those planes not yet destroyed. As he led his six-ship command *chūtai* on its first pass over the airfield, Yokoyama was flying so low that he could smell the smoke. After completing several passes, he and his pilots claimed setting fire to two B-17s and destroying another, burning or destroying four B-18s, and burning one P-40 and destroying four others. Fire from their 20-mm cannons ignited what appeared to be a fuel storage building, resulting in a huge explosion that belched fire reaching almost up to Yokoyama's plane.[6]

Although antiaircraft fire failed to hit any of the Zeros in Yokoyama's *chūtai,* others did not escape unscathed. Lieutenant Takeo Kurosawa, who led his six-ship *chūtai* on three strafing runs, found the fire coming up from the airfield to be very intense. To the leader of his other *shōtai,* FPO1c Shigeo Sugio, it looked like the tracers from the ground fire "were coming up in such wild confusion that it seemed that they would smack into one another." Due to the thick, black, rolling clouds of smoke, the whole area appeared to him "as dark as dusk." On the third pass, Kurosawa's Zero-sen took a third hit and also ran out of 20-mm ammunition. As the *buntaichō* climbed, Sugio followed behind. Looking up, he saw that his commander's ship had a hole about a foot square in its right wing. Kurosawa signaled to Sugio and the others, "I am out of it, so you fellows go down and give them the works."[7]

Sugio suddenly realized that his own ship was also damaged and that it was leaking gas from a fuel tank. He expected to crash and began heading west toward the China Sea, his CO alongside him. However, when he saluted Kurosawa and indicated his intention to ditch, the *buntaichō,* smiling back at Sugio, signaled: "Don't, don't!" Sugio felt like crying because of his defeatism, but he kept following Kurosawa, continuing to lose fuel, but making "every effort to use the remaining fuel as economically as possible."

When Kurosawa reached fourteen thousand feet, he was surprised to find a "jet black P-40" coming at him. Flustered, he reduced his prop pitch to the lowest setting and revved the engine, trying to gain power. He was too late. The enemy pilot caught up with Kurosawa and engaged the Zero pilot in a dogfight. Kurosawa, however, quickly discovered that his damaged plane's dogfighting ability was much better than that of the P-40. Within seconds he was on the American's tail, but as he was about to fire his 7.7-mm machine guns, the P-40 pilot went into a power dive, easily distancing himself from Kurosawa, whose speed had been down to begin with. To his disappointment, the American got away.[8]

Flying top cover for the strafers at fourteen thousand feet, Lieutenant Miyano and the other five pilots in his truncated *chūtai* were keeping an eye out for American ships other than those from the group they and the others had routed on arrival over Clark Field. During the twenty-five minutes they remained over Clark after their arrival at 1 P.M., they engaged P-40s at several locations, claiming a total of five shot down against no hits scored on their six Zeros.

High above all the activity below—at twenty-eight thousand feet—the pilot and observer of a C5M2 reconnaissance plane from the Tainan Kū strained to observe the results of the strafing attack. Lieutenant Masami Miza and his pilot, FPO1c Mitsuru Ōhara, had left Tainan base after Shingō's pilots departed for the attack and remained behind them on the way to Clark Field. At 1:15, Miza made a notation that they had seen six big planes, two medium-sized planes, and two small planes burning on the field. Then, out of the corner of his eye, Ōhara spotted something else and called to Miza, "Two enemy fighters are coming up to us from the left." Miza immediately broke off his observation of the field below as Ōhara headed his speedy ship in the direction of Iba.

To the west, high above the area between Clark and Iba Fields, the nine Zeros in Lieutenant Maki's *chūtai* had reached the rendezvous point for their return to Takao, their strafing of Iba Field completed. It was just before 1:10 P.M. At that moment, Hisōchō Chitoshi Isozaki, leading his three-plane *shōtai,* noticed another fighter climbing toward him, evidently in pursuit. At first he assumed that it was another Zero-sen, but in trying to make it out, he realized it was a P-40. Where did it come from? he wondered. It looked to Isozaki like the American was trying to intercept Maki's *shōtai* rather than his own. He saw the American fire at one of Maki's wingmen and stared in shock as the Zero blew up, pieces tumbling down to hit the ground. "Goddamn," Isozaki murmured. The pilot must have been napping.

As Isozaki made a turn that would put him in position to attack the P-40 from above, a glance at the oil temperature gauge on the control panel told him that his engine was overheating. He immediately opened the flaps on his engine cowling to cool the engine down. The maneuver caused his Zero-sen's speed to drop suddenly, and he found he could not get within firing range of the P-40, which was by then seven thousand feet below him in a steep dive. Isozaki broke off his chase and rejoined the others. It was 1:15 when they turned to head back to their Formosa base.[9]

DEL CARMEN FIELD, LUZON
1 P.M., DECEMBER 8, 1941

Eighteen well-worn P-35As thundered down the dirt strip at Del Carmen Field, fifteen miles due south of Clark, stirring up clouds of thick dust. Their pilots, all in the 34th Pursuit Squadron, were finally taking off after having waited in vain all morning for orders from Major Grover, spurred by the plumes of black smoke rising from Clark Field. Their commanding officer, 1st Lt. Sam Marett, had decided on his own that they should take off and attempt to intercept any enemy aircraft remaining over Clark. At the head of the formation, Marett and his wingman, 2d Lt. Frankie Bryant, were barely five hundred feet off the ground when two Japanese fighters diving out of the overcast six thousand feet above jumped them. Taking off from Del Carmen behind Marett and Bryant, 2d Lt. Stewart Robb, at the head of the third six-ship flight, thought the intruders were A-27s. He revised his identification, however, when he saw tracers streaming from their nose guns.

Startled by a burst of fire from behind, Bryant flipped his P-35A over on its back and pulled back on the stick, then almost collided with one of the other P-35As taking off. Although his ship had taken some hits, it did not seem to Bryant to be badly damaged. He regarded it as a miracle—"a blind man could have shot us down"—given their vulnerable position.[10]

Behind Bryant, in the third position, 2d Lt. Don "Shorty" Crosland was three hundred feet into his climb when he reacted to the Japanese pilot's attack on Bryant by turning his P-35A toward their adversary and firing two long bursts. Crosland then went into a tight turn but was unable to maintain it when his plane stalled out. Having straightened out and climbed up over the nimble ship, Bryant caught the Japanese in his gun sight and pulled the trigger. To his surprise and disgust, the guns did not fire.

After their frustrating encounter with the two Japanese fighters, Bryant and Crosland climbed to rejoin the other pilots, who were continuing on to Clark Field. Marett was no longer leading them, however. He had dropped out and headed back to Del Carmen when he discovered his guns were not working. First Lieutenant Ben Brown, the next most senior pilot in the squadron, took command of the formation and leveled off at eight thousand feet because their ships had no oxygen equipment, making it unsafe for them to go higher.

As they approached Clark at the base of the overcast, the 34th Pursuiters encountered six Japanese fighters. Despite being outnumbered, the enemy pilots were "very aggressive and cocky" and headed right into their formation. Brown made a ninety-degree pass at a two-ship element, his fire missing the lead plane but hitting his wingman with a deflection shot. The 34th Pursuit pilots quickly realized that they were at a clear disadvantage in a dogfight with Zeros. The Japanese ships easily outperformed their obsolete, engine-worn P-35As in every maneuver except dives, and the firepower of the Zeros cannon and machine guns was superior to their planes' two fifties and two thirties—some of which were not even working.[11]

Robb was pleased to see that he was getting good hits that caused flame and smoke to belch from the engine of one of the Zeros firing at a P-35A in front of it. A moment later he was horrified when his windshield exploded before his eyes. He had been so focused on the Japanese in front of him that he had failed to notice another one slipping up from behind. The 34th Pursuiter tried to escape his pursuer by making a tight vertical turn to the right, but to no avail. A stream of fire stitched across almost the entire length of his wing. The Zero overshot Robb's slower ship and went into a tight loop. While Robb was still in his own turn, the Japanese pilot completed his loop and came around behind the hapless American, ripping his P-35A with fire "from stem to stern." Slightly injured by glass and metal fragments, and with his engine apparently shot out, the terrified 34th Pursuiter spun out of his tight turn. Recovering moments later, he looked around but could not find his tormentor. Shaken but grateful to still be alive, he headed back to Del Carmen Field.

WEST OF CLARK FIELD
1:10 P.M., DECEMBER 8, 1941

Joe Moore glanced at his altimeter as it wound past 21,000 feet some thirty miles west of Clark Field. He had taken off from Clark in his P-40B at 12:35 and, applying full throttle, attempted to intercept the high-flying Japanese bombers that had devastated his airfield and were withdrawing to the north. His wingman, Randy Keator, was about 100 feet below and 1,200 feet behind Moore on his right. Still climbing, Ed Gilmore trailed about 2,500 feet behind and 3,000 below his CO. As Moore and Keator leveled off, they noticed a flight of planes at about their height rapidly approaching from the right. Assuming they were P-40s from Iba Field, Moore waggled his wings as a signal for them to join up with him. Closing rapidly in a tight formation of Vs, they were about even with Moore's right wing when they began a diving turn to their right. At that moment, Moore saw that there were nine of them—and that they had a "big fried egg" on their wings. They were Japanese![12]

To Moore's surprise, the fighters went after Gilmore, who by then was about five hundred feet below them. Moore led Keator in a diving right turn, intent on coming out behind and above the Zeros. As he closed with the nearest one, Moore fired his two fifties and four thirties, then continued his dive. When Keator completed his turn, he found himself face-to-face with the lead plane at the apex of the V-shaped column. Like Moore, firing his guns for the first time, Keator saw his tracers strike the Zero's engine and cockpit canopy. The enemy plane suddenly exploded, filling the sky in front of Keator with debris. The vibration he felt when he fired his guns sent shivers down his spine. Unfamiliar with the phenomenon associated with firing his P-40B's weapons, Keator had assumed the Zero pilot was shooting *him* to pieces.[13]

Pulling up after completing his pass, Keator looked back and spotted a Japanese closing in fast on his tail. Keator immediately pushed the control stick forward and pitched his ship into a near-vertical dive. His head hit the canopy and his feet left the rudder pedals: he had forgotten to fasten his seat belt and shoulder harness during their hurried takeoff. Regaining control of his fighter, he continued holding the stick forward in hopes of gaining enough speed to elude his pursuer. After descending a few thousand feet he pulled back on the stick and blacked out. Moments later, again conscious, he found that he was in a steep climb and the Zero was nowhere around. Keator leveled out after reaching nineteen thousand feet and fastened his seat belt and harness. While looking around for other Japanese, he spotted a P-40B a few thousand feet below him, diving on the tail of one of the Zeros but with another Zero on the P-40B's tail. He figured it was Joe Moore's ship.[14]

Diving down on Moore's pursuer, Keator succeeded in causing the Japanese to break off his attack. The enemy fighter went into a climbing turn to the right with Keator closing fast and following it around through part of a circle while firing tracers into the plane. But the more maneuverable Japanese plane continued to tighten the turn to a point where Keator had to break off his attack or go into a stall. When he lost sight of the enemy plane, Keator executed another diving turn, then leveled out and began a climb that took him back to the area of the original combat. He searched the sky for Moore and Gilmore, but saw no sign of either of them anywhere around. He did, however, spot three planes burning on the ground far below and thought that two of them probably belonged to his squadron mates.

Unknown to Keator, Moore was still in combat, but out of Keator's sight. He had just completed a second firing pass on the Japanese when a three-plane element broke "like a covey of quail" and went after him with a vengeance. Desperately trying to shake the enemy fighters off his tail, his head swinging from side to side, Moore angrily jerked the oxygen mask from his face. Despite using some of his favorite escape tricks, which in the past had always worked against P-40s during practice sessions at Clark, he still was unable to break away from his persistent Japanese pursuers. He was startled to see showers of tracer fire flashing past his ship. They looked like they were arcing into his cockpit but missing. Finally, giving up hope of eluding the Japanese, he put his P-40B into a steep dive and at last succeeded in leaving his tormentors behind.[15]

At a lower altitude than Moore and Keator, Gilmore faced the brunt of the attack at the initial stage of the action. Like his two squadron mates, he had turned sharply to his right in an attempted interception, but one of the Japanese got on his tail immediately and began firing at him. Gilmore immediately went into a diving turn to the left and, after building up sufficient speed, pulled up sharply to his right, causing him to black out momentarily. A check to his rear revealed that he had evaded his pursuer. Seeing no aircraft in the sky, friend or foe, and figuring that Clark Field would be too cratered to land on, Gilmore headed southeast and made for Del Carmen.

Meanwhile, Keator, flying alone at twenty-two thousand feet, concluded that the dogfight was over and started to head back to Clark. Several minutes later, he spotted a plane below him flying south on top of a solid bank of clouds at about five thousand feet. He could not tell if it was Japanese or American, so he decided to go down and check it out. Waiting until the plane passed directly under him, Keator plunged down with the sun at his back and approached from the rear. As he drew closer he was able to make out a red meatball on its wings. Keator pulled the trigger and was surprised when his adversary took no evasive action. Leveling out behind the enemy ship, he began firing at close range, observing his tracers striking the Zero's tail and canopy. The plane started to burn, then rolled upside down and entered the cloudbank inverted.[16]

At about the same time that Moore, Keator, and Gilmore intercepted the nine Japanese east of Iba, Herb Ellis arrived over Clark Field following his harrowing experience over Iba ten minutes earlier. "Scared to death" and his guns not working, Ellis had headed for Clark hoping to put his ship down safely there. However, after going through the Zambales Mountains pass and seeing the huge pall of smoke boiling up from Clark, he began to question his judgment. He could scarcely make out any of the base's features through the dense smoke. Nearing Clark Field from the west, the 3d Pursuiter noticed that the smoke was drifting southward. By flying to the north of the base, he figured he would be able to keep most of the field in sight as he attempted to make a landing. He entered a large cumulus cloud just east of Clark and took up a southerly course, keeping an eye out for any Japanese aircraft that might be lurking about on his right. Suddenly, black puffs of smoke appeared about fifty to a hundred yards in front of and slightly below his P-40E. He knew the source of the smoke: the antiaircraft boys at Clark were firing on him. To get his ship out of the line of fire, Ellis pitched violently downward. When he figured he was at a safe altitude—five thousand feet—he leveled out.

Although he was keeping a sharp lookout for Japanese on his right, he figured the thick cloud to his left would prevent anyone from approaching from that quarter. When he glanced in that direction to be double sure, he was shocked to see "baseball-sized" tracers coming straight at his ship and then curving behind his cockpit. What bad luck! It was apparent that a Japanese ship had dived through the cloudbank and by pure chance exited only about a hundred yards from Ellis and at a ninety-degree angle. It had already put a long burst into his P-40E's fuel tank behind the cockpit and into the rear fuselage. Now the Japanese pilot began a turn to follow Ellis's line of flight. Under normal circumstances, Ellis would have followed his instinct and turned into his adversary, but he resisted making such a maneuver. Instead, he pitched his plane down and out of the Zero's line of fire, knowing full well that his heavy ship could outrun any plane in the world in a dive.

A few moments later, Ellis began to smell burning paint. He looked all around but was unable to see its source. Ellis decided to crank his cockpit canopy open in order to get a better look to the rear. What he saw horrified him: The entire tail end of his ship was enveloped in flame, leaving a trail of smoke at least two hundred yards long. Ellis knew that his only option was to bail out, but first he needed to reduce speed and pull out of his dive. However, when he pulled back on the stick, the P-40E continued its dive. He knew at that moment that he was in serious trouble: the fire must have destroyed the fabric on the plane's horizontal control surfaces, which meant he would have to bail out in the dive. Pulling the canopy back, he managed to get his head and shoulders out of the cockpit, but the wind jammed him against the crash pad. Desperately digging his elbows into the canopy and the edge of the cockpit, he somehow succeeded in wiggling far enough out that the wind caught him and pulled him free.

Hurtling to the rear, he ducked his head, but the horizontal stabilizer on the tail still hit him in the small of his back. Thrown upward, he was caught behind the knees by the stabilizer, then banged his head when the wind threw him back up against the bottom of it.

Once he was clear of the aircraft, everything began to occur in slow motion as he spun through the air, a kaleidoscope of green, blue, and brown colors. When he finally pulled his parachute's ripcord, he wondered briefly if he was high enough before the canopy jerked open. In the distance he saw an aircraft diving toward him and figured he was going to be strafed. He began climbing up the risers on the left side of his parachute harness, turning the parachute half inside out, causing him to nearly free-fall. At that moment, a P-40 appeared out of nowhere and intervened, forcing the Zero to dive to the right. Ellis held onto the left-hand risers until he saw the ground rushing up and then let go, allowing the parachute to blossom out. He hit the ground standing. Still experiencing everything in slow motion, he collected his chute in the dry rice paddy in which he had landed and began to walk toward a road running off to the south.[17]

MOUNT ARAYAT, EAST OF CLARK FIELD
1:15 P.M., DECEMBER 8, 1941

Not far from where Ellis's rescuer had come—twelve miles due east of Clark Field—Earl Tash had managed to avoid drawing the attention of Japanese fighters as he flew his B-17D around the area behind Mount Arayat for thirty-five minutes following the bombing of the field. At about 1:15 he decided it was time to check out the possibility of landing at Clark. If that were not feasible, they would head for Del Monte Field on Mindanao. As Tash began the run to Clark Field, the sky appeared clear of aircraft. As they drew closer, they could see the thick smoke rising from shattered buildings on the base and make out the burning aircraft. Using field glasses, they could see planes circling low over the area, apparently American, flying in the regular landing pattern.

Tash picked out the end of the runway that looked safe to land on and ordered the copilot to lower their wheels. The ships they had seen at a distance now were clearly pursuit planes, diving in and out of the smoke billowing up from the airfield. They figured they were friendlies returning to base after chasing the Japanese bombers.

Tash ordered the bombardier, S.Sgt. Michael Bibin, who was flying as a waist gunner on the mission, to fire two red flares from a Very pistol to identify them as friendly. Just after he fired the flares, Bibin and the others were shocked to see a pursuit plane come diving through the overcast and crash straight into the ground. Instantly reassessing the situation, Tash turned to his copilot, 2d Lt. Douglas Kellar, and said tersely, "Doug, we're in the wrong damn place. Let's get the hell out of here!" Kellar whole-heartedly agreed with Tash's decision, having pointed out antiaircraft fire bursting all over the field. When Kellar responded too slowly to Tash's command, Tash himself pulled the wheels up and "smashed the throttles forward" to apply power. Just then, however, the ship's engineer, S.Sgt. John Sowa, called out that he could see three Japanese fighters coming at them from two thousand feet above, describing their approach from his position in the top dome. Kellar shot the manifold pressure up to seventy inches, although the regulations only allowed for forty-five, and within seconds the B-17D was up to 225 MPH indicated airspeed. By then, however, the Japanese pursuits were down on the deck and had started their attack run from the right rear. Kellar had wheeled the ship around and nosed it down just above the treetops to prevent the Zeros from getting under them or diving on them without smashing into the ground. Over the intercom he told the gunners to get ready to fire.

On the first pass, the Japanese pursuit cut the aileron and flap cables in half, hit one of the props, and struck Bibin. The bombardier had tried to bring the left waist gun around until it was facing the tail, but he could not get a bead on any of the pursuit ships as they were directly behind the B-17D. Bibin recalls feeling "as if someone had swung a baseball bat and hit me in the left shoulder." The next thing he knew he was sitting on the floor on the other side of the fuselage, blood running down his face and his left arm numb and hanging limply at his side. A bullet had ricocheted off the gun's armor-plated shield and gone through his parachute harness, and fragments of it hit him in the right arm, right lung, and right eye.[18]

Up in the nose, 2d Lt. Art Hoffman, the navigator, was frustrated because he was unable to bring his .30-caliber weapon to bear on the Japanese, who continued to attack from the rear. He "just sat there and watched the tracers whizzing by on each side, literally hundreds of them." So many, in fact, that it looked to him like the Japanese were shooting only tracers. Sergeant Arthur Norgaard was having better luck in the dorsal position. Manning his twin .50-caliber machine guns, Norgaard was fol-lowing the pursuits as they approached and continued firing as they passed by. He missed the first two, failing to line them up properly, but when the third made its pass, Norgaard caught him in his sights and stitched the ship from prop spinner to tail wheel. The crew watched the Japanese fighter suddenly flare smoke and dive toward the ground.

No other Japanese joined the attack after the three Zeros completed their pass. The ordeal was over within minutes. Hoffman figured that the Japanese must have used up most of their ammunition strafing the field before they pounced on their ship. That was enough for Tash, however. He had no intention of making a renewed attempt to land at Clark. Instead, he headed the bomber south toward Del Monte on Mindanao, hoping to get there in time to get medical treatment for Bibin, who lay half-conscious on the fuselage floor.[19]

John Carpenter had also been flying behind Mount Arayat trying to avoid detection by the Japanese, but he remained there when Tash attempted to land at Clark. His fuel was dwindling rapidly and he knew he would have to land soon. He did not have enough left to make it to Del Monte. It would be Clark or nothing.[20]

19TH BOMB GROUP OPERATIONS
1:20 P.M., DECEMBER 8, 1941

Although the Japanese were still shooting up the area around him, Capt. Ed Broadhurst was becoming concerned about the welfare of his B-17D, which was parked out in the open off the runway near other 30th Bomb Squadron ships. He and the others attending the Formosa mission briefing had gotten out of the 19th Group's headquarters building as soon as the bombing stopped and jumped into a slit trench behind it. They saw the craters created when a string of bombs hit right in front of the building but missed the wooden structure itself. Deciding to push his luck, Broadhurst climbed out of the trench and headed toward his bomber, ignoring the strafing Zeros overhead. Halfway to his destination, the squadron operations officer was met by his crew chief, S.Sgt. Lester Brady. He had bad news for Broadhurst. "About all we have left is the key to the airplane" he informed the captain as he handed him the key. Their ship had caught fire after several strafing passes. Broadhurst was relieved to learn, however, that all of his crewmen were safe, having taken shelter in a deep trench behind the revetment sheltering their B-17D. Unfortunately, the sandbagged walls had proven ineffective in protecting his ship from the strafers' machine-gun and cannon fire.

Near the 19th Bomb Group's mess hall, Capt. Bill McDonald was also out in the open as the Japanese strafed everything in sight. He was trying to help three fellow officers who had been severely wounded during the bombing attack and were bleeding profusely. The low-flying ships kept interrupting his efforts, however. Whenever a Zero approached his position, he had to get everyone down in a nearby ditch. By the time the strafing attack ended, all three were dead.[21]

Lying on the floor of the ambulance that had picked him up near the 19th Group's BOQ, Capt. Bill Fairfield was trying to trying to slow the blood pouring from Capt. Bill Cocke's back and chest as the ambulance set out for Fort Stotsenburg hospital. The "goon car" had not gone more than a hundred feet when the driver suddenly stopped and got out. Those passengers able to do so followed suit and clambered out, but Fairfield, unable to get up because of a bullet wound in his right leg, remained on the floor with Cocke. He suddenly realized why the driver had aborted the trip: there was a strafer overhead, firing at the ambulance, but the Japanese passed by without scoring a hit. The threat momentarily over, the driver climbed back in, joined by the other mobile wounded, and drove as fast as he could for the hospital, several thousand yards to the west.

In another ambulance headed to Fort Stotsenburg hospital on the same road and at about the same time, Sgt. Howard Harper was also stretched out on the floor with a leg wound. He was the first person the medics picked up in the smoke-induced darkness some twenty feet from where he had rolled away from his flaming B-17D. Also rescued from the site by the medics were T.Sgt. Alfred Hohimer, who was frothing at the mouth from his wound; Pvt. Jim Bibb, who was wounded in all four limbs; and an unscathed Pfc. Billy Templeton, who was looking after Bibb.

When they were barely halfway to their destination, with a total of five passengers on the seats and on the floor, someone yelled, "They're coming back!" The driver hit the brakes and everyone but Harper, held back by his leg wound, got out. After the ambulance was emptied of its passengers, Harper managed to crawl out and wiggle over to a wooden building on stilts off to the side of the road. Also under the structure was Bibb, helped out of the ambulance and to the building by Templeton, who had also crawled under the floor with his squadron mates. After getting themselves safely under the structure, they cautiously watched as the low-flying strafers continued shooting up targets in the area, including the ambulance.[22]

Overhead, John Carpenter was trying to bring his B-17D in, his fuel supply very low. From a distance, Clark Field appeared to be clear of strafing Zeros, but the sight of B-17s burning on the ground put him in a profound depression. As he approached the landing strip, he could see that the airfield was a "mess" and that it was going to be tough getting the bomber safely down without hitting any craters or wrecked planes. Nonetheless, he managed to find a section of runway stretching about fifteen hundred to two thousand feet that was not potholed, and brought the ship in for an uneventful landing. As he clambered down from his ship, he noticed Lieutenant Colonel Eubank coming toward him. Extending his hand in greeting, Eubank exclaimed, "That was a mighty fine landing, Carpenter." Eubank appeared dazed to Carpenter, who figured that his intact B-17 "probably looked awfully good to Eubank right then." Eubank was not known for praising his officers, and his compliment surprised Carpenter, who had never before received one from him.[23]

NORTHWEST OF CLARK FIELD
1:25 P.M., DECEMBER 8, 1941

As soon as the 3d Kū pilots completed their strafing attack on Clark Field they began climbing for the long return flight to Takao. Ten minutes earlier, the eight surviving Tainan Kū pilots of Lieutenant Maki's *chūtai* attached to the 3d Kū had also begun their return trip to Takao. They would all assemble at the rendezvous point some thirty miles north of Clark for the homeward journey. Halfway to Del Carmen to the south, the pilots of three Tainan Kū *chūtai* broke off their attacks between 1:20 and 1:25 and headed for the rendezvous area, too, joined by Lieutenant Asai's *chūtai,* which had remained to strafe Clark. It was about 1:30 when the first of the fighters began appearing in *shōtai* groups at fourteen thousand feet over Santa Ignacia, twenty-eight miles north northwest of Clark Field, the designated meeting point.[24]

Saburō Sakai in Hideki Shingō's *chūtai* was soaked with perspiration, his heart beating rapidly as he raced to the rendezvous area. He was also very thirsty and figured that he must have used up all his energy in his first encounter with American fighters. But he also felt somewhat sad that it was now all over. In Asai's *chūtai,* Masa-aki Shimakawa had a different sensation. Not having eaten since early that morning, he was very hungry. Now that the excitement was over, he decided to eat his lunch.

Sakai may not have noticed any American planes in the sky in the vicinity of the rendezvous point, but his *chūtaichō* did. Shingō was surprised to find a single P-40 approaching his *shōtai* from the rear. He regarded the pilot as very brave to attempt to take on his three-plane *shōtai.* Shingō and his two wingmen engaged the outclassed American in a dogfight and sent him spinning down in flames.[25]

21ST FIELD ARTILLERY REGIMENT AREA
NEAR SANTA IGNACIA, LUZON
1:20 P.M., DECEMBER 8, 1941

Down below, Col. Richard C. Mallonee, the senior American instructor for the Philippine Army's 21st Field Artillery Regiment, 21st Division, looked skyward when he heard the hum of airplane engines high over his position followed by the sound of machine-gun fire. Overhead he could see several Japanese planes working over a lone P-40. Moments later, the American ship burst into flames and fell "like a rock." As it plunged downward, the pilot bailed out and began floating slowly to earth. It appeared to Mallonee that he would hit the ground near the 21st Division command post (CP). He and the others around him continued to watch the Japanese pursuit planes as they flew north until they were no longer in sight.

Shortly afterward, a Filipino boy on a *calesa* pony rode up to the CP and excitedly announced that he had found an American aviator about two and one-half miles away, sitting on his chute in a dazed condition. Mallonee sent a doctor and litter bearers with the boy to bring the pilot back to the CP. When they returned with him about two hours later, he identified himself as 2d Lt. George Ellstrom of the 3d Pursuit Squadron. Ellstrom, who seemed to be suffering from shock, complained of severe stomach pains, but Mallonee could not find any wounds on him except for brush burns on his shoulders. His shattered watch had stopped at 1:20 P.M.

Ellstrom told Mallonee that he had been on a routine reconnaissance over the Zambales Mountains. Although he knew that the war had started, he did not know that there were any enemy planes over the Philippines until Japanese pursuit ships surrounded him. "We were tricked, we were tricked," he kept repeating. Shortly afterward, as he was being taken to the hospital, Ellstrom died.[26]

PHILIPPINE ARMY PARADE GROUND AREA
LINGAYEN, LUZON
1:15 P.M., DECEMBER 8, 1941

Thirty-two miles north of the point where Ellstrom was shot down, squadron mate Bill Powell was descending to land after having barely escaped a fate similar to Ellstrom's. He had arrived over Lingayen Field shortly after managing to outrun a Zero in level flight that had been chasing him from Iba. Powell discovered that the field was actually a Philippine Army parade ground area rather than an airstrip, but he was not going to quibble about that after his terrifying experience. Hitting the sandy ground too fast—he estimated he was going 140 MPH—he tried to slow down his P-40E before it ran off the short parade ground. His plane came to a halt just in time, out of gas. With the help of some Filipino troops, he pushed the ship under some palm trees to hide it.

ROSALES FIELD, LUZON
1:15 P.M., DECEMBER 8, 1941

At about the same time, Ellstrom's best friend, Andy Krieger, was bringing his own P-40E down safely at the 3d Pursuit's auxiliary field at Rosales, thirty miles east of Lingayen. Like Powell, his gas ran out as he was taxiing across the primitive field. Minutes earlier, he had passed high over Santa Ignacia on his Iba–Rosales route and spotted three Zeros below him, but decided not to attack them because he was so low on gas. (Krieger had apparently seen Shingō and his wingmen, who shortly after he saw them became the instruments of Ellstrom's death.) Upon climbing out of his plane, Krieger found that his CO, Hank Thorne, was already there, as were fellow 3d Pursuiters 1st Lt. Bob Hanson and 2d Lt. Howard Hardegree. They were servicing their P-40Es in dispersed positions around the twenty-five-hundred-foot strip. Several minutes later, at about 1:30, the pilots heard a plane approaching. They looked up and saw that it was another P-40, its flaps and wheels down. The plane just cleared the trees, hit the ground, and slowed down quickly because its left tire was flat. His squadron mates greeted Frank Neri warmly when he climbed out of the ship.[27]

Neri and the others examined his P-40E and were amazed that he had made it in safely. The left tire was ripped to shreds, the aileron and left wing tip were badly damaged, there were holes in the propeller, and the right side of the fuselage was stitched from stem to stern with 7.7-mm hits—with a fortunate break in the cockpit area. As he stared at his riddled fighter, Neri suddenly felt scared.

Neri described his hair-raising experience east of Iba to his squadron mates. After that combat he said he went to Clark and circled the field there for some time, but found it too badly cratered to land safely. His gas tanks were nearly empty, but he figured he had enough fuel left to make it to Rosales, fifty miles to the north. When he finished his account, they pushed his shot-up ship off the strip and under a tree. It was the only one that had landed there that was not flyable. Minutes later they heard another plane coming in low over the field. It was another P-40, but the pilot just buzzed the field and then headed south in the direction of Manila.

NEAR SAN MARCELINO, LUZON
1:15 P.M., DECEMBER 8, 1941

Along the coastline south of his devastated home field at Iba, another 3d Pursuiter, his fuel supply perilously low, was desperately trying to find a place to put down his shot-up ship. As Don Steele continued south on his search, he noticed a dried-up riverbed a few miles out, toward San Marcelino, thirty miles south of Iba. He decided to try a landing in that unlikely location. To his surprise, he managed to set the plane down in one piece. After climbing out of the "old junk heap," he examined it. He could not understand how it had continued to fly in the condition it was in. "Right then and there, I thanked the Curtiss company for building such a sturdy airplane," he recorded in his diary that evening.

Steele pushed his ship into some nearby trees to get it out of sight. Suddenly, he was shocked to see someone coming out of the bushes. To add to his surprise, he found that it was his squadron mate, 2d Lt. Gordon "Squirrely" Benson. Benson explained that he too had landed in the riverbed and rolled his P-40E into the bushes. Flabbergasted by the strange coincidence, they set out together on foot in the direction of San Marcelino to the south.[28]

Back at Iba Field, Ship Daniel was trying to find a means to fly out of the smoking base after having landed his badly shot-up ship there. When Daniel and squadron mate Glenn Cave went to check out the status of the six spare P-40Es that the 3d Pursuit had in reserve there that morning they discovered there were only five left. Ed Woolery had taken off in one earlier, following the destruction of his original ship when he landed during the bombing attack. Of the five remaining ships, all but one had been damaged or destroyed in the bombing and strafing attack.

Daniel and his Kelly Field flight-school classmate worked out a plan for Daniel to take off in the one flyable P-40E left at the bomb-pocked landing strip. Cave would stand in a bomb crater in the middle of the field and wave a torn sheet to signal to Daniel that he had to clear the field at that point or risk crashing in the craters beyond it.

After completing his preflight checks, Daniel applied maximum power to the roaring Allison engine and released the brakes. The P-40E tore down the southern end of the field and, after using up only twelve hundred feet of the airstrip, lifted off well short of the midpoint and headed north.[29]

DEL CARMEN FIELD, LUZON
EARLY AFTERNOON, DECEMBER 8, 1941

At Del Carmen Field, the pilots of the 34th Pursuit had miraculously brought their worn-out P-35As safely down after the one-sided battle south of Clark Field with the Japanese mystery ships. Not one of them had been shot down, but all were damaged. Stewart Robb had to make a wheels-down dead-stick landing with both tires flat. After their terrifying experience, 2d Lt. Jim Henry told his squadron mates that he would never again go up against a Japanese Zero in a P-35A.

As they checked out the situation at Del Carmen, the 34th Pursuiters encountered Ed Gilmore of the 20th Pursuit Squadron, who had landed there in his P-40B after evading Japanese fighters that had pursued him west of Clark Field. The pilots learned that the two Japanese that had jumped them on takeoff had afterward made a short strafing attack on Del Carmen. Fortunately, they had not done much damage, but it was enough of a warning for Sam Marett to order his men to strike their tents and disperse.[30]

CLARK FIELD, LUZON
EARLY AFTERNOON, DECEMBER 8, 1941

At about the same time Gilmore landed at Del Carmen, his squadron mate Randy Keator was approaching Clark Field to the north, trying to contact the control tower for landing instructions, but without success. From briefings he had received before on the procedures to follow for emergency landings, he knew what to do in this situation. Reducing his altitude to one thousand feet, he brought his P-40B in slowly from the east, wheels down. The dense black smoke rising from burning aircraft, oil tanks, and debris on the field obscured his view. Unable to find an undamaged strip wide enough to put down on his first pass, he went around again. Finally, on the third try, he managed to locate a clear section at the extreme edge of the airfield and set his ship down between several burning B-17s.

Played out from the day's ordeal, Keator barely managed to climb out of his ship and jump to the ground. The airfield looked deserted. Then he saw heads slowly begin to appear out of some nearby slit trenches. Apparently realizing that it was not a Japanese plane that had just landed, several men rushed over to Keator and inquired if his plane had been hit. "No, I don't think so," he replied. The men expressed surprise and exclaimed, "Well, our antiaircraft gunners were firing at you with every available gun the whole time you were circling the field!" Renewed chills went up and down Keator's spine.[31]

A few minutes later, Keator's CO started circling the field at low altitude. Joe Moore at first could not find any uncratered sections on which to land, either. Finally, after circling twice, he decided to put down on the two-thousand-foot airstrip extension near the 19th Bomb Group area, despite its pocked condition. It was not far from where Keator had landed. After taxiing between the craters and parking his P-40B, Moore was met by one of his squadron's enlisted men. "Good Lord, Lieutenant," the man exclaimed. "They've been shooting at you with everything they had!"

Moore's safe arrival was a surprise to Keator and the other 20th Pursuit pilots present. Keator had told them that Moore had been shot down. He had assumed that one of the three planes he had seen crashed and burning on the ground while in combat west of Clark was his CO's, since the last he had seen of Moore was when the squadron commander was diving straight down with Japanese fighters on his tail.[32]

Later, reflecting on the day's experiences, Keator recorded in a diary addendum: "If this is an example of what war is like and it is only the first day, I wonder what my chances are of making it all the way to the end?"

THE WRECKAGE OF A 19TH BOMB GROUP B-17 DESTROYED DURING THE ATTACK ON CLARK FIELD BURNS FURIOUSLY ON DECEMBER 8, 1941. PHOTO COURTESY G.A. VON PETERFFY.

NICHOLS FIELD, LUZON
EARLY AFTERNOON, DECEMBER 8, 1941

At Nichols Field to the south, another 24th Group pilot was more worked up than pensive after what he had gone through that day. Unlike Keator and Moore, Sam Grashio had brought his shot-up P-40E in for a safe landing at about 1:30 without being fired on, having followed the instructions that were radioed to him as he approached the field. Very popular with the 21st Pursuit's enlisted men, the warm-hearted, emotional officer was met by S.Sgt. Bryan Gibson, who hugged him joyfully. When they inspected Grashio's ship, they found that the P-40E's right aileron had nearly been completely shot off and that the wing had a hole in it "you could throw a hat through." The high-strung Grashio exclaimed, "By God, they ain't shooting spitwads, are they!"

Grashio was happy to find that Gus Williams and Johnny McCown—who had shared the terrifying combat with the Japanese fighters over Clark—were back safely, too. On landing, all three were met by their CO, Ed Dyess, who had returned to Nichols much earlier after leading the 21st Pursuit's A and B Flights on their futile patrol over Manila Bay. While the squadron's planes were being serviced, the pilots walked over to Dyess's operations tent. There were Cokes in the tubs, and olives and sandwiches had been put out for them. It was their first meal since early that morning.³³

A few minutes after Grashio landed, another P-40E approached the field and came in to land. The pilot, Ray Gehrig, of Ed Woolery's B Flight, had only three gallons of gas left in his tanks. After escaping the Japanese fighters at Iba, the senior 3d Pursuiter had first headed for Clark Field. Finding it "a smoked-covered mess," he decided that Nichols offered him the best chance of getting his ship down safely, considering his dwindling fuel supply.

Shortly afterward, yet another P-40E was spotted coming in for a landing. Ed Woolery, who had buzzed Rosales Field earlier, had had enough gas left in his tanks that he decided to try to land at Nichols rather than the primitive auxiliary airfield. After joining squadron mate Gehrig and the pilots of the 21st Pursuit Squadron on the field, Woolery regaled them with an account of his brush with death when he landed at Iba and of his escape from the devastated airfield in the spare P-40E.³⁴

CLARK FIELD, LUZON
EARLY AFTERNOON, DECEMBER 8, 1941

About halfway between where his B-17D was strafed and the hangar used by the 30th Bomb Squadron, Pvt. Mike Artukovich and the others in the big trench where they had taken shelter during the bombing and strafing attacks were calling for help. No more of the strafers seemed to be around. During the bombing, a small 132-pound bomb landed in the ditch, blowing off the 30th Squadron armorer's shoes and shirt, and sending a sliver of shrapnel into his left ear. Although the men had shifted positions from side to side to avoid the strafers' fire, several were hit, adding to the toll of those wounded by the bomb explosion. In response to their cries, a flatbed truck drove up to the trench. It was quite a sight: the windshield had been shot out and all four tires were flat. Those who were able climbed out of the trench and helped the wounded get on the truck. It proved to be a long, rough, trip for the driver and his twelve or so passengers as the battered truck bumped along the road on its rims to the hospital at Fort Stotsenburg.³⁵

Near the 28th Bomb Squadron's barracks, Cpl. Grant Adami climbed out of his trench with a friend, A. L. Ingalls, now that it appeared the strafing attacks were definitely over. They intended to head down to Adami's weather office in the Clark Field headquarters building to check out its condition after the bombing and strafing attacks, but first they walked over to the squadron's post exchange (PX) "to see what we could find in the way of ice cream." What they found was blood "about two inches deep" on the concrete floor at the entrance. The structure itself had been strafed and cut up by bomb fragments. They got no ice cream.

The 28th Bomb Squadron barracks building next to the PX had also been badly damaged. Inspecting what remained of the two-story wooden structure, they found that one bomb had struck directly in the center of the orderly room and continued down to the ground, its explosion creating a "gaping crater" and rupturing underground water lines. Another bomb had landed in one of the trenches in front of the barracks, killing several of the men sheltering in it.

Heading down in the direction of the hangar line, Adami and Ingalls saw the bodies of several men lying out in the open. Nearby, several P-40s were "still burning furiously." Black smoke billowed skyward and there was fire everywhere. As a trained weather observer, Adami noted the "strange, hot, and gusty wind" blowing from the direction of Mount Arayat to the east, which he figured was caused by the burning planes, buildings, and fuel on the base. A little farther along, the pair came across the remains of a man who had been firing a Lewis gun from one of the greens on what had been a miniature golf course. He had apparently been torn apart by a bomb. The machine gun "was twisted beyond recognition," and small pieces of his body and strips of the blue denims he had been wearing were scattered over a wide area. Some men were trying to identify the remains, but the largest body part they had found thus far was a piece of his upper trunk about six inches in width.

Continuing their sickening trek, Adami and Ingalls next noticed the body of a Filipino who had been huddling against one of the trees near the hangars, apparently the only shelter he could find during the bombing attack. When they approached to inspect the body, they found that a shell fragment had blown off the entire back of the man's head. Near the dead man by the tree lay another Filipino, his abdomen blown open and his legs twisted awkwardly.

Passing by the first two hangars on the flight line, they found only "a mass of wreckage." The wooden Clark Field headquarters building between the two pairs of hangars in which Adami had been working that morning exhibited the results of relentless strafing and near-miss bomb explosions. One bomb had landed directly on the weather office's rain gauge outside, and another had blown up "the Chinaman's" nearby cold drink stand. Checking inside his office, Adami felt a personal sense of loss when he found that nearly all of his weather instruments had been destroyed.[36]

30TH BOMB SQUADRON OPERATIONS
CLARK FIELD, LUZON
1:30 P.M., DECEMBER 8, 1941

Some distance away, 2d Lt. Austin Stitt was also headed over to his unit's location to check out the situation after the strafing attack. To the young bombardier, "everything everywhere seemed on fire or dead." Reaching the 30th Bomb Squadron's operations tent, he found his squadron mate and buddy, 2d Lt. Woodrow "Woody" Holbrook, there. Shortly afterward, they noticed a doctor collecting wounded personnel from the airfield and helped him until the truck he had with him was loaded and on its way to the Fort Stotsenburg hospital. Holbrook then suggested they go over to 19th Bomb Group headquarters and find out what they were supposed to do.

Squadron mates Jim Colovin and Ed Benham had also headed for the 30th Squadron operations tent after the strafing. Benham's eyes appeared to Colovin to be "as big as saucers" as they ran past bodies everywhere under trucks and planes. The radio operator lying near the radio station had a leg blown off and a big hole in his belly. They also saw an ambulance nearby, riddled with holes.

The two young second lieutenants found "nothing doing" around the operations tent, so they went to the orderly room tent "to make themselves useful." Along the way they ran into Eddie Oliver, who decided to join them. When they reached the tent, they found that the squadron adjutant, 2d Lt. Bill Taylor, "had things pretty well in hand" and 1st Sgt. Allen Brenner was calling the roll. After having a drink of water, Colovin, Benham, and Oliver sat down on the ground "to think the whole thing over."

Then Stitt showed up with Holbrook, stopping by on their way to group headquarters. They all agreed to go over to the BOQ, but first Stitt and Holbrook wanted to stop by headquarters. They told the others they would catch up with them later. Just outside the headquarters building, Stitt was surprised to see an old friend, Frank Bender. He had not known his fraternity brother from Hobart College in Geneva, New York, was anywhere near the Philippines. Bender had induced Stitt to join the Air Corps in the first place. "After much back-slapping and carrying on," Stitt postponed his plans to check in at headquarters and invited Bender and a fellow 27th Bomb Group lieutenant with him to join him and Holbrook over in his *sawali* quarters for a drink. Stitt had a fifth of Johnny Walker Red Label in his hut.

To get to Stitt's *sawali* quarters, they had to go behind the officers club. As they passed by, they saw many dead and wounded Filipinos who had been eating their lunch when the bombers hit the building. When he noticed the leg of a Filipina lying in the dust, he remembered the severed leg he had seen in the ditch during the attack and concluded it must have been that of squadron mate George Berkowitz. When they finally reached Stitt's *sawali* hut, the four of them nearly finished off the full fifth of scotch "in about five minutes." Bender explained that he had arrived with the 27th Bomb Group two weeks earlier, but that their planes had not yet arrived. Stitt felt that the 19th Group was in the same boat. Bender's planes were at sea, and his group's had been destroyed. They all felt "truly lost."

Holbrook decided to go to his *sawali* and collect his valuables. Meanwhile, Bender and his squadron mate said they were going to find a way to get back to Manila and left. Deciding he wanted "to die in good clothes" or at any rate needed good shoes, Stitt changed to his best pants and shirt and put on the pair of new shoes he had had made at Fort Stotsenburg. Then he set out for group headquarters, where he found that "no one knew anything." A captain told Stitt to report to 1st Lt. Sig Young on the flight line for instructions.

In the meantime, Colovin and Oliver had set out for the BOQ. On the way, they had to go around a burning B-18, its .30-caliber ammunition exploding and sending bullets off in all directions. At the rear of the first officer's hut, they saw a dead Filipina with someone else's legs lying beside her. A Filipino boy on his bicycle was searching the area for his relatives. The pair agreed that the area of the *sawali* quarters "was not a healthy place" and decided to collect blankets and sleep on the golf course.[37]

About a thousand yards to the north of the *sawali* quarters, up against the jungle, another B-18 had survived the attack without a scratch, as had the 28th Squadron enlisted man who had been assigned to guard it after it was parked there upon returning from the morning evacuation of Clark Field. When the bombers appeared overhead, Pvt. Robert W. Phillips, a twenty-one-year-old aircraft mechanic assigned to the squadron, immediately crawled under the gasoline trailer positioned next to the old bomber, foolishly figuring that it offered "the best hope for cover." Fortunately for Phillips, the B-18 and the trailer were not in the bombing pattern of the *rikkō* overhead, nor were they noticed by the low-flying Zeros, focused as they were on targets within the immediate vicinity of the base.[38]

30TH BOMB SQUADRON OPERATIONS
CLARK FIELD, LUZON
EARLY AFTERNOON, DECEMBER 8, 1941

When the strafing ended, 1st Lts. Frank Kurtz and Lee Coats and 2d Lt. Bob Meyer climbed out of their ditch from which they had been taking potshots with their forty-fives at the low-flying Japanese and headed over to the 30th Squadron operations tent to report. They had to walk around the wreckage of one of the B-17s still burning in its revetment. It was not only the intense heat that made them give the ship a wide berth, but the sadness of having to look at the B-17D in its "death agony." Its plates had weltered, "leaving only her naked skeleton shimmering in the heat and licked by the oily flame."

They were surprised to find that their operations tent had not been hit in the attack. They found their CO, Maj. Dave Gibbs, inside. Together they looked out over the airfield at the "burning or smouldering carcasses" of what they had considered "the mightiest fleet of four-motored bombers in the world." Then Gibbs said to Kurtz: "Frank, I think you'd better go over and take a look at your plane. See if by chance you can still fly her." From the tent, Kurtz could not see "Old 99" because it was positioned on the far side of the runway hump. Kurtz got on his bike and pedaled toward the rise in the runway. His heart started pounding when he saw Old 99's vertical stabilizer rising above the crest as he approached the top, but the sight that awaited him as he pedaled down the hill made it sink: All that remained of his ship was its tall, silver tail, "not even scorched or smoke-stained." Dropping his bike by the side of the runway, Kurtz walked over to its final resting place. He looked emotionally at the black and twisted ribs. The aluminum skin had melted off, leaving a naked carcass. Kurtz could see right through the fuselage into the pilots' compartment, where he and his copilot, 2d Lt. Tex Gary, used to sit side by side. Old 99's four engines had tumbled out of their nacelles in the crumpled wings and were lying on the ground. The ship was still all there, "only melted and bent and ruined and her back sagging and broken."

Then Kurtz noticed a "half burned bundle of something" lying under the wing. It was one of his crewmen. Beside that bundle lay another. Then he saw another one under Old 99's belly. Underneath the tail were the remains of Pfc. Everett Dodson. As he walked around the tail, he could see that they were "all eight in a line," from S.Sgt. Wyndolyn Burgess nearest the ship on down to Tex Gary at the very end, "with all his clothes blown off by the bomb blast." Kurtz lifted his copilot's head, "still soft and warm," and talked softly to Gary in his grief.[39]

Base Operations Building
Clark Field, Luzon
Early afternoon, December 8, 1941

Still suffering from the shock of bailing out, Herb Ellis was walking back toward Clark Field when a vehicle approached him. The driver offered him a lift to the base operations building on the hangar line. Entering the wooden structure, Ellis looked for any officer who could give him information. He finally located one, a major whom he did not know, sitting behind his desk going over some papers. Ellis waited patiently for the officer to recognize him. Finally, he looked up and asked Ellis in a surly manner what he wanted. Ellis identified himself and explained that he had been shot down and that he was looking for the 24th Pursuit Group's headquarters. The major paused for a long time before responding. "There ain't no more 24th Pursuit Group," he said flatly, then returned to his paperwork, not waiting for a reply. Ellis realized that he had been dismissed.[40]

CHAPTER 14

"What Is the Matter with the Enemy?"

High over Luzon's west coast in his C5M2 observation plane, Lt. Masami Miza was heading north to his Tainan base accompanied by the pilots of four damaged Zeros from his Tainan Kū with whom he had joined up at about 1:30 P.M. at the rendezvous point. He felt fortunate that no enemy fighters were chasing them. In one of the damaged ships, FPO2c Ryokei Shinohara was flying back with blood on his face. His Zero had been hit in the windscreen by antiaircraft fire while strafing Clark Field. The ship of his *shōtaichō*, Lt. Masao Asai, was also returning in damaged condition, having taken three hits. In Lt. Akira Wakao's hard-hit *chūtai*, a third pilot, FPO1c Keishu Kamihira had sustained twelve hits during the Clark attack. His *shōtai* leader, WO Yoshimitsu Harada, received ten hits during the Clark strafing.[1]

NICHOLS FIELD, LUZON
3 P.M., DECEMBER 8, 1941

At Nichols Field, eighteen 17th Pursuit Squadron P-40Es were coming in to land at about 3 P.M. The pilots were all just about out of gas after having patrolled for almost two and one-half hours over Manila Bay. None of them had seen enemy activity of any kind. When they reported to the 17th Pursuit's operations section, they received some upsetting news. About twenty minutes after they had taken off from Clark Field, two groups of bombers and several flights of single-engine fighters had practically destroyed the base. The radio station had been strafed, causing it to go off the air, which explained why they had not received any messages from QA-1, the call sign of 24th Group operations. They wondered how they could have circled over the Manila area throughout the fifty-minute raid and not known anything of what was happening just forty-five miles to the north. It looked like a repeat of the Tarlac patrol earlier that morning.

The 17th Pursuit pilots were a "tired and bewildered bunch" as they stood around the operations office hearing the news. "We had been flying all day and had seen nothing, yet disaster had struck all around us," Dave Obert recorded in his wartime diary. "But what now?" Obert and the other dispirited young officers wondered. It was sinking in that the 17th was the only intact, fully equipped pursuit squadron left to defend the Philippines.[2]

19TH BOMB GROUP OPERATIONS
CLARK FIELD, LUZON
MIDAFTERNOON, DECEMBER 8, 1941

At Clark Field, Lt. Col. Eugene Eubank wanted to know what remained of his 19th Bomb Group. He assigned 1st Lt. Lee Coats the job of surveying the damage to his B-17 force and finding out what planes could be put back in commission. Checking out the situation, Coats found that three were still operable. Eubank's own B-17D (40-3100) was only slightly damaged, while Al Mueller's B-17C (40-2072), hidden under trees at the edge of the field, had escaped serious damage. Earlier, 1st Lt. John Carpenter had brought his B-17D (40-3063) in safely.

Later in the afternoon, Eubank and his men saw another Flying Fortress coming in to land. They figured it must be Wheless's 40-3070, which had been out since morning patrolling to the north. They watched as the B-17D descended so low on its approach to the landing strip that its tail wheel caught on a wire fence that marked the airfield's boundary and tore out about a hundred feet of barbed wire. It slowed the big bomber down considerably, allowing it to make "a fancy short landing." The ship came to a halt before rolling onto the cratered section of the field beyond. A pleased Lieutenant Colonel Eubank was there to greet Wheless and his crew as they disembarked. Now he had at least two flyable ships.[3]

Eubank and Coats totaled up the numbers for the group. Of the 19 B-17s they had at Clark Field that morning, 12 had been destroyed, 3 were damaged but repairable, 2 were repaired and put in commission by the end of the day, 1 (Carpenter's) landed at the end of the attack, and 1 (Wheless's) had just come in, undamaged.

When Frank Kurtz reported to Lieutenant Colonel Eubank after inspecting his aircraft, the 19th Group commander asked him about his crew's status. "All dead," Kurtz replied. Eubank then sent Kurtz with the 19th Group's flight surgeon, Maj. Luther Heidger, to make an official report on the deaths. After arriving in Heidger's car at the location of what remained of Kurtz's B-17D, the pilot identified each of his dead crewmembers for Heidger, who recorded the serial numbers on the identification tags of those who were wearing them. To Kurtz, Heidger was trying "to be very businesslike about it, checking each one like it was a piece of freight." After each name, he repeated, "Killed in action" as he wrote it down. Kurtz asked Heidger for permission to take an item from each of his dead crew-members to send back to his family. "Frank, take anything you want," the flight surgeon replied. Kurtz went down the line of his dead crew and removed from each body the item Kurtz thought he had valued the most.

After returning to 19th Group operations, Heidger continued his depressing task, recording the names and serial numbers of the others in the group killed during the attack. Of the flight crews, that of Kurtz had suffered the greatest loss—four members—but six other B-17 crews had lost men, too—although only one in each case. In addition to the ten flight crewmen, twenty-one officers and men with nonflying duties had been killed.[4]

It had been a harrowing day for Heidger. During the strafing, he and his assistant, 1st Lt. Roy Day, had been out "in the middle of this hail of iron," their helmets lost, going around and tending to the wounded. When they came to a man who appeared to be dead, they would turn him over and look at him to see if he could be saved, then passed on to the next casualty, "with never a heed to their own safety." Soon, however, Heidger found himself involved in a bureaucratic dispute. The medical and quartermaster departments could not agree between them which organization was responsible for burying the dead. In the meantime, the bodies lay on the field where they had fallen. Lieutenant Carpenter and other 19th Group officers offered to take on the job themselves, but were threatened with courts-martial if they did. To Carpenter, "the whole business seemed utterly unreal."

Less controversial was the need to get the wounded to the Fort Stotsenburg hospital by any means and as fast as possible. By 2 P.M., vehicles of all sorts—ambulances, trucks, buses, carts, "anything that had wheels"—were unloading the wounded at the hospital. The men were carried in on "blood-encrusted litters, many of them still bleeding, some with shrapnel lodged in their wounds, or arms dangling, or partially-severed legs."

When Capt. Bill Fairfield arrived at the Fort Stotsenberg hospital, he, along with Lts. Bill Cocke, Jim Elder, and Jack Kaster, was lifted out of the "goon car" and put on a stretcher. They were carried up onto the hospital's veranda, where the nurses gave each of them a shot in the arm that they later found out was supposed to prevent gangrene. Fairfield saw a couple of nurses next to Bill Cocke's stretcher in the row directly ahead of him and overheard one of them say, "Mark him 'killed in action.'" He suddenly understood why Cocke had quieted down so much in the ambulance while he was trying to comfort him.[5]

With only a slight wound, 2d Lt. Lloyd Stinson of the 20th Pursuit was left sitting on the floor, waiting for a doctor to look at his foot. There were just too many wounded for the doctors to see any but the most severely wounded for the time being. He noticed that squadron mate Fred Armstrong, who had been severely burned, was also in the officers' ward, waiting his turn to go into surgery.

20TH PURSUIT SQUADRON OPERATIONS
CLARK FIELD, LUZON
MIDAFTERNOON, DECEMBER 8, 1941

Those surviving 20th Pursuit Squadron officers and men who had not been wounded were over at the squadron's operations area, where 1st Lt. Joe Moore was checking on casualties. Although the operations shack had been burned and the automobiles parked nearby had been destroyed by machine-gun fire and flames, no one who had taken refuge in the two L-shaped trenches had been killed or even injured, even though several of the 132-pound bombs had fallen within fifty yards of the trenches.

It was an entirely different story out on the airstrip. All but three of the squadron's twenty-three P-40Bs—those that had succeeded in getting airborne as the bombs began falling—were either destroyed or rendered inoperative by the attack. Those that survived the bombing had then been set ablaze by the strafing Zeros' 7.7-mm machine gun and 20-mm cannon fire.

Moore was now occupied with the grim job of identifying the bodies of the pilots of his 1st Section killed during the squadron's takeoff attempt. They had been laid out in a line near their destroyed P-40Bs. Moore confirmed to the squadron's medical officer, Capt. John Rizzolo, that the charred remains of one were those of 2d Lt. Max Louk, the first pilot killed in the Clark Field attack. They also identified the bodies of 2d Lts. Jesse Luker, Lowell "Tod" Mulcahy, and Jim Drake and marked them as having been killed in action.

Three others in Moore's eighteen-pilot section had been badly burned while attempting to take off: 1st Lt. Fred Armstrong and 2d Lts. Guy Iversen and Max Halverson. In Charley Sneed's 2d Section, only one pilot had been affected by the attack, Lloyd Stinson, with a slight wound only. Of the squadron's enlisted men, five had been killed and six wounded—7 percent of the 163 assigned to the outfit. Second Lieutenant Carl Gies wondered what the losses would have been if his squadron's officers and men had not been able to take shelter in the two L-shaped trenches.

Gies was awed by the Japanese bombers' accuracy. He estimated that not one of their bombs had hit more than two hundred feet from any border of the field. And to think that they had been told that the Japanese "couldn't hit their hats!" Gies wondered if they had stolen the Army Air Forces' super-secret Norden bombsight or perhaps perfected a better one. And what about the reports they had seen regarding the physical defects of Japanese fighter pilots and the inferior equipment they flew? Moore and Keator had put an end to such stories when they described their terrifying experiences in combat with the strange ships the Japanese were flying. Dogfighting had been emphasized throughout their training, with the best man getting on the other's tail. But Moore and Keator had quickly learned that the P-40 was no match for the Zero in a turning match, and that the only way to save your life if one got on your tail was to dive away, taking advantage of the P-40's much heavier weight.

Some distance from the 20th's operations area, 1st Lt. Herb Ellis was wandering around Clark Field, still dazed after his near-fatal encounter with one of the Japanese fighters and his high-risk bailout. Separated from his squadron, the 3d Pursuit pilot could not find anyone he knew at the airfield, which was still smoking and burning everywhere. As he passed the hangars, he observed that they appeared to be "slightly pumpkin shaped." The bombs, after penetrating the hangar roofs, had detonated on their concrete floors, tearing thousands of small holes in the corrugated iron structures. As he inspected the insides of the hangars, he thought they looked like "planetariums with star-studded skies."

Leaving the hangar area, Ellis continued walking around the airfield until he stopped in front of an antiaircraft emplacement. The sergeant in charge of the 200th Coast Artillery position offered Ellis something to eat and drink. He gladly accepted—it was his first meal since early that morning. Ellis told the sergeant that before his Air Corps days he had served with the 62d Coast Artillery (Antiaircraft) and had qualified as a master gunner. The sergeant suggested that Ellis take the place of his platoon leader, who had been wounded during the attack. Ellis accepted the offer—he was unattached and unsure if his outfit even existed anymore.[6]

Elsewhere around the base, the Provisional Tank Group commander was repositioning the 192d and 194th Tank Battalions' light tanks and half-tracks. The 194th was being shifted to a position two miles northeast of Clark Field and the 192d was moving to the vicinity of the relatively intact south airstrip, which was still under construction at the time of the attack.

Before his 192d Battalion moved out, Pfc. Bud Bardowski wanted to look for the remains of the Japanese pilot he had shot down earlier. After driving his half-track about a half-mile to the spot where he figured the crashed Zero would be, Bardowski found it, still smoldering. He saw the pilot's torso lying on the ground nearby, minus its arms, legs, and head. Looking for souvenirs, the twenty-seven-year-old Kentuckian turned the truncated body over to get at the man's sidearm.

Heavily damaged hangars at Clark Field following the December 8, 1941, attack. Photo courtesy J. M. Young.

When he finished, in a gesture of extreme contempt, he opened his fly and urinated on the corpse.[7]

Lingayen Beach, Luzon
Midafternoon, December 8, 1941

At Lingayen, northwest of Clark Field, 2d Lt. Bill Powell had managed to hide his P-40E among the palm trees off the beach, assisted by men from the Philippine Army division based there. He and two young lieutenants assigned to the division had looked over his plane once it was out of sight. The army officers were surprised to find holes in it, for they hardly knew there was a war on in the quiet of the Lingayen area. They found a technical sergeant who diagnosed why Powell's .50-caliber machine guns had jammed: it was a sticking or improperly installed solenoid. He soon fixed the problem. However, Powell still needed gas and oil if he was going to get his ship back in the air. A check of the area indicated that there was none there suitable for it. Unable to resolve the problem, Powell followed the two lieutenants to their mess, where he ate fried chicken. They offered him their bunks, too, but he was unable to take a nap, worked up as he was over the day's happenings.

Increasingly anxious to get back to his 3d Pursuit Squadron, Powell decided to make a trip over to Rosales, twenty-five miles to the southeast. He knew he could get gas and oil at the auxiliary field there, and hopefully there would be some information about his outfit. But the American colonel in charge of the division was unsympathetic to Powell's predicament and refused to help him obtain transportation to Rosales. "One plane or pilot more or less won't make any difference," he barked at Powell. However, later that afternoon one of his new lieutenant friends helped him commandeer a car in Lingayen town for the trip.

ROSALES FIELD, LUZON
MIDAFTERNOON, DECEMBER 8, 1941

At Rosales, Hank Thorne and the other pilots in the 3d Pursuit's splintered A, B, and C Flights were busily removing the five-foot-high barbed-wire fence that rimmed the twenty-five-hundred-foot strip so that they would be able to take off with the remaining flyable P-40Es they had brought to Rosales. The American sugar cane grower–custodian of the field had erected the fence to prevent his carabao from wandering onto the airfield.

Powell was correct in his assumption that there was plenty of aviation gasoline at Rosales: some ten thousand gallons had been stored at the auxiliary field. Unfortunately, there was nothing with which to pump the gas into the planes' fuel tanks. The problem was finding a way to fill the tanks of the four flyable P-40Es. Thorne decided to go into Rosales town and "beg, borrow, or steal" funnels and five-gallon cans with which they could manually refuel their ships. Thorne commandeered the first vehicle that passed by on the road. Once in town, he succeeded in locating enough funnels and gas cans to meet his needs. He also took the opportunity to send a telegram to FEAF headquarters at Nielson Field informing his superiors that he had four P-40Es and one B-18 in condition to fly out as soon as they were serviced, and that he would await further instructions.[8]

Back at the auxiliary field, Thorne pitched in to help his pilots in the time-consuming and arduous task of manually gassing up the planes. First, they had to load the fifty-five-gallon drums—each of which weighed over three hundred pounds—on the back of a truck at the fuel dump, then drive the truck to the location of the P-40Es and B-18. After transferring the gas from the drums into the five-gallon cans, they poured the gas from the cans through a funnel into each of the ships' gas tanks.

Refueling their ships was also a preoccupation with two other pilots in Thorne's squadron who were near San Marcelino south of Iba. Second Lieutenants Don Steele and Gordon Benson had reached a camp of the

Philippine Army's 31st Infantry Regiment after leaving their bone-dry P-40Es in the riverbed north of the town and setting out on the road. Their request for gas or transportation fell on deaf ears. The officer in charge of the camp told them that he was "too busy to bother with the Air Corps." Setting out on foot again, they saw a typical Filipino truck rattling along the road and decided to commandeer it. They signaled the driver to come to a halt, then pulled out their forty-fives and told the terrified native they would shoot him on the spot if he did not drive them to Olangapo, the U.S. naval base some twenty miles south of San Marcelino. The Filipino instantly acquiesced.

After arriving in Olongapo, they located a drum of gasoline and loaded it for the return trip to their P-40Es before deciding to wait until morning. The post commander had invited them to spend the night at his quarters. They concluded that the navy's hospitality was far superior to that of their own service. They also were able to get a radio message through to Thorne at Rosales, advising their commanding officer of their whereabouts.[9]

IBA FIELD, ZAMBALES, LUZON
MIDAFTERNOON, DECEMBER 8, 1941

At Iba, 1st Lt. Fred Roberts had managed to wade ashore after being extricated from his crashed P-40E in the shallow water offshore. The scene that met his eyes, one of panic and chaos, horrified him. The barracks building and gas truck were burning, the field was completely cratered from the bombing, and the radar unit had been destroyed. Shrieks emanating from wounded and terrified Filipinos in the adjacent barrio and squeals from their pigs filled his ears.

A quick check of the situation at the airfield indicated to Roberts that he was the ranking air force officer at Iba. He immediately grasped that he would need to take charge and do what he could under the circumstances. Fortunately, he had the invaluable help of 1st Lt. Frank Lloyd Richardson, the 3d Pursuit Squadron's medical officer, who had organized the squadron's medics and other men to attend to the wounded. The bespectacled doctor was working heroically to save the casualties, but it was a tough job: the squadron's dispensary had been destroyed, leaving him with practically no medical supplies.

Six to eight of the squadron's dead were taken to the small provincial hospital at Iba, and Richardson and Roberts took the squadron's wounded there, where they were placed on the floor. The building was empty, however, with no staff or medicine available, and Richardson and Roberts began trying to arrange for the men to be transported to Sternberg Hospital in Manila for treatment.[10]

The dispiriting job of identifying the squadron's dead and listing them as killed in action also fell to Roberts and Richardson. The task was made all the more difficult by the fact that many of the officers and men were not wearing their dog tags and their bodies had been badly mutilated, making positive identification nearly impossible. Lieutenant Wimer was occupied with the same job for his small Air Warning Service detachment. Four of his five dead had been killed during the bombing, at which time the power van was hit and set afire, the operations van badly damaged, the radio tent perforated by bomb fragments, and the mess hall and barracks set afire. The strafing Zeros killed the fifth man. Three men had been wounded, two seriously, and were taken to the provincial hospital, where they joined the 3d Pursuit's wounded.

Over at the coconut grove near Sergeant McBride's machine-gun emplacement, Richardson had tried to save the life of 2d Lt. Shelton Avant, but he had lost too much blood by the time Richardson arrived on the scene. Lying dead on the field were three other 3d Pursuit officers: 2d Lts. Casa O'Connell, Andy Webb, and Hawk Root. Of the squadron's 148 enlisted men, eleven were identified as having been killed in the attack.[11]

One of the 3d Pursuit's most senior pilots had a miraculous escape from death. First Lieutenant Jim Donegan had been hit several times by strafing fighters, including through the ankle, as he hunkered down in the little crow's nest of the radio tower, twenty feet above the ground, but his wounds were not fatal. Second Lieutenants Bart Passanante, John Hylton, and Jim Boone were also wounded in the attack while on the ground.

Early in the afternoon, reports of Japanese landings on the coast near Iba began circulating among the squadron's demoralized and terrified men. Most of those who could walk headed for the jungle behind the base. No one appeared to be in charge. The squadron's first sergeant was so panic-stricken he could not give an order or even talk.[12]

HEADQUARTERS, USAFFE
1 CALLE VICTORIA, MANILA
3:50 P.M., DECEMBER 8, 1941

The afternoon shadows had begun to lengthen in Manila when General Brereton appeared at the entrance to 1 Calle Victoria in Intramuros for a meeting with General MacArthur. Brereton was finally having a face-to-face meeting with his commander following two failed attempts early that morning due to General Sutherland's intervention. It had taken Brereton only eleven minutes to get to USAFFE headquarters from his own headquarters at Nielson Field. He now found MacArthur's command post equipped for total blackout.

Shortly after learning of the disaster at Clark Field—in a call at 1 P.M. from Fort Stotsenburg—Brereton had telephoned Sutherland to give him the unwelcome, but for Brereton not surprising, news. Sutherland already knew about the attack. Two minutes before Brereton's call, the USAFFE G2 had reported to Sutherland that Clark had been bombed at 12:35 by "high-flying planes."

In his 1:12 call to Sutherland, Brereton had informed MacArthur's chief of staff that he intended to bomb airdromes on southern Formosa "tonight." In addition to his B-17s, he was going to use three of his shorter-ranged B-18s. However, after learning later in the afternoon of the extent of the destruction to his B-17s and B-18s at Clark Field, Brereton now informed MacArthur that he needed to modify his attack plan to bring it in line with reality. With virtually no B-17s or even B-18s at Clark Field available for a night attack, he would have only the sixteen B-17s at Del Monte plus one survivor of the Clark attack at his disposal for the mission. Earlier in the day he had ordered the sixteen Del Monte ships up to San Marcelino for a night arrival, but he now proposed that they arrive at daybreak on December 9 instead. Rather than San Marcelino, they would come directly to Clark Field, where they would be bombed up for a morning attack on southern Formosa. MacArthur approved Brereton's revised plan.[13]

After his meeting with Brereton, Sutherland drafted a radiogram for his chief to send to Washington based on the information he had received about the Clark Field attack and indicating MacArthur's planned response. The adjutant general was informed that "52 two-engined bombers" had bombed Clark Field from high altitude in a coordinated attack with "40 dive bombers." The FEAF's air losses were "heavy," and the enemy's were "medium." MacArthur indicated he now had "17 heavy bombers, 50–54 P-40s, and 15 P-35s." Appropriating Brereton's plan as his own, he disclosed in his secret message that "I am launching a heavy bombardment counter attack tomorrow morning on enemy airdromes in southern Formosa."

After returning to FEAF headquarters at Nielson Field following his meeting with MacArthur, Brereton was informed of a 3:50 telephone call from Lieutenant Colonel Eubank at Clark Field. Eubank indicated that he had received a coded message from Captain O'Donnell at Del Monte requesting verification of the message that FEAF headquarters had sent O'Donnell to move his B-17s to San Marcelino that evening. Because the message was sent to O'Donnell in the clear, he suspected it might be a Japanese trick.

Eubank also informed FEAF headquarters that Clark Field could be ready for landing B-17s the following day. At the end of the call, it was agreed that a coded radiogram should be sent to O'Donnell instructing him to fly to Clark at daybreak, at which time his B-17s would be loaded with bombs and sent out to bomb Japanese airdromes on southern Formosa as indicated in FEAF Field Order 2. Immediately after the phone call from Eubank, FEAF headquarters—now more sensitive to communications security—sent him a coded message confirming the telephone conversation.[14]

HEADQUARTERS, FAR EAST AIR FORCE
NIELSON FIELD, MANILA
LATE AFTERNOON, DECEMBER 8, 1941

About forty minutes later, Capt. Bud Sprague landed at Nielson Field with the results of the special reconnaissance of Clark, Del Carmen, and San Marcelino Fields that FEAF headquarters had ordered. The 5th Interceptor Command operations officer reported that Clark Field was still available for landing aircraft, but light planes only. He had seen six or seven B-17s and B-18s still on fire, but "apparently not many airplanes destroyed on the ground." There were many craters on the field and several buildings were still on fire. The airfields at Del Carmen and San Marcelino appeared to be untouched.

27TH BOMB GROUP TENT AREA
FORT MCKINLEY, MANILA
LATE AFTERNOON, DECEMBER 8, 1941

Over at Fort McKinley, the pilots of the planeless 27th Bomb Group were relieved that the earlier planned night bombing of Formosa had been canceled. They had been assigned three B-18s at about noon from the 19th Bomb Group, which 2d Lts. Bob Ruegg, Frank Bender, and Alexander Salvatore were ordered by their CO, Maj. John Davies, to fly up to Formosa from Nielson Field that night. Second Lieutenant Roland Birrn felt that "having to use B-18s would be suicide." Fortunately for the pilots, the destruction of almost all of the B-18s in the Clark Field attack put a finish to the plan.

Earlier that afternoon, following the news of the Clark Field attack, Major Davies had called a meeting of the group's officers to discuss what they were supposed to do now. Some of the less senior pilots without bimotor training were being sent to Nichols Field to fly pursuits, while 2d Lt. Madsen Kokjer and three other very junior Class 41-G flying school graduates were being assigned to nonflying duties with the AWS at FEAF headquarters. Eight senior pilots had earlier been ordered to go to Nielson to fly B-18s, but that was out now. They found themselves left with no recourse but to curse "whoever was responsible for shipping the 27th Group to the Philippines without planes."[15]

NICHOLS FIELD, LUZON
5:30 P.M., DECEMBER 8, 1941

At Nichols Field, orders directing the 17th and 21st Pursuit Squadrons to shift their aircraft up to Clark Field were received at 5:30 P.M. Brereton's headquarters figured that the Japanese would hit Nichols next—probably that night—and did not want to run the risk of losing any more of its reduced P-40 force. According to Bud Sprague, Clark Field was in adequate shape for light planes to land there. The pilots of the two squadrons took off singly as there was to be no formation on the mass exodus flight. At the head of the thirty-five P-40Es were the 21st Pursuit's eighteen ships, with seventeen from Buzz Wagner's squadron bringing up the rear. Three others from his squadron were being left behind, requiring minor repairs after having flown two long patrols earlier in the day. The 21st also was obliged to leave some of its aircraft behind. Those flown by Joe Cole, Bob Clark, and Jimmy May had thrown oil while flying over Clark Field, and Sam Grashio's had been damaged beyond repair in combat over Clark.[16]

ROSALES FIELD, LUZON
LATE AFTERNOON, DECEMBER 8, 1941

At Rosales, Hank Thorne finally received the orders he was expecting as the sun was setting. The telegram from FEAF headquarters directed him to take the four flyable P-40Es on the auxiliary field there to Nichols without delay. The FEAF brass by then had apparently changed their view that Nichols was an unsafe place for pursuit ships. Thorne turned over responsibility for activities at Rosales to Frank Neri, who was being left behind because his ship was too badly damaged to fly out. Shortly after dark, Thorne took off in his P-40E, followed by Bob Hanson, Andy Krieger, and Howard Hardegree. Also remaining behind with Neri were two other 3d Pursuit pilots who were instructed to fly to Nichols early the following morning.[17]

CLARK FIELD, LUZON
LATE AFTERNOON, DECEMBER 8, 1941

At Clark Field, officers and men of the 20th Pursuit Squadron—most still dazed from the bombing and strafing they had gone through—lugged blankets, web belts, equipment, and gas masks into the jungle to a location about four miles from the field. They were going to set up a base camp at this sheltered spot. Joe Moore had left a few of the men behind on the field to service and rearm any P-40s that arrived Clark later that day or night.[18]

Some of the officers and many of the men of the 19th Bomb Group had taken off for the hills just after the attack on Clark Field. However, their CO, Lieutenant Colonel Eubank, was not overly concerned. Late that afternoon he assembled those who had stayed and tried to calm them down. Climbing up on a tractor, he announced, "Gentlemen, we're just like a good bird dog that's been shot too close to on its first time out." Referred to as "Pappy" by the men, Eubank was well known for treating his enlisted men better than the officers. Afterward, the mess sergeant, George Robinett, prepared a late lunch for members of the 30th Squadron who had remained. Toward sunset, it was decided to move the 30th Squadron's officers and men to a sugarcane field about a mile and a half from the airfield, where they would spend the evening and establish a camp. They were relieved to get off the base, fully expecting another Japanese attack at any time.[19]

Overhead, the light of late afternoon was fading as Ed Dyess and his squadron's pilots approached Clark Field after their short flight from Nichols. They wondered how they were supposed to land. Towering pillars of smoke were still rising from the base. Lowering their altitude, they saw that the field was covered with bomb craters, wrecked aircraft strewn about, and structures everywhere were burning. The few men they could see on the airfield were still busy marking holes for them. Dyess suddenly spotted an auxiliary strip that seemed intact enough to land on, although it appeared to him to be "little better than a country road."

Dyess's P-40E touched down and rolled to a halt, it stirring up clouds of dust. The *cogan* grass covering the airstrip had been burned off during the attack, leaving a soft pumice undersurface. In order to allow the dust to settle between landings, Dyess radioed his pilots to wait several minutes after the aircraft ahead of them landed before attempting to put down. He did not want to risk any accidents because of poor visibility due to the dust.

Waiting overhead for the 21st Pursuit's pilots to complete the sloweddown process of landing, the 17th Pursuiters were becoming increasingly restless. Darkness was falling fast. It looked to Wagner like it would be a long time before his pilots would be able to land. The 17th Pursuit's commanding officer decided to abort the arrangement to land at Clark and radioed his squadron mates to follow him to nearby Del Carmen Field instead.[20]

Over at the 28th Bomb Squadron barracks, Cpl. Grant Adami and the others had collected their gear from the partially wrecked structure and were heading out to the jungle to set up for sleeping in the open when they noticed aircraft coming toward Clark from the east. One of the jittery men failed to identify the ships as their own P-40s and yelled "Japs!" triggering a stampede. Out on the airfield, Sam Grashio climbed out of his ship and looked around, not realizing that his squadron had caused such a scare among the 28th Squadron's men. The whole base appeared deserted. Then he noticed something near a pile of burning debris that made him feel sick. It was a helmet with a hole in it and a piece of bone protruding from the hole. John Posten—who had inadvertently landed with the 21st Pursuit when a malfunctioning radio caused him to miss Wagner's call—was similarly traumatized by what he saw as he wandered around the field. "Automobiles, trucks and planes were wrecked and burning all over the place," he recorded in his diary that night. The sight of dead men still lying where they had fallen, including a B-17 crew next to its burning ship, upset him. Every few minutes, Posten jumped when ammunition exploded nearby.

The 21st Pursuiters were looking for men to service their P-40Es, but no one seemed to be around. They finally located an old master sergeant who eventually succeeded in rounding up enough men for the job. Then Dyess and his pilots made their way over to the 24th Pursuit Group operations hangar, but there was no one there except a lone soldier, who informed them that group operations had moved into the jungle not far from the airfield. When Dyess was finally able to locate Major Grover, the 24th Group commander gave Dyess his squadron's orders. They were to be ready early in the morning to provide cover for B-17s that would be coming up to Clark from Del Monte on Mindanao to land at daybreak.[21]

Elsewhere in the jungle, 1st Lt. John Carpenter, the ranking officer among those from the 93d Squadron that had been left behind at Clark, was setting up sleeping arrangements for his crew and himself. The foliage was so thick that it made an impenetrable cover, but the men would not even put up a mosquito cover for fear that the white material would show up under the trees to any Japanese pilots passing by overhead. First Lieutenant George Verity, a nonflying officer in the squadron, led the rest of the 93d's personnel to another jungle area adjacent to a recently cleared airfield extension. He had his mess sergeant set up his kitchens where the jungle was not too thick and serve the men a hot meal before they bedded down.

Just after sunset, 2d Lts. Austin Stitt and Woodrow Holbrook of the 30th Squadron were sitting along the edge of the road leading west to Fort Stotsenburg after helping Lt. Ray Cox to salvage engines and instruments from the wrecked B-17s that afternoon. With darkness beginning to cover the area, Cox told them to move away from the flight line—in case the Japanese came back that night—and report to him at dawn. As they watched the tanks and other army units pulling out of the area, the two young officers felt "nothing but abject defeat." They knew that the Japanese had won the air battle. "Clark Field was dead and so probably was Nichols," and without aircraft, the army "would be of no consequence."

What a difference in mood from that of six hours earlier, when they had been walking back to the operations area with Lieutenant Berkowitz after lunch. "We were all comedians," Stitt recalled years later. In that innocent time before the first bombs fell, they had put on their gas masks and "made faces at each other, horsed around, and generally played the fools we were." Now, completely crushed in spirit, they did not even bother to go off to the 30th Squadron's camp, instead just curling up by the side of the road for the night.

Thanks to the efforts of Stitt, Holbrook, Cox, and others of the group scavenging for parts, Lieutenant Colonel Eubank hoped to salvage three B-17s from the five aircraft on the field that had been damaged but not destroyed. By "replacing a wing here, a tail there, and taking two undamaged engines from a third," he figured he would soon have five operational B-17s, including the two Carpenter and Wheless had gotten off in before the attack. In addition, Eubank still had at last one B-18 on the field late that afternoon that had not been damaged. First Lieutenant Sam Maddux and 2d Lt. Hal McAuliff of the 30th Squadron had spotted it and decided to take it up and check out the situation over at Iba Field. However, they had barely climbed aboard the old twin-engine bomber and started its engines than Eubank appeared on the scene. He told the pair to get out of the ship because they "didn't stand a chance in that thing."[22]

Eubank would need an operational field for his heavy bombers. Fortunately "every available officer and man" of the resident 803d Aviation Engineers' Headquarters Company had gone to work immediately after the Clark Field attack to clear wrecked aircraft from and repair the cratered runways. By dusk, they had succeeded in getting a single landing strip ready.

DEL CARMEN FIELD, LUZON
EARLY EVENING, DECEMBER 8, 1941

At nearby Del Carmen, the field was nearly unusable—but not as a result of enemy attacks. When Wagner brought his 17th Pursuit Squadron pilots in at sunset after having tired of waiting to land at Clark Field, the adverse field conditions obliged them to allow two to three minutes between landings so the several inches of pure dust stirred up by the P-40Es could settle. It was with a profound relief that 17th Pursuit's commanding officer watched the last of his seventeen ships touch down without incident. After the 17th Pursuiters parked their ships and climbed out, the 34th Pursuit pilots based there greeted them. Also on the field was Ed Gilmore of the 20th Pursuit, who had landed at Del Carmen in the early afternoon after his narrow escape from Japanese fighters west of Clark Field.

Landing conditions were also difficult at Nichols Field early in the evening. Upon arriving over the field after his flight from Rosales with Bob Hanson, Andy Krieger, and Howard Hardegree, Hank Thorne was unable to contact the control tower to ask for the field, runway, or obstruction lights to be turned on. Nevertheless, they decided to try to land without lights since they were all very familiar with the field. When the time came, they lined up with the single runway that had been left open and began their approaches. Unable to switch on their ships' wing lights, Thorne and Hanson would be making a landing in the pitch dark. Just as he touched down, Hanson went into a ground loop, damaging his P-40E's left wing and propeller. Thorne and the others managed to land without incident. Taxiing their ships over to the hangar, they climbed out and turned their planes over to ground crewmen from the resident 17th Pursuit Squadron for servicing and dispersal.

Satisfied that the planes were being tended to properly, Thorne rushed to the nearest telephone and placed a call to FEAF headquarters at nearby Nielson Field. When Colonel George got on the line, the 5th Interceptor Command's chief of staff asked how Thorne's squadron had fared. Thorne, not knowing what most of his pilots had experienced, could not give him complete information on their status. However, if the colonel was interested in Iba's potential for use as an operational field, Thorne told him, "you might as well try to land in a quarry." After talking to Colonel George, Thorne looked for Maj. Billy Maverick, his predecessor as CO of the 3d Pursuit and now commander of the 20th Air Base Group at Nichols. Maverick was delighted to see Thorne. He had heard that the entire 3d Pursuit had been wiped out.[23]

Thorne also was reunited with two of his B Flight pilots who had landed that afternoon at Nichols. Ray Gehrig had come in with only three gallons of gas left in his tanks after narrowly escaping Iba and subsequently flying over Clark in vain hope of landing there. Ed Woolery told Thorne that he was the pilot of the P-40E that had buzzed Rosales that afternoon. Thorne and the other 3d Pursuiters at Nichols tried to piece together what had happened to the squadron's eighteen pilots from the time they had taken off from Iba at 11:45 that morning in three different flights. It was no easy task, as the three flights had become splintered during the day's confused events. In his own B Flight, Woolery knew that Hawk Root—Gehrig's wingman—had been killed as he tried to land back at Iba, and that Ship Daniel had landed at Rosales. Daniel's element leader, Don Steele, had radioed Thorne that he was at Olongapo. In Herb Ellis's

C Flight, there were reports from Clark that Ellis had been shot down but had safely bailed out. George Ellstrom, on the other hand, was believed to have been killed after bailing out. Frank Neri was safe at Rosales, but they had no news about Bill Powell, Fred Roberts, or Dana "Chubby" Allen. From Thorne's A Flight, Clark Field had reported that Vern Ireland had been shot down and killed when he crashed into Mount Arayat to the east. Missing element leader Gary Keenan had landed at Rosales, and Gordon Benson was reported safe at Olongapo.

It would be days before Thorne would get the final reckoning of his squadron's pilot and aircraft losses. He knew that Ireland, Root, and Ell-strom were dead, but he later learned that none of the other fifteen pilots flying that day had been killed or even wounded. Materiel losses were heavy, though: thirteen of the 3d Pursuit's twenty-four P-40Es had been destroyed or damaged beyond repair.[24]

APPROACHING DEL MONTE, MINDANAO
5 P.M., DECEMBER 8, 1941

Second Lieutenant Earl Tash and his crew were all under heavy strain that afternoon as they continued flying south toward Mindanao in a heavily damaged bomber with a seriously wounded man aboard. The B-17D's aileron control cables had been shot away, the superchargers damaged, and propellers punctured with bullet holes. Tash was relying heavily on his navigator's skill to get them safely back to Del Monte Field. Second Lieutenant Arthur Hoffman claimed that he was the "best under-the-table navigator in the Air Force" and Tash hoped that his boast was not an idle one. At one point on the long trip, they flew through a narrow pass at half the altitude of the surrounding peaks.

As the B-17D approached Del Monte at five in the afternoon, Tash instructed his radioman to call the base and ask them to have an ambulance meet them. Looking out the windows, the crew saw a great cloud of smoke billowing up from the vicinity of the base. Their hearts began pounding. Had the secret field been discovered and hit by the Japanese? Whatever the case, they had no choice; they had to put down there.

Captain "Rosie" O'Donnell responded to Tash's call for an ambulance. He also ordered the flying area cleared of all personnel except for his own staff and necessary equipment. A badly wounded man would be the first sight of war for the men at the Del Monte base, and he did not want it to make them squeamish.

Watching the ship as it made its approach, 2d Lt. Ed Jacquet thought that it was "wobbling all over the sky" and "making awfully big circles to get into the field." Much to the relief of all, however, it made a "beautiful landing with no ailerons and no flaps." Jacquet and the others watched as the "meat wagon" approached the big bomber. They could see sunlight coming through its side: bullet holes! Someone spotted something drip from the bottom of the fuselage: blood! The stunned bystanders watched as Sgt. Mike Bibin was eased out of the ship and put in the ambulance for the trip to the base hospital. It looked like almost all of his left shoulder had been blown off. Then it dawned on Jacquet and the others: "we were at war!"

While O'Donnell's reception committee may have been in a state of shock, Tash and his crew were relieved—not only to make a safe landing, but also to find out that the smoke they had seen was from a brushfire near the airfield. En route to the Del Monte plantation for a meal and night accommodations, they were bombarded with questions about their experience trying to land at Clark during the attack.

But the sight of Mike Bibin had made 2d Lt. Francis Cappelletti feel "pretty glum." The 93d Squadron navigator had disliked being sent to the isolated Mindanao base in the first place, and their stay now looked like it was going to be "very indefinite." With a war on now, he figured the 93d might never get back to Clark Field.[25]

HEADQUARTERS, ELEVENTH AIR FLEET
TAKAO, FORMOSA
3:40 P.M., DECEMBER 8, 1941

At Takao, Lt. Comdr. Koichi Shimada was at the base's wide airstrip with other staff officers from Eleventh Air Fleet headquarters, watching as the first *rikkō* made their landing approach. The tail markings on the twin-engine G4M1s told him that the first group consisted of Takao Kū ships. Shimada was relieved to see that all twenty-seven had made it back safely.

After climbing out of their bombers, the crew members excitedly commented to Eleventh Air Fleet and 23d Kōkūsentai staff officers about their attack on Clark Field. "Are we really at war?" one asked. "We met no opposition." Another exclaimed, "What is the matter with the enemy?" Similar views were expressed by the crews of the second group of twenty-seven Takao Kū *rikkō* that landed ten minutes later, after their attack on Iba.

Twenty minutes later—at 4:10 P.M.—Lt. Tamotsu Yokoyama and forty 3d Kōkūtai Zero-sen began landing at the field, which had been cleared of the Takao Kū's *rikkō*. Admiral Tsukahara and his chief of staff, Admiral Ōnishi, and other staff officers from Eleventh Air Fleet, plus Captain Kamei and Comdr. Takeo Shibata from his own 3d Kū, were on hand to greet him. Overwhelmed with emotion by the success of their attack,

Yokoyama made similar comments about the weakness of the American opposition at Iba and Clark Fields. The spirits of the 3d Kū pilots were very high. They were surprised to find that the P-40 performed so poorly. Lieutenant Takeo Kurosawa thought there would be "no problem" in the future "if the enemy is like that."[26]

Ground fire was altogether another matter. Kurosawa's Zero-sen had a big hole in the right wing, and his *shōtaichō*, FPO1c Shigeo Sugio, had barely managed to get back to base with fuel leaking from his ship from three hits sustained over Clark. His gas gauge read empty when he touched down at Takao.

The 3d Kū pilots could not speak for Lt. Yukio Maki's attached Tainan Kū *chūtai*, which had been operating independently of the 3d Kū during the Iba attack. Three of his Zero-sen had landed at Takao earlier, at 3:45 P.M., the pilot of one of them badly injured. Shōtaichō FPO1c Yoshio Koike, hit in the face by a bullet through his windshield, had been escorted back to Takao by his two wingmen. On being assisted out of his Zero-sen, Koike fainted, blinded in one eye and only able to distinguish light and darkness with the other. Low on gas, Maki and the other four surviving pilots of his *chūtai* had landed at 3:20 P.M. at Koshun, an army airfield on Formosa's southern tip, forty-eight miles south of Takao. Flying Petty Officer First Class Otojirō Sakaguchi and FPO3c Kiyotake Fukuyama, flying on CFPO Chitoshi Isozaki's wing, had taken three and two hits, respectively, in their ships. The ninth member of the *chūtai*—Maki's wingman, FPO2c Yoshio Hirose—did not return with the others. He had been shot down and killed between Iba and Clark.[27]

Just before entering Eleventh Air Fleet headquarters to report the 3d Kū's attack results, Yokoyama noticed the famous "Z flag" flying from a nearby pole. He knew the significance of that. Admiral Heihachirō Tōgō had unfurled it at the 1905 battle of Tsushima to signal his message: "The fate of the empire rests upon this one battle . . . let every man do his utmost!"[28]

Outside, the Kanoya Kū's *rikkō* began landing at 4:30 P.M. One of its twenty-seven aircraft had been forced to return with engine trouble shortly after departing the field, but now it appeared only twenty-four were returning from their attack on Iba. After landing, Comdr. Toshii Irisa reported that one of his bombers had flown on to the Tainan base and another had crash-landed short of Takao, heavily damaging its fuselage. Three of its crewmembers died and four were seriously injured.

As was the case in the Takao and 3d Kū, the Kanoya Kū's crews commented about the lack of opposition they met over Iba. Shimada began to wonder if Iba had been cleared of planes in advance, as so often was the situation on Chinese airfields prior to their bombing attacks. He would have to await the reports of damage inflicted on Iba Field before coming to that conclusion.[29]

TAINAN NAVAL AIR BASE, FORMOSA
4 P.M., DECEMBER 8, 1941

At Tainan Field, located north of Takao, twenty-six of the 1st Kū's G3M3 *rikkō* returned at 2:45 P.M. Except for the ship they lost in take-off, they had not suffered any losses on their attack mission to Clark Field and back. Just before 4 P.M., twenty-nine Zero-sen from the Tainan Kū began approaching the base. In formation with the others, Masa-aki Shimakawa passed low over the field and looked down at the headquarters building, then broke off to land, along with the others. Shimakawa felt relieved; he had not expected to see Formosa again after taking off that morning.

After landing, Shimakawa waved at the bystanders and talked to his maintenance crew before going over to his *shōtaichō,* Gitarō Miyazaki, to give him the results of his day's operations and report on the condition of his plane, including how the engine had performed on the long mission. Just before he headed toward Tainan Kū headquarters to report in, he stopped before his V-135 and patted it. "Thank you very much," he whispered to his ship in appreciation. "We have to work again tomorrow."[30]

Of the thirty-six Zero-sens that had left Tainan that morning on the mission, only thirty made it back to the airfield. Two had been obliged to return before reaching Luzon and thus missed the attack on Clark Field. Four were now reported missing: *shōtaichō* Ryōichi Nakamizo in Seto's 2d Chūtai, *shōtaichō* Yasuhisa Satō and wingmen Yasujirō Kawano and Yoshio Aoki in Wakao's 4th Chūtai. Only one pilot among the thirty survivors who participated in the attack returned nonstop to Tainan. Shimakawa and twenty-eight others had been obliged to land at the army's Koshun airfield, seventy-five miles short of their destination, to refuel before continuing on back to Tainan. With them was Lieutenant Miza in his C5M2 reconnaissance plane, having guided the four damaged Zero-sen of Lieutenant Asai and his wingman Ryokei Shinohara of Asai's 3d Chūtai and *shōtaichō* Yoshimitsu Harada and his wingman Keishu Kamihira of Wakao's 4th Chūtai to a safe landing back on Formosa. Wakao's *chūtai* had been hit harder than any other in the Clark attack: three Zero-sen were missing and two were heavily damaged—more than half of his nine ships.[31]

After taking their wingmen's statements, Miyazaki and the other eight surviving *shōtaichō* reported their *shōtai's* claims for the day to their commander, Lieutenant Shingō. Toting up the results, it appeared that the Tainan Kū had shot down six aircraft, with an additional four unconfirmed, in the aerial combat over Clark and between Clark and Del Carmen. They reported destroying six aircraft and burning thirteen others during their strafing attacks on Clark.[32]

HEADQUARTERS, ELEVENTH AIR FLEET
TAKAO, FORMOSA
EARLY EVENING, DECEMBER 8, 1941

Back at Eleventh Air Fleet headquarters at Takao early that evening, Shimada and the other staff officers were going over the after-action reports submitted by each *kōkūtai* participating in the attacks on Clark and Iba Fields. It was apparent that the Zero-sen and the *rikkō* alike had scored great successes. It was now clear to Shimada and the others that the airfields had not been evacuated of aircraft, as he had earlier assumed, and that the lack of opposition was not intentional, as had been the case in China. The bombers had met some antiaircraft fire, but no enemy fighters intercepted them. What was most astonishing to Shimada was that they had found the American planes lined up on the targeted fields as if in peacetime. It seemed to Shimada and his fellow staff officers "almost as if the enemy did not know the war had started." They wondered if the Philippines had received no warning from Pearl Harbor following the attack there.

As they studied the reports received from the Tainan- and Takao-based air units to prepare a final assessment of the results of the Clark and Iba attacks, the Eleventh Air Fleet staff officers were alert to the possibility of claims exaggeration due to double-counting the number of enemy aircraft destroyed. They also had the reports of the Tainan and 3d Kū's C5M2 reconnaissance planes, which had attempted to determine at the conclusion of the attacks exactly how much damage had been inflicted on the two airfields. These did not jibe with the fighter pilots' claims when comparisons could be made.[33]

The 3d Kū's reconnaissance plane had surveyed the results of the Iba attack at 1 P.M. and indicated in its report that of the ten small planes that were on the field, three were burning and seven were heavily damaged. The Tainan Kū's reconnaissance plane reported that at Clark Field at 1:15 six large planes, two medium-sized, and two other planes were burning, while at Del Carmen at 1:20 there was one plane in the air and twelve on the ground, one of which was burning. These results were much less than the claims of the fighter pilots and also took into account damage inflicted by the *rikkō*. The 3d Kū pilots reported shooting down ten P-40s and one P-35A in air combat, while their strafing attacks destroyed two B-17s, three medium-sized planes, and four small planes, and left six B-17s, six medium-sized planes, and one small plane burning at Iba and Clark. Not distinguishing by types of aircraft, the Tainan Kū pilots claimed six planes shot down and four others unconfirmed, six destroyed, and thirteen left burning.[34]

In the end, Eleventh Air Fleet headquarters concluded that the total American losses at Clark and Iba Fields from the bombing and strafing attacks amounted to 102 planes. These included heavily damaged planes as well as those that were destroyed. A report of the total claimed aircraft lost by the Americans in the day's operations, as well as the losses sustained by the Eleventh Air Fleet during the attack—seven Zero-sen and one *rikkō*— was sent to IGHQ in Tokyo. Anxious to know the outcome of the first attack on the Philippines—all the more so because it knew it had been carried out behind schedule—IGHQ had been bombarding Takao with urgent inquiries.

Early that evening, Eleventh Air Fleet headquarters staff officers were busily modifying the attack plan for December 9 because of the changes made in the original plan for the December 8 opening offensive against the Philippines. Nichols Field—which had been included in the original plan but was dropped in favor of Iba Field—was now designated the primary target for the December 9 attack. The Eleventh Air Fleet planners decided to open the offensive on Nichols with a small-scale night raid, to be followed with heavier attacks after daylight. Assigned the night-bombing mission was a *chūtai* of nine G3M3s commanded by Lt. Yoshirō Kaneko, the 1st Kōkūtai's combat-hardened senior *buntaichō*.[35]

Fort Stotsenburg Hospital, Luzon
Evening, December 8, 1941

The numbers of wounded requiring treatment that evening overwhelmed the doctors and nurses at the Fort Stotsenburg hospital. The Clark Field flight surgeon estimated that there were 250 troops jammed in the building, plus Filipino civilians who had been working at Clark. Major William Kennard was staying late in the operating room, working on the most seriously wounded, when a young lieutenant called him out so that he could put a dressing on Kennard's head, which had a piece of shrapnel in it. He was so bloodied from performing operations that he decided to go back to Clark Field for a while to check out the situation there.

Captain Bill Fairfield was resting comfortably when he was surprised to see Maj. Gen. Jonathan Wainwright coming through the wards. The North Luzon Force commander was spending a few moments with each of the wounded, saying something of encouragement as he shook their hands. "Don't give up, we're going to lick them yet," he asserted. It was close to midnight when Fairfield's turn to be operated on came. As the nurses lifted him out of bed, one of those standing by with a flashlight exclaimed, "Look at that bed!" Fairfield looked at the sheet. It was black. He realized then that he had been bleeding quite profusely. Fairfield was pushed into the operating room, where he noticed that two tables were being used. The doctors were moving from one table to the other while the chief nurse, 1st Lt. Florence MacDonald, was giving anesthetic. The smell of the operating room and of sweat and blood was unpleasant to Fairfield, but he was soon unconscious from the anesthetic.

As he approached Clark Field after his walk back from the hospital, Kennard found it eerie to see the bombers' twisted frames in the moon-light and to experience such complete silence after what had happened there that afternoon. The whole base was blacked out. He seemed to be the only person around. He walked over to his quarters without meeting a soul on the way. The structure was a wreck. After a few minutes' delib-eration, he decided to go back to the hospital for the night. Collecting his clothes, he set out for Fort Stotsenburg again.

CLARK FIELD, LUZON
EVENING, DECEMBER 8, 1941

Second Lieutenant Ed Whitcomb was back at work at 19th Group headquarters, making copies of Formosa maps for the B-17 crews that would be mounting the mission ordered for early the next morning. Fellow officers Warner Croxton and Walter Seamon were there, too, all working by candlelight, tracing the secret maps they had never seen before that showed all the airdromes and naval bases on Formosa. After several hours, the three 19th Group officers made their last tracing and walked out of the building, which now looked "more like a haunted house than the headquarters of a bomb group." They found their barracks across the street completely deserted, certainly no place to spend the night. Each took a blanket from his quarters and headed off to a location northwest of the base, behind the old "Officer's Row." Stretching out on the blankets in the middle of an open field, their gas masks, steel helmets, and .45-caliber pistols beside them, they tried to catch some sleep. Their efforts were frus-trated by the bursting of flares in the darkness, shot up from all directions around Clark Field. Several times, Whitcomb or one of the others went looking for the suspected enemy sympathizers with forty-five in hand, but they were never able to find anyone.[36]

In the jungle back of Clark Field, Ed Dyess and his 21st Pursuit pilots had been given a cold meal of pork, beans, bread, blackberry jam, and cof-fee before spreading themselves out on the hard ground in the hope of catching some sleep before their early morning mission to fly cover for the B-17s due in at daybreak. South of the field, the pilots and enlisted men of the 20th Pursuit Squadron were lying in some underbrush on each side of a dirt road, their blankets over them. Lieutenant Randy Keator was having difficulty sleeping, but not due to the rude conditions. He was preoccupied with thoughts about the two or three men he had killed that day. "Even though they were Japs, it worried me," he recorded in his diary.

DEL CARMEN FIELD, LUZON
EVENING, DECEMBER 8, 1941

Just to the south, at Del Carmen, the 17th Pursuit's pilots were obliged to bed down in a gully beside the airstrip after having finished eating a couple of hot dogs each that passed for dinner. Lieutenant John Brownewell had pulled a big, heavy engine cover over himself in order to obtain some warmth on what turned out to be an unusually cold night for the Philippines. "It was probably the most uncomfortable night of my life," he recalled later.[37]

BETWEEN IBA AND SAN MARCELINO, LUZON
EVENING, DECEMBER 8, 1941

First Lieutenant Fred Roberts had commandeered a Filipino bus in Iba that afternoon for evacuating the 3d Pursuit's and AWS detachment's wounded to Manila's Sternberg Hospital. To make enough room to accommodate all of the casualties, including Iba natives injured during the attack, the men had ripped out all of the seats. Packed together on the floor of the open-sided vehicle, they were being driven south under blackout conditions over the bumpy road. San Marcelino was to be their first stop. Other commandeered vehicles carrying most of the remaining wounded would leave Iba at midnight and follow the same route.[38]

Facing even more trying circumstances, 2d Lt. Glenn Cave and twenty-nine enlisted men from the 3d Pursuit Squadron were hiking that evening along the trail leading to the Zambales Mountains. They were going to attempt to cross over the mountains and reach Clark Field, thirty-seven miles to the east, on foot. However, they had no food, lacked suitable clothing, and had no knowledge about conditions along the route. Late that afternoon, Cave had spontaneously decided to head for Clark rather than take the bus south along the coastline when an excited enlisted man announced to him that the Japanese were landing offshore. The enlisted men on the trek with him had reacted to the terrifying news in the same way.

Also out on the road that night, 2d Lt. Bill Powell was headed back to Lingayen from Rosales field after having obtained two fifty-five-gallon drums of aviation gas and cans of oil for his beached P-40E. Frank Neri had put a truck at his disposal for the return trip and informed Powell that he and the other two pilots at Rosales would be flying to Nichols early the next morning. Powell had decided to bring his ship into Rosales before daybreak so that he could join them and not have to fly alone in skies he figured would be full of Japanese the next day. Despite the total blackout in force, Powell had turned on the headlights. As he crossed bridges and passed through towns and barrios, he was fired at several times by patrols enforcing the blackout, but he did not get hit. Finally, at about 11 P.M., he arrived back at Lingayen with his precious cargo of gas and oil.

POST EXCHANGE
NICHOLS FIELD, LUZON
9 P.M., DECEMBER 8, 1941

It was about nine o'clock when Hank Thorne, Billy Maverick, and the other 3d Pursuit pilots at Nichols Field began to dig into a late supper in the base's PX—their first meal since the sandwiches they had eaten at Iba late that morning. Suddenly, there was a "terrific blast" outside. "Another damn bombing attack," they surmised, and dived to the floor. Moments later, they realized that they were alone in the building. All of the others had fled outside. Thorne and his company got up, ran outside, and dove headlong into a ditch. Crouching in the mud, they waited for the next bombs to hit. But all was quiet. A few minutes later, they heard a group of soldiers running along the road above them. Climbing back up to the road, Thorne and Woolery asked the next passerby if the bombing was over. They were informed that there had been no bombing. The noise they had heard was the Nichols Field salute cannon, which was now serving as an air-raid warning for the base. Feeling very sheepish, Thorne and Woolery walked over to Thorne's house off of Nichols Field. Thorne's houseboy prepared them a plate of sandwiches to substitute for their aborted meal at the PX.[39]

DEL MONTE FIELD, MINDANAO
LATE EVENING, DECEMBER 8, 1941

The 14th and 93D Bomb Squadrons' flight crews talked excitedly late into the night with Earl Tash and his crew about their experiences over Clark Field. Ed Jacquet and the others were not going to let Tash's boys rest until they had dug out all the details. No one was sleepy.

Late that night, a coded radiogram came in from Lt. Stan Nanney at 19th Group headquarters at Clark Field. The message contained orders for one of the two B-17 squadrons at Del Monte to mount a six-ship armed reconnaissance mission to look for an aircraft carrier reported to be east of Catanduanes Island and then land at Clark Field. Each ship was to be loaded with twenty one-hundred-pound demolition bombs. Jacquet and his bombardier, Lt. Donald C. Miller, could not sleep for the rest of the night, agitated as they were by the strange orders. "What could 100-pound bombs do to a carrier?" Jacquet wondered. It would be "like sticking an elephant with a pin."[40]

WEST OF CLARK FIELD
LATE EVENING, DECEMBER 8, 1941

Ed Whitcomb, lying in an open field west of Clark Field, could not sleep either, being equally troubled by circumstances beyond his control. "What had happened?" he asked himself. "What had happened to the air warning net about the island which was to give us two hours' notice before any enemy reached Clark? What had happened to our fighters and our anti-aircraft which would keep enemy planes so high they could not bomb with any degree of accuracy? What had happened to the orders we should have received to unleash our many bombers against the enemy installations on Formosa?" It seemed to the young Headquarters Squadron navigator that no one knew the answers to those questions. Things apparently just did not work out the way they should have.[41]

After receiving a warning message that Japanese bombers were headed south in the direction of the base, Captain Colin P. Kelly's B-17C (serial 40-2045) is hurriedly serviced and readied for take-off from Clark Field at 9:25 on the morning of Wednesday, December 10, 1941. Kelly and his men were ordered to attack a Japanese carrier that was reported off Aparri, at the northern tip of Luzon. This would be Kelly's last mission. Original oil painting, "In Alis Vincimus" (On Wings We conquer), by Gil Cohen, in the collection of Eugene Eisenberg. Copyright 1998 by Eugene eisenberg.

Epilogue

I n carrying out their strategy of destroying American air strength in the Philippines before attempting to land invasion forces, the Japanese achieved greater success on the first day of their effort to gain air superiority in the skies over Luzon than they had imagined possible. In materiel terms, they destroyed twelve of the Far East Air Force's nineteen Clark-based B-17s (of a total Philippines force of thirty-five) and thirty-four of its ninety-two P-40Es, the only modern bombers and pursuit ships in the American arsenal. Two of the five pursuit squadrons were eliminated as fighting units in a single stroke, and of the three remaining, one was equipped with an obsolete aircraft proven to be incapable of staying in the sky with the Zero-sen. The one operational radar set was destroyed, leaving USAFFE blind to subsequent Japanese air raids.

The destruction was also heavy in human terms. Nine of the 24th Pursuit Group's pilots were killed in action, plus 26 enlisted men and a ground officer, while the 19th Bomb Group lost 10 flight crewmen and 21 ground personnel. The 7th Materiel Squadron attached to the 19th Group lost 4 enlisted men and its commanding officer. Five of the 30 men in the Iba Air Warning Service detachment were killed in the attack on Iba. Although the total loss of life in all units based at Clark has never been definitively tallied, MacArthur on December 9 reported losing "about 55 killed and 110 wounded" at Clark Field and at Iba "3 officers and 19 enlisted men killed and 16 officers and 22 enlisted men wounded."[1]

Another casualty of the Japanese attack was the spirit of the young men in the FEAF, so many of whom that morning had been carefree and confident that the Japanese posed no serious threat to American airpower, despite warnings to the contrary by their pursuit commander. By that afternoon, their morale had sunk to the bottom, their belief in American superiority crushed.

Was the Japanese attack on Clark and Iba Fields on December 8, 1941, "another Pearl Harbor"? MacArthur's Philippines intelligence chief thought not. In a 1954 biography of his commander, Col. (later Maj. Gen.) Charles A. Willoughby criticized "the attempt . . . made to equate the loss of 17 bombers at Clark Field with the loss of the battleships at Pearl Harbor. But there really is no comparison. Brereton's pitiful number of planes was never enough to affect the issue in the Philippines and they would soon have disappeared through attrition even with the most careful husbanding." Historians, however, do not support the opinion of Willoughby, who was not exactly a disinterested evaluator of the attack or of MacArthur's responsibility for it. As Rear Adm. Edwin Layton, John Costello, and Roger Pineau have maintained, "Compared to this strategic disaster [Clark Field], the loss of the five battleships at Pearl Harbor had relatively little influence on the course of the war." Costello, in contrast, asserts that the entire "Anglo-American strategy in the Far East hinged on MacArthur's airpower." With its near-destruction in one blow, not only was the defense of the Philippines doomed, that of Malaya and the Dutch East Indies was also greatly weakened, he maintains. Indeed, in my view, Louis Morton's conclusion that "the Japanese had removed in one stroke the greatest single obstacle to their advance southward" is as valid today as when he recorded it fifty years ago.[2]

This is not to contest Willoughby's assertion that Brereton's air force would, in any event, have been destroyed "through attrition." That would have been the fate of any force—American, British, or Dutch—that opposed the Japanese in the early months of the Pacific War. While neither it nor any other force in place at the time could have reversed the inevitable outcome, the FEAF could have significantly increased the cost of seizing the Philippines and the Japanese' other southern objectives and upset their timetable of conquest if it (and its radar capability) had not been crippled on the first day of the war. Over the next five months, the Philippines campaign was fought as a delaying action. MacArthur's announced intention to strike Formosa on the morning of December 9 never, for reasons that remain unclear, materialized. In any event, the surviving B-17s never attacked Formosa.[3]

Yet the question of who was responsible for the disaster at Clark Field remains. It attracted considerable attention following the publication of Brereton's *Diaries* in 1946 and the sharp reaction the book elicited immediately afterward from MacArthur. Brereton maintained that MacArthur and Sutherland turned down his early morning requests to attack Formosa and that he was not authorized to mount any bombing missions until "11:00 A.M." Then, while his B-17s were being loaded with bombs and the crews briefed for the Formosa mission after Brereton issued his order, Clark Field was hit. The implication was that USAFFE's delay in authorizing the Formosa strike was the operative factor in his B-17 force being caught on the ground.[4]

In a September, 1946, statement to the *New York Times,* MacArthur attempted to shift blame for the disaster to Brereton. In a point-by-point pronouncement, he maintained

1. That General Brereton never recommended an attack on Formosa to me and I know nothing of such a recommendation having been made; that my first knowledge of it was contained in yesterday's press statement.
2. That it must have been of a most nebulous and superficial character, as no official record exists of it at headquarters.
3. That such a proposal, if intended seriously, should have been made to me in person by him; he has never spoken of the matter to me either before or after the Clark Field attack.
4. That an attack on Formosa with its heavy air concentrations by his small bomber force without fighter support, which because of the great distance involved, was impossible, would have had no chance of success.
5. That in the short interval of time involved, it is doubtful that an attack could have been set up and mounted before the enemy's arrival.
6. That the enemy's bombers from Formosa had fighter protection available in their attack on Clark Field from their air carriers, an entirely different condition than our own.
7. That I had given orders several days before to withdraw the heavy bombers from Clark Field to Mindanao, several hundred miles to the south, to get them out of range of enemy land-based air.
8. That half of the bombers, 18, had already been so withdrawn when war broke.
9. That General Brereton was fully alerted on the morning of December 8 (1941) and his fighters took to the air to protect Clark Field but failed to intercept the enemy.
10. That tactical handling of his air force, including all measures for its protection against air attack of his planes on the ground, was entirely in his own hands.
11. That the over-all strategic mission of the Philippine command was to defend the Philippines, not to initiate an outside attack.[5]

I have shown in an earlier evaluation of MacArthur's attempt to exonerate himself from responsibility for the Clark Field disaster that each of the points he makes is factually incorrect or irrelevant. Thus, in response to the number sequence above, consider the following:

1. Even on the highly unlikely assumption that Sutherland never checked with MacArthur on Brereton's many requests beginning early that morning, the FEAF headquarters diary documents that MacArthur *himself* called Brereton at 10:14 A.M. and authorized a B-17 strike on Formosa late that afternoon.

2. Contrary to MacArthur's assertion, an official record of Brereton's attack request *did* exist at USAFFE headquarters: in Sutherland's office diary. According to his "Brief Summary of Action in the Office of the Chief of Staff," Sutherland called Brereton at 8:50 A.M. to "Hold off bombing of Formosa for present."

3. Brereton *tried* to meet with MacArthur to request authority to attack Formosa, but was rebuffed during his visits to USAFFE headquarters at 5 and 7:15 A.M., and was obliged to receive instructions from Sutherland instead. Colonel William Morse, an impartial observer, overheard Sutherland and Brereton discussing that subject during the second visit. The 10:14 call aside, Brereton was forced to submit his urgent requests for an air strike to Sutherland rather than deal directly with MacArthur.

4. If an attack on Formosa "would have no chance of success," why did MacArthur inform the War Department late on December 8 that he was "launching a heavy bombardment counter attack on enemy airdromes in southern Formosa" when the chances of success would have been even less?

5. If MacArthur had authorized Brereton at their 5 A.M. meeting to mount a B-17 attack on Formosa, had opted for airfields as targets, and if the bombers had been airborne by 6:30 A.M., they could have reached the Japanese naval air base at Takao—the prime target— while the field was recovering from being fogged in and caught the main part of the Japanese navy's attack force on the ground, being loaded with fuel and bombs, before its takeoff beginning at 9:30 A.M. Indeed, the Eleventh Air Fleet staff at Takao was in a state of high anxiety, fearing that a B-17 strike had been ordered after news of the Pearl Harbor attack reached USAFFE headquarters and that the B-17s could reach Formosa as early as 7 A.M. Japanese defenses against such an attack "were far from complete." Their air-raid warning system and antiaircraft defenses were "totally inadequate," and they had little air strength left "which would have been ineffective against a determined enemy attack," an Eleventh Air Fleet staff member maintained.[6]

Contrary to MacArthur's assertion, an attack "could have been set up and mounted" before the enemy's arrival, provided that MacArthur had approved the strike at least an hour and a half—to allow time for loading up with bombs—before the B-17s at Clark were obliged to go aloft for protection at about 8:45 A.M. After they were called back and landed at about 11 A.M., it was indeed too late to have them refueled and bombed up for takeoff before the Japanese struck at 12:35 P.M.

6. The Japanese bombers were not protected by carrier-based, but rather *land-based* fighters: the long-range Zero fighter. No one at FEAF believed the nimble pursuit planes could fly nonstop to central Luzon and return and still have enough fuel to engage in attacks on American bases. Carriers were *not* an alleged advantage for the Japanese.

7. The only record extant that relates to any formal order by MacArthur (or Sutherland) to transfer the thirty-five B-17s to Mindanao is USAFFE Special Orders 83 issued on November 29, which ordered the 19th Bomb Group's ground echelon to Del Monte on or after December 8. Furthermore, on December 2, Special Orders 85 rescinded even that limited transfer order. As noted in chapter 7, it was Brereton who ordered half of the B-17s to Del Monte on November 28, not MacArthur or Sutherland.

8. Indeed, sixteen of the thirty-five bombers—not eighteen—had been relocated, albeit temporarily, to Del Monte.

9. MacArthur is evidently referring to the Japanese army air force's bombing mission headed toward Clark Field early in the morning on December 8, which subsequently bombed Baguio and Tuguegarao. Those bombers' targets were north of the patrol area assigned to the pursuit pilots who had taken off to intercept the Japanese, who the Americans erroneously believed were intending to bomb Clark. Failure to intercept the enemy was thus not the pilots' fault, as implied by MacArthur.

10. Tactical handling of Brereton's air force was indeed Brereton's responsibility, but Sutherland ordered him not to use his B-17 force offensively or even for reconnaissance purposes without first obtaining Sutherland's permission.

11. MacArthur misconstrues his role here. His strategic mission was indeed defensive, but once hostilities commenced, he was under orders to execute the Rainbow 5 plan, which called for offensive tactical operations while on the strategic defense. The plan specifically included the "mounting of air raids against Japanese forces and installations within tactical operating radius." Those targets obviously included the Japanese airfields on southern Formosa.[7]

In attempting to allocate responsibility for the disaster at Clark and Iba Fields in a more methodical way, one needs to distinguish between decisions made at the tactical and strategic levels of command. Brereton and his bomber and pursuit commanders were responsible for the former, as influenced by MacArthur, the commander of all U.S. Army forces in the Philippines. Decisions of a strategic nature were the responsibility of high officials in Washington, notably Arnold and his superior, Marshall, but also at the highest level, Stimson. Due to his high standing with the War Department, MacArthur himself was able to influence broad strategic decisions made by the Joint Board pertaining to the Philippines and the rest of the Far East, but that is not a relevant consideration here, focused as we are on the more limited question of the role of MacArthur's airpower and its employment on December 8, 1941.

In addition to those points evident in MacArthur's exchange with Brereton as covered above, there are other factors related to the USAFFE commander's reasoning and attitudes that should be examined. They may help to explain why MacArthur failed to take immediate offensive action against the Japanese on Formosa once he knew not only about the attack on Pearl Harbor but also had been informed by his staff of early morning attacks on Philippines soil: the 6 A.M. raid on Davao and the 8:30 A.M. bombing attacks on Baguio and Tuguegarao. His stated argument that a B-17 attack on Formosa would have had "no chance of success" conflicts with his decision later that morning, and again after the Clark Field raid, to mount such an attack. MacArthur never revealed what his real rationale was for holding his B-17 force on the ground that morning against his air commander's wishes.[8]

Some have speculated that MacArthur may have hesitated to attack Formosa in deference to Pres. Manuel Quezon's alleged hope that the Japanese would not attack the Philippines if MacArthur did not attack them first. On the other hand, Quezon reportedly told Maj. Gen. Dwight Eisenhower in Washington in 1942: "when the Japanese attacked Pearl Harbor, MacArthur was convinced for some strange reason that the Philippines would remain neutral and would not be attacked by the Japanese." However, MacArthur asserted in 1954: "I personally had not the slightest doubt we would be attacked."[9] Yet, these statements still do not address the relevant question: Why did MacArthur take no offensive action when whatever hope the Philippines might have remained neutral was dashed by the Japanese raids on Davao, Baguio, and Tuguegarao early on December 8?

MacArthur should indeed have had no doubt that the Japanese would attack the Philippines. He had intelligence information that pointed to such an attack to lead off their southern operations aimed at the conquest of Southeast Asia. From MAGIC messages intercepted by his own Signal Intelligence Service (SIS) Station 6, decrypted by the navy's Intercept Station C (CAST) on Corregidor, and passed on to him, MacArthur knew the Japanese consul in Manila was sending Tokyo reports on the size and composition of his air force. Such intelligence could only indicate hostile intentions toward the Philippines and specifically toward his B-17 force at Clark Field, about which the Japanese navy was seeking information. In addition to the diplomatic messages, MacArthur also benefited from intelligence reports based on traffic analysis by CAST regarding Japanese naval (including air force) movements for southern operations, copies of which were provided to him.[10]

Air Force historian Robert F. Futrell has suggested that MacArthur's "unfamiliarity with strategic air capabilities" may have been a factor in his decision not to send his B-17s to Formosa. Another historian has noted that while MacArthur was serving as Quezon's military adviser in the late 1930s, "it was common knowledge that MacArthur was not air-minded." As late as September, 1941, Admiral Hart, who knew him well, maintained that MacArthur's "own ideas and real interests are confined to ground forces." The initiative for deploying B-17s to the Philippines as a strategic airpower weapon came from the War Department, not MacArthur, who was a passive player as decisions were being made on the size of the force to be sent to him and on the objectives of their use. Furthermore, once the bombers arrived in the Philippines, MacArthur was more concerned with decisions regarding their location, particularly in terms of providing ground defenses for them, than in their mission. Although he referred to his B-17 force in early December, 1941, as his "ace unit" that would "smash invasion fleets before they landed," he never mentioned its more logical role of attacking air bases on Formosa (as expected under the Rainbow Five plan). Nor is there any record of discussions about the strategic use of B-17s with his air chief, Brereton, to whom he deferred on decisions involving the FEAF (with the notable exception of its use on the morning of December 8, 1941).[11]

MacArthur can also be faulted for not conferring with Brereton early in the morning on December 8, when his air commander twice tried to meet with him to discuss Brereton's proposed strike on Formosa. He should not have allowed Sutherland to block access to him on such a critical matter, nor permitted his chief of staff to make decisions on his behalf that morning. Indeed, one might argue that MacArthur should have taken the initiative and sought out Brereton for a meeting, rather than vice versa.

To what extent can Brereton be held accountable for the Clark and Iba Fields disaster? If the analysis presented here is accepted, then it would appear the FEAF commander did all within his power to launch an all-out bombing strike on Japanese air bases on Formosa on the morning of December 8, which the men under his command expected of him. He might be faulted for not having objected to MacArthur's diplomatic missions for him to Australia and (as planned) to Malaya and the Dutch East

Indies at a time when his presence was vitally needed for the buildup of his air force in the Philippines. Although MacArthur had been instructed by the War Department to carry out such missions, he might have asked Brereton to select a senior FEAF staff officer whose services were less critical to the buildup effort.

Brereton has been judged "a capable commander and an effective leader" as well as "a competent planner and administrator" by his biographer. Brereton himself thought MacArthur had picked him to take over his growing air force mainly on the basis of his administrative skills—"someone with supply and maintenance knowledge." In its early stages, the buildup of the FEAF "would largely be one of preparing services and facilities," which made his selection appear logical to him. On the other hand, Arnold saw in Brereton more than just administrative abilities. He informed MacArthur that Brereton was "specially qualified to satisfy your air command requirements, since he has a keen appreciation and understanding of the employment of air forces and the potentialities of air power."

However, Brereton's successor as MacArthur's air commander, Maj. Gen. George Kenney, was of the opinion that—based on Brereton's brief Philippines record—he "lacked the attention to detail" required of a great commander. Indeed, Brereton may have deferred too much to his pursuit and bomber commanders on operational matters on December 8, perhaps due to his "limited experience with pursuit aircraft and heavy bombers," as noted by his biographer.[12]

Regarding a particular tactical matter, it is not clear why Brereton ordered a photoreconnaissance mission over Formosa (FEAF Field Order 1) at the same time as the bombing strike (FEAF Field Order 2) if he already had adequate information on Japanese air bases on the island. The three photorecon B-17s could have been put to better use as part of the bombing group. The pilots themselves wondered why a photorecon was necessary since they were being provided detailed maps of their Formosa targets copied for them by 19th Group headquarters officers. It is possible that Brereton was merely responding to Sutherland's criticism that Brereton had inadequate target information for mounting an attack on Formosa.

This leads us to the question of how well Colonel George and Major Grover of the V Interceptor Command and Lieutenant Colonel Eubank, head of the V Bomber Command, performed that fateful day. The nominal head of the V Interceptor Command, General Clagett, was not involved in tactical decisions at the time, having sidelined himself (or been sidelined) while awaiting transfer out of the Philippines.

Eubank's 19th Bomb Group took the worst hit on December 8, a blow that wrote *finis* to the War Department's strategy for employing it as a deterrent to Japan's southward expansion. The destruction of one-third of its

FROM RIGHT: Far East Air Force commander Maj. Gen. Lewis H. Brereton poses with Lt. Gen. George H. Brett, deputy commanding general of Allied forces in the Southwest Pacific; Adm. Thomas C. Hart, commander of the U.S. Asiatic Fleet; and Hart's chief of staff, Rear Adm. William R. Purnell, on January 10, 1942, at Batavia, Dutch East Indies, following Brereton's departure from the Philippines on December 24, 1941. U.S. Army Signal Corps photo no. 130486 courtesy National Archives and Records Administration.

B-17 force in the Clark Field attack has always been the focus of analysis of the December 8 attack on the Philippines. To what extent can Eubank be held responsible for the catastrophe that befell his command? The forty-nine-year-old Eubank was a highly experienced and capable officer in bombardment operations, having progressed from squadron commander in 1931 to group commander in 1940.[13] How could the seventeen B-17s under his control at Clark Field have been caught on the ground and almost all destroyed in one blow? As he and every officer and man of the 19th Group interviewed after the disaster maintain, they had no warning of the Japanese bomber and fighter force bearing down on Clark just before 12:35.

If the above assertion is correct, a basic question arises: What procedures were in effect at Clark Field for alerting the 19th Group of an impending attack? Although I have found no documentation nor gained information from interviews or correspondence providing a definitive answer, it appears from a 1951 statement by the head of the Air Warning

Service at the time, Lt. Col. Alexander Campbell, that the "Clark Field Communication Center" (which has been identified as being located in the 24th Group's operations hangar) on receipt of Teletype warning messages from the AWS at FEAF headquarters was to inform Eubank's V Bomber Command (19th Bomb Group) of the warnings, evidently by telephone. As the former AWS chief maintained, "We had direct teletype to the Clark Field Communication Center, and if the bomber command was not notified [about the warning message dispatched to the center at 11:45], internal administration was at fault."

Did Grover's staff fail to contact 19th Group headquarters about the warning message? There is no record of any such warning being relayed to Eubank's command, and no member of the group has ever indicated receiving such a message from 24th Group operations. Earlier, in response to an AWS message to Clark Field received at about 8:30, it appears that 24th Group operations did not inform 19th Group headquarters of the incoming Japanese aircraft at that time, either. Instead, it appears the Clark Field CO did so (as noted in chapter 9).

Colonel Campbell also indicated that in addition to directly transmitting the 11:45 warning message to the Clark Field communication center, it was radioed or transmitted (where Teletype machines were installed) to "all units of the FEAF."[14] Was the message sent to the 19th Bomb Group headquarters, too? If so, by what means was it dispatched?

The communications setup at 19th Group headquarters on December 8 is not totally clear. An SCR-197 radio communications van operated by 19th Group headquarters personnel was located outside the wooden, two-story building, but it reportedly was used only for ground-to-air and air-to-ground radio messages. The officer on duty in the van at the time maintains that no radio messages were received from the AWS on December 8, as noted in Chapter 10. Did the 19th Group have a Teletype machine in its headquarters building? No 19th Group officer or enlisted man recalls there being one. However, group headquarters *did* receive Teletype messages that morning, including FEAF Field Order 1. If 19th Group headquarters received that and other Teletype messages *indirectly,* where had they been sent? An enlisted man working in the message center at group headquarters indicates that he picked up and delivered messages to and from the 19th Group, including at Clark Field headquarters—which did have a Teletype machine. However, as Campbell stated in 1951, it sent the December 8 warning message by Teletype only to those FEAF units with *direct* Teletype connections to the AWS.[15]

What can one conclude on this question of a warning message being received or not by 19th Group headquarters? Campbell states that, at the very least, a *radio* message was sent. Yet the 19th Group officer on duty that

SERGEANT JOE SCHOEBERT OF THE CLARK FIELD OPERATIONS SECTION SENDING
A TELETYPE MESSAGE IN SEPTEMBER, 1941. PHOTO COURTESY JAMES H. COOKE VIA
KATHLEEN COOKE.

day in the radio van maintains that no such message was received. There is
no indication of a telephoned warning message from 24th Group operations in response to the Teletype message it received. Should a message
of such dire import for the group—with its B-17 force exposed on the
ground like sitting ducks—have been received at 19th Group headquarters, regardless of format, it is inconceivable that it would not have been
passed immediately by the recipient to Lieutenant Colonel Eubank or a
member of his staff, who were only a few yards away.

Shifting now to the question of possible dereliction of duty on the
part of the V Interceptor Command headquarters at Nielson Field, one
necessarily must focus on its chief of staff, Col. Harold George. He shared
responsibility with the FEAF's Air Warning Service to ensure that warning
messages of approaching Japanese aircraft were sent to Major Grover's 24th

Group operations at Clark Field. Their progress would then be monitored on the plotting board in the group's hangar. Furthermore, he was responsible for ordering the interception of any enemy force by the pursuit squadrons under Grover's immediate command.

Colonel Campbell has documented the actions of Colonel George and his operations officer, Captain Sprague, from the time the radar unit at Iba Field began picking up (at 11:20) the two groups of bogies headed south from Formosa toward the Philippines. According to Campbell, the three officers monitored the course of the Clark-bound flight "for a considerable length of time." Campbell was urging Colonel George and Captain Sprague to send an interception order to Grover, "but they insisted on waiting until they reached a certain distance from the field." It was not until about 12:15 that Sprague wrote out an interception message, which was then Teletyped to Grover at about 12:20, or fifteen minutes before the bombing attack on Clark Field commenced.[16]

Both Colonel George and Sprague knew that the P-40 was a poor interceptor, too heavy and underpowered to reach the altitude required in less than half an hour to pounce on high-flying Japanese bombers.[17] Why then did they give the P-40s at Clark Field only fifteen minutes in which to take off and intercept the attack force? They evidently overestimated the Clark-bound bombers' arrival time.

At Clark Field, Grover's performance was a source of bewilderment to his pilots, who were ordered from one patrol area to another from the time the 24th Group received the first warning of approaching Japanese aircraft. He mistook the Iba-bound bombers' target as Manila instead, which he also did with the second group coming down central Luzon, despite warnings that it was headed in his direction, and for that reason directed his pursuit aircraft to the Manila area. Only when V Interceptor Command ordered him at 12:15 to intercept over Clark Field did he realize that the second group was indeed bound for his airfield, triggering frantic calls for his patrolling P-40s to head for Clark (leaving Iba undefended). Yet even as he was ordering the other squadrons to Clark posthaste, he left the Clark-based 20th Pursuit on the ground for no discernible reason and thus doomed it to destruction. Why did he not order it aloft when he received Sprague's interception order?

Grover's derelict behavior was not only the cause of the destruction of his own 20th Pursuit Squadron but apparently was responsible for the loss of Eubank's B-17 force on the field, if we can confirm that his 24th Group operations should have notified 19th Group headquarters of the warning message sent to him via Teletype at 11:45 and failed to do so.

It is difficult to account for Grover's egregious performance during the hour leading up to the attack on Clark Field. The thirty-seven-year-old officer was highly experienced in pursuit operations, commanding his first pursuit squadron in 1934 and eventually rising to group commander in 1941. After the Philippines, however, he never again commanded a tactical unit and was instead assigned to staff jobs of increasing responsibility.[18]

Why is it that Grover's responsibility for the Clark Field disaster has gone unnoticed in the literature on the Philippines campaign? In my opinion, it is largely because his self-serving 1942 narrative on the operations of the 24th Group in the campaign misrepresented his actions during the hour when the fate of Clark Field hung on his decisions. He does not mention ordering his squadrons to switch to Manila from their originally assigned Clark and Iba Field patrol areas, or afterward radioing them to return to Clark posthaste. Nor does he mention holding the 20th Pursuit Squadron on the ground after he received Sprague's Teletype order to intercept the attackers over Clark. To account for his most serious error, he falsely blames a "communications breakdown" for failing to accept warnings that the second group of Japanese bombers was headed for Clark Field.[19] Because his narrative was the only official document prepared by a high-ranking officer who participated in the events, it is not surprising that he has been "let off the hook" by historians. Hopefully the detailed reconstruction of events in this book, which is based on the experiences of many individual officers and enlisted men who were present, will set the historical record straight.

Decisions of a *strategic* nature made by the War Department in Washington beginning in late July, 1941, provided the conditions for the disaster of December 8 at Clark and Iba Fields. We can identify three that characterize the poor judgment shown by Stimson, Marshall, and Arnold in their efforts to respond to the rising aggression of the Japanese in the Far East:

1. Opting to deter further Japanese aggression through the threat of application of American airpower against Japan proper.
2. Emphasizing an offensive airpower stance over a defensive one.
3. Rushing the buildup of American airpower in the Philippines without adequate provision for airfield defense

Beginning with the formulation of the so-called Victory Program in July, 1941, Secretary of War Stimson became enamored of the capabilities of the new "five-engine" bomber as a means of changing U.S. strategy in the Far East. No longer would the United States be helpless in responding to the mounting Japanese expansionism in the Far East. The threat posed by the new B-17 "Flying Fortress" would deter the Japanese from further efforts at expanding their empire. This view was adopted by Marshall in the War Department and by his air force commander, Hap Arnold, and a new strategy for the defense of the region was predicated on the new weapon. Unfortunately, the Japanese were unimpressed and proceeded on according to their own timetable for "Southern Operations."

In support of this deterrent approach, the decision was then made to emphasize *offensive* operations from the Philippines over defensive efforts. Major Laurence Kuter expressed his misgivings about this approach to Marshall in November, 1941, but his view was ignored. Hoyt Vandenberg's efforts to introduce a Battle of Britain–style defense of the Philippines based on an adequate P-40 interceptor force never gained War Department acceptance, even after the July decision to build up Philippines airpower. The focus of the buildup was the shipment of virtually all B-17s coming off the production lines to the islands. Recall that Marshall, in his secret November press conference, threatened to "set the paper cities of Japan on fire" with B-17s that would land in Vladivostok, and longer-ranged B-24s that he maintained could make the round-trip from Philippine bases.

In implementing the new strategy, the War Department decided to rush the airpower buildup before the Philippines had been strengthened adequately to defend the precious bomber fleet. In addition to materiel, pilots were to be rushed to the Philippines, regardless of their experience. As a result, pursuit pilots fresh from flying school—who should have remained stateside to receive some operational training first—were transferred to the Philippines. Dive-bomber pilots were sent on a troop transport minus their aircraft in the rush to reinforce the islands, never to receive the aircraft that might have made a difference in the campaign's outcome.

The War Department admitted it was taking a gamble by not expecting the Japanese to attack the Philippines before April, 1942. In his October briefing at the War Department before assuming command of the FEAF, Brereton had warned Marshall and Arnold of the risk, but they were willing to run it. In a radiogram to Arnold in March, 1942, in which Brereton tried to explain how his FEAF command had suffered such a loss, he maintained:

> Losses have been due mainly to failure to provide combat air forces with proper and adequate anti-aircraft defense, including air warning service equipment, personnel and anti-aircraft artillery. Prior to my departure from Washington, I stated that in the event of war it was almost certain to incur destruction of a bomber force put in the Philippine Islands without providing adequate anti-aircraft defense. . . . Against determined and well-executed attacks by low-

flying fighter-bombers and ground-strafing pursuit, passive defense measures, such as dispersion, protection by pens and camouflage are futile. . . . I protest against the implication that failure to use every means available for protection on the ground has been responsible for losses. These are in my opinion due to failure to provide combat commanders with the properly balanced components of an air force with which to wage war against a well-led enemy of superior strength and not, repeat not, due to shortcomings of local commanders.[20]

Considerations of a *political* nature lie at the root of the War Department's pre-July, 1941, policy against any buildup of the Philippines defense capabilities and subsequently resulted in the unsystematic rush to reinforce the islands when the policy was reversed. If Vandenberg's proposed Battle of Britain–style air defense system had been adopted by the War Department in February, 1941, following Air Chief Marshal Dowding's visit to Washington, the islands probably would have been ready and able to effectively oppose a Japanese air offensive. President Roosevelt, however, opposed reinforcement of the Philippines before July, 1941, for political reasons, including the priority given to the "Germany first" approach in planning for the war, as argued by the British. Only ad hoc, piecemeal, efforts were sanctioned, occasioned by the urging of the Navy Department, which was concerned about the aerial defense of its Asiatic Fleet in Manila Bay.

However, even if the War Department had supported a policy to build up the Philippines defensive capabilities, it would have been hard-pressed to supply the modern weapons and experienced aircrews needed to deter sustained Japanese aerial attacks. The American people's isolationist stance during the prewar period had translated into niggardly budget allocations for the armed services by Congress, reflecting the will of its constituents and resulting in a third-rate military arsenal that could spare little for the legitimate needs of Philippines defense, despite the pleas of General Grunert.

Unlike the case of the Pearl Harbor attack, no official investigation was ever conducted to determine the causes and allocate responsibility for the Clark and Iba Fields disaster, despite an enormity of loss no less than that in Hawaii. Conducting such an inquiry would not have been possible in the months after the attack, since the Philippines were an active war zone. It would have been inappropriate to call the USAFFE commander to Washington to testify while he was engaged in a military campaign. At any rate, MacArthur had become a hero to the American people for his resistance to the Japanese onslaught in the Philippines (largely attributable to his self-glorifying communiqués, of course). As historian John Costello noted, MacArthur's appointment in 1945 as Supreme Commander of Allied Powers in the occupation of Japan made it "politically impossible" to hold him accountable in the early years after the war for the Philippines disaster. Such an action would have been seen by the American public as a mean-spirited attempt to "tarnish the reputation of the heroic American general."[21]

APPENDIX A

JAPANESE NAVAL AIR STRENGTH FOR THE PHILIPPINES OPERATION, DECEMBER 8, 1941

Base	Unit	Number and Type of Aircraft
Takao, Formosa	Takao Kōkūtai	54 Type 1 Attack Bombers ("Betty")[a]
	Kanoya Kōkūtai	27 Type 1 Attack Bombers ("Betty")
	3d Kōkūtai	45 Type 0 Carrier Fighters ("Zero")
		12 Type 96 Carrier Fighters ("Claude")
		7 Type 98 Reconnaissance Planes ("Babs")[b]
	Tainan Kōkūtai (detached)	9 Type 0 Carrier Fighters ("Zero")
Tainan, Formosa	1st Kōkūtai	27 Type 96 Attack Bombers ("Nell")
	Tainan Kōkūtai	36 Type 0 Carrier Fighters ("Zero")
		12 Type 96 Carrier Fighters ("Claude")
		6 Type 98 Reconnaissance Aircraft ("Babs")
Palau	Toko Kōkūtai	18 Type 97 Flying Boats ("Mavis")
At Sea	*Ryūjō*	12 Type 96 Carrier Fighters ("Claude")
		13 Type 97 Carrier Attack Bombers ("Kate")
	Sanuki Maru	20 Type 95 Reconnaissance Seaplanes ("Dave")
		and Type 0 Observation Seaplanes ("Pete")
	Mizuhō	20 Type 95 Reconnaissance Seaplanes ("Dave")
		and Type 0 Observation Seaplanes ("Pete")
	Chitose	22 Type 95 Reconnaissance Seaplanes ("Dave")
		and Type 0 Observation Seaplanes ("Pete")

Source: Ikuhiko Hata and Yasuho Izawa, *Japanese Naval Aces and Fighter Units in World War II*, 123, 132; *Senshi Sōsho*, vol. 24, 160, 173; WDC 160541.

[a] Allied code names are given in parentheses for each aircraft type.

[b] The Imperial Navy's Type 98 reconnaissance plane ("Babs") was the navy version of the Imperial Army's Type 97 reconnaissance plane with the same Allied code name.

APPENDIX B

Japanese Army Air Strength for the Philippines Operation, Formosa, December 8, 1941

Base	Unit	Number and Type of Aircraft
Heito	24th Sentai	12 Type 97 Fighters ("Nate")[a]
	52d Dokoritsu Chūtai	9 Type 97 Command Reconnaissance Planes ("Babs")b
	74th Dokoritsu Chūtai	12 Type 98 Direct Cooperation Planes ("Ida")
	76th Dokoritsu Chūtai	9 Type 97 Headquarters Reconnaissance Planes ("Babs")
Choshu	14th Sentai	27 Type 97 Heavy Bombers ("Sally")
	24th Sentai	24 Type 97 Fighters ("Nate")
Kato	8th Sentai	27 Type 99 Twin-engine Light Bombers ("Lily")
		9 Type 97 Command Reconnaissance Planes ("Babs")
	16th Sentai	27 Type 97 Light Bombers ("Ann")
Koshun	50th Sentai	36 Type 97 Fighters ("Nate")

Source: Headquarters Army Forces Far East, Military History Section, "Philippines Air Operations Record: Phase One," Japanese Monograph no. 11, 8; Koichi Shimada, "The Opening Air Offensive against the Philippines," chap. 3 in David C. Evans, ed., *The Japanese Navy in World War II,* 79–80 (as corrected); Takushiro Hattori, *The Complete History of the Greater East Asia War,* 2:31.

[a]Allied code names are given in parentheses for each aircraft type.

[b]The Imperial Navy's Type 97 reconnaissance plane ("Babs") was the army version of the Imperial Navy's Type 97 reconnaissance plane with the same Allied code name.

APPENDIX C

FAR EAST AIR FORCE STRENGTH IN THE PHILIPPINES, DECEMBER 8, 1941

Location	Unit	Number and Type of Aircraft
Clark Field, Luzon	Headquarters Squadron, 24th Pursuit Group	1 P-40B
	20th Pursuit Squadron	23 P-40Bs
	19th Bomb Group (Heavy)	4 B-17Cs
	(Headquarters Squadron,	15 B-17Ds
	30th Bomb Squadron,	10 B-18s
	28th Bomb Squadron)	
Del Carmen Field, Luzon	34th Pursuit Squadron	22 P-35As
Iba Field, Luzon	3d Pursuit Squadron	24 P-40Es
		4 P-35As
		1 A-27
Nichols Field, Luzon	17th Pursuit Squadron	21 P-40Es
	21st Pursuit Squadron	22 P-40Es
	2d Observation Squadron	11 O-52s
		2 0-46As
Nielson Field, Luzon	27th Bomb Group	3 B-18s
Del Monte Field, Mindanao	14th Bomb Squadron	1 B-17C
		7 B-17Ds
	93d Bomb Squadron	1 B-17C
		7 B-17Ds
	5th Air Base Group	2 B-18s

Source: William H. Bartsch, *Doomed at the Start,* 43, 44, 46, 48, 49 (for pursuit squadrons); Appendix I (for 19th Bomb Group); "The 27th Reports," 16–17 (for 27th Bomb Group); radiogram, Brereton to Adjutant General, November, 1941, "Status Report of Airplanes in the USAFFE October 31, 1941" (for B-18s in 28th Bomb Squadron).

APPENDIX D

ORDER OF BATTLE, TAINAN KŌKŪTAI, TAINAN, FORMOSA, DECEMBER 8, 1941

Chūtai	Shōtai	Number	Rank and Name	Remarks
	11	1	Tai-i Hideki Shingō	
		2	1-Hisō Kuniyoshi Tanaka	
		3	3-Hisō Hiroshi Kuratomi	
1st	12	1	Tokumu Shō-i Mitsuo Toyoda	
		2	1-Hisō Toyo-o Sakai	
		3	2-Hisō Tsunehiro Yamakami	
	13	1	1-Hisō Saburō Sakai	
		2	2-Hisō Kazuo Yokokawa	1 hit
		3	3-Hisō Toshiaki Honda	
	21	1	Tai-i Masuzō Setō	
		2	1-Hisō Toshio Kikuchi	
		3	3-Hisō Saburō Nozawa	
2d	22	1	Hisōchō Ryōichi Nakamizo	Missing
		2	2-Hisō Hideo Izumi	
		3	3-Hisō Kosaku Minato	1 hit
	23	1	1-Hisō Yoshimichi Saeki	
		2	2-Hisō Yoshimi Hidaka	Aborted
		3	3-Hisō Shizuo Ishii	Aborted
	31	1	Tai-i Masao Asai	3 hits
		2	2-Hisō Ryokei Shinohara	2 hits
		3	1-Hisō Masaharu Higa	
3d	32	1	Hisōchō Gitarō Miyazaki	
		2	2-Hisō Toshio Ōta	
		3	1-Hi Masa-aki Shimakawa	
	33	1	1-Hisō Toshiyuki Sakai	
		2	2-Hisō Yoshisuke Arita	
		3	1-Hi Yoshio Motokichi	

Chūtai	Shōtai	Number	Rank and Name	Remarks
		1	Tai-i Akira Wakao	
	41	2	2-Hisō Yasujirō Kawano	Missing
		3	3-Hisō Yoshio Aoki	Missing
		1	Hisōchō Yoshimitsu Harada	10 hits
4th	42	2	1-Hisō Keishu Kamihira	12 hits
		3	1-Hi Haruo Fujibayashi	
		1	1-Hisō Yasuhisa Satō	Missing
	43	2	2-Hisō Susumu Ishihara	
		3	1-Hi Shizuki Nishiyama	

Source: War History Section, Japan Defense Agency, via Hideki Shingō.

APPENDIX E

ORDER OF BATTLE, 3D KŌKŪTAI, TAKAO, FORMOSA, DECEMBER 8, 1941

Daitai	Chūtai	Shōtai	Number	Rank and Name	Remarks
		1	1	Tai-i Tamotsu Yokoyama	
			2	2-Hisō Kaneyoshi Mutō	
			3	3-Hisō Yasunobu Nahara	
	Command (Yokoyama)	2	1	Hisōchō Sadaaki Akamatsu	
			2	1-Hisō Shigeru Yano	
			3	3-Hisō Masakichi Sonoyama	
		1	1	Tai-i Takeo Kurosawa	1 hit
			2	1-Hisō Yoshinao Tokuji	
			3	2-Hisō Hatsumasa Yamaya	
	1st (Kurosawa)	2	1	1-Hisō Shigeo Sugio	3 hits
			2	2-Hisō Katsujirō Nakano	3 hits
			3	1-Hi Masao Masuyama	2 hits
1st (Kurosawa)		1	1	Shō-i Tsuneo Nakahara	
			2	1-Hisō Hisashi Hide	
			3	3-Hisō Isaburō Yawata	
	2d (Nakahara)	2	1	1-Hisō Masayuki Nakase	
			2	1-Hisō Yoshiaki Hatakeyama	
			3	2-Hisō Kaneo Suzuki	
		1	1	Tai-i Ichirō Mukai	2 hits
			2	2-Hisō Yukiharu Ōzeki.	2 hits
			3	2-Hisō Nobutoshi Furukawa	
	1st (Mukai)	2	1	1-Hisō Yoshihiko Takenaka	4 hits
			2	2-Hisō Kunimori Nakakariya	
			3	3-Hisō Fumio Itō	Missing

Daitai	Chūtai	Shōtai	Number	Rank and Name	Remarks
2d (Mukai)			1	Hisōchō Fujikazu Koizumi	
		1	2	1-Hisō Kiyoharu Tezuka	
			3	1-Hi Katsutaro Kobayashi	
	2d (Koizumi)		1	1-Hisō Yoshikane Sasaki	
		2	2	2-Hisō Shigeo Okazaki	
			3	1-Hi Seiji Tajiri	
			1	Tai-i Zenjirō Miyano	
		1	2	2-Hisō Tamotsu Kojima	
			3	1-Hi Zenpei Matsumoto	Aborted
			1	Hisōchō Osamu Kudō	Aborted
	1st (Miyano)	2	2	1-Hisō Masayoshi Okazaki	
			3	3-Hisō Takashi Kurauchi	
		3	1	1-Hisō Jūzō Okamoto	
			2	3-Hisō Yashiro Hashiguchi	
3d (Miyano)			1	Tai-i Yukio Maki	
		1	2	2-Hisō Yoshio Hirose	Missing
			3	1-Hi Mibuichi Shimada	
			1	Hisōchō Chitoshi Isozaki	
	2d (Maki)	2	2	1-Hisō Otojirō Sakaguchi	3 hits
			3	3-Hisō Kiyotake Fukuyama	2 hits
			1	1-Hisō Yoshio Koike	
		3	2	2-Hisō Kunimatsu Nishiura	
			3	1-Hi Haruo Kawanishi	
			1	Tai-i Takaichi Hasuo	
		1	2	2-Hisō Bunkichi Nakajima	
	Rear Defense (Hasuo)		3	3-Hisō Shō-ichi Shōji	
			1	Hisōchō Kazuo Kubo	
		2	2	1-Hisō Fumio Ōzumi	3 hits
			3	3-Hisō Saburō Yoshii	Missing

Source: Tamotsu Yokoyama to author, March 28, 1980; 3rd Kōkūtai Hikōtai Sentō Kodo Chosho, December 8, 1941.

APPENDIX F

Officers of the 24th Pursuit Group, December 8, 1941

Headquarters and Headquarters Squadron

Maj.   Orrin S. Grover
1st Lt. William J. Cummings
        Ross N. Huguet
        Walter B. Putnam

2d Lt. Albert H. Chestnut
        Joe DeGraftenreid
        John G. Griffith
        Ridgley L. Hall
        Forrest S. O'Brien
        William A. Parsons

3d Pursuit Squadron

1st Lt. Henry G. Thorne
        James J. Donegan Jr.
        Herbert S. Ellis
        Raymond M. Gehrig
        Reuben W. Hager
        Robert T. Hanson
        Gerald M. Keenan
        Frank V. Neri
        Frank L. Richardson
        Frederick C. J. Roberts Jr.
        Edward R. Woolery
2d Lt. Dana H. Allen
        James E. Alsobrook
        Shelton E. Avant
        Gordon S. Benson
        James E. Boone
        William H. Brewster
        Joseph L. Burke
        Glenn E. Cave
        C. Philip Christie
        John Ship Daniel
        George O. Ellstrom
        James R. Field
        Harold E. Finley

2d Lt. Cleitus R. Garrett
        Howard P. Hardegree
        Robert James Hinson
        John T. Hylton Jr.
        Vernon R. Ireland
        Lycurgus W. Johnson
        Andrew E. Krieger
        Marston D. Langholf
        William L. Longmire
        James E. Mackey
        Donald H. Miller
        Paul O. Mock
        Robert W. Newman
        John F. O'Connell
        Bart A. Passanante
        James H. Pate
        William H. Powell
        Paul Racicot
        Burton R. Richard
        Richard L. Root
        Charles A. Sheeley
        Edgar B. Smith Jr.
        Donald D. Steele
        Andrew F. Webb

17th Pursuit Squadron

1st Lt.	Boyd D. Wagner	2d Lt.	Maurice G. Hughett
	GEORGE H. Armstrong		Earl H. Hulsey
	Theodore T. Bronk		George E. Kiser
	John L. Brownewell		Robert A. Krantz
	Russel M. Church		Joseph J. Kruzel
	Howard B. Connor		Robert J. Leyrer
	Walter L. Coss		Lawrence K. Lodin
	William D. Feallock		Truett J. Majors
	William A. Sheppard		Joseph L. McClellan
	Raymond A. Sloan		Hiram A. Messmore
	Allison W. Strauss		David L. Obert
2d Lt.	A. W. Balfanz Jr.		Charles W. Page
	Nathaniel H. Blanton		James A. Phillips
	Jerry O. Brezina		John H. Posten Jr.
	Charles W. Burris		Elmer B. Powell
	Stephen H. Crosby		James M. Ross
	Willis P. Culp III		William M. Rowe
	Jack D. Dale		James M. Rowland
	Edward A. Erickson		Earl R. Stone Jr.
	John P. Gillespie		John E. Vogel
	R. LaMar Gillett		Walter V. Wilcox
	Wilson Glover		Silas C. Wolf
	William J. Hennon		Oscar D. Wyatt
	Forrest M. Hobrecht		

20th Pursuit Squadron

1st Lt.	Joseph H. Moore	2d Lt.	Frank A. Ansley
	Glen M. Alder		Daniel L. Blass
	Marshall J. Anderson		Frederick B. Browne
	Frederick M. Armstrong Jr.		William B. Carter
	James E. Garrett		Erwin B. Crellin
	Joseph P. McLaughlin		James T. Drake
	Hugh H. Marble Jr.		Robert P. Duncan
	John Rizzolo		W. James Fossey
	Robert F. Roberts		James W. Fulks
	Kenneth B. Shelton		J. Jack Gates
	Charles R. Sneed		Carl Parker Gies
	William Tom Akins		Edwin B. Gilmore

2d Lt. Max B. Halvorson
        Edward Houseman
        Harrison S. Hughes
        Guy W. Iversen
        Randall D. Keator
        Max Louk
        Jesse A. Luker
        Morgan S. McCowan
        Melvin E. McKnight
        Lowell J. Mulcahy
        James E. Mullen

2d Lt. Thomas W. Patrick
        Percy E. Ramsey
        Henry C. Rancke
        Harlan F. Rousseau
        Eugene B. Shevlin
        Fred L. Siler
        Lloyd H. Stinson
        Edward J. Tremblay
        Custer E. Wake
        Varian Kiefer White
        Milton H. Woodside

21st Pursuit Squadron

1st Lt. William Edwin Dyess
         Herbert H. Ball
         William R. Brenner
         Lawrence W. Parcher
2d Lt.   Leo A. Boelens
         John P. Burns
         Robert D. Clark
         Joseph P. Cole
         Lloyd A. Coleman
         I. B. Jack Donalson

2d Lt.   Leo B. Golden Jr.
         Samuel C. Grashio
         Robert S. Ibold
         Ben S. Irvin
         Harold Johnson
         James E. May
         John L. McCown
         Linus L. Schramski
         Augustus F. Williams

34th Pursuit Squadron

1st Lt. Samuel H. Marett
         Ben S. Brown
         Jack H. Jennings
         Daniel A. Shapiro
2d Lt.   William L. Baker Jr.
         Frankie M. Bryant
         William G. Coleman
         Donald M. Crosland
         Charles E. Gaskell
         Jack W. Hall

2d Lt.   Abraham L. Hankin
         James M. Henry
         Arthur B. Knackstedt
         Lawrence E. McDaniel
         James C. Nicol
         Donald E. Pagel
         Claude W. Paulger
         John N. Raker
         Stewart W. Robb

Source: William H. Bartsch, *Doomed at the Start,* app. B, 434–40 (for flying officers); O. L. Grover, "Narrative of the Activities of the 24th Pursuit Group in the Philippine Islands," appendix: Roster of the 24th Pursuit Group as of December 8, 1941 (for nonflying officers).

APPENDIX G

OFFICERS OF THE 19TH BOMB GROUP (HEAVY)
DECEMBER 8, 1941

*Headquarters and
Headquarters Squadron*

Lt. Col. Eugene L. Eubank
Maj.   Birrell Walsh
Capt.   John A. E. Bergstrom
       Cornelius B. Cosgrove Jr.
       William E. McDonald
       Charles W. Miller
       William C. Shamblin Jr.
1st Lt.   Edgar B. Burgess
       Lee B. Coats
       William A. Cocke
       Warner W. Croxton Jr.
       Edwin S. Green
       Kenneth R. Kreps
       Wayne Livergood
       Ray W. McDuffee

1st Lt.   Patrick W. McIntyre
       Arthur W. Schmitt Jr.
       John H. M. Smith
       Kenneth F. Wetzel
2d Lt.   Glenn H. Boes
       John W. Chiles
       Roy H. Davidson
       James J. Dey
       James. C. Donahoe
       Edwin H. Graham
       Edgar H. Heald
       Jay M. Horowitz
       Walter A. Kelso
       Melvin A. McKenzie
       Edgar D. Whitcomb

14th Bomb Squadron

Maj.   Emmett O'Donnell Jr.
Capt.   William K. Horrigan
       Colin P. Kelly Jr.
1st Lt.   Henry C. Godman
       Donald McK. Keiser
       Sam Maddux Jr.
       Guilford R. Montgomery
       George E. Schaetzel
       Weldon H. Smith
       Edward C. Teats
2d Lt.   Kenneth A. Bandy
       Joe M. Bean
       Gleneth B. Berry
       Charles L. Bowman

2d Lt.   Kenneth A. Brady
       Thomas J. Burke
       Wallace F. Churchill
       Robert S. Clinkscales
       Stanley Cottage
       Henry Dittman
       Courtney R. Draper
       Guilford E. Evans
       James P. Ferrey
       Morris N. Friedman
       Theodore S. Greene
       Eddie W. Hayman
       Curtis J. Holdridge
       Jacques P. Jamal

2d Lt.   James S. Kale
          Lawrence H. Keyes
          Edgar V. Markley
          Francis K. McAllister
          Gerald W. McClune
          Paul S. Miller
          Milton E. Moore
          Donald D. Robins

2d Lt   Edson J. Sponable Jr.
          Paul R. Tarbutton
          Chandler B. Thomas
          Francis R. Thompson
          John J. Valkenaar
          Ernest C. Wade
          Robert F. Wasson
          John B. Wright

28th Bomb Squadron

Capt.   William P. Fisher
          Russell B. Patch
          Andrew G. Russell
1st Lt.   Clyde Box
          James R. Bruce Jr.
          Thomas J. Christian Jr.
          Fred T. Crimmins Jr.
          Ted B. Fisch
          Perry L. Franks
          Thomas H. Hubbard
          Alvin J. H. Mueller
          William D. Strong
2d Lt.   Theodore Arter III
          Oscar L. Black
          Alton H. Bryant
          Richard T. Carlisle
          Frank W. Carroll
          David M. Conley
          John W. Cox Jr.
          William K. Culp
          Everett Davis
          Robert D. Downes
          Leslie W. E. Duvall

2d Lt.   Lewis A. Edwards
          Willis J. Gary
          John H. Geer
          Earl C. Foster
          Herbert F. Glover
          Hugh T. Halbert
          Richard P. Haney
          Oscar St. J. Hillberg Jr.
          James A. Hilton
          Victor J. Howard
          Robert D. Lanier
          Donald L. Larson
          Basil H. Lewis
          William F. Lovegreen
          George M. Markovich
          Charles L. Mathis
          Robert E. L. Michie
          Joseph C. Milligan
          Reade R. Pickler
          Charles E. Rogers
          Roy D. Russell
          Dorwood C. Stephens
          Lonnie B. Wimberley

30th Bomb Squadron

Maj.	David R. Gibbs	2d Lt.	Lee H. Hall
Capt.	Edwin B. Broadhurst		James Harris
1st Lt.	Jack Adams		Woodrow Holbrook
	Elmore G. Brown		Dwight N. Holmes
	Ray L. Cox		Ralph Howard
	Clyde E. Fleming		Butler H. Lauterbach
	John E. L. Huse		Harold C. McAuliff
	Frank A. Kurtz		Robert R. Meyer
	Glenn Rice		Donald C. Mitchell
	Raymond V. Schwanbeck		Cuthbert L. Mosely
	Hewitt T. Wheless		Marne Noelke
	Sig R. Young		Anthony E. Oliver
2d Lt.	William H. Ambrosius		William M. Railing
	Edward J. Bechtold		John I. Renka Jr.
	Edward D. Benham		Alvino V. Reyes
	George B. Berkowitz		Robert E. Richards
	Harry A. Blitch		Harry J. Schreiber
	George J. Breindel		Walter E. Seamon
	Thomas A. Caswell		Richard F. Smith
	William T. Chesser		Arthur F. Sorrell
	James E. Colovin		Charles J. Stevens
	Dayton L. Drachenberg		Austin W. Stitt Jr.
	Carl E. Epperson		William M. Taylor
	Arthur E. Gary		Raymond G. Teborek
	Eugene R. Greeson		

93d Bomb Squadron

Capt.	Cecil E. Combs	2d Lt.	Philip H. Ashe
1st Lt.	William J. Bohnaker		Reuben A. Baxter
	John H. Carpenter III		Milton R. Beekman
	James T. Connally		Francis R. Cappelletti
	Walter R. Ford		William M. Carrithers
	Dean C. Hoevet		William F. Clapp
	Elmer L. Parsel		James A. Elder
	Morris H. Shedd		George C. Faulkner Jr.
	Elliott J. Vandevanter		Owen R. Graham
	George L. Verity		Cecil E. Gregg

2d Lt.	Purcell S. Harrington	2d Lt.	John W. Norvell
	Jack H. Heinzel		Carey Law O'Bryan
	PERCY M. HINTON		Charles H. O'Neil
	Arthur E. Hoffman		Harl Pease Jr.
	Melvin H. Hunt		John S. Pryor
	Edward M. Jacquet		Vincent L. Snyder
	Jack E. Jones		Maxwell D. Stone
	Douglas H. Kellar		Earl R. Tash
	William G. Mahoney		Jerome M. Triolo
	William F. Meenagh		William S. Warner
	Donald C. Miller		Byron R. Work
	Stancill M. Nanney		

Source: Compiled by the author from "Roster 19th Bombardment Group as of December 8, 1941" (unofficial document of 19th Bomb Group Association) and "Alphabetical Casualty Listing of Officers who Were in the Philippine Islands Area as of 7 Dec. 1941" (RG 407, Philippine Records, box 6, NARA).

APPENDIX H

FAR EAST AIR FORCE PERSONNEL KILLED IN ACTION DECEMBER 8, 1941

Clark Field

Headquarters and Headquarters Squadron, 24th Pursuit Group

	T.Sgt. Joseph Ambrose	06079279
	S.Sgt. William E. Asbury	06556087
★	Sgt. James E. Quinn	06067645
	Pfc. John R. Gagliardi	06291419
★	Pfc. Robert E. Lamb	06980086
★	Pfc. Wade H. Williams Jr.	06993789
	Pvt. Joseph N. Bowman Jr.	19020144
	Pvt. Albert E. Herron	07031214
★	Pvt. Theodore Koocherook	06142788
★	Pvt. Michael Seelig Jr.	06298748

20th Pursuit Squadron, 24th Pursuit Group

2d Lt. James T. Drake	0-418430
2d Lt. Max Louk	0-417114
2d Lt. Jesse A. Luker	0-412524
2d Lt. Lowell J. Mulcahy	0-426571
S.Sgt. William A. Hainer	06920045
S.Sgt. Andrew F. Kapalko	06913518
Pvt. Cornelius Bumbar	16027768
Pvt. Edwin W. Wissing	19016241
Pvt. Vernon E. Wyatt	19013073

Headquarters and Headquarters Squadron, 19th Bomb Group (Heavy)

	Capt. John A. E. Bergstrom	0-260949
	1st Lt. William A. Cocke Jr.	0-22801
	Sgt. Russell Cornford	6559720
	Sgt. William C. Jones	6268715
	Sgt. Otto E. Wellman	06859377
★	Pfc. LeRoy R. Carpenter	19018122
	Pfc. Robert G. Menzie	06296374
	Pvt. Wayne C. Gerron	19028874
	Pvt. Leslie V. Long	19032138

Pvt. Chester J. Pokrzywa	16003426
Pvt. Greeley B. Williams	17003441

28th Bomb Squadron, 19th Bomb Group (Heavy)

2d Lt. Leslie W. E. Duvall	0-418431
2d Lt. Lonnie B. Wimberley	0-397830
Cpl. Joseph Hriczko	06982033
Pvt. Darrell I. Edwards	17029512
Pvt. Robert L. Jennings	19020893
Pvt. Edward E. Van Dyke	19019921

30th Bomb Squadron, 19th Bomb Group (Heavy)

2d Lt. Arthur E. Gary	0-398704
S.Sgt. Wyndolyn E. Burgess	06246578
Sgt. Stanley A. Domin	06915684
Sgt. Lionel Lowe	06855137
Sgt. Everett A. Pond	06296460
Pfc. Everett W. Dodson	06938453
★ Pfc. Robert L. Palmer	06915639
★ Pvt. Ernest M. Abreen	19002910
Pvt. Austin F. Bittner	13030356
Pvt. Frank D. Borchers	06938053
Pvt. Wayne C. Gerron	19028874
Pvt. Leslie D. Meyers	12024659
Pvt. Hugh P. Rice Jr.	19050636
Pvt. Andrew V. Slane	06281975

7th Materiel Squadron, 19th Bomb Group (Heavy)

Maj. Clarence R. Davis	0-238423
Sgt. George F. Loritz	06911518
Pfc. William R. Briggs	unknown
Pvt. Robert R. McLennan	unknown
Pvt. Russell W. Smith	19013384

Near Clark Field

3d Pursuit Squadron, 24th Pursuit Group

2d Lt. Vernon R. Ireland	0-406684

Near Santa Ignacia

3d Pursuit Squadron, 24th Pursuit Group
    2d Lt. George O. Ellstrom   0-401152

Iba Field

3d Pursuit Squadron, 24th Pursuit Group

	2d Lt. Shelton E. Avant	0-367768
	2d Lt. John F. O'Connell Jr	0-411725
	2d Lt. Richard L. Root	0-407094
	2d Lt. Andrew F. Webb	0-408872
★	S.Sgt. Cecil M. Commander	06379224
★	S.Sgt Walter T. Foster	06262497
	Cpl. Gerald Dumais	06139330
	Cpl. John Jurcsak	06879158
	Pfc. Orin H. Gillett	06980536
	Pfc. Leo A. Mack	06933681
	Pvt. Henry M. Colvin	07024421
	Pvt. Joseph Deschambeau	06110627
	Pvt. Kenneth H. Messenger	06147406
★	Pvt. Karl Santschi	06627142
★	Pvt. Arthur F. Space	11019684

Air Warning Company, Iba Detachment

Pfc. Wash C. Shaffron	12023627
Pfc. Orville M. Street	13011429
Pfc. William L. Todd	13022713
Pvt. John M. Harler	12023627
Pvt. Jarriet T. Moore	15047892

★December 8, 1941, not confirmed as date of death.

Source: American Battle Monuments Commission, "The World War II Honor Roll," http://www.abmc.gov; U.S. Total Army Personnel Command (for those reinterred in the United States); Ray Thompson, "Roster of the 7th Squadron, 19th Bomb Group," in *19th Bomb Group,* 24–30; author's research for others (including those for whom December 8, 1941, is not confirmed as the date of death).

APPENDIX I

B-17s of the 19th Bomb Group (Heavy), December 8, 1941

At Clark Field

B-17Cs

40-2048 Destroyed in attack
40-2067 Destroyed in attack
40-2072 Undamaged in attack
40-2077 Destroyed in attack

B-17Ds

40-3059 Destroyed in attack
40-3063 On reconnaissance during attack
40-3068 Destroyed in attack
40-3069 Destroyed in attack
40-3070 On reconnaissance during attack
40-3075 Destroyed in attack
40-3076 Destroyed in attack
40-3088 Destroyed in attack
40-3093 Damaged in September landing;
   survived the attack
40-3094 Destroyed in attack
40-3095 Destroyed in attack
40-3096 Damaged during attack; repaired later
40-3098 Damaged during attack; repaired later
40-3099 Destroyed in attack
40-3100 Slightly damaged during attack;
   repaired later

At Del Monte Field

B-17Cs

40-2045 14th Squadron
40-2062 93d Squadron

B-17Ds

40-3061 14th Squadron
40-3062 93d Squadron
40-3064 93d Squadron
40-3066 14th Squadron
40-3067 93d Squadron
40-3072 93d Squadron
40-3073 93d Squadron
40-3074 93d Squadron
40-3078 14th Squadron
40-3079 14th Squadron
40-3086 14th Squadron
40-3087 93d Squadron
40-3091 14th Squadron
40-3097 14th Squadron

Source: John H. Mitchell, *On Wings We Conquer,* apps. A-1, A-4, and A-5 (modified by author to correct for errors on 40-3066 and 40-3070).

APPENDIX J

Japanese Naval Terminology

Naval Air Organization

Kōkūkantai	Air Fleet
Kōkūsentai	Air Flotilla
Kōkūtai	Air Group
Buntai	Air Division (personnel only)
Chūtai	Air Division (of aircraft, usually 9)
Shōtai	Air Section (3 aircraft)

Naval Aircraft

Rikujō Kogeki-ki (Rikkō)	Land-based attack aircraft

Naval Air Ranks

Taisa	Captain
Chūsa	Commander
Shōsa	Lieutenant Commander
Tai-i	Lieutenant
Chū-i	Lieutenant (junior grade)
Shō-i	Ensign
Hikō Heisōchō (Hisōchō)	Chief Flight Petty Officer
Ittō Hikōheisō (1-Hisō)	Flight Petty Officer 1st Class
Nitō Hikōheisō (2-Hisō)	Flight Petty Officer 2d Class
Santo Hikōheisō (3-Hisō)	Flight Petty Officer 3d Class
Ittō Hikōhei (1-Hi)	Flight Seaman 1st Class

Source: Ikuhiko Hata and Yasuo Izawa, *Japanese Naval Aces and Fighter Units in World War II,* xiii–xiv; Osamu Tagaya, *Mitsubishi Type 1 Rikkō "Betty" Units of World War 2,* 6, 16–17; Osamu Tagaya to author, Nov. 26, 1978.

Notes

ABBREVIATIONS USED IN NOTES AND SOURCES

AAF	Army Air Forces
AAG	Air Adjutant General
ABMC	American Battle Monuments Commission
AC	Air Corps
AC/S	Assistant Chief of Staff
AFCC	Air Force Combat Command
AFHRA	Air Force Historical Research Agency, Maxwell Air Force Base, Ala.
AFSHRC	Albert F. Simpson Historical Research Center, Maxwell Air Force Base, Ala.
AG	Adjutant General
AGWAR	Adjutant General, War Department
AS	Air Staff
AWPD	Air War Plans Division
CAC	Chief of Air Corps
CG	Commanding General
CINC	Commander in Chief
CNO	Chief of Naval Operations
CO	Commanding Officer
C/S	Chief of Staff
FEAF	Far East Air Force
GCMF	George C. Marshall Foundation, Lexington, Va.
GHQ	General Headquarters
GHQFE	General Headquarters, Far East
GS	General Staff
HQ	Headquarters
IGHQ	Imperial General Headquarters
LOC	Library of Congress, Washington, D.C.
MMA	MacArthur Memorial Archives, Norfolk, Va.
NARA D.C.	National Archives and Records Administration, Washington, D.C.
NARA C. P.	National Archives and Records Administration, College Park, Md.

NASM	National Air and Space Museum, Washington, D.C.
NHC	Naval Historical Center, Washington, D.C.
NPRC	National Personnel Records Center, St. Louis, Mo.
OCAC	Office of the Chief of the Air Corps
OCMH	Office of the Chief of Military History, Washington, D.C.
OC/S	Office of the Chief of Staff
PD	Philippine Department
PDAF	Philippine Department Air Force
RG	Record Group
RAAF	Royal Australian Air Force
RAFM	Royal Air Force Museum, London
USAFA	U.S. Air Force Academy, Colorado Springs, Colo.
USAFFE	U.S. Army Forces in the Far East
USAMHI	U.S. Army Military History Institute, Carlisle Barracks, Pa.
USSBS	U.S. Strategic Bombing Survey
WD	War Department
WPD	War Plans Division

PROLOGUE: "SEIZE THIS GOLDEN OPPORTUNITY"

1. George V. Strong to George C. Marshall, memo, Aug. 21, 1939, "Military Policy as to the Philippines, WPD 4192, RG 165, WPD General Correspondence, 1940–42, NARA D.C.

2. Brian McAllister Linn, *Guardians of Empire: The U.S. Army and the Pacific, 1902–1940,* 220.

3. Strong to Marshall, Aug. 21, 1939; idem., memo, Oct. 10, 1940, "War Department Policy Reference Defense of the Philippines," WPD 3251-37, RG 165, WPD General Correspondence, 1940–42, NARA D.C.; Linn, *Guardians of Empire,* 235. Linn offers a detailed discussion of WD policy regarding the defense of the Philippines dating back to 1902.

4. AG to CAC, memo, Mar. 23, 1939, "Aviation in the National Defense," 381 War Plans, box 207, RG 18, Central Decimal Files, ser. 2, 1939–42, NARA D.C.; annex to memo for AG, Oct. 18, 1940, "Review and Revision of War Department Air Board Report," Tab A, ibid.; "Air Defense of the Philippine Islands," entry 422, executive 8, RG 165, Executive Group Files, WPD, 1939–42, NARA D.C.

5. Carl Spaatz to Henry H. Arnold, memo, Sept. 1, 1939, "Strategically Offensive Operations in the Far East," 381 War Plans, "Bulkies," box 183, RG 18, Central Decimal Files, 1939–42, NARA D.C.

6. Henry H. Arnold to AC C/S, WPD, memo, Oct. 19, 1939, WPD 3748-18, RG 165, WPD General Correspondence, 1940–42, NARA D.C.; Army War College, Course at the Army War College 1938–39, War Plans, Report of Committee no. 4, "Philippine Department (Military Policy in the Western Pacific)," Apr. 5, 1939, USAMHI, 2.

7. Spaatz to Arnold, Sept. 1, 1939. The calculation of the number of aircraft is mine, based on the standard Air Corps group's table of organization and equipment (TO&E).

8. Peter Bowers, *Fortress in the Sky,* 57–59, 241. Pursuit plane totals are based on a listing prepared by the OCAC for the WD, "Army Pursuit Airplanes on Hand, Nov. 30, 1939," entry 422, executive 4, RG 165, WPD Executive Group Files, 1939–42, NARA D.C.

9. DeWitt S. Copp, *Forged in Fire: Strategy and Decisions in the Air War over Europe, 1940–45,* vii, x.

10. By the end of April, 1941, only 134 B, C, and D model B-17s had been delivered to the AC, of which twenty had been turned over to the RAF (Bowers, *Fortress in the Sky,* 59–66, 241).

11. Table submitted to the WD by the OCAC, Nov. 30, 1939, entry 422, executive 4, RG

165, WPD Executive Group Files, 1939–42, NARA D.C. Vandenberg's calculations were based on distances from Clark Field in central Luzon.

12. Alan G. Blue, *The B-24 Liberator,* 12, 214. Vandenberg may have had in mind the long-range heavy bomber recommended by the Kilner Board in June, 1939. Arnold established the board to determine AC procurement needs, which resulted the following year in the selection of Boeing's proposed XB-29 with a range of seven thousand miles (an operating radius of thirty-five-hundred miles) carrying a two-thousand-pound bomb load. However, the B-29 did not enter service until April, 1944 (Carl Berger, *B-29: The Superfortress,* 23–25, 59.)

13. Arnold to AC C/S, WPD, Oct. 19, 1939; WPD Tally and OK sheet, "Implementation of the Board Report," Oct. 20, 1939, WPD 3748-18; and George V. Strong to George C. Marshall, memo, Mar. 2, 1940, "Practicability of Increasing Army Aviation Strength in the Philippines," WPD 4192-3, both in RG 165, WPD General Correspondence, 1940–42, NARA D.C.

14. Henry H. Arnold to George V. Strong, memo, Feb. 26, 1940, "Estimates for Aviation Reinforcement for the Philippine Department," WPD 4192-2, RG 165, WPD General Correspondence, 1940–42, NARA D.C.; Strong to Marshall, Mar. 2, 1940; Mark S. Watson, *Chief of Staff: Prewar Plans and Preparations,* 416.

15. "National Policies Set at Liaison Conference," *Japan Times and Mail,* July 29, 1940. A *tsubo* is a unit of measure equal to 1.8 meters by 1.8 meters, which means the room was seventy-eight square meters in size.

16. Emperor Hirohito established the Imperial Headquarters in the palace in November, 1937, on the recommendation of Konoe, thus allowing Hirohito to exercise his constitutional role as supreme commander and facilitate coordination between the army and navy. Through the instrument of the Imperial Headquarters, Hirohito exercised command over both the army and navy (Herbert P. Bix, *Hirohito and the Making of Modern Japan,* 327, 329).

17. "National Policies"; Robert J. C. Butow, *Tōjō and the Coming of War,* 170. Konoe introduced Imperial Headquarters–Government Liaison Conferences in November, 1937, as a means of bringing the army and navy chiefs and vice chiefs of staff into closer consultation with the government regarding the integration of decisions and the armed services' needs with government policies and resources (Bix, *Hirohito,* 327).

18. "National Policies"; James B. Crowley, "Japan's Military Foreign Policies," in *Japan's Foreign Policy, 1868–1941: A Research Guide,* ed. James W. Morley, 83, 85.

19. Butow, *Tōjō,* 139, 151, 246; Jun Tsunoda, "The Navy's Role in the Southern Strategy," in *The Fateful Choice: Japan's Advance into Southeast Asia, 1939–1941,* ed. James W. Morley, 246; Crowley, "Japan's Military," 84–85. Although there is no record of it, the army chief of staff most likely presented the paper since it was his staff that drafted it.

20. Takushirō Hattori, *The Complete History of the Greater East Asia War,* 1:33–37; Butow, *Tōjō,* 151–53; Tsunoda, "Navy's Role," 248, 253–54; Chihirō Hosoya, "The Tripartite Pact 1939–1940," in *Deterrent Diplomacy: Japan, Germany, and the USSR, 1935–1940,* ed. James W. Morley, 207.

21. Hattori, "Complete History," 1:33; Crowley, "Japan's Military," 85.

22. "National Policies"; Hattori, *Complete History,* 1:35–36.

23. John Toland, *The Rising Sun,* 51–52; Hattori, *Complete History,* 1:38; Crowley, "Japan's Military," 86–87.

24. "National Policies"; Bix, *Hirohito,* 368, 375.

25. Tamotsu Yokoyama, *Ah Zero-sen Ichidai* (*Oh, My Life in the Zero Fighter*), 74; Robert C. Mikesh, *Zero,* 36; Masataka Okumiya and Jirō Horikoshi, with Martin Caidin, *Zero!* 156–57; Jirō Horikoshi, *Eagles of Mitsubishi,* 98; Ikuhiko Hata and Yasuho Izawa, *Japanese Naval Aces and Fighter Units in World War II,* 91.

26. Yokoyama, *Ah Zero-sen,* 77; Mikesh, *Zero,* 36.

27. Col. D. H. Torrey, AG, PD, to AGWAR, 1st Indorsement, Jan. 3, 1940; and Lawrence Churchill, PDAF, to CG, PD, memo, Dec. 8, 1939, both in 210.31-B, Philippines, box 1112,

RG 18, Project Files, Departments, 1939–42, NARA D.C.; William H. Crom, PDAF, to Ira Eaker, OCAC, Aug. 4, 1939, 321.9-B, Miscellaneous, Philippines, box 1114, ibid.

28. Crom to Eaker.

29. Lawrence Churchill, PDAF, to George Stratemeyer, OCAC, Mar. 26, 1940, 210.31-B, Philippines, box 1112, RG 18, Project Files, Departments, 1939–42, NARA D.C.

30. Linn, *Guardians of Empire,* 234, 235, 238.

31. Francis Sayre to George C. Marshall, Nov. 30, 1940, Francis Sayre Papers, LOC (hereafter Sayre Papers).

32. George Grunert to AG, July 10, 1940, PD 660.2, box 1021, RG 407, AG Central Decimal Files, 1940–42, NARA D.C.

33. George Grunert to AG, memo, July 22, 1940, 145.93 AC/AS Plans Collection, Philippine Department, reel A 1449, AFHRA; and as compiled from NASM aircraft history cards for P-26As and B-10Bs.

34. Grunert to AG, July 22, 1940; Churchill to Stratemeyer.

35. George Grunert to George C. Marshall, Sept. 1, 1940, in *The Papers of George Catlett Marshall,* vol. 2, *"We Cannot Delay,"* ed. Larry I. Bland, 315 n 1.

36. George V. Strong to George C. Marshall, memo, July 29, 1940, PD (7-10-40), box 1021, RG 407, AG Central Decimal Files, 1940–42, NARA D.C.

37. Henry H. Arnold to George V. Strong, memo, Aug. 8, 1940, 145.93, AC/AS Plans Collection, reel 1449, AFHRA.

38. F. S. Clark to AG, memo, Sept. 7, 1940, "Status of Air Corps Officers and Airplanes in the Philippine Department," WPD 3633-11, RG 165, WPD General Correspondence, 1940–42, NARA D.C.; George C. Marshall to George Grunert, Sept. 20, 1940, in *Papers of George Catlett Marshall,* ed. Bland, 2:314–15.

39. George Grunert to AG, radiogram, Sept. 9, 1940, PD 660.2 (9-9-40), box 1021, RG 407, AG Central Decimal Files, 1940–42, NARA D.C.

40. Hattori, *Complete History,* 1:39; Tsunoda, "Navy's Role," 241, 252.

41. Tsunoda, "Navy's Role," 243–46, 252–53, 255, 258; 259.

42. Ibid., 255; Bix, *Hirohito,* 376.

43. Ikuhiko Hata, "The Army's Move into Northern Indochina," in Morley, *Fateful Choice,* 159, 160, 162, 175, 176; 177, 178–79.

44. Okumiya and Horikoshi, with Caidin, *Zero!* 34–35

45. Ibid., 37; Horikoshi, *Eagles of Mitsubishi,* 96–97.

46. Bix, *Hirohito,* 329.

47. Nobutaka Ike, *Japan's Decision for War,* 4; Tsunoda, "Navy's Role," 266, 267, 269, 273; Ike, *Japan's Decision,* 9, 12, 13; Hattori, *Complete History,* 1:43. The Philippines were not cited in the list as being within Japan's sphere of influence.

48. Ike, *Japan's Decision,* 9, 12, 13.

49. As translated in Bix, *Hirohito,* 383.

50. Hata, "Army's Move," 192, 203.

Part 1: "By God, It Is Destiny That Brings Me Here!"

1. Frank L. Kluckhohn, "Hull Deplores Attack on Indochina as Blow to Pacific Status Quo," *New York Times,* Sept. 24, 1940; idem., "U.S. Embargoes Scrap Iron, Hitting Japan," *New York Times,* Sept. 27, 1940; Maurice Matloff and Edwin M. Snell, *Strategic Planning for Coalition Warfare, 1941–1942,* 64.

2. George V. Strong to C/S, memo, Oct. 10, 1940, "War Department Policy Reference Defense of the Philippine Islands," WPD 3251-37, RG 165, WPD General Correspondence, 1940–42, NARA D.C.

3. Henry L. Stimson Diary, Oct. 2 and Oct. 18, 1940, reel 6, vol. 31, Henry L. Stimson

Papers, LOC (hereafter Stimson Papers); "Memorandum of Army/Navy Conference, Dec. 16, 1940," and "Notes on General Council Meeting, 10:00, Feb. 19, 1941," both in RG 165, OC/S Minutes and Notes of Conferences 1938–42, NARA D.C.; "Navy Families to Leave," *New York Times,* Oct. 22, 1940; James Leutze, *A Different Kind of Victory,* 177, 179.

4. Strong to Marshall, Mar. 2, 1940; Forrest C. Pogue, *George C. Marshall: Ordeal and Hope,* 178; Stimson Diary, Oct. 18, 1940; George Stratemeyer, WPD, to Major Upston, memo, Oct. 16, 1940, 381 Philippine Department, RG 18, AAG 800-Miscellaneous A (Philippines), NARA D.C.; Marshall to Grunert, Sept. 20, 1940.

5. Henry H. Arnold to C/S, memo, Oct. 17, 1940, "Additional Pursuit Units for the Philippine Department," 381 Philippine Department, RG 18, AAG 800-Miscellaneous A (Philippines), NARA D.C.; "Status of Reinforcement of Pacific Garrison," Oct. 23, 1940; and memo, Plans to Exec, Oct. 17, 1940, both in Stimson Top Secret File, RG 107, NARA D.C.; memo to CGs, Hamilton and Selfridge Fields, Oct. 19, 1940, 370.5 Assignments, RG 18, Central Decimal Files, ser. 2, 1939–42, NARA D.C.

6. Harold Denny, "U.S. Will Dispatch Air Reinforcements to the Philippines," *New York Times,* Oct. 24, 1940; John G. Norris, "U.S. Warns She'll Protect Philippines," *Washington Post,* Oct. 24, 1940.

7. Hanson W. Baldwin, "Strategy of Change," *New York Times,* Oct. 26, 1940.

8. Matloff and Snell, *Strategic Planning,* 25–28.

9. Tsunoda, "Navy's Role," 243–46, 261, 277–78.

10. As quoted in Tsunoda, "Navy's Role," 281.

11. Theodore H. White, *In Search of History,* 113–14; draft dispatch to *Time* in the Theodore White Collection, Harvard University Archives, Pusey Library, Cambridge, Mass.

12. Ricardo T. Jose, *The Philippine Army, 1935–1942,* 137; Linn, *Guardians of Empire,* 234.

13. George Grunert to George C. Marshall, Nov. 2, 1940; and Leonard T. Gerow to C/S, memo, Nov. 20, 1940, both in WPD 3251-37, RG 165, WPD General Correspondence, 1939–1942, NARA D.C. Grunert's intention was to seek War Department approval to call the Philippine Army to active duty for training under his Philippine Department in order to ensure its effectiveness in time of war. See Richard B. Meixsel, "Major General George Grunert, WPO-3, and the Philippine Army, 1940–1941," *Journal of Military History* 59, no. 2 (Apr., 1995): 312.

14. Yamamoto to Vice Adm. Shigetaro Yamada, Dec. 10, 1940, quoted in Gordon W. Prange, *At Dawn We Slept,* 11–12.

15. Yamamoto to Navy Minister Koshirō Oikawa, Jan., 1941, quoted in Prange, *At Dawn We Slept,* 15, 17.

16. Hattori, *Complete History,* 2:326–27; Imperial General Headquarters, Army Directive 810, Jan. 16, 1941, Japanese Naval Records, vol. 1, box 40, Operational Archives Division, NHC.

17. Tsunoda, "Navy's Role," 288–89.

18. C/S to General Gerow, memo, Jan. 17, 1941, "White House Conference of Thursday, Jan. 16, 1941," reproduced as Exhibit D in William R. Burt, *Adventures with Warlords,* 212–13.

19. Memo for the AC/S, WPD, "Staff Conversations with British," n.d. (evidently late Jan., 1941), reproduced in Burt, *Adventures with Warlords,* 214.

20. Matloff and Snell, *Strategic Planning,* 34–37.

21. Henry H. Arnold to AC/S, WPD, memo, Feb. 27, 1941, Chief of Staff Conference File; and "Conference in Office of the Chief of Staff at 10:00 A.M., Tuesday, Feb. 25, 1941," both in RG 165, OC/S Minutes and Notes on Conferences, 1938–42, NARA D.C.; George C. Marshall to Leonard T. Gerow, memo, Feb. 26, 1941, WPD 4175-18, reproduced in Bland, ed., *Marshall Papers,* 2:430–32.

22. George C. Marshall's acceptance of Hugh Dowding's dinner invitation, Mar. 22, 1941, Dowding Correspondence, box 58, folder 41, Papers of George C. Marshall, GCMF (hereafter

Marshall Papers); Hugh Dowding, "Visit to Canada and the U.S.A." (daily activity log), Jan. 5, 1941, RAFM; "Dowding to Confer on Plane-Building," *New York Times,* Jan. 6, 1941.

23. Copp, *Forged in Fire,* viii, ix, x; Lt. Col. William H. Walker to Senior Army Member, Joint Planning Committee, memo, June 28, 1940, "Review and Revision of the War Department Air Board Report," entry 422, executive 4; and memo for the AG, Oct. 18, 1940, "Review and Revision of War Department Air Board Report," entry 422, executive 8, both in RG 165, WPD Executive Group Files, 1939–42, NARA D.C.

24. Leonard T. Gerow to C/S, memo, Feb. 21, 1941, "Development of Air Base Facilities in Mid-Pacific Islands," WPD 2550-20, RG 165, WPD General Correspondence, 1940–42, NARA D.C.

25. George Grunert to George C. Marshall, Mar. 6, 1941; and Marshall to Grunert, Mar. 28, 1941, both in box 69, folder 34 (Grunert Correspondence), Marshall Papers.

26. H. Ford Wilkins, "Three Power Talk on Orient Defense Is Set for Manila," *New York Times,* Apr. 5, 1941; "Weekly Summary of Philippine News," nos. 9 and 14, box 1885, RG 165, Military Intelligence—Philippine Islands, NARA C. P.

27. Matloff and Snell, *Strategic Planning,* 65–67; "Draft Agreement on the Outline Plan for Employment of American, Dutch, and British Forces in the Far East Area in the Event of War with Japan," Aug., 1941, WPD 4402-18, RG 165, WPD General Correspondence, 1940–42, NARA D.C.

28. Matloff and Snell, *Strategic Planning,* 44–46, 66–67.

29. Hattori, *Complete History,* 1:93, 120; Tsunoda, "Navy's Role," 295. As noted by one observer, what was "desired" in 1940 as part of the future new order had by April, 1941, "become essential" to the security of the Japanese empire (Crowley, "Japan's Military," 91–92).

30. Otto D. Tolischus, "Japanese Report U.S. Is in a Secret Accord to Defend Southeast Asia Against Drive," *New York Times,* Apr. 21, 1941.

31. Referred to in Leonard T. Gerow to George C. Marshall, memo, June 6, 1941, WPD 3251-50, RG 165, WPD General Correspondence, 1940–42, NARA D.C.

32. George C. Marshall to Douglas MacArthur, June 20, 1941, WPD 3251-50, reproduced in Bland, ed., *Marshall Papers,* 2:540–41.

CHAPTER 1: "THEY HAVE REALLY RIPPED THE 17TH ALL TO HELL"

1. George Armstrong to author, Oct. 13, 1996; idem., taped narrative provided to author, May, 1977; James Hight to author, Jan. 6, 1997; Edward T. Maloney, *Boeing P-26 Peashooter,* 20.

2. Walter Coss to author, Dec. 31, 1996; Armstrong to author, Oct. 13, 1996.

3. Kirtley J. Gregg to wife, Dec. 18, 1940.

4. George Armstrong to author, Sept. 29, 1977; Maj. Carl Spaatz, Hensley Field, to CO, March Field, radiogram, Oct. 17, 1932, copy in author's collection; Armstrong narrative.

5. Kirtley J. Gregg to wife, Dec. 18, 24, and 26, 1940; and Jan. 29, Feb. 2, and Mar. 26, 1941.

6. Ibid., Nov. 15 and Dec. 18, 1940.

7. Ibid., Dec. 18, 1940.

8. Grant Mahony to mother, Dec. 7, 1940. Mori later changed his occupation and became Colonel Mori, commander of the Cabanatuan POW camp, where prisoners were incarcerated following the fall of the Philippines (George Armstrong to author, Apr. 18, 1997).

9. Mahony to mother, Dec. 7 and 9, 1940; HQ, PD, *Telephone Directory, Manila and Vicinity: Directory of All Officers Stationed within the Philippine Department, July 16, 1941.*

10. William Sheppard to parents, Feb. 19, 1941; Norman Ernst to author, Mar. 6, 1980.

11. Burt, *Adventures with Warlords,* 39; WD, *Officers of the Army Stationed in or Near the District of Columbia, Oct. 1, 1940,* 59.

12. Peter Flint, *Dowding and Headquarters Fighter Command,* 186–87; "Dowding to Confer on Plane-Building," *New York Times,* Jan. 6, 1941; Philip S. Meilinger, *Hoyt S. Vandenberg: The Life of a General,* 26.

13. Meilinger, *Vandenberg,* 18–19; Burt, *Adventures with Warlords,* 4, 10, 15.

14. "Report of a Board of Officers Appointed to Make a Study on Air Defense Problems," Oct. 30, 1940, 381 War Plans, "Bulkies," box 183, RG 18, Central Decimal Files, ser. 2, 1939–42, NARA D.C.; G. H. Brett to AG, memo, Nov. 14, 1940, "Air Defense Organisation," 381 War Plans, box 207, RG 18, Central Decimal Files, ser. 2, 1939–42, NARA D.C.; Burt, *Adventures with Warlords,* 78.

15. Army War College, Fort Humphreys, D.C., "Course at the Army War College 1938–39: War Plans, Report of Committee No. 4, Group No. 4, Subject: Philippine Department," archives, USAMHI; Burt, *Adventures with Warlords,* 59; Spaatz to Arnold, Sept. 1, 1939.

16. Copp, *Forged in Fire,* vii; Burt, *Adventures with Warlords,* 63, 68.

17. Dowding, "Visit to Canada and the U.S.A.," 10 A.M., Jan. 13, 1941; Arnold Visitors Log, ser. 5, box 90, envelope 4, 9:50 A.M. and 12:10 P.M., Jan. 13, 1941, Hap Arnold–Murray Green Collection, Special Collections, Academy Libraries, USAFA (hereafter Arnold-Green Collection).

18. William T. Sexton, OC/S, "Substance of Remarks Made by Chief Air Marshal Sir Hugh Dowding to a Group of Officers at 10:00 A.M. Saturday, Jan. 11, 1941," box 888, RG 165, OC/S Minutes and Notes of Conferences, 1938–42, NARA D.C.; Burt, *Adventures with Warlords,* 76. It is assumed that Dowding repeated the observations he made at this meeting to his Air Corps audience at the Army War College two days later, although there is no record of this meeting. Similarly, it cannot be documented that Vandenberg attended the meeting, but it is inconceivable that as a major in the OCAC Plans Division with a close relationship to Spaatz he would not have been invited.

19. Dowding's and Arnold's departure time is from Arnold's Visitor's Log. In the log covering his activities while in the United States, Dowding makes no mention of meeting with Vandenberg in any of the daily entries he meticulously recorded hour by hour. However, Burt informed Vandenberg's biographer that the two did discuss Vandenberg's aerial defense plan for Luzon (William R. Burt to Philip S. Meilinger, Oct. 20 and Nov. 12, 1984, copy in author's possession). If that assertion is correct, then they must have talked within a group situation rather than one on one. The only opportunity for such a group discussion would have been at the AWC meeting on January 13 (as I have assumed here), with the outside possibility that it could also have occurred during the dinner party Air Commodore Pirie put on for Dowding on January 14, to which he might have invited Vandenberg, given their close working relationship.

20. Burt, *Adventures with Warlords,* 63–65.

21. Ibid., 13–14. Burt does not recall the date he was briefed about Vandenberg's discussions with Dowding, but it would certainly have taken place immediately after Vandenberg returned to his office, given their close working relationship. Burt himself was evidently too junior an officer to have been invited to hear Dowding at the War College.

22. Ibid., 14, 51, 61–62.

23. Memorandum reproduced as Exhibit D, ibid., 212–13.

24. Burt, *Adventures with Warlords,* 43.

25. *Nichols News,* Dec. 25, 1939; William Sheppard to sister, Jan. 6, 1941.

26. Kirtley J. Gregg to wife, Dec. 30, 1941 and Jan. 7, 1941.

27. Grant Mahony to mother, Jan. 10, 1941.

28. Edward Maloney and Frank Ryan, *P-26,* 8–9; Grant Mahony to brother, Jan. 10, 1941.

29. Mahony to brother, Jan. 10, 1941.

30. Kirtley J. Gregg to wife, Jan. 23, Feb. 11, and Mar. 20, 1941. The four assigned to the 17th Pursuit were Nathaniel "Cy" Blanton, Jack Dale, George Kiser, and David Obert. I erroneously included Joseph Kruzel in the group assigned to the 17th in *Doomed at the Start.*

31. Gregg to wife, Feb. 11 and 12, 1941.

32. Grant Mahony to mother, Jan. 25, 1941.

33. Gregg to wife, Feb. 11, 1941.

34. George Grunert to AG, radiogram 057, Feb. 8, 1941, RG 18, AAG 452.1-A (Philippines), NARA D.C.

35. George C. Marshall to George Grunert, Feb. 8, 1941, box 69, folder 3 (Grunert Correspondence), Marshall Papers.

CHAPTER 2: "A TROOP OF BOY SCOUTS FLYING KITES COULD TAKE THESE DAMNED ISLANDS"

1. William R. Burt to Robert A. Lovett, June 17, 1983, copy in author's collection; Burt, telephone interview with author, Dec. 15, 2000; WD, *Officers of the Army in or Near the District of Columbia, Apr. 1, 1941*. The meeting's exact date is not known, but it would have been shortly after Chauncey's February 12 assignment to the WPD, as indicated in the April, 1941, directory of army officers in the Washington area.

2. Brett to AC/S, WPD, memo, Feb. 11, 1941, "Estimates for Defensive Installations, Philippine Department," WPD 3251-42, RG 165, WPD General Correspondence, 1940–42, NARA D.C.

3. Burt to Lovett, June 17, 1983; Burt, *Adventures with Warlords*, 25.

4. George Grunert to AG, radiogram 58, Feb. 10, 1941; and Leonard T. Gerow's request for a reply, Feb. 12, 1941, both in Project Geographic, 320.2, PD (2-10-41), RG 407, AG Classified Decimal Files, 1940–42, NARA D.C.

5. "Conference in the Office of the Chief of Staff at 10:00 A.M., Tuesday Feb. 25, 1941," RG 165, OC/S Minutes and Notes of Conferences, 1938–42, NARA D.C.; George C. Marshall to Leonard T. Gerow, memo, Feb. 26, 1941, item 11, executive 4, RG 165, OPD Executive Files, 1939–42, NARA D.C.

6. Carl Spaatz to AC/S, WPD, memo, Jan. 28, 1941, "Considerations Governing the Omission of Certain Pursuit Types from Rainbow No. 5," 381 War Plans, RG 18, Central Decimal Files, ser. 2, 1939–42, NARA D.C.

7. William Sheppard to parents, Mar. 8, 1941; Grant Mahony to mother, Apr. 28, 1941. By February 28, fourteen P-35As were operational and twenty-two were nonoperational (George Grunert to AG, radiogram 582, Mar. 8, 1941, RG 18, AAG 452.1-A [Philippines], NARA D.C.). A month later, forty-two were operational (PD to AG, radiogram 748, Apr. 7, 1941, RG 18, AAG 452.1-A [Philippines], NARA D.C.).

8. George Armstrong, as quoted in Joe Mizrahi, "P-35: Seversky's Cadillac in the Air," *Wings*, Oct., 1971, 40, 44; Grant Mahony to brother, Mar. 3, 1941.

9. Sheppard to parents, Mar. 8, 1941.

10. Andrew E. Krieger to father, Mar. 4, 1941.

11. Grant Mahony to mother, Jan. 25, Feb. 22, and Mar. 3, 1941; Robert L. Scott, *Damned to Glory*, 149.

12. HQ, PD, *Telephone Directory*, 20; Gregg to wife, Dec. 18, 1940; Maurer Maurer, *Combat Squadrons of the Air Force in World War II: History and Insignia*, 15–16, 22–23, 141–42.

13. Miriam Pachacki to author, Dec. 21, 1996.

14. Reid H. Brock, taped narrative, Oct. 1, 1993. Maitland's chauffeur was dubbed "the Little Pig." Maitland allowed him only one beer for every two he drank himself at each of the many stops they made at the post exchanges while driving between Fort Stotsenburg and Clark Field. When Biggs asked Maitland following one such round-trip why he got such unequal treatment, Maitland is said to have replied, "Dammit, Biggs, you've got to drive!" (Ibid.)

15. George Grunert to George C. Marshall, Mar. 6, 1941, box 69, folder 34 (Grunert Correspondence), Marshall Papers. Grunert received a radiogram from the War Department the following week announcing Maitland's promotion to lieutenant colonel (Gregg to wife, Mar. 13, 1941).

16. Gregg to wife, Mar. 25 and 26, 1941.

17. Ibid., Mar. 20, 1941. This is the report cited in footnote 4 above.

18. Ibid., Mar. 11, 1941.

19. Ibid., Mar. 20, 1941; George Grunert to George C. Marshall, Apr. 11, 1941, AG 660.2, PD Decimal Files, RG 407, Army-AG Classified Decimal Files, Project Geographic, 1940–42, NARA D.C. I could find no copy of Gregg's report in the records of the Philippine Department, the Army Air Corps, or the War Department.

CHAPTER 3: "THEY WILL BE SHOT DOWN AS FAST AS THEY ARE PUT IN THE AIR"

1. "List of Students, Air Defense Orientation and Indoctrination Course, Hq Air Defense Command, Mitchel Field, N.Y.," enclosure to James E. Chaney to George C. Marshall, Mar. 27, 1941; and idem., Apr. 1, 1941, both in box 60, folder 28 (J. E. Chaney Correspondence), Marshall Papers.

2. Orlando Ward to George C. Marshall, memo, Mar. 25, 1941, RG 165, OC/S Minutes and Notes of Conferences, 1938–42, NARA D.C.; Henry H. Arnold to Orlando Ward, handwritten memo, Mar. n.d., 1941; and George C. Marshall to George Grunert, radiogram, Mar. 28, 1941, both in box 69, folder 34 (Grunert Correspondence), Marshall Papers.

3. Air Defense School, Mitchel Field, N.Y., Apr. 5, 1941, "Preliminary Plans for the Air Defense of the Hawaiian Islands," Exhibit M in Burt, *Adventures with Warlords*, 250–53.

4. "History of the Air Defense Command, Feb. 26, 1940–June 2, 1941," microfilm reel A4000, 410.01, AFHRA, 192.

5. Kirtley J. Gregg to wife, Apr. 1, 1941; George C. Marshall to George Grunert, Mar. 28, 1941, box 69, folder 34 (Grunert Correspondence), Marshall Papers.

6. "Staff Group Assignments," HQ Air Defense Command, Mitchel Field, N.Y., enclosure to Chaney to Marshall, Mar. 27, 1941; Kirtley J. Gregg to wife, May 7, 1941; Maurer Maurer, ed., *Air Force Combat Units of World War II*, 85.

7. Stimson Diary, Mar. 27, 1941, reel 6, vol. 33, Stimson Papers; George C. Marshall to Henry H. Arnold, memo, Mar. 28, 1941, reproduced in Bland, ed., *Marshall Papers*, 2:458–59.

8. Marshall to Grunert, Mar. 28, 1941; miscellaneous official papers regarding the service of Henry B. Clagett in the collection of Henry B. Clagett III, Atlantic Highlands, N.J. (Hereafter Clagett Collection.)

9. Grunert to Marshall, Apr. 11, 1941.

10. Kirtley J. Gregg to wife, Apr. 10 and 28, and May 6, 1941

11. Ibid., May 6, 1941; Andrew E. Krieger to father, May 4, 1941.

12. Gregg to wife, May 7, 1941.

13. William H. Bartsch, *Doomed at the Start*, 11–12.

14. Allison Ind, *Bataan: The Judgment Seat*, 7–8.

15. Gregg to wife, May 7, 1941; Ind, *Bataan*, 24–25, 68; Henry Clagett to George Brett, OCAC, July 9, 1941, 300-B-MISC, RG 18, Project Files, Philippine Department, 1939–42, NARA D.C.

16. Gregg to wife, May 7, 1941; Ind, *Bataan*, 8–9.

17. Ind, *Bataan*, 11–12.

18. Kirtley J. Gregg to wife, May 13, 1941; William Maverick to wife, May 12 and July 8, 1941.

19. Bartsch, *Doomed*, 11; Maverick to wife, May 12 and 21, 1941; Maverick to mother, May 22, 1941; Laura Maverick Griswold to author, May 8, 1995.

20. Maverick to wife, May 21, 1941; Kirtley J. Gregg to wife, May 7 and 16, 1941.

21. Gregg to wife, May 13, 1941.

22. Ibid., June 12, 1941; Carlos Baker, *Ernest Hemingway: A Life Story*, 364–65; Jeffrey Meyers, *Hemingway: A Biography*, 356–61.

23. Baker, *Hemingway;* Gregg to wife, May 13, 1941; Maverick to wife, May 12, 1941.

24. Gregg to wife, May 13 and 16, 1941; Maverick to wife, May 21, 1941.

25. Ted Fisch to wife, May 15 and 20, 1941; HQ, PD, *Telephone Directory,* 22; Christmas, 1940, Menu, 28th Bomb Squadron; Gregg to wife, Mar. 13, 1941. Maitland's promotion made him ineligible for command of a tactical squadron, a position that at that time called for a major.

26. Fisch to wife, May 20, 1941; Andrew E. Krieger to father, May 30, 1941.

27. Lt. Gen. Delos Emmons to C/S, memo, May 28, 1941, "Status of Condition of Combat Aircraft Assigned to GHQ Air Force on May 27, 1941," Secret Correspondence, 1936–42, 381 War Plans Statistics, RG 18, HQ, AFCC, 1935–42, NARA D.C.; AG to CG, PD, radiogram, Apr. 15, 1941, RG 18, AAG 452.1-A (Philippines), NARA D.C.; George Grunert to AG, radiogram 632, Mar. 14, 1941; and OCAC to AG, 2d indorsement, Apr. 7, 1941, both in microfilms 2084 and 2080-81, AFHRA. Only thirty-eight B-23s (redesigned B-18s) were produced and delivered to the Army Air Corps (John M. Andrade, *U.S. Military Aircraft Designations and Serials Since 1909,* 45–46.)

28. Emmons to C/S; Ind, *Bataan,* 16, 18–19, 141–42; George Grunert to AG, radiogram 1061, June 5, 1941, RG 18, AAG 452.1-A (Philippines), NARA D.C.

29. Maverick to wife, May 21, 1941; idem. to mother, May 22, 1941; Bartsch, *Doomed,* 11.

30. Kirtley J. Gregg to wife, May 22, 1941.

31. Maverick to wife, May 21 and June 28, 1941.

32. Gregg to wife, May 22, 1941.

33. Ind, *Bataan,* 22; "Comments on Current Events, May 29–June 25, 1941," box 1851, RG 165, Military Intelligence—Philippine Islands, NARA C. P.

34. "Comments on Current Events."

35. Ind, *Bataan,* 22–23.

36. Ibid., 24. The U.S. Naval Observer, Singapore, forwarded Darvall's six-page secret report, "Notes on the Defense Problem of Luzon," to the CNO (War Plans) on Aug. 5, 1941. It was passed to General Gerow in the WPD on October 5, and a copy was sent to General MacArthur in Manila on October 14 (WPD 4192-4, box 191, RG 165, WPD General Correspondence, 1940–42, NARA D.C.).

37. "Air Corps Annex, Philippine Defense Project," box 1853, RG 165, Military Intelligence—Philippine Islands, NARA C. P. In July, 1941, Clagett acknowledged to General Brett at AC HQ that "we will have to disperse the depot." He also expressed the need for "at least 18 landing fields for dispersion" and some "dummy fields" (Clagett to Brett, July 9, 1941).

38. Ind, *Bataan,* 17–18; Leonard T. Gerow to George C. Marshall, memo, n.d. (ca. Jan. 15, 1941), RG 18, AAG 600-Miscellaneous-A (Philippines), NARA D.C.; idem., Jan. 27, 1941, "Defense of the Philippine Islands," WPD 3251-39, RG 165, WPD General Correspondence, 1939–42, NARA D.C.

39. AG to George Grunert, radiogram, June 6, 1941, microfilm 2052, AFHRA; Grunert to AG, radiogram, Mar. 14, 1941, microfilm 2084, AFHRA; Grunert to George C. Marshall, Mar. 13, 1941, reel 34, item 1422, GCMF; Grunert to AG, radiogram, May 10, 1941, microfilm 2054, AFHRA; AG to Grunert, radiogram, Apr. 15, 1941, RG 18, AAG 452.1 (Philippines), NARA.

40. Burt, *Adventures with Warlords,* 61–62. Dowding left for England on May 4, 1941, via Canada ("Visit to Canada and the U.S.A.," May 4, 1941).

41. Brett to AC/S, WPD, memo, June 5, 1941, "Air Force Requirements," 381 War Plans, RG 18, Central Decimal Files, ser. 2, 1939–42, NARA D.C.

42. Ind, *Bataan,* 25, 26; Gregg to wife, June 12, 1941. Seven months later, while in Australia, Clagett informed the RAAF hospital that he had flown at seventeen thousand feet without oxygen during his China mission, "and as a result had a circular pain in his head for 7 days" (RAAF, "Hospital or Sick List—Record Card, Henry B. Clagett, Jan. 19, 1942," Clagett Collection).

43. Gregg to wife, June 12, 1941.

44. Ind, *Bataan,* 29; Henry Clagett to George C. Marshall (via George Grunert), "Air Mission to China," June 12, 1941, file 380.3, RG 407, AG Central Decimal Files, 1940–42, NARA D.C.

45. Gregg to wife, June 12, 1941.

46. Charts dated Feb. 25 and Oct. 5, 1941, box 1852, RG 165, Military Intelligence—Philippine Islands, NARA C. P.

47. "Philippine Defense Project (1940 Revision), Headquarters Philippine Department, May 1, 1941," box 1853, ibid.

48. Ind, *Bataan,* 20–21.

49. Col. D. H. Torrey, AG, PD, to AG, memo, Jan. 9, 1941, RG 18, AAG 600-A (Philippines), NARA D.C.; Gerow to Marshall, memo, n.d. (ca. Jan. 15, 1941).

50. George Grunert to George C. Marshall, June 2, 1941, AG 660.2, PD Decimal Files, RG 407, Army-AG Classified Decimal Files, Project Geographic, 1940–42, NARA D.C.

51. Ted Fisch to wife, May 29 and June 11, 1941.

52. "The Hair Corps at Clark Field Raise a Bumper Crop of Beards," *Sunday Tribune (Manila),* magazine section, Aug. 10, 1941; Ted Fisch to wife, June 3 and 11, 1941; James Cooke to parents, Sept. 7, 1941.

53. Grunert to AG, radiogram 1378, July 14, 1941, RG 18, 452.1-A (Philippines), NARA D.C.; Fisch to wife, May 29, and June 11 and 23, 1941.

PART II: "IF WE MAKE OUR ATTACK NOW, THE WAR IS NOT HOPELESS"

1. Bix, *Hirohito,* 395; Hattori, *Complete History,* 1:125, 128, 129; Prange, *At Dawn We Slept,* 103.

2. Bix, *Hirohito,* 397–99; Crowley, "Japan's Military," 94.

3. Prange, *At Dawn We Slept,* 29, 166; Osamu Tagaya, "Technical Development and Operational History of the Type 1 Rikkō," unpublished manuscript, 2000, copy in author's collection.

4. Edwin T. Layton et al., *And I Was There,* 121; Bix, *Hirohito,* 400–402.

5. Matloff and Snell, *Strategic Planning,* 64, 65; Layton et al., *And I Was There,* 121.

6. George C. Marshall to Henry H. Arnold, memo, July 16, 1941, reproduced in Bland, *Marshall Papers,* 2:567–68.

7. Matloff and Snell, *Strategic Planning,* 67; Layton et al., *And I Was There,* 121; Marshall to MacArthur, June 20, 1941.

8. Bix, *Hirohito,* 403, 405; Hattori, *Complete History,* 1:166.

9. H. Ford Wilkins, "M'Arthur Calls Manila Meeting," *New York Times,* July 28, 1941; Linn, *Guardians of Empire,* 245.

10. Bix, *Hirohito,* 407.

11. As quoted ibid., 406.

12. Hattori, *Complete History,* 1:157, 2:301; Prange, *At Dawn We Slept,* 177; Hiroyuki Ogawa, *The Reluctant Admiral: Yamamoto and the Imperial Navy,* 226; Bōeichō Bōekenshūsho Senshishitsu (Japanese Defense Agency, War History Section), *Hitō Malay Hōmen Kaigun Shinkō Sakusen (Philippines and Malaya Area Navy Offensive Operations), Senshi Sōsho,* 24:36.

13. *Senshi Sōsho,* 24:35–36.

14. Pogue, *Marshall,* 185–86.

15. Henry H. Arnold, *Global Mission,* 248–49; Michael S. Sherry, *The Rise of American Air Power,* 105; Matloff and Snell, *Strategic Planning,* 70.

16. Matloff and Snell, *Strategic Planning,* 38; AWPD, AS, Aug. 12, 1941, "Munitions Requirements of the AAF to Defeat our Potential Enemies," A-WPD/1, tab 7, "Bombardment Aviation Required for Strategic Defense in Asia," copy 13, Special Collections Branch, Academy Libraries, USAFA (hereafter Special Collections).

17. Stimson Diary, Sept. 12, 1941, Stimson Papers.

18. Minutes of Joint Board meeting of Sept. 19, 1941, quoted in Layton et al., *And I Was There,* 170; George C. Marshall to Harold R. Stark, memo, Sept. 12, 1941, reproduced in Bland, *Marshall Papers,* 2:605–606.

19. Hattori, *Complete History,* 1:173; Bix, *Hirohito,* 409, 413–14.

20. Ibid., 414. As presented to the U.S. government by Ambassador Kichisaburō Nomura, these demands included that the United States abandon its aid to China, recognize Japan's status in Indochina, resume free trade with Japan, and stop reinforcing the Philippines. In return, Japan would agree not to advance beyond Indochina, evacuate Indochina when the "China Incident" was terminated, and guarantee the Philippines neutrality (Matloff and Snell, *Strategic Planning,* 68).

21. Bix, *Hirohito,* 416; Agawa, *Reluctant Admiral,* 232.

22. Saburō Hayashi, *Kogun: The Japanese Army in the Pacific War,* 29; Hattori, *Complete History,* 1:188–89; Bix, *Hirohito,* 415; Bōeichō Bōekenshūsho Senshishitsu, *Hitō Koryaku Sakusen (Philippine Invasion Operations), Senshi Sōsho,* 2:50.

23. Hattori, *Complete History,* 1:188, 2:301; Prange, *At Dawn We Slept,* 223–31.

24. Prange, *At Dawn We Slept,* 234, 261.

25. "Conversation between Admiral Hart and General MacArthur," Sept. 22, 1941, ser. 1, "Java Papers," Hart Personal Papers, Operational Archives, NHC (hereafter Hart Papers).

26. Douglas MacArthur to AG, Oct. 1, 1941, "Operations Plan R-5," as quoted in Watson, *Chief of Staff,* 433.

27. George C. Marshall to Douglas MacArthur, radiogram, Oct. 3, 1941, Stimson Top Secret File, RG 107, Records of the Office of the Secretary of War, NARA D.C.

28. "Diary, General Douglas MacArthur, Commanding General USAFFE," entries for Oct. 3, 4, 6, RG 2, MMA (hereafter MacArthur Diary).

29. GHQFE, memo, Sept. 19, 1941, "The Problem of Defeating Japan—Review of the Subject," RG 2, MMA; Robert Brooke-Popham to Lord Ismay, Oct. 10, 1941, file 6/2/18, Robert Brooke-Popham Papers, Liddell Hart Centre for Military Archives, King's College, London; Leutze, *Different Kind of Victory,* 213.

30. MacArthur Diary, Oct. 13, 1941; "Indies Army Head Dies in Air Crash," *New York Times,* Oct. 14, 1941.

31. Map and covering note, Henry L. Stimson to Cordell Hull, Oct. 4, 1941, Stimson Top Secret File, RG 107, Records of the Office of the Secretary of War, NARA; Jeffrey S. Underwood, *The Wings of Democracy,* 175.

32. Leonard T. Gerow to secretary of war, memo, Oct. 8, 1941, "Strategic Concept of the Philippine Islands," WPD 3251-60; Henry H. Arnold for the secretary of war, memo, Oct. 8, 1941, "Airplanes to the Philippines"; and idem., memo, Oct. 16, 1941, "Diversion of Additional Heavy Bombers," all in Stimson Top Secret File, RG 107, Records of the Office of the Secretary of War, NARA D.C.

33. Henry L. Stimson to Franklin D. Roosevelt, Oct. 21, 1941, included in Stimson Diary, Stimson Papers.

34. "Memorandum of Conference between Secretary Hull and Secretary Stimson, Oct. 6, 1941," and Oct. 28, 1941, entry, both in Stimson Diary, Stimson Papers; Sherry, *Rise of American Air Power,* 107.

35. George C. Marshall to Douglas MacArthur, memo, Oct. 18, 1941, "U.S. Army Forces in the Far East," WPD 4175-18, microfilm reel 32, item 1308, GCMF; Watson, *Chief of Staff,* 445–46. General Brereton evidently hand-carried the memo and gave it to MacArthur on November 5, when Brereton arrived to assume command of the FEAF.

36. Bix, *Hirohito,* 417–19; Hattori, *Complete History,* 1:195.

37. Hattori, *Complete History,* 2:302; *Senshi Sōsho,* 2:51.

38. Prange, *At Dawn We Slept,* 281–82; Agawa, *Reluctant Admiral,* 230–31.

39. Prange, *At Dawn We Slept,* 297, 299; *Senshi Sōsho,* 24:48, 53.

40. Prange, *At Dawn We Slept,* 285, 325.

CHAPTER 4: "WHY SEND OVER THESE NINETY-DAY WONDERS?"

1. Kirtley J. Gregg to wife, June 27, 1941; Forrest Hobrecht to parents, June 25, 1941; Bartsch, *Doomed,* 13.

2. William Maverick, interview by William Priestley, Cabanatuan POW Camp, 1943, William Priestley Papers, Philippines Records, RG 407, NARA D.C. (hereafter Priestley Papers); Ind, *Bataan,* 80; Bartsch, *Doomed,* 14; Torrey, AG, PD, to AG, memo, Jan. 9, 1941, "Construction for Defensive Installations and Air Fields, Philippine Department," RG 18, AAG 600-Miscellaneous-A (Philippines), NARA D.C.

3. Bartsch, *Doomed,* 14-15.

4. Gregg to wife, June 19 and 26, 1941; Maverick to wife, June 27, 1941; Bartsch, *Doomed,* 14.

5. Maverick to wife, June 27 and 28, 1941; Gregg to wife, June 27, 1941. Gregg did not mention this incident to his wife, but one of his pilots wrote about it to his parents (William Sheppard to parents, June 30, 1941).

6. Clagett to Brett, July 9, 1941.

7. Gregg to wife, June 27, 1941. Clagett spent ten days in the hospital following his return to Manila on June 10 ("Hospital or Sick List"). On June 28, the Nichols Field flight surgeon advised the OCAC Medical Division in Washington that while Clagett "has made excellent recovery from his recent illness," he had a "mild coronary" problem and that he was not to fly above ten thousand feet (Capt. Charles H. Morhouse, Nichols Field, to chief, Medical Division, OCAC, memo, June 28, 1941, Clagett Collection).

8. Bartsch, *Doomed,* 15; William Maverick to wife, July 7, 1941; Carl Gies to parents, July 6, 1941; Lawrence Lodin to parents, July 3, 1941; Individual Flight Record of Bill Rowe, July, 1941, copy in author's collection.

9. Maverick to wife, June 28 and July 7, 1941.

10. James E. Brown, Apr. 10, 1978; Glenn Bowers, Jan. 9, 1979; and Orville Roland, Oct. 30, 1980, personal narratives provided to author.

11. Bartsch, *Doomed,* 15; Kirtley J. Gregg to wife, July 9, 1941.

12. Andrew E. Krieger to father, July 13, 1941; Randall Keator Diary (hereafter Keator Diary), July 15, 1941, copy in author's collection.

13. Ted Fisch to wife, July 6 and 9, 1941.

14. Maverick to wife, July 7, 1941.

15. Wilson Glover to parents, July 6, 1941, Lawrence Lodin to parents, July 4, 1941, and John Gillespie to author, Oct. 30, 1979, and Feb. 14, 1980; Forrest Hobrecht to parents, July 10, 1941.

16. Lawrence Lodin to parents, July 6, 1941; Glover to parents, July 6, 1941.

17. Forrest Hobrecht to parents, July 26, 1941.

18. Frank Neri to wife, July 25, 1941; Hobrecht to parents, July 26, 1941; Jerry Brezina to parents, July 29, 1941.

19. Neri to wife, July 25, 1941; Albert Bland, interview by author, Jan. 30, 1983.

20. Carl Gies to parents, July 31, 1941; Ted Fisch to wife, July 30, 1941.

21. William Maverick to wife, July 30, 1941; Kirtley J. Gregg to wife, July 30, 1941.

21. Gies to parents, July 31, 1941.

22. Maverick to wife, July 30, 1941.

23. William Ambrosius to wife, July 25, 1941

24. Ted Fisch to wife, July 9 and 18, 1941; William Maverick to wife, Oct. 1, 1941. The PD telephone directory for July 16, 1941, listed Nichols as S4 and aide to Clagett.

25. Fisch to wife, July 30, 1941.

26. Gregg to wife, July 30, 1941; Bartsch, *Doomed,* 18-20.

27. Ind, *Bataan,* 39-40; Gregg to wife, July 21, 22, and 29, Aug. 9, and Sept. 13, 1941; James Cooke to parents, Sept. 7, 1941.

28. Gregg to wife, July 30, 1941.

29. USAFFE General Orders 4, Aug. 4, 1941, RG 2, MMA.

30. Leonard T. Gerow to AG, memo, July 31, 1941, item 1737, reel 50, NARA records in GCMF; (Maj. Gen. Emory S.) Adams to CG, USAFFE, radiogram, 10:28 A.M., Aug. 12, 1941, RG 2, MMA.

31. Douglas MacArthur to George C. Marshall, Nov. 29, 1941, item 1553, reel 39, NARA records in GCMF. MacArthur indicates he asked Clagett to prepare the study, but Clagett was away from July 22–August 20.

32. Henry Clagett to CG, USAFFE, memo, Sept. 11, 1941, "Study of Air Force for United States Army Forces in the Far East," RG 2, MMA.

33. Adams to CG Philippine Department (*sic*), radiogram, 7:50 P.M., Aug. 12, 1941; and Douglas MacArthur to AG, radiogram, Aug. 19, 1941, both in RG 2, MMA.

34. MacArthur to AG, Aug. 19, 1941; Clagett to CG, USAAFE, Sept. 11, 1941.

35. "Emergency Aircraft Warning Service," 1st indorsement, HQ, AF USAFFE, to CG, USAFFE, Aug. 28, 1941, Decimal File, SAS 660.2, Air Warning Service, box 142, folder 6, Henry H. Arnold Papers, Manuscript Division, LOC (hereafter Arnold Papers).

36. William Seckinger to author, Mar. 6, 1984; Robert Arnold to author, Apr. 26, 1980.

37. Arvid Seeborg to brother, July 10, 1941; idem. to parents, Aug. 7, 1941; idem. to sister, Sept. 1, 1941; "Blackout of Manila Staged by Civilians," *New York Times,* July 11, 1941.

38. Seeborg to sister.

39. James C. Gaston, *Planning the American Air War: Four Men and Nine Days in 1941,* 22; Harold L. George, memo, Aug. 8, 1941, "A-WPD/1," A-WPD/1 Scrap Book, 27–28; idem., memo, Aug. 4, 1941, "Outline of Basic Requirements and Coordinating Instructions Relative to A-WPD/1," A-WPD/1 Scrap Book, 4–6; and President Roosevelt to Secretary of War Stimson, July 9, 1941, A-WPD/1 Scrap Book, 1, all in Special Collections.

40. Burt, *Adventures with Warlords,* 52, 68–69.

41. Copp, *Forged in Fire,* 151–52; Martha Byrd, *Kenneth N. Walker: Airpower's Untempered Crusader,* 65–67.

42. George, memo, Aug. 8, 1941.

43. Ibid., Aug. 4, 1941, tab 10, 16.

44. AWPD, AS, "A-WPD/1: Munitions Requirements of the Army Air Forces to Defeat Our Potential Enemies," tab 10, "Pursuit Aviation Required for Strategic Defensive in Asia," Special Collections.

45. George, memo, Aug. 4, 1941, 5; AWPD, AS, "A-WPD/1," tab 7, "Bombardment Aviation Required for Strategic Defense in Asia," Special Collections.

46. AWPD, AS, "A-WPD/1," tab 7. In September, 1940, Boeing was awarded a contract to produce an experimental model, the XB-29, which the company indicated would have a range of seven thousand miles with a two-thousand-pound bomb load. A contract calling for the production of 250 such aircraft was signed a year later. Production models had a range of only 5,830 miles (Berger, *B-29,* 25–26, 33, 102).

47. AWPD, AS, "A-WPD/1," tab 12, "Air Support Aviation Required for Support of Ground Forces," Special Collections.

48. Copp, *Forged in Fire,* 153; "Col. Bissell's Comments on Study," A-WPD/1 Scrap Book, 35, Special Collections. Evidently Bissell was unaware that a contract was being issued the following month for the production of B-29s, which were no longer in the experimental stage. Kuter and Walker did not regard them as experimental when they included them in their part of the air annex.

49. Gen. Laurence S. Kuter, Oral History K 239.0512-810, 1974, AFSHRC, 204, 206; "Daily Diary of the Chief of the Air Staff, 23 June–6 December 1941" (hereafter Spaatz Diary), Aug. 19 and July 26, 1941, entries, Bulkies, box 150, RG 18, Central Decimal Files, ser. 2, 1939–42, NARA D.C.

50. Robert P. Fogerty, *Biographical Study of USAF General Officers,* Orvil Anderson entry;

Maj. Gen. Orvil Anderson, Oral History K239.0512-898, Oct. 27, 1959, AFSHRC, 22; AWPD to Muir Fairchild, memo, Nov. 13, 1941, microfilm page 1036, AFHRA.

51. Orville A. Anderson for the Chief of the Air Staff, memo, Aug. 30, 1941, "Plan for Reinforcing Philippine Department Air Force," microfilm pages 1982–85, AFHRA.

52. Indorsement, AAF Chief of Air Staff, to CAC, Sept. 5, 1941, microfilm page 1974, AFHRA.

53. Kirtley J. Gregg to wife, Aug. 17, 1941; Ind, *Bataan,* 47, 49.

54. Gregg to wife, Aug. 19, 1941.

55. George Armstrong to wife, Aug. 17, 1941; Lawrence Lodin to parents, Aug. 13, 1941; Bill Hennon to parents, Aug. 19, 1941; William Rowe to author, Sept. 27, 1983; idem., interview by author, May 9, 1986.

56. Rowe to author, Sept. 27, 1983; Rowe interview.

57. Ted Fisch to wife, Sept. 1, 1941.

58. HQ, AF USAFFE, to CG, PD, memo, Oct. 1, 1941, "Report of Trip Made by Brig. Gen. H. B. Clagett, Lt. Col. Lester Maitland, and Capt. Allison W. Ind, July 22–Aug. 20, 1941," RG 2, MMA, 11; Ind, *Bataan,* 50. Clagett self-diagnosed his illness in Java as "malaria," and so reported it to the RAAF hospital in January, 1942 ("Hospital or Sick List").

59. "Diary, General Douglas MacArthur, Commanding General, United States Army Forces in the Far East" Aug. 21 and 23, 1941 entries (hereafter MacArthur Diary), RG 2, MMA.

60. Ind, *Bataan,* 51, 52.

61. Kirtley J. Gregg to wife, Aug. 23 and 25, 1941. Gregg still felt that taking him out of the group was "a slap in the face."

62. Ibid., Aug. 25, 29, and 30, 1941; Maverick to wife, Aug. 30, 1941; Frank Neri to wife, Aug. 27, 1941; Don Miller to parents, Aug. 28, 1941; USAFFE General Orders 13, Oct. 1, 1941, RG 2, MMA; Enrique B. Santos, *Trails in Philippine Skies,* 187 and photograph between 150, 151; Ind, *Bataan,* 50, 52; Bernard Anderson to author, Feb. 3, 1980; Allison Ind to Courtney Whitney, Aug. 3, 1943; Pete Legg to mother, Aug. 17 and 29, 1941; William Maverick to parents, Aug. 30, 1941.

CHAPTER 5: "THE CREATION OF THE FIVE-ENGINE BOMBER HAS COMPLETELY CHANGED THE STRATEGY IN THE PACIFIC"

1. Ind, *Bataan,* 53–55. I assume that the Sept. 11, 1941, document in the MacArthur Memorial Archives is the final version of the plan originally prepared by George, although the clipped style seems to reflect Clagett as described by Ind.

2. "Emergency Aircraft Warning Service Project," 1st indorsement. As the AWS was his responsibility, Colonel Campbell, assisted by his staff, most likely drew up the project document.

3. AG to CG, PD, "Air Defense Organization," Sept. 2, 1941, Decimal File, SAS 320.2, Air Warning Service, box 86, folder 4, Arnold Papers; George C. Marshall to Douglas MacArthur, telegram, Sept. 9, 1941, NARA microfilm reel 317, item 4996, GCMF; "Emergency Aircraft Warning Service Project."

5. John Legg to mother, Aug. 17 and 29, 1941.

6. Arvid Seeborg to brother, Sept. 1, 1941; idem. to parents, Aug. 7, 1941.

7. Herbert Ellis to author, Sept. 17 and Dec. 18, 1979, and Nov. 12, 1980. Ind describes what appears to be this particular failed exercise in *Bataan,* 21–22.

8. Harold L. George to Carl Spaatz, memo, Sept. 15, 1941, "Information Reference A-WPD/1," A-WPD/1 Scrap Book, item 65, Special Collections; Maj. Gen. Haywood S. Hansell, interview, Jan. 2, 1970, Arnold-Green Collection; Gaston, *Planning,* 92.

9. Gaston, *Planning,* 92; George to Spaatz, Sept. 15, 1941; Stimson Diary, Sept. 11, 1941, Stimson Papers.

10. Gaston, *Planning,* 92; George to Stimson, memo, Sept. 12, 1941, A-WPD/1 Scrap Book, item 64, Special Collections.

11. Stimson Diary, Sept. 12, 1941, Stimson Papers. Stimson's erroneous description of the new four-engined B-17s and B-24s as "five-engine" bombers is an indication of his ignorance regarding the characteristics of individual aircraft in the air force's arsenal.

12. George to Stimson, memo, Sept. 12, 1941; Stimson Diary, Sept. 16, 1941, Stimson Papers.

13. Stimson Diary, Sept. 16, 1941; Spaatz Diary, Sept. 16, 1941.

14. Spaatz Diary, Staff Meeting, Sept. 16, 1941; Spaatz Diary, Sept. 19, 1941.

15. Emmett O'Donnell Jr., interview, Mar. 27, 1970, Arnold-Green Collection; James Cooke to parents, Sept. 22, 1941.

16. Andrew E. Krieger to father, Sept. 17, 1941; Edward C. Teats, as told to John M. McCullough, "Turn of the Tide," *Philadelphia Inquirer,* Dec. 31, 1942; Historical Division, AAF, "Army Air Action in the Philippines and Netherlands East Indies, 1941–1942," 19; Francis R. Thompson to author, Feb. 9, 1994. One of the copilots told Krieger that a P-40 had come down to meet the lead B-17 and guide it through the mountains to Clark. The pilot was apparently Bud Sprague, the Air Force, USAFFE, operations officer (Charles Sprague obituary, USMA *Assembly,* Mar., 1992, 157; Ind, *Bataan,* 59).

17. O'Donnell interview, Mar. 27, 1970.

18. Lt. Col. J. G. Taylor, chief, AC Intelligence Division, memo to CG, Hawaiian Department Air Force, n.d. (but apparently late August, 1941), RG 18, AAG 686-A (Philippines), NARA D.C.

19. George Armstrong to wife, Sept. 23, 1941; General Orders 10, Headquarters, USAFFE, Sept. 16, 1941, RG 2, MMA; War Department to CG, USAFFE, Aug. 16, 1941, "Constitution and Reorganization of Air Force Units," cited in ibid.; AG to CG, PD, "Air Defense Organization."

20. Bartsch, *Doomed,* 21; Neri to wife, Aug. 27, 1941; Kirtley J. Gregg to wife, Sept. 20 and 23, and Oct. 11, 1941.

21. William Maverick to parents, Oct. 3, 1941; Andrew E. Krieger to father, Oct. 2, 1941; Herbert Ellis, narrative provided to author, Jan. 13, 1980, 23.

22. Ellis narrative, Jan. 13, 1980, 23. Putnam recalled that only six planes were involved, the same number Krieger cited in a letter to his father describing the incident (Walter B. Putnam to author, Apr. 30, 1979; Krieger to father, Oct. 2, 1941).

23. Ellis narrative, Jan. 13, 1980, 23; Krieger to father, Oct. 2, 1941; Putnam to author, Apr. 30, 1979; Frank Neri to wife, Oct. 6, 1941; Andrew E. Krieger to father, Oct. 11, 1941; Raymond Gehrig to author, June 30, 1980.

24. Krieger to father, Oct. 2, 1941. At the end of the month, of the twenty-three on hand, eight were out of commission and five were in the depot for maintenance or repairs (Brereton to AGWAR, radiogram, Nov. n.d., 1941, "Aircraft Status Report," AG 452.1 [5-21-40], RG 407, AG Central Decimal Files, 1940–42, NARA D.C.).

25. Masa-aki Shimakawa, *Zero-sen Kusen Kyroku (The Air Battle Record of a Zero Fighter),* 16, 75, 250. The *kōkūtai*—often abbreviated to *kū*—was the main tactical unit of the Japanese naval air force. It was composed of *chūtai* of nine planes each (plus three in reserve).

26. Ibid., 250; Saburō Sakai, *Ohzora no Samurai (Samurai of the Skies),* 99.

27. Shirō Mori (pseudonym for Masaru Nakai), *Kaigun Sentōkitai (Navy Fighter Groups),* 1: 190; list of Tainan Kū pilots participating in the Dec. 8, 1941, mission prepared by Bureau of War History, Self-Defense Ministry, Tokyo, n.d. (hereafter Tainan Kū list); Hideki Shingō to author, Feb. 8, 1982; Kuniyoshi Tanaka interview in Naoki Kohdachi, *Reisen Saigo no Shogen (Zero Fighter: Final Testimony),* 1:92.

28. Shimakawa, *Zero-sen,* 76, 78; SRN 117264, Oct. 1, 1941, RG 457, Translations of Intercepted Japanese Naval Messages, NARA C.P. Shimakawa and Itō were graduates of the fifty-third class of enlisted trainees for carrier fighters, February–August, 1940 (Hata and Izawa, *Japanese Naval Aces,* 414).

29. Mori, *Kaigun,* 1:190;Tanaka interview, 93.

30. Lewis H. Brereton, *The Brereton Diaries,* 3–5; Arnold Visitors Log, Oct. 6, 1941. Brereton erroneously gives the date of this meeting with Arnold as October 5, a Sunday. Indeed, all the dates in the coverage in his *Diaries* of his Washington briefing are incorrect—not surprising considering that he reconstructed these dates from memory because he did not keep a personal diary.

31. Brereton draft diary, box 201, folder 4, Arnold Papers, 1; idem., *Diaries,* 5; Douglas MacArthur to George C. Marshall, radiogram, Oct. 2, 1941, RG 2, MMA. On September 30, Marshall had radioed MacArthur that he was to be provided with a "properly qualified commander to take over your increased Air Force units' extended field of operations and proposed as candidates Brereton, Maj. Gen. Jacob Fickel, and Brig. Gen. Walter Frank (Marshall to MacArthur, radiogram, Sept. 30, 1941, ibid.). Arnold most likely made the decision to replace Clagett as MacArthur's air force commander, although there is no documentary evidence supporting this assumption.

32. George C. Marshall to Douglas MacArthur, Sept. 9, 1941, radiogram, microfilm reel 317, item 4996, NARA records in GCMF; Adams to Douglas MacArthur, radiogram A-3-108, Sept. 29, 1941, Air AG 452.1, PD, Arnold Papers.

33. Brereton draft diary, 1; idem., *Diaries,* 6. Relying on his memory, Brereton mentioned four pursuit groups, but such a number was never envisaged for the Philippines. While he does not mention it specifically, Colonel George told Brereton on October 15 about the A-WPD/1 plan as the basis for the numbers given him of aircraft ultimately to be based in the Philippines (see chapter 6).

34. Brereton draft diary, 2; idem., *Diaries,* 6. In reviewing the draft of Brereton's manuscript, Arnold had deleted his name from a list of those to whom Brereton said he told of his objections to the plan. Nevertheless, Brereton restored it in the published version. Arnold was obviously sensitive about being associated with any responsibility on the part of his AAF headquarters for the disaster at Clark Field on December 8, 1941.

35. Brereton draft diary, 2. Brereton noted that the "fighter forces" to be sent also needed to be formed and trained. The decision to proceed with the dispatch of heavy bombers despite the risk would have originated with the WPD and been cleared on up to Marshall and Stimson, both of whom were ultimately responsible for such a determination.

36. Gerow to secretary of war, memo, Oct. 8, 1941. The map—Tab A—is not attached to the memorandum copy, but is included without any covering document in the Stimson Top Secret File.

37. Ibid.; map, Tab A to ibid. Stimson forwarded the map to Secretary of State Cordell Hull under cover of a letter dated Oct. 4, 1941, also in the Stimson Top Secret File. The radii of operation were not associated with any particular bomb load for the aircraft.

38. WD to Douglas MacArthur, draft radiogram prepared by Leonard T. Gerow, Sept. 30, 1941, reel 51, item 1827, NARA microfilm records at GCMF.

39. A. L. Valencia, "Talks Begin," *Manila Daily Bulletin,* Oct. 4, 1941; Jorge T. Teodoro, "Sir Robert, Clagett Make 3-Hour Aerial Tour of Vital Areas," *Philippines Herald,* Oct. 4, 1941; "Weekly Summary of Philippine News," no. 33, Oct. 2–14, 1941, box 1888, RG 165, Military Intelligence—Philippine Islands, NARA C. P.; MacArthur Diary, Oct. 3, 1941.

40. Brooke-Popham to Ismay, Oct. 10, 1941, Brooke-Popham Papers, 6/2/18, Liddell Hart Centre, London; Teodoro, "Sir Robert, Clagett"; MacArthur Diary, Oct. 4, 1941.

41. Henry Clagett to Douglas MacArthur, Oct. 5, 1941, memo, "Consultation with Group Captain Darvall," RG 2, MMA; Kirtley J. Gregg to wife, Oct. 7, 1941.

42. Gregg to wife, Oct. 7, 11, and 21, 1941; memo for Gen. Marshall, Oct. 8, 1941, box 92, folder 12, Appointments Memos 1941, Marshall Papers, GCMF.

43. Clagett to Brett, July 9, 1941; Gregg to wife, Oct. 21, 1941; Ind, *Bataan,* 62.

44. Ind, *Bataan,* 62; Gregg to wife, Oct. 21, 1941. Since mid-September, despite his recovery from malaria, Clagett had felt "knocked out, no energy, breathless when exerting himself," or so he told an Australian medic three months later. He also mentioned that he had been

working and drinking hard during this period ("Hospital or Sick List"). Clagett allegedly was so drunk at an official banquet in China that the State Department wanted him recalled. However, there is no documentary evidence to support this allegation (Geoffrey Perret, "My Search for General MacArthur," *American Heritage,* Feb.–Mar., 1996, 81; William H. Bartsch, "Was MacArthur Ill-Served by his Air Force Commanders in the Philippines?" *Air Power History* 44, no. 2 [summer, 1997]: 47.)

45. Gregg to wife, Oct. 21, 1941.

46. MacArthur Diary, Oct. 13 and 14, 1941; Edward P. King Diary, Oct. 11, 13, and 14, 1941; idem. to wife, Oct. 14, 1941, both in the archives, USAMHI.

47. Mori, *Kaigun,* 1:177; *Senshi Sōsho,* 24:45; Osamu Tagaya, *Mitsubishi Type 1 Rikkō "Betty" Units of World War II,* 34.

48. Prange, *At Dawn We Slept,* 261–63, 280; Mori, *Kaigun,* 1:179; *Senshi Sōsho,* 24:46.

49. Mori, *Kaigun,* 1:179; *Senshi Sōsho,* 24:39, 41.

50. Mori, *Kaigun,* 1:179; Masatake Okumiya and Jirō Horikoshi, with Martin Caidin, *The Zero Fighter,* 120–22.

51. Mori, *Kaigun,* 1:180.

52. Ibid., 1:182, 192; *Senshi Sōsho,* 24:47.

53. Hata and Izawa, *Japanese Naval Aces,* 123; Yokoyama, *Ah Zero-sen,* 97; SRN 117310, Oct. 1, 1941, RG 457, Translations of Intercepted Japanese Naval Messages, NARA C.P.

54. Yokoyama, *Ah Zero-sen,* 99.

55. SRN 117792 and 117810, RG 457, Translations of Intercepted Japanese Naval Messages, NARA C. P. Yokoyama, *Ah Zero-sen,* 102. In his autobiography, Yokoyama claims that he succeeded in changing the Eleventh Air Fleet's plan stipulating carrier training for the 3d *kōkūtai,* but the documentary evidence does not bear him out. Intercepted Japanese navy coded messages indicate that the 3d Kōkūtai practiced carrier landings on the *Ryūjō* from October 10–19 while the 3d Kū was still based at Kanoya (SRN 116520, Oct. 1, 1941, and SRN 116101, Oct. 4, 1941, RG 457, Translations of Intercepted Japanese Naval Messages, NARA C. P.). His senior *buntaichō* also recalls that the 3d Kū undertook such carrier training (Takeo Kurosawa interview in Kohdachi, *Reisen Saigo,* 1:108). However, he maintains that the 3d Kū was not informed of the training's purpose.

56. George Armstrong to wife, Oct. 8, 1941; Ted Fisch to wife, Oct. 10, 1941; USAFFE to HQ, AF USAFFE, memo, Oct. 5, 1941, and HQ, AF USAFFE, to MacArthur, memo, Oct. 9, 1941, both in RG 2, MMA.

57. Mamerow, HQ, AF USAFFE, to MacArthur, memo, Oct. 11, 1941, "Movement of Troops," in RG 2, MMA.

CHAPTER 6: "FEASIBILITY OF DIRECT ATTACK ON LUZON IN THE PHILIPPINES"

1. Brereton mentions meeting with Marshall on October 7 (*Diaries,* 8), but the documentation indicates he did not meet with the chief of staff until October 15. He indicates he was back in Tampa on October 12 (*Diaries,* 9), but without noting the purpose of his return, which is assumed here.

2. Arnold Visitor's Log, Oct. 15, 1941; letter orders, War Department, Oct. 7, 1941, as noted in USAFFE Special Orders 61, Nov. 4, 1941, RG 2, MMA.

3. HQ, AAF, AWPD, A-WPD/1 Scrap Book; "Notes on AWPD Meeting," Oct. 16, 1941, microfilm reel 1489, item 1023, AFHRA. Brady was Brereton's acting chief of staff at Third Air Force headquarters in Tampa, and Caldwell was his AC/S for personnel there. Several days before, Brereton had recommended that Brady be given command of the new Third Air Force Service Command, and Brady expressed disappointment that he would be going out to the Philippines for yet another staff assignment at the age of forty-five (Francis Brady to Frank Andrews, Oct. 6, 1941, box 1, folder 5, Francis Brady Papers, USAFA).

NOTES TO PAGES 153–55

4. "Notes on AWPD Meeting"; William T. Sexton to George C. Marshall, memo, Oct. 15, 1941, box 2, folder 41, Marshall Papers, GCMF.

5. Brereton, *Diaries,* 8–9; Joseph A. Green to George C. Marshall, memo, Nov. 5, 1941, "Anti-Aircraft Requirements of the Philippine Department," 320.2, RG 407, AG Central Decimal Files, 1940–42, NARA D.C.; Brereton draft diary, 3–4.

6. Brereton, *Diaries,* 8.

7. Brady receipt for WPD memo of Oct. 16, 1941, for Brereton, Oct. 18, 1941, WPD 3251–62, RG 165, WPD General Correspondence, 1940–42, NARA D.C.; Spaatz Diary, Oct. 17, 1941. In his *Diaries,* Brereton indicates he was given a "secret directive" and "certain confidential instructions" to pass on to MacArthur. However, it appears they were given to Brady on October 18 to hand over to Brereton for delivery to MacArthur—assuming the document in question is Marshall's secret memo to MacArthur dated Oct. 18, 1941, which lists USAFFE's new tasks under the revised Rainbow Five plan.

8. Lt. Col. Claude E. Duncan to George C. Marshall, memo, Oct. 22, 1941, "Augmentation of Arms and Services with the Air Forces, Plum," 320.2, RG 407, AG Central Decimal Files, 1940–42, NARA D.C.

9. Maj. Edward P. Curtis to AG, memo, Oct. 20, 1941, "Activation of Air Corps Units," 320.2, RG 407, AG Central Decimal Files, 1940–42, NARA D.C.; Henry H. Arnold to Douglas MacArthur, Oct. 14, 1941, RG 2, MMA. Strangely enough, no reference to the activation of an interceptor command was mentioned, although a "5th Interceptor Command" is cited in the memo as one of the units of the new Far East Air Force.

10. Arnold to MacArthur, Oct. 14, 1941. MacArthur may have informed the PD G2 about Arnold's interest in the possibility of bombing attacks on Japan, for on October 30, Lt. Col. Joseph K. Evans, the PD's assistant G2, cabled the WD requesting that "the exact locations of aircraft factories and other important objectives in Japan be furnished" (quoted in Spaatz Diary, Nov. 4, 1941). Evidently in response to Arnold's October 14 communication to MacArthur, Ind's S2 section in Manila prepared bombing objective folders covering targets on Hainan, Formosa, and the Japanese home islands. Calculations were made of how much gasoline was required by the heavy bombers on the route Clark–Aparri–Formosa/Japan and back. (Ind, *Bataan,* 53). His section may also have prepared the undated (October, 1941) three-page note found in the MMA files covering a mission to bomb Tokyo with B-17s from Clark and indicating bomb loads and amount of gasoline required, but concluding it could only be carried out from bases in Vladivostok, given the B-17's range limitations. The note was apparently based on the map given to Stimson in early October, 1941, and referred to in chapter 5.

11. Memo for Arnold, Oct. 15, 1941, "Equipment Necessary for Daylight Penetration of Organized Defenses by Bomber Units," 381 War Plans "Bulkies," RG 18, Central Decimal Files, ser. 2, 1939–42, NARA D.C.

12. Laurence S. Kuter to secretary, GS, memo, "Air Offensive Against Japan," Nov. 21, 1941, WDCSA/381/Philipines (12-4-41), RG 165, Top Secret General Correspondence, 1941–47, NARA D.C. In outlining his plans to Brereton, Arnold did not refer to an ongoing disagreement with the navy over what the sea service regarded as the proper use of airpower in the Philippines, which would have had the effect of eliminating an independent offensive role for the B-17s. In a draft secret letter prepared October 14 to be sent to MacArthur and his naval counterpart, Adm. Thomas Hart, by Marshall and Chief of Naval Operations Harold Stark, it was proposed that the army's air strength be relegated solely "to support naval operations" against Japanese sea communications under a revision of the Rainbow Five war plan. Colonel George, in a memo to Spaatz a week later, asked the WD not to send the letter. The augmentation of Philippines air strength was primarily needed to enable the army "to participate in the strategic offensive, not just support naval operations," he argued. Indeed, the proposal had it backward, Colonel George observed. The Asiatic Fleet's operations necessarily "will primarily be in support of Army air operations, as it is

incapable of coping with the Japanese fleet," he maintained. The AWPD regarded such a draft proposal as another example of the WPD's refusal to give the AWPD any planning responsibilities whatsoever in the formulation of joint army/navy strategic plans or even army plans. The ongoing revision of Rainbow Five was not even mentioned (CNO and C/S to CINC Asiatic Fleet and CG, USAFFE, Oct. 14, 1941, draft, "Preparations for Joint Operations," 381 War Plans, RG 18, Central Decimal Files, ser. 2, 1939–42, NARA D.C.; Harold L. George to Carl Spaatz, Oct. 21, 1941, ibid.; "Notes on A-WPD-1 Officers' Meeting," Oct. 14, 1941, microfilm 1029, AFHRA).

13. Lt. Col. Carey L. O'Bryan, interview, Mar. 5, 1945, Walter D. Edmonds Collection, AFHRA (hereafter Edmonds Collection).

14. Edward M. Jacquet, diary provided to author (hereafter Jacquet Diary); HQ, 19th Bomb Group, Albuquerque, N.M., Special Orders 1, Oct. 17, 1941, Edmonds Collection.

15. Henry H. Arnold to George C. Marshall, memos, Oct. 20 and 21, 1941, "Flight of B-17s to Hawaii," RG 107, Stimson Top Secret File, NARA, D.C.

16. Ted Fisch to Mimi Fisch, Oct. 17, 1941.

17. Leonard T. Gerow for secretary of war, memo, Oct. 2, 1941, "Reinforcements and Movement of Troops," pt. 1, 370.5 (8-1-41), RG 407, AG Central Decimal Files, 1940–42, NARA D.C.; Krieger to father, Oct. 11, 1941.

18. George Armstrong to wife, Oct. 18, 1941.

19. Arnold to author; Capt. C. J. Wimer, "History of Signal Corps Radar Units in the Philippine Islands, 1 Aug. 1941–6 May 1942," quoted in George R. Thompson, Dixie R. Harris, Pauline M. Oakes, and Dulany Terrett, *The Signal Corps: The Test,* 11. The two fixed-location SCR-271s received earlier in the month with three SCR-270Bs were put in storage, as they had to be mounted on permanent towers at prepared sites (Charles H. Bogart, "Radar in the Philippines, 1941–1942," *Journal of America's Military Past,* fall, 1999, 27–30).

20. Melvin E. Thomas, interview by author, May 1, 1996; WD, Technical Manual 11-1100, *Radio Set SCR-270B,* 2–3; WD, Technical Bulletin SIG 106, *Radio Sets SCR-270 and SCR-271,* 4–5; Roland narrative.

21. Robert J. Hinson, interview by author, Jan. 12, 1981.

22. Shimakawa, *Zero-sen,* 78.

23. SRN 117810, Sept. 26, 1941; SRN 115763, Oct. 1, 1941; SRN 116138, Oct. 15, 1941, RG 457, Translations of Intercepted Japanese Naval Messages, NARA C.P.

24. SRN 117810, Sept. 26, 1941; SRN 116101, Oct. 4, 1941; and SRN 116134, Oct. 21, 1941, RG 457, Translations of Intercepted Japanese Naval Messages, NARA C. P. The *rikkō*—short for Rikujō Kogeki-ki—were twin-engine naval bombers whose primary mission was to attack with aerial torpedos or bombs (Tagaya, "Techical Development," 2).

25. Yokoyama, *Ah Zero-Sen,* 100.

26. Ibid.; Kurosawa interview, 1:108–10. It is assumed that the 3d Kū had the same number of Zeros that it had on October 1: a total of forty-one (SRN 117310, Oct. 1, 1941).

27. George Armstrong to wife, Oct. 26, 1941.

28. "Army Pilot Lands Plane on Highway," *Manila Daily Bulletin,* Oct. 24, 1941.

29. Armstrong to wife, Oct. 26, 1941; Andrew E. Krieger to father, Nov. 2 and 7, 1941.

30. Ted Fisch to wife, Oct. 30, 1941.

31. Thomas Caswell to author, Feb. 19, 1994. I identified the fifteen Class 41-G pilots by their serial numbers, which are included on the 19th Bomb Group roster.

32. Officers and men listed individually in Air Base Headquarters, Albuquerque, N.M., Special Orders 135, Sept. 20, 1941, AFCC 340.5, RG 18, NARA D.C.; Stancill M. Nanney, interview, May 19, 1945; and George R. Robinett, interview, Apr. 9, 1945, both in the Edmonds Collection.

33. Harold George to Hugh Casey, memo, Oct. 17, 1941; and USAFFE to CG, AF USAFFE, memo, Oct. 31, 1941; and Douglas MacArthur to AGWAR, radiogram, Oct. 23, 1941, all in RG

2, MMA. One wonders where the 28th Bomb and 20th Pursuit were to have stayed if they had been transferred in mid-October to Cabanatuan and Rosales Fields, respectively.

34. Harold George to Hugh Casey, Oct. 29, 1941; and 1st indorsement, Douglas MacArthur to Hugh Casey, both in RG 2, MMA.

35. AG to Douglas MacArthur, radiogram, Oct. 21, 1941, 452.1, Arnold Papers; Spaatz Diary, Oct. 21, 1941.

36. Air Base Headquarters, Fort Douglas, Special Orders 251, Nov. 8, 1941; Table, "Reinforcement of the Philippines—to Include Sailings Dec. 8, 1941," executive 8-4, RG 165, OPD Executive Group Files, 1939–42, NARA D.C.

37. Douglas MacArthur to George C. Marshall, Oct. 28, 1941, RG 2, MMA. The target of 165 heavy bombers was considerably fewer than the 272 recommended in A-WPD/1, but was based on the realities of expected production of B-17s and B-24s through February, 1942. Arnold had indicated in October that 95 B-17s and 35 B-24s expected from production by the end of February, 1942, would be allocated to the Philippines, yielding—with the 9 B-17s delivered in September and the 26 to be delivered in October—a total of 165 (Arnold for the secretary of war, memo, Oct. 8, 1941).

38. Mori, *Kaigun,* 1:190.

39. SRN 116134, Oct. 21, 1941. Mori gives the date as October 2, but that is an error, as the Eleventh Air Fleet did not move to Takao until October 21 (*Kaigun,* 1:191).

40. Mori, *Kaigun,* 1:191. Mori notes that Japanese records indicate Shingō was informed of the 3d Ku's attack plan, but that he opposed it because the likelihood of success was uncertain at the time. In his postwar interview with Mori, Shingō denied being informed of the plan. The *Senshi Sōsho* records that neither the Eleventh Air Fleet headquarters nor the Tainan Kū believed it was possible for the Zero-sen to fly nonstop to Luzon and back (24:50).

41. Mori, *Kaigun,* 1:192.

42. Ibid., 1:192, 194–95; *Senshi Sōsho,* 24:48; Prange, *At Dawn We Slept,* 297; Koichi Shimada, "The Opening Air Offensive Against the Philippines," in *The Japanese Navy in World War II,* ed. David C. Evans, 77–78. The *Zuihō* had a capacity of 27 aircraft, the *Ryūjō* 36, and the *Taiyō* (formerly the *Kasuga Maru*) 23. Shimada notes that the three small carriers accommodated only 75 aircraft, but the standard volume on Japanese warships agrees with Mori's total of 86, excluding spares (A. J. Watts and B. G. Gordon, *The Imperial Japanese Navy,* 178, 186, 188).

43. Mori, *Kaigun,* 1:195–96, 198.

44. The fuselage tank had a capacity of 145 liters and each wing tank a capacity of 195 liters, for a total of 535 liters. Total capacity thus equaled 855 liters (I converted the fuselage and wing tank figures from gallon figures given in Mikesh, *Zero,* 121). *Senshi Sōsho* summarizes the fuel-savings argument (24:51).

45. Mori, *Kaigun,* 1:198. Evidently the plan for the use of small carriers called for the Zeros to fly on to their Formosa airfields after combat.

46. Ibid.; *Senshi Sōsho,* 24:52.

47. Mori, *Kaigun,* 1:198–200; *Senshi Sōsho,* 24:52.

48. Mori, *Kaigun,* 1:159, 200; Richard Fuller, *Shokan: Hirohito's Samurai,* 280–81.

49. Mori, *Kaigun,* 2:163; *Senshi Sōsho,* 24:52; SRN 116481, Nov. 5, 1941.

50. Jacquet Diary; Eugene L. Eubank, interview, Nov. 29, 1945, Edmonds Collection; John L. Mitchell, *On Wings We Conquer,* 169.

51. Edgar D. Whitcomb, *Escape from Corregidor,* 4; Henry H. Arnold to George C. Marshall, memos, Oct. 31 and Nov. 5, 1941, both in Philippine File, RG 107, NARA D.C.; O'Bryan interview; Michael Bibin to author, July 28, 1981; Melvin McKenzie to author, Mar. 31, 1994.

52. Ted Fisch to Mimi Fisch, Nov. 6, 1941.

53. Jacquet Diary; Melvin McKenzie Diary, Nov. 13, 1941 (hereafter McKenzie Diary); James Cooke to parents, Oct. 27, 1941; C. L. Moseley Jr. to author, Mar. 14, 1994; Whitcomb, *Escape from Corregidor,* 4; McKenzie to author; Fisch to wife, Nov. 6, 1941.

54. Fisch to wife, Nov. 6, 1941.

55. HQ, 19th Bomb Group (H), Special Orders 1, Oct. 17, 1941.

56. "Two Top-Flight War Experts Arrive by Air to Help Guide P.I. Defense," *Manila Tribune,* Nov. 5, 1941.

57. Krieger to father, Nov. 2 and 7, 1941; George Armstrong to wife, Nov. 4, 1941.

58. Brereton draft diary, chap. 3; "Two Top-Flight War Experts Arrive." In his published *Diaries,* Brereton erroneously gives his date of arrival as November 3.

59. MacArthur Diary, Nov. 4, 1941; Brereton draft diary, chap. 3; idem., *Diaries,* 18.

60. Brereton, *Diaries,* 18–19; idem. draft diary, chap. 3. Brereton recalled in his *Diaries* that he was asked to report at 8 A.M., but MacArthur's office diary records that their meeting took place at ten.

61. George C. Marshall to Douglas MacArthur, Oct. 18, 1941, WPD 4175-18, item 1308, reel 32; and Bryden to MacArthur, memo, Nov. 21, 1941, "U.S.–British Commonwealth Cooperation in the Far East," item 1372, reel 33, both in the GCMF. In a radio to MacArthur from Marshall on Nov. 27, Marshall mentions that Brereton delivered the revised Rainbow Five plan to MacArthur (Brereton, *Diaries,* 33 n 7).

62. Brereton, *Diaries,* 19.

63. Marshall to MacArthur, Oct. 18, 1941.

64. Bryden to MacArthur, Nov. 21, 1941.

65. Brereton draft diary, chap. 3; idem., *Diaries,* 19–20; HQ, FEAF, memo, Dec. 18, 1941, "Reference Activities in the Philippine Islands," container 201, folder 4, Arnold Papers; Ind, *Bataan,* 64–65.

66. Brereton, *Diaries,* 20; HQ, FEAF, memo, Dec. 18, 1941; Ind, *Bataan,* 65, 66. Although not indicated in Ind's account, it is obvious that the Air Warning Service was represented at the meeting. Noteworthy is the fact that the meeting was not held in Clagett's office. He evidently did not attend.

67. Air Force USAFFE, General Orders 6, Nov. 6, 1941, RG 2, MMA; Ind, *Bataan,* 66, 67. Staffs at division level and above are classified as G staffs, whereas those of battalions, regiments, and brigades are S staffs.

68. Ind indicates that Clagett was announced as commander of the V Interceptor Command, but that the unit had not yet been officially activated (*Bataan,* 67).

69. Kirtley J. Gregg to wife, Nov. 7, 1941; Bryden to AG, memo, Oct. 21, 1941, item 1821, reel 51, GCMF. Clagett did indeed request to return to the United States (Henry Clagett to AG, memo, Nov. 12, 1941, "Relief from Foreign Duty," Clagett Collection). He based his request on "a definite loss of prestige" following his replacement by Brereton, which detracted from his "value as a commander." Brereton endorsed Clagett's request the same day on the grounds of his poor physical condition and recommended "steps be taken to expedite Gen. Clagett's departure from this command." MacArthur recommended approval of the request the same day (ibid.).

70. Ind, *Bataan,* 67; Gregg to wife, Oct. 11 and Nov. 7, 1941.

PART III: "THE INABILITY OF AN ENEMY TO LAUNCH HIS AIR ATTACK ON THESE ISLANDS IS OUR GREATEST SECURITY"

1. Bix, *Hirohito,* 424, 425–26, 427

2. Hattori, *Complete History,* 1:223, 2:1–2, 7; Department of the Army, *Reports of General MacArthur: Japanese Operations in the Southwest Pacific Area,* vol. 2, pt. 1, 70; Ogawa, *Reluctant Admiral,* 237.

3. Pogue, *Marshall,* 194–95; Marshall and Stark, "Memorandum for the President—Estimate Concerning Far Eastern Situation," Nov. 5, 1941, WPD 4389-29, RG 165, WPD General Correspondence, 1939–42, NARA D.C.

4. Henry H. Arnold to secretary of war, Oct. 20, 21, 24, 25, 26, and 31, and Nov. 1 and 5, Stimson Top Secret File, RG 107, NARA D.C.

5. Bix, *Hirohito,* 421–22; Hattori, *Complete History,* 1:223, 278, and 2:4; Fuller, *Shokan,* 216.

6. Hattori, *Complete History,* 2:2–3; Arthur Swinson, *Four Samurai,* 47; Fuller, *Shokan,* 216; Prange, *At Dawn We Slept,* 340; Ogawa, *Reluctant Admiral,* 237–38; *Senshi Sōsho,* 24:142.

7. Eiichirō Sekigawa, *Japanese Military Aviation,* 114; Fuller, *Shokan,* 198; Sadatoshi Tomioka, *Kaisen to Chusen (The Beginning and End of the War),* 91; Hattori, *Complete History,* 2:30; Swinson, *Four Samurai,* 47; *Senshi Sōsho,* 24:150; Bōeichō BōekenshūshoSenshishitsu (Japanese Defense Agency, War History Section), *Nampo Shinkō Rikūgun Kōkū Sakusen (Southern Offensive Army Air Operations), Senshi Sōsho,* 34:203.

8. *Senshi Sōsho,* 24:150; Prange, *At Dawn We Slept,* 435; Swinson, *Four Samurai,* 34–35. Hattori indicates the Imperial GHQ/Army estimated Manila could be taken within thirty days (*Complete History,* 1:279).

9. Matloff and Snell, *Strategic Planning,* 76; U.S. secretary for collaboration to joint secretaries, British Joint Staff Mission, Nov. 11, 1941, WPD 4402-18, RG 165, WPD General Correspondence, 1940–42, NARA D.C..

10. Robert L. Sherrod to David W. Hurlburd Jr., memo, Nov. 15, 1941, "General Marshall's Conference Today," reproduced in Bland, *Marshall Papers,* 2:676–81. Marshall was overoptimistic in maintaining a B-17 had the range to bomb Tokyo from the Philippines and land in Vladivostok. A study prepared by the Air Force, USAFFE, staff (see chapter 6, note 10) concluded that even with only half a bomb load, a B-17 flying from Clark Field would go down 440 nautical miles short of Vladivostok after passing over Tokyo.

11. Stimson Diary, Nov. 25, 1941, Stimson Papers.

12. "Conference in the Office of Chief of Staff, 10:40 A.M., Nov. 26, 1941," WDCSA/381/Philippines (12-4-41), RG 165, Top Secret General Correspondence, 1941–42, NARA D.C. General Arnold proposed a photorecon of the Japanese mandates with a pair of high-flying B-24s that would subsequently be turned over to MacArthur for further reconnaissance, even over Japan—a plan Marshall approved on the spot. Lieutenant Colonel Thomas T. Handy of the WPD was leary of recon flights over Japanese territory and told the conferees that allowing planes to fly over Formosa would likely be considered an overt act.

13. Pogue, *Marshall,* 206; Stimson Diary, Nov. 27, 1941, Stimson Papers.

14. Bix, *Hirohito,* 428–29; Prange, *At Dawn We Slept,* 390; Paul S. Dull, *A Battle History of the Imperial Japanese Navy, 1941–1945,* 10. Bix erroneously gives the date as November 27 (*Hirohito,* 430).

15. Crowley, "Japan's Military," 102–103; Fuller, *Shokan,* 278, 305–306; Bix, *Hirohito,* 432–33.

16. Ike, *Japan's Decision,* 271–72, 283

17. Swinson, *Four Samurai,* 49.

18. Matome Ugaki, *Fading Victory: The Diary of Admiral Matome Ugaki, 1941–1945,* 32.

19. George C. Marshall to CG, USAFFE, cablegram 624, Nov. 27, 1941, AG 381 (11-27-41), RG 407, AG Central Decimal Files, 1940–42, NARA D.C.

20. George C. Marshall and Harold R. Stark, Nov. 27, 1941, "Memorandum for the President: Subject, Far Eastern Situation," WDCSA/381/Philippines (12-4-41), RG 165, Top Secret General Correspondence, 1941–42, NARA D.C.

21. Stimson Diary, Nov. 27 and 28, 1941. The force was actually heading for Japanese-occupied Hainan Island off southern China, where it would assemble for the Malaya invasion (Hattori, *Complete History,* 2:25).

22. Matloff and Snell, *Strategic Planning,* 76–77; Adams to CG, USAFFE, secret telegram 650, Nov. 29, 1941, AG 381 (11-27-1941), RG 407, AG Central Decimal Files, 1940–42, NARA D.C.

23. Adams to CG, USAFFE. Marshall and Stark were misinformed about Phillips's arrival date in Singapore. When he reached Ceylon, he was ordered not to wait for his entire departing force to arrive in Singapore but rather to fly on to Singapore on November 29 (Martin Middlebrook and Patrick Mahoney, *Battleship: The Loss of the Prince of Wales and the Repulse,* 69–72).

24. Douglas MacArthur to George C. Marshall, radiogram 1045, Dec. 2, 1941; and Marshall to MacArthur, telegram 656, Nov. 29, 1941, both in AG 381 (11-27-41), RG 407, AG Central Decimal Files, 1940–42, NARA D.C.

25. Bix, *Hirohito,* 433–35. The text of the imperial rescript issued on December 8 is reproduced in Edwin P. Hoyt, *Japan's War: The Great Pacific Conflict,* 229–31. Curiously enough, the Japanese declared war on the United States and Great Britain but not on the Netherlands, even though the Dutch East Indies was the prime target of their southern operations.

26. Hattori, *Complete History,* 1:260; Ugaki, *Fading Victory,* 34; *Senshi Sōsho,* 24:170; Prange, *At Dawn We Slept,* 445.

27. Hattori, *Complete History,* 2:6, 25; Toland, *Rising Sun,* 187. Toland gives the departure time from Hainan as dawn rather than in the afternoon.

28. "No Need to Fear ABCD Encircling," *Japan Times and Advertiser,* Dec. 5, 1941. The "Consolidated PBY-28 heavy bomber" Rear Adm. Toshio Matsunaga referred to was actually the Consolidated B-24 Liberator, which, as previously noted, had the range to hit southern Japan from northern Luzon. It is not known if Matsunaga was reflecting IGHQ's reaction to information "leaked" by the White House or State Department of the offensive threat MacArthur's B-17 force posed to the Japanese homeland (as per Marshall's press conference) or to intelligence information about the B-17s in the Philippines made available by the Japanese consul in Manila (as indicated in Magic intercepts).

29. Douglas MacArthur to George C. Marshall, cablegram 1004, Nov. 28, 1941, AG 381 (11-27-41), RG 407, AG Central Decimal Files, 1940–42, NARA D.C.

30. "Conference in Manila," *New York Times,* Nov. 28, 1941; original manuscript for "Glad Adventure," box 23, Sayre Papers; MacArthur Diary, entries for Nov. 27 and 28, 1941.

31. Marshall to MacArthur, telegram 656, Nov. 29, 1941, and MacArthur to Marshall, radiogram 1045, Dec. 2, 1941. In his response to MacArthur's radiogram, Marshall on December 3 held to the WD's position that "in accordance with quote joint action Army and Navy unquote . . . it is intended that Army air units would be placed under Navy unity of command for specific tasks of temporary and definitely naval character" (Marshall to MacArthur, telegram 693, Dec. 3, 1941, AG 381 [11-27-41], RG 407, AG Central Decimal Files, 1940–42, NARA D.C.).

32. Middlebrook and Mahoney, *Battleship,* 72–73, 89; Leutze, *Different Kind of Victory,* 224. According to Middlebrook and Mahoney, Phillips left Singapore by air on December 4 (*Battleship,* 89). The fifteen-hundred-mile trip would have taken at least ten hours by flying boat, which means Phillips most likely reached Cavite early on December 5.

33. "Report of Conference," Manila, Dec. 6, 1941, ser. 1, Subject Files, item 12, Hart Papers; Leutze, *Different Kind of Victory,* 224–25. There is no mention of this meeting in MacArthur's office diary. Since MacArthur held a press conference at 9:45 A.M. on December 5, according to his office diary, the meeting with Hart and Phillips must have taken place in late morning or early afternoon.

34. Middlebrook and Mahoney, *Battleship,* 89–90; Leutze, *Different Kind of Victory,* 225.

35. Adams to CG, USAFFE, cablegram 647, Nov. 28, 1941; and Douglas MacArthur to AGWAR, radiogram, 11:05 A.M., Dec. 6, 1941, both in AG 381 (11-27-41), RG 407, AG Central Decimal Files, 1940–42, NARA D.C. It has been suggested that this sabotage warning was Washington's "last message," and that it also mentioned that the WD intelligence staff "had calculated that Japanese aircraft did not have sufficient range to bomb Manila from Formosa." However, no such information is included in the November 28 cablegram (D. Clayton James,

"The Other Pearl Harbor," *MHQ: The Quarterly Journal of Military History* 7, no. 2 [winter, 1995]: 27–28).

36. Middlebrook and Mahoney, *Battleship,* 90–91; Leutze, *Different Kind of Victory,* 226.

37. Douglas MacArthur to George C. Marshall, radiogram 1112, Dec. 7, 1941 (received by the WD at 4:47 P.M., December 6), reel 78, item 2171, microfilmed NARA records, GCMF.

38. Pogue, *Marshall,* 219–20; Stimson Diary, Dec. 6, 1941, Stimson Papers; Col. Robert W. Crawford to Leonard T. Gerow, memo, Dec. 1, 1941, "Airplanes for the Philippine Islands," executive 8-4, RG 165, OPD Group Executive Files, 1939–42, NARA D.C.; WPD memos for the secretary of war, Nov. 26 and Dec. 5 and 6, 1941, Stimson Top Secret File, RG 107, NARA D.C.

39. Pogue, *Marshall,* 221–22; Matloff and Snell, *Strategic Planning,* 79.

40. John Keegan, ed., *The Times Atlas of the Second World War,* 70–71.

41. *Reports of General MacArthur,* vol. 2, pt. 1, 89; *Senshi Sōsho,* 34:294–96; Military History Section, HQ, Army Forces Far East, "Philippines Air Operations Record: Phase One," Japanese Monograph no. 11, 10.

42. Military History Section, HQ, Army Forces Far East, "Philippines Air Operations," 9; *Senshi Sōsho,* 34:200, 294. See appendix B for the disposition of the 5th Hikōshidan's aircraft on Formosa on Dec. 8, 1941. See appendix A for details on numbers, types, and locations of navy aircraft for the Philippines operation.

43. *Senshi Sōsho,* 24:162, 164; Hata and Izawa, *Japanese Naval Aces,* 143. The Eleventh Air Fleet's intelligence information on the B-17 force was quite accurate, except that half had been dispersed to Mindanao since December 5. Nonetheless, its knowledge of types and disposition of fighters was way off the mark, with nine-tenths of the FEAF's fighters being P-40s based at Iba, Clark, and Nichols Fields, and only one squadron of P-35s, which was deployed at Del Carmen.

44. Prange, *At Dawn We Slept,* 438.

Chapter 7: "We Are Going Much Too Far on the Offensive Side"

1. Brereton draft diary, 11; idem., *Diaries,* 21.

2. Brereton draft diary, 12; idem., *Diaries,* 22; HQ, FEAF, memo, Dec. 18, 1941. After arriving at Clark Field on September 26, the 200th Coast Artillery (Antiaircraft) unpacked its guns, set up ammo dumps, and began digging gun emplacements around Clark Field and Fort Stotsenburg. The latter activity was hindered by the closure of many suitable sites by private landowners (Charles H. Bogart, "200th Coast Artillery [AA]," *The Quan,* Apr., 1983, 9; Brig.Gen. Charles G. Sage, "Report of Operations of the Philippine Provisional Coast Artillery Brigade (AA) in the Philippines Campaign," Annex IX to Jonathan M. Wainwright, "Report of Operations of USAFFE and USFIL in the Philippine Islands, 1941–1942," Fort Sam Houston, Tex., 1946, 2, reproduced in Celedonia A. Ancheta, ed., *The Wainwright Papers,* vol. 2; Dorothy Cave, *Beyond Courage,* 51).

3. Brereton draft diary, 11; idem., *Diaries,* 21; George to Casey, Oct. 29, 1941; Norman J. Lewellyn to wife, Nov. 6, 1941; William H. Montgomery, "I Hired Out to Fight," unpublished memoir, archives, USAMHI.

4. Brereton draft diary, 12; idem., *Diaries,* 23. Brereton stated that the new orders were issued on November 6, but the date clearly was later. I have been unable to locate any documents covering the new schedule.

5. George Armstrong to wife, Nov. 11, 1941; HQ, AF USAFFE, memo, Nov. 10, 1941, "Preparation for Emergency," RG 2, MMA.

6. Douglas MacArthur to AG, radiogram 812, Nov. 12, 1941, RG 2, MMA; Francis Brady to Carl Spaatz, Nov. 17, 1941, Project Files 1939–42, Philippine Department, RG 18, NARA D.C.

7. AG to Douglas MacArthur, telegram 536, Nov. 15, 1941, 320.2, Philippines, RG 407, AG Central Decimal Files, 1940–42, NARA.

8. Max Louk to parents, Nov. 23, 1941; George Armstrong to wife, Nov. 16, 1941; Forrest Hobrecht to parents, Nov. 14, 1941.

9. Francis Cappelletti, "My Overseas Log: A Navigator's Experience in the Far East," unpublished memoir, n.d. (hereafter "Overseas Log"); Max Louk to sister, Nov. 22, 1941; Carl Gies Diary, Dec. 8, 1941 (hereafter Gies Diary). Cappelletti noted that his 93d Squadron B-17s "could fly circles around the P-40s at 20,000 feet" ("Overseas Log").

10. Carl Gies to parents, Nov. 12, 1941; Frank Neri to wife, Nov. 27, 1941; Joseph H. Moore to author, June 16, 1979, and Feb. 29, 1988; idem., interview by John Toland (n.d., but ca. 1958), Toland Papers, LOC, 2.

11. SRN 116044, Oct. 13, 1941; SRN 115547, Nov. 3, 1941; SRN 116308, Oct. 29, 1941; and SRN 116310, Oct. 29, 1941, all in RG 457, Translations of Intercepted Japanese Naval Messages, NARA C. P.

12. Sakai, *Ohzora,* 100; idem., with Martin Caidin and Fred Saito, *Samurai!* 67. The protest note is reproduced in Exhibit 130, 2942, *Hearings before the Joint Committee on the Investigation of the Pearl Harbor Attack,* 79th Cong., 2d sess., pt. 18. The November 27 protest note did not identify the type of aircraft involved, but until December 1, Patrol Wing 10 (which operated PBYs) was solely responsible for flying reconnaissance missions in the Formosa area. Although there is no documentation on the U.S. side referring to overflights of Formosa by Patrol Wing 10, such flights may not have been recorded because of their sensitive nature. Two surviving enlisted men who served with Patrol Wing 10's VP-101 recall flying over Formosa, but they have no recollection of dates or other details (Russell N. Rawlins, taped narrative provided to author, Nov. 10, 2000; Walter E. Mount, telephone interview by author, Sept. 2, 2000). Another former enlisted man, Emanuel Kundert, recalls that although his PBY did not fly over Formosa, others did (telephone interview by author, Sept. 26, 2000).

13. Sakai, *Samurai!* 67; idem., *Ohzora,* 102; Imperial Japanese Army Directive 1045, Dec. 2, 1941, and Imperial Japanese Naval Order 5, Nov. 21, 1941, both in NHC; Hideki Shingō to author, May 9, 1980.

14. Yokoyama, *Ah Zero-sen,* 102, 104

15. Ind, *Bataan,* 70; Norman Lewellyn to wife, Nov. 21, 1941; photo of McKenzie's B-17D no. 67 at Archerfield, Australia, copy in author's collection; Brereton draft diary, 13; MacArthur to Marshall, Nov. 29, 1941; MacArthur Diary, Nov. 17, 1941; WD to MacArthur, radiogram, Oct. 22, 1941; USAFFE Special Orders 52, Oct. 24, 1941; WD to MacArthur, radiogram, Nov. 3, 1941; and MacArthur to (Col. Van S.) Merle-Smith, radiogram, Nov. 11, 1941, all in RG 2, MMA. Ind indicates that the postponement was due to the fact that Air Force, USAFFE,"could ill [afford to] spare" Colonel George (*Bataan,* 69–70). The WD's November 3 radiogram includes authorization for USAFFE to arrange for air training facilities in Australia.

16. McKenzie Diary, Nov. 10 and 16, 1941; Ind, *Bataan,* 70. Brereton erroneously gives the time of departure as 1 A.M. on November 11 (draft diary, 13).

17. USAFFE General Orders 28, Nov. 14, 1941, RG 2, MMA. The 14th Bomb Squadron maintained its separate status until it joined the 19th Group on December 2 ("Army Air Action," 34.)

18. Henry H. Arnold to AG, memo, Oct. 20, 1941, and WD to USAFFE, Oct. 28, 1941, both in 320.2, RG 407, AG Central Decimal Files, 1940–42, NARA D.C.; "Brereton Organizes His Staff," and "Brereton Names Staff for Air Force," *Manila Tribune,* Nov. 7 and 14, 1941, respectively. Although the 5th Interceptor Command is referred to specifically in a November 21 memorandum (Francis Brady to Douglas MacArthur, "Proposed Installations and Facilities for Far East Air Force," RG 2, MMA), no authorization for its activation in the Philippines has been found in official orders ("Army Air Action," 211 n 3).

19. "Brereton Names Staff"; Kirtley J. Gregg to wife, Nov. 22, 1941; John H. M. Smith, interview with AAF historians, 1943, Appendix A, "19th Bombardment Group (H) History,"

n.d., Edmonds Collection. Horrigan took over the 28th Bomb Squadron at the end of October, after being replaced as commander of the 3d Pursuit by 1st Lt. Hank Thorne (Frank Neri to wife, Nov. 2, 1941).

20. Gregg to wife, Nov. 22, 1941; William Maverick to wife, Nov. 16 and Dec. 1, 1941.

21. USAFFE Special Orders 74, Nov. 19, 1941, RG 2, MMA; Maverick interview; memo to Henry H. Arnold, Oct. 14, 1941, microfilm reel 208, Arnold Papers.

22. HQ, FEAF, memo, Dec. 18, 1941; Francis Brady to Carl Spaatz, Nov. 13 and 17, 1941, 210.31-B and 686-B, respectively, both in Project Files 1939–42, Philippine Department, RG 18, NARA D.C.. The unit working on the field was Company B, 803d Engineer Aviation Battalion, which arrived in the Philippines on October 23, 1941 (Karl C. Dod, *The Corps of Engineers: The War against Japan,* 63). Brady may have overestimated the length of the strip. A military intelligence report gives the length of the field at that date as 880 yards, or 2,640 feet only ("Provisional List of Aerodrome Landing Grounds and Seaplane Facilities, 5 Dec. 1941," folder 15, box 1864, RG 165, Military Intelligence—Philippine Islands, NARA C. P.).

23. George C. Marshall to Henry H. Arnold, memo, Nov. 13, 1941, "Philippines 1941 Correspondence," box 80, folder 16, Marshall Papers, GCMF; Douglas MacArthur to George C. Marshall, telegram, Nov. 18, 1941, RG 2, MMA.

24. "Brereton Names Staff"; Dod, *Corps of Engineers,* 64.

25. McKenzie Diary, Nov. 13, 1941; idem. to author; caption on Jacquet photo.

26. George L. Verity, *From Bataan to Victory,* 10, 12.

27. Spaatz Diary, Nov. 19 (instructing his A3 to inform MacArthur of his decision) and Nov. 14, 1941; Lewis Brereton to Henry H. Arnold, Nov. 7, 1941, Decimal File 1940–45, 320.2, box 91, folder 4, Arnold Papers. Brady reiterated his chief's concerns about the inexperienced pursuit pilots being sent to the Philippines (Brady to Spaatz, Nov. 13, 1941).

28. William Sheppard to parents, Nov. 20, 1941; Bartsch, *Doomed,* 28.

29. Ted Fisch to wife, Nov. 21, 1941; 28th Bomb Squadron roster, Oct. 31, 1941, NPRC.

30. Gaston, *Planning,* 38–39, 91; Laurence S. Kuter, "Growth of Air Power," unpublished manuscript, 1979, Special Collections; Lt. Gen. Harold L. George, interview, Mar. 16, 1970, Arnold-Green Collection.

31. Kuter to secretary, GS. For a report on Marshall's conference, see Sherrod to Hulburd Jr., Nov. 15, 1941.

32. Brereton, *Diaries,* 31–32; HQ, FEAF, memo, Dec. 18, 1941; Francis Brady to Douglas MacArthur, memo, Nov. 21, 1941, "Proposed Installations and Facilities for Far East Air Force"; and attachment, "Proposed Development of Facilities for Air Force Operation within the Philippine Islands," Nov. 20, 1941, both in RG 2, MMA.

33. MacArthur to Marshall, Nov. 29, 1941; Marshall to MacArthur, telegram, Sept. 9, 1941; AG to Douglas MacArthur, radiogram, Oct. 21, 1941, 452.1, Arnold Papers.

34. Attachment, "Proposed Development." Colonel George had Mindanao in mind as a major base for heavy bomber operations at least as early as October, as suggested by his October 29 request to USAFFE for massive housing construction at Del Monte (George to Casey, Oct. 29, 1941).

35. Brady to MacArthur, Nov. 21, 1941; attachment, "Proposed Development."

36. Attachment, "Proposed Development." Interestingly enough, the northern Luzon fields to be developed did not include Aparri or any other field at Luzon's northern tip from which AAF HQ wanted B-24s positioned to strike Japan. Aparri was apparently deemed unsuitable for development. Instead, Iguig and Amalung, some forty miles south of Aparri, as well as Tuguegarao, fifty miles south of Aparri—where a field already existed—were to be developed as auxiliary airdromes for limited operations by all types of aircraft, to include B-24s.

37. Brereton, *Diaries,* 32–33. Brady briefed Brereton on his discussions with Sutherland following Brereton's return from Australia. The 5th Air Base Group's HQ Squadron was temporarily assigned to Fort McKinley by USAFFE General Orders 29.

39. MacArthur to Marshall, Nov. 29, 1941. I have assumed that the *Brereton Diaries'* description of Brady's discussions with Brereton regarding Brady's meetings with Sutherland is accurate.

40. Francis Brady to Douglas MacArthur, memo, Dec. 3, 1941, "Priority in Airdrome Construction," container 201, folder 4, Philippines 1941, Arnold Papers; Bartsch, *Doomed,* 179; USAFFE General Orders 29. The A-24s were shipped on the cargo ship *Meigs,* which was not due in Manila until December 19, later changed to January 4 (A3 to Henry H. Arnold, memo, Nov. 24, 1941, 452.1, Arnold Papers; Crawford to Gerow).

41. "Provisional List of Aerodrome Landing Grounds and Seaplane Facilities, 5 Dec. 1941"; Brady to MacArthur, Dec. 3, 1941; USAFFE General Orders 29; A3 to Arnold, Nov. 24, 1941; Bartsch, *Doomed,* 30–32; "The 27th Reports: History of the 27th Bomb Group (L) in the Philippines, Java, Australia, and New Guinea," pt. 7, "Nov. 1–Dec. 7, 1941," copy in author's collection. I have been unable to find any documents regarding the 34th Pursuit's transfer to Del Carmen.

42. Interview of Capt. Chihaya Takahashi, USSBS interrogation no. 74, Oct. 20, 1945, in USSBS (Pacific), *Interrogations of Japanese Officials,* 1:74–76; Katsumi Nihro to Tokyo, secret radio message 722, Nov. 1, 1941; and Tokyo (Shigenori Togo) to Manila, secret radio message 349, Nov. 5, 1941, both translated in Department of Defense, *The "Magic" Background of Pearl Harbor,* vol. 4, app. A-157, A-160; Yasuho Izawa, "Rikkō and Ginga: Japanese Navy Twin Bomber Units," unpublished manuscript, n.d., copy in author's collection, 49; Richard M. Bueschel, *Mitsubishi-Nakajima G3M1/2/3 in Japanese Naval Air Service,* 10–11. The top-secret mission known as "A Sagyo" to mount high-altitude photoreconnaissance flights over much of Southeast Asia and the Pacific was carried out by Type 96 *rikkō* between April and September, 1941 (Tagaya, "Technical Development," 34).

43. Masami Miza, "Meritorious Deeds of the Secret Reconnoitering Unit which Became the Shadow Strength of the Zero Fighter Squadrons" (in Japanese), *Maru,* Feb., 1962, 126–29; Jim Sawruk to author, Aug. 1, 2, and 5, 2002; Andrew Obluski to author, Aug. 5, 2002; Shingō to author, Feb. 8, 1982; Rene J. Francillon, *Japanese Aircraft of the Pacific War,* 154–55.

44. P-40s sometimes managed to get up to thirty thousand feet, but their performance was sluggish at that altitude. The two pursuing P-40s must have been from the HQ or 20th Pursuit Squadrons based at Clark, but there is no record of who was flying them. The pilots may have been Benny Putnam, commander of the 24th Group's HQ Squadron, and Billy Maverick, the group operations officer, who about three weeks before the war, as Putnam recalled, spotted nine planes ten thousand feet above and tried to catch up with them, but failed (Capt. Walter B. Putnam, interview, Feb. 23, 1945, Edmonds Collection).

45. Miza, "Meritorious Deeds," 126–29; Takahashi interrogation.

46. Sakai, *Ohzora,* 102, 103; Shingō to author, Feb. 8, 1982. Sakai maintains that his was the only one of the Tainan Kū's fifteen *shōtai* that had no officers assigned. However, at the time of the attack on the Philippines two weeks later, there were, including Sakai's, *five shōtai* composed only of noncommissioned officers. Flight Petty Officers 1st Class Toshiyuki Sakai, Yoshimichi Saeki, Yasuhisa Sato, and Yoshio Koike led the others (Hideki Shingō to author, June 16, 1982).

47. Shingō recalled that his Tainan Kū had forty-five first-line pilots organized into fifteen *shōtai* at the time of the strafing contest (Shingō to author, Feb. 8, 1982). On Nov. 20, the Tainan Kū had been expanded from three *buntai* of Zero fighters (a total of twenty-seven) to four (totaling thirty-six). See SRN 115840, Nov. 20, 1941, RG 457, Translations of Intercepted Japanese Naval Messages, NARA C. P. A fifth *buntai* evidently was added prior to the competition in late November.

48. Sakai, *Ohzora,* 103, 104; Shingō to author, Feb. 8, 1982.

49. Kurosawa interview, 1:109; Yokoyama, *Ah Zero-sen,* 102–105; Hata and Izawa, *Japanese Naval Aces,* 123.

50. Yokoyama, *Ah Zero-sen,* 105.

51. McKenzie Diary, Nov. 26, 1941; Ind, *Bataan,* 76–77. Brereton erroneously reports his return date as November 28 (*Diaries,* 30–31). The numbers of P-40Bs and B-18s in commission are as of October 31 (Lewis Brereton to AGWAR, radiogram, Nov. n.d., 1941, AG 452.1 (5-21-40), RG 407, AG Central Decimal Files, 1940–42, NARA.

52. Eubank interview; American Ex-Prisoners of War, "The 200th Coast Artillery (AA) and its 'Child,' the 515th Coast Artillery (AA)," Arlington, Tex., 1976, copy in author's collection, 2.

53. MacArthur Diary, Nov. 27, 1941; Brereton, *Diaries,* 30–31; MacArthur to Marshall, Nov. 29, 1941; Lewellyn to wife, Nov. 27, 1941. Although Brereton recalled in his *Diaries* that he had asked MacArthur for "a delay of a week" and accordingly had scheduled his departure for Monday, December 8, MacArthur informed Marshall in his letter of November 29 that "I am sending him immediately" on the new mission, a statement that is in accord with Lewellyn's starting date as indicated to his wife.

54. Brereton, *Diaries,* 31, 33; HQ, FEAF to COs, memo, Nov. 28, 1941, "Readiness Status of Far East Air Force," RG 2, MMA. There is no documentation to confirm the decision to cancel Brereton's mission to Singapore and the Dutch East Indies, but with a Japanese attack considered to be a distinct likelihood, MacArthur would not have wanted his air force commander away at such a critical time. It is most likely that the question of Brereton's mission would have come up during their discussions that day, and I have so assumed here.

55. HQ, FEAF, to COs, Nov. 28, 1941.

56. Brereton was adhering to the agreement reached with Sutherland and MacArthur that only part of his bomber force would be located at Del Monte—and even then only temporarily (Brereton, *Diaries,* 32). See also Bartsch, "Was MacArthur Ill-Served?" 50–51.

57. HQ, FEAF, memo, Dec. 18, 1941; Reginald Vance, narrative provided to author, July 22, 1980; Brereton, *Diaries,* 33; Eubank interview. These command changes probably occurred before November 29, although there is no documentation of them. By December 8, the changes involving George and Gregg were definitely in effect (Walter D. Edmonds, *They Fought with What They Had,* 37–38). Gregg's last letter home was dated November 22, when he was still incapacitated following the removal of teeth. Maverick's position is referred to in his December 1, 1941, letter to his wife. In the narrative he provided to me, Vance indicated that Brereton made him his G2 because the FEAF commander wanted a rated pilot in every staff position. He appointed Vance commander of the 27th Group just for the trip to the Philippines in order to get him into the G2 position.

58. USAFFE Special Orders 83, Nov. 29, 1941; and Special Orders 82, Nov. 28, 1941, both in RG 2, MMA; Courtney Kruger, telephone interview by author, Dec. 10, 2001. According to Kruger, 2d Lt. Edgar H. Heald, HQ Squadron, 19th Bomb Group, led the detachment. MacArthur indicated to Marshall "the initial location of the Bomber Command will be in the vicinity of Del Monte, Mindanao" (letter, Nov. 29, 1941). Special Orders 83, issued the same day MacArthur wrote to Marshall, was evidently intended to set in motion this decision reached between FEAF HQ and USAFFE by first sending the 19th Group's ground echelon (minus one squadron), and following up with the dispatch of the B-17s and their flight crews (Bartsch, "Was MacArthur Ill-Served?" 51). Curiously enough, the order indicates the *full strength* of the 19th Group and the two pursuit squadrons subject to the move, rather than of the ground echelon only. However, MacArthur changed his mind three days later and canceled the order dispatching the ground echelons of the 19th Group and the 3d and 17th Pursuit Squadrons to Del Monte (USAFFE Special Orders 85, Dec. 2, 1941, RG 2, MMA). It is not known whether this new order was initiated by Brereton or MacArthur.

59. Fisch to wife, Nov. 30, 1941; "27th Reports"; "Annual 'Big Game' Party at Army-Navy Club Nov. 29/30," *Manila Tribune,* Nov. 27, 1941.

60. "27th Reports," 13; *Manila Tribune,* Nov. 27, 1941.

61. George Armstrong to wife, Nov. 30, 1941; Sheppard to parents, Nov. 25, 1941.

62. Arthur E. Hoffmann, interview, Mar. 23, 1946, Edmonds Collection; Thomas Caswell to author, Feb. 19, 1994; Cappelletti, "Overseas Log"; idem., interview by author, June 27, 1982. The exact date of the meeting is not documented, but Hoffmann refers to it as coming "after Brereton's speech to commanding officers in Manila" and Cappelletti as "towards the end of November."

63. Caswell to author; Norman Lewellyn to parents, Nov. 28, 1941; Cappelletti, "Overseas Log."

64. Cappelletti, "Overseas Log"; Hofmann interview; Eugene Greeson to author, Sept. 23, 1981.

65. William P. Fisher, interview by AAF historians, 1942, Edmonds Collection; Maverick interview; William Mason, interview by William Priestley, Cabanatuan POW Camp, 1943, Priestley Papers; John Smith interview; Fisher to author, Oct. 12, 1981. Fisher was one of the pilots with B-17 experience transferred to the 28th, along with squadron mates Dick Carlisle, Clyde Box, and Fred Crimmins of the 93d, and Al Mueller of the 30th. I ascertained the names of transferred pilots by comparing the October 31 28th Bomb Squadron roster with the 19th Bomb Group Association's December 8 roster. No documentation exists on the exact number of B-17s transferred to the 28th Squadron for transition training. Its commander at the time recalls there were five, which matches the number of B-17 first pilots reassigned to the 28th (William P. Fisher to author, Oct. 12, 1981).

66. Cecil Combs, interview, Apr. 25, 1945, Edmonds Collection.

67. Robert Michie to author, Aug. 15, 1982; William Ambrosius to wife, Nov. 28, 1941. Michie recalled that five others also passed, but they were from Class 41-B (Willis Gary, Herb Glover, Dick Haney, and Jim Hilton) and 40-H (Hugh Halbert), who evidently had been tested earlier. The six recently arrived Class 41-G pilots were not tested because of their inexperience and remained with the 28th Squadron.

68. Ambrosius to wife, Nov. 28, 1941; Fisch to wife, Nov. 6, 1941.

69. Krieger to father, Nov. 2 and 7, 1941; Ellis to author, Sept. 17, 1979, and Nov. 12, 1980.

70. Ellis narrative, Jan. 13, 1980; Neri to wife, Nov. 2, 1941; Krieger to father, Nov. 2, 1941.

71. C. J. Wimer, "Report on Enemy Air Activities over the Philippines up to and Including the First Day of War, As Observed by S.C. Radar," quoted in Thompson et al., *Signal Corps,* 13; Henry Brodginski, interview no. 2 by William Priestley, Cabanatuan POW Camp, 1943, Priestley Papers.

72. WD, Technical Manual 11-1100, 1–8.

73. Jack Rogers and James Bitner, taped memoir provided to author, June 15, 1986.

74. Brodginski interview no. 2; Charles Heffron, interview by William Priestley, Cabanatuan POW Camp, 1943, Priestley Papers. The Japanese navy's Takao communications unit on Formosa, which had been monitoring radio messages from Clark-based B-17s and Patrol Wing 10 PBYs on its radio direction finding equipment since November 17, also noted the falloff in flights from Clark ("Takao Special Intelligence Report No. 1," SRN 116645, Nov. 18, 1941, RG 457, Translations of Intercepted Japanese Naval Messages, NARA C. P.

CHAPTER 8: "STRUCK BY ITS RESEMBLANCE TO A RAILROAD TIMETABLE"

1. Cappelletti, "Overseas Log"; O'Bryan, interview. The exact date of the alert is not given, but it would have been between when the 19th Group went on alert (November 28) and when the 93d departed for Del Monte (December 5). The 93d was down to eight B-17s from its original ten following the late November transfers.

2. Edson Sponable, interview by author, July 23, 1993; anonymous, "Personal Diary" (probably maintained by 2d Lt. James Colovin of the 30th Squadron), Edmonds Collection. Kurtz won a bronze medal in diving at the 1932 summer Olympics.

3. Brereton, *Diaries,* 34–35; Brereton draft diary, 19; Douglas MacArthur to George C.

Marshall, radiogram, Nov. 28, 1941; and Francis Brady to Richard K. Sutherland, memo, Dec. 1, 1941, USAFFE G3 Journal, both in RG 2, MMA; HQ, FEAF, memo, Dec. 18, 1941. Admiral Hart apparently did not consider reconnoitering Formosa an overt act, however, having sent PATWING 10's PBYs over the Japanese-occupied island as noted in chapter 7. Such reconnaissance was carried out in October and November—*before* Marshall's "war warning" message was received.

4. AG to Douglas MacArthur, radiogram 618, Nov. 26, 1941, WPD 4544-9, RG 165, NARA D.C.; idem., radiogram 679, Dec. 3, 1941, Project Geographic, 580, PD (12-3-41), RG 407, AG Classified Decimal Files, 1940–42, NARA D.C.; Douglas MacArthur to (Lt. Col. Francis G.) Brink, Singapore, radiogram, Dec. 2, 1941, RG 2, MMA; Maurer Maurer, "A Delicate Mission: Aerial Reconnaissance of Japanese Islands before World War II," *Military Affairs* 26, no. 2 (summer, 1962): 66–68, 69. The plan to send B-24s on high-altitude photorecon missions over Japanese territory originated with Arnold in a morning conference with Marshall and his top three WPD officers on November 26. Arnold proposed sending the two B-24s and Marshall agreed. Marshall clearly was not really concerned about the risk of being caught in an "overt act" against the Japanese. In making this decision, the advice of Col. Charles Bundy, a WPD staff member who told the conference attendees "allowing planes to fly over Formosa constituted an overt act," was discounted ("Conference in the Office of the Chief of Staff, 10:40 A.M., Nov. 26, 1941," WDCSA/381, Philippines [12-4-41], RG 165, Top Secret General Correspondence 1941–47, NARA D.C.).

5. Sakai, *Ohzora,* 104–105; Tainan Kōkūtai Hikōtai Sentō Kodo Chosho (Tainan Kū Aircraft Echelon Combat Log) (hereafter Tainan Kū SKC), Dec. 2, 1941; SRN 116768, Nov. 27, 1941; and SRN 116840, Dec. 3, 1941, RG 457, Translations of Intercepted Japanese Naval Messages, NARA C. P.; Shimakawa, *Zero-sen,* 81, 104.

6. Mori, *Kaigun,* 2:165; Sakai, *Ohzora,* 105; Seiji Ozaki to author, Dec. 29, 1980. Sakai recalled that the Tainan base commander called the meeting for bomber and fighter crews alike, but Mori indicates it was for fighter pilots only and provides more convincing detail.

7. Izawa, "Rikkō and Ginga," 46, app. 1; Francillon, *Japanese Aircraft,* 386; Seiji Ozaki to author, Dec. 29, 1980; SRN 115535, Nov. 16, 1941, RG 457, Translations of Intercepted Japanese Naval Messages, NARA C. P. Ozaki indicates that the training was completed November 23, but the intercepted radio message says the special bombing training was to be completed by November 18.

8. *Senshi Sōsho,* 24:158–59, 163; SRN 116608, Oct. 12, 1941; SRN 116585, Oct. 13, 1941; SRN 116265, Oct. 18, 1941; SRN 116267, Oct. 31, 1941; SRN 117140, Nov. 6, 1941; SRN 117052, Nov. 8, 1941, and SRN 115535, Nov. 16, 1941; Izawa, "Rikkō and Ginga," 51; Tagaya, "Technical Development," 36–37; idem. to author, Apr. 9, 2001.

9. Interview of Capt. Bunzo Shibata, USSBS interrogation no. 424, Nov. 18, 1945, in USSBS (Pacific), *Interrogations of Japanese Officials,* 2:379; Izawa, "Rikkō and Ginga," 52; Tagaya, "Technical Development," 37; Rene J. Francillon, *Mitsubishi G4M "Betty" and Ohka Bomb,* Aircraft Profile no. 210, 109, 112.

10. Lewis Brereton to Henry H. Arnold, Dec. 1, 1941, RG 18, AAG 400-Miscellaneous-A (Philippines), NARA D.C.; Bartsch, *Doomed,* 42, 43, 47; Crawford to Gerow; Duncan (A4) to AG, memo, Nov. 27, 1941 (approved by Arnold, Nov. 29, 1941), 254 Philippines, Arnold Papers.

11. George C. Marshall to Henry H. Arnold, memo, Dec. 1, 1941, 254 Philippines, Arnold Papers; Spaatz Diary, Air Staff meeting, Dec. 1, 1941; Maj. Edward P. Curtis to AC/S, G4, Dec. 10, 1941, Decimal Files, 1940–45, SAS 471.6, Arnold Papers; Spaatz Diary, Nov. 5, 1941; Duncan (A4) to AG, memo, Nov. 27, 1941.

12. Laurence Kuter to secretary, GS, secret memo, Dec. 4, 1941, "Air Objectives in Japan," WDCSA/381/Philippines, RG 165, Top Secret Correspondence, 1941–42, NARA D.C.

13. Spaatz Diary, Air Staff meeting, Dec. 4, 1941; Carl Spaatz to A1, A2, A3, and A4, memo, Dec. 5, 1941, 381 War Plans, RG 18, Central Decimal Files, ser. 2, 1939–42, NARA D.C.; Crawford to Gerow. I have assumed that this "Strategical Estimate" is the plan to which Colonel George referred the previous day.

14. "Philippine Narrative of Henry G. Thorne, Jr.," n.d., 1947, Edmonds Collection, 1–2; Bogart, "Radar in the Philippines," 27; Brodginski interview no. 2; Bartsch, Doomed, 38–39. It has not been possible to match these bogies with references from Japanese records. The Eleventh Air Fleet was patrolling from Formosa during this period, however (Senshi Sōsho, 24:171).

15. Thorne, "Philippine Narrative," 2–3; Bartsch, Doomed, 39; Richard K. Sutherland, interview, June 4, 1945, Edmonds Collection; (Lt. Col. William F.) Marquat, USAFFE, to CG, Harbor Defenses, Fort Mills, radiogram, Dec. 5, 1941, RG 2, MMA. I have been unable to identify who made these night intrusions. The reconnaissance planes of the Tainan and 3d Kōkūtai flew only daylight missions, as noted earlier.

16. Thorne, "Philippine Narrative," 3; Bartsch, Doomed, 39–40.

17. Joe Bean (Kelly's navigator), interview by Richard Haney, Dec. 13, 1991; Robert Altman, telephone interview by author, May 6, 1997.

18. James Halkyard, telephone interview by author, May 7, 1997. Lieutenant Colonel Eubank most likely sanctioned the intrusion into Formosa airspace before takeoff, but there is no documentation that such permission was given. In a 1945 interview, Eubank did not acknowledge ordering any flights over Formosa. However, he stated that "some fliers were supposed to have exceeded the letter of their orders" not to cross the international boundary (Eubank interview). A B-17 from the 93d Squadron also flew near Formosa about the same time, and when it dipped below the cloud cover at about a thousand feet found itself over a "Japanese invasion fleet" (Vincent Snyder, interview by author, Feb. 11, 1994). The B-17 apparently flew near Mako in the Pescadores, fifty miles northwest of the Japanese base at Tainan, where transports, cruisers, and destroyers were preparing to deliver troops for landings at Vigan and Aparri scheduled for December 10 (Reports of General MacArthur, vol. 2, pt. 1, plate 18, 89; Hattori, Complete History, 2:32–34. A private in the 30th Bomb Squadron recalled years later that B-17s were flying over Formosa at the time and that "reports started to trickle down from the crews that there appeared to be many airfields on the island and that they were saturated with aircraft" (Lyle G. Knudson, "Things I Remember," memoir, n.d., 16–17).

19. The floatplane was probably from one of the cruisers anchored in Takao Bay. Kelly's three surviving crewmembers gave different accounts of this incident, but all agreed that their ship flew up to and over at least the southern tip of Formosa. Joe Bean agreed with Halkyard that a Japanese plane attacked their ship, but while Bean claims that it "shot some holes in the left wing and fuselage," Halkyard maintains that no hits were scored (Bean and Halkyard interviews). Radioman Bob Altman denied that a Japanese plane attacked them. Both Altman and Halkyard also deny that photographs were taken, as maintained by Bean (Altman, Bean, and Halkyard interviews).

20. Jacquet Diary. Eubank's attitude toward overflights of Formosa is speculative on my part. To add to his woes that day, Eubank suffered a broken left wrist when a taxi struck his staff car while he was on his way to (from?) FEAF HQ (ibid.).

21. Brereton, Diaries, 36; Edmonds, They Fought, 34–35; Lawrence Churchill to CO Del Monte HQ, radiogram, Dec. 5, 1941, 6:07 P.M., Emmett O'Donnell Papers, Special Collections (hereafter O'Donnell Papers); Courtney Kruger, telephone interview by author, Dec. 10, 2001; Ed Jackfert, "The History of the U.S. Army Air Corps in the Philippine Islands," in 19th Bomb Group Association, 19th Bomb Group, 10–11.

22. USAFFE Special Orders 85, Dec. 2, 1941; Eubank interview; O'Donnell interview, July 2, 1945.

23. Jacquet Diary; Jacquet to author, Apr. 22, 1981; Cappelletti, "Overseas Log"; O'Bryan interview; Bibin to author; Teats, "Turn of the Tide"; Arthur E. Norgaard, interview, Mar. 2, 1945; Earl R. Tash, interview, Feb. 26, 1945; and Raymond T. Elsmore, interview, June 2, 1945, all three in the Edmonds Collection. Cappelletti recorded there were 8 B-17s from the 93d Squadron and 7 from the 14th Squadron in the flight, whereas O'Bryan recalled there being 8 from the 14th and 7 from the 93d. Bibin remembered that each squadron sent 8, as did Eubank.

24. Sakai, *Ohzora,* 105. Shimada indicates the final plan was issued on December 6 and also apparently set the date and time ("Opening Air Offensive," 86). It appears the Eleventh Air Fleet HQ left out the date and time in copies distributed to the officers of the *kōkūtai* participating in the attacks.

25. Shimada, "Opening Air Offensive," 86; 3d Kū SKC, Dec. 8, 1941; Shimakawa, *Zero-sen,* 81–82; Mori, *Kaigun,* 2:175; Hideki Shingō to author, Feb. 27, 1979.

26. Sakai, *Ohzora,* 104; idem. to author, Aug. 10, 1982; "3d Kōkūtai Hikōtai Sentō Kodo Chosho" (3d Kū Aircraft Echelon Flight Log), (hereafter 3d Kū SKC), Dec. 5, 1941

27. Bartsch, *Doomed,* 40–42

28. Brereton, *Diaries,* 37; Jacquet Diary; diary of William A. Fairfield, 7th Materiel Squadron (hereafter Fairfield Diary); Cappelletti, "Overseas Log"; Hoffmann interview; William Marrocco Diary, 4. Brereton gives December 6 as the date of his talk, but most of the attendees recalled that it was in late November. Despite Brereton's assertion that he did not, there is some question as to whether the FEAF had photos of southern Formosa bases in its possession (see chapter 11).

29. Robert H. Arnold, *A Rock and a Fortress,* 4–9; idem. to author, Apr. 26, 1980; Jack Rogers, interview by author, May 10, 1986; Thomas interview; Samuel E. Goldy, interview by William Priestley, Cabanatuan POW Camp, 1943, Priestley Papers; Louis Goldbrum to author, Apr. 11, 1984.

30. Wimer, "Signal Corps Radar Units," 12–13; USAFFE Special Orders 84, Dec. 1, 1941, RG 2, MMA; Ted Williams, *Rogues of Bataan,* 11–14; Bogart, "Radar in the Philippines," 29–31.

31. Wesley F. Craven and James L. Cate, eds., *The AAF in World War II,* vol. 1, *Plans and Early Operations,* 193; Arnold, *Global Mission,* 268; "Telegram from General Arnold re Status of B-17s Scheduled for the Far East," entry 422, executive 4, RG 165, WPD Executive Files, 1939–42, NARA D.C.; Crawford to Gerow; Spaatz Diary, Air Staff meetings, Nov. 26 and Dec. 4, 1941.

32. Arnold, *Global Mission,* 268; Maurer, "Delicate Mission," 72–73, 74; Edmonds, *They Fought,* 7; Craven and Cate, eds., *Plans and Early Operations,* 1:268.

33. Tash interview; Norgaard interview; Floyd Deterding, taped narrative provided to author, Aug. 11, 1993 (fixing the date of the mission). Eubank could not confirm whether Gibbs flew over Formosa or not (Eubank interview). Deterding, at the time a staff sergeant serving as radio operator on the flight, later recalled coming within sight of Formosa, but not flying over it. Both Tash and Norgaard were from the 93d Squadron and based at Del Monte at the time.

34. Bartsch, *Doomed,* 48; Gerow to secretary of war, memo, Oct. 2, 1941, "Personnel and Supplies for the Philippines," WPD 4561-2, Stimson Top Secret File, RG 107, NARA D.C.; Cave, *Beyond Courage,* 51; Nov. 29, 1941 USAFFE order to CO, 200th Coast Artillery Regiment (Antiaircraft), cited in Richard Connaughton, *MacArthur and Defeat in the Philippines,* 153–54; Zenon Bardowski to author, Dec. 6, 1982; Ernest B. Miller, *Bataan Uncensored,* 65.

35. Benjamin F. Kimmerle, undated (1946?) memoir, Special Collections, Research Division, U.S. Air Force Museum, Wright-Patterson Air Force Base, Ohio (hereafter Kimmerle memoir); Eubank interview; Kenneth R. Kreps, interview, Jan. 17, 1945, Edmonds Collection; Edgar D. Whitcomb to author, May 21, 1994; Howard Harper, telephone interview by author, Dec. 28, 2001.

36. James E. Madden to author, Dec. 9, 1981, Jan. 28, 1982, and Feb. 20, 1982; idem., taped narrative provided to author, Feb. 20, 1982; Eugene Franklin to author, Feb. 6, 1982; Ronald Dickson to author, Nov. 1 and Dec. 23, 1981; George Armstrong to author, Apr. 24, 1979; Thorne, "Philippine Narrative," 3; William Sheppard and Edwin Gilmore, narrative, Nov. 1, 1944–Feb. 1, 1945, Edmonds Collection. Madden, Franklin, and Dickson confirmed the existence of a Teletype machine in the group operations hangar.

37. Moore to author, Mar. 8, 1979; idem., interview by Toland; idem., interview by author, June 11, 1981; Milton Woodside, interview by William Priestley, Cabanatuan POW Camp, 1943, Priestley Papers; Samuel A. Goldblith, "The 803rd Engineers in the Philippine Defense," *Military Engineer,* Aug., 1942, 323–25.

38. Michie to author, Aug. 15 and Sept. 10, 1982; Hugh Halbert to author, Nov. 29, 1993; Maverick interview.

39. Bartsch, *Doomed,* 46–47; Ellis to author, Sept. 17, 1979; idem., narrative provided to author, 1979; William Sheppard to author, Nov. 26, 1988.

40. Bartsch, *Doomed,* 43–45. There is disagreement on the number of P-40Es delivered to the 21st Pursuit Squadron by December 8. The author accepts the figure of twenty-two, as indicated by Dyess in a 1943 interview (Ed Dyess, interview by William Priestley, Cabanatuan POW Camp, 1943, Priestley Papers). Twenty-four, serial numbers 40-615 through 40-658, had been delivered to the Philippines.

41. Dyess interview; Samuel C. Grashio to author, May 19, 1981; Maj. Ben Brown, "Statement," Oct. 25, 1944, Edmonds Collection; Frankie Bryant to author, Jan. 10, 1979; Thomas Gage to author, Oct. 6, 1978; Claude Paulger, interview by Calvin Chunn, Cabanatuan POW Camp, n.d., 1942, box 1443, RG 407, Philippines Records, NARA D.C..

42. "Softball at Forbes Field," *Manila Sunday Tribune,* Dec. 7, 1941; "27th Reports," 15; Maurer, ed., *Air Force Combat Units,* 385–86; Bert Schwarz, telephone interview by author, May 20, 1997; Norman Tant, interview by William Priestley, Cabanatuan POW Camp, 1943, Priestley Papers. For a thorough analysis of Brereton's professional and personal traits, see Roger G. Miller, "A 'Pretty Damn Able Commander'—Lewis Hyde Brereton," pt. 1, *Air Power History* 47, no. 4 (winter, 2000); and pt. 2, *Air Power History* 48, no. 1 (spring, 2001). A telephone call from the AWS to Brereton at the party was most likely the reason for his visit to the AWS later that night, although Brereton does not refer to it in his autobiography. Tant, a private in the 409th Signal (Aviation) Company assigned to the cryptography section of the message center, was on duty at the time and recalled Brereton's presence during the plotting operation that evening (Norman Tant to author, June 4, 1981).

43. Brereton, *Diaries,* 38. According to Brereton, a "combat alert" required the bombers to be bombed up and crews briefed and ready for takeoff "in a little over an hour," while the pursuit pilots were to be briefed, assembled, and ready for takeoff "in a little under an hour." (Brereton, *Diaries,* 38 n 9). Brereton indicates that the "combat alert" order he gave derived from a meeting he had with Sutherland that evening at which he was informed war might break out at any moment (*Diaries,* 38). He does not mention being at the 27th Group party that night, nor being at AWS to track Japanese intruders. There is no other documentation suggesting that Brereton met with his staff that evening.

44. Shimakawa, *Zero-sen,* 82; Sakai, *Ohzora,* 106. Sakai says forty-five pilots were at the meeting, but Maki's *buntai* of nine pilots had been sent over to Takao to fly with the 3d Air Group for the December 8 mission. In addition, the Tainan Kū had fifteen reserve pilots (Shingō to author, Feb. 8, 1982). The commanders of all five *kōkūtai* of *rikkō* taking part in the Philippines attack met with their flying personnel to announce the date of the attack (Tagaya, "Technical Development," 38).

45. Sakai, *Ohzora,* 106; Shimakawa, *Zero-sen,* 83–84, 85.

46. Yokoyama, *Ah Zero-sen,* 106; Mori, *Kaigun,* 2:175. Details of the battle plan provided to Yokoyama have been added here, based on Shimada ("Opening Air Offensive," 90), including takeoff time, and the 3d Kū SKC, Dec. 8, 1941 entry, with regard to targets.

47. Kurosawa interview, 1:110; Tagaya, "Technical Development," 38; *Senshi Sōsho,* 24:173–74; Izawa, "Rikkō and Ginga," 54. The *Senshi Sōsho* indicates the takeoff time for all Philippine attack groups was 1:30 A.M., but Shimada maintains their takeoff was at 2:30 ("Opening Air Offensive," 90). The *Senshi Sōsho* must be referring to the extra hour the 1st Ku's slower *rikkō* needed to reach their target and thus would have had to depart much earlier than the other attack groups. Shimada is referring to the *Takao-based* groups, which would require only four hours to reach their targets—including the time-consuming positioning in night formation after takeoff.

48. Shimada, "Opening Air Offensive," 89, 90; *Senshi Sōsho,* 24:174; Mori, *Kaigun,* 2:163; Miza, "Meritorius Deeds," 126–29. Shimada recalled only one plane on each of the two recon missions, but the *Senshi Sōsho* and Mori cite two each. The hours cited are Philippines time, which is an hour earlier than Tokyo time. Japanese naval forces on Formosa followed Tokyo time.

49. Mori, *Kaigun,* 2:182; Hata and Izawa, *Japanese Naval Aces,* 31–32; *Senshi Sōsho,* 24:52.

50. SRN 116328, Nov. 11, 1941; SRN 117029, Nov. 11, 1941; SRN 117740, Nov. 18, 1941; SRN 116784, Nov. 22, 1941; SRN 115492, Nov. 24, 1941; SRN 116734, Nov. 28, 1941; and SRN 116969, Dec. 2, 1941; *Senshi Sōsho,* 24:52, 155, 171; Mori, *Kaigun,* 2:182.

51. Wimer, "Enemy Air Activities," 13; Record of phone conversation between Gerow and MacArthur, Dec. 7, 1941, WPD 4622, RG 165, WPD General Correspondence, 1940–42, NARA D.C.; Bartsch, *Doomed,* 48. Wimer later recalled that the pickup was made "before midnight," while MacArthur told Gerow that the radar had detected "a bomber squadron" off the Luzon coast between 11:30 P.M. and midnight on December 7. Hank Thorne recalled it as being about 1 A.M., but that appears to have been too late. Considering that the two 1st Weather Reconnaissance planes left Takao at 8:30 P.M., and allowing for a three-hour flight in the slow G3Ms, they would have arrived north of Iba around 11:30 P.M. and were evidently the bogies picked up (Shimada, "Opening Air Offensive," 90; Mori, *Kaigun,* 2:163; *Senshi Sōsho,* 24:174). According to the *Senshi Sōsho,* by 12:30 they had reached a point twenty-five nautical miles off Corregidor (24:175).

Part IV: "I Shall Die Only for the Emperor, I Shall Never Look Back"

1. Prange, *At Dawn We Slept,* 486–87, 488–89, 493–95.

2. Leonard T. Gerow for the AG (through the SGS), memo, Dec. 7, 1941, Subject: Far East Situation (instructing dispatch of the message), AG 381 (12-7-41), RG 407, AG Central Decimal Files, 1940–42, NARA D.C.

3. Prange, *At Dawn We Slept,* 504; John Prados, *Combined Fleet Decoded,* 185; John Lundstrom to author, July 27, 2001; Toland, *Rising Sun,* 222. Prange says Fuchida's signal was a voice message, but Prados, more logically given the transmission distances involved, says it was sent by key. Lundstrom confirms the message was sent out by key by Fuchida's radio operator, POIc Mizuki Tokunobu. I assume the relayed message was received right after Fuchida sent it out.

4. Toland, *Rising Sun,* 204; Hattori, *Complete History,* 2:1. Prange indicates that the originally scheduled attack time was 6:30 and was later changed to 8 A.M. (*At Dawn We Slept,* 322). *Senshi Sōsho* (24:398) indicates that the landing operation only began at 1:35 and that the troops went ashore "shortly after 0200" rather than at 1:30 as per an IGHQ/Army message. The Singora and Patani landings took place at 4:12 A.M. and "about 0430," respectively—after the Pearl Harbor attack (24:403, 406).

5. Gerow for the AG, Dec. 7, 1941. The air raid on Pearl Harbor commenced at 1:25 P.M. Washington time, equivalent to 7:55 A.M. Hawaii time.

6. John J. Beck, *MacArthur and Wainwright: Sacrifice of the Philippines,* 11; Paul P. Rogers, *The Good Years: MacArthur and Sutherland,* 94; MacArthur Diary, Dec. 8, 1941; Douglas MacArthur to George C. Marshall, radiogram, Dec. 8, 1941, RG 2, MMA. The message to which MacArthur referred was radiogram 733 from Marshall, sent out at 12:05 P.M. Washington time. The

"unnumbered RCA message" would have been cablegram 736 recorded by the WD as going out of its message room, but apparently passed to RCA for transmission. Citing the copy of this message marked WPD 4544-20, Beck indicates it was received by MacArthur at 7:30 A.M., rather than 5:30, as MacArthur indicated in the message (*MacArthur and Wainright,* 12).

7. "Record of Telephone Conversation between Gen. Gerow, WPD, and Gen. MacArthur in Manila, P.I., about 7:00 P.M.," Dec. 7, 1941, WPD 4622, RG 165, WPD General Correspondence, 1940–42, NARA D.C. MacArthur was responding off the top of his head on the times the two messages were received. In a subsequent radiogram to Washington (see note 9 below) he indicated they were received at 4:30 and 5:30 A.M., respectively (MacArthur to Marshall, Dec. 8, 1941).

8. "Record of Telephone Conversation." MacArthur failed to inform Gerow that his G2 had received a message at 6:15 A.M. advising that Davao on Mindanao had been attacked (USAFFE G2 Journal, 6:15 A.M. entry, RG 2, MMA). At dawn, a Japanese naval landing force went ashore on Batan Island, midway between Formosa and Luzon, and seized the airfield there. This act of aggression had not been reported to USAFFE headquarters, probably due to the inadequacy of communications facilities on the tiny island ("An Account of the Imperial Japanese Navy's Activities in the Philippines at the Beginning of War," ATIS 1969C, May 15, 1946, NHC).

9. MacArthur to Marshall, radiogram, Dec. 8, 1941. The time the radiogram was dispatched is my own estimate, based on the fact that Baguio was bombed at 8:25 A.M. (USAFFE G2 Journal, 8:25 A.M. entry). MacArthur is in error regarding interceptors being in contact with Japanese aircraft north of Clark Field. His patrolling P-40s completely missed finding the Japanese bombers (see chap. 10).

10. *Reports of General MacArthur,* vol. 2, pt. 1, 43, and plate 1, xiv.

11. Ibid., 43.

12. HQ, FEAF, "General Brereton's Headquarters Diary: Summary of the Activities for the Period from 8th Dec. '41–24th Feb. '42" (hereafter cited as FEAF Activities Summary), 1 P.M., Dec. 8, 1941, Brereton Papers, Dwight D. Eisenhower Library, Abilene, Kans.; Richard K. Sutherland, "Brief Summary of Action in the Office of the Chief of Staff, Headquarters, U.S. Army Forces in the Far East, 8:58 A.M. Dec. 8, 1941 to 11:00 P.M., Feb. 22, 1942," (hereafter cited as Sutherland Summary), 1:10 P.M. entry, RG 2, MMA.

13. Leonard T. Gerow for the AG, memo, Subject: Philippine Situation (sent as radiogram 746 to CG, USAFFE, Dec. 8, 1941), AG 381 (12-8-41), RG 407, NARA D.C. I have assumed this radiogram was sent in the early morning of December 8 and thus would have reached MacArthur in the early evening of the same day.

14. Adams to CG, USAFFE, radiogram 749, Dec. 8, 1941, AG 381 (12-8-41), RG 407, NARA D.C.

15. Douglas MacArthur to AG, radiogram 1133, Dec. 8, 1941, AG 381 (12-8-41), RG 407, NARA D.C. Beck (*MacArthur and Wainright,* 16) indicates the message was sent "later that night." A time of 12:14 P.M., December 8, is recorded by the WD Message Center on its decoded copy—equivalent to 1:14 A.M., December 9, in Manila.

16. Douglas MacArthur to AGWAR, unnumbered radiogram, Dec. 10, 1941, RG 2, MMA; Arnold, *Global Mission,* 272.

CHAPTER 9: "WHAT A FOG!"

1. Brodginski interview no. 2; Wimer, "Enemy Air Activities," 13; "Report of Phone Conversation between Gerow and MacArthur, Dec. 7, 1941." The identity of the scope operator on duty before Brodginski is unknown.

2. Thorne, "Philippine Narrative," 4; Andrew E. Krieger interview, Jan. 28, 1945; and idem., narrative, n.d. (ca. 1945), both in the Edmonds Collection, AFHRA, 3; 16th Naval District War

Diary, Dec. 8, 1941, RG 2, MMA (hereafter 16th Naval District Diary); Brodginski interview no. 2; Bogart, "Radar in the Philippines," 27.

3. Frank Neri, interview by author, Mar. 29, 1980; Ellis narrative, 1979; Thorne, "Philippine Narrative," 4; Neri interview; Andrew Krieger to Walter D. Edmonds, Nov. 9, 1945, Edmonds Collection, AFHRA.

4. Wimer, "Enemy Air Activities," 13; Neri interview; Ellis narrative, 1979; Andrew E. Krieger, interviews, Jan. 28 and Feb. 23, 1945, Edmonds Collection, AFHRA. At 2 A.M., the 16th Naval District communications center at Cavite received a message stating that the unidentified planes first reported to it at 1:30 were withdrawing (16th Naval District Diary, 2 A.M., Dec. 8, 1941). The aircraft must have been the two Type 96 bombers that had taken off from Takao (*Senshi Sōsho* indicates Tainan, apparently erroneously) at 8:35 P.M. They made a U-turn at a point twenty-five miles from Corregidor to return to base (Mori, *Kaigun*, 2:163; *Senshi Sōsho*, 24:175).

5. Bartsch, *Doomed*, 53; Ind, *Bataan*, 90. Ind says the pickup was at 4 A.M., much later than it actually was.

6. Sheppard and Gilmore narrative, 5; Moore, interview by Toland, 5; Keator Diary, Dec. 8, 1941; Moore, interview by author; Wimer, "Enemy Air Activities," 11-15.

7. Mori, *Kaigun*, 2:162, 163; *Senshi Sōsho*, 24:174; Shimada, "Opening Air Offensive," 86, 90. The Japanese navy on Formosa operated on Japan time, which was one hour later than in the Philippines and on Formosa. All times cited in Japanese accounts of activities on Formosa in Japan time have been converted here to local Formosa/Philippines time. Shimada gives 2:30 A.M. Formosa/Philippines time as the scheduled takeoff time versus 1:30 (2:30 Japan time) in the *Senshi Sōsho* and in Mori's account, which, as explained in chapter 8, refers to the departure of the 1st Ku's slow *rikkō* only, with the others set to follow at 2:30.

8. Japanese sources give different accounts of the substance of the radio messages intercepted by the Takao unit. Mori notes that Manila ordered Iba and Clark Fields to go on fifteen-minute standby at 11:15 P.M., and that at midnight Iba was instructed to shoot down the unidentified planes approaching the field (*Kaigun*, 2:163). Calls from Manila warning Iba and Clark Fields allegedly were picked up at 11:15 (Shimada, "Opening Air Offensive," 90). The *Senshi Sōsho* cites the radio interception message reporting the takeoff of the six P-40s (24:174). This message is the one that most nearly corresponds to the Americans' actual activity.

9. Mori, *Kaigun*, 2:164. On Formosa, 2:30 A.M. on December 8 corresponded to 8 A.M. on December 7 in Hawaii. The Hawaii attack force's takeoff was to commence at 5:50 A.M. Honolulu time, equivalent to 12:20 A.M. on Formosa (Prange, *At Dawn We Slept*, 490).

10. Mori, *Kaigun*, 2:164. This radio intercept implies that Thorne radioed Grover at Clark of the results of the attempted interception, or that the Iba radar detachment radioed the air warning section at Nielson with the same message. Either would appear likely, but there are no American records documenting such a call.

11. Mori, *Kaigun*, 2:164, 168; Shimada, "Opening Air Offensive," 90.

12. Sakai, *Ohzora*, 107; Shimakawa, *Zero-sen*, 85, 87-88. Although Shimakawa recalled that Shingō stated they would have only *ten minutes* of combat time over Clark, Shingō indicated that he allowed for *thirty minutes* (Hideki Shingō to author, Oct. 27, 1980). By removing the forty-four-pound weight of the Zeros' "almost unusable" radios, his pilots would cut gasoline consumption even more, as well as enhance their climbing capability (idem. to author, Sept. 26, 1980).

13. Shimakawa, *Zero-sen*, 88-89; Sakai, *Ohzora*, 107. Apparently Shingō knew that a Japanese force was scheduled to land at Aparri on the morning of December 10.

14. Mori, *Kaigun*, 2:177; Sakai, *Ohzora*, 108; Shimakawa, *Zero-sen*, 89.

15. Mori, *Kaigun*, 2:175; *Senshi Sōsho*, 24:174, 177; Shimada, "Opening Air Offensive," 86, 90. The 4 A.M. hour evidently was for the slow *rikkō* of the 1st Kū at Tainan, with the rest of the Philippines attack force to begin taking off an hour later. Eleventh Air Fleet headquarters erroneously believed that half of the B-17 force was based at Nichols Field, evidently due

to the faulty assumption that the two B-17 squadrons that had left Clark on the evening of December 5–6 were now based at Nichols.

16. Although the change of targets for the 3d and Tainan Kū's Zero-sen is not mentioned in the Eleventh Air Fleet's plans as described by Shimada—or by Mori or the *Senshi Sōsho*—it must have been at this time that Iba replaced Nichols as the objective of the *rikkō's* attack. My assumption corresponds with what actually happened.

17. Shimada, "Opening Air Offensive," 91; *Senshi Sōsho*, 24:177–78. Shimada indicates that the feint plan was not dropped until the takeoff time was reset after the fog finally cleared, but the *Senshi Sōsho* notes that the decision was made when the fog became thick again at 5 A.M., which seems more logical.

18. Mori, *Kaigun*, 2:176; *Senshi Sōsho*, 14:177, 178; Shimada, "Opening Air Offensive," 92; Mori, *Kaigun*, 2:176; Sakai, *Ohzora*, 108; Hata and Izawa, *Japanese Naval Aces*, 123, 132; Military History Section, HQ Army Forces Far East, "Philippines Air Operations," 6–8.

19. Shimada, "Opening Air Offensive," 91, 92; Mori, *Kaigun*, 2:177; Tagaya, "Technical Development," 39–40; idem. to author, Feb. 9, 2001. Shimada says the fog began to lift at 7 A.M., but I have accepted Mori's time of 7:50.

20. Yoshiaki Kubo, *97 Jubaku Ku-sen Ki* (*The Air Combat Saga of the Type 97 Heavy Bomber*), 8–9; Yasuho Izawa, *Nippon Rikūgun Jubaku Tai* (*Japanese Heavy Bomber Units*), 170. Kubo recalled that takeoff was at 4:30 A.M., but Izawa's time is more exact. The Ki-21 could carry up to ten one-hundred-kilogram (220-pound) bombs (Francillon, *Japanese Aircraft*, 163). I have assumed that each 14th Sentai aircraft carried the maximum bomb load.

21. Osahirō Gotō, "Konpeki No Sora Goh Goh To" ("Roar in the Deep Blue Sky"), *Kōkū Fan*, Jan., 1967, 83–84; *Senshi Sōsho*, 34:294. Gotō recalled that thirty-six Ki-48s were assigned the mission, twelve planes to each *chūtai*, but the *Senshi Sōsho* indicates that only twenty-five of the bombers participated in the mission (34:294). The times of the reconnaissance plane's return and the subsequent takeoff of the 8th Sentai bombers are not documented. However, assuming a 2:30 A.M. takeoff, the Ki-15-II would have returned to Formosa at about 5:30 A.M. after making the 730-mile round-trip, Kato–Tuguegarao–Kato.

22. Gotō, "Konpeki," 83–84. Gotō's first name was Kyosato; Osahirō is evidently a pen name (Osamu Tagaya to author, Mar. 31, 2001). The takeoff time is not documented. Gotō recalled that it was "as scheduled at 04:00," but the Ki-15 reconnaissance plane did not return until about 5:30 A.M.

23. Kubo, *97 Jubaku*, 9.

24. Mori, *Kaigun*, 2:182; Hata and Izawa, *Japanese Naval Aces*, 31.

25. Tant interview; idem. to author. Tant recalled the time as being "after 0130," but the Pearl Harbor attack did not commence until 2:30 A.M. Philippines time. He also recalled the message as having been sent by the "Hawaiian Department Commander" (Lt. Gen. Walter Short). However, since it was sent to FEAF HQ rather than to USAFFE HQ, it would appear more likely that Maj. Gen. Frederick L. Martin, the Hawaiian Air Force CG, sent it. There is no documentary evidence of the message in USAFFE records. Tant also recalled giving a copy directly to Colonel George of the 5th Interceptor Command, but George was asleep in his quarters at that hour, as were the G3—Lieutenant Colonell Caldwell—and Brereton himself. I assume Tant gave the message to night duty officers.

26. Harold E. Eads, interview, Aug. 7, 1945, Edmonds Collection; Ind, *Bataan*, 79, 86–87. Eads recollects the call as being received at 3 A.M., but Ind's time (4:17 at the end of the call) appears more logical. I have assumed here that Tant's message was picked up and telephoned to Sprague by a 5th Interceptor Command duty officer.

27. Brereton, *Diaries*, 38–39. Sutherland called MacArthur earlier, at 3:30 A.M., with news of the Pearl Harbor attack (Rogers, *Good Years*, 94). Although there is no documentary evidence of it, Colonel George most likely called Brereton with Sprague's 4:15 message and found that Sutherland had already informed him.

28. Eubank interview; idem. to Mrs. Sky Beaven Phillips, Aug. 13, 1980; and William J. Kennard, interview, Apr. 3, 1945; Edwin B. Broadhurst, interview, Jan. 15, 1945; and William E. McDonald, interview, Jan. 18, 1945, all in the Edmonds Collection. Brereton evidently decided to call Eubank himself, as Eubank later said the call was from Brereton. Kennard does not indicate who the caller was.

29. Brereton, *Diaries*, 38–39; Clark Lee, *They Call It Pacific*, 35–37; Rogers, *Good Years*, 11; William Manchester, *American Caesar*, 207; John Toland, *But Not in Shame*, 40–41. There is no official record of Brereton's visit to USAFFE HQ at that hour. Lieutenant Colonel Francis Wilson, Sutherland's assistant who kept the daily record of Sutherland's activities, did not report in at USAFFE until after 8 A.M., and made his first entry in the "Brief Summary of Action in the Office of the Chief of Staff" that he started that day at 8:58 A.M. (Rogers, *Good Years*, 53, 95). Similarly, the record of events kept at FEAF HQ from December 8 (believed to have been maintained by Brereton's aide, Capt. Norman J. Lewellyn) begins with a 7:15 A.M. entry. Brereton believed that MacArthur was in conference with Admiral Hart, but there is no indication in either MacArthur's office diary or in Hart's papers that the two met that morning (Brereton, *Diaries*, 38).

30. Brereton, *Diaries*, 38–39; Toland, *But Not in Shame*, 40–41. Brereton recalled going to his HQ after visiting USAFFE, but that was not until after his *second* visit to MacArthur's HQ.

31. John W. Carpenter, interview, Jan. 9, 1945, Edmonds Collection; Broadhurst, Eubank, Kreps, and McDonald interviews; anonymous diary (Colovin ?).

32. Raymond Teborek, interview by author, June 2, 1994; idem. to author, Mar. 27, 1981, and June 2, 1994; W. L. White, *Queens Die Proudly*, 16–17.

33. Bartsch, *Doomed*, 60, 61–62.

34. David Obert to author, June 25, 1981; Walter Coss to author, May 6, 1978; Samuel C. Grashio and Jack N. Donahoe, interview, Apr. 2, 1945, Edmonds Collection.

35. Mori, *Kaigun*, 2:184.; Hata and Izawa, *Japanese Naval Aces*, 31–32; Dwight R. Messimer, *In the Hands of Fate: The Story of Patrol Wing Ten, 8 Dec. 1941–11 May 1942*, 41. The seaplane tender was the *William B. Preston* of the Asiatic Fleet, mother ship to three PBYs of PATWING 10, one of which was on patrol at the time. In P-7, a 7.7-mm shell in the head killed the pilot, Ens. Robert G. Tills, instantly. He was the first American killed in the initial attack on the Philippines (Messimer, *In the Hands of Fate*, 40–41).

36. Hata and Izawa, *Japanese Naval Aces*, 32; WDC 161733, "*Ryūjō* Operations," Operational Archives, NHC; Tameichi Hara, *Japanese Destroyer Captain*, 55. Evidently the pilots of the two lost planes were not killed.

37. Ind, *Bataan*, 98. Eubank's arrival time at Nielson assumes a half-hour flight from Clark at sunrise. Eubank later recalled that he flew to Nichols Field, but he must have meant Nielson, where FEAF headquarters was located.

38. Ind, *Bataan*, 91, 92, 93; Eads interview, Aug. 7, 1945; idem., interview, Apr. 6, 1944, Edmonds Collection.

39. Toland, *But Not in Shame*, 41; FEAF Activities Summary, 7:15 A.M. entry. Brereton does not mention this second visit to USAFFE headquarters in his *Diaries*, although it is cited in the FEAF Activities Summary. Toland's source for the visit is Lt. Col. William P. Morse, a USAFFE staff officer who overheard the heated exchange between Sutherland and Brereton (William Morse, interview by John Toland, ca.1958, Toland Papers, LOC). Toland logically assumes this was Brereton's second visit to USAFFE headquarters.

40. Toland, *But Not in Shame*, 41. Brereton, who apparently had not been informed that the Japanese had bombed Davao earlier that morning, which was reported to USAFFE at 6:15 A.M. MacArthur and Sutherland, however, knew about the attack on Davao (G2 Journal, USAFFE, 6:15 A.M. entry, RG 2, MMA). What is not known is why Sutherland and MacArthur did not consider this an overt act against the Philippines and give Brereton the green light to launch an attack on Formosa.

41. Eads interview, Aug. 7, 1945; Ind, *Bataan,* 92; Brereton, *Diaries,* 39.

42. Brereton, *Diaries,* 39; Ind, *Bataan,* 93; HQ, FEAF, Field Order 1, Dec. 8, 1941, RG 2, MMA; FEAF Activities Summary, 11:20 A.M., Dec. 8, 1941. While not specifically mentioned, the Tainan base would also have been included, being located below 23 degrees, 10 minutes north latitude.

43. Arnold, *Global Mission,* 272; Toland, *But Not in Shame,* 42. There is no documentation of this call in Arnold's papers, Brereton's *Diaries,* the FEAF Activities Summary, or other records. Arnold *did* send a message (via the adjutant general) with such a warning to the Philippines, but it was a December 8 radiogram rather than a phone call; MacArthur was the recipient, not Brereton; and it would have been received in the Philippines on the evening of December 8—not during the FEAF morning meeting ([Emory S.] Adams to CG, USAFFE, Dec. 8, 1941).

44. Ind, *Bataan,* 94; Eads interview, Aug. 7, 1945. The 16th Naval District communications center in Manila had received a message at 8:15 A.M. that seventeen unidentified planes had been sighted over San Fernando, headed toward Manila (16th Naval District Diary, Dec. 8, 1941). They would have been the seventeen Type 97 army bombers heading for Baguio, just thirty miles to the southeast. Considering that San Fernando is only ninety-three miles north-northeast of Iba, it appears that the pickup was made by the SCR-270B at Iba, easily within its range of about 150 miles. After being informed by the Iba radar detachment, AWS at Nielson would have alerted Clark Field. MacArthur's office diary records that "high flying planes" were reported to USAFFE "about 08:30" (MacArthur Diary, Dec. 8, 1941). Brereton indicates that he ordered Colonel George to "undertake fighter cover of Clark and Nichols fields" at 9 A.M., but it is more likely that George (in response to the report of approaching planes from the north) made this decision on his own—most likely between 8:15 and 8:30, given the timing of the Iba pickup and transmission to the AWS at FEAF HQ (*Diaries,* 40).

45. Sutherland Summary, 8:50 A.M. entry. A message from Sutherland recorded in the FEAF Activities Summary at 9 A.M.—"Planes not authorized to carry bombs at this time"—evidently refers to Sutherland's 8:50 call.

46. Arnold, *Rock and a Fortress,* 4–6, 8–9; Louis Goldbrum to author, Apr. 22, 1984. Arnold claims that the set *was* operational by the morning of December 8, but four men from his detachment, including the scope operator, say it was not (Goldy interview; George Benedum to author, May 25, 1984; Louis Goldbrum to author, Apr. 11 and June 3, 1984; John Chernitsky [citing William Snyder, the scope operator] to author, June 6, 1994.) The sighting time is my estimate, based on the report that the bombers were over San Fernando at 8:15 A.M., 130 miles due south of Bojeador (USAFFE G2 Journal, 8:15 A.M., Dec. 8, 1941). Arnold recalled seeing "35 Jap bombers," but they must have been the seventeen heading south along the Luzon coastline toward Baguio.

47. Arnold, *Rock and a Fortress,* 9; Heffron interview; Maurice Chartoff to author, Sept. 1, 1994; FEAF Activities Summary, 9:23 A.M., Dec. 8, 1941. Arnold recalled that he then succeeded in telephoning the report in, using Philippine long-distance telephone services that relayed his call to Manila (Arnold to author, Apr. 26, 1980). There is no documentation of any such call being received by the AWS at FEAF HQ.

48. Bartsch, *Doomed,* 62. There is no documentation specifically indicating that these three pursuit squadrons were ordered to intercept, but a 9:10 A.M. entry in the FEAF Activities Summary notes that Colonel George had reported fifty-four airplanes in the air and that no contact had been made with hostile aircraft. The fifty-four planes would have been the eighteen each from the 20th, 17th, and 34th Pursuit Squadrons. Grover's 1942 report on the operations of the 24th Pursuit Group in the Philippines mentions only that the 20th and 17th Pursuit were ordered to intercept (Col. O. L. Grover, HQ, Allied Air Forces Southwest Pacific Area, Brisbane, to chief of staff, GHQ, Southwest Pacific Area, memo, Oct. 7, 1942, "Narrative of the Activities of the 24th Pursuit Group in the Philippine Islands," Edmonds Collection),

but since it is known that the 21st and 3d Pursuit remained on the ground, the third pursuit squadron in the air at the time must have been the 34th. Some of its pilots recall patrolling over Clark Field at this time.

49. Kreps interview. Ind indicates that while Eubank was at FEAF HQ, he made an "emergency call" to Clark Field after being informed of the approach of enemy aircraft, but gave no indication to whom he was speaking (*Bataan,* 94). It apparently was not Gibbs, however, since Eubank later said Gibbs had ordered the 19th Group's bombers aloft on his own (Eubank interview).

50. Whitcomb, *Escape from Corregidor,* 18–19; idem., interview, Mar. 20, 1945, Edmonds Collection; Thompson to author, Feb. 9, 1994; Kreps interview; Hewitt T. Wheless, interview by AAF historians, Apr. 4, 1942, AFHRA; Ray Teborek, taped narrative, Mar. 27, 1981; idem. to author, Aug. 24, 1981.

51. Fairfield Diary; Austin Stitt to Sky Phillips Beaven, Apr. 6, 1974, in *Air Power History* 47, no. 3 (fall, 2000): 28–33; Carpenter interview; idem. to author, Oct. 31, 1982; Francis R. Thompson to author, June 7 and July 16, 1994.

52. Moore to author, Mar. 8, 1979; J. Jack Gates to author, July 4, 1978; Joseph Moore to James E. Brown, Mar. 19, 1978; Whitcomb interview; David L. Obert, *Philippines Defender: A Fighter Pilot's Diary, 1941–42,* 11–12.

53. Tash interview; 19th Bomb Group Diary, Dec. 8, 1941; Eugene L. Eubank to Emmett O'Donnell Jr., Dec. 8, 1941, 5:55 and 8:35 A.M. radiograms, O'Donnell Papers. Tash recalled taking off between 8:30 and 8:35, but the group diary cites his takeoff time as 9:45.

54. Mori, *Kaigun,* 2:177. A B-17 attack was still feared at Takao base, however. An American radio message indicating that an attack on Formosa was being considered was intercepted at 7 A.M. The message said B-17s would arrive over the island at 9:10. When a Japanese army pilot falsely reported at the time specified in the intercepted message that B-17s were approaching Takao, base personnel put on gas masks and prepared for the attack (interview of Comdr. Ryōsuke Nomura, 23d Air Flotilla air operations officer, USSBS interrogation no. 601, Nov. 28, 1945, USSBS (Pacific), *Interrogations of Japanese Officials,* 2:531).

55. Mori, *Kaigun,* 2:177; Shimakawa, *Zero-sen,* 90; Sakai, *Ohzora,* 108. The plane apparently blew a tire during the takeoff roll (Mori, *Kaigun,* 2:177).

56. Mori, *Kaigun,* 2:177; Sakai, *Ohzora,* 109; Shimakawa, *Zero-sen,* 90.

57. Kubo, *97 Jubaku,* 12; G2 Journal, USAFFE, 8:25 A.M. entry; *Senshi Sōsho,* 34:294. Neither Kubo nor the *Senshi Sōsho* indicate the time of the bombing, but the G2 Journal message reported that it occurred at 8:25.

58. Gotō, "Konpeki," 84; *Senshi Sōsho,* 34:294. The USAFFE G2 received a message at 9:30 A.M. stating that Tuguegarao was being raided, while FEAF HQ recorded a 9:23 message from Colonel George reporting that twenty-four twin-engine bombers were near Tuguegarao. These times record when the messages were received, however, not when the events occurred (G2 Journal, USAFFE, 9:30 A.M., Dec. 8, 1941; FEAF Activities Summary, 9:23 A.M., Dec. 8, 1941).

59. *Senshi Sōsho,* 24:181; Shimakawa, *Zero-sen,* 90, 91; Sakai, *Ohzora,* 109; Mori, *Kaigun,* 2:177; Shingō to author, Sept. 26, 1980, and Oct. 17, 1981; Robert C. Mikesh, *Zero Fighter,* 28–29. Shingō assured me that all of his pilots brought their parachutes and sat on them. However, he did not indicate whether they also brought their parachute harnesses (Hideki Shingō to author, Aug. 8, 1981).

60. Mori, *Kaigun,* 2:178; Shimakawa, *Zero-sen,* 9, 85–86, 91.

61. Sakai, *Ohzora,* 108; Hata and Izawa, *Japanese Naval Aces,* 132 (for an illustration of Sakai's Zero); *Senshi Sōsho,* 24:180–81. The list of 3d Kū pilots participating in the December 8 mission (hereafter referred to as 3d Kū pilot list) was provided to me by Maj. Gen. Tamotsu Yokoyama, Japan Self-Defense Force (Ret.), as an attachment to his letter of March 28, 1980.

62. Yokoyama, *Ah Zero-sen,* 107.

CHAPTER 10: "GO GET 'EM!"

1. John L. Brownewell, interview, June 2, 1945, Edmonds Collection; David L. Obert Diary (hereafter Obert Diary); idem. to author, Feb. 5, 1988.

2. Obert Diary; idem. to author, Jan. 25, 1981; idem., "Activities of Fighter Units in the Philippines," Apr. 25, 1945, Edmonds Collection, 1.

3. Lloyd Stinson, narrative provided to author, June 8, 1978; idem., interview by William Priestley, Cabanatuan POW Camp, 1943, Priestley Papers; idem. to author, July 19, 1978; Gates to author, July 4, 1978; Neri interview; William H. Powell Diary (hereafter Powell Diary), copy in author's possession; Thorne, "Philippine Narrative," 6. At 9:31 A.M., FEAF HQ informed the 16th Naval District in Manila that the patrol had made "contact with hostile forces over Clark Field," but this information was incorrect (16th Naval District Diary, 9:31 A.M., Dec. 8, 1941). This report is not cited in the FEAF Activities Summary for December 8.

4. Grashio and Donahoe interview; Samuel C. Grashio and Bernard Norling, *Return to Freedom*, 3; William E. Dyess, *The Dyess Story*, 29–30; Augustus Williams, taped narrative provided to author, May, 1978.

5. Brereton, *Diaries*, 40; Eubank interview; idem. to Mrs. Sky Beaven, Aug. 13, 1980; FEAF Activities Summary, 9:23, 10, and 10:10 A.M., Dec. 8, 1941. The Tarlac and Tuguegarao attacks were reported to USAFFE HQ at 9:30 (USAFFE G2 Journal, 9:30 A.M., Dec. 8, 1941). In his 1945 interview, Eubank does not mention Brereton ordering him to mount the recon mission when they met, but that he received instructions to that effect from Brereton *after* his return to Clark. I have assumed that Sutherland's consent to allow the photorecon mission (as cited in Brereton, *Diaries*, 40, but with no time indicated) was given during Brereton's 10 A.M. conversation with Sutherland. Sutherland's office diary records no exchanges between Brereton and Sutherland between 8:50 and 11:55 A.M.

6. FEAF Activities Summary, 10:10 A.M., Dec. 8, 1941; Kreps interview; Maj. William P. Fisher, interview by AAF historians, May 27, 1942, AFHRA; McKenzie Diary, Dec. 8, 1941; Capt. Lee B. Coats, interview by AAF historians, Apr. 3, 1942, AFHRA; diary of John Geer, Dec. 8, 1941 (hereafter Geer Diary); Edwin S. Green, interview by AAF historians, Apr. 4, 1942, AFHRA; Bean interview; Mason interview.

7. Mason interview; Bean interview; Thomas Hubbard to author, Aug. 18, 1982; Wheless interview; Raymond Teborek, narrative provided to author, Mar. 27, 1981; idem., interview by author, June 2, 1994; idem. to author, Aug. 24 and Oct. 19, 1981.

8. Carpenter interview; idem. to author, Oct. 31, 1982; "Operations Journal, 19th Bomb Group," pt. 1, "Philippine Operations, Dec. 7, 1941 to Dec. 16, 1941," AFHRA, 1–2; Kreps and Broadhurst interviews; Fisher and Green interviews; Coats interview; Richard T. Carlisle, interview, Feb. 27, 1945, Edmonds Collection; Geer Diary, Dec. 8, 1941; Teborek, taped narrative; Stancill M. Nanney to author, July 11 and 20, 1982; William Williams to author, Aug. 5, 1993. Times ranging from 9:30–11 A.M. are given for the order for the B-17s and B-18s to return, but I have accepted Geer as a contemporary source as he was backed up by Broadhurst.

9. Sakai, *Ohzora*, 110; Shimakawa, *Zero-sen*, 9. One of the thirty-six Zero pilots of the Tainan Kū who had taken off—FPO2c Yoshimi Hidaka in Lieutenant Seto's *chūtai*—dropped out and returned to base when his landing gear failed to retract (Hideki Shingō to author, Apr. 4, 1979). The Garampi watch station reported to Eleventh Air Fleet HQ that a force of unidentified aircraft was approaching. Believing them to be B-17s on their way to bomb his bases, Vice Admiral Tsukahara issued an air-raid alarm. He also ordered his remaining fighters—obsolete Type 96 carrier fighters—to take off and intercept. The 5th Hikōshidan (Air Division)—whose twin-engine bombers had attacked Baguio and Tuguegarao earlier that morning—also took defensive measures at its bases on Formosa (*Senshi Sōsho*, 24:178–79).

10. Sakai, *Ohzora,* 110. That evening, a report from Fourteenth Army HQ revealed that the planes were army bombers returning to their base after having attacked their targets as ordered (*Senshi Sōsho,* 24:179). When the nine Zeros came straight at them, the 14th Sentai's seventeen Ki-21-IIA bombers "frantically rocked their wings to signal they were friendly" (Kubo, *97 Jubaku,* 12).

11. *Senshi Sōsho,* 24:181; Saeki to author, Sept. 8, 1980; Shingō to author, Apr. 4, 1979, and Dec. 30, 1980. The other seven pilot in the aborted interception have not been identified. Sakai indicates the nine designated pilots were in three *shōtai* of three pilots each, including his own, but Ishii's *shōtai* leader maintains he himself was not included (Yoshimichi Saeki to author, Sept. 8, 1980).

12. Shimakawa, *Zero-sen,* 10; Miza, "Meritorious Deeds," 126–29; Sakai, *Ohzora,* 110.

13. Mori, *Kaigun,* 2:164, 186; Tanaka interview, 1:92.

14. FEAF Activities Summary, 10:14, 10:20 and 10:45 A.M., Dec. 8, 1941; Brereton, *Diaries,* 41; HQ, FEAF, Field Order 2, Dec. 8, 1941, RG 2, MMA. This order has "1315" annotated next to the date, which indicates it was issued at 1:15 P.M. However, the substance of the order was sent to 19th Group HQ at about 11:30 A.M., according to Capt. Charles Miller, who received it (Miller, interview by William Priestley, Cabanatuan POW Camp, 1943, Priestley Papers).

15. Eubank and Kreps interviews; FEAF Activities Summary, 11:20 A.M., Dec. 8, 1941. Brereton indicates that Eubank sent a coded message recalling the bombers, but the evidence is that they had been recalled *prior* to Eubank's return to Clark (*Diaries,* 41). The pilots recollect receiving a *voice* message to return in the clear, not a coded message.

16. Coats interview; Carlisle interview; Harold C. McAuliff to author, June 18, 1994; Whitcomb to author, May 21, 1994; Eugene Greeson, narrative provided to author, Apr. 9, 1981. James Collier, then a major serving as assistant G3 at USAFFE HQ, maintained on the basis of secondhand information that all the bombers that landed were left practically in line or near hangars for ground crew inspection and gassing (Col. James V. Collier, POW Notebooks, OCMH collection, archives, USAMHI, 1:48). However, the 19th Group's Lt. Eugene Greeson believes that such claims in the case of the B-17s may refer to about five dummy B-17s made of wood that were parked in front of the officers' quarters as decoys (Greeson narrative). No 19th Group source indicates that the B-17s were lined up after landing.

17. Gates to author; Moore to author, Mar. 8, 1979; Stinson narrative; Moore, interview by Toland; idem., interview by author.

18. Obert Diary; David Obert, "Activities of Fighter Units in the Philippines," Apr. 25, 1945, Edmonds Collection, 1; Moore, interview by author; Stinson interview; Gies Diary. Actually, Baguio and Tuguegarao were bombed before they even began their patrol (see chapter 9). Not until Japanese records were made public after the war was it made known that the army-navy agreement limited the two groups of Japanese bombers to striking targets north of sixteen degrees latitude due to the relatively short range of the army's bombers (*Senshi Sōsho,* 24:203–204; Military History Section, HQ, Army Forces Far East, "Philippines Air Operations," 9)

19. Shimakawa, *Zero-sen,* 10. Shimakawa's arrival time over Luzon is based on my estimate of a cruising speed of 207 miles per hour and a distance of 302 miles to the tip of northern Luzon from Tainan following takeoff at 9:45 A.M. and allowing ten minutes to climb to altitude. Shingō claims the agreed cruising speed for his Zeros was 180 knots per hour (207 miles per hour; Shingō to author, May 9, 1980).

20. The estimated positions of the Takao and 1st Kū *rikkō* are mine, based on the Takao Kū's Type 1 *rikkō* covering the 503 miles to Clark from Takao in two hours and forty-five minutes following takeoff at 9:30, and the Type 96 *rikkō* covering the 527 miles to Clark from Tainan in four hours following takeoff at 8:18 and allowing fifteen minutes for the climb to altitude in each case. The indicated average speed for the Type 1s would be 183 miles per hour, and 132 miles per hour for the Type 96 *rikkō*.

21. The maximum range of the SCR-270B under the best conditions was 150 miles. (Thompson et al., *Signal Corps,* 94; Bogart, "Radar in Philippines," 27; Everett Roseen to author, May 1, 1984).

22. Thomas Lloyd, interview by William Priestley, Cabanatuan POW Camp, 1943, Priestley Papers; FEAF Activities Summary, 11:37 A.M., Dec. 8, 1941, (reporting an 11:27 pickup, which I have assumed to be that of the Iba-bound bombers); Ind, *Bataan,* 97–98; J. Fred Moran, interview by William Priestley, Cabanatuan POW Camp, 1943, Priestley Papers; Wimer, "Enemy Air Activities," 14; Howard W. Brown, "Reminiscences," Aug. 4, 1945, SRH-045, RG 457, Records of the National Security Agency, NARA C. P., 17–18; Maurice Chartoff to author, Apr. 11, 1983, and Sept. 11, 1984; Melvin Thomas, interview by author, May 1, 1996.

23. Lloyd interview; Brodginski interviews no. 1 and 2; Wimer, "Enemy Air Activities," 14. The Lingayen Valley group had also been sighted earlier by the Cape Bojeador radar detachment as the bombers and fighters flew overhead, but—as noted earlier—the AWS could not be contacted by radio. The detachment commander maintains that he telephoned the sighting to FEAF HQ—but it is an assertion that I have been unable to document (Arnold, *Rock and a Fortress,* 4–9).

24. Col. Alexander H. Campbell to Maj. Gen. Orlando Ward, Office of the Chief of Military History, Washington, D.C., Dec. 4, 1951, Louis Morton Papers, USAMHI (hereafter Morton Papers); Ind, *Bataan,* 20–21, 98; Moran interview; Roseen to author, May 31, 1984. Campbell apparently acted based on the 11:27 A.M. pickup of aircraft west of Lingayen Gulf and over Luzon. Contrary to Grover (see note 27), he did not recall sending an 11:30 A.M. message. Although there is no documentation that the Clark Field communicatins center was located on the 24th Group's hangar, two men maintain that it was sighted there. (Thurman Matthews, telephone interview by author, Dec. 2, 1984; John Koot, interview by author, May 10, 1986.)

25. Sutherland Summary, 11:55 A.M., Dec. 8, 1941; FEAF Activities Summary, 10:45 and 11:56 A.M., Dec. 8, 1941; Brereton, *Diaries,* 41. Brereton claims that *he* called Sutherland, but his headquarters diary does not identify the call's originator. Sutherland's office diary, which I accept as the authoritative documentation, states that *Sutherland* called Brereton at MacArthur's request.

26. Matthews telephone interview; Madden to author, Dec. 9, 1981, and Jan. 28, 1982; Eugene Franklin to author, Feb. 6, 1982; Madden narrative; George Armstrong to author, Feb. 16, Mar. 26, and Apr. 24, 1979, and Apr. 18, 1980; Joseph Moore to author, Mar. 8 and May 18, 1979, and June 11, 1981; William Cummings, interview by author, Mar. 30, 1980.

27. Grover, "Narrative," 2, 4; Walter B. Putnam to author, May 29, 1979; Cummings interview; Thorne, "Philippine Narrative," 6. Grover does not specifically indicate in his report that the two warning messages received were by *Teletype* from the AWS at Nielson, but he does mention that the system provided for warning reports to be relayed by Teletype from the AWS to the 24th Group's plotting board at Clark Field. It is not clear on what basis he assumed the Japanese force reported to him in the first message was heading for Manila when the Iba radar unit had reported it to the AWS as coming toward Iba. However, Ind, who was at FEAF HQ, also thought it was headed for Manila (*Bataan,* 98). The second report of aircraft heading south over the Lingayen Gulf was sent to him via Teletype by the AWS at 11:45 A.M. Grover later noted that "communications breakdown prevented proper identification" of this report, but there is no indication of any such breakdown, and the report clearly originated with the Iba radar unit (Grover narrative, 4).

28. Grover narrative, 4; Dyess, *Dyess Story,* 30; Walter B. Putnam to author, Apr. 30, 1979. Grover failed to mention in his report that the 17th Pursuit was also at Clark and available to him.

29. Thorne, "Philippine Narrative," 6; Ellis narrative, 1979; idem. to author, Nov. 12, 1980.

30. Powell Diary, 3; idem. to author, July 26, 1979; Krieger interview, Jan. 28, 1945; idem. narrative, 5; idem. to author, May 14 and June 22, 1981; Raymond Gehrig to author, June 6, 1981; Fred Roberts, interview by author, Mar. 23, 1980. In his narrative on 24th Group operations, Grover makes no mention of radioing new orders to the 3d Pursuit. For details on the takeoff mixup at Iba, see Bartsch, *Doomed,* 67–68.

31. Grashio and Donahoe interview; Dyess, *Dyess Story,* 29–30; Augustus Williams, taped narrative; Grashio and Norling, *Return to Freedom,* 4–5; Joe Cole to father, Jan. 22, 1942.

32. Dyess, *Dyess Story,* 29–30; Augustus Williams, taped narrative; Charles Burris to author, Dec. 11, 1978; Grashio and Norling, *Return to Freedom,* 3; Grashio and Donahoe interview; Cole to father. In his 1942 narrative of 24th Group operations, Grover does not mention radioing the new orders to the 21st Pursuit. In switching the 21st and 3d Squadrons to the Manila area, it appears he had discounted the 11:45 warning that Japanese bombers were headed south in Clark's direction and was instead concentrating on the group identified in the 11:30 warning as seemingly headed for Manila.

33. Capt. John E. Lester, "Air Corps in the War," ca. 1945, archives, USAMHI; Cole to father; Grashio and Donahoe interview; Grashio and Norling, *Return to Freedom,* 3–4; Augustus Williams, taped narrative. While Dyess and Williams recall the original orders to go to Clark, Grashio does not remember any mission order at all, just indicating in his accounts that he decided to take the four ships to Clark Field after Bob Clark was forced to abort (Samuel C. Grashio, telephone interview with author, Jan. 16, 1987).

34. Carlisle interview; Maj. William P. Fisher, interview by AAF historians, May 27, 1942, AFHRA; Coats interview; 1st Lt. Harold C. McAuliff and 1st Lt. Alexander D. DeShago, "The 30th Squadron," Pyote Field, Tex., Feb. 2, 1943, 4; FEAF Activities Summary, 11:20 A.M., Dec. 8, 1941; Miller and Maverick interviews; McKenzie Diary, Dec. 8, 1941; Eubank interview. Eubank recalled the second mission order to attack Formosa arriving "just before 12:00 noon," while Maverick (who was not present at 19th Group HQ) was told the message arrived "about 11:45." Miller was obviously relaying FEAF Field Order 2, but he recalled that sixteen B-17s were to attack, instead of the two squadrons specified in the field order.

35. Broadhurst and McDonald interviews; Sig R. Young and Ignatius B. Sargent, interview, May 8–9, 1945, Edmonds Collection; McAuliff to author, June 18, 1994; Raymond Schwanbeck to author, Jan. 13, 1982. Frank Kurtz, then a first pilot in the 30th Squadron, maintained he was also assigned the photoreconnaissance mission (White, *Queens Die Proudly,* 18, 20–21), but most of his account of December 8 events cannot be reconciled with other 19th Group officers' recollections.

36. Charles Miller interview; FEAF Field Order 2; Philip McKee, *Warriors with Wings,* 2. A B-17D could carry a maximum of fourteen three-hundred-pound bombs (Roger A. Freeman, *B-17 Fortress at War,* 120). Field Order 2 called for the strike mission to carry a mix of one-hundred- and three-hundred-pound bombs, but Charles Miller recalled that the order he received specified three-hundred pounders only.

37. Broadhurst and McDonald interviews; Brereton, *Diaries,* 42; Fairfield Diary, 1; McAuliff to author, June 18 and July 22, 1994, Schwanbeck to author; Eugene Greeson to author, Apr. 9 and May 20, 1981; Douglas Logan, interview by John Toland, ca. 1958, Toland Papers, LOC.

38. Miller and Maverick interviews; Coats interview; Carlisle interview; Green interview; Fred T. Crimmins Jr., interview, Mar. 1, 1945, Edmonds Collection. Carlisle must have been watching the 17th Pursuit taking off at about 12:10. While not documented, the attack mission crews were probably scheduled to meet again before 2 P.M. for a briefing.

39. McKenzie Diary, Dec. 8, 1941; Melvin McKenzie, memoir, Dec. 20, 1993, 5; idem. to author, Mar. 31, 1994; McAuliff to author, June 18, 1994; Whitcomb interview. These sketches/maps may have been sent from FEAF HQ after being extracted from the objective folders Ind's section had prepared. It is not clear why Brereton ordered the photorecon mission, unless Sutherland—who was skeptical of Brereton's intelligence on Japanese air bases on Formosa—insisted on it.

40. Whitcomb, *Escape from Corregidor,* 15; Nanney to author; Teborek, taped narrative; Carpenter interview. Although the 11:45 warning message sent out from Nielson's AWS "went to all units of the FEAF by radio or direct teletype, where available" (Campbell to Ward, memo, Dec. 4, 1951), the SCR-197 at 19th Group HQ apparently did not receive it, as the SCR-197 was reportedly used only for ground-to-air and air-to-ground radio calls. Not a single 19th Group officer or enlisted man with whom I have been in contact recalls any warning message being sent to the group.

41. Sakai, *Ohzora,* 110; Shingō to author, July 4, 1981; Shimakawa, *Zero-sen,* 10–11; idem. to author, Feb. 25, 1980. The Zeros' location is my estimate, based on a crusing speed of 207 miles per hour. Shimakawa states that the Zeros climbed to six thousand meters, not seven thousand (*Zero-sen,* 12).

42. Miza, "Meritorious Deeds," 128.

43. Brodginski no. 2 and Lloyd interviews; WD, Technical Manual 11-1100, 2–3, 7–8; Brown, "Reminiscences," 17–18; Wimer, "Enemy Air Activities," 14.

44. Alexander H. Campbell, "Notebook," n.d. (ca. 1942), Morton Papers; idem. to Ward, Dec. 4, 1951. Colonel Campbell indicated in his notebook that Sprague took the intercept order into the Teletype room for transmission to 24th Group Operations "about 15 minutes before bombing," which would make it 12:20, given that the bombing began at 12:35 (see chapter 11).

45. Powell Diary; 16th Naval District Diary, message received 12:15 P.M., Dec. 8, 1941. I have assumed that the ten planes spotted were those of Woolery's group, as his was the only aircraft formation heading for Manila at 12:10 (and allowing for a five-minute delay in the report reaching the 16th District).

46. Krieger interviews; idem. narrative, 5; idem. to author, Apr. 15, 1979, May 13 and June 24, 1980, and June 22, 1981; Powell Diary; Donald D. Steele Diary (hereafter Steele Diary); idem., telephone interviews by author, Oct. 19, 1989, and Jan. 9, 1982. Neither Powell in C Flight nor Gehrig in B Flight remembers receiving this call. It appears it was made from the SCR-197 communications van at 24th Group operations at Clark.

47. William Feallock to author, Feb. 27, 1978. I have assumed that this message is the one referred to in Campbell's notebook as Teletyped to Clark Field at 11:45 A.M., and that it was the last one from Iba to AWS that was relayed to the 24th Group.

48. Walter B. Putnam, interviews, Feb. 23 and 27, 1945, Edmonds Collection; William Feallock to author, Feb. 27, 1978; David Obert to author, spring and June 2, 1979, and Feb. 5, 1988; John L. Brownewell, journal, Dec. 8, 1941; Stinson interview; Obert Diary, 2.

49. In 1951, former AWS chief Campbell estimated the order was sent "about 15 minutes" before Clark was bombed (Campbell to Ward, memo, Dec. 4, 1951). Although neither Grover in his 1942 narrative of events nor his staff officers acknowledged receiving it—nor did anyone (except Grover) even recall having a Teletype machine in the hangar—this critical message must have been one of those Sgt. James Madden of the operations section recalled receiving late that morning, just before the attack (Madden narrative). Furthermore, Lieutenant Colonel Campbell later asserted that the AWS had "perfect communication with Clark and no mention was made about any difficulty in getting this second message through at the time by Sprague or anyone else" (Campbell to Ward, Dec. 4, 1951).

50. Madden narrative. Grover does not mention in his 1942 narrative having given such orders by radio. Only the 3d Pursuit pilots flying over Manila picked up the call.

51. Gies Diary, Dec. 8, 1941; Stinson interview; Moore, interview by Toland, 7–8; idem., interview by author; idem. to author, Mar. 8 and May 18, 1979; James E. Brown narrative, Apr. 10, 1978. Grover erroneously maintains in his 1942 narrative that the 20th Pursuit's ships were being refueled until five minutes before the attack, and thus were unable to take off to "investigate" a "bombardment formation reported over Lingayen Gulf, headed south" (narrative, 4). Apparently unknown to him, Grover also had the 34th Pursuit at Del Carmen at his disposal.

According to squadron survivors, the 34th received no orders from 24th Group operations after their return from a morning patrol over Clark Field.

52. Garry Anloff to author, Apr. 5 and May 16, 1979; FEAF Activities Summary, 12:55 P. M., Dec. 8, 1941, recording the 12:25 sighting report. No one knows what Johnson did with the report.

53. Krieger narrative, 5; idem., interview, Jan. 28 and Feb. 23, 1945; Powell Diary, 3. The two unidentified pilots must have been from Hank Thorne's A Flight, which had broken up while on the high-altitude patrol over Iba at about 12:15.

54. Grashio and Norling, *Return to Freedom,* 4; Grashio and Donahoe interview; John Cole to father; Augustus Williams, taped narrative; Powell Diary; Gehrig to author, June 6, 1981.

CHAPTER 11: "NAVY, HELL, IT'S THE JAPS!"

1. Moore to author, Mar. 8, 1979; idem., interview by author; Toland, *But Not in Shame,* 47; Keator Diary, Dec. 8, 1941; idem., supplement, 1; Gies Diary, Dec. 8, 1941; Edwin Gilmore to author, Dec. 30, 1977.

2. Gates to author; Kimmerle memoir, 7; Gies Diary, Dec. 8, 1941. There were actually fifty-three in the two formations. Photo evidence indicates the two groups bombed parallel to rather than directly behind each other.

3. Arnold H. "Bill" King to author, Apr. 5 and June 4, 1979; Putnam to author, Apr. 30, 1979; George Armstrong to author, Mar. 26 and May 29, 1979; Cummings interview. Allison Ind indicates that Colonel George was on the phone with Grover as the bombs fell, but his account does not jibe with the recollections of those around him at the time, as described here (*Bataan,* 99).

4. Leroy Cookingham, telephone interview by author, Dec. 3, 2001; Jackfert, "History," 13–14; idem. to author, Jan. 14, 2002. Jackfert's account is based on what he was told about Strathern's action. Cookingham did not recall the operations officer's name, but Strathern held that position. No one knows where Major Johnson, who had received the warning call from Anloff minutes earlier in the operations section, was at the time (see chapter 10).

5. Broadhurst and Eubank interviews; Whitcomb interview; idem., *Escape from Corregidor,* 20; Broadhurst interview; Schwanbeck to author, Jan. 13, 1982; Fairfield Diary; Verity, *From Bataan to Victory,* 10; Sponable interview.

6. Fairfield Diary; Verity, *From Bataan to Victory,* 11; Grant E. Adami Jr., memoir, Nov., 1946; Grant E. Adami III, telephone interview by author, Dec. 10, 2001; Howard Harper, telephone interview by author, Dec. 20, 2001. Private Greeley Williams was the man Harper saw climbing into the B-17, intent on manning one of the ship's machine guns (posthumous DSC citation for Pvt. Greeley B. Williams, "SWPA Awards and Decorations," Edmonds Collection; James Bibb, telephone interview by author, Dec. 28, 2001).

7. Bibb telephone interviews, Dec. 28 and 30, 2001; Crimmins interview; McKee, *Warriors with Wings,* 2; John Cox and Bob Barnard, "We Smote their Wickedness," in 19th Bomb Group Association, *19th Bomb Group,* 88–90; John Cox, telephone interview by author, Feb. 6, 2002.

8. Stitt to Beaven (Stitt discovered later that the leg was Berkowitz's); Carlisle interview; Thompson to author, Feb. 9, 1994. Carlisle did not indicate who his two dead lunch partners were. The most likely candidates are Leslie Duvall and Lonnie Wimberley, the only two 28th Squadron officers killed during the raid. Francis Thompson, on the other hand, recalls that he was the only casualty in the bombing of their quarters.

9. McDonald interview.

10. Sakai, *Ohzora,* 111; Kunio Yanagida, *Moyuru Zero-Sen (Burning Zeros),* 84–88; Shingō to author, Jan. 2, 1982; Kuniyoshi Tanaka to author via Noboru Jyoko, June 10, 1979. The P-40s they spotted must have been the six from Woolery's group that had been circling low over

Clark Field and were now climbing for the return to their Iba base rather than to intercept the Japanese, as Sakai and the others erroneously assumed. Woolery's group most likely was concentrating on the situation at Clark Field below and apparently did not notice the Japanese six thousand feet above them.

11. Yanagida, *Moyuru Zero-sen,* 84–88; Sakai, *Ohzora,* 111–12; Haruo Fujibayashi to author, Oct. 6, 1980. The pilots of Shingō's *shōtai* evidently did not drop their tanks. Information is lacking on the actions of *shōtai* other than Sakai's and Harada's.

12. Takeo Ozaki to author, Jan. 17, 1981; Seiji Ozaki to author, Dec. 29, 1980; Fumio Iwaya, *Chūkō (Medium Attack Bomber),* 210; *Senshi Sōsho,* 24:181. Takeo Ozaki recalled that his altitude was 5,500 meters, but another source maintains the bombers were at 7,000 meters (Tagaya, "Technical Development," 41). However, they must have been below 7,000 meters, which was the altitude at which Sakai and the other Zeros were flying top cover. Sakai indicates that the *rikkō* were at 6,000 meters (Sakai, *Ohzora,* 112).

13. Sakai, *Ohzora,* 112; *Senshi Sōsho,* 24:181. The photo on page 319 indicates that the Takao Kū bombed parallel to and slightly south of the 1st Kū rather than behind it.

14. Moore to Brown; Moore to author, Mar. 8, 1979; idem., interview by author; Keator Diary, Dec. 8, 1941, and supplement, 2; Gies Diary; Gilmore to author; Stinson interview; Fred Armstrong, telephone interview with author, Oct. 17, 1982.

15. W. James Fossey, narrative provided to author, June 14, 1978; Gies Diary; Stinson interview; Fred Siler to author, Sept. 27 and Oct. 12, 1983; W. James Fossey to author, Jan. 9, 1982.

16. Mason interview; Thorne, "Philippine Narrative," 8.

17. Grashio and Donahoe interview; Cole to father; Augustus Williams, taped narrative; Grashio and Norling, *Return to Freedom,* 4; Thorne, "Philippine Narrative," 6; idem., taped narrative provided to author, 1979; Steele Diary; Bartsch, *Doomed,* 76.

18. Tash interview; Arthur Hoffman to "Little Bum," May 26, 1942, Edmonds Collection; Carpenter interview; idem. to author, Dec. 27, 1981.

19. Putnam to author, Apr. 30, 1979; Armstrong to author, Mar. 26 and May 29, 1979, and Apr. 18, 1980; Cummings interview; Bowers narrative; Gates to author; Lester Maitland to Walter D. Edmonds, Nov. 20, 1950, Edmonds Collection.

20. Cave, *Beyond Courage,* 66; James M. Hamilton, *Rainbow over the Philippines,* 4; Bogart, "200th Coast Artillery (AA)," 9; idem. to author, Sept. 7, 1998; American Ex-POWs, "200th Coast Artillery (AA)"; Sage, "Report of Operations," 2.

21. Albert L. Allen, "Absurd Order Calms Soldier During Danger," *(Mansfield, Ohio) News Journal,* Dec. 6, 1991; Gates to author; Miller, *Bataan Uncensored,* 67; McDonald interview.

22. Whitcomb, *Escape from Corregidor,* 20; idem. interview; Eubank and Broadhurst interviews. Eubank's driver had gone over to the group commander's quarters expecting to pick him up there. A bomb hit the quarters, demolishing the car and killing the driver.

23. Crimmins interview; McKee, *Warriors with Wings,* 2; Stitt to Beaven; Floyd Deterding taped narratives provided to author, Aug. 11 and Nov. 12, 1993; McAuliff and DeShago, "30th Squadron," 6.

24. Sakai, *Ohzora,* 112; idem. et al., *Samurai!* 73; Takeo Ozaki to author; Tainan Kū SKC, Dec. 8, 1941; Shingō to author, Mar. 31, Sept. 26, and Oct. 27, 1980, Aug. 8, 1981, and Jan. 2, 1982; Haruo Fujibayashi to author, Jan. 12, 1981; Tanaka to author via Noboru Jyoko, June 10, 1979. Shingō and Tanaka recalled that the arrangement was for the 1st and 2d Chūtai to strafe while the 3d and 4th Chūtai provided top cover. However, the SKC indicates otherwise and is, I believe, correct, corresponding as it does with the recollections of all the other Tainan Kū pilots.

25. Saeki to author; Sakai, *Ohzora,* 112–13. Saeki recalls heading north to the assembly point rather than taking up high-altitude cover for the strafing runs by Asao's and Wakao's *chūtai.*

26. Fujibayashi to author, Oct. 6, 1980; Shimakawa, *Zero-sen,* 12. I have assumed that when one *chūtai* completed its pass and began the climb to prepare for its second run, the other

chūtai began its strafing run. The total time for completion of three strafing runs by both *chūtai* was apparently about ten to twelve minutes.

27. Grashio and Donahoe interview; Cole to father; Augustus Williams, taped narrative; Grashio and Norling, *Return to Freedom,* 5; Grashio to author, Nov. 3, 1977; Augustus Williams, taped narrative.

28. Kimmerle memoir, 13–14; Cole to father. McCown evidently related his experience to Kimmerle while in a POW camp. It is unlikely that McCown downed the Zero, as he was not credited with a victory in the 24th Group's records.

29. Grashio and Donahoe interview; Cole to father; Kimmerle memoir, 14; Powell Diary; idem. to author, July 26, 1979, and June 15, 1984; Fred Roberts, interview by John Toland, ca. 1958, Toland Papers, LOC; idem., interview by author, Mar. 23, 1980; Steele Diary. The Japanese must have been in the two *shōtai* from Lieutenant Asai's *chūtai,* as Wakao's *chūtai* was evidently flying top cover for Shingō's and Seto's *chūtai.* Asai's *chūtai* reportedly engaged in aerial combat during its attack on Clark. Shimakawa was the sole member of Asai's *chūtai* to survive the war and leave documentation of their combat that day.

30. Steele Diary; Bartsch, *Doomed,* 80. Tainan Kū survivors do not believe any of their four losses over Clark that day were the result of aerial combat.

31. Thorne, "Philippine Narrative," 6–7; Carpenter interview; idem. to author, Dec. 27, 1981; Tash interview; Hoffman to "Little Bum." The call that Thorne heard most likely was from Andy Krieger, who had radioed while flying over Iba at about 12:50 P.M. after the field was bombed (Krieger narrative, 6–7). Later, at the end of the day, the 3d Pursuit Squadron learned that Ireland had spun out of control and crashed into Mount Arayat, ten miles east of Clark Field, evidently shot down by Zeros (ibid., 10).

32. Sakai, *Ohzora,* 112. The time is my own estimate.

33. Mori, *Kaigun,* 2:196; Sakai, *Ohzora,* 112–13. Sakai's assessment of the wingmen's capabilities is curious, considering that Tanaka said all of the pilots in Shingō's *chūtai* had a minimum of one thousand hours' flying time.

34. Sakai, *Ohzora,* 112–13. The list of Tainan Kū pilots on this mission confirms that Sakai individually burned an aircraft on the ground.

35. Ibid., 114–15; idem. et al., *Samurai!* 74; Hideki Shingō to author, May 16, 1981. Although Sakai's wingman Honda confirmed that the P-40 Sakai attacked hit the ground, none of the P-40 pilots in combat with the Japanese at this time was shot down (Sakai, *Ohzora,* 115). Sakai's *shōtai* missed the subsequent combat with the P-35As coming up from Del Carmen (see chapter 13). Sakai mentions that after his combat, "other Zero pilots caught a group of planes in the air," evidently referring to the engagement with the P-35As (idem. et al., *Samurai!* 74).

36. Shimakawa, *Zero-sen,* 12, 13; idem. to author.

37. Stitt to Beaven; Crimmins interview; McKee, *Warriors with Wings,* 3–4, 5; Charles Bogart to author, Sept. 7, 1998; Joe Smith, "We Shoot Down the First Japs," *Life,* Dec. 22, 1941, 30. Crimmins may have been exaggerating when he claimed he gave the 37-mm gunners instructions on how to operate their gun, as they were fully trained in its operatation.

38. Cave, *Beyond Courage,* 68, 70; Smith, "We Shoot Down," 29–30; Bardowski to author; Alvin C. Poweleit, *Kentucky's Fighting 192nd Light GHQ Tank Battalion,* 32, 209.

39. Gies Diary; Stinson interview; Moore to author, June 16, 1979; Stinson narrative, 4; McKenzie memoir, 6; Armstrong to author, Mar. 26 and Apr. 24, 1979, and Apr. 18, 1980; Bernard Pothier to author, Apr. 17, 1997; Madden narrative; William Jones, taped narrative provided to author, Feb. 28, 1981. The courageous pursuit pilot remains unidentified.

40. Whitcomb, *Escape from Corregidor,* 20–21; idem. and Eubank interview; White, *Queens Die Proudly,* 26–28; McAuliff and DeShago, "30th Squadron," 5.

41. Anthony Holub, "Clark Field, Dec. 8, 1941," in 19th Bomb Group Association, *19th Bomb Group,* 107; DSC citation for T.Sgt. Anthony Holub, "SWPA Awards and Decorations,"

Edmonds Collection. Holub's B-17D was probably 40-3096 of HQ Squadron. Holub was credited with shooting down two Zeros, although he did not claim them himself (Holub, "Clark Field," 107).

42. Bibb telephone interviews, Dec. 28 and 30, 2001; Greeley Williams DSC citation; Billy Templeton, telephone interview by author, Jan. 17, 2002; Edgar D. Whitcomb, E-mail to author, Jan. 17, 2002; Harper telephone interview, Dec. 20, 2001.

43. Mason interview; DSC citation for Pfc. Joseph McElroy, "SWPA Awards and Decorations," Edmonds Collection. One of the strafers was unofficially reported as having crashed in flames.

44. Jacquet Diary; Adami memoir; Fairfield Diary.

45. 16th Naval District Diary, Dec. 8, 1941; Obert Diary; Walter Coss to author, Jan. 31, 1980. The damaged SCR-197 had been taken out of service at about 12:47. None of the 17th Pursuiters picked up its distress call just before it went off the air, although 1st Lt. Bill Feallock recalled hearing "a lot of chattering and yelling" on the frequency before it fell silent. He was unable to make out what was said, however (Feallock to author). Nor did they pick up the "Tally Ho! Clark Field!" message called out over the SCR-197 just before the Japanese bombers reached Clark Field.

46. Grashio and Donahoe interview; Lester narrative.

CHAPTER 12: "WHATEVER YOU DO, DON'T GET UNDER THE DAMNED TRUCK!"

1. Brodginski interviews no. 1 and 2; Thomas interview. Brodginksi recalled that Nelms and Street were in the power van at the time. This seems unlikely, however, given that Nelms was responsible for radioing to AWS the reports telephoned to him from the operations van.

2. Woodrow McBride to author, Mar. 5, 1981; Eric Schramm to author, Apr. 6, 1981; Orville Roland to author, Sept. 8 and Oct. 18, 1981.

3. Yokoyama, *Ah Zero-sen,* 108; Kurosawa interview, 1:108–10; Chitoshi Isozaki to author, Apr. n.d., 1979. Two of his original 53 had to abort.

4. Iwaya, *Chūkō,* 209; *Senshi Sōsho,* 24:180; Fumio Iwaya to author, Mar. 15 and May 5, 1980; Seiji Ozaki to author, Dec. 29, 1980.

5. Seiji Ozaki to author, Dec. 29, 1980; Kokichi Nakahara quoted in Tagaya, "Technical Development," 40; *Senshi Sōsho,* 24:180. The Japanese did not know there were no 37-mm or 3-inch antiaircraft guns defending Iba. They had planned a high-level attack based on the assumption that antiaircraft guns capable of reaching them at lower altitudes guarded the airfield.

6. *Senshi Sōsho,* 24:180; Iwaya, *Chūkō,* 209; idem. to author, Mar. 15, 1980. One of the Kanoya Kū *rikkō* had to return to Formosa with mechanical problems.

7. Ellis narratives, n.d. (1979), and Jan. 13, 1980; Krieger interview, Jan. 28, 1945; Neri interview; Woodrow McBride to author, Feb. 11 and Mar. 5, 1981; Lester narrative, 2; Edgar B. Smith, interview by William Priestley, Cabanatuan POW Camp, 1943, Priestley Papers.

8. Raymond Gehrig to author, Feb. 15, 1978; Bland interview; Gehrig to author, June 6, 1981. Gehrig, Krieger, and Lester all believe that Zeros shot down Root while he was attempting to land, but none of them saw him crash. The Zeros did not begin strafing until *after* the 3d Pursuiters attempted to land.

9. Neri interview; Krieger narrative, 5–6; idem. to author, June 22, 1981.

10. Glenn Cave, interview by John Toland, ca. 1958, Toland Papers, LOC; idem., taped narrative for author, Apr. 4, 1981; Floyd Grow, interview by John Toland, ca. 1958, Toland Papers, LOC; Kelly Davis to Mike Drake, n.d. (Dec., 1981); Hardy Bradley to author, May 3, 1983.

11. Hardy Bradley, narrative provided to author, Apr. 18, 1983; Herb Tyson to author, Feb. 12, 1979.

12. Hinson interview; McBride to author, Mar. 5, 1981.

13. Brodginski interview no. 1; Lloyd interview.

14. Thomas interview; Brodginski interview no. 1; Lloyd interview; Thomas interview; Krieger narrative, 11; Steele Diary, 8.

15.Yanagida, *Moyuru Zero-sen,* 84–88; *Senshi Sōsho,* 24:180; Isozaki to author. One Zero was lost in the Iba attack, but the pilot's identity is not known, nor is the cause of his demise.

16.Yanagida, *Moyuru Zero-sen,* 84–88.The *Senshi Sōsho* (24:180) indicates the 3d Kū arrived at Clark at 1 P.M. Manila time, as does Yokoyama (*Ah Zero-sen,* 198), but that would have been too early, since it would have taken ten to fifteen minutes to reach Clark from Iba, and they had been allowed fifteen minutes over Iba from their arrival time of 12:40.

17. Krieger narrative, 6–7; idem., interview, Jan. 28, 1945; idem. to author, Oct. 3, 1981; Ellis to author, June 2, 1978.The call Krieger heard must have been from a P-40E pilot in combat over Clark, since it was about that time (12:47) that the SCR-197 communications van at 24th Group headquarters went off the air.

18. Krieger narrative, 7; idem. to author, Oct. 3 and June 22, 1981; Thorne, taped narrative; Ellis narrative, 1979; idem. to author, June 2, 1978, and Nov. 12, 1980. Ellis apparently engaged the Zeros after Krieger broke off his attack, as neither 3d Pursuiter ever saw the other and Ellis had not been in on the start of the strafing attack, as was Krieger.

19. Ellis narrative, 1979; idem. to author, Nov. 12, 1980. According to Japanese accounts, Yokoyama's Zero force lost only three aircraft in its combined attacks on Iba and Clark, of which just one was over Iba (*Senshi Sōsho,* 24:180; Yanagida, *Moyuru Zero-Sen,* 84–88).

20. Powell Diary, 3; idem. to author, Mar. 22, 1978; Roberts, interview by Toland; idem., interview by author; Bland interview; Cave narrative. Roberts and Powell both recalled that the rear gunner of a two-seat plane shot Roberts down, but the Japanese employed only single-seat Zeros over Iba during the strafing attack.

21. Powell Diary, 3; Steele Diary; Thorne, "Philippine Narrative," 7; idem., taped narrative; idem. to author, Jan. 20, 1980. They did not notice any aircraft over the field. Evidently the 3d Kū pilots had broken off their strafing attack by the time Thorne arrived. The bombers Thorne spotted most likely were the fifty-three *rikkō* that had bombed Iba some fifteen minutes earlier and were passing north over the Iba area again on their homeward flight at high altitude, evidently not lowering to 16,000 feet until clear of Luzon. (Seiji Ozaki to author, Mar. 16, 1981).The identity of the two pilots with Thorne is not known.

22.Thorne, "Philippine Narrative," 7; idem., taped narrative.The estimate of the time taken to reach twenty-one thousand feet is mine, based on rate-of-climb data from fifteen thousand feet for a combat-loaded P-40E as derived from the P-40E operations manual and communications from Herb Ellis (to author, Sept. 17, 1979, and narrative, Jan. 13, 1980).

23.Thorne, "Philippine Narrative," 7; Neri interview. Allen eventually landed at O'Donnell Field, east of Rosales, instead (Gies Diary, Dec. 8, 1941). Neri recalled that he had climbed to 23,000 feet and found the Japanese some 5,000 feet above him. He must have been at 18,000 feet, however, as the Iba bombers were at 23,000.

24. McBride to author, Feb. 11 and Mar. 5, 1981; Enoch "Red" Pitts to author, Nov. 11 and 14, 1978. McBride believes he was struck by a fragment from a bomb dropped by an aircraft making what he and many others erroneously thought was a second attack on the field. However, strafing fighters most likely hit him with a 7.7-mm bullet.

25. Hinson interview; McBride to author, Feb. 11 and Mar. 5, 1981.

26. Bradley narrative; Bart Passanante, interview by author, Jan. 29, 1983.

27.Thomas interview; Brodginski interview no. 1; Brown, "Reminiscences"; Lloyd interview.

28. Cave interview. Cave, like several others who survived the attack, recalled that bombers reappeared over the field after it was strafed, this time flying south to north on their bombing run. A second strafing attack soon followed. Such a scenario is at odds with Japanese accounts, which record only a single bomb run followed by a single strafing attack. As noted earlier, the second group of bombers appears to have been made up of the *rikkō* that attacked Iba Field earlier and passed by Iba on their way home. It is possible that the Zeros cut short their

strafing attack when the bombers passed overhead because of the risk of being hit by falling bombs.

29. Neri interview; Ellis narrative, 1979; idem. to author, Oct. 3, 1981. Mount Pinatuba is twenty-seven miles southeast of Iba, between Iba and Clark Fields.

30. Neri interview. Maki's chūtai heading east to Clark Field after strafing Iba must have attacked Neri and Keenan.

31. Steele Diary, 6. He would have arrived over Iba after the 3d Kū had left for Clark Field.

32. Edgar Smith interview; Lester narrative, 2; Herbert Ellis, interview by author, Nov. 22, 1986; Krieger interview, Jan. 28, 1945; idem. to author, Oct. 3, 1981; McBride to author, Feb. 11 and Mar. 5, 1981; Bland interview. The 3d Pursuit men evidently rescued Roberts immediately after the Japanese stopped strafing the airfield.

Chapter 13: "All We've Got Left Is the Key to the Airplane"

1. *Senshi Sōsho,* 24:181; Tainan Kū SKC, Dec. 5 and 8, 1941. The time of departure for Del Carmen is not indicated, but it was immediately after completion of the attack on Clark, which is believed to have been about 1 P.M.

2. Hideki Shingō to author, Mar. 13, 1979; Fujibayashi to author, Oct. 6, 1980. Fujibayashi recalled that the three ships in his *shōtai* were engaged, but I believe that Harada and Kamihira, who were badly shot up while strafing Clark, did not participate in this encounter (see chapter 11). Sakai indicates that he was not in this engagement, although he notes that others "caught a group of planes in the air"—which evidently were the P-35As coming up from Del Carmen. (*Samurai!* 74.) According to the Tainan Kū SKC, Asai's 3d Chūtai did not leave for Del Carmen.

3. Tainan Kū SKC, Dec. 8, 1941. It does not specifically state that the three were missing after being shot down by American pursuits, but the implication is clear. The alternative is that they were hit by antiaircraft fire, but that is unlikely as they were somewhat beyond Clark Field at the time they were hit. Because the P-35A pilots in the 34th Pursuit did not claim any victories, it is likely that P-40s also were involved in the combat, as Shingō recalled. Wakao's *chūtai* lost a third pilot in the Clark–Del Carmen attack—FPO1c Yasuhisa Satō—but the SKC does not indicate the circumstances or time of loss. Because the Tainan Kū's exaggerated aerial victory claims for the day—six P-35As or P-40s confirmed as shot down and five unconfirmed—do not distinguish between the Clark- and Del Carmen–based pursuit, it is not possible to ascertain how many of either aircraft type were shot down (Shingō to author, Mar. 13, 1979).

4. Yokoyama, *Ah Zero-sen,* 108; *Senshi Sōsho,* 24:182; 3d Kū SKC, Dec. 8, 1941. Yokoyama and the SKC are in conflict on the distribution of the attack force over Clark, which here is based on my interpretation. Two of Miyano's eight-ship *chūtai* aborted prior to reaching Clark. It appears that Yokoyama was taking on the same P-35As being attacked by the Tainan Kū as they approached Clark from Del Carmen.

5. Yokoyama, *Ah Zero- Sen,* 108–109. Yokoyama claimed only one P-40 shot down in this engagement. FPO1c Yoshikane Sasaki's *shōtai* in CFPO Fujikazu Koizumi's 2d Chūtai, 2d Daitai, claimed the only P-35A shot down (3d Kū SKC, Dec. 8, 1941).

6. Yokoyama, *Ah Zero-sen,* 109; 3d Kū SKC, Dec. 8, 1941. The 3d Kū SKC indicates that Ens. Tsuneo Nakahara's six-ship *chūtai* (1st Daitai) remained outside the attack area where it could provide support and watch.

7. Kurosawa interview, 1:108–10; 3d Kū SKC, Dec. 8, 1941; *Hawaii-Malay Oki Kaisen* (*Sea Battles Off Hawaii and the Malay Peninsula*), interview I, 77. Kurosawa was the 3d Kū's senior *buntaichō* and was renowned for his strafing ability. The *Bungei Shunjū* interview does not identify Shigeo Sugio by name due to wartime censorship, but all nine of the pilots interviewed for the book's section on the Philippines are, based on circumstantial evidence, 3d Kū

pilots. Sugio confirmed that he was hit in the gas tank while strafing Clark (see note 8 below); he is the only 3d Kū pilot whose experience fits the description of the interviewed pilot.

8. *Hawaii-Malay Oki Kaisen,* interview 1, 77; Shigeo Sugio to author via Noboru Jyoko, June 10, 1979; Kurosawa interview, 1:110. Kurosawa says that although he was hit three times by ground fire, he still was able to engage in a dogfight with the P-40.

9. 3d Kū SKC, Dec. 8, 1941; Miza, "Meritorious Deeds," 126–29; Tainan Kū SKC, Dec. 8, 1941; *Senshi Sōsho,* 24:182; Yanagida, *Moyuru Zero-Sen,* 84–88; Isozaki to author, Apr. n.d., 1979, and Jan. 8, 1982. Isozaki later learned that the pilot was Yoshio Hirose.

10. Maj. Stewart W. Robb, "Statement," Nov. 30, 1944, 2–3; Brown, "Statement," 1; Robert Reynolds, *Of Rice and Men,* 18–19; Frankie Bryant to author, Jan. 10 and Feb. 18, 1979. The 34th Pursuit had evidently never received the 11:30 order from group to take off and patrol over Manila Bay. The 1 P.M. takeoff time is my own estimate, given that the Tainan Kū pilots left Clark Field to strafe Del Carmen at that hour. The number of pilots taking off from Del Carmen is subject to disagreement. Brown indicated there were 18 in his 1944 statement, but Robb in 1944 recalled only 16—as did Brown in 1979. Bryant in 1979 recalled 16–18, and Reynolds mentioned 14 in 1947. In accepting a figure of 18, I am assuming that three pilots from other squadrons were detached to the 34th on that day.

11. Bryant to author, Jan. 10 and Feb. 18, 1979; Donald Crosland to author, Mar. 6, 1979; Brown, "Statement," 1–2; Robb statement, 2–3; Ben Brown, interview by Lloyd Stinson for author, Mar. 3, 1979.

12. Robb statement, 2–3; Moore, interview by Toland; idem. to author, Mar. 8, 1979; Keator Diary, Dec. 8, 1941; idem., supplement. Moore, when interviewed by Toland in 1958, estimated that his position was about fifty miles west of Clark Field. Iba, however, is only thirty-seven miles west of Clark, and he had not yet reached Iba.

13. Keator Diary, Dec. 8, 1941; idem., supplement; idem. to author, May 22, 1979. Circumstances indicate that his victim was FPO2c Yoshio Hirose of Maki's *chūtai.*

14. Keator, supplement. His pursuer evidently was CFPO Chitoshi Isozaki.

15. Ibid.; Keator Diary, Dec. 8, 1941; Moore to author, Mar. 8, May 18, June 16, and July 28, 1979. Moore's ship did not sustain any damage in this action. He believed he shot down two of the Japanese, but Japanese records indicate that only Hirose was lost. However, both of Isozaki's wingmen had been hit: FPO1c Otojirō Sakaguchi's ship sustained three hits, and FPO3c Kiyotake Fukuyama's was hit twice (Tainan Kū list).

16. Gilmore to author; Keator Diary, Dec. 8, 1941; idem., supplement.

17. Ellis narrative, 1979; idem. to author, Mar. 28 and June 2, 1978, Nov. 12, 1980, and Nov. 14, 1985. Ellis most likely arrived over Clark at about 1:10, roughly ten minutes after the Japanese finished strafing Iba Field. He later found out that it was Johnny McCown of Grashio's flight, flying alone near Mount Arayat twelve miles east of Clark, who had spotted his predicament and come to his rescue (Ellis to author, June 2, 1978; Grashio and Donahoe interview).

18. Tash interview; Hoffman to "Little Bum"; Bibin to author. It is possible that the P-40 they saw hit the ground was Ellis's. Vern Ireland's P-40E also dove into the ground, but reportedly into Mount Arayat to the east—and with fatal consequences (Krieger narrative, 10).

19. Ibid. The crew believed Norgaard was the first American in World War II to score a victory over an enemy aircraft from a bomber. They did not, however, see the Japanese ship crash.

20. Carpenter to author, Dec. 27, 1981.

21. Broadhurst interview; McDonald interview; idem., Purple Heart citation, Edmonds Collection. According to McDonald, two of the three were Maj. "Buck" Davis of the 7th Materiel Squadron and 2d Lt. Lonnie Wimberley of the 28th Bomb Squadron.

22. Fairfield Diary; Harper telephone interview, Dec. 20, 2001; Bibb telephone interviews, Dec. 28 and 30, 2001; Howard Harper, telephone interviews by author, Jan. 4 and Feb. 9, 2002. The strafers were probably 3d Kōkūtai Zeros that had taken up the attack on Clark Field

shortly after the Tainan Kōkūtai Zeros withdrew. The wooden building that sheltered Harper, Bibb, and Templeton was probably the 28th Bomb Squadron's barracks, located off to the right of the road.

23. Carpenter interview; idem. to author, Dec. 27, 1981. The 19th Bomb Group Diary records in a retrospective entry that Carpenter landed at 4 p.m., but that appears to be about two and one-half hours too late since he brought his B-17D in just after the strafers left at 1:25.

24. 3d Kū SKC, Dec. 8, 1941; Yanagida, *Moyuru Zero-Sen*, 84–88; Mori, *Kaigun*, 2:198; Tainan Kū SKC, Dec. 8, 1941; Shimakawa, *Zero-sen*, 14; Sakai, *Ohzora*, 115; Bartsch, *Doomed*, 105. The arrival time over Santa Ignacia is my estimate.

25. Shimakawa, *Zero-sen*, 14; Sakai, *Ohzora*, 115; Shingō to author, May 16, 1981.

26. Richard C. Mallonee II, *The Naked Flagpole: Battle for Bataan from the Diary of Richard C. Mallonee*, 20; Richard C. Mallonee diary, copy in Richard C. Mallonee II's collection, 62. The time on the watch suggests that Shingō's *shōtai* was at the rendezvous point about fifteen minutes earlier than my estimate based on the SKC documentation. Ellstrom became separated from the others in Herb Ellis's C Flight on takeoff from Iba at 11:45 A.M. He must have flown around the general area of Zambales for about an hour after being left behind. It was his bad luck that he happened to be over the rendezvous point at Santa Ignacia at the same time Shingō and his wingmen arrived after their attack on Clark Field. Ellstrom allegedly was strafed and killed in his chute, but Mallonee's documentation shows otherwise. Shingō insisted that none of his pilots ever fired on American pilots after they bailed out (Shingō to author, May 16, 1981).

27. Powell Diary, 3; Bartsch, *Doomed*, 105; Krieger narrative, 7–8; Thorne, "Philippine Narrative," 7–9.

28. Neri interview; Thorne, "Philippine Narrative," 7–8; Krieger narrative, 7–8; idem. to author, Oct. 3, 1981; Steele Diary, 6–7.

29. Edgar Smith interview; Lester narrative, 2; Ellis interview; McBride to author, Feb. 11 and Mar. 5, 1981; Krieger interview, Jan. 28, 1945; idem. to author, Oct. 3, 1981; Cave interview; idem. to author, Sept. 22, 1981. It is not explicitly documented that Daniel's P-40E was too badly damaged to fly out, but it is implicit.

30. Robb statement, 3; Thomas Gage to author, Sept. 20, 1978, and Mar. 18, July 10, and Aug. 10, 1981; Gilmore to author; Frankie Bryant to author, Feb. 18 and Apr. 8, 1979; *Senshi Sōsho*, 24:181–83; Robert Reynolds to author, Dec. 1, 1980.

31. Keator Diary, Dec. 8, 1941; idem., supplement, 3–4; Stinson interview.

32. Moore, interview by author; idem. to author, May 18 and June 16, 1979; Stinson interview.

33. Keator supplement, 4; Grashio and Donahoe interview; Grashio and Norling, *Return to Freedom*, 5–6; Augustus Williams, taped narrative; Dyess, *Dyess Story*, 30. Based on a comparison of the two pilots' experiences, I believe it was Saburō Sakai who shot up Grashio's ship.

34. Gehrig to author, Feb. 15, 1978, and June 6, 1981; Krieger interview, Jan. 28, 1945; idem. to author, Oct. 3, 1981.

35. Mike Artukovich, telephone interview by author, Jan. 6, 2002. The bomb that landed in the trench was most likely one of the small sixty-kilogram (132-pound) ones dropped by the Japanese bombers.

36. Adami memoir.

37. Stitt to Beaven; anonymous diary (Colovin?).

38. Robert Phillips, E-mails to author, Dec. 26 and 28, 2001;

39. White, *Queens Die Proudly*, 7–9, 31–32. In recounting his experiences to William White, Kurtz overdramatized his crew's losses. Four of his men, rather than eight, were lying dead under his ship: Burgess, Dodson, Gary, and Sgt. Stanley Domin. His bombardier, 2d Lt. Arthur

Sorrell, and Pfcs. Herbert Arthur and William Killin survived the bombing, and his navigator, 2d Lt. Eddie Oliver, was not at the ship during the attack.

40. Ellis to author, June 2, 1978. The major Ellis found was apparently Maj. Lee Johnson, the Clark Field adjutant general.

CHAPTER 14: "WHAT IS THE MATTER WITH THE ENEMY?"

1. Miza, "Meritorious Deeds, 129; Yanagida, *Moyuru Zero-Sen,* 88; Shimakawa, *Zero-sen,* 15; Tainan Kū list. According to Shimakawa, Shinohara had been hit above the left eye.

2. Obert Diary; idem. to author, June 2, 1979; diary of Leo Arhutick. At least four of the pilots recalled seeing dust and smoke over Clark Field, but evidently did not report what they had seen to anyone else. Dave Obert, for one, was concentrating on the plane ahead of him in the formation the whole time in order not to lose his position (Brownewell interview; Kiser statement; Nathaniel Blanton, taped narrative provided to author, Nov. n.d., 1980; Coss to author, May 6, 1978; Obert to author, June 2, 1979). In his wartime diary, Col. James V. Collier, a G3 officer at USAFFE HQ, faults the 17th Pursuit's CO for making no effort to investigate the situation at Clark, which he alleges Wagner must have seen smoking while patrolling over Manila Bay (Collier, POW Notebooks, 1:58).

3. Coats interview; "Letter from the Front, No. 10," broadcast from Station WOAI, San Antonio, Tex., Aug. 2, 1942; John N. Mitchell, "Flying Fortresses of the 19th Bomb Group," *AAHS Journal,* winter, 1984, 289 (re: aircraft no. 40-3100); Eubank interview; William Williams to author, Aug. 5, 1993; Raymond Teborek, telephone interview by author, Mar. 17, 2001.

4. Mitchell, *On Wings We Conquer,* 34, and Appendix A-1, 164; White, *Queens Die Proudly,* 32–33. As noted earlier, Kurtz misstated the number of his crewmen who were killed. I derived the casualty totals from individual World War II death records listed on the ABMC's Internet site (for those whose remains were not subsequently returned to the United States) and the "Individual Deceased Personnel File" records of the U.S. Total Army Personnel Command (for those reinterred in the United States). The six crewmen were 1st Lt. William Cocke, Sgt. William Jones, and Pfc. Robert G. Menzie (HQ Squadron), and Sgt. Lionel Lowe and Pvts. Frank Borchers and Andrew Slane (30th Bomb Squadron). See Appendix H for the names of all 19th Group personnel killed in the Clark Field attack. I have been unable to determine if any 28th Bomb Squadron personnel killed were flight crew.

5. Fairfield Diary; Carpenter interview; Schultz, *Hero of Bataan,* 79. Heidger, who was awarded the DSC for his actions that day, maintained that all of the wounded were initially brought to either the Clark Field dispensary or the 19th Bomb Group dispensary for first aid, then sent to the Fort Stotsenburg hospital for further treatment (notes from William Kennard's material, Edmonds Collection). However, I have found no documentary evidence indicating that any of the Clark casualties were taken anywhere other than the Fort Stotsenburg hospital.

6. Stinson narrative, 4; Kennard interview; A. V. H. Hartendorp, *The Japanese Occupation of the Philippines,* 175; Gies Diary, Dec. 8, 1941; Moore to author, Mar. 8 and June 16, 1979; Keator, supplement, 4; Ellis to author, June 2, 1978.

7. OCMH, U.S. Army, "Operations of the Provisional Tank Group, U.S. Army Forces in the Far East, 1941–1942," http//:www.terracom.net/~vfwpost/provisionaltank2.htm; Bardowski to author. The pilot's identity remains unknown.

8. Powell Diary; Thorne, "Philippine Narrative," 7–9; FEAF Activities Summary, 3:25 P.M., Dec. 8, 1941. The B-18 had been flown into Rosales from Clark Field during the attack on Clark.

9. Thorne, "Philippine Narrative," 9; Steele Diary. The 31st Regiment, with the rest of the Philippine Army's 31st Division, was guarding the beaches on the Zambales coast (Jose, *The Philippine Army, 1935–1942,* 211).

10. Roberts and Cave interviews by Toland; Davis to Drake; Passanante interview; Krieger interview, Jan. 28, 1945. See Appendix H for a list of those killed.

11. Thorne, "Philippine Narrative," 14–15; Roberts and Cave interviews by Toland; Brodginski interviews no. 1 and 2; Thomas interview; McBride to author, Mar. 5, 1981; ABMC records. See Appendix H for the names of those killed.

12. Steele Diary; Cave interview; Thorne, "Philippine Narrative," 14–15; Tyson to author; Hardy Bradley to author, Apr. 18, 1988. There are no records indicating how many of the 3d Pursuit's enlisted men were wounded during the attack, but one source estimates as many as twenty-five (Grow, interview by Toland). Eight were evacuated to Australia on the hospital ship *Mactan* on Dec. 31, 1941, along with Donegan, Passanante, and Hylton (William L. Noyer, *Mactan: Ship of Destiny,* Appendix I, 79–84).

13. MacArthur Diary, Dec. 8, 1941; Sutherland Summary, 1:10, 1:12, and 3:39 P.M., Dec. 8, 1941; "27th Reports"; Roland J. Birrn, "A War Diary," *Airpower Historian,* Oct., 1956, 196; FEAF Activities Summary, 1:00 P.M., Dec. 8, 1941; Douglas MacArthur to AGWAR, radiogram, Dec. 8, 1941, box 2, RG 2, MMA. There is no documentation of what Brereton and MacArthur discussed at their 3:50 meeting, but since the radiogram was sent afterward, it can be surmised that it reflects the substance of what was said. It had to have been sent sometime after 3:35 P.M.—when Sutherland was informed of the casualties at Clark, which MacArthur cited verbatim in his radiogram (Sutherland Summary, 3:35 P.M., Dec. 8, 1941).

14. MacArthur to AGWAR, Dec. 8, 1941; FEAF Activities Summary, 3:50 P.M., Dec. 8, 1941. The FEAF message to O'Donnell was apparently based on FEAF Field Order 2 issued at 1:15 P.M. directing the movement of the two B-17 squadrons at Del Monte to San Marcelino at the "earliest practicable moment." Prior to departing for his meeting with MacArthur, Brereton had evidently discussed with his staff the changed plans regarding the proposed attack on Formosa.

15. FEAF Activities Summary, 4:37 P.M., Dec. 8, 1941; "27th Reports," 16–17; Birrn, "War Diary," 196; James B. McAfee and Madsen Cobb Kokjer Diaries, Dec. 8, 1941; Thomas P. Gerrity Diary, Dec. 8, 1941, published in the *Philadelphia Evening Bulletin,* June 15, 1942, There is no official FEAF correspondence referring to this order. It is not clear why the FEAF did not plan to use the 28th Bomb Squadron's pilots for such a mission, given their qualification with B-18s.

16. John Posten Diary (hereafter Posten Diary); idem., interview, Feb. 23, 1945, Edmonds Collection; Steve Crosby Diary; Lester narrative, 2; Grashio and Norling, *Return to Freedom,* 7; Dyess, *Dyess Story,* 30; Grashio and Donahoe interview; FEAF Activities Summary, 4:37 P.M., Dec. 8, 1941; Blanton, taped narrative; Bill Rowe Diary, Dec. 8, 1941 (hereafter Rowe Diary); Obert to author, June 2, 1979, and Feb. 5, 1988; Cole to father; Brownewell interview.

17. Thorne, "Philippine Narrative," 9; Powell Diary; Krieger narrative, 9. Although FEAF HQ did not order it, the B-18 at Rosales was also going to be flown out. Ted Fisch was on his way to Rosales to evacuate it (Mason interview). The identity of the two pilots staying with Neri is not known, but candidates would be Gerry Keenan and Ship Daniel.

18. Keator Diary, Dec. 8, 1941; Gies Diary, Dec. 8, 1941; Fossey narrative, 3; Brown narrative, 19; Bowers narrative; Jones, taped narrative.

19. Carpenter interview; Arthur Hoffman to Walter D. Edmonds, Jan. 15, 1946, Edmonds Collection; Logan interview; White, *Queens Die Proudly,* 35–36; Robinett interview; McAuliff and DeShago, "30th Squadron," 6; Pvt. Richard Osborn, HQ Squadron, 19th Bomb Group, interview by Eric Morris, n.d., Accession no. 005033, Department of Sound Records, Imperial War Museum, London.

20. Posten Diary; Dyess, *Dyess Story,* 30–31; Grashio and Norling, *Return to Freedom,* 7; Grashio and Donahoe interview; Brownewell interview; Rowe Diary, Dec. 8, 1941; idem. to author, Sept. 15, 1984.

21. Adami memoir; Grashio and Donahoe interview; Posten Diary; idem. interview; Dyess, *Dyess Story,* 31; Jack Donalson, quoted in Jerry Valencia, *Knights of the Sky,* 91; Lester narrative, 2. The dead B-17 crewmen he saw must have been Kurtz's.

22. Carpenter interview; Verity, *From Bataan to Victory,* 13; Stitt to Beaven; White, *Queens Die Proudly,* 35; Kreps interview; McAuliff to author, June 18, 1994. The B-18 probably was the one Pvt. Bob Phillips had been guarding that was not hit during the bombing and strafing attacks (see chapter 13).

23. Samuel A. Goldblith, "The 803rd Aviation Engineers in the Philippines Defense," *Military Engineer,* Aug., 1946, 323; White, *Queens Die Proudly,* 25; Rowe Diary, Dec. 8, 1941; Brownewell interview; Gilmore to author; Thorne, "Philippine Narrative," 9–10.

24. Krieger narrative, 8, 10–12; Gehrig to author, Feb. 15, 1978. Ireland, Ellstrom, Ellis, and Roberts all were shot down. Woolery's original ship and Root's were destroyed while landing at Iba; Neri's P-40E and Daniel's original aircraft were severely damaged and written off at Rosales and Iba, respectively; and Powell's P-40E was a wreck at Lingayen after an unsuccessful takeoff attempt early in the morning on December 9 (Bartsch, *Doomed,* 127–28). Four of the six spare P-40Es at Iba were destroyed in the Japanese attack there.

25. Tash interview; Hoffman to "Little Bum"; 19th Bomb Group Diary, Dec. 8, 1941; Jacquet Diary; Cappelletti, "Overseas Log."

26. Shimada, "Opening Air Offensive," 92, 93; *Senshi Sōsho,* 24:180, 183; 3d Kū SKC, Dec. 8, 1941; Yokoyama, *Ah Zero-sen,* 109; Kurosawa interview, 1:110. The *Senshi Sōsho* and SKC indicate that 48 Zeros landed, but of the 53 that Yokoyama set out with, 2 were forced to return because of malfunctions and 2 were missing, while the 8 surviving Zeros in Maki's attached 9-ship *chūtai* did not land with Yokoyama.

27. Hata and Izawa, *Japanese Naval Aces,* 255; 3d Kū SKC, Dec. 8, 1941; Sugio to author; Tainan Kū SKC, Dec. 8, 1941; *Senshi Sōsho,* 24:180; Tainan Kū list. Koike must have been hit either while strafing Iba or in the subsequent combat with Moore and Keator. The two other pilots landing at Takao with him were most likely his wingmen, given that a *shōtai* operated as a unit.

28. Yokoyama, *Ah Zero-Sen,* 109; David C. Evans and Mark R. Peattie, *Kaigun: Strategy, Tactics and Technology in the Imperial Japanese Navy, 1887–1941,* 118.

29. *Senshi Sōsho,* 24:180, 182; Shimada, "Opening Air Offensive," 93. The *Senshi Sōsho* does not mention why one *rikkō* went past Takao base to Tainan, nor the cause of the other's crash.

30. *Senshi Sōsho,* 24:182; Tainan Kū SKC, Dec. 8, 1941; Shimakawa, *Zero-sen,* 14, 15. Although the *Senshi Sōsho* gives 2:45 P.M. as the 1st Kū *rikkō*'s return time, this seems too early for the slow Type 96 bombers, implying a return flight of only two hours and ten minutes after their 12:35 bombing of Clark Field.

31. Tainan Kū list; Tainan Kū SKC, Dec. 8, 1941; *Senshi rikkō,* 24:182; Miza, "Meritorius Deeds," 129. Miza does not identify the four pilots, but the pilots indicated here flew the four damaged Zero-sen that returned.

32. My compilation of individual pilot claims is as reported on the list of Tainan Kū pilots for the Dec. 8, 1941 mission. Aircraft types are not indicated.

33. Shimada, "Opening Air Offensive," 93. Shimada must be referring to the six P-40Bs of the 20th Pursuit's A Flight, which were lined up in position for takeoff from Clark Field while awaiting the order. The B and C Flight ships were in the squadron's dispersal area (Bartsch, *Doomed,* 72). The B-17s were scattered around the field being serviced and bombed up. The reference to the discrepancy between the two types of reports is mine.

34. Numbers derived from December 8, 1941, lists of Tainan and 3d Kū pilots. The *Senshi Sōsho* indicates that the 3d Kū reported shooting down 9 planes, plus 5 others unconfirmed, and setting fire to 6 big planes, 6 medium-sized planes, and 5 small planes, while the Tainan Kū reported shooting down 7 planes, plus 5 others unconfirmed "at Del Carmen"; setting fire to 5 four-engine planes, 3 twin-engine planes, and 3 other types at Clark; and damaging

or burning 21 planes on the ground at Del Carmen (*Senshi Sōsho*, 24:182). The Del Carmen ground claim is particularly curious since the Tainan Kū's pilots claimed a total of only 20 aircraft destroyed or burned on the ground at both Clark and Del Carmen. Moreover, the men at Del Carmen recall only a short strafing attack by two Zeros, with little damage inflicted (Bartsch, *Doomed*, 107).

35. Shimada, "Opening Air Offensive," 93, 94; *Senshi Sōsho*, 24:184; Izawa, "Rikkō and Ginga," 52. The Takao and Kanoya Kū reported destroying thirty aircraft on the ground at Iba, plus setting fire to one big plane and five small planes. The 1st and Takao Kū claimed the destruction of sixty-two planes on the ground at Clark (*Senshi Sōsho*, 24:180, 182).

36. Kennard interview; Fairfield Diary; Whitcomb, *Escape from Corregidor*, 24; idem. interview.

37. Dyess, *Dyess Story*, 32; Grashio and Norling, *Return to Freedom*, 7; Grashio and Donahoe interview; Donalson, quoted in Valencia, *Knights*, 92; Augustus Williams, taped narrative; Brown narrative, 19; Keator Diary, Dec. 8, 1941; Gies Diary, Dec. 8, 1941; Rowe Diary, Dec. 8, 1941; Gilmore to author; John L. Brownewell to author, Aug. 29, 1977.

38. Glen Cave to author, Feb. 26, 1981; McBride to author, Feb. 11 and Mar. 5, 1981; James Boone to author, Mar. 6, 1979; Tyson to author; Schramm to author, Apr. 6, 1981; Passanante interview; Roland narrative, 7–8; Brodginski interviews no. 1 and 2; Thorne, "Philippine Narrative," 14–15; Roberts, interview by Toland.

39. Cave and Roberts interviews; Cave to author, Feb. 26, 1981; idem. narrative; Davis to Drake; Powell Diary; idem. to author, Mar. 22, 1978; Thorne, "Philippine Narrative," 10–11.

40. Jacquet Diary; idem. to author, Sept. 16, 1981; 19th Bomb Group Diary, Dec. 8, 1941; (Eugene Eubank) radiogram to Del Monte Field, 2:22 A.M., Dec. 9, 1941, O'Donnell Papers. Eubank's 2:22 radiogram did not specify which of the two squadrons should carry out the attack, nor did it indicate the number of B-17s that should participate. O'Donnell apparently selected the 93d Squadron. Earlier, USAFFE HQ had received a message from Legaspi stating that a Japanese carrier had been spotted about fifty miles off Catanduanes (G2 Journal, USAFFE, 11:45 P.M., Dec. 8, 1941, RG 2, MMA). Someone at USAFFE then must have passed it to FEAF HQ. Catanduanes Island is located 350 miles north of Del Monte, off southern Luzon's east coast. The carrier would have been the *Ryūjō*, which was moving toward Legaspi after launching its early morning attack on Davao. Meanwhile, the 24th Pursuit Group HQ and 19th Bomb Group HQ at Clark Field were expecting B-17s from the 14th and 93d Squadrons to land at daybreak for a bombing mission against Japanese airfields on southern Formosa, as noted earlier in this chapter.

41. Whitcomb, *Escape from Corregidor*, 22.

Epilogue

1. MacArthur to AGWAR, radiogram, Dec. 9, 1941, RG 2, MMA. The figures of the dead closely correspond to those I calculated, as shown in Appendix H: fifty-seven killed at Clark and its environs, and twenty killed at Iba. However, my tally does not include fatalities in the non–FEAF units at Clark Field.

2. Charles A. Willoughby and John Chamberlain, *MacArthur, 1941–1951*, 26; Layton et al., *And I Was There*, 507; John Costello, *Days of Infamy*, 3, 245; Louis Morton, *The Fall of the Philippines*, 90.

3. Brereton says the reason the Del Monte B-17s did not move up to Clark after dark for the planned strike on Formosa early on December 9 was the "hazards of takeoff at night" (*Diaries*, 43). However, that explanation seems implausible. Evidently, attacking the Japanese carrier sighted off Catanduanes that evening took priority over the Formosa mission.

4. Brereton, *Diaries*, 38–41. It was actually 10:14 when MacArthur authorized the missions (FEAF Activities Summary, 10:14 A.M., Dec. 8, 1941).

5. "M'Arthur Denies Brereton Report," *New York Times*, Sept. 28, 1946. See also Bartsch, "Was MacArthur Ill-Served?" 58–59.

6. Shimada, "Opening Air Offensive," 92.

7. Bartsch, "Was MacArthur Ill-Served?" 59–60.

8. Robert F. Futrell speculated that the decision was probably due to "the incubus of a long period of defensive thinking, unfamiliarity with strategic air capabilities, and the hesitation arising from the directive that the Japanese should attack first" ("Air Hostilities in the Philippines 8 Dec. 1941," *Air University Review*, Jan.–Feb., 1965, 41). However, the third factor can be discounted, as MacArthur knew about the attacks not only on Pearl Harbor but also on the Philippines.

9. Quoted in Costello, *Days of Infamy*, 271; and D. Clayton James, *The Years of MacArthur*, vol. 2, *1941–1945*, 11, 15.

10. Costello, *Days of Infamy*, 5, 19, 63, 261; Ronald H. Spector, *Eagle Against the Sun*, 447; Edward J. Drea, *MacArthur's ULTRA: Codebreaking and the War against Japan, 1942–1945*, 11; Jack Finnegan, "Grim Fate for Station 6," *Military History*, Oct., 1986, 10; Frederick D. Parker, *Pearl Harbor Revisited: United States Navy Communications Intelligence, 1924–1941*, 18, 20, 45–48. Intercept Station C was also intercepting Japanese navy messages in the JN-25 code that contained detailed information about naval air force activities on Formosa, but could only exploit them for their "externals": addresses, call signs, association with others (ibid., 42).

11. Futrell, "Air Hostilities," 41; Connaughton, *MacArthur*, 82; "Conversation between Admiral Hart and General MacArthur"; "Report of Conference."

12. Miller, "'Pretty Damn Able Commander,'" pt. 2, 40–41; Brereton, *Diaries*, 5–6; Arnold to MacArthur, Oct. 14, 1941.

13. Fogerty, *Biographical Study*, Eugene Eubank entry.

14. Col. Alexander H. Campbell to Maj. Gen. Orlando Ward, Dec. 4, 1951, Morton Papers; Matthews telephone interview.

15. Ibid.; FEAF Activities Summary, 11:20 A.M., Dec. 8, 1941; Robert D. Haines, E-mails to author, Jan. 5, 7, and 8, 2002; Cooke to parents, Sept. 22, 1941. Cooke indicated that the Teletype was "used primarily for administration and air traffic."

16. Campbell to Ward.

17. It took Joe Moore thirty-five minutes to climb to twenty-one thousand feet in his P-40B, as noted in chapter 13.

18. Fogerty, *Biographical Study*, Orrin L. Grover entry.

19. Grover, "Narrative," 4.

20. Lewis Brereton to Henry Arnold, radiogram, paraphrased in radiogram ABDA 522 to AGWAR, Mar. 1, 1942, doc. A-1832, microfilm reel A7385, AFHRA.

21. Costello, *Days of Infamy*, 7.

Sources

In identifying the sources used in the preparation of this book, it is useful to distinguish between four levels of textual coverage:

1. The personal experiences of American combat personnel in the FEAF (and its predecessors) in the Philippines preparing for and participating in the islands' defense, and of staff officers in the FEAF and at AAF HQ in Washington, D.C., charged with building up the Philippines' aerial defense capabilities and providing for their aerial reinforcement, respectively.
2. The personal experiences of Imperial Japanese Navy and Army air force combat personnel on Formosa training for and carrying out the aerial attack on the Philippines, and of Eleventh Air Fleet staff officers at Takao, Formosa, who planned the attack.
3. The efforts of high-level War and Navy Department staff officers in Washington as they planned and arranged for the buildup of airpower in the Philippines, subject to the Roosevelt administration's political decisions, and the efforts of the commanding general and his staff at USAFFE (and its predecessor, the Philippine Department) HQ in Manila to the same end.
4. The Japanese government's political decision to engage in war, and the plans and strategies of high-level Imperial Japanese Army and Navy staff officers to launch the war with southern operations, including those in the Philippines.

This multifaceted story is most heavily weighted toward the experiences of American combat and staff officers in the FEAF. For the experiences of the pilots and enlisted men of the 24th Pursuit Group (and the pursuit squadrons of its predecessor, the 4th Composite Group), I have again tapped the sources used in the preparation of my book *Doomed at the Start,* including the interviews conducted in 1945 for Walter Edmonds's *They Fought with What They Had* (at the AFHRA), in 1943 by William Priestley (the "Philippine Collection" in RG 407, NARA), in 1958 by John Toland (the Toland Papers in the Manuscript Division of the LOC), and by me in 1979–86, as well as narratives prepared for me by the participants and their correspondence with me from 1976–89. I have again used pilots' personal diaries and their prewar correspondence to families and friends. In expanding the coverage of participants to include members of the 19th Bomb Group (H), the 27th Bomb Group (L), the Air Warning Company, and to a limited extent the 200th Coast Artillery (Antiaircraft) and the Provisional Tank Group, I have again referred to the 1943 Priestley and 1945 Edmonds interviews, and augmented them with those I conducted in 1994–2002. Prewar correspondence with friends and family and letters to me from 19th Bomb Group and Air Warning Company personnel from 1981–2002 have also been tapped.

The book's coverage of what transpired at the staff level in the FEAF and its predecessors, the USAFFE and PD air forces in the prewar period, is heavily dependent on the detailed letters sent home by Maj. Kirtley J. Gregg and, to a lesser extent, by Maj. William H. Maverick, copies of which were made available to me by their families. Allison Ind's *Bataan: The Judgment Seat* (1944) also provided insight into the operations of FEAF HQ, as, of course, did Lewis H. Brereton's *The Brereton Diaries* (1946), although the latter contains slight factual errors regarding times and places. Brereton's office diary (a copy is available at the Eisenhower Library) is an invaluable source for details on FEAF HQ operations on December 8, 1941.

For the plans and preparations of staff officers at AAF HQ (and its predecessor, the Army Air Corps) in Washington, I have exhaustively explored the National Archives's holdings—particularly RG 18—for the period 1939–41. The late Bill Burt's recollections of his experiences in the OCAC Plans Division, as shared in correspondence with me and as published in his *Adventures with Warlords* (1994), was the starting point for understanding the situation during that period. Particularly useful is the day-to-day accounting of plans and arrangements for the aerial reinforcement of the Philippines in the Air Staff office diary maintained by Brig. Gen. Carl Spaatz during the July–December 7, 1941, period (RG 18, NARA). The Henry H. "Hap" Arnold papers in the Manuscript Division at the LOC helped fill in gaps with memoranda and other official items relating to this subject. The Air Force Academy has a copy of the air war plan annex to the War Department's 1941 "Victory Program" that includes the plan for the Philippines aerial buildup.

I was fortunate to have the cooperation of most of the surviving Zero pilots who participated in the December 8 attack in writing my account of Japanese preparations for and conduct of air operations against the Philippines. They related to me their recollections in correspondence during the period 1979–82. Three of them—Saburō Sakai, Tamotsu Yokoyama, and Masa-aki Shimakawa—published memoirs in Japan of their wartime experiences. A particularly valuable supplement to these accounts was the information collected by Shirō Mori (Masaru Nakai's pen name) through interviews that he included in his four-volume account of Zero operations in the Pacific War, *Kaigun Sentōkitai* (1973). Unpublished Japanese navy reports covering the Tainan and 3d Kōkūtai given to me by Osamu Tagaya provided a detailed record of the two Zero units' operations in the December 8 attack. I also relied on volume twenty-four of the *Senshi Sōsho*. Hata and Izawa's *Japanese Naval Aces and Fighter Units in World War II* (1989) offers valuable information on the two units in English.

For the experiences of Japanese navy *rikkō* units participating in the December 8 attack, I briefly corresponded with two of the crewmembers (Seiji and Takeo Ozaki) in 1980–81 and relied on the Japanese-language description of their preparations and attack operations in volume twenty-four of the *Senshi Sōsho,* and Fumio Iwaya's *Chūkō* (1976). Useful details about their training are found in translations of intercepted Japanese naval messages during the period September–November, 1941, included in RG 457, NARA. Two personal accounts by participants in the little-known operations of the two army units that bombed northern Luzon on December 8 have been published in a Japanese periodical (*Kōkū Fan* [January, 1967]) and in a book by a bomber pilot (Yoshiaki Kubo, 1984).

Volume twenty-four of the *Senshi Sōsho* is a valuable source of information about the activities of the Eleventh Air Fleet's headquarters in preparation for the Japanese navy's attack on the Philippines. Similarly, volume thirty-four of the *Senshi Sōsho* covers the army's 5th Hikōshidan's plans and preparations for its bombing attacks on Tuguegarao and Baguio preceding the Eleventh Air Fleet's main operation. At a more personal level, an Eleventh Air Fleet staff officer offered an account of Philippine operation plans and preparations for the December 8, 1941, attack (Koichi Shimada, *Naval Institute Proceedings,* January, 1955; reprinted in *The Japanese Navy in World War II,* ed. David C. Evans, 1986). However, the best account of activity in the Eleventh Air Fleet HQ on Formosa prior to the attack is found in Mori's *Kaigun Sentōkitai.* Intercepted navy messages (RG 457, NARA) help fill in details as to exact dates and places of preparatory activities.

Details of high-level U.S. government deliberations regarding the question of reinforcing the Philippines, as well as the planning and preparation to that end once the decision was made to build up Philippines airpower as a deterrent to Japanese aggression, are found in War Department records (RG 165, NARA). The WPD's memoranda are particularly useful. Mark S. Watson's *Chief of Staff: Prewar Plans and Preparations* (1950) taps into these records and is a readable account. Secretary of War Henry L. Stimson's diary (Stimson Papers, LOC) and his secret records (collected in RG 107, NARA) document his increasing enthusiasm for introducing offensive airpower into the Philippines and his discussions with President Franklin D. Roosevelt, Navy Secretary Frank Knox, and Secretary of State Cordell Hull (as well as WD and AAF planners) on that subject. For the efforts to attempt to mesh American plans and strategy for the Philippines with those of the British for their Far East territories, Maurice Matloff and Edwin M. Snell's *Strategic Planning for Coalition Warfare, 1941–42* (1953) remains the most useful source.

On the receiving end of presidential and WD decisions affecting the Philippines, the PD and—from July, 1941—USAFFE also generated considerable documentation covering reinforcement of the islands. National Archives Record Group 407 includes exchanges of radiograms, letters, and memoranda between the PD and USAFFE commanders and the WD relating to the question of aerial reinforcement. Chief of Staff Marshall's papers at the George C. Marshall Foundation in Lexington, Virginia, include correspondence between Marshall and George Grunert and Douglas MacArthur, as well as microfilmed records not always available in the NARA files, while RG 2 at the MacArthur Memorial Archives in Norfolk, Virginia, has copies of many other USAFFE records, including general and special orders not found elsewhere. MacArthur's office diary (also included in RG 2) identifies specific activities by time and place and helps fill in gaps in knowledge. For activities of December 8, 1941, Richard K. Sutherland's office diary (also in RG 2) documents USAFFE HQ's actions related to air operations and supplements Lewis H. Brereton's FEAF HQ diary.

For the Japanese government's top-level political decision to engage in hostilities against the United States, Great Britain, and the Netherlands by launching southern operations, I have relied heavily on Herbert Bix's well-documented *Hirohito and the Making of Modern Japan* (2000), which places the emperor in the thick of the decision-making process. Particularly valuable in following the Japanese military's strategic decision making and war planning during the period 1939–41 as it developed in tandem with the emperor's thinking is Takushirō Hattori's *Dai Tōa Senso Zenshi (Complete History of the Greater East Asia War),* available in English at the LOC. The three *Senshi Sōsho* volumes covering the army's and navy's plans, preparations, and operations for seizing the Philippines (vols. 2 and 34 and 24, respectively) provide the most comprehensive accounts, but they are not available in English. Jun Tsunoda's chapter in *The Fateful Choice* (1980), a volume edited by James Morley, is the most detailed account of the navy's role in the southern strategy available in English. As a sidelight to the Pearl Harbor operation on which it focuses, Gordon Prange's *At Dawn We Slept* (1981) offers additional useful, scattered information on the Imperial Navy's Combined Fleet's plans and preparations for Philippine operations.

ORAL HISTORY

Interviews Conducted by Author

Bland, Albert. Jan. 30, 1983
Cappelletti., Francis. June 27, 1982
Cummings, William. March 30, 1980
Ellis, Herbert. November 22, 1986
Hinson, Robert James. January 12, 1981
Koot, John. May 10, 1986
Moore, Joseph. June 11, 1981
Neri, Frank. March 29, 1980
Passanante, Bart. January 29, 1983
Roberts, Fred. March 23, 1980
Rowe, William. May 9, 1986
Sponable, Edson. July 23, 1993
Teborek, Raymond. June 2, 1994
Thomas, Melvin E. May 1, 1996

Interviews by Walter D. Edmonds, G. A. McCulloch, or E. R. Emmett, Walter D. Edmonds Collection, AFHRA

Broadhurst, Edwin B. January 15, 1945
Brownewell, John L. June 2, 1945
Carlisle, Richard T. February 27, 1945
Carpenter, John W. January 9, 1945
Combs, Cecil E. April 25, 1945
Crimmins, Fred T., Jr. March 1, 1945
Eads, Harold E. April 6, 1944, and August 7, 1945
Elsmore, Raymond T. June 2, 1945
Eubank, Eugene L. November 29, 1945
Grashio, Samuel C., and Jack Donahoe. Apr. 2, 3–4, and 7, 1945
Hoffmann, Arthur E. March 23, 1946

Kennard, William J. April 3, 1945
Kreps, Kenneth R. January 17, 1945
Krieger, Andrew E. January 28 and February 23, 1945
McDonald, William E. January 18, 1945
Nanney, Stancill M. May 19, 1945
Norgaard, Arthur E. March 2, 1945
O'Bryan, Carey Law. March 5, 1945
O'Donnell, Emmett, Jr. July 2, 1945
Posten, John H., Jr. February 23, 1945
Putnam, Walter B. February 23 and 27, 1945
Robinett, George R. April 9, 1945
Sutherland, Richard K. June 4, 1945
Tash, Earl R. February 26, 1945
Whitcomb, Edgar D. March 20, 1945
Young, Sig R., and Ignatius B. Sargent. May 8–9, 1945.

Interviews by AAF Historians, AFHRA

Coats, Lee B. April 3, 1942
Fisher, William P. May 27, 1942
Green, Edwin S. April 4, 1942
Smith, John H. M. N.d., 1943
Wheless, Hewitt T. April 4, 1942

Interviews by William Priestley, Cabanatuan POW Camp, 1943, Philippine Records, RG 407, NARA

Brodginski, Henry (two interviews)
Dyess, W. Edwin
Goldy, Samuel
Heffron, Charles
Lloyd, Thomas
Mason, William
Maverick, William
Miller, Charles
Moran, J. Fred
Smith, Edgar B.
Stinson, Lloyd
Tant, Norman
Woodside, Milton

Interviews by John Toland, ca. 1958, John Toland Papers, Manuscript Division, LOC

Cave, Glenn
Grow, Floyd
Logan, Douglas
Moore, Joseph
Morse, William
Roberts, Fred

Miscellaneous Interviews

Brown, Ben. By Lloyd Stinson for author, March 3, 1979.
Kenney, George C. By D. Clayton James, 1971. MMA.
Osborn, Richard. By Eric Morris, n.d. Accession no. 005033, Department of Sound Recording, Imperial War Museum, London.
Paulger, Claude. By Calvin Chunn, Cabanatuan POW Camp, n.d., 1942, box 1443, RG 407, "Philippines Records, NARA.

Telephone Interviews by Author

Adami, Grant, III. December 10, 2001
Altman, Robert. May 6, 1997
Armstrong, Fred. October 17, 1982
Artukovich, Mike. January 6, 2002
Bibb, James. December 28 and 30, 2001
Burt, William R. December 15, 2000
Chiles, John. December 6, 2001
Cookingham, Leroy. December 8, 2001
Cox, John. February 6, 2002
Grashio, Samuel C. January 16, 1987
Halkyard, James. May 7, 1997
Harper, Howard. December 20 and 28, 2001; January 4 and February 9, 2002
Kruger, Courtney. December 10, 2001
Kundert, Emanuel. September 26, 2000
Matthews, Thurman. December 2, 1984
Mount, Walter E. September 2, 2000
Rogers, Jack. May 10, 1986
Schwarz, Bert. May 20, 1997
Snyder, Vincent. Feb. 11, 1994
Steele, Donald D. October 19, 1982; January 9, 1989

Teborek, Raymond. March 27, 1981; March 17, 2001
Templeton, Billy. January 17, 2002
Whitcomb, Edgar D. January 15, 2002

Taped Narratives Provided to Author

Armstrong, George. N.d. (May, 1977)
Blanton, Nathaniel. N.d. (November, 1980)
Cave, Glenn. April 4, 1981
Deterding, Floyd. August 11 and November 12, 1993
Jones, William. February 28, 1981
Madden, James E. February 20, 1982
Rawlins, Russell N. November 10, 2000
Rogers, Jack, and James Bitner. June 15, 1986
Teborek, Raymond. March 27, 1981
Thorne, Henry G., Jr. May 4, 1979
Williams, Augustus. May 7, 1978

Taped Narratives Provided to Others

Bean, Joe. Interview by Richard Haney, December 13, 1991. Copy in author's collection.
Brock, Reid H. October 1, 1993. Provided to Reid H. Brock Jr. Copy in author's collection.

U.S. Air Force Oral Histories

Anderson, Maj. Gen. Orvil. Oral History K239.0512-898, October 27, 1959, AFSHRC.
George, Lt. Gen. Harold L. March 16, 1970. Hap Arnold–Murray Green Collection, Special Collections, Academy Libraries, USAFA (hereafter Arnold-Green Collection).
Hansell, Maj. Gen. Haywood S. January 2, 1970. Arnold-Green Collection.
Kuter, Gen. Laurence S. Oral History K 239.0512-810, 1974, AFSHRC.
O'Donnell, Maj. Gen. Emmett, Jr. March 27, 1970. Arnold-Green Collection.

CORRESPONDENCE

Between the PD/USAFFE and the War Department and Army Air Corps

Arnold, Henry H., OCAC, and Douglas MacArthur, CG, USAFFE. 1941.
Brady, Francis, FEAF, and Frank Andrews. 1941.

————, and Carl Spaatz, OCAC. 1941.

Brereton, Lewis H., CG, FEAF, and Henry H. Arnold, OCAC. 1941.

Churchill, Lawrence, PDAF, and George Stratemeyer, OCAC. 1940.

Clagett, Henry, CG, AF USAFFE, and George Brett, OCAC. 1941

Crom, William H., PDAF, and Ira Eaker, OCAC. 1939

Grunert, George, CG, PD, and George C. Marshall, C/S, WD. 1940–41

MacArthur, Douglas, CG, USAFFE, and George C. Marshall, C/S, WD. 1941

Other U.S. Government Correspondence

Roosevelt, Pres. Franklin D., and Secretary of War Henry L. Stimson. 1941

Sayre, Francis, Philippines High Commissioner, and George C. Marshall, C/S, WD. 1940

U.S. Secretary for Collaboration and Joint Secretary, British Joint Staff Mission. 1941

Imperial Japanese Navy Correspondence

Yamamoto, Isoroku, CINC, Combined Fleet, and Adm. Shigetaro Yamada. 1941

————, and Navy Minister Koshirō Oikawa. 1941

FEAF Officers and Enlisted Men to Their Families, 1941–42

Ambrosius, William
Armstrong, George
Brezina, Jerry
Cole, Joseph
Cooke, James
Fisch, Ted
Gies, Carl Parker
Glover, Wilson
Gregg, Kirtley J.
Hennon, William
Hobrecht, Forrest
Hoffmann, Arthur
Krieger, Andrew
Legg, John "Pete"
Lewellyn, Norman J.
Lodin, Lawrence
Louk, Max
Mahony, Grant

Maverick, William
Miller, Donald
Neri, Frank
Seeborg, Arvid
Sheppard, William

FEAF Officers and Enlisted Men to Author

Anderson, Bernard. February 3, 1980
Armstrong, George. September 29, 1977; February 16, March 26, April 24,
    and May 29, 1979; April 18, 1980; October 13, 1996; April 18, 1997
Bibin, Michael. July 28, 1981
Boone, James. March 6, 1979
Bradley, Hardy. May 3, 1983; April 18, 1988
Brown, James E. January 8, 9, 10, and 13, 2002 (all via E-mail)
Brownewell, John L. August 29, 1977
Bryant, Frankie. January 10, February 18, and April 8, 1979
Burris, Charles. December 11, 1978
Carpenter, John. December 27, 1981, October 31, 1982
Caswell, Thomas. February 19, 1994
Cave, Glenn. February 26 and September 22, 1981
Coss, Walter. May 6, 1978; January 31, 1980; December 31, 1996
Crosland, Donald "Shorty." March 6, 1979
Ellis, Herbert. March 28 and June 2, 1978; September 17 and December 18,
    1979; January 13 and November 12, 1980, October 3, 1981; November 14,
    1985
Ernst, Norman L. March 6, 1980
Feallock, William. February 27, 1978
Fisher, William P. October 12, 1981
Fossey. W. James. January 9, 1982
Franklin, Eugene. February 6, 1982
Gage, Thomas. September 20 and October 6, 1978; March 18, July 10, and
    August 10, 1981
Gates, J. Jack. July 4, 1978
Gehrig, Raymond. February 15, 1978; June 30, 1980; June 6, 1981
Gillespie, John. October 30, 1979; February 14, 1980
Gilmore, Edwin. December 30, 1977
Grashio, Samuel C. November 3, 1977; May 19, 1981
Greeson, Eugene. April 9, May 20, and September 23, 1981
Haines, Robert D. January 5, 7, and 8, 2002 (all via E-mail).
Halbert, Hugh. November 29, 1993
Hubbard, Thomas "Speed." August 18, 1982
Jackfert, Edward. January 14, 2002

Jacquet, Edward M. April 22 and September 16, 1981

Keator, Randall. May 22, 1979.

King, Arnold H. "Bill." April 5 and June 4, 1979

Krieger, Andrew. April 15, 1979; May 13 and June 24, 1980; May 14, June 22, and October 3, 1981

Madden, James E. December 9, 1981; January 28 and February 20, 1982

McAuliff, Harold C. June 18 and July 22, 1994

McBride, Woodrow "Woody." February 11 and March 5, 1981

McKenzie, Melvin. March 31, 1994

Michie, Robert. August 15, 1982

Moore, Joseph H. March 8, May 18, June 16, and July 28, 1979; June 11, 1981; February 29, 1988

Moseley, C. L., Jr. March 14, 1994

Nanney, Stancill M. July 11 and 20, 1982

Obert, David. Spring and June 2, 1979; January 25, June 25, 1981; February 5, 1988

Phillips, Robert W. December 26 and 28, 2001 (both via E-mail)

Pitts, Enoch "Red." November 11 and 14, 1978

Powell, William H. July 26, 1979; June 15, 1984

Putnam, Walter B. "Benny." April 30 and May 29, 1979

Reynolds, Robert. December 1, 1980

Roland, Orville. September 8, 1980; October 18, 1981

Rowe, William. September 27, 1983; September 15, 1984

Schramm, Eric. April 6, 1981

Schwanbeck, Raymond. January 13, 1982

Sheppard, William. November 26, 1988

Siler, Fred. September 27 and October 12, 1983

Stinson, Lloyd. July 19, 1978

Teborek, Raymond. March 27, August 24, and October 19, 1981; June 2, 1994

Thompson, Francis R. February 9, June 7, and July 16, 1994

Tyson, Herbert. February 12, 1979

Whitcomb, Edgar D. May 21, 1994, and January 17, 2002 (via E-mail)

Williams, William. August 5, 1993

Japanese Naval Air Officers to Author

Fujibayashi, Haruo. October 6, 1980; January 12, 1981

Isozaki, Chitoshi. N.d. (April, 1979); January 8, 1982

Iwaya, Fumio. March 15 and May 5, 1980

Ozaki, Seiji. December 29, 1980; March 16, 1981

Ozaki, Takeo. January 17, 1981

Saeki, Yoshimichi. September 8, 1980

Sakai, Saburō. August 10, 1982
Shimakawa, Masa-aki. February 25, 1980
Shingō, Hideki. February 27, March 13, and April 4, 1979; May 9, September 26, October 27, and December 30, 1980; May 16, July 4, August 8, and October 17, 1981; February 8 and June 16, 1982
Sugio, Shigeo. June 10, 1979
Tanaka, Kuniyoshi. June 10, 1979
Yokoyama, Tamotsu. N.d. (April, 1980).

Other USAFFE Personnel to Author

Anloff, Garry. April 5 and May 16, 1979
Arnold, Robert. April 26, 1980
Bardowski, Zenon "Bud." December 6, 1982
Benedum, George. May 25, 1984
Chartoff, Maurice. April 11, 1983; September 11, 1984; September 1, 1994
Chernitsky, John. June 6, 1994
Dickson, Ronald. November 1 and December 23, 1981
Goldbrum, Louis. April 11 and 22, and June 3, 1984
Pothier, Bernard. April 17, 1997
Roseen, Everett. May 1, 1984
Seckinger, William. March 6, 1984
Tant, Norman. June 4, 1981

Other Persons to Author

Bogart, Charles. September 7, 1998
Griswold, Laura Maverick. May 8, 1995
Hight, James. January 6, 1997
Lundstrom, John. July 27, 2001
Obluski, Andrew. August 5, 2002 (via E-mail)
Pachacki, Miriam. December 21, 1996
Sawruk, Jim. August 1, 2, and 5, 2002 (via E-mail)
Tagaya, Osamu. February 9, March 31, and April 9, 2001 (all via E-mail)

Other Correspondence

Brooke-Popham, Robert, to Lord Ismay. October 10, 1941
Burt, William R., to Robert A. Lovett. June 17, 1983
————, to Philip S. Meilinger. October 20 and November 12, 1984
Campbell, Alexander H., to Orlando Ward, December 4, 1951
Chaney, James E., to George C. Marshall. March 27 and April 1, 1941

Davis, Kelly to Mike Drake. N.d. (December, 1981)
Eubank, Eugene, to Sky Phillips Beaven. August 13, 1980
Hoffmann, Arthur, to Walter D. Edmonds. January 15, 1946
Ind, Allison, to Courtney Whitney. 1943
Krieger, Andrew, to Walter D. Edmonds. November 9, 1945
Maitland, Lester, to Walter D. Edmonds. November 20, 1950
Moore, Joseph H., to James E. Brown. March 19, 1978
Stitt, Austin, to Sky Phillips Beaven, April 6, 1974

UNPUBLISHED MATERIALS

Reports and Statements

Brown, Maj. Ben. "Statement." October 25, 1944
Kiser, Lt. Col. George E. "Statement." N.d., ca. 1944
Obert, Maj. David L. "Activities of Fighter Units in the Philippines." April 25, 1945
Robb, Maj. Stewart W. "Statement." November 30, 1944
Wimer, Capt. C. J. (excerpts from) "History of Signal Corps Radar Units in the Philippine Islands, 1 August 1941–6 May 1942." 1946.
———. "Report on Enemy Air Activities over the Philippines up to and Including the First Day of War, As Observed by S.C. Radar." 1946.

Unit and Office Diaries and Official Narratives

"Army Air Action in the Philippines and Netherlands East Indies, 1941–42." USAAF Historical Study no. 111. Washington, D.C.: Assistant Chief of Air Staff, Intelligence, Historical Division, March, 1945.
"Battle Report no. 2, *Sanuki Maru*." WDC 160541. N.d.
"Daily Diary of the Chief of the Air Staff, 23 June–6 December 1941."
"Diary, General Douglas MacArthur, Commanding General, USAFFE." (21 July 1941–23 February 1942).
Grover, Col. O. L., HQ, Allied Air Forces Southwest Pacific Area, Brisbane, to chief of staff, GHQ, Southwest Pacific Area, memo, Oct. 7, 1942. "Narrative of the Activities of the 24th Pursuit Group in the Philippine Islands."
HQ, FEAF. "General Brereton's Headquarters Diary: Summary of the Activities for the Period 8th Dec. 1941–24th Feb. 1942."
"History of the Air Defense Command, Feb. 26, 1940–June 2, 1941"
McAuliff, Harold C., and Alexander D. DeShago. "The 30th Squadron." Pyote Field, Texas, February 2, 1943.
"19th Bomb Group Diary." N.d.

"19th Bombardment Group (H) History." N.d.

"*Ryūjō* Operations." WDC 161733. N.d.

Sage, Brig. Gen. Charles G. "Report of Operations of the Philippine Provisional Coast Artillery Brigade (AA) in the Philippines Campaign." Annex IX to Jonathan M. Wainwright, "Report of Operations of USAFFE and USFIL in the Philippine Islands, 1941–1942." Fort Sam Houston, Texas, 1946.

"16th Naval District War Diary." N.d.

Sutherland, Maj. Gen. Richard K. "Brief Summary of Action in the Office of the Chief of Staff, Headquarters, U.S. Army Forces in the Far East, 8: 58 A.M. December 8, 1941 to 11:00 P.M., February 22, 1942."

"The 27th Reports: History of the 27th Bomb Group (L) in the Philippines, Java, Australia, and New Guinea."

"USAFFE G2 Journal."

Official Japanese Navy Unit Records

"Tainan Kōkūtai Hikōtai Sentō Kodo Chosho" (Tainan Kōkūtai Aircraft Echelon Combat Log). December, 1941, entries.

"3d Kōkūtai Hikōtai Sentō Kodo Chosho" (3d Kōkūtai Aircraft Echelon Combat Log). December, 1941, entries.

Personal Diaries and Journals of FEAF Personnel, 1941–42

Anonymous Diary (James Colovin?)

Arhutick, Leo

Brownewell, John L. Journal

Cappelletti, Francis. "My Overseas Log: A Navigator's Experience in the Far East." N.d.

Crosby, Stephen

Fairfield, William A.

Geer, John

Gerrity, Thomas P.

Gies, Carl Parker

Jacquet, Edward M.

Keator, Randall. Diary and supplement, April 5, 1974.

King, Edward P.

Kokjer, Madsen Cobb

Marrocco, William

McAfee, James B.

McKenzie, Melvin

Obert, David L.

Posten, John
Powell, William H.
Rowe, William
Steele, Donald D.

Personal Diaries and Logs of Others, 1941–42

Dowding, Sir Hugh. "Visit to Canada and the U.S.A."
Mallonee, Richard C.
Stimson, Henry L.

Personal Narratives of FEAF Personnel Provided to Author

Bowers, Glenn. January 9, 1979
Bradley, Hardy. April 18, 1983
Brown, James E. April 10, 1978
Ellis, Herbert. N.d. (1979); January 13, 1980
Fossey, W. James. June 14, 1978.
Greeson, Eugene. April 9, 1981
Roland, Orville. October 30, 1980
Stinson, Lloyd. June 8, 1978
Vance, Reginald. July 22, 1980

Other Personal Narratives and Memoirs of USAFFE Personnel

Adami, Grant E., Jr. Memoir. November, 1946
Brown, Howard W. "Reminiscences." SRH-045. August 4, 1945
Campbell, Alexander H. "Notebook." N.d. (ca. 1942)
Collier, James V. POW Notebooks. N.d. (ca. 1943)
Kimmerle, Benjamin F. Memoir. N.d. (1946?)
Knudson, Lyle G. "Things I Remember." N.d.
Krieger, Andrew E. Narrative. N.d. (ca. 1945)
McKenzie, Melvin. Memoir. December 20, 1993
Montgomery, William H. "I Hired out to Fight." N.d.
Sheppard, William, and Edwin Gilmore. November 1, 1944–February 1, 1945
Thorne, Henry G., Jr. "Philippine Narrative, 1941–1942." N.d. (1947)

Admiral Hart's Personal Papers

"Conversation between Admiral Hart and General MacArthur." September 22, 1941. Series 1, "Java Papers."
"Report of Conference, Manila, December 6, 1941." Series 1 (Subject Files).

War Department Memoranda

Chief of Staff, 1940–41
Chief of Staff to Chief of Naval Operations, 1941
Adjutant General, 1939–41
War Plans Division, 1939–41
Office of the Chief of the Air Corps, 1939–41
Office of the Chief of the Air Staff, HQ, Army Air Forces, 1941
Air War Plans Division, HQ, Army Air Forces, 1941

Other War Department Documents

Minutes and Notes, Office of the Chief of Staff, 1941
Record of Telephone Conversation, Leonard T. Gerow to Douglas
    MacArthur, December 7, 1941

Philippine Department and USAFFE Memoranda

HQ, Philippine Department, 1940–41
HQ, Philippine Department Air Force, 1939–41
HQ, 4th Composite Group, 1939
HQ, USAFFE, 1941
HQ, Air Force, USAFFE, 1941
HQ, FEAF, 1941

USAFFE General, Field, and Special Orders

General Orders 4, August 4, 1941
General Orders 10, September 16, 1941
General Orders 13, October 1, 1941
General Orders 28, November 14, 1941
General Orders 29, November 21, 1941
Special Orders 61, November 4, 1941
Special Orders 74, November 19, 1941
Special Orders 82, November 28, 1941
Special Orders 83, November 29, 1941
Special Orders 84, December 1, 1941
Special Orders 85, December 2, 1941
HQ, Air Force, USAFFE, General Orders 6, November 6, 1941
HQ, FEAF, Field Orders 1, December 8, 1941
HQ, FEAF, Field Orders 2, December 8, 1941

Army Air Forces Orders

Air Base HQ, Albuquerque, N.M. Special Orders 135, September 20, 1941
HQ, 19th Bombardment Group (H), Air Force Combat Command, Special Orders 1, October 17, 1941
Air Base HQ, Fort Douglas, Ariz., Special Orders 251, November 8, 1941

Imperial Japanese Army Directives

Directive 810, January 16, 1941
Directive 1045, December 2, 1941
Imperial Japanese Navy Orders, Order 5, November 21, 1941

War Department, Philippine Department, and USAFFE Radiograms, Cablegrams, and Telegrams

Adjutant General, War Department, to Grunert and MacArthur, 1941
Chief of Staff, War Department, to Grunert and MacArthur, 1941
HQ, Army Air Forces, to MacArthur, 1941
HQ, Philippine Department (Grunert), to Adjutant General, 1940–41
HQ, USAFFE (MacArthur), to Adjutant General, 1941
HQ, USAFFE (MacArthur), to Brink, Singapore, 1941
HQ, FEAF (Brereton), to Adjutant General, 1941
HQ, USAFFE (Marquat), to Commanding General, Harbor Defense, Fort Mills, 1941
HQ, Far East Air Service Command (Churchill), to Commanding Officer, Del Monte Air Base HQ, 1941
HQ, 5th Bomber Command, to O'Donnell (Del Monte), 1941

Translations of Intercepted Japanese Naval Radio Messages

SRN 115492, November 24, 1941
SRN 115547, November 3, 1941
SRN 115840, November 20, 1941
SRN 116101, October 4, 1941
SRN 116138, October 15, 1941
SRN 116267, October 31, 1941
SRN 116310, October 29, 1941
SRN 116481, November 5, 1941
SRN 116585, October 13, 1941
SRN 116645, November 18, 1941
SRN 116768, November 27, 1941
SRN 115535, November 16, 1941
SRN 115763, October 1, 1941
SRN 116044, October 13, 1941
SRN 116134, October 21, 1941
SRN 116265, October 18, 1941
SRN 116308, October 29, 1941
SRN 116328, November 11, 1941
SRN 116520, October 1, 1941
SRN 116608, October 12, 1941
SRN 116734, November 28, 1941
SRN 116784, November 22, 1941

SRN 116840, December 3, 1941   SRN 116969, December 2, 1941
SRN 117029, November 11, 1941   SRN 117052, November 8, 1941
SRN 117140, November 6, 1941   SRN 117264, October 1, 1941
SRN 117310, October 1, 1941   SRN 117740, November 18, 1941
SRN 117792, September 26, 1941   SRN 117810, September 26, 1941

Other Documents

(Air Defense Command, Mitchel Field). "History of the Air Defense Command, Feb. 26, 1940—June 2, 1941."

Air Defense School, Mitchel Field, N.Y. Memo. 1941.

"Alphabetical Casualty Listing of Officers Who Were in the Philippine Islands Area as of 7 December, 1941." N.d.

American Ex-Prisoners of War. "The 200th Coast Artillery (AA) and its 'Child,' the 515th Coast Artillery (AA)." Arlington, Texas, n.d., 1976.

American Battle Monuments Commission. "The World War II Honor Roll." Available at http://www.abmc.gov.

"An Account of the Imperial Japanese Navy's Activities in the Philippines at the Beginning of War." May 15, 1946.

Army War College. Courses, 1938–39.

Darvall, Group Captain Lawrence. "Notes on the Defense Problem of Luzon." 1941.

Distinguished Service Cross Citations for T. Sgt. Anthony Holub, Pfc. Joseph G. McElroy, and Pvt. Greeley B. Williams. "SWPA Awards and Decorations." Walter D. Edmonds Collection, AFHRA.

HQ, Army Forces Far East, Military History Section. "Philippines Air Operations Record: Phase One." Japanese Monograph no. 11. Tokyo: February 1, 1952.

(HQ, Army Air Forces). "Air Defense Organization." September 2, 1941.

(HQ, Army Air Forces. Air War Plans Division). "A/WPD Notebook." N.d. [1941].

————"A-WPD/1: Munitions Requirements of the Army Air Forces to Defeat Our Potential Enemies." N.d. [1941].

(HQ, Philippine Department). "Weekly Summary of Philippine News." 1941.

Izawa, Yasuho. "Rikko and Ginga: Japanese Navy Twin [Engine] Bomber Units." Unpublished manuscript. N.d.

Kuter, Laurence S. "Growth of Air Power." Unpublished manuscript. 1979.

Lester, John E. "Air Corps in the War." N.d., ca. 1945.

(Office of the Chief of the Air Corps). "Arnold Visitors Log." 1941.

"Operations of the Provisional Tank Group, U.S. Armed Forces in the Far East, 1941–1942." Available at http//:www.terracom.net/~vfwpost/provisionatank2.htm.

RAAF, "Hospital or Sick List-Record Card, Henry B. Clagett, January 19, 1942."
Sayre, Francis. Manuscript for *Glad Adventure*. N.d.
Sherrod, Robert L. Memo to David Hurlburd. November 15, 1941.
Station WOAI, San Antonio, Texas. "Letters to the Front, no. 10." August 2, 1942.
Tagaya, Osamu. "Technical Development and Operational History of the Type 1 Rikko." Unpublished manuscript, 2000.
(USAFFE). "Emergency Aircraft Warning Service Project." 1941.
(USAFFE). "Provisional List of Aerodrome Landing Grounds and Seaplane Facilities, 5 December 1941."
U.S. Total Army Personnel Command. "Individual Deceased Personnel File."
White, Theodore H. Draft dispatch to *Time*. Theodore White Collection. Archives, Pusey Library. Harvard University. Cambridge, Mass.

PUBLISHED MATERIALS

Newspapers

Japan Times and Advertiser. 1940, 1941
Manila Daily Bulletin. 1941
Manila Tribune, 1941
Philippines Herald. 1941
New York Times. 1940, 1941
Nichols News (Manila). 1939
Washington Post. 1940, 1941

Magazine and Newspaper Articles

Allen, Albert L., Jr., "Absurd Order Calms Soldier during Danger." *(Mansfield, Ohio) News Journal*, December 6, 1991.
Baldwin, Hanson W. "Strategy of Change." *New York Times*, October 26, 1940.
Bartsch, William H. "Was MacArthur Ill-Served by his Air Force Commanders in the Philippines?" *Air Power History* 44, no. 2 (summer, 1997): 44–63.
Birrn, Roland J. "A War Diary." *The Airpower Historian* 3, no. 4 (October, 1956): 195–202.
Bogart, Charles H. "Radar in the Philippines, 1941–1942." *Journal of America's Military Past*, fall, 1999, 27–30.

————. "200th Coast Artillery (AA)." *The Quan,* April, 1983, 9.

Cook, Charles O. "The Strange Case of Rainbow-5." *U.S. Naval Institute Proceedings* 104, no. 8 (August, 1978): 66–73.

Denny, Harold. "U.S. Will Dispatch Air Reinforcements to the Philippines." *New York Times,* October 24, 1940.

"Dowding to Confer on Plane-Building." *New York Times,* January 6, 1941.

Finnegan, Jack. "Grim Fate for Station 6." *Military History,* October, 1986, 10, 63–66.

Futrell, Robert F. "Air Hostilities in the Philippines, 8 December 1941." *Air University Review,* January-February, 1965, 33–45.

Goldblith, Samuel A. "The 803d Engineers in the Philippine Defense." *Military Engineer,* August, 1946, 323–25.

Gotō, Osahirō. "Konpeki No Sora Goh Goh To" ("Roar in the Deep Blue Sky"). *Kōkū Fan,* January, 1967, 83–88.

Harrington, Daniel F. "A Careless Hope: American Air Power and Japan, 1941." *Pacific Historical Review* 45, no. 2 (May, 1979): 217–38.

Harvey, A. D. "Army Air Force and Navy Air Force: Japanese Aviation and the Opening Phase of the War in the Far East." *War in History* 6, no. 2 (1999): 174–204.

"Indies Army Head Dies in Air Crash." *New York Times,* October 14, 1941.

Jacquet, Edward M. "Flight into History." *Daedalus Flyer,* winter, 1985, 12–23.

James, D. Clayton. "The Other Pearl Harbor." *MHQ: The Quarterly Journal of Military History* 7, no. 2 (winter, 1995): 22–29.

Kluckhohn, Frank L. "Hull Deplores Attack on Indochina as Blow to Pacific Status Quo." *New York Times,* September 24, 1940.

————. "U.S. Embargoes Scrap Iron, Hitting Japan." *New York Times,* September 27, 1940.

"M'Arthur Denies Brereton Report." *New York Times,* September 28, 1946.

Maurer, Maurer. "A Delicate Mission: Aerial Reconnaissance of Japanese Islands before World War II." *Military Affairs* 26, no. 2 (summer, 1962): 66–75.

Meigs, Montgomery C. "This Must Mean the Philippines!" *U.S. Naval Institute Proceedings* 111, no. 8 (August, 1985): 72–78.

Meixsel, Richard B. "Major General George Grunert, WPO-3, and the Philippine Army, 1940–1941." *Journal of Military History* 59, no. 2 (April, 1995): 303–24.

Miller, Roger G. "A 'Pretty Damn Able' Commander—Lewis Hyde Brereton." Pt. 1, *Air Power History* 47, no. 4 (winter, 2000): 4–27.

————. "A 'Pretty Damn Able' Commander—Lewis Hyde Brereton." Pt. 2, *Air Power History* 48, no. 1 (spring, 2001): 22–45.

Mitchell, John N. "Flying Fortresses of the 19th Bomb Group." *AAHS Journal,* winter, 1984, 287–93.

Miza, Masami. "Meritorious Deeds of the Secret Reconnoitering Unit which Became the Shadow Strength of the Zero Fighter Squadrons." (In Japanese.) *Maru,* February, 1962, 126–29.

Mizrahi, Joe. "P-35: Seversky's Cadillac in the Air." *Wings,* October, 1971, 39–46.

"No Need to Fear ABCD Encircling." *Japan Times and Advertiser,* December 5, 1941.

Norris, John G. "U.S. Warns She'll Protect Philippines." *Washington Post,* October 24, 1940.

Obituary for Charles Sprague. *U.S. Military Academy Assembly,* March, 1992.

Perret, Geoffrey. "My Search for General MacArthur." *American Heritage,* February–March, 1996, 75–84.

Shimada, Koichi. "Japanese Naval Air Operations in the Philippines Invasion." *U.S. Naval Institute Proceedings* 81, no. 1 (January, 1955): 1–17.

Smith, Joe. "We Shoot Down the First Japs." *Life,* December 22, 1941, 30.

Teats, Edward C., as told to John M. McCullough. "Turn of the Tide." Pt. 1. *Philadelphia Inquirer,* December 31, 1942.

"The Hair Corps at Clark Field Raise a Bumper Crop of Beards." *Sunday Tribune (Manila),* Magazine Section, August 10, 1941.

Tolischus, Otto D. "Japanese Report U.S. Is in a Secret Accord to Defend Southeast Asia against Drive." *New York Times,* April 21, 1941.

Wilkins, H. Ford. "Three Power Talk on Orient Defense is Set for Manila." *New York Times,* April 5, 1941.

———. "M'Arthur Calls Manila Meeting." *New York Times,* July 28, 1941.

Books and Chapters / Sections of Books

Ancheta, Celedonia A., ed. *The Wainwright Papers.* Vol. 2. Quezon City, P.I.: New Day, 1980.

Andrade, John M. *U.S. Military Aircraft Designations and Serials Since 1909.* East Shilton, UK: Midland Counties (Aerophile), 1979.

Arnold, Henry H. *Global Mission.* New York: Harper and Brothers, 1949.

Arnold, Robert H. *A Rock and a Fortress.* Sarasota: Blue Horizons Press, 1979.

Baker, Carlos. *Ernest Hemingway: A Life Story.* New York: Scribner's, 1969.

Bartsch, William H. *Doomed at the Start.* College Station: Texas A&M University Press, 1992.

Beck, John J. *MacArthur and Wainwright: Sacrifice of the Philippines.* Albuquerque: University of New Mexico Press, 1974.

Berger, Carl. *B-29: The Superfortress.* London: Purnell, 1970.

Bix, Herbert P. *Hirohito and the Making of Modern Japan.* New York: HarperCollins, 2000.

Bland, Larry I., ed. *The Papers of George Catlett Marshall.* Vol. 2, *"We Cannot Delay."* Baltimore: Johns Hopkins University Press, 1986.

Blue, Alan G. *The B-24 Liberator.* New York: Charles Scribner's Sons, 1975.

Bōeichō Bōekenshūsho Senshishitsu (Japanese Defense Agency, War History Section). *Senshi Sōsho.* Vol. 2, *Hitō Koryaku Sakusen (Philippine Invasion Operations).* Tokyo: Asagumo Shimbun-sha, 1966.

———. *Senshi Sōsho.* Vol. 24, *Hitō Malay Hōmen Kaigun Shinkō Sakusen (Philippines and Malaya Area Navy Offensive Operations).* Tokyo: Asagumo Shimbun-sha, 1969.

———. *Senshi Sōsho.* Vol. 34, *Nampo Shinkō Rikūgun Kōkū Sakusen (Southern Offensive Army Air Operations).* Tokyo: Asagumo Shimbun-sha, 1970.

Bowers, Peter. *Fortress in the Sky.* Granada Hills, Calif.: Sentry Books, 1976

Brereton, Lewis H. *The Brereton Diaries.* New York: William Morrow, 1946.

Bueschel, Richard M. *Mitsubishi-Nakajima G3M1/2/3 in Japanese Naval Air Service.* Reading, Pa.: Osprey, 1972.

Burt, William R. *Adventures with Warlords.* New York: Vantage Press, 1994.

Butow, Robert J. C. *Tōjō and the Coming of War.* Princeton, N.J.: Princeton University Press, 1961.

Byrd, Martha. *Kenneth N. Walker: Airpower's Untempered Crusader.* Maxwell AFB, Ala.: Air University Press, 1997.

Cave, Dorothy. *Beyond Courage.* Las Cruces: Yucca Tree Press, 1992.

Connaughton, Richard. *MacArthur and Defeat in the Philippines.* New York: Overlook Press, 2001.

Copp, DeWitt S. *Forged in Fire: Strategy and Decisions in the Air War over Europe, 1940–45.* New York: Doubleday, 1982.

Costello, John. *Days of Infamy.* New York: Pocketbooks, 1994.

Cox, John, and Bob Barnard. "We Smote their Wickedness." In 19th Bomb Group Association, *19th Bomb Group.* Paducah, Ky.: Turner, 2000.

Craven, Wesley F., and James L. Cate, eds. *The Army Air Forces in World War II.* Vol. 1, *Plans and Early Operations.* Chicago: University of Chicago Press, 1948.

Crowley, James B. "Japan's Military Foreign Policies." In *Japan's Foreign Policy, 1868–1941: A Research Guide,* ed. James W. Morley. New York: Columbia University Press, 1974.

Department of Defense. *The "Magic" Background of Pearl Harbor.* Vol. 4. Washington, D.C.: USGPO, 1977.

Department of the Army. *Reports of General MacArthur: Japanese Operations in the Southwest Pacific Area.* Vol. 2, pt. 1. Washington, D.C.: USGPO, 1966.

Dod, Karl C. *The Corps of Engineers: The War against Japan.* Washington, D.C.: USGPO, 1966.

Drea, Edward J. *MacArthur's ULTRA: Codebreaking and the War Against Japan, 1942–1945*. Lawrence: University Press of Kansas, 1992.

Dull, Paul S. *A Battle History of the Imperial Japanese Navy, 1941–1945*. Annapolis, Md.: Naval Institute Press, 1978.

Dyess, William E. *The Dyess Story*. New York: G. P. Putnam's Sons, 1944.

Edmonds, Walter D. *They Fought with What They Had*. Boston: Little, Brown, 1951.

Evans, David C., and Mark R. Peattie. *Kaigun: Strategy, Tactics and Technology in the Imperial Japanese Navy, 1887–1941*. Annapolis, Md.: Naval Institute Press, 1997.

Flint, Peter. *Dowding and Headquarters Fighter Command*. London: Airlife, 1976.

Fogerty, Robert P. *Biographical Study of USAF General Officers*. Manhattan, Kans.: MA/AH, n.d.

Francillon, Rene J. *Japanese Aircraft of the Pacific War*. London: Putnam, 1970.

———. *Mitsubishi G4M "Betty" and Ohka Bomb*. Aircraft Profile no. 210. Windsor: Profile Publications, n.d.

Freeman, Roger A. *B-17 Fortress at War*. London: Ian Allan, 1977.

Fuller, Richard. *Shokan: Hirohito's Samurai*. London: Arms and Armour, 1992.

Gaston, James C. *Planning the American Air War: Four Men and Nine Days in 1941*. Washington, D.C.: National Defense University Press, 1982.

Grashio, Samuel C., and Bernard Norling. *Return to Freedom*. Tulsa, Okla.: MCN Press, 1982.

Hamilton, James M. *Rainbow over the Philippines*. Chicago: Adams Press, 1974.

Hartendorp, A.V.H. *The Japanese Occupation of the Philippines*. Manila: Bookmark, 1967.

Hara, Tameichi. *Japanese Destroyer Captain*. New York: Ballantine Books, 1961.

Hata, Ikuhiko. "The Army's Move into Northern Indochina." In *The Fateful Choice: Japan's Advance into Southeast Asia, 1939–1941*, ed. James W. Morley. New York: Columbia University Press, 1980.

———, and Yasuho Izawa. *Japanese Naval Aces and Fighter Units in World War II*. Annapolis, Md.: Naval Institute Press, 1989.

Hattori, Takushirō. *Dai Tōa Sensō Zenshi (The Complete History of the Greater East Asia War)*. 2 vols. Tokyo: Masu Shobo, 1953. English translation available in the LOC.

Hawaii-Malay Oki Kaisen (Sea Battles Off Hawaii and the Malaya Peninsula). Tokyo: Bungei Shunjū, 1942.

Hayashi, Saburō. *Kogun: The Japanese Army in the Pacific War*. Quantico, Va.: Marine Corps Association, 1959.

Headquarters, Philippine Department. *Telephone Directory Manila and Vicinity: Directory of All Officers Stationed within the Philippine Department, July 16, 1941.* Manila: Philippine Department, 1941.

Hearings before the Joint Committee on the Investigation of the Pearl Harbor Attack. 79th Cong., 2d sess., pt. 18. Washington, D.C.: USGPO, n.d.

Holub, Anthony. "Clark Field, Dec. 8, 1941." In 19th Bomb Group Association, *19th Bomb Group.* Paducah, Ky.: Turner, 2000.

Horikoshi, Jirō. *Eagles of Mitsubishi.* Seattle: University of Washington Press, 1981.

Hosoya, Chihirō. "The Tripartite Pact, 1939–1940." In *Deterrent Diplomacy: Japan, Germany, and the USSR, 1935–1940,* ed. James W. Morley. New York: Columbia University Press, 1976.

Hoyt, Edwin P. *Japan's War: The Great Pacific Conflict.* New York: McGraw-Hill, 1986.

Ike, Nobutaka, ed. *Japan's Decision for War.* Stanford, Calif.: Stanford University Press, 1967.

Ind, Allison. *Bataan: The Judgment Seat.* New York: Macmillan, 1944.

Iwaya, Fumio. *Chūkō (Medium Attack Bomber).* Tokyo: Hara Shobō, 1976.

Izawa, Yasuho. *Nippon Rikūgun Jubaku Tai (Japanese Heavy Bomber Units).* Tokyo: Gendai Shi Shuppan Kai, 1982.

Jackfert, Ed. "The History of the U.S. Army Air Corps in the Philippine Islands." In 19th Bomb Group Association, *19th Bomb Group.* Paducah, Ky.: Turner, 2000.

James, D. Clayton. *The Years of MacArthur.* Vol. 2, *1941–1945.* Boston: Houghton Mifflin, 1975.

Jose, Ricardo T. *The Philippine Army, 1935–1942.* Manila: Ateneo de Manila Press, 1992.

Keegan, John, ed. *The Times Atlas of the Second World War.* London: Times Books, 1989.

Kohdachi, Naoki. *Reisen Saigo no Shogen (Zero Fighter: Final Testimony).* 2 vols. Tokyo: Kojinsha, 2000.

Kubo, Yoshiaki. *97 Jubaku Ku-sen Ki (The Air Combat Saga of the Type 97 Heavy Bomber).* Tokyo: Kojinsha, 1984.

Layton, Edwin S., with Roger Pineau and John Costello. *And I Was There.* New York: William Morrow, 1985.

Lee, Clark. *They Call It Pacific.* New York: Viking, 1943.

Leutze, James. *A Different Kind of Victory.* Annapolis, Md.: Naval Institute Press, 1981.

Linn, Brian McAllister. *Guardians of Empire: The U.S. Army and the Pacific, 1902–1940.* Chapel Hill: University of North Carolina Press, 1997.

Mallonee, Richard C. II. *The Naked Flagpole: Battle for Bataan from the Diary of Richard C. Mallonee.* Novato, Calif.: Presidio Press, 1980.

Maloney, Edward, and Frank Ryan. *P-26*. North Hollywood: Challenge, 1965.

Maloney, Edward T. *Boeing P-26 Peashooter*. Fallbrook, Calif.: Aero, 1973.

Manchester, William. *American Caesar*. New York: Little, Brown, 1978.

Matloff, Maurice, and Edwin M. Snell. *Strategic Planning for Coalition Warfare, 1941–1942*. Washington, D.C.: Center for Military History, U.S. Army, 1953.

Maurer, Maurer, ed. *Air Force Combat Units of World War II*. Washington, D.C.: Zenger, 1980.

———, ed. *Combat Squadrons of the Air Force. World War II*. Washington, D.C.: Department of the Air Force, 1969.

McKee, Philip. *Warriors with Wings*. New York: Crowell, 1947.

Meilinger, Philip S. *Hoyt S. Vandenberg: The Life of a General*. Bloomington: Indiana University Press, 1989.

Messimer, Dwight R. *In the Hands of Fate: The Story of Patrol Wing Ten, 8 December 1941–11 May 1942*. Annapolis, Md.: Naval Institute Press, 1985.

Meyers, Jeffrey. *Hemingway: A Biography*. New York: Harper and Row, 1985.

Middlebrook, Martin, and Patrick Mahoney. *Battleship: The Loss of the Prince of Wales and the Repulse*. London: Allen Lane, 1977.

Mikesh, Robert C. *Zero*. Osceola: Motorbooks International, 1994.

———. *Zero Fighter*. New York: Crown, 1981.

Miller, Ernest B. *Bataan Uncensored*. Long Prairie, Minn.: Hart, 1949.

Mitchell, John L. *On Wings We Conquer*. Springfield, Mo.: Gem, 1990.

Mori, Shirō. *Kaigun Sentōkitai (Navy Fighter Groups)*. Vols. 1 and 2. Tokyo: R. Shuppan, 1973.

Morton, Louis. *The Fall of the Philippines*. U.S. Army in World War II. Pacific Theater of Operations. Washington, D.C.: OCMH, U.S. Army, 1953.

Noyer, William L. *Mactan: Ship of Destiny*. Fresno, Calif.: Rainbow Press, 1979.

Obert, David L. *Philippines Defender: A Fighter Pilot's Diary, 1941–42*. Norman, Okla.: Levite of Apache, 1992.

Ogawa, Hiroyuki. *The Reluctant Admiral: Yamamoto and the Imperial Navy*. Tokyo: Kodansha International, 1979.

Okumiya, Masatake, and Jiro Horikoshi, with Martin Caidin. *Zero!* New York: E. P. Dutton, 1956.

———. *The Zero Fighter*. London: Cassell, 1958.

Parker, Frederick D. *Pearl Harbor Revisited: United States Navy Communications Intelligence, 1924–1941*. Washington, D.C.: Center for Cryptologic History, National Security Agency, 1994.

Pogue, Forrest C. *George C. Marshall: Ordeal and Hope*. New York: Viking, 1966.

Poweleit, Alvin C. *Kentucky's Fighting 192nd Light GHQ Tank Battalion.* Newport, Ky.: Quality Lithographing, 1981.

Prados, John. *Combined Fleet Decoded.* New York: Random House, 1995.

Prange, Gordon W. *At Dawn We Slept.* New York: McGraw-Hill, 1981.

Reynolds, Robert. *Of Rice and Men.* Philadelphia: Dorrance, 1947.

Rogers, Paul P. *The Good Years: MacArthur and Sutherland.* New York: Praeger, 1990.

Sakai, Saburō. *Ohzora no Samurai (Samurai of the Skies).* Tokyo: Kojinsha, 1970.

————, with Martin Caidin and Fred Saito. *Samurai!* New York: E. P. Dutton, 1957.

Santos, Enrique B. *Trails in Philippine Skies.* Manila: Philippine Airlines, 1981.

Schultz, Duane. *Hero of Bataan: The Story of General Jonathan M. Wainwright.* New York: St. Martin's Press, 1981.

Scott, Robert L. *Damned to Glory.* New York: Charles Scribners' and Sons, 1944.

Sekigawa, Eiichirō. *Pictorial History of Japanese Military Aviation.* London: Ian Allan, 1974.

Sherry, Michael S. *The Rise of American Air Power.* New Haven, Conn.: Yale University Press, 1987.

Shimada, Koichi. "The Opening Air Offensive against the Philippines." In *The Japanese Navy in World War II,* ed. David C. Evans. Annapolis, Md.: Naval Institute Press, 1986

Shimakawa, Masa-aki. *Zerosen Kusen Kyroku (The Air Battle Record of a Zero Fighter).* Tokyo: Kojinsha, 1989.

Spector, Ronald H. *Eagle Against the Sun.* New York: Free Press, 1985.

Swinson, Arthur. *Four Samurai.* London: Hutchinson, 1968.

Tagaya, Osamu. *Mitsubishi Type 1 Rikko "Betty" Units of World War II.* Osprey Combat Aircraft Series, no. 22. Oxford: Osprey, 2001.

Thompson, George R., Dixie F. Harris, Pauline M. Oakes, and Dulany Terrett. *The Signal Corps: The Test.* Washington, D.C.: OCMH, Department of the Army, 1957.

Toland, John. *But Not in Shame.* New York: Random House, 1961.

————. *The Rising Sun.* New York: Random House, 1970.

Tomioka, Sadatoshi. *Kaisen to Chusen (The Beginning and End of the War).* Tokyo: Mainichi Shimbun-sha, 1968.

Tsunoda, Jun. "The Navy's Role in the Southern Strategy." In *The Fateful Choice: Japan's Advance into Southeast Asia, 1939–1941,* ed. James W. Morley. New York: Columbia University Press, 1980.

Ugaki, Matome. *Fading Victory: The Diary of Admiral Matome Ugaki, 1941–1945.* Pittsburgh: University of Pittsburgh Press, 1991.

Underwood, Jeffrey S. *The Wings of Democracy.* College Station: Texas A&M University Press, 1991.

U.S. Strategic Bombing Survey (Pacific). *Interrogations of Japanese Officials.* Vols. 1 and 2. Tokyo: n.p., 1945. (No. 74, Capt. Chihaya Takahashi; no. 424, Capt. Bunzo Shibata; no. 601, Cdr. Ryosuke Nomura).

Valencia, Jerry. *Knights of the Sky.* San Diego: Reed Enterprises, 1980.

Verity, George L. *From Bataan to Victory.* New York: Carlton Press, 1992.

War Department. *Officers of the Army Stationed in or Near the District of Columbia, Oct. 1, 1940.* Washington, D.C.: USGPO, 1940.

———. *Officers of the Army Stationed in or Near the District of Columbia, April 1, 1941.* Washington, D.C.: USGPO, 1941.

———. *Radio Set SCR-270B.* Technical Manual 11-1100. Washington, D.C.: War Department, December 3, 1942.

———. *Radio Sets SCR-270 and SCR-271.* Technical Bulletin SIG 106. Washington, D.C.: War Department, October 21, 1944.

Watson, Mark S. *Chief of Staff: Prewar Plans and Preparations.* Washington, D.C.: Historical Division, U.S. Army, 1950.

Watts, A. J., and B. G. Gordon. *The Imperial Japanese Navy.* London: Macdonald, 1971.

Whitcomb, Edgar D. *Escape from Corregidor.* London: Allan Wingate, 1959.

White, Theodore H. *In Search of History.* New York: Harper and Row, 1978.

White, W. L. *Queens Die Proudly.* New York: Harcourt, Brace, 1943.

Williams, Ted. *Rogues of Bataan.* New York: Carlton Press, 1970.

Willoughby, Charles A., and John Chamberlain. *MacArthur, 1941–1951.* New York: McGraw-Hill, 1954.

Yanagida, Kunio. *Moyuru Zero-Sen (Burning Zeros).* Tokyo: Shukan Bunshun, 1984.

Yokoyama, Tamotsu. *Ah Zero-sen Ichidai (Oh, My Life in the Zero Fighter).* Tokyo: Kojinsha, 1969.

Index